THE WORLD'S MOST
INFAMOUS
CRIMES
AND
CRIMINALS

THE WORLD'S MOST INFAMOUS CRIMES AND CRIMINALS

GALLERY BOOKS
An Imprint of W. H. Smith Publishers Inc.
112 Madison Avenue
New York City 10016

Acknowledgements

The publishers wish to thank the following for their kind permission to reproduce the pictures used in this book:

John Topham Picture Library 11, 12, 13, 40, 52, 57, 61, 101, 103, 104, 107, 109, 119, 130, 131, 157, 161, 165, 172, 177, 191, 210, 347, 361, 423, 469, 471, 490, 498, 523, 527, 530, 544, 555, 569, 574, 577, 585, 589, 602, 611, 624, 634, 643, 644, 665, 668, 683, 684, 687, 689, 693, 696, 701, 702, 704, 717, 729, 732, 735; Mary Evans Picture Library 27, 48, 217, 228, 233, 247, 254, 266, 271, 300, 324, 337, 369, 379, 547, 647, 673, 710; Keystone Press Agency 189, 205, 213, 277, 285, 286, 373, 387, 393, 401, 406, 410, 452, 454, 471, 476, 535; Radio Times Hulton Picture Library 47, 67, 85, 147, 155, 350, 351; Syndication International 18, 22, 41, 79, 86, 90, 110, 178, 447; Popperfoto Limited 93, 114, 307, 312, 391, 419, 677; The Mansell Collection 321, 345, 416, 431; The Robin May Collection 513, (Pinkertons) 515, (Wells Fargo Bank) 517; Associated Press 39, 97; National Portrait Gallery 707, 708; Fox Photos 280; Central Press Photos 291; Culver Pictures 364; Tim Healey 486; The Photo Source 460; The Bettmann Archive 541; Thames Television Ltd 550;

First published in 1987 by
Octopus Books Limited
59 Grosvenor Street, London W1

This edition published in 1987 by Gallery Books
An imprint of W.H. Smith Publishers Inc.
112 Madison Avenue, New York, New York 10016

ISBN 0 8317 9677 4

Printed in Great Britain

Contents

Introduction   7

I   Murder Most Foul   8

II   Twentieth-Century Killers   76

III   Tyrants and Despots   184

IV   Deadlier Than The Male   314

V   Frauds and Swindlers   384

VI   Thieves and Villains   444

VII   Spies and Spymasters   538

VIII   Unsolved Crimes   606

IX   Crimes of Passion   680

Charles Manson. Inset: Sharon Tate with Roman Polanski

Introduction

Perhaps the reason why crime holds such a high degree of fascination for everyone is simply because most of us are quite capable of committing some serious misdeed ourselves. In the majority of cases, however, innate good sense and civilized behaviour prevents people stepping over the line and breaking the law. There is also, of course, the fear of punishment thrown in for good measure.

Unfortunately there are a number of people who, for whatever reason, are unable to hold back from committing petty, malicious and even heinous crimes ranging from theft to cold-blooded murder. Assembled in this volume is a catalogue of crime and corruption, an intriguing line-up of the most notorious crooks and criminals. The stories take a penetrating look at the merciless murderers, notorious villains, thieves and swindlers, terrifying tyrants and snooping spies who parade through these pages. This is a compilation of true stories, revealing astonishing facts about real acts of criminal intrigue, so what follows, although never laudable, makes for compelling reading.

Chapter one

MURDER MOST FOUL

Life is very frail, death very final and murder often a simple crime to commit. Which is perhaps why such fearful crime fascinates us all. The foulest of murders are the premeditated ones, inspired by greed, envy or hatred and those which are the sadistic product of a twisted mind. No one can hope to explain the savage slaughters of Jack the Ripper or the callous cold-blooded murders committed by George Smith, the lethal romeo – no one will forget these most evil of murders.

East End Terror

JACK THE RIPPER

On 25 September, 1888, a letter was delivered to the Central News Agency in London's Fleet Street. It read:

'Dear Boss, I keep on hearing that the police have caught me. But they won't fix me yet . . . I am down on certain types of women and I won't stop ripping them until I do get buckled.

Grand job, that last job was. I gave the lady no time to squeal. I love my work and want to start again. You will soon hear from me, with my funny little game.

I saved some of the proper red stuff in a ginger beer bottle after my last job to write with, but it went thick like glue and I can't use it. Red ink is fit enought, I hope. Ha, ha!

Next time I shall clip the ears off and send them to the police just for jolly.'

The letter was signed 'Jack the Ripper'. It was the first time the name had ever been used. And it immortalized this twisted and mysterious killer who lurked in London's backstreets.

Jack the Ripper's reign of terror was a short one. He first struck on a warm night in August 1888. On a chill, foggy night three months later he claimed his last victim. He is known to have slaughtered at least five women – and some criminologists have credited him with 11 murders.

All that is known for certain about Jack the Ripper is that he had some medical knowledge and that he was left-handed – a fact obvious to police surgeons who examined the grisly remains of his victims. He was probably a tall, slim, pale man with a black moustache. This was the description given by witnesses, including one policeman who saw someone hurrying away from the vicinity of one of the crimes. Each time, he wore a cap and a long coat, and he walked with the vigorous stride of a young man.

But it is unlikely that anyone will ever be able to identify him. Even in 1992, when the secret Scotland Yard files on the case are finally made public, they are expected to cast little new light on the case.

The story of London's most mysterious and ferocious mass-murderer began shortly after 05.00 on the morning of 7 August, 1888. A man hurried down the stairs of the Whitechapel hovel in which he had a room – to be confronted by a

The face of Jack the Ripper

Daniel Farson has already told how he discovered that Sir Melville Macnaghten, head of the CID soon after the Jack the Ripper murders, left papers naming as a prime suspect a man called M. J. Druitt.

Later research had discovered that Montague John Druitt was an unsuccessful barrister, whose father, uncle and cousin were all doctors. Before finally emigrating to Australia Lionel Druitt, the cousin, had a surgery in the Minories, close to the scene of the murders. Montague Druitt would have been familiar with the surgery. There was some evidence that Montague himself had lived in the Minories.

Sir Melville had written that he had little doubt that Druitt's family suspected Montague. A subsequent witness wrote of having seen, in Australia, a document entitled "The East End Murderer—I knew him," written by a Lionel Druitt or Drewett.

Montague Druitt drowned himself in the Thames soon after the last murder. There was evidence that his mother had gone mad and that he feared for his own sanity.

WE can now build up "the case against M. J. Druitt."

As far as physical description and personality is concerned Druitt is closer to the Ripper than the concept of a black-bearded Russian lunatic.

by **DANIEL FARSON**

The eye-witness

Sharp knife

From the Evening News

bundle lying on the first floor landing. He tried to push the bundle out of his way, then recoiled with horror when he realized that what lay at his feet were the bloody remains of a woman. She was identified as Martha Turner, a prostitute. Her throat had been slit, she had been stabbed several times, and bestial mutilations had been carried out on her body.

As the murder of prostitutes was no rare thing in those days, the case was soon shelved. But when a second, similar murder was committed 24 days later, fear and panic began to sweep the mean streets of the East End. The mutilated body of 42-year-old Mary Ann Nicholls – or Pretty Polly as she was known – was found in the early hours of 31 August.

Mary had probably taken no heed of the grisly fate of Martha Turner. She was desperate for money. She needed fourpence for a doss-house bed, and when a tall, pale man approached her she looked forward to the chance of making a few coppers, with perhaps something left over for a couple of tots of gin.

The man drew her into the shadows. If she finally realized there was anything wrong, it was too late. The Ripper put a hand over her mouth and dexterously slit her throat. Then the crazed killer set about his savage butchery. A detective who examined the body said: 'Only a madman could have done this.' And a police surgeon said: 'I have never seen so horrible a case. She was ripped about in a manner that only a person skilled in the use of a knife could have achieved.'

Two extracts from *The Illustrated Police News*

It was just one week before the Ripper struck again. His prey was 'Dark Annie' Chapman, 47 years old and dying of tuberculosis when she was hacked down. When found in Hanbury Street by a porter from nearby Spitalfields Market, her few pitiful possessions had been neatly laid out beside her disembowelled corpse.

The next victim was Elizabeth 'Long Liz' Stride. On the evening of Sunday, 30 September, a police constable spotted a white-stockinged leg sticking out from a factory gate. Unlike earlier cases, Elizabeth Stride's body had not been mutilated – which led police to surmise that the Ripper had been disturbed in his grisly task. But, to satisfy his bloodlust, he soon found another victim. And it was during this killing that he left the only clue to his identity.

Just 15 minutes walk from the spot where Long Liz's body had been found was discovered the bloody remains of 40-year-old Catherine Eddowes. Her body was the most terribly mutilated so far – the Ripper had even cut off her ears. And from the corpse a trail of blood led to a message scrawled in chalk on a wall: 'The Jewes are not men to be blamed for nothing.' But this vital piece of evidence was never studied properly. Sir Charles Warren, head of the Metropolitan Police, perhaps fearing a violent backlash of hatred aimed at the Jews, ordered the slogan to be rubbed out and kept a secret.

Rumours now began to sweep like wildfire through the sleazy streets of London's East End. . . . . . The Ripper carried his instruments of death in a little black bag – and terror-crazed crowds chased any innocent passer-by carrying such a bag. He was a foreign seaman – and anyone with a foreign accent went in fear of opening his mouth for fear of being set upon. He was a Jewish butcher – and latent anti-Semitism already simmering because of the influx of Jewish immigrants fleeing the Russian and Polish pogroms began bubbling to the surface.

An even wilder theory, popular in the most squalid areas where there was no love lost between the inhabitants and the police, was that the killer was a policeman. How else would he be able to prowl the streets at night without creating suspicion?

The killer was in turn thought to be a mad doctor, a homicidal Russian sent by the Czar's secret police trying to cause unrest in London, a puritan obsessed with cleansing the East End of vice, and a crazed midwife with a hatred of prostitutes.

On 9 November, the Ripper struck again. Mary Kelly was unlike any of the other victims. She was younger – only 25 – blonde and she was attractive. The last person to see her alive was George Hutchinson whom she had asked for money to pay her rent. When he said he could not help she approached a slim, well-dressed man with a trim moustache and a deerstalker hat. She was never seen alive again.

Early next morning, Henry Bowers knocked impatiently at her door for his unpaid rent. Finally he went to the window of Mary's room and pushed aside the sacking curtain. The sickening sight within made him forget all about the rent and sent him running for the police. Later, he was to say: 'I shall be haunted by this for the rest of my life.'

With Mary Kelly's death, the Ripper's reign ended as suddenly and mysteriously as it began.

Two convicted murderers claimed to be the Ripper. One, who poisoned his mistress, said when arrested: 'You've got Jack the Ripper at last.' But there is little evidence to suggest that he was telling the truth. The second cried out as the trapdoor on the gallows opened 'I am Jack the . . .' But it was later proved that he was in America when the Ripper crimes were committed.

Some members of the police force were sure they knew who the Ripper was. In 1908, the assistant commissioner of police said flatly: 'In stating that he was a Polish Jew, I am merely stating a definitely established fact.'

But Inspector Robert Sagar, who played a leading part in the Ripper investigations and who died in 1924, said in his memoirs:

'We had good reason to suspect a man who lived in Butcher's Row, Aldgate. We watched him carefully. There was no doubt that this man was insane, and, after a time, his friends thought it advisable to have him removed to a private asylum. After he was removed, there were no more Ripper atrocities.'

Even Queen Victoria's eldest grandson has been named as a suspect. He was Prince Albert Victor, Duke of Clarence, who, if he had lived, would have become king when his father, Edward VII, died.

But perhaps the most likely solution is the one arrived at by author and broadcaster Daniel Farson. He pointed the finger of suspicion at Montagu John Druitt, a failed barrister who had both medical connections and a history of mental instability in his family.

Farson based his accusation on the notes of Sir Melville Macnaghten, who joined Scotland Yard in 1889 and became head of the Criminal Investigation Department in 1903. Macnaghten named three Ripper suspects – a Polish tradesman, who hated women and was probably Jewish, a homicidal Russian doctor, and Druitt.

The soundest basis for blaming Druitt for the murders is that a few weeks after the death of Mary Kelly, Druitt's body was found floating in the River Thames. After that, there were no further attacks by Jack the Ripper

Caught By A New Invention

DR CRIPPEN

No name in the annals of murder is more notorious than that of Dr Hawley Harvey Crippen. Yet Crippen killed only once and, but for three fatal errors, might have got away with it. He was a quiet, inoffensive little man, intelligent, courteous and kind with a touch of nobility about his actions. Perhaps that only served to enhance the horror of his ghastly crime.

Born in Coldwater, Michigan, in 1862, he studied long and hard for his medical degrees in Cleveland, Ohio, London and New York. He practised in several big American cities, and was already a widower when, at 31, he became assistant to a doctor in Brooklyn, New York. Among the patients there was a 17-year-old girl who called herself Cora Turner. Attractive and lively, she was the mistress of a stove manufacturer by whom she was pregnant. She miscarried.

Despite her circumstances, Crippen fell in love with her, and began trying to win her affections. He found that her real name was Kunigunde Mackamotzki, that her father was a Russian Pole and her mother a German, and that the girl wanted to be an opera singer. Crippen paid for singing lessons, though he must have known her dreams were bigger than her talent. They married in 1893.

In 1900, Crippen, now consultant physician to Munyon's, a company selling mail-order medicines, was transferred to England as manager of the head office in London. Later that year Cora joined him, and decided to switch her singing aspirations to music hall performances. She changed her name to Belle Elmore, and Crippen too took a new name. He dropped Hawley Harvey and called himself Peter.

Cora cultivated a large circle of Bohemian friends, dressing gaudily, bleaching her hair, and acquiring false blonde curls. She was extrovert and popular, particularly with men, and for a time her insignificant husband, small, slight and with an over-sized sandy moustache, was happy to observe her gay social whirl through his gold-rimmed spectacles, occasionally buying her furs or jewellery which he loved to present in front of her friends. The finery contrasted with the squalor of their home – neither had much inclination for household chores, and both were content to live in a dingy back kitchen, surrounded by dirty crockery, piles of clothes, and two cats that were never let out.

Any bliss that there had been in this marriage of apparent opposites vanished while Crippen was away on the company's business in Philadelphia. He returned after several months to be told by Cora that she had been seeing an American music hall singer called Bruce Miller, and that they were fond of each other.

In September, 1905, the Crippens moved to 39 Hilltop Crescent, off Camden Road, in north London. It was a leafy street of large Victorian houses, enjoying its heyday as a good address, and cost £52 50p (£52 10s) rent a year – a large slice out of Crippen's £3 a week salary. But the new home did nothing to heal the growing rift between husband and wife. Crippen was to recall: 'Although we apparently lived very happily together, there were very frequent occasions when she got into the most violent tempers and often threatened she would leave me, saying she had a man she would go to and she would end it all. She went in and out just as she liked and did as she liked. I was rather a lonely man and rather miserable.' Soon they were sleeping in separate rooms.

Cora threw herself into working for the Music Hall Ladies Guild, pretending to be a big star helping the less lucky members of her profession via the charity organization. She also took a succession of lovers, some of whom gave her gifts and money. Crippen found consolation too, in the form of Ethel Le Neve, a secretary at Munyon's offices in New Oxford Street. She could not have been less like Cora. Quiet, lady-like, she craved respectability, and the doctor had to use all his powers of persuasion before she at last agreed to accompany him to a discreet hotel room for the first time. Thoughts of her kept Crippen's spirits up as life at home became even worse. His wife began taking in 'paying guests', and when he returned from work, he was expected to clean their boots, bring in their coal, and help with cleaning.

By 1909, Crippen was also a paying partner in a dental clinic, and his expenses, with two women to support, were strained. That November, he lost his job as Munyon's manager, and was paid only a commission for sales. The following month, Cora gave their bank 12 months notice that she was withdrawing the £600 in their joint deposit account. She did not need her husband's consent for that. Cora had also learnt of Crippen's affair with Ethel, and told friends she would leave him if he did not give the girl up.

On 17 January, 1910, Crippen ordered five grains of hyoscine from a chemist's shop near his office. The drug, a powerful narcotic used as a depressant in cases of mental or physical suffering, was then virtually unknown in Britain, and the chemist had none in stock. He delivered it to the doctor two days later.

On 31 January, the Crippens entertained two retired music hall friends to dinner and whist. It was, according to one of the guests, Clara Martinetti, 'quite

Dr. Crippen's wife

a nice evening and Belle was very jolly.' Clara and her husband Paul left at 01.30. Then, according to Crippen's later statements, Cora exploded with fury, threatening to leave home next day because he, Crippen, had failed to accompany elderly Mr Martinetti to the upstairs lavatory.

Cora Crippen was never seen alive again. On 2 February her husband pawned some of her rings for £80 and had Ethel Le Neve deliver a letter to the Music Hall Ladies Guild, saying that Cora, by now treasurer, would miss their next few meetings. She had rushed to America because a relative was seriously ill. On 9 February Crippen pawned more of his wife's gems, receiving £115. And soon her friends noticed still more of her jewels and clothes – being worn by Ethel Le Neve. She even went to the Guild's benevolent ball with Crippen, and wore one of Cora's brooches.

Inquiring friends started to get increasingly bad news about Belle Elmore from her husband. First she was uncontactable, 'right up in the wilds of the mountains of California.' Then she was seriously ill with pneumonia. And on 24 March, Crippen sent Mrs Martinetti a telegram just before he and Ethel left for a five-day Easter trip to Dieppe. It read: 'Belle died yesterday at six o'clock.' Two days later, notice of the death appeared in *The Era* magazine. Her body, according to Crippen, had been cremated in America.

Meanwhile, Ethel Le Neve had moved into 39 Hilldrop Crescent as housekeeper, bringing a French maid with her. She told her own landlady that Crippen's wife had gone to America. Clearly she was not likely to come back – Ethel left half her wardrobe behind, expecting to use Cora's clothes.

Crippen had given his own landlord notice of quitting, but he grew more confident as the constant questions about Cora tailed off, and so extended his lease until September. Then, on 28 June, came the first of what would prove fatal blows. A couple called Nash arrived back from touring American theatres, and told Crippen they had heard nothing of Cora's death while in California. Unhappy with his answers, they spoke to a highly-placed friend of theirs in Scotland Yard.

In 1914 society beauty Henriette Caillaux, wife of the French finance minister, shot dead Gaston Calmette, editor of the newspaper *Le Figaro*. Henriette had become enraged over a campaign against her husband by Calmette, who in two months had written 130 vitriolic articles about the minister. The final straw came when *Le Figaro* printed a revealing love letter written to Henriette by Caillaux before their marriage. The trial jury obviously sympathized with her. Henriette, who claimed her gun had fired by mistake, was acquitted.

Brian Donald Hume, a 39-year-old racketeer and psychopath, knew that he could not be tried for murder twice. He had been arrested for chopping up his business partner, Stanley Setty, and throwing the bits from a plane over the English Channel. He was cleared of murder but admitted to being an accessory and collected a 12-year sentence.

In 1958 Hume sold his confession to a Sunday newspaper and went off to Switzerland where he began a new career as a bank robber. In Zurich he murdered a taxi driver and, while awaiting trial, penned a novel *The Dead Stay Dumb*. Sentenced to life imprisonment in 1976, Hume was sent back to Britain where he was declared insane and despatched to Broadmoor.

On Friday 8 July, Chief Inspector Walter Dew and a sergeant called at Crippen's office, and asked to know more about Cora. Did her husband have a death certificate? Crippen admitted that the story of her death was a lie, designed to protect her reputation. She had, in fact, run off to America to join another man, probably her old flame Bruce Miller. The doctor dictated a long statement over five hours, broken only for amicable lunch with the policemen at a nearby restaurant. He readily agreed to accompany the officers back to Hilldrop Crescent for a search of the house. Dew was mildly puzzled that Mrs Crippen had left behind all her finest dresses, but he left satisfied nothing was amiss.

Crippen did not know that, however. He panicked, and made what would prove to be his biggest mistake. Overnight, he persuaded Ethel to leave with him for a new life in America. Early next morning, he asked his dental assistant to clear up his business and domestic affairs, then sent him out to buy some boy's clothes. That afternoon Crippen and Ethel left for Europe.

On the following Monday, Chief Inspector Dew returned to ask Crippen to clarify a few minor points in the statement, and discovered what had happened. Alarmed, he instantly ordered a more thorough search of Crippen's house and garden. At the end of the second day, Dew himself discovered a loose stone in the floor of the coal-cellar. Under it he found rotting human flesh, skin and hair, but no bones.

A team of top pathologists from St Mary's hospital, Paddington, painstakingly examined the remains, and decided they were of a plump female who bleached her hair. Part of the skin came from the lower abdomen, and included an old surgical scar in a position where Mrs Crippen was known to have one. The remains also contained huge traces of hyoscine, which kills within 12 hours if taken in excess. On 16 July, warrants for the arrest of Crippen and Ethel were issued. They were wanted for murder and mutilation.

Crippen had made two errors. He had carved out the bones of the body, and presumably burned them in his kitchen stove. But he had treated the fleshy remains with wet quicklime, a corrosive substance only effective when dry. And he had wrapped them before burial in a pyjama jacket with the label 'Shirtmakers, Jones Brothers, Holloway.' All might still have been well but for his third error, fleeing.

The discovery of the body aroused horrified indignation in the British press, but the two runaways, staying in Rotterdam and Brussels, did not realize the storm had broken. On 20 July, they left Antwerp in the liner *SS Montrose*, bound for Quebec. Crippen had shaved off his moustache and discarded his glasses, and was posing as John Philo Robinson, while Ethel, dressed in the boy's clothes Crippen's assistant had bought, pretended to be his 16-year-old son, John. But if they thought they were safe, they were wrong.

The ship's commander, Captain Kendall, had read all about the gruesome findings at Hilldrop Crescent, and was aware that the *Daily Mail* had offered £100 for information about the couple the police were hunting. Kendall noticed an inordinate amount of hand-touching between Mr Robinson and his son. The boy's suit fitted badly, and he seemed almost lady-like when eating meals, when his father would crack nuts for him or offer him half his salad.

Kendall surreptitiously collected up all the English-language papers on board so as not to alarm the couple. He checked Crippen's lack of reaction when he called him Robinson, and invited the couple to dine at his table. After two days at sea, he sent a message to the ship's owners over the newly-installed wireless telegraph, reporting his suspicions. On 23 July, Chief Inspector Dew and his sergeant set sail from Liverpool in the *Laurentic*, a faster trans-atlantic liner, which would overtake the *Montrose* just before it reached Quebec.

Then followed eight bizarre days. Crippen sat on deck, admiring the 'wonderful invention' of the wireless telegraph, not realizing that he was the subject of the crackling messages. Kendall's daily reports were avidly printed by the *Daily Mail*, whose readers relished every word as the net closed in on the unsuspecting doctor.

It was 08.30 on 31 July when Dew, accompanied by a Canadian policeman, boarded the *Montrose* disguised as a pilot. The ship was in the St Lawrence, and only 16 hours from Quebec. After reporting to Captain Kendall, Dew walked down to the deck and approached his suspect. 'Good morning, Dr Crippen,' he said. 'I am Chief Inspector Dew,' Crippen said only: 'Good morning, Mr Dew.' Ethel, reading in her cabin, screamed, then fainted, when a similar introduction was made. Crippen said later: 'I am not sorry, the anxiety has been too much. It is only fair to say that she knows nothing about it. I never told her anything.' He described Ethel as 'my only comfort for these past three years.'

Dr. Hawley Harvey Crippen, with inset of Ethel,
dressed as a boy

Ivan the Terrible claimed to have seduced 1,000 virgins, killed
1,000 of his own illegitimate offspring, poisoned three of his eight
wives, together with their families, and speared to death his own
son. Having done away with so many of his own children, he died
of syphillis in 1584 leaving only one direct heir, an imbecile called
Feodor.

Extradition formalities took less than three weeks, and on 20 August, Dew set
sail for England with his celebrated prisoners aboard the liner *SS Megantic*.
Dew, who was travelling as Mr Doyle, kept Crippen, now known as Mr Nield,
apart from Ethel, though on one evening he did allow the two to gaze silently at
each other from their cabin doors, after a request from Crippen. Huge, angry
crowds greeted the two at every stage of their rail journey from Liverpool to
London. And public feeling was still at fever pitch when their trials began.
Crippen was charged with murder, Ethel with being an accessory, and wisely
they elected to be tried separately.

The doctor refused to plead guilty, even though he knew he had no credible
defence. Seven days before his hearing began, at the Old Bailey on 10 October,
the remains found at Hilldrop Crescent were buried at Finchley as those of Cora
Crippen. Yet her husband claimed in court that they could have been there
when he bought the house in 1905. That argument fell when a buyer for Jones
Brothers swore that the pyjama material in which the remains were wrapped
was not available until 1908. Two suits in it had been delivered to Crippen in
January, 1909.

Crippen had no answer to questions about why he had made no effort to
search for his wife after she vanished on 1 February, why no-one had seen her
leave the house, why he had then pawned her possessions or given them to
Ethel. Bruce Miller, now married and an estate agent in Chicago, said he last
saw Cora in 1904, and denied ever having an affair with her.

On the fifth day of the trial, the jury found Crippen guilty after a 27-minute
retirement, and Lord Chief Justice Alverstone, who had been scrupulously fair
throughout the proceedings, sentenced him to death. Crippen, who had stood
up remarkably well to cross-examination, declared: 'I still protest my
innocence.'

A curious story, that Crippen had rejected a suggested defence because it
would compromise Ethel, began circulating. The line, allegedly suggested by
eminent barrister Edward Marshall Hall, was that the doctor had given his
nymphomaniac wife hyoscine to calm her demands on him, because he was also
making love to Ethel, and that Cora had died through an accidental overdose.
Crippen was wise to reject the story, if he did so. For if death was accidental,

why go to so much trouble to chop up the body, remove the bones, and to hide the flesh?

All along, he had been anxious to clear Ethel Le Neve's name, and on 25 October the Old Bailey did so after a one-day trial dominated by a brilliant speech by her defence lawyer, F. E. Smith, later Lord Birkenhead. He asked the jury if they could really believe that Crippen would take such care to hide all the traces of the murder, then risk the 'aversion, revulsion and disgust' of a young, nervous woman by telling her: 'This is how I treated the woman who last shared my home, and I invite you to come and share it with me now.' Ethel was found not guilty and discharged.

But she did not desert her lover, and as he waited for execution, he thought only of her, continually proclaiming her innocence, kissing her photograph, and writing touching love letters to her. He also wrote in a statement: 'As I face enternity, I say that Ethel Le Neve has loved me as few women love men . . . surely such love as hers for me will be rewarded.'

The man whose name has become synonymous with murder was hanged in Pentonville Prison on 23 November, 1910, still protesting that he had murdered no-one. His last request was that Ethel's letters and photograph be buried with him. They were. A curious kind of sympathy had grown for the quiet, considerate little man, both among prison staff and those who came into contact with him. F. E. Smith called him 'a brave man and a true lover.' And there were many who agreed with Max Beerbohm Tree's verdict on the day of execution: 'Poor old Crippen.'

Ethel Le Neve slipped quickly into obscurity. Some say she emigrated to Australia, and died there in 1950, others that she went to Canada or America. Another report was that, for 45 years, she ran a tea-room near Bournemouth under an assumed name. And there have been rumours that she wrote her version of the Crippen affair, to be published after her death. But all the theories could be as wide of the mark as the wild legends that have turned her mild-mannered lover into the most monstrous murderer the world has even seen.

The Marquis de Sade

When police raided the house of 'Moors Murderers' Ian Brady and Myra Hindley in 1965, they found, along with the remains of one of their victims, the collected works of the Marquis de Sade. De Sade and Adolf Hitler's *Mein Kampf* were read as 'Bibles' in the killers' household. Although Hitler's philosophy is political and de Sade's sexual, both are in their own way equally dangerous. Both are able to snare the weak-minded. Both can turn mild men and women into monsters.

De Sade's distorted view of life, morality and sexual fulfilment is flaunted in books like *Justine, Juliette, Philosophy In The Bedroom* and *120 Days Of Sodom*. Stories of sexual deviation are told with relish. The extent of the perversions are limited only by de Sade's imagination – and that is considerable.

The man who gave his name to sadism was born Donatien Alphonse François De Sade on 2 June, 1740 in pre-Revolutionary Paris, which was a hotbed of vice and corruption. Related to the royal house of Condé, his father was a court diplomat and his mother a lady-in-waiting to the Princesse de Condé. Educated by his uncle, the Abbé de Sade of Ebreuil, he grew up good-looking, wealthy and spoilt. By the age of 18 he had experimented in every form of sexual adventure he could devise. But it was not enough. His over-fertile imagination began to invent new and terrible perversions to fuel his fantasies. The principal tenet of his philosophy was that the finest form of sexual pleasure is achieved through cruelty and pain.

De Sade served in the army during the Seven Years' War, leaving in 1763 and marrying the daughter of a judge. But within a month he was having an affair with an actress known as La Beauvoisin and was inviting prostitutes into the marital home at Arceuil. There he put his sadistic theories into practice with numerous victims, many of them strangely willing to subject themselves to his cruel whims. But some complained about their sexual abuse and de Sade was ordered to be detained in jail at Vincennes.

Within weeks he was freed and, despite having fathered two sons and a daughter by his long-suffering wife, he returned to his old ways. This time, his activities created a national scandal. In 1768 he hired a Paris prostitute called Rose Keller whom he locked up and tortured to such a degree that she complained to the authorities. De Sade was sent to jail in Lyons.

Possibly because of his family connections, he again secured an early release and in 1772 moved to Marseilles where in the busy port his pockmarked valet,

Latour, found for him a ready supply of prostitutes. But, as ever, his sensual experimentation was his undoing. De Sade fed the girls sweetmeats laced with various supposed aphrodisiacs. The girls were sick, believed they had been poisoned and complained to the police. The marquis and Latour fled.

At Aix, master and servant were sentenced to death in their absence and were executed 'in effigy'. The fugitives were finally captured and thrown into the fortress of Miolans. But de Sade still seemed to have the ability to get out of prison as easily he had got himself in. He escaped and hid away with his wife at their château. By now she too was debauched, both were in debt and further trouble with the authorities was inevitable. His wife became an enthusiastic partner in his perversions and when a new scandal broke involving young boys, both husband and wife fled.

The Marquise de Sade sought refuge in a convent while her husband bolted to Italy with his latest mistress – his wife's own sister, the Canoness de Launay. A year later, in 1777, they foolishly risked returning to France and de Sade was arrested in Paris. Thrown into the dungeons at Vincennes and then into the notorious Bastille, he suffered at the hands of harsh warders and fellow prisoners. The cruelty he had always been ready to mete out to others was now his lot.

His enforced isolation did, however, allow him to develop his blasphemous philosophy through his writing. In de Sade's eyes, there was no god but nature – and nature was not only the creator of beauty but also of destruction, through earthquake, flood, fire and tempest. Man's destiny, he believed, ran parallel with nature, and man's destructive impulses had to be obeyed in the same way as his more gentle ones were. So a truly 'complete' man should fulfil himself by becoming a monster.

De Sade propounded such lofty thinking as a camouflage for his real designs which are clear to see in books like his elegantly titled *120 Days Of Sodom* which was written in the Bastille on a single roll of paper about 12 metres (39 ft) long.

Ex-monk Joseph Vacher was committed to an asylum in 1893 and was released, supposedly cured, a year later at the age of 25. A series of mutilation murders followed across a wide area of south-east France. Vacher, who was leading the life of a tramp, killed and disembowelled eleven victims, five of them young boys. The 'French Ripper' was arrested in 1897 for an assault on a woman and was jailed for three months. In prison, he wrote to the authorities admitting all his crimes and asking to be sent back to the asylum. Judges accepted his confessions but not his plea to be treated as insane; he was executed in 1898.

The Marquis de Sade (based on contemporary descriptions)

He would probably have spent the rest of his days in prison but for a strange quirk of fate. In the chaos of the French Revolution – the Bastille itself was stormed on 14 July, 1789 – De Sade was freed.

Despite his aristocratic background, he became 'Citizen Sade', head of one of Paris's ruling revolutionary committees. As such, he managed to save his father-in-law from the guillotine – but only just escaped it himself. Strange as it may seem, 'Citizen Sade' began to deplore the unbridled brutality of France's new rulers and was accused of being a 'moderate'. He was sentenced to be guillotined but was overlooked in the prison line-up on his day of execution. The following day, Robespierre, hard-line leader of the revolutionary Convention, was overthrown and de Sade was safe once more.

In desperate poverty, he set up home with a young, widowed actress, Marie-Constance Quesnet, and wrote, among other books, *Justine* and *Juliette*. But it was these works that finally ended his freedom for ever. In 1801, on the basis of his writings, he was judged insane and locked up in Charenton asylum. Napoleon Bonaparte himself ordered that he never be released.

Visited by his actress mistress, he continued writing books and plays, which were performed by the asylum inmates. On 2 December, 1814 he died. His son visited Charenton, collected 13 years of his work and burned the lot.

A will was discovered. Written nine years previously, it instructed that his body was to be buried in the midst of a particular thicket on his old estate and the grave sown with acorns so that over the years it would be obliterated. He wrote: 'The traces of my grave must disappear from the face of the earth as I flatter myself that my memory will be effaced from the minds of men'. His wishes were ignored and de Sade the atheist was given a Christian burial, a stone cross being erected above his grave. Shortly afterwards the grave was broken into and the body stolen. The skull later came into the possession of a leading phrenologist who read de Sade's bumps and declared that he was a man of 'tender character and love of children'.

The contribution de Sade left to the world of literature is slight – but his contribution to criminality is considerable. The sickening philosophies he propounded have taken seed in the minds of the bad and the mad, the weak and the willing, murderers and mutilators from the beginning of the nineteenth century to the present day. Because he could so well express the fantasies of his own evil mind, others who followed him have been encouraged to act out their own. Indirectly, he may have been responsible for more murders than any other individual in peacetime history. The name of the Marquis de Sade is synonymous with evil.

The 'Monster in Human Shape'

MARY ANN COTTON

Welfare worker Thomas Riley walked briskly through the early morning summer sunshine. It was 06.00 and he was on his way to another day's duties at the village workhouse in West Auckland. Times were hard for the people of County Durham, and Riley was kept busy trying to care for those who could not cope. As he turned into Front Street, he recalled the widow at No 13. She had come to him only six days earlier, asking if he had room in the workhouse for her seven-year-old stepson, Charles Edward. 'It is hard to keep him when he is not my own, and he is stopping me from taking in a respectable lodger,' she said. Riley joked about the identity of the lodger. Was it the excise officer village gossips said she wanted to marry? 'It may be so,' the woman had replied, 'but the boy is in the way.'

Now, as he walked to work, Riley noticed the widow in the doorway of her three-room stone cottage. She was clearly upset, and he crossed the road to ask why. He could not believe his ears at what she told him: 'My boy is dead.'

Riley went straight to the police and the local doctor. What he told them was the first step in an investigation that was to brand the widow, Mary Ann Cotton, the worst mass murderer Britain had ever seen.

Riley was suspicious about the death because the lad had seemed in perfect health when he saw him six days earlier. Dr Kilburn was also surprised to hear of the tragedy. He and his assistant Dr Chambers had seen the boy five times that week for what they thought were symptoms of gastro-enteritis, but they never thought the illness could be fatal. Dr Kilburn decided to withhold a death certificate and asked for permission to carry out a post-mortem examination. The coroner agreed to the request, and arranged an inquest for the following afternoon, Saturday, 13 July, 1872.

The pressures of their practice meant the two doctors could not start their post-mortem until an hour before the hearing. After a cursory examination, Dr Kilburn told the jury in the Rose and Crown Inn, next to Cotton's house: 'I have found nothing to suggest poisoning. Death could have been from natural causes, possibly gastro-enteritis.' The jury returned a verdict of natural death, and Charles Edward was buried in a pauper's grave.

But Dr Kilburn had taken the precaution of preserving the contents of the boy's stomach in a bottle. On the following Wednesday he at last had time to put them to proper chemical tests. He went straight back to the police with the results. There were distinct traces of arsenic. Next morning, widow Cotton was arrested and charged with murder. The boy's body was dug up and sent to Leeds School of Medicine, where Dr Thomas Scattergood, lecturer in forensic medicine and toxicology, discovered more arsenic, in the bowels, liver, lungs, heart and kidneys.

Meanwhile, Thomas Riley was pointing out to the authorities that the death of Charles Edward was not the first in the family. In fact, there had been four in the two years since Mary Ann Cotton, a former nurse, had arrived in West Auckland. Her fourth husband, coal miner Frederick Cotton, died from 'gastric fever' on 19 September, 1871, two days after their first wedding anniversary. He was 39. Then, between 10 March and 1 April, 1872 10-year-old Frederick, Cotton's son by a previous marriage, Robert, Mary Ann's 14-month-old son, and Mary Ann's former lover, Joseph Nattrass, who had moved in with her again, all died. Gastric fever was again the cause of death on their certificates, except for the baby, who died from 'teething convulsions.'

Those three bodies were exhumed while Mary Ann waited for her trial in Durham Jail, and Dr Scattergood found traces of arsenic in all of them. Newspapers began looking more closely at the life of the miner's daughter from the Durham pit village of Low Moorsley. They unearthed a horrifying dossier of an apparently kind, good-natured and devout Methodist who seemed to spread death wherever she went.

In 1852, aged 20, she had married a labourer called William Mowbray, and moved to Devon. She had five children there, but four died. The couple returned to the north-east, moving from house to house in the Sunderland area, while Mary Ann worked at the town's infirmary. They had three more children. All died. Then Mowbray died. Mary Ann married again. Her husband, an engineer called George Wood, died in October 1866, 14 months after the wedding.

A month later, Mary Ann moved in as housekeeper to widower James Robinson and his three children. She soon became pregnant and married Robinson. But within weeks of her arrival in the household, Robinson's 10-month-old son John was dead. On 21 April, 1867, Robinson's son James, six, went to his grave. Five days later, his sister Elizabeth, eight, followed him. And on 2 May, nine-year-old Isabella, the only survivor of Mary Ann's marriage to Mowbray, lost her life.

Mary Ann had two daughters by Robinson. The first died within days of birth. The second was given away to a friend when the marriage broke up. Robinson survived, possibly because he resisted his wife's pleas to take out insurance on his life. But others who knew Mary Ann were not so lucky. She went to visit her mother because she feared she 'might be about to die'. No-one

Morbid American cannibal Albert Fish enjoyed a variety of dishes. The quiet painter and decorator confessed to having slaughtered six children – although the true total may have been 15. Most of the tender little bodies he swooped on were carefully cut up and stewed with vegetables. In the electric chair at Sing Sing in 1936, Fish seemed quite excited about being roasted himself – and even helped the executioner fix the electrodes.

else was worried about the apparently sprightly 54-year-old, but within nine days she was dead. Mary Ann moved on, laden with clothes and bed linen.

She met and became friends with Margaret Cotton, and was introduced to her brother Frederick. Mary Ann quickly became pregnant, and married her new lover bigamously – her third husband, Robinson, was still alive. The wedding was slightly marred by the unexpected death of Margaret, whose £60 bank account went to the newly-weds. In all, 21 people close to Mary Ann lost their lives in less than 20 years. She had given birth to 11 children, yet only one survived – the girl she gave away. Small wonder, then, that on the morning of her trial, a local newspaper, unfettered by today's laws of libel and contempt, ran the headline: 'The Great Poisoning Case At West Auckland – Horrible Revelations'. But when she stepped into the courtroom at Durham Assizes shortly before 10.00 on 5 March, 1873, she was charged only with one killing, that of her stepson, Charles Edward.

The prosecution, led by Sir Charles Russell, later to become Lord Chief Justice, alleged the 40-year-old widow had poisoned the boy because there was a Prudential Insurance policy on his life worth £8, and because he was an impediment to her marraige to her excise officer lover, a man called Quick-Manning, by whom she was already pregnant. 'She was badly off and Charles Edward was a tie and burden to her,' said Sir Charles.

Mary Ann Dodds, a former neighbour of the accused, told the court she had bought a mixture of arsenic and soft soap from one of the village's chemist's shops in May 1872, two months before the boy's death. 'The mixture was needed to remove bugs from a bed in Mary Ann's home,' she said. 'I rubbed most of it into the joints of the bed and the iron crosspieces underneath.'

Chemist John Townend said the mixture would have contained about an ounce of arsenic – about 480 grains. Three grains were enough to kill an adult. He also thought it significant that his shop was not the closest chemist's to widow Cotton's home.

Thomas Riley gave his evidence about Mary Ann's eagerness to get the boy off her hands, and Dr Kilburn explained the medical steps he had taken. It was then that controversy entered the trial. The prosecution wanted to introduce evidence of earlier deaths in the family. Defence lawyer Thomas Campbell Foster, appointed only two days before the trial because Cotton could not afford her own legal representation, protested that his client was charged with only one death, which he maintained was an accident caused by arsenic impregnation of some green floral wallpaper. To discuss the earlier deaths would prejudice a fair trial, he said.

But Judge Sir Thomas Archibald ruled against him, citing legal precedent. From that moment on, the verdict was a foregone conclusion. The defence introduced no witnesses, and at 18.50 on the third day of the trial, the jury returned after only an hour's deliberations to pronounce Mary Ann Cotton guilty of murder.

The judge donned his black cap to sentence her to death, saying: 'You seem to have given way to that most awful of all delusions, which sometimes takes possession of persons wanting in proper moral and religious sense, that you could carry out your wicked designs without detection. But while murder by poison is the most detestable of all crimes, and one at which human nature shudders, it is one the nature of which, in the order of God's providence, always leaves behind it complete and incontestable traces of guilt. Poisoning, as it were, in the very act of crime writes an indelible record of guilt.'

They were fine words, but not strictly true. The state of medical knowledge in the 1870s was not as sophisticated as it is today. In an unsanitary age, gastric fever was a common killer, and overworked doctors could not examine every corpse without strong reasons. Though the final toll of deaths in Mary Ann's circle was high, she avoided suspicion by moving house frequently, and always calling in local doctors when her victims began complaining of stomach pains. The fact that she had once been a nurse, and was well known for caring for sick neighbours, also made people trust her.

No-one will ever know how many of the 21 unlucky people around her were poisoned either for insurance money, possessions, or because they stood in the way of a new marriage. Most people put the number of murders at 14 or 15. But despite the horror at what the *Newcastle Journal* newspaper described as 'a monster in human shape', many people had misgivings about her death sentence. There were doubts about hanging a woman, doubts about the way

---

Fugitive Leonard T. Fristoe was on the run from the law for 46 years. Jailed for life in 1920 for killing two deputy sheriffs, he served only three years of his sentence before escaping. His luck ran out when, at the ripe old age of 77, he was recaptured at Compton, California, after being turned in by his own son.

her defence in court had been organized, doubts about whether evidence of earlier deaths should have been allowed, doubts about the lack of any witnesses for the defence.

The *Newcastle Journal* admitted:

'Perhaps the most astounding thought of all is that a woman could act thus without becoming horrible and repulsive. Mary Ann Cotton, on the contrary, seems to have possessed the faculty of getting a new husband whenever she wanted one. To her other children and her lodger, even when she was deliberately poisoning them, she is said to have maintained a rather kindly manner.' The paper felt instinctively that the earth should be rid of her, but added: 'Pity cannot be withheld, though it must be mingled with horror.'

Mary Ann spent her last few days in jail trying to win support for a petition for a reprieve. She gave birth to Quick-Manning's daughter, Margaret, and arranged for her to go to a married couple who could not have children. Five days before her execution, the baby was forcibly taken from her. On 24 March, 1873, still maintaining her innocence, she went to the scaffold at Durham. It was three minutes before the convulsions of her body stopped.

Within eight days, a stage play, *The Life and Death of Mary Ann Cotton*, was being performed in theatres, labelled 'a great moral drama'. Mothers threatened recalcitrant children with the prospect of a visit from the West Auckland widow, and youngsters made up a skipping rhyme which began: 'Mary Ann Cotton, she's dead and rotten.' But she remains today one of the most enigmatic figures in the gallery of killers – a simple-minded mass murderer who evoked revulsion and sympathy in equal measures.

Herman Mudgett and the Chicago 'Torture Castle'

I f there were a league table of mass killers, the name of Herman Webster Mudgett would be high on the list. He is reckoned to have murdered at least 200 victims – mainly young ladies – for the sheer pleasure of cutting up their bodies.

Mudgett researched his dreadful pastime at America's Ann Arbor medical school. An expert in acid burns, he boosted his student allowance by body snatching. He would steal corpses, render them unrecognizable, then claim on life insurance policies he had previously taken out under fictitious names. He got away with several of these frauds before a nightwatchman caught him removing a female corpse and the errant student fled.

Mudgett next turned up in Chicago where, under the alias 'Dr H. H. Holmes', he ran a respectable pharmacy without a hint of scandal. So successful was he that in 1890 he bought a vacant lot and set about building a grand house.

But this was no ordinary home. It contained a maze of secret passages, trap doors, chutes, dungeons and shafts. Suspicion was averted during the construction of what later became known as the 'Torture Castle' by the expedient of hiring a different builder for each small section of the house.

The house was finished in time for the great Chicago Exposition of 1893 when the city filled with visitors, many of whom were to be Mudgett's prey. He lured girls and young ladies to his 'castle' where he attempted to seduce them before drugging them. They were then popped into one of the empty shafts that ran through the building. The hapless girls would come round only to find themselves trapped behind a glass panel in an airtight death chamber into which would be pumped lethal gas.

The bodies would be sent down a chute to the basement which contained vast vats of acid and lime and, in the centre of the room, a dissecting table. Here Mudgett would cut up the corpses, removing particular organs which took his fancy and disposing of the rest in the vats.

Mudgett later admitted to having murdered 200 girls during the Chicago Exposition alone, and the orgy of bloodletting might have continued for much longer but for the phoney doctor's greed. He had murdered two visiting Texan sisters and, rather than quietly dispose of their remains, he set fire to the house in an attempt to gain the insurance money and make good his escape from Chicago.

The insurance company refused to pay and the police began an investigation into the blaze. Strangely, the police work was not pursued vigorously enough to produce any evidence of Mudgett's bloody activities – but the killer did not know this, and he fled.

This time he went south to Texas, where he traced relatives of the sisters he had so clumsily murdered. Having ingratiated himself with them, he tried to swindle them out of a $60,000 fortune. They were suspicious so Mudgett again took to the road, this time on a stolen horse. Police caught up with him in Missouri, where, using the name H. M. Howard, he was charged with a further fraud attempt. With the help of a crooked lawyer, he was granted bail – and promptly absconded.

Mudgett next turned up in Philadelphia where an associate in crime had been operating insurance frauds at the mass killer's behest. In an apparent accident one day in 1894, this co-conspirator blew himself up. In fact, he had been murdered by Mudgett who ran off to Toronto with his victim's wife and their three children. Their young bodies were later found in the basements of two rented houses.

It was not any of his many murders that finally brought Mudgett to justice but the jumping of bail in Missouri and the theft of a horse, a capital offence in Texas at that time. Detectives traced Mudgett through his aged mother who was happy to give them the whereabouts of the son of whom she was so proud.

The mass killer was arrested with his mistress in Boston and was charged with horse stealing and fraud. It was only at this stage that police searched the burned-out Chicago Torture Castle. They pieced together the remains of 200 corpses. Mudgett confessed to the murders of all of them. He was hanged on 7 May, 1896.

The Heartless Husband

JOHANN HOCH

Johann Otto Hoch had never believed in very long courtships or in long marriages. He had at least 24 wives in 15 years – and he brutally murdered all of them. The diabolical 'Bluebeard' even proposed to his sister-in-law over the deathbed of his wife, who was dying from a massive dose of arsenic. She accepted. 'Life is for the living.' Hoch told her. 'The dead are for the dead.'

Throughout Hoch's bizarre years of marriage and murder in the United States between 1892 and 1905, a tough Chicago cop named George Shippy stalked him relentlessly. Shippy knew Hoch was cutting a bloody trail of murder but was never able to prove it.

Born Johann Schmidt in 1862, Hoch had emigrated from Germany at 25 leaving his wife and three children behind. A big, jovial man with a sweeping handlebar moustache, he found work in the country as an itinerant bartender.

From 1887 to 1895 it was anybody's guess how many women he murdered. In April 1895 he found a woman in a saloon in Wheeling, West Virginia. Using the name Jacob Huff, he married her and then killed her three months later.

As with his other murders, the doctor thought the woman died of kidney disease for which there was no cure. But the lady's pastor knew better and Hoch fled from the town after converting his wife's estate to cash. Leaving his clothes and a suicide note behind, he walked naked into the River Ohio. A hundred yards up he had anchored a boat with new clothing in it. He clambered aboard and rowed to the Ohio side.

In 1898, using the name Martin Dotz, the murderer ran foul of Inspector George Shippy. The killer was arrested in Chicago on a minor swindling charge. But the Wheeling preacher saw a newspaper photo, recognized Jacob Huff and contacted Shippy.

Hoch breezed through a year in the Cook County jail while Shippy backtracked the man's elusive trail and investigated dozens of unsolved cases of murdered women. The determined cop went to Wheeling and had the body of Hoch's ex-wife exhumed, only to find that Hoch had removed many of the woman's vital organs.

After serving his sentence, Hoch married and murdered another 15 women between 1900 and 1905. His weapon was always arsenic, which was easily available in any drugstore. The victims were always lonely but wealthy women overwhelmed by Hoch's animal charm. And slipshod doctors were always too quick with the wrong diagnoses.

By now Hoch was acting like a man possessed. He slipped like a ghost from city to city, murdering in record time. Frequently he married and murdered in less than a week.

In 1904 he buried his last victim, Marie Walcker, and promptly married her sister. He fled with his new wife's savings account and the enraged woman contacted Shippy. Her sister's body was exhumed and this time the medical examiner found enough arsenic to kill a dozen women.

Shippy then made his long-awaited arrest.

Throughout the trial Hoch maintained an air of boyish innocence. Even after the guilty verdict, Hoch was confident he would never swing from the gallows.

As guards led him to the scaffold on 23 February, 1906, the killer joked and said: 'You see, boys, I don't look like a monster, now do I?' Nobody answered the question as Hoch's massive hulk fell through the trapdoor.

The Lonely Hearts Killers
RAYMOND FERNANDEZ AND MARTHA BECK

Raymond Fernandez and Martha Beck were two social misfits whose crimes outraged the society that had scorned them. Both had at one stage led almost normal, useful lives, but fate had played cruel tricks on them. After they teamed up in 1947, it was they who played the cruel tricks. And they paid for them with their lives.

Fernandez, born in Hawaii of Spanish parents, moved to Spain in the 1930s and married a Spanish woman. After serving in Franco's forces during the Civil War, and gaining the reputation of a war hero, he worked with distinction for British intelligence in the Gibraltar docks. In 1945, he sailed for America, working his passage on an oil tanker. During the voyage, a hatch cover fell on his head. He recovered in hospital at Curaçao, but his personality had changed radically. He became a cunning, ruthless swindler, convinced that he had supernatural powers over women, and determined to use them to the utmost.

He began advertizing in lonely hearts magazines, and fleecing the gullible people who answered his pleas. By 1947 he had claimed more than 100 victims. He was just back from Spain, where his latest dupe had died mysteriously during their holiday, when he decided to follow up an intriguing letter from a woman in Florida with a personal visit.

Martha Beck's name had been forwarded to the lonely hearts club as a joke by one of her friends. Martha was an outsize woman of 280lb whose bulk and sexuality constantly made her a figure of fun to others. At 13 she had been raped by her own brother, who continued the incestuous relationship until she complained to her mother. For reasons which Martha never understood, she was blamed for the sordid affair, and forced to live a cloistered existence which deprived her of normal relationships as a teenager.

She became a nurse, moving to California and an army hospital. But the scandals of her nymphomaniac sex life forced her to return east, where she became superintendent of a home for crippled children at Pensacola, Florida. There she met Fernandez, who was using his business name, Charles Martin.

A torrid affair quickly began, Fernandez introducing Martha to new perversions which satisfied her sexually for the first time in her life. She gave up her job and left behind her two children, one illegitimate, the other the product

Raymond Fernandez (second from left) and Martha Beck examined at court in Michigan

of a disastrous marriage, to follow Fernandez. When he explained his line of business, she agreed to become his accomplice, posing as his sister. But she loved him too much to allow him a free hand. He could woo and wed women – but she would not allow him to consummate the marriages.

Such jealousy hampered the romantic con-man. The first joint effort resulted in the victim claiming back her car and $500, and refusing to sign over her insurance policies. The ill-starred lovers moved on to Cook County, Illinois, and Fernandez married Myrtle Young in August 1948. But again there were violent rows when the bride expected to sleep alone with her husband, and Martha refused to allow it. Myrtle was given an overdose of barbiturates, and put on a bus to Little Rock, Arkansas. She collapsed and died there. Fernandez and Beck made $4,000 and gained a car.

In Albany, New York, that December, Fernandez charmed a naive widow, Janet Fay, 66, into signing over all her assets and her $6,000 insurance policy to him. Then she was strangled and battered to death with a hammer. The body was stuffed into a trunk, and the couple took it with them to New York City, where they rented a house in Queens, and buried the makeshift coffin under cement in the cellar.

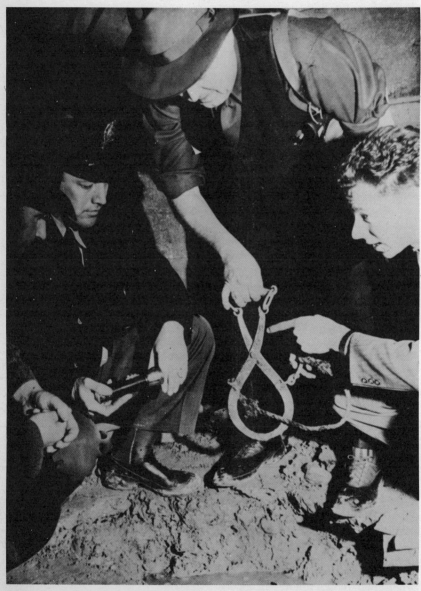

Bloodstained tongs discovered in the cellar where Mrs Downing and daughter were found

The following year Fernandez and Beck were in Grand Rapids, Michigan, trying to fleece a 28-year-old widow called Delphine Downing. Once again, Martha reacted angrily when Fernandez started sleeping with her. Then Delphine saw her husband without his toupe, and threatened to leave him. Fernandez and Beck were out at the cinema, found the two bodies, and arrested Rainelle. Both bodies were cemented into the cellar floor, and curious neighbours were told that Delphine and her daughter were away on holiday.

But suspicious relatives called the police. They searched the house while Fernandez and beck were out at the cinema, found the two bodies, and arrested the couple on their return. A curious tug-of-war between two states now began. Michigan did not have the death penalty, but New York did. The murder of Janet Fay had been discovered, and New York asked for the couple to be sent there for trial. Public fury at the couple's evil exploits played some part in New York getting its way.

Fernandez and Beck were charged with three murders, and suspected of 17 more, including that of Myrtle Young. The trial began in July 1949, and lasted 44 days. Press coverage of the proceedings was unprecendented in its hatred and intolerance, and every intimate detail of the sordid sex life of the couple created sensational headlines. Crowds flocked to the courtroom to catch a glimpse of the 'monster' and his 'overweight ogress'.

The verdict was never in doubt. Fernandez and Beck were found guilty of first-degree murder, and sentenced to death on 29 August. Their appeals were dismissed and on 8 March, 1951, they went to the electric chair at Sing-Sing Prison.

Two hours before the execution, Fernandez sent Martha a message of love. She said: 'Now that I know Raymond loves me, I can go to my death bursting with joy.' But there was nothing joyful about the death. Newspapers gleefully reported the struggle to fit her huge bulk into the chair, and the·prolonged writhing as the electric shocks struggled to have an impact through her flabby body. Such was public distaste for the Lonely Hearts Killers that more people laughed at that last ordeal than felt pity for its victim.

The Vampire Killer

JOHN HAIGH

Donald McSwann entered a den of death when he followed his friend John Haigh into his basement workshop. McSwann operated a pinball arcade in London where Haigh sometimes worked as a mechanic. Haigh boasted about his workshop and it was, indeed, a basement to be proud of. There was equipment for every kind of craftsman . . . for the carpenter, the welder, the sheet metal worker – and the murderer.

McSwann stared at the 40-gallon vat of sulphuric acid in one corner. His curiosity drove him to ask about the need for such a strange array of equipment. His questions were never answered. Crouching behind him, Haigh viciously swung a hammer in a deadly arc . . . and he had slaughtered his first victim.

According to Haigh, when he later confessed to the crime, he drank some of McSwann's blood. Then he spent the night methodically dismembering his body and feeding it into the vat. The sulphuric acid bubbled and smoked, occasionally forcing him to escape outdoors for a breath of fresh air. By the next afternoon, McSwann's remains had dissolved into a mass of sludge. Haigh disposed of it, bucket by bucket, sloshing the ghastly residue into a basement manhole connected to the sewer system.

It was September 1944 and no one thought anything of McSwann's disappearance. Haigh's murder-for-profit scheme was succeeding to perfection.

He assured McSwann's aging parents that their son was hiding out in Scotland until the end of the war. Haigh even went to Scotland once a week to post a letter to them signing McSwann's name.

In between the trips, he ran the pinball arcade business that had belonged to his victim. Wartime crowds poured into the arcade and Haigh was taking in money hand over fist. But it was still not enough to buy the lifestyle he wanted, and greed drove him to his next murder for profit.

His victims were to be McSwann's parents. He wrote to them, again forging their son's name, and begged them to meet him at the home of his dear friend, John Haigh.

On the night of 10 July, 1945, Haigh bludgeoned them to death in his workshop. Afterwards he dissolved their bodies in the vat of acid and poured the reeking sludge down the drain.

Using forged documents Haigh helped himself to the entire estate – five

The kidnapping of the 20-month-old son of world-famous aviator Charles Lindbergh scandalized America on 1 March, 1932. The boy was taken from his luxury New Jersey home, and the anguished father was desperate enough to pay a $75,000 ransom, but there was no child in return. On 12 May the boy's body was found in a shallow grave near Lindbergh's home. But it was September before the killer was found – he handed in a note from the ransom money at a petrol station, and was traced through his car registration number. Bruno Hauptmann, 36, a former German soldier who had entered America illegally in 1923, went to the electric chair at Trenton, New Jersey, on 3 April, 1936.

houses and a fortune in securities and later transferred it to his own name.

Because of his inveterate gambling, self-indulgence and a string of bad investments, he was broke again by February 1948. He decided to invite a young marrried couple, Rosalie and Dr Archie Henderson, to look at his new workshop at Crawley, south of London. Both went into the acid bath.

Although the Henderson's estate had been profitably disposed of in 1949 Haigh found that he needed one more victim. Still convinced he was living a charmed life, he chose this one with little caution.

She was Mrs Olive Durand-Deacon, a 69-year-old widow whose husband had left her £40,000. She lived at the same London residential hotel as Haigh, who had not paid his bills for months and who was desperate for money.

Mrs Durand-Deacon believed that, apart from having a private income, Haigh had made money by patenting inventions. She put to him an idea for false plastic fingernails. Haigh showed interest, invited her to visit his Crawley workshop and in February 1949 drove her down there.

What happened next was described by Haigh in a statement he made to police and which was read at his trial:

> She was inveigled by me into going to Crawley in view of her interest in artificial fingernails. Having taken her into the storeroom, I shot her through the back of the head while she was examining some materials.
>
> Then I went out to the car and fetched a drinking glass and made an incision – I think with a penknife – in the side of her throat. I collected a glass of blood, which I drank.
>
> I removed her coat and jewellery (rings, necklace, earrings and crucifix) and put her in a 45-gallon tank.
>
> Before I put her handbag in the tank, I took from it about 30 shillings and a fountain pen. I then filled the tank with sulphuric acid, by means of a stirrup-pump. I then left it to react.

As an afterthrought, Haid added: 'I should have said that, in between having her in the tank and pumping in the acid, I went round to the Ancient Prior's [a local teashop] for a cup of tea.'

It took some days and two further trips to Crawley to check on the acid tank before Mrs Durand-Deacon's body appeared to have been entirely dissolved. Meantime, the police had questioned her fellow guests at the hotel, including Haigh.

The killer's glib, over-helpful manner made one detective particularly suspicious and he checked on the 39-year-old suspects background. He unearthed a prison record for minor frauds and arrested Haigh. The murderer confessed, but claimed that he could never be proven guilty because police could never find any of his victims' remains.

He was wrong. Forensic scientists examined the foul sludge that had been emptied from the tank onto the ground in the yard of the Crawley workshop. They were able to identify a gallstone, part of a foot, remains of a handbag and an almost complete set of false teeth. These were shown to Mrs Durand-Deacon's dentist, who confirmed that they had belonged to the trusting widow.

In court Haigh's lawyers claimed that the killer was insane. They pointed to a strict and unhappy childhood – his parents belonged to the Plymouth Brethren – and to his claimed habit of drinking his victims' blood. But although the British press labelled him The Vampire Killer, the judge and jury failed to accept this bloody trait as evidence of insanity. After a trial of only two days, he was found guilty of murdering Mrs Durand-Deacon and sentenced to death. Asked if he had anything to say, Haigh replied airily: 'Nothing at all.'

On 6 August, 1949, he was hanged at Wandsworth Prison.

The Murderous Musician

CHARLES PEACE

What kind of man could sit calmly in a court's public gallery and watch another condemned to die for a murder he had committed? Charles Peace could. And it was only after his arrest, two years later, for another murder, that he made a full confession to a chaplain and saved the innocent prisoner's life. For stony-hearted Peace lived his criminal life by the maxim, 'If I make up my mind to a thing, I am bound to have it.' And for 20 years, he had made up his mind to be one of England's most cunning crooks.

Peace was a small, wiry man who walked with a limp and used an artificial hook arm to conceal the loss of two fingers in a childhood accident. He played the violin well enough to be billed at local concerts as 'The Modern Paganini'. But at night, he turned into an expert cat-burglar, carrying his tools in a violin case and using his monkey-like agility and phenomenal strength to plunder from the rooftops. For many years he wandered from town to town, until 1872, when he returned to his native Sheffield with his wife Hannah and their son Willie, and set up shop as a picture framer and bric-a-brac dealer in Darnall.

He was then 40, an ugly man whose tongue seemed too big for his mis-shaped mouth. Yet he seems to have had a way with certain women. He began an illicit affair with Mrs Katherine Dyson, the buxom wife of one of his neighbours in Britannia Road, visiting pubs to satisfy her craving for drink, then going to the attic of a nearby empty house to satisfy his own cravings. Soon Peace grew less cautious, calling on the Dysons whenever the fancy took him, and eventually Katherine's husband Arthur, a giant of over 2 metres in height, banned him from the house.

But Peace could not stand rebuffs. Mrs Dyson recalled later: 'I can hardly describe all that he did to annoy us . . . he would come and stand outside the window at night and look in, leering all the while. He had a way of creeping and crawling about, and of coming on you suddenly unawares.' The Dysons went to the police after their persecutor made threats at gunpoint in July 1876, but he fled to Hull to escape the arrest warrant that was issued. The Dysons decided to move home, to Banner Cross Terrace, Ecclesall Road, but when they arrived at what they thought would be their haven, Peace walked out of the front door, declaring: 'I am here to annoy you and I will annoy you wherever you go.'

On the evening of 29 November, Mrs Dyson left the house to visit the outside

WC. Peace was waiting in the shadows, holding a gun. Her shriek brought her husband running from the parlour, and he chased Peace down the alleyway that ran behind the terraced houses. When they reached the street, two shots were heard in rapid succession, and Dyson fell dying, a bullet in his head. Peace fled, dropping as he went a bundle of notes Mrs Dyson had written him. And though a reward of £100 was put on his head by police, he evaded capture, burgling his way from town to town until he reached London, and set up home in Evelina Road, Peckham.

It was a strange household. His wife Hannah and their son lived in the basement, while Peace and his mistress masqueraded as Mr and Mrs Thompson on the floor above, throwing musical parties for new friends and neighbours, and attending church every Sunday. Eventually the 'Thompsons' had a baby boy.

Peace cultivated a respectable image quite deliberately, saying: 'The police never think of suspecting anyone who wears good clothes.' He dyed his grey hair black, shaved off his beard. By day he drove his cart round south London, ostensibly collecting other people's unwanted possession. At night he went out and stole the possessions they were not so keen to lose. Though his exploits made the newspapers, police had no idea who the daring raider was, and Peace made the most of their ignorance. He delighted in chatting to policemen he met on trains, and even shared lodgings with an officer while staying briefly in Bristol.

But on 10 October, 1878, his luck ran out. Police were waiting in force outside a house in Blackheath when Peace emerged at 02.00 carrying a silver flask, a letter case and a cheque book. The cornered villain threatened them with a gun, and fired four shots, but the officers ignored him. The fifth shot struck PC Edward Robinson in the arm, but he still managed to overpower the gunman with colleagues, inflicting quite a beating-up in the process.

Peace was tried under the false name he gave, John Ward, for attempted murder, and the Old Bailey jury took four minutes to find him guilty. Despite a whining personal plea for mercy from the 'most wretched, miserable man,' he was jailed for life. Then his mistress revealed his true identity so she could collect the £100 murder reward still on offer at Sheffield. Police brought Mrs Dyson from her native America, where she had gone after the death of her husband, and charged Peace.

On 22 January, 1879, two warders accompanied the handcuffed prisoner on to the 05.00 express from London to Sheffield. He proved troublesome throughout the journey, and when the train reached Yorkshire, he flung himself out of a window. The warders stopped the train and ran back a mile to find him unconscious in the snow, having landed on his head. Committal proceedings were held outside his cell in Sheffield, and Peace was sent for trial at Leeds.

The jury took 12 minutes to find Peace guilty, and he was condemned to

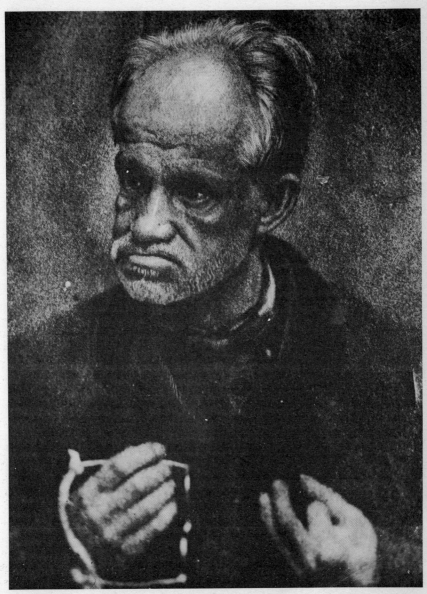

Engraved portrait of Charles Peace at his trial

An artist's impression of Charles Peace escaping from the train

death. He spent the days before the execution writing moralistic letters and praying. And he also revealed to the chaplain, the Rev J. H. Littlewood, that four months before the death of Dyson he had shot and killed a policeman who disturbed him during a robbery at Whalley Range, Manchester.

Even more chillingly, he confessed that he had sat in the gallery at Manchester Assizes when two Irish brothers were charged with the death, and had watched 18-year-old William Habron be sentenced to death on 28 November just 24 hours before he shot Dyson. 'What man would have done otherwise in my position?' he said when asked why he had remained silent at such a blatant miscarriage of justice.

Habron was pardoned and given £800 compensation, and at 08.00 on 25 February, 1879, aged 46, Charles Peace took his place on the scaffold at Armley Jail, Leeds, after complaining bitterly about the 'bloody rotten bacon' he was served for his last breakfast. Though he pretended contrition and trust in God in an odious final speech, he confessed to the chaplain: 'My great mistake, sir, has been this: in all my career I have used ball cartridge; I ought to have used blank.' His last words before Marwood the executioner pulled the trapdoor lever were: 'I should like a drink; have you a drink to give me?' And he left his own epitaph in his cell. He was executed, he wrote, 'for what I done but never intended.'

A Miscarriage of Justice?

JOHN CHRISTIE

John Reginald Halliday Christie was regarded by his neighbours as hard-working and respectable, although not particularly likeable. They often took his advice on medical matters, of which he affected a knowledge. It was also rumoured that he could help a girl terminate a pregnancy which may be why he apparently found it so easy to lure prostitutes to his home . . . and to their deaths.

For 14 years Christie lived in a run-down terraced house at 10 Rillington Place in London's decaying Notting Hill district. Christie and his wife Ethel had taken the ground-floor flat in 1938 at a time when he was trying to play down his five criminal convictions, one of which was for assaulting a woman. During the war he applied for a job as a reserve policeman and, because his record was never checked, he got it. After the war he worked briefly in a factory, then took a job as a post office clerk.

Christie's wife disappeared while the couple were living at number 10, and the solitary widower finally moved to another flat in 1952.

In March 1953 a prospective tenant was looking over the ground floor flat at 10 Rillington Place when he detected a foul smell which seemed to be emanating from a papered-over kitchen cupboard. Thinking that a rat had found its way inside and died, he ripped open the cupboard. What he found made him rush to the nearest telephone box and dial 999.

When the police arrived, they stripped the flat. In the kitchen cupboard they found the bodies of three prostitutes. Two more bodies were found buried in the back-yard. And beneath the sitting-room floor was the body of Ethel Christie.

Christie confessed to the six murders. In one of the most sensational and horrifying trials in history, it was said that he could gain sexual satisfaction only with dead women. Christie hoped to be found guilty but insane, and his life spared, but he was sentenced to death by hanging.

That, however, was far from being the end of the story. For as well as the six bodies found at 10 Rillington Place, Christie also confessed to murdering Beryl Evans, the wife of an ex-neighbour, Timothy Evans. The confession, however, came too late to help poor Timothy Evans, for in 1950 he had been sentenced to death by hanging – for murder.

To this day, no-one knows for sure which of the two men killed Beryl Evans.

Bible-loving Earle Leonard Nelson claimed he was 'a very religious man of high ideals'. But in less than two years, he raped and strangled at least 22 landladies across the United States and Canada in a trail of terror that began in San Francisco in February 1926, and ended in Winnipeg, Canada, in June 1927.

He was finally captured after changing his clothes at a secondhand store, and leaving behind a fountain pen taken from the home of his last victim, Mrs Emily Paterson. At his trial in Winnipeg, accused of her murder, he pleaded insanity. However, the jury decided that a man who kept on the move, changing his clothes and name after each killing, was not insane. He was hanged on 13 January, 1928, aged 36.

What is certain is that no jury today could possibly convict Timothy Evans of the crime.

Evan's confession was made on the spur of the moment when he walked into a police station in Merthyr Tydfil, South Wales, on 30 November, 1949, and told the officer at the desk: 'I would like to give myself up. I have disposed of the body of my wife.'

Evans, a gullible, illiterate van driver who ws largely under the spell of the evil Christie, told detectives that they would find his wife's body in a drain at 10 Rillington Place, where the Evans family had occupied the top-floor flat.

Police searched the house but could not find the dead woman in the drains. A later search, however, revealed the body in a small wash-house at the back of Number 10. She had been strangled, the same means of death meted out by Christie to all his victims. But more horrifying still was the discovery of a second corpse in the wash-house. It was the body of Evans's baby daughter, Geraldine. Evans appeared to be shattered by the discovery of his daughter. He at first admitted both murders but at his trial he accused Christie of the crimes.

The unfortunate Evans said that his wife was pregnant for the second time and that Christie had offered to give her an abortion. Evans agreed and left the two together. Afterwards, Christie showed Evans the woman's body and said that she had died during the abortion. He advised Evans to get rid of all his wife's clothes and other possessions and to leave London for a while. Meanwhile, Christie would arrange for little Geraldine to be unofficially adopted by a couple he knew. But apparently he decided to get rid of her, too.

That was Evans's story but the jury did not believe him. In court Christie, the ex-policeman, was a much more convincing witness. His previous conviction for viciously assaulting a woman was not mentioned to the jury. The prosecution described Christie as 'this perfectly innocent man'.

Above left: 10 Rillington Place. Victims from left to right: Beryl Evans, Hectorina
MacLennan, Muriel Amelia Eady, Kathleen Maloney, Rita Nelson, Ruth Fuerst
Above right: John and Ethel Christie

The simple-minded Evans was convicted – technically for murder of his baby only – and hanged. Christie stayed free for another three years . . . free to commit another four murders. He murdered his wife and then three prostitutes in close succession. Their bodies were added to those of the two women whom Christie had murdered in 1943 and 1944 and buried in the back-yard.

Christie was brought to justice in June 1953. He was tried for the murder of his wife and hanged at Pentonville Prison on 15 July, 1953.

But that was not the end of the story. Public outcry grew over the years for an inquiry into what was seen as a ghastly miscarriage of justice over the execution of Timothy Evans. But it was not until 1966 that pressure for an official review of the case succeeded in prompting the government to authorize an inquiry under Mr Justice Brabin. He ruled: 'It is more probable than not that Evans killed Beryl Evans, and it is more probable than not that Evans did not kill Geraldine.'

The ruling fell short of the sort of verdict that the pro-Evans campaigners had fought for over the years. But it did mean that Evans, whose conviction was for killing his daughter, could receive a posthumous royal pardon. His body was exhumed from Pentonville Prison and reburied in consecrated ground.

What the ruling did not do was to answer some extremely pertinent questions about the efficiency of the police, who failed to turn up the evidence that would, right from the start, have pointed the finger clearly at scheming, glib, persuasive mass-strangler Christie.

Why, when investigating Evan's allegations, did they fail to take note of Christie's previous record, happily accepting his wartime police service as evidence of his good character? Why did they unquestionably accept Christie's claim that he could not have helped dispose of Beryl Evans's body because his fibrositis prevented his lifting any heavy weight?

Why, on the first two occasions that police searched 10 Rillington Place for the body of Mrs Evans, did they not look in the wash-house? It was only on the third visit that they made their grisly discovery. And then only after standing with Christie in his back-yard and discussing with him the possibility of digging up his tiny garden to find out whether Beryl Evans was buried there.

If they had decided to dig up the yard, the detectives would have found the shallow grave of, not Mrs Evans, but the two other women who had been lured to the house, murdered and buried by Christie. As they chatted to Christie on that chill December morning in 1949, the detectives were standing on top of the two bodies. While the men spoke, Christie's small mongrel dog dug in the earth around their feet – and uncovered a woman's skull. Christie shooed the dog away and kicked earth over the evidence. The detectives noticed nothing.

If they had been more observant, four women might have been saved from murder, and Timothy Evans saved from the gallows.

The Prince of Poisoners
WILLIAM PALMER

William Palmer has gone down in history as the Prince of Poisoners, a murderer so notorious that the town where he practised his evil arts applied to the prime minister for permission to change its name. Palmer's trial has been hailed as the most sensational of the nineteenth century. What made it so was not that he was the first prisoner to use strychnine, but the incredible story of debauchery and lust that unfolded. For Palmer and his wretched relatives were leftovers from an earlier age. And an England trying to get used to the puritanism of Queen Victoria lapped up each lurid detail of Palmer's Regency lifestyle – sex, gambling, drinking, scandal . . . and murder.

Palmer was born in Rugeley, Staffordshire, in 1824, the second son of a sawyer who had swindled his employer, the Marquess of Anglesey, out of £70,000 by selling his timber, and a woman whose uncle had fathered an incestuous granddaughter by his own illegitimate daughter. Such a heritage need not have brought out the worst in young William – four of his brothers and sisters led perfectly normal lives. But his eldest sister, Mary Ann, turned to promiscuity, taking after her mother; his brother Walter became an alcoholic; and William himself turned to a life of wine, women and gambling – funded by theft and fraud.

His father died when he was 12, but any hopes William had of enjoying a life of leisure on his legacy were dashed when he received only a £7,000 share of the ill-gotten fortune. When Palmer left school, he was apprenticed to a Liverpool firm of chemists, Evans and Evans, but the demands of his heavy flutters on the horses, entertaining the ladies, and keeping up with the rich, idle circle of friends he formed soon exhausted his allowance. Palmer began stealing money sent with orders he collected for the firm from the Post Office. He was soon discovered and sacked.

His mother settled the bill for the missing cash and sent him to work for a surgeon, Edward Tylecote. Though outwardly industrious and ambitious, Palmer was more intent on profit and profligacy than medicine. He stole from his employer and took advantage of his position to seduce his patients. It is estimated that he fathered 14 illegitimate children during the five years he worked for Tylecote. Eventually the surgeon lost patience with his troublesome assistant, and enrolled him as a 'walking pupil' at Stafford Infirmary. Palmer quickly found that this in no way lessened his opportunities for sex and stealing, and he also grabbed the chance to indulge a new passion – poisons. The hospital authorities were so alarmed by his activities that they barred him from the dispensary, but Palmer was not so easily rebuffed.

In 1846, an inquest was held at Stafford into the death of a man called Abley. He had been unwise enough to accept a challenge to a drinking bout from Palmer, who was having an affair with his wife. After only two tumblers of brandy, Abley was violently sick, and died within minutes. Though the authorities were suspicious, nothing could be proved against Palmer, who left shortly after the death to continue his studies at St Bartholomew's Hospital in London. In retrospect, most experts believe Abley was the poisoner's first victim in what may have been a toxicological experiment.

Palmer squandered more than £2,000 during a riotous year in London – an enormous sum in those days – and only just managed to qualify as a doctor. But in one subject he was top of his class. The only note he made in one of his textbooks was: 'Strychnine kills by causing tetanic fixing of the respiratory muscles.'

In August 1846, Palmer was back in Rugeley, setting up his practice in a large house opposite the Talbot Arms Inn. The lascivious reputation of both his widowed mother and himself made the locals far from eager to put their lives in his hands, and Palmer had few patients to keep him away from his first love, the race track. But already he was tumbling into debt, and was anxious to cut his expenditure in other directions. One day he asked to see the illegitimate daughter he had fathered by a maid he had known when working for Dr Tylecote. She died shortly after returning to her mother the same evening. Soon other illegitimate offspring unaccountably suffered fatal convulsions after licking the honey their fond father spread on his finger.

In 1847, Palmer took himself a wife. Ann Brookes was herself illegitimate. Her father, an Indian Army colonel, had committed suicide, and her mother, the colonel's former housekeeper, had taken refuge in drink. Both were well provided for, the widow inheriting property worth £12,000, the daughter living on the interest of £8,000 capital as a ward of court. One of her two guardians was a cousin of Palmer's former employer, Dr Tylecote, and was opposed to the marriage, but Palmer successfully asked the courts for permission to wed their charge. From all accounts, the two were very much in love, and their happiness was clouded only by the way their children kept dying. Four were killed by mysterious convulsions when only days or weeks old between 1851 and 1854. Only the eldest boy, Willy, survived.

Several of Palmer's relatives and racing companions were not so lucky. He called on his uncle, Joseph Bentley, a drunken degenerate, and suggested a trial

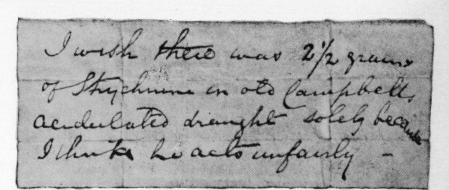

A note written by William Palmer to his council while in the dock at the Old Bailey

of drinking strength. Again, sharing brandy with Palmer proved a sickening experience. The uncle died three days later, leaving his nephew a few hundred pounds. In 1848, Palmer invited his mother-in-law to stay at Rugeley. Though an alcoholic, she still had enough of her wits about her to detest her daughter's husband. She confided to a friend before the journey to Rugeley: 'I know I shan't live a fortnight.' She died ten days after arriving.

That nobody found anything suspicious in the deaths of those around Palmer was due in large measures to his performance as an actor. To the community, he was a respected, church-going, unctious man, charming, pious, kind and generous. His wife believed he was doing his best to save her mother when he gave her medication and personally prepared her food.

Palmer also allayed suspicion by calling in a second opinion, a good-hearted, doddering local doctor named Bamford, who was over 80 and prepared to agree with his young friend's diagnoses. When Palmer told him death was due to apoplexy or English cholera, Bamford obligingly signed death certificates to that effect.

The death of Palmer's mother-in-law was not as profitable as he expected. Her property was tied up, and what little money accrued to the grieving newly-weds was only a drop in the ocean of the doctor's gambling debts. Already he owed thousands of pounds to a dubious Mayfair lawyer, Thomas Pratt, and lesser sums to Midlands' moneylenders called Padwick and Wright. His attempts to remove his own relatives continued, but when the wife of another uncle became ill while paying him a visit, she refused to take the pills he proferred, throwing them out of a window instead. Palmer managed to explain away the fact that chickens who pecked at the pills were dead next morning.

He turned his attentions to his racing companions. He owed a man called Leonard Bladen £800 after a run of back luck. He invited him to Rugeley, and after a convivial evening, the guest took to his bed with a stomach upset. Within a week he was dead. Bladen's wife, who heard about the illness from a third party, arrived just before the end, but was upset at not being allowed to see the body. She was also perturbed to be told that her husband had only £15 on him, and that Palmer expected £59 from the man's estate to settle a gambling debt. Her friends urged her to go to the police, but she refused, out of consideration for Mrs Palmer. Another gambler called Bly also learned how lethal it could be to win money from Palmer. Mrs Palmer was becoming upset at the string of deaths in the house. 'My mother died here last year, now these men,' she wailed. 'What will people say?'

Towards the end of 1853, Palmer's finances were in a more hopeless state than ever. He backed one of his own horses, Nettle, to win £10,000 in the Oaks. It lost. Twice he was declared a defaulter on bets, and barred from Tattersalls, the Mecca of the racing establishment. Pratt, Padwick and Wright were all becoming increasingly strident in their demands for payment – and interest on his gambling debts was now running into thousands of pounds. Palmer needed money desperately – desperately enough to kill the wife he loved.

In January 1854, the month he poisoned his fourth child, he took out three life insurance policies on Mrs Palmer, for a total of £13,000. They were arranged with the help of Pratt and a local attorney, Jeremiah Smith. Smith was having an affair with Palmer's mother, now aged over 60, but was not anxious for the news to be broadcast. Palmer knew of the liaison, and had used it to pressure Smith into helping him forge his mother's signature on guarantees for his own debts. Now Smith helped to fix up the three life policies – two, with Norwich Union and Sun Insurance, for £5,000 each, one, with the Prince of Wales company, for £3,000. The premium was a total of £760 a year, and apparently none of the companies bothered to ask how a country doctor with little income and a penchant for betting could afford to pay so much. In fact, Palmer borrowed the money from Pratt.

The Roman Emperor Tiberius was incredibly strong – he could poke his finger through an apple – but his weaknesses were even more dramatic. His lusts knew no bounds. He once broke the legs of two priests when they did not react favourably to his advances. And he would often have his lovers tortured and murdered when he no longer found them amusing.

Palmer managed to tide himself over during the summer, but a fresh cash crisis hit him in September. As luck would have it, his wife returned from visiting relatives in Liverpool with a chill. She took to her bed, and Palmer's devoted care soon turned a minor ailment into chronic antimony poisoning.

This time, he took the precaution of calling in not only Dr Bamford, but also his wife's former guardian, the once-suspicious Dr Knight. He too was now an octogenarian, and, like Bamford, was prepared to concur with Palmer's diagnosis. All three signed a death certificate citing English cholera. Palmer seemed distraught at the death, weeping and sobbing inconsolably. But he still managed to spend that night with his maid, Eliza Tharm, who gave birth to a child exactly nine months later.

At first the insurance companies were reluctant to settle the policies Palmer had taken out such a short time before. They were suspicious at such a sudden death in a seemingly healthy woman of 27. But faced with the verdicts of two doctors of good repute, they decided not to call for an inquest, and Palmer was given his money. He immediately gave £8,000 to Pratt and £5,000 to Wright. But Padwick stepped up his demands, and Pratt was soon insisting on further efforts to settle Palmer's account. Shrugging off the suspicions of the insurance .companies, Palmer decided they were the best policy for saving him from ruin.

With Pratt's help, he devised a scheme to cover the life of his brother Walter, a bankrupt dipsomaniac, for an astonishing £82,000. The total was split between six companies, and Palmer persuaded Walter to co-operate by promising to lend him £400, and by offering to provide him with the drinks that Walter's wife was rationing.

The insurance companies, once bitten, were shy about dealing with the Palmer family again. Walter's doctor, a man called Waddell, signed one application form, declaring that his patient was 'healthy, robust and temperate'. But he added in a covering note: 'Most confidential. His life has been rejected in two offices. I am told he drinks. His brother insured his late wife's life for many thousands, and after the first payment she died. Be cautious.'

Palmer finally secured policies to a total of £13,000, invited his brother to Rugeley, and for five months plied him with gin. It has been estimated that Walter drank 19 gallons of the spirit before leaving for home in July, 1855. Palmer arranged to meet his brother at Wolverhampton races on 14 August, and prepared for the encounter by buying some prussic acid. Again Walter embarked on a gin binge, but this time the drinks were laced. Two days later he was dead of an apoplectic fit. By the time his widow learned of his demise, the body was already in its coffin.

Palmer instantly applied for the life insurance policies to be paid up, but the companies delayed settlement until they had investigated further. Palmer would have been wise to wait, but Pratt, who had been assigned the policy on

Walter as security for loans of £11,500, would not let him. In September, he demanded a £6,000 payment. Palmer desperately tried to take out new insurance policies on George Bate, whom he described as a 'gentleman farmer'. When the companies investigated, they found they were being asked to take a £25,000 risk on a penniless undergroom at Palmer's stables.

Palmer was told there would be no policy on Bate's life – and no payment on the insurance for Walter. If he went to court to claim his £13,000, they said, they would counter claim with a charge of murder. Palmer was now in desperate straits. Pratt was threatening to sue for his money by issuing writs against Palmer's mother, the unwitting guarantor. Palmer knew that the penalty for forging signatures was transportation. He also had a new problem to contend with. Some years earlier he had arranged an abortion for a Stafford girl, Jane Burgess, whom he had made pregnant. He unwisely sent her passionate love letters, described by one author who read them as 'too coarse to print'. Palmer had urged the girl to burn them, but she was not that foolish. Now she wrote to him, threatening blackmail.

On 13 November, 1855, Palmer went to Shrewsbury races with his pal John Parsons Cook, a 27-year-old rake who had squandered a £12,000 legacy from his father, but aimed to recoup some of it on his horse Polestar in the Shrewsbury Handicap. To the delight of both men, Polestar won. Cook collected £800 in cash from bets on the course, and unwisely showed Palmer a betting slip from Tattersalls for a further £1,200.

Cook, like Palmer, was generous in sharing his successes. He and a party of friends celebrated the victory with a slap-up champagne supper at the Raven Hotel in Shrewsbury. But after accepting a glass of brandy from Palmer, he was violently ill. He handed over his cash winnings to another man, saying: 'I believe that damned Palmer has dosed me.' Yet he agreed to Palmer's suggestion next morning that he come back to Rugeley for medical treatment.

Cook took rooms in the Talbot Arms, where Palmer, living just across the road, could keep a careful eye on him. On Friday, 16 November, Cook dined with Palmer and Jeremiah Smith. Next morning, he was again violently sick. Palmer kept popping in with medicines, and on the Sunday sent some broth across to the inn. A chambermaid who tasted it while heating it retched for the next five hours, but nobody blamed the broth, and Palmer was allowed to take a bowl up to his friend. Dr Bamford had already been called in for consultations, and by the Monday Cook was feeling a little better. This could have been because Palmer had gone up to London to cash Cook's betting slip at Tattersalls, and pay £450 of it to Pratt.

There could now be no turning back for Palmer. He returned to Rugeley at 22.00, and bought three grains of strychnine from the local surgeon's assistant on his way to the Talbot Arms. That night, Cook went through agony.

Above: The trial of
William Palmer 1856

Right: extract
from Palmer's
diary

Chambermaid Elizabeth Mills was with him. She said later: 'He was sitting up beating the bedclothes with his hands. His body, his hands and his neck were moving then – a sort of jumping or jerking. Sometimes he would throw himself back on the pillow and then raise himself up again. He screamed three or four times and called out "Murder" '.

Next day, Cook refused to take any more medication. But Palmer had summoned Cook's own physician, Dr William Jones, from Lutterworth, and he, Bamford and Palmer persuaded the patient to take some pills made up by Dr Bamford. He agreed, not realizing that Bamford had given the pills to Palmer, who had bought more strychnine that morning, along with some prussic acid.

Cook's long ordeal was almost over. At midnight on Tuesday, the jangling bell in his room sent Elizabeth and her fellow chambermaid Lavinia Barnes hurrying upstairs. The patient was arched in excruciatingly painful contortions, resting only on his head and heels, as Dr Jones massaged his neck. Curiously, Cook was screaming for Palmer. One of the girls ran to the doctor's house, and found him fully dressed and ready. He forced two more pills through Cook's clenched teeth, and the poor man writhed in new agonies before slumping, lifeless, on the bed. The two chambermaids had watched the death scene in the errie candlelight with terrified awe. Now Elizabeth was amazed to see Palmer going through the dead man's pockets.

Desperation had forced the maniacal medic to throw all caution to the wind. he had already persuaded the Rugeley postmaster, Samuel Cheshire, to help him forge a cheque for £350 from Cook to Palmer. Now he asked him to witness a document saying Cook owed him another £4,000. Cheshire refused.

More trouble was in store for Palmer. On Friday, 23 November, Cook's stepfather, William Stevens, arrived in Rugeley. The appearance of the body, the haste with which it had been given to an undertaker, the search of Cook's pockets, and the claim for money from Cook's estate all made him suspicious. Unhappy with the stated cause of death, apoplexy, he ordered that the room where the body lay be locked, and left for London to see a solicitor, and demand a post-mortem.

It was held at the Talbot Arms on the following Monday morning, under the direction of a Dr Harland. Both Palmer and Bamford were present – one of the rare occasions a murderer has taken part in the search for clues to his murder. Palmer did all he could to obstruct that search. As the medical students cutting the body lifted out the stomach, Palmer brushed against them, and much of the vital contents spilled irretrievably back into abdomen. Harland reprimanded Palmer, assuming the doctor was playing a joke, and Palmer whispered to Bamford: 'They won't hang us yet.'

The stomach and intestines were sealed into a bottle, to be sent for analysis in

London. Then the bottle disappeared. Harland angrily demanded to know where it was, and Palmer produced it from behind his back. There were two cuts in the air-proof lid. Still Palmer would not admit defeat. He offered the post-boy £10 if he would upset the carriage taking Stevens and the bottle to Stafford to catch the London train. The boy refused.

Palmer waited impatiently for the results of the London autopsy. He learned them before anyone else. Postmaster Cheshire was in the habit of allowing his friend to read any mail that interested him, and Palmer was delighted to intercept the report from the analyst. No poison had been found, apart from slight traces of antimony.

Palmer now took leave of his senses. He wrote two letters to the coroner, saying he was confident of a 'death by natural causes' verdict at the inquest – and enclosing the gift of some game and a £5 note. The coroner handed both letters and gifts to the police and recorded a verdict of wilful murder. Palmer, already in the custody of the sherrif's officer because of his debts, was arrested and taken to Stafford jail.

The bodies of his wife Ann and brother Walter were exhumed for post-mortems, and soon all England was talking of the Rugeley poisoner, attributing him with even more grisly deeds than those that were suspected. A special Act of Parliament, still known as 'Palmer's Law', had to be passed to transfer the trial from Stafford to the Old Bailey in London. Local prejudice was the given reason – and according to one of Palmer's defence team, Edward Kenealy, it was the fear that a local jury would never convict him. Kenealy wrote in his memoirs: 'Palmer was such a general favourite and had so many personal friends and acquaintances that no verdict of guilty could have been obtained.'

The Crown had no such problems at the Old Bailey. The trial, which began on 14 May, 1856, attracted intense attention from high society. The courtroom was packed each day, and outside throngs of spectators blocked the pavements to watch the protagonists arrive and leave. Bound volumes of verbatim evidence sold in their thousands, even though much of it was conflicting technical jargon from medical men.

The prosecution, led by Attorney-General Sir Alexander Cockburn made problems for itself by specifying that Cook was murdered by strychnine. Though Palmer was known to have bought it, no traces were found in Cook's corpse. Both sides brought in batteries of experts to try to explain this. Palmer's attorney, Serjeant Shee, berated one doctor for cruelty to animals after he spoke of the effects of strychnine on rabbits. Another man said the state of Cook's stomach when it reached London would have made establishing cause of death virtually impossible, 'if I had not been informed that there was a considerable quantity of strychnine present.'

Medical science knew little about the relatively new poison, or how to detect it, and some experts were prepared to swear that Palmer had found ways of disguising it. If so, he was not about to share the secret. There was little doubt that Palmer was guilty of poisoning Cook, and the jury and three judges were happy to go along with the Attorney-General's convenient theory: that Cook had been softened up with other poisons, then finished off by strychnine in an almost imperceptible dose. On 27 May, having listened to a masterly closing oration from Sir Alexander Cockburn, and a strong recommendation to convict from Lord Chief Justic Campbell, the jury took one hour to find Palmer guilty of murder.

He accepted sentence of death philosophically, and was taken back to Stafford under strong escort. He showed little sign of conscience or depression in prison, except when news that the Home Secretary had rejected his appeal came through, and to the end refused to make any confession, beyond saying, ambiguously: 'I am innocent of poisoning Cook by strychnine.'

Nearly 30,000 people were outside Stafford Jail on the morning of 14 June, 1856. Packed trains arrived in the town from the early hours, and spectators paid up to a guinea to take their places on the 23 platforms erected to give them a better view. When Palmer arrived, apparently indifferent to and amused by his fate, police had trouble controlling the mob as it surged forward. The sensational details of his sordid life had enthralled the nation, but there was nothing exceptional about his death at the end of the rope.

Few murderers have rivalled William Palmer for cold-hearted, premeditated callousness and cruelty. Though convicted and hanged for only one killing, he was suspected of at least 15 more, many of the victims being innocent children he fathered through debauched lechery. But even his horrific story has two wry postcripts. The moneylenders who hounded him received nothing after his death, because his mother refused to honour forged guarantees. And when the town of Rugeley, shamed by the notoriety brought on it by its infamous son, applied to change its name, the prime minister is alleged to have replied: 'By all means, provided you name your town after me.' His name was Lord Palmerston.

The Lethal Romeo

GEORGE SMITH

Many men have made a living by playing with the affections of plain, naive, lovelorn spinsters, then abandoning them once they have handed over their savings. The public often find the foolish victims of such romantic con-men comic rather than tragic figures, and found reasons for amusement even at the trial of Henri Landru, who was accused of killing ten such dupes. But nobody found anything remotely funny about the exploits of another wicked womaniser, George Joseph Smith.

Smith was born in London's Bethnal Green in 1872, and was soon the despair of his parents. His mother predicted he would 'die with his boots on', and she was hardly surprised when, at the age of only nine, he was sentenced to eight years in a Gravesend reformatory. But the sentence merely helped train him for a life of crime, and, apart from three years as a soldier in the Northamptonshire Regiment, he became a full-time thief, constantly in and out of prison.

Smith was cunning. He realized he was having little success stealing for himself, so he decided to get others to do it for him. Though his bony face was not really attractive, he had small, dark mesmerising eyes that seemed to have an extraordinarily magnetic power for some women. 'They were little eyes that seemed to rob you of your will,' one of his victims told police later.

Smith found it easy to persuade women to work with him, and not to implicate him if they were caught. Using the proceeds of one woman's raids, he opened a baker's shop in Russell Square, Leicester, in 1897, and a year later married an 18-year-old bootmaker's daughter, Caroline Beatrice Thornhill, despite her family's disapproval. He was then 26 and calling himself George Love.

They moved to London, and Smith found his wife employment as a servant with a succession of wealthy families in Brighton, Hove and Hastings. She had no trouble getting work. She had impeccable references from a past employer – Smith. But late in 1899 she was arrested trying to pawn the loot from one theft, some silver spoons, and was jailed for a year. Smith abandoned her, which increased her bitterness, and after her release, she spotted him by chance in London, and alerted the police. In January 1901, he was jailed for two years for receiving stolen goods. Revenge was in his mind, too, once the sentence ended. He travelled to Leicester, bent on killing his wife. But her family beat him up, and Caroline later emigrated to safety in Canada.

Smith had already discovered a new way of making women work for his living. In 1899 he had bigamously married a middle-aged boarding-house keeper, milking her of what money she had while living rent free at her lodgings. Now he began to tour the south coast, particularly seaside resorts, wooing, wedding and walking out on his brides, who were often too humiliated to reveal the truth to police or their friends·and relations.

He did it all in the cheapest way possible – third-class rail travel, meagre lodgings, outings to places of free entertainment. In that way, he made the maximum of profit from each of them. In June 1908 he met Florence Wilson, a Worthing widow with £30 in her Post Office savings account. They married in London after a whirlwind three-week affair. On 3 July, he took her to the White City exhibition and left her there, claiming he was going out to buy a newspaper. In fact he dashed back to their rooms in Camden Town and sold all her belongings.

In October 1909, calling himself George Rose, Smith married Southampton spinster Sarah Freeman and they set up home in Clapham, South London. Smith played the charming gent, in smart frock coat and top hat, and his bride did not demur when he said he needed money to set up an antiques business. She withdrew her savings, and sold her Government stocks. On 5 November he took her to the National Gallery, excused himself to go to the lavatory, and scuttled back to their rooms, clearing out everything, and leaving his deserted bride destitute. In less than a month he had made £400, four times the average annual wage.

In between these two coups, Smith had taken another wife, Edith Mabel Pegler. Dark-haired, round-faced and plump, she was 28 when she answered his advertisement for a housekeeper in a local newspaper at Bristol, where he had opened a shop in Gloucester Road. But for once Smith, who used his own name this time, was not after money. What he took from others, he gave to Edith. And though he left her from time to time, claiming he was travelling in search of antiques, he always returned after his matrimonial adventures.

Those adventures now took a more sinister turn. In August 1910, he met 33-year-old spinster Beatrice Constance Anne Mundy while strolling in Clifton, a resort near Bristol. The ardent wooer could hardly believe his luck when she told him of the £2,500 in securities her father, a Wiltshire bank manager, had left her when he died. The legacy, managed by a trust of relatives, paid her £8 a month. Smith, now going under the name of Henry Williams, whisked her off to Weymouth, where they set up home in Rodwell Avenue. They married on 26 August and began to flood the relatives with reassuring letters.

But the relatives had more sense than bride Bessie. They did not like the look of Williams, suspecting that he was a fortune hunter, and it was December before they finally sent £134 owed in interest. Smith, despairing of collecting

George Smith and Beatrice Mundy

Gangster, racketeer and murderer Al Capone did not die with a
bullet in his back. He died an ungentlemanly death of
neurosyphilis. The man whose Twenties crime empire brought in
$5 million a year and left 1,000 bodies on the streets of Chicago
died in Florida in 1947, an ex-jailbird with hardly a dime in his
pocket.

the capital, abandoned Bessie on 13 December in an especially heartless way.
He left her a letter claiming she had 'blighted all my bright hopes of a happy
future' by infecting him with venereal disease, and accusing her of not being
'morally clean.' He was off to London to be cured, 'which will cost me a great
deal of money.' So he took the £134, advising her to tell her relatives it was
stolen while she was asleep on the beach.

Poor Bessie resumed her spinster life, telling friends, on Smith's advice, that
her husband had gone to France. Smith went back to Edith Pegler, moving to
Southend, then London, and back to Bristol again. The VD accusation had
only been an excuse, though it must have upset a woman who was far from
worldly-wise.

That she missed her adoring husband was only too clear when, 18 months
later, they met again by sheer chance in Weston-super-Mare. Bessie, staying
with a friend, popped out to buy daffodils one morning in March 1912, and
spotted Smith on the seafront. The smooth-talking Casanova had an explanation for his note, his long absence, and the fact that he had spent all her
money, and by mid-afternoon the besotted girl was ready to ignore her friend's
pleas and leave with her husband, taking none of her belongings.

They travelled across country, and in May set up a modest home at 80 High
Street, Herne Bay, Kent. Smith had been asking expert advice on how he could
get at Bessie's £2,500 nest-egg, and in July a lawyer told him that it was only
possible if she left it to him in her will. The wily bigamist wasted no time – and
seemingly had no qualms about turning to murder to feather his nest. On 8 July
the couple signed wills, leaving their wordly possessions to each other should
they die. On 9 July, Smith bought a tapless zinc bath, haggling 12½p (half-a-
crown) off the ironmonger's price of £2.

On 10 July, he took Bessie to a young, inexperienced doctor, claiming she had
had a fit. Two days later the doctor called at their home after another fit was
reported. He found Bessie in bed, flushed but seemingly well, and left a
prescription for sedatives. That night, Bessie wrote to her uncle, telling him of
her attacks, of how her husband was looking after her well, and of how they had
both made their wills.

At 08.00 next morning, Saturday 13 July, the doctor received a note saying: 'Can you come at once? I am afraid my wife is dead.' He arrived to find Bessie submerged in the bath. She was naked and lying on her back, a bar of soap clasped in her right hand. Smith said his wife had filled the bath herself, making 20 trips downstairs to the kitchen to fetch water for it. He had gone out to buy some fish, and returned to find her dead. The police were called, but saw no reason to think the death was suspicious. Smith wept throughout the inquest on the following Monday, and was offered words of comfort by the coroner, who recorded a verdict of misadventure.

No-one asked why Bessie had drowned in a bath far shorter than her full height, or why Smith had left her lying under the water until the doctor arrived, instead of trying to resuscitate her. Nor was it found suspicious that she had just made a will, a point Smith was foolish enough to mention to the estate agent when he cancelled the letting of their home.

He had been careful to time the murder for a Saturday. Although he wired news of the death to Bessie's uncle, saying a letter would follow, there was no time for relatives to get to the inquest, or the economy-version funeral which followed just 24 hours later. Trustees of Bessie's legacy asked in vain for a post-mortem examination, and tried to stop Smith getting her money. But he had been too clever for them, and reluctantly they handed over £2,591 13s 6d.

Smith had one last piece of business to attend to. He took the bath back to the ironmonger to avoid having to pay for it. Then he left for Margate, and summoned Edith Pegler to join him. He told her he had made a nice profit selling antiques in Canada, but lost his temper when she revealed that she had been looking for him in Woolwich and Ramsgate. 'He said he did not believe in women knowing his business,' she was to recall. 'He remarked that if I interfered I should never have another happy day.'

Smith was one of the few big-time bigamists not to squander his earnings. He bought eight houses in Bristol with Bessie's money and opened a shop, and also invested in an annuity for himself. By October 1913, he was anxious for more cash, and there seemed no reason why a once-successful scheme should not work again.

Alice Burnham was short, plump and 25, a private nurse to an elderly invalid, when she met a tall, charming stranger at Southsea. Her father, a Buckinghamshire fruit-grower, took an instant dislike to the man, but that did

---

Dr Edward William Pritchard was the last person to be publicly hanged in Scotland. He had murdered his wife and mother-in-law by poisoning them with antimony. No fewer than 100,000 people watched the doctor go to his death in 1865.

not stop her marrying him at Portsmouth on 4 November, one day after he took out a £500 insurance policy on her life. Nor did it stop Smith writing immediately to her father, demanding £104 he was holding for his daughter, and withdrawing £27 from his bride's savings account.

Then he decided to take his new wife on holiday. It was Wednesday, 10 December when they arrived in breezy Blackpool for their bracing, out-of-season break. They called first at a boarding house in Adelaide Street, but Smith rejected the offered rooms – there was no bath. Mrs Crossley at 16 Regent Road had one, however, and the couple booked in there for ten shillings a week. A local doctor was consulted about Mrs Smith's headaches, and the dutiful wife wrote to her father, saying she had 'the best husband in the world.'

On the Friday evening, the couple asked for a bath to be prepared for Mrs Smith while they went for a walk. At 20.15 the Crossleys were having a meal downstairs when they noticed water staining the ceiling. They were about to investigate when a dishevelled Smith appeared at the door carrying two eggs which he said he had just bought for next day's breakfast. Then he went upstairs, and shouted down: 'Fetch the doctor, my wife cannot speak to me.'

Alice had gone the same way as Bessie, and though Smith was asked at the inquest next day why he had not lifted her from the bath, or pulled the plug out of it, an accidental death verdict was recorded. Again Smith wept copiously throughout the hearing, but at least one person was not impressed by his tears. Mrs Crossley was so appalled at his seeming indifference to his wife's death that she refused to let him sleep in her house that Friday night. She also noted that, while waiting for the inquest on the Saturday afternoon, he played the piano in her front room and drank a bottle of whisky.

Even worse was to come. Smith refused to have an expensive coffin for the burial, which took place at noon on Monday. He said: 'When they are dead, they are done with.' He left by train for Southsea – to clear out and sell all Alice's belongings – immediately after the funeral, and Mrs Crossley shouted 'Crippen' at him as he left the house. She also wrote on the address card he gave her: 'Wife died in bath. We shall see him again.' She could not know how prophetic those words were.

Smith rejoined the faithful Edith Pegler at Bristol in time for Christmas and used the £500 insurance money to increase his annuity. By August they were in Bournemouth, via London Cheltenham and Torquay. Smith announced he was going up to London again, alone, for a few days. He had met and wooed a maid called Alice Reavil while listening to a band on the seafront. They married at Woolwich on 17 September, but Smith did not stay long. He was back in Bristol with the girl's £80 savings and some of her clothes – a gift for Edith – by late autumn.

The callous truth was that Alice was so poor she was not worth killing. Smith

Blood-shedding Mongol leader Genghis Khan never let up on his bouts of mayhem and murder – even when he was in his coffin. He left orders that if anyone looked at his coffin, his funeral guards were to ensure that the next coffin would be theirs.

Genghis Khan once had 70 enemy chiefs stewed alive. He did not believe in taking prisoners and tore open victims' bellies in case they were hiding jewels. His prisoners' heads would be cut and banked up in sickly pyramids.

Genghis Khan is reputed to have been the biggest mass killer in history. He is believed to have been responsible for the deaths of 20 million people – one-tenth of the world's population at that time. He died in 1227.

abandoned her in some public gardens after a long tram ride. But he already had a third murder victim in mind. He had met Miss Margaret Lofty, a 38-year-old clergyman's daughter, in Bath the previous June. She worked as a lady's companion, living between jobs with her elderly widowed mother. And she was ripe for exploitation – she had discovered earlier in the year that her 'fiance' was a married man.

Smith was now calling himself John Lloyd and posing as an estate agent. He took her out to tea on 15 December and two days later they were married in secret. Smith had taken the precaution of persuading his beloved to insure her life for £700 and had even generously paid the first premium. They moved to London, taking rooms at 14 Bismarck Road, Highgate. Naturally they had a bath. But Smith seemed to have grown over-confident after the success of his two previous killings. This time he was amazingly impatient.

He took Margaret to see a local doctor on their evening of arrival, 17 December. Next morning, he took her to a solicitor to make her will – leaving everything to him. Then she wrote to her mother, describing her husband as 'a thorough Christian man.' By 20.00 on 18 December, she was having a bath. Her landlady, ironing downstairs, later recalled a splashing sound, and a noise 'as of someone putting wet hands or arms on the side of the bath.' Then there was a sigh, followed by the strains of the hymn Nearer My Go To Thee on the harmonium in the front room. Ten minutes later the landlady answered the doorbell and found 'Mr Lloyd' standing outside, saying he had forgotten his key after popping out to buy tomatoes for his wife's supper. Sadly, Mrs Lloyd was not alive to eat them.

Though Margaret was buried on the following Monday morning, the inquest was held over until after Christmas. Smith hurried home to Bristol again, and even had the cheek to tell Edith to beware of taking a bath, adding:

'It is known that women have often lost their lives through weak hearts and fainting in the bath.' That had been the coroner's verdict on Alice Burnham, and the Highgate coroner saw no reason to think differently when he considered the death of Margaret 'Lloyd' on 1 January, 1915.

But it was to be no happy new year for George Joseph Smith. His impatience to get rid of Margaret proved his undoing. The previous deaths had not attracted too much press attention. But this one had all the ingredients of a front page story. 'Found dead in bath,' said the headline in the *News Of The World*. A second headline read: 'Bride's Tragic Fate On Day After Wedding.'

Two readers, miles apart, noticed the story and thought it was too much of a coincidence. In Buckinghamshire, Alice Burnham's father contacted his solicitor, who went to the police. And in Blackpool, landlady Mrs Crossley also passed on her fears to the authorities. They began investigating possible connections between John Lloyd, estate agent, and George Smith, bachelor of independent means, and pieced together the incredible story of Smith's bigamous philanderings. On 1 February, a detective inspector and two sergeants arrested the deadly bridegroom as he left his solicitor's office, where he was making arrangements to collect the £700 insurance on his third victim.

Though the bodies of all three women were exhumed, and examined by famous pathologist Sir Bernard Spilsbury, there were no obvious signs of how they had drowned. And though Smith was charged with all three murders, he could only be tried, under English law, with one, that of Bessie Mundy. Smith denied strenuously that he had murdered anyone. He described the deaths of three brides in the same way as a 'phenomenal coincidence.' Any jury might have been prepared to accept that one such death was just an unfortunate accident. The prosecution therefore had to apply for permission to produce evidence about all three killings to show proof of a 'system.' Smith's attorney, Sir Edward Marshall Hall, protested, realizing that his only hope of a successful defence would be destroyed. But Mr Justice Scrutton agreed to consider all three deaths.

Marshall Hall, who believed privately that Smith used hypnotic powers to persuade all three wives to kill themselves, had another setback before the trial. Some newspapers had agreed to foot the defence bill in return for Smith's

---

In 1880, at the age of 26, Australian bushranger Ned Kelly was hanged at the end of a rope, watched by a huge crowd outside Melbourne jail. Kelly and his gang had killed at least four troopers in their flight from the law. Ned Kelly's last words on the scaffold were: 'Such is life!'

exclusive life story. But the Home Office vetoed the plan, and since all Smith's money was tied up in annuities, Marshall Hall received only a paltry fee under the Poor Persons Defence Act.

He received no help at all from his client. Smith repeatedly soured opinions, both at committals and at his trial, which began at the Old Bailey on 22 June, 1915, with bad-tempered outbursts at witnesses, his own lawyers and the judge. At one stage he screamed: 'It's a disgrace to a Christian country, this is. I'm not a murderer, though I may be a bit peculiar.'

The irony of the timing of the trial during World War One was not lost on Mr Justice Scrutton. A month before it, 1,198 lives were lost when a German submarine torpedoed the *Lusitania*. On the morning the trial began, *The Times* listed 3,100 men killed in the trenches. 'And yet,' said the judge in his summing-up, 'while this wholesale destruction of human life is going on, for some days all the apparatus of justice in England has been considering whether the prosecution are right in saying that one man should die.'

It took the jury only 22 minutes on 1 July to decide that he should. They had heard pathologist Spilsbury explain how Smith could have lifted his brides' legs with his left arm while pushing their heads under water with his right. And they had watched a dramatic reconstruction of such a possibility, carried out by a detective and a nurse in a bathing costume in an ante-room of the court. Even though the nurse knew what was about to happen, she still needed artificial respiration after her ordeal.

Smith was taken from Pentonville Jail to Maidstone Prison, still protesting his innocence. He remained unrepentant, though he turned to religion and was confirmed by the Bishop of Croydon, who was said to be impressed with his sincerity. On the eve of his execution, Smith wrote to Edith Pegler, who had wept for him outside the Old Bailey, saying: 'May an old age, serene and bright, and as lovely as a Lapland night, lead thee to thy grave. Now, my true love, goodbye until we meet again.'

Edith alone mourned on Friday, 13 August, when Smith was led to his execution. One day later, his first and only legal wife, Caroline Thornhill, took advantage of her widowhood to marry a Canadian soldier in Leicester.

The Teenage Monster
JESSE POMEROY

Horrified vacationers stumbled across the body of four-year-old Horace Millen on the beach at Dorchester Bay, near Boston, in April 1874. The child's throat has been cut and he had been stabbed no fewer than 15 times. Before he died, the boy had been savagely beaten. It was the work of a monster, and police immediately launched a full-scale hunt for the killer.

They were looking for a grown man, but some cross-referencing in the official files produced the name Jesse Harding Pomeroy: a lad of 14 who has been reprimanded and sent to a special reform school two years earlier for beating up young children. Fights among youngsters were commonplace, but the name of young Pomeroy, only just out of primary school, had been remembered by the authorities because of the extraordinary amount of unnecessary force he had used.

When police called on Jesse Pomeroy, his answers to questioning immediately aroused suspicion. He was arrested, brought to court and convicted. But Pomeroy's was one of the most remarkable murder cases ever. For, though sentenced to die, he was to live for another 58 years and the first 40 years – until he was 55 – were spent in solitary confinement.

The American public refused to take a chance on someone who had already displayed the most vicious cruelty. When arrested, he had been at liberty only 60 days after spending 18 months in the Westboro Reformatory. The magistrate who sent him there remarked on the savagery of the beatings he had handled out to children younger than himself and a short while after his trial for the Millen killing, it was established that just five weeks earlier he had killed nine-year-old Katie Curran. He had buried her body in the cellar of a shop.

At the Millen trial, Jesse Pomeroy pleaded innocence by way of insanity but it did him no good. He was convicted and sentenced to death. There were those who, because of his age, urged that his death sentence be commuted to life imprisonment but they were shouted down by the masses who demanded a swift execution. As it turned out, Pomeroy's life was spared only because of the legal complexities governing death sentences in the state of Massachusetts.

Although a judge had passed a sentence of death on him, the law required that the state governor of Massachusetts set the date of execution and sign the death warrant. Governor Gaston, in office at the time, refused possibly for political reasons to do anything at all: he would neither sign the death warrant nor commute young Pomeroy's sentence. He compromised with an order, signed and sealed, that Pomeroy must spend the rest of his natural days in solitary confinement. That order stood until long after Governor Gaston had passed away himself.

It was 1916, when Pomeroy was 54, before he was finally released from solitary and allowed to mix with other prisoners at Charlestown Prison. He had survived what must have been a superhuman ordeal by burying himself in studies. He read an immense number of books, and he wrote a lot himself.

If he had been mad at the time of the beatings, there was no longer any sign of it in his writings in these later years. One of the manuscripts he spawned was an autobiography which chronicled his early life, the crimes of which he had been convicted and an attempt he made to break out of jail.

Pomeroy died in the prison in which he had spent all his life, on 29 September, 1932. He was 73 and had spent more than 60 of those years behind bars.

Chapter two

TWENTIETH-CENTURY KILLERS

Most people have, at one time or another, thought or said, 'I'd like to murder him' (or her). They don't usually mean it – but occasionally, someone has sufficient malice to put that thought into practice. Assembled in this chapter are the most infamous twentieth-century killings; the callous child slayings of the moors murders, and the maniacal fervour of Wayne Williams, Atlanta's most feared killer.

The Sadistic Romeo

NEVILLE HEATH

Neville George Clevely Heath had the looks that boys' comic heroes are made of. His wide, blue eyes and fair, wavy hair set off a fresh-complexioned face which had women swooning. And his suave charm around the clubs and restaurants of London ensured that he was never short of a pretty companion when the evening ended. Girls fell for his impeccable manners, and his tales of derring-do in the war that had just finished. But Heath's handsome face hid a terrible secret. Possibly bored with the conventional sex that was so readily available to him, he began pandering to a sadistic streak. And in the summer of 1946, that perversion turned him into a ladykiller in every sense of the word.

Heath was then 29, and well known to both the police and the armed forces. He had served time in civilian jails for theft, fraud and false pretences. He had been court-martialled by the British RAF in 1937 (absent without leave, escaping while under arrest and stealing a car), the British Army in 1941 (issuing dishonoured cheques and going absent without leave) and the South African Air Force in 1945 (undisciplined conduct and wearing unauthorized decorations). In April 1946, he was fined £10 by magistrates at Wimbledon, London, for wearing medals and a uniform to which he was not entitled. By then, unknown to the authorities, he was also indulging in much more sinister fantasies.

A month earlier, the house detective at a hotel in London's Strand burst into a locked room after other guests reported hearing screams. He found Heath standing over a naked girl who was bound hand and foot, and being savagely whipped. Neither she nor the hotel wanted any publicity, and Heath was allowed to slink away. But in May he was at it again. This time he had a more willing victim, a 32-year-old masochist called Margery Gardner. She was a film extra, separated from her husband, and known as Ocelot Margie to doormen at the clubs where she turned up in an ocelot fur coat, looking for men prepared to satisfy her craving for bondage and flagellation. Heath was more than ready to oblige, but when he took her to the Pembridge Court Hotel in Notting Hill Gate the hotel detective again intervened after hearing the sound of flesh being thrashed.

Ocelot Margie did not learn from her escape. When Heath phoned her a few

Margery Gardner with inset of Neville Heath

weeks later, she agreed to meet him on Thursday, 20 June. After drinks at one of Heath's favourite haunts, the Panama Club in South Kensington, they took a taxi back to the Pembridge Court, where Heath had booked in four days earlier with another girl who had since left. It was after midnight when they arrived. Guests in adjoining rooms heard nothing to disturb their slumbers that night.

At 14.00 next day, a chambermaid entered Room 4 on the first floor of the 19-bedroom hotel and recoiled with horror when she drew back the curtains. The two single beds were bloodied and disordered. And in one of them lay the lifeless body of Ocelot Margie. She was naked, her ankles bound tightly together with a handkerchief. Her face and chin were bruised, as if someone had used intense force to hold her mouth closed. There were 17 criss-cross slash marks on her face, front and back. Her breasts had been badly bitten. And she had been bleeding profusely from the vagina.

Police forensic experts quickly built up a grisly picture of the indignities inflicted on the woman before her death from suffocation. Her wrists also showed signs of being tied together, though the bond had been removed and was missing. The killer had washed the face of the corpse, but left dried blood in the nostrils and eyelashes.

On Saturday Heath was in Worthing, Sussex, wining and dining the girl with whom he had first occupied the room in Notting Hill. She was Yvonne Symonds, a 19-year-old who had met the chilling charmer at a dance in Chelsea seven days earlier, and only consented to spend the following night with him after accepting his whirlwind proposal of marriage. Now she was back at her parents' home. Heath booked into the nearby Ocean Hotel, and took her for dinner at a club at Angmering.

There he told her his version of the murder in the room they had shared. He said he met the victim on the evening of 20 June, and she asked to borrow his room to entertain another man, since they had nowhere else to go. Heath claimed he slept elsewhere, and was taken to the room by an Inspector Barratt next day and shown the body. It was, he told Yvonne, 'a very gruesome sight.' He added that the killer must be 'a sexual maniac.'

Both Yvonne and her parents were puzzled next morning to read in the Sunday papers that police were looking for Neville George Clevely Heath. Surely they had already seen him? Yvonne rang Heath at the Ocean Hotel, and he told her he was going back to London to clear up what must be a misunderstanding. He did indeed leave Worthing – but not for London. He went further down the south coast, to Bournemouth, where he booked in at the Tollard Royal Hotel as Group Captain Rupert Brooke.

Before he left Worthing, he posted a letter to Inspector Barratt at Scotland Yard. The two had never met, but Heath, who signed the letter with his real name, said he felt duty bound to report what he knew of the murder in his room.

He again said Margery Gardner asked for his keys, but said she was obliged to sleep with the other man for mainly financial reasons. She hinted that, if Heath arrived back at 02.00 she would spend the rest of the night with him. He arrived at the appointed time, found her 'in the condition of which you are aware', then panicked and fled because of his 'invidious position'.

Heath gave a fictitious description of the other man – a slim, dark-haired character called Jack – and curiously added: 'I have the instrument with which Mrs Gardner was beaten and am forwarding this to you today. You will find my fingerprints on it, but you should also find others as well.'

The instrument never arrived, though Inspector Barratt was not surprised by that. Yet despite his suspicions, increased by the letter, Scotland Yard did not issue a photograph of the wanted man. Heath was thus able to enjoy himself in Bournemouth for 13 days, drinking freely, going to shows, and chatting up holidaymaking girls at dances. On 3 July, he invited the friend of one of his dancing partners to tea, and they got on so well that a dinner date was fixed for that night at his hotel. Just after midnight, Heath left to walk her home along the promenade. He was asleep in his own bed at 04.30 when the night porter checked, not having seen him return.

Two days later, the manager of the nearby Norfolk Hotel reported one of his guests missing. Miss Doreen Marshall, a 21-year-old from Pinner, Middlesex, had last been seen leaving for dinner at the Tollard Royal. The manager there asked 'Group Captain Brooke' about his guest, and suggested he contact the police. Heath duly called at the station, identified the girl from photographs, and consoled her anguished father and sister.

But an alert detective constable thought the handsome six-footer fitted a description Scotland Yard had sent them. Heath was asked if he was the man wanted for questioning about a murder in London. He denied it, but was delayed long enough for other officers to take a good look at him. When he complained of feeling cold as the evening drew in, an inspector went to the Tollard Royal to collect Heath's jacket. And in the pockets was all the evidence the police needed.

As well as a single artificial pearl and the return half of a first class rail ticket from London to Bournemouth, there was a left-luggage ticket issued at Bournemouth West station on 23 June. It was for a suitcase which contained clothes labelled Heath, a bloodstained neckerchief, a scarf with human female hairs stuck to it, and a vicious-looking leather-bound riding crop, with a criss-cross weave. The end had worn away, and there was blood on the exposed wires.

Heath was taken to London and charged with the murder of Margery Gardner. On the same evening, 8 July, the body of his second victim was discovered. A woman walking her dog in a deep, wooded valley called

Branksome Chine, a mile west of the Tollard Royal, noticed swarms of flies around a rhododendron bush. She called the police, having read of the missing girl. And officers found a sickening sight.

Doreen Marshall was naked except for one shoe. Her battered body had been covered with her underwear, her inside-out black dress and yellow jacket. Her ripped stockings, broken pearl necklace and powder compact were discarded close by. Her wrists were tied and the inside of her hands ripped, as if she had been trying to avert the blade of a knife. One of her ribs was broken and sticking into her lung, as if someone had knelt on her. And her flesh had been mutilated – mercifully, as forensic experts later proved, after she had been killed with two deep cuts across the throat.

Heath told police that he left Doreen near Bournemouth pier, and watched her walk towards her hotel through some public gardens. He then returned to his own hotel at around 00.30, and because he knew the night porter would be waiting for him, decided to play a practical joke on him, climbing to his room via a builder's ladder left outside. He described it as 'a small deception'. The police dismissed the whole statement as a great deception. And on Thursday 24 September, Heath was charged at the Old Bailey, London, with the murder of Margery Gardner.

His guilt was easily proved. And because he had subsequently killed again, Heath was unable to use what might have been a plausible defence – that Ocelot Margie willingly submitted to whipping and beating, and died accidentally when things got out of hand. Heath knew the game was up, and wanted to plead guilty and accept his punishment coolly and calmly. But his defence counsel persuaded him, against his better judgement, to plead insanity. The attempts of a psychiatrist called on his behalf to try to prove that insanity provided the only memorable moments of the two-day trial.

Dr William Henry de Bargue Hubert, a former psychotherapist at Wormwood Scrubs jail, and one of the leading practising psychiatrists of the day, was utterly discredited by the prosecution cross-examination. A year later, he committed suicide.

Under close questioning from Mr Anthony Hawke for the prosecution, Dr Hubert claimed Heath knew what he was doing when he tied up and lashed Mrs Gardner, but did not consider or know it to be wrong. Did he then think it was right, Dr Hubert was asked. Yes came the reply. 'Are you saying, with your responsibility, that a person in that frame of mind is free from criminal responsibility if what he does causes grievous bodily harm or death?' asked the astounded Hawke. Hubert said he was, because sexual perverts often showed no regret or remorse.

Hawke then asked: 'Would it be your view that a person who finds it convenient at the moment to forge a cheque in order to free himself from financial responsibility is entitled to say that he thought it was right, and therefore he is free from the responsibility of what he does?' Hubert: 'He may think so, yes.'

Hawke: 'With great respect, I did not ask you what he thought. I asked whether you thought he was entitled to claim exemption from responsibility on the grounds of insanity.' Hubert: 'Yes, I do.'

Hawke: 'You are saying that a person who does a thing he wants to do, because it suits him at the moment to do it, is entitled, if that thing is a crime, to claim that he is insane and therefore free from responsibility?' Hubert: 'If the crime and the circumstances are so abnormal to the ordinary person, I do.'

It was an extraordinary thing to claim, and even Heath knew the doctor was harming, not helping, his case. He passed anguished notes to his own counsel, urging him to drop the insanity ploy.

In 1946 the dividing line between the noose and being confined in a mental hospital was the difference between psychopath and psychotic. Psychopaths were considered able to control their evil urges, psychotics were not. In Heath's case, two Home Office prison doctors said he was certainly abnormal, a sadistic sex pervert, but as a psychopath, he was not insane.

The jury of 11 men and one woman found him guilty after only an hour's consideration, and Heath was sentenced to death. He did not bother to appeal, expressed no remorse or sympathy for the families of his victims, and refused to discuss his life or beliefs with any of the experts sent to examine him. He spent most of his last days writing letters, one of which was to his parents: 'My only regret at leaving the world is that I have been damned unworthy of you both.'

He was hanged at Pentonville Prison in London on 26 october, 1946.

The Moors Murders
IAN BRADY AND MYRA HINDLEY

It was the Swinging Sixties and everyone was into wild fashion, weird cults and *The Beatles*. But it wasn't long before Britain was stunned by what were labelled the most cold-blooded killings of the century. Even 20 years later, the horror was still etched in peoples' minds. A country could not forget Myra Hindley and Ian Brady, perpetrators of the notorious Moors Murders.

The 27-year-old stock clerk and 22-year-old typist committed some of the most macabre crimes ever recounted before a British jury. Britain of the sixties was hypnotised by the couple's blood-lust, of how they enticed young children back to their home, sadistically tortured them, murdered them and then buried their bodies on the desolate Pennine moors.

The couple's terrible crimes were committed while capital punishment was still in force but they were found guilty after its abolition. A short year separated them from the gallows and sentenced them to a life behind bars.

Many years later, reformers, such as Lord Longford, were to argue for Hindley's release. The brassy blonde, once infatuated by her lover was said to have undergone a startling change. In her 20 years in Holloway Prison she had turned to religion and taken and passed an Open University degree in humanities. She had, said Longford and his supporters, reached the point where she was no longer a danger to the public.

In 1973, Hindley was given her first taste of freedom since her life sentence – 'life' in Britain normally being 10 years with the possibility of release on licence at the Home Secretary's approval after a third had been served. Along with a prison officer, she was taken on early morning excursions to a London park, but her bouts of freedom raised a howl of protest from the public who could neither forgive or forget the killing of the innocents.

It was Myra Hindley's brother-in-law, David Smith, who eventually gave away the perverted couple's secrets. On 7 October, 1965 at 6.20 am, he contacted the police. The realization of what was going on at number 16, Wardle Brook Avenue on the Hattersley council estate, Manchester, was too strong for him to bear. Shaking, he walked to a public telephone kiosk and rang nearby Stalybridge police station. Within minutes, a young patrol car officer found Smith quaking beside the telephone box. He was so agitated that he could hardly wait to bundle himself into the officer's car.

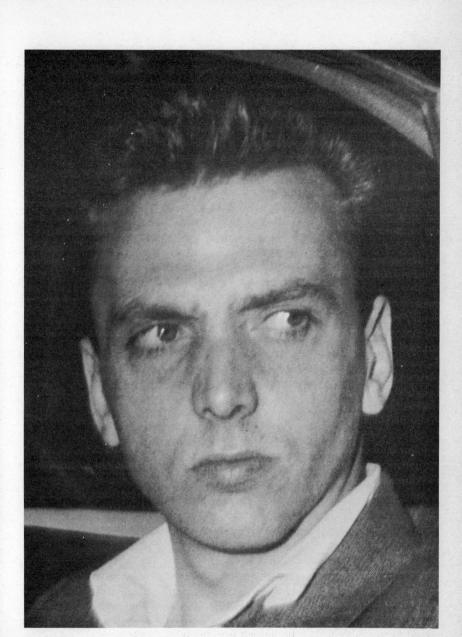

Ian Brady

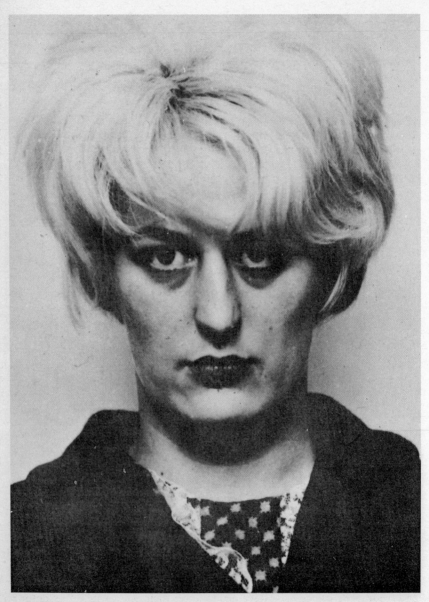

Myra Hindley

Alfred Stratton, 22, and his brother Albert, 20, were the first British murderers to be convicted by their fingerprints. It happened in May 1905, after the battered bodies of Thomas Farrow and his wife were found in the flat above their paint shop in south-east London. A right thumbprint was discovered on the forced cashbox, and after extensive inquiries the police found that it belonged to Alfred who, with his brother, was known to be a burglar.

At the Old Bailey trial, the defence argued strongly that fingerprints were inadmissible evidence, but the judge ruled otherwise. The two brothers were hanged.

As David Smith blurted out his tales of horror, one of the biggest searches ever seen in Britain was begun. Hundreds of police spent weeks scouring the desolate moors for the graves of 10-year-old Lesley Ann Downey and 12-year-old John Kilbride. John had vanished on 23 November, 1963 and Lesley had disappeared a year later, on Boxing Day, 1964.

But first the police had to gain entry to the house in Wardle Brook Avenue where the children had met their deaths. A police superintendent borrowed a white coat and basket from a bread roundsman and approached the house, which belonged to Hindley's grandmother. He knocked on the door which was opened by Hindley.

Brady was lying on a divan bed writing a letter. The note was to his employers saying he wouldn't be at work that day because he had injured his leg. At his trial, it was revealed he had planned to spend the day back on the moors – digging another grave.

With Brady and Hindley separated and safely behind bars, police concentrated all efforts on the moorland search. There they found the grave of 12-year-old John Kilbride. A few yards away, on the other side of a road which split the wild moorland in two, they found the remains of tiny Lesley Ann Downey. They were helped in their search by 'souvenir' photographs, taken by the couple, of Hindley standing over the two graves.

Then came the trial at Chester Assizes – and a courtroom and country shaken by tales of horror and torture. Brady and Hindley, it was revealed, kept vile photographs of their mutilated victims.

But nothing shocked the courtroom more than the playing of a tape. On it were the pleadings, the screams and last dying moments of Lesley Ann Downey.

It took the jury – all male – 18 days to listen to the most horrific evidence ever put before a British court. All seemed to lower their heads when prosecutor Sir Elwyn Jones, the Attorney General, played the tape of young Lesley Ann

> **Cicero's tongue finally got the better of him in AD 43. The Roman orator was assassinated after vexing Mark Anthony with his caustic speeches. As a result, he lost his head and hands, which were displayed in Rome.**
>
> **Anthony's wife, Fulvia, took great glee in ripping Cicero's tongue out of his head and repeatedly stabbed it with a hairpin. She could never match his wit in life – but in death he could not answer back.**

Downey's last moments. People in the court swayed with disgust and onlookers buried faces in their hands.

Brady, quizzed in the witness box, could only say that he was 'embarrassed' when he heard the tape. Hindley did not have her partner in crime's arrogance, but she still held her poise and confidence in the witness box. As her part in the killings became clear she kept uttering 'I was cruel. I was cruel'.

At precisely 2.40 pm on Friday, 6 May, the jury retired. For two hours and 20 minutes, they considered the verdict in 'the trial of the century'. Brady was given concurrent life-sentences for 'these calculated, cruel, cold-blooded murders'. Then came the final words that put Brady behind bars: 'Put him down'. Myra Hindley, for the first time, stood alone in the dock as the judge turned to her. She swayed, as if to faint as she too, was given life-sentences.

The Murderous 'Family'

CHARLES MANSON

Charles Manson preached bloody revolution and ruled a satanic cult who killed at his bidding. He was sentenced to die in the gas chamber, but with the death sentence now abolished in California he is serving nine life sentences for nine murders. On his orders, his followers slaughtered the actress Sharon Tate, the wife of film producer Roman Polanski, and three friends at her Hollywood home in August, 1969.

Two nights later he sent his followers into action again to butcher close neighbours of the Polanskis, supermarket owner Leno la Bianca and his wife Rosemary. He was also found guilty of beheading stuntman Donald Shea and of ordering the execution of musician Gary Hinman.

Manson, 48, is the illegitimate son of a prostitute. When he was young his mother and brother were jailed for beating and robbing men she picked up.

At 11, Manson fell foul of the law and was sent to reform school. He spent the next 21 years in penal institutions, emerging at 32 never having slept with a woman or drunk a glass of beer. Confused by freedom, he caught a long-distance bus chosen at random and alighted at San Francisco's Haight-Ashbury district, centre of the world hippie movement.

It was 1967, the height of the peace-and-love flower-power era. Manson grew his hair long, wore a beard and played the guitar. Soon he had a circle of admirers. Girls came to kneel at his feet. One said: 'The first time I heard him sing, it was like an angel. He was magnetic.' Another, Lynette 'Squeaky' Fromme, said: 'With Charlie, I was riding on the wind. Making love with Charlie was guiltless, like a baby.'

But Manson had little respect for women. At the commune he set up in the Hollywood hills, they outnumbered men four-to-one. One of the rules of his 'family' was that the dogs had to be fed before the women. Girls had to submit instantly to the men Manson named. He banned contraceptives, alcohol and the wearing of spectacles. Questions by the girls were forbidden and they could not use the word 'Why?' But they worshipped him as a god.

Women would travel miles to ask him to sleep with them. A film actress who begged for his favours was told to first climb a nearby mountain. Another woman brought along her 15-year-old daughter. Manson told the mother to go because she was too old, and to leave her daughter. She obeyed.

Charles Manson, in the chapel of Vacaville jail, California

Manson's incredible magnetism gave him an entry to the wilder fringe of the Hollywood party circuit. It is almost certain he and some of his followers had been entertained by the Polanskis before the night Sharon and her friends died.

The slaughter was the culmination of months of testing to which Manson had subjected his disciples. Bored with their simple adoration of him, he started to organize law-breaking exercises. He made them steal cars, commit petty thefts and prowl round people's homes in 'creepy-crawling' black clothes. Then he ordered them to Sharon Tate's house to terrorize a man whom he said had broken several promises to him.

Polanski was in Europe making a film, and he asked an old friend, Voytek Frykowski and his girlfriend Abigail Folger, to move in with Sharon to keep her company.

On the evening of 8 August, Jay Sebring, Sharon's ex-lover and now a friend, had dropped in too. They and an 18-year-old youth visiting Frykowski, were to die horribly that night at the hands of three girls and an ex-football star, trusted members of Manson's inner circle. Sharon, who was eight months pregnant, was stabbed 16 times. The word 'Pig' was written in her blood on the front door.

Today the man whose reign of bloody terror stunned the world is serving out his sentence as caretaker of the prison chapel at Vacaville, in southern California. He is unrepentant about the past, claiming to feel no guilt for the bestial crimes committed at his command. He told the British photographer Albert Foster: 'I am not ashamed or sorry. If it takes fear and violence to open the eyes of the dollar-conscious society, the name Charles Manson can be that fear.'

Inset: Sharon Tate with Roman Polanski at their wedding, 1968

The Son of Sam

DAVID BERKOWITZ

Son of Sam killer David Berkowitz cold-bloodedly murdered six people and wounded another seven during the year he terrorized New York. He shot five women and one man dead in a series of vicious killings which spread panic round the city during 1977. Son of Sam struck at courting couples and lone women. The killer also turned his gun on two dogs. When the spate of killings were linked, hysteria mounted. Discos and restaurants were deserted as the frightened population made sure they were home before dark.

It was in the last few months Berkowitz was at large that he became known as Son of Sam. Police found a letter lying in the road just a few yards from the dead bodies of two young lovers. The letter read: 'Dear Captain Joseph Borelli, I am deeply hurt by your calling me a woman hater. I am not. But I am a monster. I am the Son of Sam.' Berkowitz left the letter in the road after he fired at a couple as they embraced in a car.

He had already killed three people and wounded four, but after the chilling letter was published New York's Mayor Beame ordered police: 'Catch this man.' A special squad of 200 detectives was formed. Every rumour and tip-off was followed up but the identity of the killer remained a mystery. More than 100 police were put on nightly patrols in areas of the Bronx and Queens where it was thought he might strike again.

Police described the killer as 'neurotic, schizophrenic and paranoid'. They came up with the theory that he might believe himself the victim of demonic possession. Because of the uncanny way Berkowitz escaped detection, it was believed at one time that he might be a policeman using inside information to vanish undetected. Meanwhile the killings continued.

One night a high-school girl and her boyfriend were shot as they got into their car. Berkowitz fired through the windscreen, hitting the boy in the arm and the girl in the head, neck and shoulder. A month later he struck again. Two 20-year-olds on their first date together were shot as they kissed in a car. Bobby Violante was just telling Stacy Moskowitz how much he cared for her when the bullet which was to blind him smashed into his face. Stacy was also shot in the head, and she died 38 hours later on a hospital operating table.

Berkowitz was caught eventually because of a parking ticket. He watched from the shadows while police stuck a ticket on his car. When they had gone he

David Berkowitz with inset of 17-year-old victim, Judy Placido

walked over and screwed up the ticket. But he was seen by a woman walking her dog. She thought he had a strange smile on his face and when he came close to her she saw he had a gun in his hand. She called the police the next day and told them about the parking ticket. They traced the car through their records. The next day police lay in wait for Berkowitz. He walked to his car with the .44 calibre gun in a paper bag. When challenged he told police in his soft voice: 'I'm Sam.' The officers remember that he had a peculiar, child-like smile on his face. At his trial he claimed bloodthirsty demons made him kill. He said that one of the dogs he shot had the spirit of a 6,000-year-old man who ordered him to kill.

Berkowitz, now 28, was sentenced to 30 years in jail after he pleaded guilty to the series of attacks and killings. Since his trial he has claimed that he was a member of a New York satanic cult and other men were involved in the murders. Now he passes his days writing letters to girlfriends, newspapers, congressmen and journalists.

Police still believe that Berkowitz acted alone. But other people take seriously his claims that more people were involved. Eyewitness descriptions of the killer varied markedly in height and appearance. And none of the four different police sketches of the murderer closely resembled Berkowitz. Nor does the handwriting on many of the messages sent to police and newspapers by Son of Sam match up with Berkowitz's. The most intriguing riddle involves Sam Carr, who owned the dog that Berkowitz claimed bewitched him. Carr's two sons, John and Michael, both died in suspicious circumstances after Berkowitz was arrested. John Carr was found shot to death in his girlfriend's apartment and Michael died when his car crashed for no apparent reason. These factors have led some lawyers to claim that Berkowitz was only a lookout for a group involved in the murder conspiracy.

People who knew Berkowitz before his arrest say he was a loner without any personal charms. He loved to gorge himself on junk food. His favourite meal

---

Mentally deranged sex-maniac, German-born Bruno Ludke, had committed no fewer than 85 murders before his arrest in 1943. From the age of 18 he raped, robbed, stabbed or strangled his prey for pleasure. When humans were not available he resorted to torturing animals. Finally, when Ludke was arrested for sexual assault, Himmler's SS sterilised him. When he confessed to all his crimes, his prosecutors realized that, in several cases, other people had been executed for Ludke's killings. The scandal was hushed up and Ludke was sent to hospital in Vienna, where he became the guinea pig for medical and psychiatric experiments. He died there in 1944.

was hamburgers followed by chocolate ice-cream. When he was arrested, police at first took him to be retarded. Two guns were pressed against his head and he was ordered to 'freeze', but his only response was to keep smiling. Arresting officer John Falotico remembers: 'He had that stupid smile on his face, like it was a kid's game.'

Nobody knows why Berkowitz started to kill. But after the first killing of Donna Lauria, the murders became an addiction. He drove around New York night after night looking for victims. He also liked to return to the scene of his murders. One night after shooting a courting couple, instead of fleeing the scene he drove on a few blocks to catch a glimpse of the apartment block where his first victim Donna had lived. He told police that after a murder he felt 'flushed with power'. After a killing he would go to a late night snack bar to eat his favourite chocolate desserts.

It was Berkowitz's ordinariness that helped him escape capture. At one place where he lodged, all that the family could remember of him was that he was a 'regular sort of guy who used to take his car out in the middle of the night'.

Since he has been in prison Berkowitz has gone some way to achieving his ambition of becoming a celebrity. He has unlimited letter writing privileges and conducts torrid pen-pal romances with women. Berkowitz has made more than $200,000 from various articles, a book and film rights to his life. A court battle by the relatives of his victims to prevent him getting any of the money failed.

The Boston Strangler

ALBERT DESALVO

I t was a hot steamy night in June, 1962, when police were called to a run-down apartment building in the centre of Boston. In the bedroom, they found the body of a young woman. Partially clothed, with her limbs arranged in an obscene posture, the woman had been strangled with one of her own stockings.

Although, on that sticky, humid night, the killing seemed only to be a random sex murder, the discovery was the beginning of a reign of terror that was to grip the city and capture the morbid imagination of the nation for more than 18 months. For the murder was the first carried out by one of the most notorious mass murderers of the century . . . 'The Boston Strangler'.

For a year-and-a-half, police sought in vain to unmask the fiend who left his trademark on 11 of the 13 bodies: a single stocking tied tightly around the neck of his victim. Of the two other victims, one was stabbed to death, and another died of a heart attack, allegedly in the arms of the Strangler.

The man behind the mass murders was former US Army boxing champion, Albert DeSalvo. In a twist as bizarre as the killings themselves, DeSalvo was never tried for the Strangler murders, but for an assorted series of robberies and sex attacks on women whom he did not kill.

Although some still express doubt that DeSalvo was the Boston Strangler, the thick-set handyman, who always wore his black hair slicked back and had an obsession for dressing in neat, freshly laundered white shirts, did make a confession to the killings. Facts which only came to light after he was sentenced to life imprisonment seemed to confirm that DeSalvo was indeed the Strangler.

Albert DeSalvo had been in trouble with the law since his childhood, mostly for breaking into homes – a skill that was to be put to terrifying use when he began his killing spree. As a young man he served with the US Army's occupation force in Germany, where he married a local girl, Irmgard. But after having two children, the couple were divorced. He became the Army's middleweight boxing champion, but left the service on his return to America and became a handyman.

DeSalvo had a sexual drive that some doctors described as 'uncontrollable'. Back in his army days, according to one psychiatrist who gave evidence at his trial, his wife constantly complained about his sexual demands. 'She refused

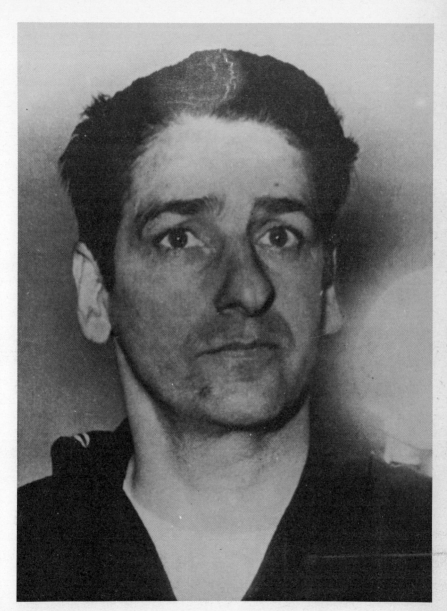

Albert DeSalvo, aged 35

him sex', said Dr James Brussel, 'because he made excessive demands on her. She did not want to submit to his type of kissing which was extensive as far as the body was concerned.'

He added that during his off-duty hours in the army, DeSalvo would engage in wild orgies with the wives of officers who were absent.

'DeSalvo was without doubt, the victim of one of the most crushing sexual drives that psychiatric science has ever encountered', said his lawyer, the famous defence attorney, F. Lee Bailey. 'He was without doubt schizophrenic.'

The wave of killings began in 1962 and, despite the setting up of a special 'Strangler Squad' by law enforcement officers, they continued unabated until 1964. In each case, the women who fell victim to the Strangler were killed in their own homes. DeSalvo gained access to their apartments by posing as a delivery man or by claiming he had been sent by the superintendent of the building to check a leaking waterpipe.

Many of the Strangler's victims were sexually molested, which was in keeping with DeSalvo's insatiable sex drive. They were nearly all undressed, and their bodies arranged in obscene poses.

As the murders continued unabated, so the fear and panic among the citizens of Boston increased. Few took to the streets by themselves at night. Husbands going away on business left their wives loaded guns at their bedsides. Police patrols reached an unprecedented level. But despite the rising death toll, and the almost daily arrest – and release – of possible suspects, Albert DeSalvo, then 32 was never once interviewed by police. He should have been a prime target for investigation . . . having only just been released from prison after serving six months for sex offences. He had posed as an agent for a top modelling agency, and persuaded young women to allow him to take their measurements. But it was just an excuse to molest them, and he was arrested for what became known as the 'Measuring Man' attacks.

Then in 1964 he was arrested for the 'Green Man' attacks. He was nick-named the 'Green Man' because of his love for green trousers, which he always wore when he broke into the homes of single women. He would strip his victims at knife-point and kiss them all over, before making his escape. A description given by one of the victims, however, was matched by a detective, as being an exact description of the 'Measuring Man', and DeSalvo was brought in.

After his arrest, he was taken to the Bridgewater Mental Institute in Massachusetts, where the terrible truth was to come out.

At his trial for the 'Green Man' offences, psychiatrist Robert Mezer stunned the court when he revealed that DeSalvo had admitted to him in hospital that he was the Strangler. He said that during an interview at Bridgewater, DeSalvo had confessed he strangled 13 women. 'He went into details about some of them, telling me some of the intimate acts he had committed.'

But by Massachusetts' law no doctor who takes information from a suspect in a case can give it as evidence in a courtroom, so the full story never came out at DeSalvo's trial. However, there is little doubt in the minds of most experts that DeSalvo was the Boston Strangler. Probably the most telling revelations came from his defence lawyer, F. Lee Bailey, in his book, *The Defence Never Rests*. He explained that that DeSalvo had made another confession, this time to doctors and law enforcement officers, in a dramatic meeting in July 1965. But because of a special deal between the police and the defence, the evidence was never used.

'I wanted DeSalvo studied by experts, and the authorities wanted to be able to end their investigation. In both cases, DeSalvo's identification as the Boston Strangler had to be irrefutably established. That was only possible if the police interviewed him and matched his memory against the myriad of details of the 13 murders.'

After striking the bargain that the conversations with DeSalvo would not be used in court, the meeting took place at the Bridgewater Mental Institute. It was supposed to take only 15 minutes. Instead it took more than five hours, as more and more damning evidence that DeSalvo was the Strangler was to emerge. He revealed information about the victims that only the real murderer could possibly have known. He said there was a notebook under the bed of victim number eight, brunette Beverly Samans. He was also able to draw floor plans of the apartments of his victims, and could give clear descriptions of the furnishings and decoration.

These and other details added up to more than 50 hours of tapes made at subsequent interviews with DeSalvo and more than 2000 pages of transcript. All details were checked and all were correct.

But the dramatic details that could have convicted DeSalvo as the Boston Strangler were never fully revealed until after his trial for the other offences. And the only man who could know with certainty whether he had killed 13 women, Albert DeSalvo, is now silenced for ever. In 1973, six years after he was sent to Walpole State Prison, in Massachusetts, DeSalvo was stabbed to death by three other inmates, in a row over drugs.

The Yorkshire Ripper

PETER SUTCLIFFE

When the savagely-mutilated body of Wilma McCann, a 28-year-old prostitute, was found on 30 October, 1975, on playing fields in Leeds, no-one but the police took much notice. The newspapers dismissed her murder with a few paragraphs, and her neighbours, while shocked by the tragedy, explained that 'Hotpants' McCann was 'no better than she ought to have been'.

Only Wilma's four children and a handful of friends mourned her wretched end. The honest citizens of Leeds, long angered by the vice which flourished in the Chapeltown district where Wilma lived, quickly forgot about her death.

However, Dennis Hoban, the 48-year-old head of Leeds area CID could not forget the horrific injuries he had seen on McCann's body – the skull smashed in with a blunt instrument, the trunk punctured by 15 stab wounds. 'The attack was savage and frenzied,' Chief Superintendent Hoban told a press conference. 'It suggested the work of a psychopath and, with this kind of person, there is always the likelihood that he will strike again.' His words were grimly prophetic.

During the next five years the man who came to be known as 'the Yorkshire Ripper' struck many times, killing 12 more women and maiming seven – a terrifying, shadowy figure who brought near hysteria to the cobbled streets of West Yorkshire and who sparked off the biggest police hunt of the century.

His grim nickname, reminiscent of London's Jack the Ripper of 1888, did not hit the headlines until his second murder – that of part-time prostitute Mrs Emily Jackson, 42, in a Chapeltown alleyway on 20 January, 1976 – less than three months after the McCann killing.

Mrs Jackson's body, too, was dreadfully mutilated. Repeated blows from a blunt instrument had stove in the back of the skull and the bloodstained trunk was punctured by 50 cruciform-shaped stab wounds, caused by a sharpened Phillip's-type screwdriver.

Chief Superintendent Hoban appealed to the public: 'I can't stress strongly enough that it is vital we catch this brutal killer before he brings tragedy to another family.'

If the first murder had been virtually ignored, the second was given big play by the press. And it was George Hill, of the *Daily Express* who coined the soubriquet 'the Yorkshire Ripper'.

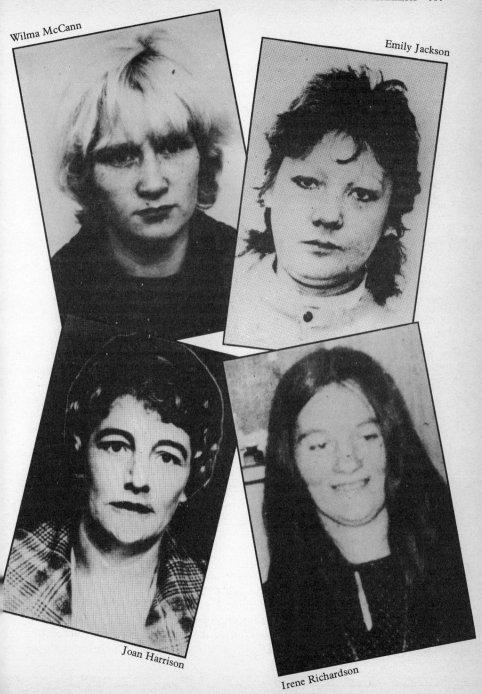

Wilma McCann

Emily Jackson

Joan Harrison

Irene Richardson

On 8 February, 1977, the Ripper killed again. His victim, another prostitute, was 28-year-old Irene Richardson, whose stabbed body was found in Roundhay Park, Leeds. Although Roundhay is a highly-respectable, middle-class suburb, it is little more than a mile from the edge of the Chapeltown district where McCann and Jackson had died.

Less than three months later the Ripper's grim 'score' rose to four and, once again, the victim was a prostitute, Tina Atkinson, aged 32, who was found battered to death on 24 April. She was on the bed of her flat in the Lumb Lane area of Bradford, a 'red light' district smaller than Leeds's Chapeltown, but with an equally bad reputation.

As in the three previous killings, the Ripper had left precious few clues for the police beyond his 'trademark' of hammerblows to the skull. Of the few clues, however, one was vital: the footprint made by a boot, which exactly matched a print found at the scene of Emily Jackson's murder.

It was a useful break for the weary and bewildered CID men, but they were still being hampered by lack of public concern. What they needed was something that would bring forward witnesses who, up to then, had refused to get involved on the grounds that the victims were 'only prostitutes'.

They got what they wanted on the morning of Sunday 26 June, 1977, but there was not a policeman in the West Yorkshire force who did not wish that it could have happened some other way.

Jayne MacDonald was found battered and stabbed to death in a children's playground in the heart of Chapeltown. But Jayne, just 16, blonde and with filmstar good looks, was no prostitute – just a happy teenager, ruthlessly cut down by the Ripper while walking home after a night out with a boyfriend. Now, at last, after almost two years of working against public apathy, the police had an 'innocent' victim on their hands.

From that moment there was no shortage of information. On the contrary, the Ripper Squad began slowly to founder under the weight of facts, theories and suppositions from the general public.

There is no doubt that the slaying of Jayne MacDonald led to the death of her father, railwayman Wilf MacDonald, two years later. Soon after Jayne's killing he told reporters how his daughter had bent to kiss him on the head before going out on that fateful night. 'She was so sweet and clean,' said Mr MacDonald. 'She was untouched and perfect, just like a flower.'

The next time he saw her was on a mortuary slab. He said: 'The pain of seeing her blonde hair, which had been so shiny and clean the night before, now caked in blood was so indescribable it haunts my every waking moment.'

From that moment Wilf MacDonald waited for death, praying for the moment when he would be released from the horror that the Ripper had visited upon him. When he died broken-hearted on 11 October, 1979, he was a Ripper

Patricia Atkinson

Jayne MacDonald

Jean Jordan

Yvonne Pearson

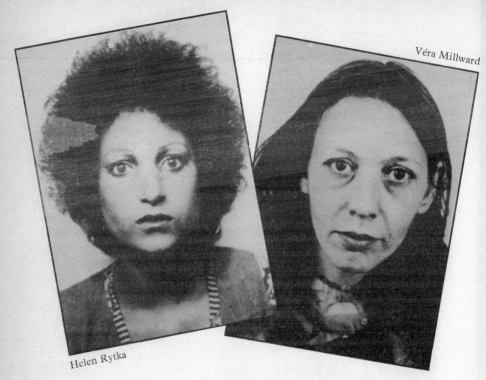

Véra Millward

Helen Rytka

victim just as surely as if he had been killed by a blow from a ball-pein hammer.

By then six more women had been murdered: Jean Jordan, aged 21, prostitute, murdered and hideously mutilated on allotments in Manchester, on 1 October, 1977. Yvonne Pearson, aged 22, prostitute, murdered on 21 January, 1978, on waste ground in Bradford. Her badly decomposed body was not found until 26 March. Helen Rytka, aged 18, prostitute, murdered beneath a railway viaduct in Huddersfield, West Yorkshire, on 31 January 1978. Vera Millward, aged 41, prostitute, murdered in the grounds of Manchester Royal Infirmary on 17 May, 1978. Josephine Whitaker, aged 19, a respectable building society clerk, bludgeoned to death near her home in Halifax, Yorkshire, while taking a short cut through Savile Park on the night of 4 April, 1979. Barbara Leach, aged 20, a respectable student at Bradford University, killed near Bradford city centre in the early hours of 2 September, 1979.

Three months before the slaying of 'Babs' Leach, a sensational twist to the Ripper inquiry had echoed all round the world, giving newspapers, television and radio one of the most bizarre crime stories ever to hit the headlines. It was in the form of a cassette tape, played at a press conference on 26 June by Assistant Chief Constable George Oldfield, head of West Yorkshire CID.

'I'm Jack,' said the voice on the tape in a chilling monotone. 'I see you are still having no luck catching me. I have the greatest respect for you, George, but, Lord, you are no nearer catching me than four years ago when I started. I reckon your boys are letting you down, George. you can't be much good, can ya? The only time they came near catching me was a few months back in Chapeltown when I was disturbed. Even then it was a uniform copper, not a detective.

I warned you in March that I'd strike again. Sorry it wasn't Bradford. I did promise you that, but I couldn't get there. I'm not quite sure when I will strike again, but it will be definitely some time this year, maybe September or October, even sooner if I get the chance. I am not sure where, maybe Manchester. I like it there, there's plenty of them knocking about. They never learn, do they, George. I bet you've warned them, but they never listen.

At the rate I'm going I should be in the book of records. I think it's up to eleven now, isn't it. Well, I'll keep on going for quite a while yet. I can't see myself being nicked just yet. Even if you do get near I'll probably top myself first.

'Well, it's been nice chatting to you, George. Yours, Jack the Ripper.

No good looking for fingerprints. You should know by now it's as clean as a whistle. See you soon. Bye. Hope you like the catchy tune at the end. Ha. Ha. Ha.'

The music that followed was the six-line reprise of 'Thank You For Being a Friend', a 1978 song by Californian musician Andrew Gold.

As the music faded, George Oldfield said: 'I believe that we have now got the break we have been waiting for.'

But that was where it all started to go wrong. The Ripper inquiry went off course at a tragic tangent. For the voice on the tape was identified by dialect experts as belonging to someone from the Castletown district of Sunderland. From that moment detectives manning the £4,000,000 hunt for the Ripper began looking for a man with a Geordie accent. . .

Peter William Sutcliffe did not have a Geordie accent. His voice, slightly high-pitched and hesitant, was flat with the broad vowels of his native town of Bingley, a few miles to the west of Bradford.

There, on the fringes of the Brontë country, Sutcliffe was born on 2 June, 1946, the first child of John and Kathleen Sutcliffe who lived in a one-up, one-down cottage in Heaton Row, close by the edge of the wild moors above Bingley.

Peter was a shy boy, prone to blushing in the company of girls, though his polite good manners were much admired by his parents' neighbours. He left

Cottingley Manor School, Bingley, at the end of spring term in 1961, aged 15, and for three years drifted through a variety of undistinguished jobs before starting work as a gravedigger in Bingley Cemetery in 1964. With the exception of a short break in 1965, he remained at the job until he was sacked for bad timekeeping in 1967 . . . and loved every minute of it.

Sutcliffe's gravedigging career is littered with revolting stories of desecration and grave-robbing that tell of the dark shadows that were already gathering in his mind. Often he outraged his workmates by interfering with corpses, sometimes to steal rings or gold teeth, but other times simply because he seemed to enjoy handling dead bodies.

Eventually he managed to get himself attached to the mortuary as an attendant and would regale his friends with descriptions of the cadavers he had seen cut open for post-mortem examination. Often, after a night in the pub, he would rattle the mortuary keys and ask if anyone wanted to see the latest body. There were never any takers.

Sutcliffe was married on 10 August, 1974, at Clayton Baptist Chapel, Bradford. It was a double celebration for that day was also the birthday of his bride, Sonia Szurma, an attractive 24-year-old teacher, daughter of eastern European refugees. A shy girl, Sonia looked even more demure than usual at her wedding. She could not have known that her groom had ended the previous evening's stag night celebrations by taking himself down to Bradford's red light district of Lumb Lane. But the darkly-handsome, sallow-faced Sutcliffe was a frequent visitor to Lumb Lane, and to Leeds's Chapeltown, and to Manchester's Moss Side.

Fourteen months after marrying Sonia, Sutcliffe killed Wilma McCann, and those infamous districts became a slaughterhouse where women lived in terror and police sought desperately for a murderer with a Geordie accent.

They had one gift of a clue – a brand new £5 note found in the handbag of the Ripper's first Manchester victim, Jean Jordan, murdered on 1 October, 1977. The serial number, AW51 121565, was traced to the Midland Bank at Shipley, a suburb of Bradford. The manager explained to detectives that the note had been issued only five days before it had been handed over to Jordan – probably in the pay-roll of a local firm.

Manchester police sent a team over to Shipley to join their West Yorkshire colleagues, and thousands of local men were interviewed. Among them was the entire workforce of T. and W. H. Clark, an engineering and haulage firm, based in Canal Road, Shipley.

One of the men interviewed was a lorry driver called Sutcliffe. In the cab of his lorry was pinned this handwritten notice: 'In this truck is a man whose latent genius, if unleashed, would rock the nation, whose dynamic energy would overpower those around him. Better let him sleep.'

Josephine Whitaker

Barbara Leach

Jacqueline Hill

Olivia Reivers and Denise Hall

If the detectives trying to trace the owner of the £5 note saw the notice they did not read any significance into it for Peter Sutcliffe was questioned and cleared.

He was to be interviewed another eight times throughout the remaining span of the Ripper enquiry . . . and each time he was cleared and released. His workmates at Clark's even joked about the number of times he was questioned and gave him the nickname 'the Ripper'.

By now, under the influence of the intelligent, well-educated Sonia, Sutcliffe was busy bettering himself. Always immaculately dressed in crisp, fresh overalls, he had a reputation as one of Clark's top drivers. And he and Sonia moved into the decidedly middle-class Heaton district of Bradford, buying a four-bedroomed detached house in Garden Lane.

But strange things happened behind the respectable lace curtains at Number 6. There was domestic friction with the tiny, frail Sonia often heard ranting and shouting at her embarrassed husband, ignoring his pleas to keep her voice down 'in case the neighbours hear'.

It is a bizarre concept – the monstrously evil killer as a henpecked husband, but in Sutcliffe's case it was true. More than one detective on the Ripper Squad has said: 'Every time he killed, he was really killing Sonia.'

The faithful and devoted husband, the loyal and hardworking employee, the polite and helpful friend, these were the faces that Peter Sutcliffe showed to the rest of the world. The face of the fiend was one he reserved for darkness – and his victims. At first they had been prostitutes and, in a perverted way, he could try to justify their deaths, as did the original Jack the Ripper, by claiming that he was ridding the streets of 'filth'.

But then had come the murder of Jayne MacDonald. She had been no whore. Nor had Jo Whitaker or Babs Leach, victims number ten and eleven. Nor had several of the women who had survived his attacks. So now there could be no pretence of being a crusading 'street-cleaner'.

Was he seeking to punish the domineering Sonia? Or was he seeking revenge on all womankind? For in 1972 Sutcliffe, his two sisters and two brothers, had been astounded and horrified to discover that their mother, Kathleen, the woman they called 'the Angel', had been having a secret affair. Highly religious, even prudish, Kathleen had slipped from the pedestal on which her doting children had placed her.

Perhaps it is significant that the twelfth victim was, like the late Mrs Sutcliffe (she died in November 1978), middle-aged and highly respectable. Margo Walls was 47, a former sergeant in the WRAC, an unmarried civil servant who lived alone in Pudsey, a small town between Leeds and Bradford.

After working late on 22 August, 1980, she set off to walk the half mile from her office to her home – and met Sutcliffe. He reared out of the dark shadows of a gateway and aimed a blow at her head. Although stunned, Miss Walls fought

Peter Sutcliff and Sonia on their wedding day

Peter Sutcliffe's fantasy woman, Theresa Douglas

back savagely, punching and clawing at her attacker. But the slightly built Sutcliffe was strong and managed to get a garotte around her neck. When Margo was dead, Sutcliffe stripped her body, dragged her up the driveway – that of a local magistrate – and buried her beneath a pile of grass cuttings.

Police investigating the murder decided that it was not the work of the Ripper. The garotte, they said, was not his style. But three months later, on Monday 17 November, 1980, the Ripper struck again and this time there was no doubt in the minds of the investigating detectives.

The victim was Jacqueline Hill, a 20-year-old student at Leeds University. At 21.23 that fateful Monday night she alighted from a bus outside the Arndale shopping centre in the residential district of Headingley, Leeds, and began walking the 200 metres up Alma Road towards her hall of residence.

Sutcliffe, who minutes before had been eating chicken and chips from a nearby Kentucky Fried Chicken shop, leapt out of his parked Rover and rained hammerblows on the back of her head. She went down without a sound, laying limply as her attacker dragged her across Alma Road into some bushes behind the Arndale Centre. There, with a sharpened screwdriver, he set about inflicting his terrible trademark on her body. The final wound was the worst of all – a stab through the retina of the eye 'because', Sutcliffe explained after his arrest, 'she seemed to be staring at me.'

The killing of yet another respectable victim, particularly in the straight-laced heart of middle-class Headingley, caused a more violent eruption of public fury and indignation than before. West Yorkshire's Chief Constable, Mr Ronald Gregory, was being pressed hard by the public and local politicians who demanded action fast.

On 25 November he announced the formation of a 'super squad' – a think-tank of senior officers drawn from other forces. Assistant Chief Constable George Oldfield was, effectively, taken off the case, although he remained head of West Yorkshire CID.

It must have been a bitter blow for Oldfield who had lived, day and night, with the case almost from the start. The hunt for the Ripper had become a personal crusade, especially since that tape recording had arrived to taunt him.

In his place, with the temporary acting rank of Assistant Chief Constable, Mr Gregory appointed Jim Hobson, head of Leeds area CID, successor to Chief Superintendent Dennis Hoban who had begun the inquiry and who had died suddenly at the age of 51 in March 1978.

Hobson and Oldfield did not see eye to eye. Their relationship was correct rather than cordial and Hobson lost no time in getting rid of the albatross of the 'Geordie accent' that had hung round the neck of the inquiry for so long. Oldfield, who had virtually staked his reputation on the tape, could only watch.

Then Hobson, in a statement that was almost clairvoyant, announced that if the Ripper was caught 'it will be by an ordinary uniformed copper, going about his normal duties'.

That is exactly what happened on the night of Friday, 2 January, 1981, as Peter Sutcliffe prepared to kill his fourteenth victim – a coloured Sheffield prostitute called Ava Reivers. The two of them were sitting in Sutcliffe's Rover V8 in the driveway of an office block in Melbourne Drive, Sheffield. Sutcliffe had handed over a £10 note for sex, but had failed to get an erection. On the back seat were a hammer, a garotte and a sharpened screwdriver.

The man who had called himself 'Dave' suddenly whispered to Ava: 'I'm scared – really scared.' But it was Ava who was scared; somehow she knew beyond doubt that this 'punter' intended her harm.

At that moment the police arrived, a sergeant and a PC in a panda car, making a routine check on the cars parked in the leafy lovers' lane. 'Dave' was reduced to near panic.

Ava, pleased for the first time in her life to see a policeman, was relieved to be taken to the police station for questioning about her 'lover's' identity and for him to be quizzed as to why the Rover was carrying false number plates.

It was during that interview that Sergeant Arthur Armitage, after studying the man who claimed to be 'Peter Williams', suddenly spoke up. In his broad South Yorkshire accent he said: 'Tha's t' Ripper, thee!'

The nightmare was over.

On Friday, 22 May, 1981, Peter William Sutcliffe stood in the dock at the Old Bailey's Number One court and listened impassively as the jury found him guilty of 13 murders and seven attempted murders.

Mr Justice Boreham sentenced him to life imprisonment on each count, adding: 'I shall recommend to the Home Secretary that the minimum period which should elapse before he orders your release shall be 30 years. That is a long period, an unusually long period in my judgement, but you, I believe, are an unusually dangerous man. I express the hope that, when I have said life imprisonment, it will mean precisely that.'

Sutcliffe is currently serving that sentence in the maximum security wing of Parkhurst Prison on the Isle of Wight.

The cruel hoaxer who threw the whole Ripper hunt awry with his mocking Geordie voice – and so helped kill three woman – remains free.

The Killer Clown

JOHN WAYNE GACY

When they christened him with the name of their favourite film star, John Wayne Gacy's parents had high hopes that their little boy would one day become famous. In a way they saw their dreams realized – although not quite as wished.

John Wayne Gacy today is a name that conjures up revulsion among millions of Americans. He is one of the country's most sadistic and prolific mass murderers, and known as the Killer Clown. When he was finally tracked down and tackled by the Chicago police in 1978, Gacy readily admitted to murdering no fewer than 33 young men and boys. Before strangling and stabbing them to death, he had brutally raped them.

Gacy was a fat, lonely homosexual with an insatiable sexual appetite. He longed to be loved by the neighbours who regarded him as 'a wierdo'. And he had aspirations of becoming somebody in local politics. To that end, he began a deliberate campaign to win over the local populace in the Chicago suburb of Norwood Park Township. A friend with connections in the Democratic Party showed him how: he would have to become a local benefactor with particular emphasis on the neighbourhood children.

Gacy set about this task with gusto. He designed three clown outfits himself, then set about creating a character. Very soon he was a local celebrity as Pogo the Clown, performing in the streets, at children's parties and other functions. He was so successful that President Carter's wife Rosalynn posed with him for a photograph, then sent him an autographed copy. He treasured that.

But while 38-year-old Gacy clowned for the kids and posed for posterity, the Chicago police were baffled by the mysterious disappearance of a number of local youths. On their files were also several missing persons from other states.

It took the police six years to nail Gacy. When they did, they met with a torrent of abuse from residents of Northwood Park for the appalling record of overlooked clues and bungled detective work. Had they been more efficient, people argued, at least some of the Killer Clown's victims might have lived. In fact, on four occasions between 1972 and 1978, Gacy's name had appeared on police files as a suspect in the missing persons cases. He had also been convicted twice for sex assaults on young men.

Interviewed at police headquarters, Gacy drew a detailed map of his

Above: Police search John
Wayne Gacy's home for more
bodies

Right: John Wayne Gacy,
convicted of killing 33
men and boys

property, pinpointing the location of 28 of the bodies. After raping and killing his victims, he had methodically buried them in the extensive, landscaped garden of his neat and modern ranch house. The bodies of five other boys had been thrown into the Des Plaines river, near his home.

Gacy had been heavily influenced by his mother since childhood. His older sister also seemed to dominate him. He was a weak-willed man who carried his resentment towards women with him through later life. Nevertheless, he was determined to succeed in business. And that much he did. From humble beginnings, he built up a construction business that flourished.

Gacy took advantage of the rising unemployment in Chicago and offered jobs to young unskilled men who stood the least chance of finding employment. His local lads were all under 20 and receiving unemployment benefit. Others he picked up from the Greyhound Bus station in Chicago: these were often drifters heading for California hoping to find their pot of gold. Instead they found death.

'I wanted to give these young people a chance' he told police during questioning. 'Young people always get a raw deal. But if you give them responsibility they rise to the occasion. They're hard workers and proud of their work.'

Gacy's teenage workforce were well-paid and happy. As the contracts continued to pour in, he needed more labourers. At the end of a hard day – for he put in many hours himself – Gacy would get into his Oldsmobile and head for the Greyhound Station, looking for more employees among the itinerants. He always found somebody.

He had been married in 1967 and again five years after that. His first wife, who divorced him in 1969, bore him two children. She said of him. 'He was a likeable salesman who could charm anything right out of you.' Wife number two, Carole Hoff, said her husband 'started bringing home a lot of pictures of

Unrepentant sex assaulter, robber and murderer Carl Panzram could not wait to be hanged. He told his executioner at Fort Leavenworth, Texas, in 1930: 'While you're fooling around, I could hang a dozen men.' Panzram's life was one of insatiable hatred. 'I hate the whole darn race, including myself,' he said. And he had proved it by murdering more than 21 people and committing thousands of burglaries.

Sentenced to 25 years at Fort Leavenworth, he threatened to kill the first man who angered him. He carried out the threat shortly afterwards by murdering a prison laundry worker. When sentenced to be executed, he said he looked forward to it as 'a pleasure and a great relief'.

> **John Wesley Hardin started out as a Texas Sunday school teacher and ended up a cold, calculating killer. From the age of 15, when he murdered a negro slave and shot two soldiers who tried to catch him, he continued his rampage of slaughter until his death in 1895 at the age of 42. He was reputed to have murdered between 24 and 40 people, most of them black.**

naked men' just before they separated. They were divorced in 1976. Both his wives described him as 'mysterious' and said he had been a normal husband for the first few months of marriage, but then began staying out at night in his car. He beat his wives.

Where did Gacy go? Later it emerged that he would frequent 'Bughouse Square', a notorious corner of Chicago populated at night by legions of young homosexuals and male prostitutes. He picked up young men and they, like the itinerants and the local boys who worked for his building company, were among the dead found later by police.

All this time, Gacy was winning friends and influencing people with his Pogo The Clown antics. He made hefty contributions to the Democratic Party, which he supported wholeheartedly. In the three years before his capture, Gacy funded and organized an annual political summer fete with beer, hamburgers and music and attended by five hundred local dignitaries and business bigwigs. The proceeds went to President Carter's re-election fund, and for his efforts he was lauded by the White House.

A pure coincidence led to his arrest. One of Gacy's political contacts during this time had known one of the victims, and harried police into mounting an extraordinarily intensive search for the missing youngster. Once again, as had happened on several occasions years before, the trail seemed to lead to Gacy. Police raided his luxury ranch house in December 1978. They placed Gacy under arrest and a team of forensic experts moved in, combing the place for clues.

As the horrified neighbours watched, police systematically dug up the garden. By the third day, the remains of 28 different bodies had been unearthed. Gacy had at first denied murdering anyone, but gradually admitted the first few, then finally drew a detailed map of his garden for police. The five remaining corpses were fished out of the Des Plaines river by police frogmen in a massive dredging operation.

Details of Gacy's *modus operandi* emerged over the ensuing months. Since boyhood, he had had a fixation for police matters. He loved to play policeman, and owned guns and other paraphernalia, including handcuffs. When he got a

A German tailor was hanged for Britain's first murder on a train, mainly because he picked up the wrong hat at the scene of the crime. Bank clerk Thomas Briggs, 70, was found dead on the railway line between Hackney Wick and Bow, London, on 9 July, 1864. His gold watch and hat were among the items missing, and a silk hat found near the body was identified as belonging to Franz Muller, 25. Police discovered that Muller had set sail for America on the *SS Victoria*. They took a faster liner, and were waiting to arrest him at New York. Despite a personal plea to Queen Victoria from the Prussian king, Muller was hanged on 14 November, 1864.

young man back to his house he would show the unsuspecting fellow the 'handcuff trick', assuring him that he would be released after only a few seconds. Instead, of course, once the victim was in Gacy's power, he would become the subject of a wild homosexual rape. Instead of learning, as Gacy had promised, how to get free from the handcuffs, the victim would hear Gacy say: 'The way to get out of these handcuffs is to have the key. That's the real trick.'

The handcuff trick was quickly followed by the 'rope trick' and this always spelled the end for the victim. Gacy would throw a piece of cord around the victim's neck, and tie two knots in it. Then he would push a piece of wood through the loop and slowly turn. Within seconds the victim was unconscious: a few seconds more and he was dead.

At his trial in 1979, Chicago District Attorney William Kunkle described him as a sick man who methodically planned and executed his many murders. Kunkle asked for the death penalty; the State of Illinois was then debating whether to reintroduce execution for certain types of murder.

Defence attorney Sam Amirante pleaded that Cary was insane at the time he committed the murders. But there had been so many, and over such a long period of time that Gacy was convicted and given life imprisonment.

Atlanta's Streets of Fear

WAYNE WILLIAMS

The 'Missing and Murdered Children' file in the Atlanta Police headquarters had 26 unsolved cases by late spring of 1981. Throughout the two previous years black children had been snatched from the streets or simply disappeared in this town in America's deep south and it was sometimes months before their bodies were discovered hidden in undergrowth or dumped in a river. Murder had reached epidemic proportions in Atlanta. The victims were always coloured and often too young to have had any chance to defend themselves. Death was usually due to strangulation. Forensic experts believed the children, one of whom was aged only seven, were being attacked from behind by a man who squeezed the life out of them by locking his arm around their necks.

A shroud of fear fell over the town while the homicidal maniac stalked the streets. At night the roads and the pavements were deserted. Parents too scared to let their children out of their sight for more than a few seconds were locking their doors to keep them inside. Vigilante parent patrols were formed. Fathers often armed themselves with baseball bats.. And over everything hung suspicion. Was a white man carrying out his own macabre mission against blacks or was a crazy cult killer on the loose?

The two-year search for the killer had broken the health of many senior police officers, stretched the resources of the whole town and even caused the State Justice Department to set up a special unit to join in the hunt. Every time another child went missing the efforts were intensified. But despite millions of dollars spent, the murders continued.

FBI officers had to be drafted in to Atlanta to help police chief Lee Brown who was under universal attack from the townspeople. And hordes of cranks arrived in town eager to pick up the $100,000 reward for information leading to the arrest of the killer. It was a frightening and macabre mystery – made the worse by the fact that the police believed the killer was taunting them.

After November 1980, when the eleventh killing occurred, children were being murdered at intervals of about three and a half weeks. The bodies, instead of being hidden, were left conspicuously in parks. And despite all precautions the parents were taking, the killer was still finding victims.

As he stepped up his campaign of death, a grisly pattern was beginning to

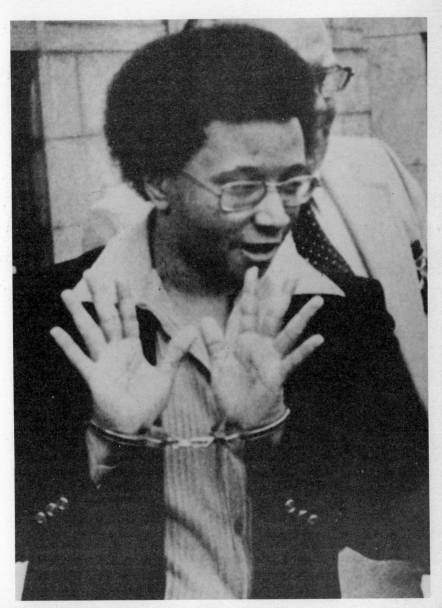

Wayne Williams leaving Fulton County Court, August 1981

emerge. All the children had been aged between 7 and 14 years and all but two were boys. Yet despite fears of a crazed pervert being on the loose, there was no evidence that any of the children had been sexually assaulted. Worse, the police were worried that if just one person was responsible for all the deaths then other psychopaths may be encouraged by the apparent ease and lack of detection. The desperate hunt for the killer was one of the biggest police operations ever launched in the United States. Twenty-thousand citizens were interviewed by officers, another 150,000 were questioned over the telephone. Tens of thousands of children were spoken to because the police believed that at sometime the killer could have tried to abduct a child unsuccessfully. Thirty-five FBI agents were permanently stationed in Atlanta and had been told they would stay there until the investigation was over.

Then one night in May 1981 there was a dramatic breakthrough. Two police officers and two FBI agents were huddled in a corner under the arches of the four-lane South Drive Bridge. They were one of dozens of teams which undertook around-the-clock vigils in the city. Ironically they were not watching the river on that misty night. They were merely covering the bridge because it formed one of the main routes to and from the town and they could quickly be on the road to join in any chase or stop any suspect leaving Atlanta. But as they chatted in whispers they were startled by something splashing into the water only a metre or so away. Two of the men went into the water to try to help whoever had gone in, and two sprinted up to the road and were there within a few seconds. They radioed ahead and a patrol car arrived almost instantly at the end of the bridge and stopped the traffice coming off it. Drivers were questioned briefly and then allowed to go on their ways.

Two days later police frogmen fished out of the river the body of Nathaniel Cater a 27-year-old negro. Strangulation was given as the cause of death.

If the same killer had struck again, then he had broken his pattern. The victim was black and had died from strangulation . . . but he was an adult. There

---

John Lee was the man they could not hang. Lee, a 19-year-old servant with a previous conviction for theft, was controversially found guilty of murdering his employer, Miss Emma Keyse, who had her throat cut and skull crushed in November 1884. Three times, he took his place on the scaffold, but each time the trapdoor refused to open, though it worked perfectly when tested with weights in between. Lee, who said: 'It was the Lord's hand which would not let the law take away my life,' was given a prison sentence instead, and released in 1907 after serving 22 years. He then married, emigrated to America, and died there in 1933.

Anna Maria Zwanziger took a terrible revenge on the legal profession after her husband, an alcoholic lawyer, died leaving her only debts. She took housekeeping jobs in the homes of judges, then proceeded to poison her employers and their families.
    She is known to have murdered one judge who refused to marry her, the wives of two more, and the child of one of them. Altogether, she poisoned an estimated 80 people, though most escaped with violent illness. After her arrest, police noticed that she trembled with pleasure when confronted with arsenic powder. She was executed by the sword in Bavaria in 1811.

were enough similarities for the police to suspect that Cater was number 27 in the chain of killings. The 'Missing and Murdered Children' file was renamed 'Missing and Murdered People'.

A few days later the body of a second victim, 21-year-old Ray Payne, also a negro, was recovered from the river. He had been thrown in at the same time as Cater and had also died from strangulation. Knowing that four of the child victims had previously been recovered from the river, the investigation team went back to the drivers they had stopped on the night the surveillance team had been under the bridge.

One of the men they questioned was Wayne Bertram Williams a 23-year-old black who lived quietly with his parents, both retired school-teachers, in a modest single-storey house in north-west Atlanta. He was taken to the city police headquarters and held overnight but was released despite the police discovery that he lived a bizarre lifestyle and considered himself a genius. Williams was a self-described 'media groupie'. He used to sit around in his car with a short-wave radio and tune in to police and fire services listening out for crimes or fires. Then, equipped with a camera, he would rush to the scene, usually arriving ahead of reporters and television crews and sell his exclusive pictures to the highest bidder. At the age of 14 he had started broadcasting on his own small pirate radio station in Atlanta. An only and lonely child, he had been convicted at 18 of impersonating a police officer. All his friends were shocked and surprised when they learnt that he was a police suspect.

On 3 June he was again taken in for questioning by police and given a 12-hour grilling. The next day, he rang newspapers and TV stations and held a press conference. Professing his innocence, he claimed the police had told him he was the prime suspect in some of the slayings. He said: 'One cop told me "You killed Nathaniel Cater. It's just a matter of time before we get you." I never killed anybody and I never threw anything from the bridge.'

For the next two and a half weeks Williams was under constant surveillance.

Charles Whitman went to pieces after his parents split up in March 1966. The 25-year-old student complained of headaches, showed violent temper tantrums, and became convinced he had a growth in his brain which was making him mentally ill. In the early hours of 1 August, he stabbed and shot his mother, then stabbed his wife. Taking several pistols, a radio and sandwiches, he climbed a 100 metres high observation tower at the University of Texas in Austin, clubbing a receptionist to death and barricading the stairway.

Two people climbing to the tower were shot, and at 11.40, Whitman, an expert shot after Marine service, began shooting indiscriminately at students. He killed 16 and wounded 30 in the next 90 minutes, defying attempts by police and low-flying aircraft to dislodge him. Finally police stormed the barricade he had built, and shot him to pieces. They later found a note from him saying: 'Life is not worth living.'

And then the results of tests on fibres taken from his car came from the laboratory. The fibres matched those on clothing of murder victims Cater and Payne. Williams was arrested and indicted on the charge of murdering Cater. The Payne charge was added later.

The police then faced up to the real problem of trying to get Williams convicted. Their evidence was not good. They had no witnesses either to the killings or the dumping of the bodies. All their hopes were pinned on the wizardry of the forensic scientists.

Their fears were justified as the nine-week trial got under way. Firstly, there was no motive, though prosecution lawyers suggested that Williams was 'a frustrated man driven by a desire to purify the black race by murdering poor young blacks'. Defending the accused man was Alvin Binder a well-known Mississippi trial lawyer, who was clearly scoring points as he tore the prosecution's evidence into shreds. Then the trial took a remarkable turn when the judge made a surprise ruling after a plea from the prosecution. With their case literally hanging by threads, the lawyers persuaded him to allow them to introduce evidence linking Williams to the deaths of ten other victims. The assistant District Attorney, Joseph Drolet, said: 'He has not been formally charged with the killings but the cases will reveal a pattern and bent of mind.'

The evidence brought to life a case that had slipped into a repetition of complicated forensic evidence. A boy aged 15 said he had been fondled by Williams who he later saw with 14-year-old Lubie Geter whose decomposed body was found clad only in underpants. Other witnesses said they had spotted him with more of the victims. One music business contact of Williams' said the accused man had once passed him a note which said: 'I could be a mayor – I could even be a killer.'

When Williams took the stand he denied everything. No, he had not stopped his car on the bridge, nor even slowed down. No, he had not thrown Cater's body over nor did he believe he would have had the strength to lift it. No, he was not a homosexual. Yes, all the witnesses and even the police had lied. He told the jury: 'I never met any of the victims. I feel just as sorry for them as anybody else in the world. I am 23 years old and I could have been one of the people killed out there.'

Later, under persistent cross-examination, he accused the prosecutor of being a fool and he described two FBI men who had interviewed him as 'goons'.

Finally the jury of eight blacks and four whites retired. They deliberated for 12 hours before returning a verdict of 'Guilty'.

As he was being led away to start two consecutive life terms Williams turned with tears streaming down his face, and protested his innocence 'from my heart'. His father, Homer Williams, cried out: 'It's impossible to find a young man like this guilty.' But guilty he was found and he went to jail knowing that it would be 14 years before he could be eligible for parole.

His lawyers immediately made plans to appeal – a process which many expected to take years.

The One Who Got Away

BELA KISS

I f the term 'kiss of death' had not already existed, headline writers would have invented it to describe Bela Kiss. For the well-to-do, middle-aged Hungarian murdered at least 23 people before 'dying' on a battlefield during World War One, and escaping to freedom in America. He is one of the few mass murderers to evade·justice.

Kiss was 40 when he arrived in the Hungarian village of Czinkota in 1913 with his beautiful, 25 year-old bride Maria. He had bought a large house and taken on servants, and the locals soon warmed to the man who collected stamps, grew roses, and did a little writing, especially on astrology. From time to time he would drive to Budapest on business in his smart red car, and the village policeman, Adolph Trauber, readily agreed to keep an eye on the home of the man with whom he had struck up a close friendship.

War was clearly only months away, and Constable Trauber was not surprised when his friend started returning from Budapest with oil drums. Kiss explained they were full of petrol so that he could continue his business trips when fuel became scarce. Trauber decided to keep quiet about the fact that, while Kiss was away, his wife was entertaining a young artist called Paul Bihari. But the affair was common knowledge among villagers and servants at the house. And they sympathized when, after another trip to Budapest the distraught husband emerged from his empty home to show them a note, saying the couple had eloped together.

For several months, Kiss shut himself away, refusing to see anyone, even Trauber. But in the spring of 1914, the constable persuaded him to rejoin the world, and found him an elderly widow to act as housekeeper. Kiss resumed his journeys to the Hungarian capital, returning each time with more oil drums. He told Trauber that the petrol was in payment of a debt owed to him by a Budapest garage owner. But Kiss brought other things from Budapest – women, not young like Maria, but sometimes even older than himself. Several times his housekeeper stormed out when her kitchen was invaded, only to return when Kiss told her the offending female had left.

Kiss and Constable Trauber spent many evenings together in conversation, and during one of their chats, the policeman mentioned the disappearance of two widows in Budapest. They had vanished after answering a lonely hearts advertisement in a newspaper, placed by a man named Hofmann. Both had drawn heavily on their savings after meeting him. Kiss joked that he too had had some unsuccessful affairs with middle-aged widows, and both men laughed.

War broke out that August, but Kiss was not among the first to be called up. He continued his trips to Budapest, returning with more oil drums and more women. When he was eventually conscripted, he left the house and his petrol stockpile in Trauber's care. And the constable continued to look after them after May 1916, when news arrived that Bela Kiss had been killed in action.

Later that summer, soldiers arrived in Czinkota looking for petrol. Trauber remembered the oil drums, and led the way to where they were stood. But a horrific discovery awaited him. Instead of petrol, each of the seven drums in the house contained alcohol. And each contained the doubled-up body of a naked woman.

Detectives called in from Budapest combed the gardens, and dug up yet more drums, each containing a grisly secret. In all, there were 23 tin-can coffins. The victims, who included faithless Maria and her lover, had all been garotted. Letters found in the house made it clear that Kiss and lonely-heart Hofmann were the same person, and that he had taken money or possessions from each of his fatal conquests. But there was nothing police could do: Their quarry had died at the front. The file was closed.

Then, in 1919, a friend of one of the victims recognized Bela Kiss crossing Margaret Bridge in Budapest, and reported the sighting to police. Shocked detectives discovered that Kiss had exchanged identities with a fallen colleague during the war, but before they could find him, he vanished again.

In 1924, a deserter from the French Foreign Legion told French police of a colleague called Hofmann, who had boasted of garotting exploits. But by then Hofmann, too, had deserted. It was ten years before he was again recognized, in Times Square, New York. And in 1936, he was reportedly working as a janitor at a Sixth Avenue apartment block. Fellow Hungarians there described him as a small, plain, inoffensive man in his middle sixties, a man with a bleak future. Bela Kiss did not talk about his even bleaker past.

The Monster of the Andes

PEDRO LOPEZ

The guards fingered their pistols and watched nervously as the steel door to cell 14 was unlocked. There, in Ambato Jail, high up in the Andes mountains in Ecuador, was the man who held the world's most horrible distinction.

Inside, cowering in a corner of his cell in the women's section of the prison, was Pedro Alonzo Lopez. He was petrified that he might be burned alive, or castrated, by the other inmates or the guards themselves. Lopez, known in South America as 'the Monster of the Andes' had admitted to murdering 300 young girls. Lopez has been credited with being the world's worst mass sex killer, with the highest ever tally of victims.

Like most mass killers, Lopez' motive was sex. Before the 300 were strangled, they were first raped. Lopez did away with girls in this fashion at the rate of two a week for the three years he was on the rampage.

In Ambato alone, nestling 3,000 metres up in the Andes, the killer took police to the secret graves of the bodies of the 53 girls all aged between 8 and 12. At 28 other sites he described to police, bodies could not be found because the graves had been robbed by prowling animals. Some of the girls' bodies were buried at construction sites, and police have had to assume that they are now encased in concrete, perhaps never to resurface. Others are under roads.

In his confessions, Lopez admitted to killing 110 girls in Ecuador, another 100 in neighbouring Colombia and 'many more than 100' in Peru. Retired Major of Police, Victor Hugo Lascano, director of Ambato prison, said: 'We may never know exactly how many young girls Lopez killed. I believe his estimate of 300 is very low, because in the beginning he co-operated and took us each day to three or four hidden corpses. But then he tired, changed his mind and stopped helping.'

Lopez was eventually charged with 53 of the murders but another charge listed 110 more bodies named in his confession. Major Lascano said: 'If someone confesses to 53 you find, and hundreds more that you don't, you tend to believe what he says. What can he possibly invent that will save him from the law?'

In his cell in the women's section of Ambato Prison, Lopez was kept out of immediate danger from enraged guards and male prisoners. The women prisoners were considered to be in no danger themselves 'because his sex drive was geared only to young children.'

This mass child-killer was born the seventh son in a family of 13 children. His mother was a prostitute in the small Colombian town of Tolima, who threw him out onto the streets when he was eight for sexually fondling one of his younger sisters. A stranger found the boy crying and hungry, took him in his arms and promised to be his new father and care for him. Instead, the stranger took young Pedro to a deserted building and raped him. For the rest of his life, Lopez would be afraid to sleep indoors.

'I slept on the stairs of market places and plazas', he told police. 'I would look up and if I could see a star, I knew I was under the protection of God.'

In Bogota, an American family fed and clothed the street urchin, and enrolled him in a Colombian day school for orphans. When he was 12 he stole money from the school and ran away with a middle-aged woman teacher who wanted to have sex with him.

At 18 he stole a car and drove across Colombia. He was caught and jailed. On his second day in prison he was raped in his cell by four male prisoners. Lopez made himself a crude knife. Within two weeks, according to the story he told police, he had murdered three of the men: the fourth stumbled across their bodies and ran screaming through the prison. Lopez was given an additional two-year sentence for the killings, which were deemed self-defence.

Released from jail, Lopez found himself excited by pornographic magazines and movies. But he was afraid of women and therefore unable to communicate with them. 'I lost my innocence at the age of eight', he told police, 'so I decided to do the same to as many young girls as I could.'

By 1978, Lopez had killed more than 100 Peruvian girls, many of them belonging to indian tribes.

His crimes first came to light when he was caught by Ayacucho indians in the northern sector of Peru as he carried off a nine-year-old girl. They stripped and tortured him, then put him in a deep hole . . . they were going to bury him alive.

An American woman missionary saved his life. She convinced the indians that they should not commit murder. She took Lopez in her jeep to the police outpost. Within days he had been deported; the police did not want to bother with dead indian girls at that time. Only later, when the full story emerged, was a proper investigation begun.

Across the border in Ecuador the real killing spree then began. 'I liked the girls in Ecuador' Lopez told police. 'They are more gentle and trusting, and more innocent. They are not as suspicious of strangers as Colombian girls.'

Lopez would walk through market squares seeking out his victims. He said he deliberately sought out young girls with 'a certain look of innocence'. In graphic detail he told police how he would first introduce the children to sex, then strangle them.

> I would become very excited watching them die.' 'I would stare into their eyes until I saw the light in them go out. The girls never really struggled – they didn't have time. I would bury a girl, then go out immediately and look for another one. I never killed any of them at night, because I wanted to watch them die by daylight.'

Police in the three countries were by now collating information, but they still did not realize they were looking for a mass killer. Their main theory was that an organization had been kidnapping the girls and transporting them to work as maids and prostitutes in large cities.

In April 1980, a rain-swollen river overflowed its banks near Ambato and horrified townspeople discovered the remains of four missing girls. Police launched a manhunt, but it was unsuccessful.

Days later, Carlina Ramon Poveda, working in the Plaza Rosa market, discovered her 12-year-old daughter Maria was missing. Frantically, she ran through the plaza, calling for her. She saw her walking out of the market, holding a stranger's hand.

Carlina followed her daughter and the tall man to the edge of town and then called for help. A dozen local indians jumped on Lopez and pulled him to the ground. They held him until the police arrived.

In jail awaiting trial, Lopez was tricked by police into making a confession. A priest, Pastor Cordoba Gudino, masqueraded as a fellow prisoner. For a month he stayed locked in the same cell as Lopez, and developed a behind-bars friendship with him. From the information he gave Gudino, the Ecuadoran police were able to extract a full confession from Lopez. Subsequent liaison with the police forces of Colombia and Peru substantiated Lopez's story.

Convicted of the murders in Ecuador, Lopez received a life sentence, which, in that country, means a maximum of 16 years, with good behaviour he could be a free man by 1990. Had he been convicted in Colombia, Lopez would be dead. There, the penalty for murder is death by firing squad.

Death of a President

The Mafia organization is America's 'Public Enemy Number One'. But for a long time the Mafia itself also had its own very public enemy . . . The Kennedy Clan.

The feud went back half a century to the days when, according to mobsters' stories, the Kennedy patriarch, Joseph, made a fortune from the profits of Prohibition whiskey illegally imported from Ireland to Boston.

In 1927 one of the Irish cargoes was hijacked by The Mob and 11 smugglers were killed in the shoot-out. It was, believe the Mafia, the start of a long campaign, instigated by Joseph Kennedy and continued by his children – principally John, who became President of the United States, and Robert, who became Attorney General.

Robert Kennedy was responsible for pursuing Teamsters union boss Jimmy Hoffa to jail in the U.S. Justice Department's relentless drive to crush Mafia influence within the organized labour movement. It was elder brother John who, as President, failed to give full backing to the disastrous Bay of Pigs invasion attempt of Cuba, planned by the CIA with Mafia assistance.

Many years later, after the assassination of both men, the question was being asked: was the Mafia linked with the killing of the U.S. President in 1963? At one time, such a question would have been unthinkable. But when dealing with organized crime in the USA, the unthinkable often becomes the perfectly feasible.

That was what happened in 1979 when a committee set up by the U.S. House of Representatives suggested it was likely that a contract killer was involved in the assassination that shocked the world, in Dallas, Texas, on 22 November 1963. After a $3 million investigation lasting two years, the committee's experts reported: 'An individual crime leader or a small combination of leaders might have participated in a conspiracy to assassinate President Kennedy.'

The report went on to name the 'most likely family bosses of organized crime to have participated in such a unilateral assassination plan' – Carlos Marcello of New Orleans and Santos Trafficante of Miami. Both men immediately issued the strongest denials of any involvement with Kennedy's death.

The circumstantial evidence to back a conspiracy theory was that Lee Harvey Oswald, who is presumed to have fired the shots that killed the President, had some links with underworld figures. So had Jack Ruby, the man who gunned down Oswald before the latter could be brought to court.

Oswald's connection was through his uncle, Charles Murret, and an acquaintance, David Ferrie – both of whom worked for Carlos Marcello.

Murret took Oswald under his wing when his favourite nephew moved from Dallas to New Orleans in 1963. He gave Oswald a home, a job in his book-making business and treated him like a son. The investigative committee described Murret as 'a top deputy for a top man in Carlos Marcello's gambling apparatus.' Murret died in 1964.

David Ferrie also worked for Marcello, as a pilot. He had flown him back to the U.S. after he was deported to Guatemala in 1961 by Robert Kennedy. Ferrie had also had secret connections with the CIA and had trained pilots who later took part in the Bay of Pigs invasion. Oswald's New Orleans work address in 1963 was the same as Ferrie's, and Oswald was in the same air club in which Ferrie was a pilot.

Such evidence, quoted in the House of Representatives committee's report, is circumstantial in the extreme. But judged alongside the evidence linking Oswald's executioner, Jack Ruby, to the Mafia, the conspiracy theory becomes stronger.

Club-owner Ruby's connections with underworld figures were well-established. His telephone records showed that he had been in contact with Mob

Moments before the fatal shot on 22 November, 1963 . . .

personalities in Miami, New Orleans and Chicago. He had visited Santos Trafficante. And on 21 November, the day before Kennedy's death, Ruby was seen drinking with a friend of pilot David Ferrie.

Whoever may have been pulling the strings, the evidence points to Ruby's public execution of Oswald being a certain way of keeping him quiet and preventing him naming accomplices during his trial. Ruby's own life would not have been of high account . . . he died in prison shortly afterwards of cancer.

Ruby's connection with Santos Trafficante brings the amazing web full circle.

When Meyer Lansky, 'Lucky' Luciano and their associates ran the Havana hotel and casino business under corrupt Cuban dictator Fulgencio Batista, Trafficante was a small cog in the business. Fidel Castro overthrew the Batista regime in 1959 and threw the Mob's men either into jail or out of the country. Among them was Trafficante.

The fact that Trafficante's pilot, David Ferrie, worked for the CIA may not have been known to his boss. If he did know, he might not have been concerned. He may even have approved of the connection. For the CIA, the Mafia and big business interests had all been involved in various plots to overthrow Castro and return Cuba to 'democratic' – and capitalist – rule. The CIA, with the unpublicized but tacit agreement of the U.S. government, wanted to remove the

and moments after

communist threat from the Caribbean. The Mafia and big business wanted to restore Cuba's profitable tourist industry, complete with acquiescent officials, politicians susceptible to bribes plus gambling and vice interests.

The CIA and the Mafia had previously worked together successfully, even launching joint military operations before and during the allied invasion of Sicily. A similar link-up made sound sense in the organizing of the Bay of Pigs invasion.

Even the world's richest businessman was involved. The eccentric Howard Hughes was said to have volunteered to fund one particular part of the Cuban invasion – the assassination of Fidel Castro. The plan was discussed by the CIA. Through their connections in Las Vegas, where Hughes had interests in 17 casinos, his aides recruited two Mafia hoodlums. But the invasion was a debacle, the assassination never took place – and the hoodlums died under mysterious circumstances in the 1970s.

Another sensational case in which politics and crime are sinisterly intertwined is the death of Marilyn Monroe. Again, the central characters are John and Robert Kennedy, both of whom were rumoured to have had affairs with the world's leading sex symbol. But this time the government agency suspected of being involved was not the CIA but the FBI.

J. Edgar Hoover, chief of the FBI, had long been hampered by the Kennedys in his autocratic handling of the agency's affairs. Attorney-General Robert, with his brother's White House backing, clipped the wings of the all-powerful Hoover – and earned himself an unforgiving enemy.

Hoover's agents collected every scrap of information about the private lives of every leading politician in the country. It was one of the reasons that Hoover's eccentric handling of the FBI had previously gone unchallenged. In the Kennedys' case, the FBI's personal files bulged with scandal.

Neither John nor his younger brother had been suitably secretive in their extra-marital activities. They had both known Marilyn Monroe and, in her developing state of depression and nervous disorder, it was thought that she might make public some of their indiscretions.

Such stories, which were no more than rumours at the time of Monroe's death, have since become common currency. And in 1981 a reformed criminal, Ronald 'Sonny' Gibson, wrote a book adding some startling new allegations.

In the book, *Mafia Kingpin*, Gibson said that while working for the Mob, he had been told that Marilyn had been murdered by a Mafia hit-man. J. Edgar Hoover, he said, had been furious about the actress's affairs with top politicians. So the Mafia had taken upon themselves the task of silencing her as a means of repaying favours done for them by the FBI.

Gibson is not alone in his assertion that Marilyn died not because she had swallowed an overdose of barbiturates, but because drugs had been injected into her. Even top pathologists who investigated the case have since gone into print to say the same.

Was Marilyn Monroe murdered by the Mafia? Was John F. Kennedy assassinated with the help of the Mob? The theories sound preposterous . . . Almost as preposterous an idea as that the U.S. government and the Mafia would collaboate in a Caribbean invasion. But it happened . . .

There are rich pickings for crooks along France's glittering south coast, sun-soaked playground of millionaires and 'beautiful people'. In the early 1980s police estimated that more than £70 million a year was being raked in from drugs, casino rackets, prostitution and extortion.

Chicago-style gang warfare arrived on the Riviera in 1970 when more than 100 people died in a wave of shootings which began with the jailing of crime czar 'Mimi' Guerini, 70, for his part in a gangland murder.

The spate of killings was stepped up in February 1977 after the shooting of ex-jockey Jacques 'Tomcat' Imbert. Imbert, who owed his nickname to his reputation for having nine lives, ran a nightclub in the small Riviera resort of Cassis. He was believed to have clashed with a gang who had taken over the Marseilles end of the 'French Connection' drug ring after the former boss had been jailed. Living up to his nickname, Imbert survived the shooting – though he lost an eye – spent six months in hospital and was permanently crippled.

A month after Imbert's shooting, one of his three attackers was shot dead while leaving a cemetery after visiting his son's grave. Next day the second man was killed in the street. The third man was murdered a few weeks later, shot as his car stopped at traffic lights.

The battle for power on the Riviera erupted into bloody violence again in October 1978 when nine people were gunned down in a Marseilles bar. They were riddled with 91 bullets. Five of the victims had police records, but the other four were thought to be innocent customers, shot to keep them quiet. Police, who were working closely with the FBI, said they believed the killings were 'Mafia-linked'.

The A6 Lay-By Murder

JAMES HANRATTY

The A6 murder has led to more controversy than almost any other killing in Britain. An illiterate, feeble-minded petty criminal called James Hanratty was hanged for it after the longest murder trial in English legal history. Ever since, an extensive and distinguished lobby of authors has campaigned to persuade the public that British justice executed the wrong man.

At dusk on 22 August, 1961, two scientific workers at the Road Research Laboratory in Slough, Buckinghamshire, were cuddling in the front seat of a grey Morris Minor saloon in a cornfield at Dorney Reach, beside the river Thames between Windsor and Maidenhead. Michael Gregsten was 38, a married man with two children. Valerie Storie was an attractive, single 23-year-old who had been his mistress for three years.

They were interrupted by a tap on the driver's side window. Gregsten wound down the window, and the man standing there pointed a gun at him. The terrified couple thought it was a hold-up. They offered the man their money, watches, even the car. He sat in the back seat, warning them not to look at him, toying with the gun. He told them he was on the run, and that every policeman in Britain was on the look-out for him. But he seemed undecided about what he was going to do.

Finally, at about 23.30, he ordered Gregsten to start driving. There followed a bizarre 30-mile drive through the northern suburbs of London, Slough, Hayes and Stanmore, broken only by stops to buy petrol and cigarettes. Gregsten, nervous already, was put further on edge by the back-seat driving of his captor, issuing instructions about the route and urging care at blackspots. They turned on to the A5 towards St Albans, Gregsten occasionally flashing his reversing lights to try to attract attention, and keeping an eye out for policemen, so he could stage a crash. He saw none.

On the A6, between St Albans and Luton, the gunman ordered Gregsten to pull into a lay-by. He said he wanted 'a kip', and made an attempt to tie Miss Storie to a door handle. He asked Gregsten to hand him a duffle bag, but as the driver reached for it, he was shot twice in the head. 'He moved too quick, he frightened me,' the gunman said as the girl screamed: 'You bastard.'

As blood flowed from her lover's wounds, Miss Storie was forced into the back seat, ordered to remove some of her clothes, then raped. The man then made Miss Storie pull Gregsten's body from the car to the edge of the concrete lay-by. She sat beside the body, too stunned to cry, while the man continued to dither about what to do next.

Eventually, Miss Storie gave him a £1 note if he would leave quickly. He took it, and seemed to be going. But as he approached the car, he unexpectedly turned, and pumped five bullets at the girl. One pierced her neck, close to the spinal cord. She lay still, pretending to be dead, as he strode over to inspect his work. Convinced he had eliminated the only witness to his earlier killing, he drove off.

Passing drivers failed to hear Miss Storie's screams. She took off and waved her petticoat, but no-one saw it in the dark. At last she passed out, and was found at around 06.30 by a teenager arriving for a traffic census. She recovered consciousness in hospital, and began giving waiting police officers extremely detailed descriptions of all that had happened. Her wounds had paralyzed her, consigning her to life in a wheelchair, but her mind was unaffected.

Two identikit pictures were issued, based on her descriptions, and those of witnesses who saw Gregsten's car being driven before it was abandoned in Ilford, Essex. Police were following a confusing trail of clues. At first they suspected Peter Louis Alphon. Two .38 bullets were found in the hotel room at the Vienna Hotel, Maida Vale, where he spent the night after the murder. Ballistics experts matched them with those that had killed Gregsten. But when Alphon was put in an identity parade, Valerie Storie failed to pick him out. She selected one of the stooges who could not possibly have been the murderer. Alphon did not match the identikit descriptions, nor did James Hanratty. And the police did not suspect him because he was known to them only as a petty and none-too-successful villain. But then he seemed to go out of his way to attract attention.

Police were already puzzled by anonymous calls to the hospital where Valerie Storie was recovering, threatening her life. They moved her to a fresh

---

Twice-convicted murderer Walter Graham Rowland almost cheated the gallows before his luck finally ran out. Rowland strangled his two-year-old daughter and killed a 40-year-old prostitute, Olive Balchin, with a hammer. He was convicted of the child's murder, sentenced, then reprieved.

It seemed as if he would escape the gallows a second time when a prisoner in Walton Jail, Liverpool, confessed to the prostitute's murder. But the statement was found to be false and Rowland was hanged in 1947.

Bugsy Siegel was a cunning killer who mixed with the Hollywood stars and thought there was nothing more important than a touch of class. From the squalor of Brooklyn, he graduated to racketeering and bootlegging and became New York's top hit man. In 1945 he borrowed $3 million to build a hotel in Las Vegas. Siegel refused to repay the money and was murdered in his home by an unknown gunman in 1947.

bed every night, and reinforced the guard on her. Then Hanratty phoned Detective Superintendent Acott, the man in charge of the hunt, saying he was anxious about being suspected for the A6 murder, and denying his involvement. Since the call was completely unsolicited, Hanratty immediately became a prime suspect.

Police discovered that he had asked an associate, Charles France, whether the back seat of a London bus was a good place to hide a gun. Hanratty was known to have acquired a .38 Enfield revolver earlier in the year. A similar gun was found behind the rear seat on the top deck of a No 36 bus. Police also discovered that Hanratty had booked into the Vienna Hotel the night before Alphon, staying in the same room as J. Ryan. And Gregsten's widow named him as the likely killer of her husband, though many wondered how she could possibly know.

Hanratty was arrested in Blackpool on 9 October and put in an identity parade. Valerie Storie again failed to pick him out, though she had now mentioned piercing blue eyes in her description of the killer. Hanratty had such eyes. She then asked each of the line-up to say the words the murderer had used several times: 'Be quiet, will you, I am thinking.' Hanratty always pronounced the last work 'finking'. And it was then that Miss Storie indentified him.

The trial began on 22 January, 1962. The police were given a hard time by the defence, who accused them of concentrating on implicating Hanratty instead of hunting down the truth. Much was also made of Miss Storie's identity parade failures, and the changes in her description of the killer.

But the defence was not helped by Hanratty himself. Though he pleaded not guilty, he was cocky and insolent throughout. A fellow prisoner who had been in custody with Hanratty swore that he had confessed to the killing and gave details of it known only to police and Miss Storie. Hanratty claimed that at the time of the murder he was in Liverpool with friends. But he refused to name them, saying to do so would break their trust in him. Then, inexplicably, he changed his alibi, and said he was in Rhyl, North Wales. Again he could not prove it.

There were enough doubts about both the prosecution and defence cases to keep the jury out for nine-and-a-half hours on 11 February. Once they returned for guidance from the judge. Then they filed back to court to return a verdict of guilty. He said only: 'I an innocent.' Every appeal was rejected. Hanratty, aged 25, was hanged at Bedford Prison on 4 April, 1962.

But even today, there are those who say there was too much 'reasonable doubt' about the affair to condemn any man. Peter Alphon made a series of sensational confessions to newspapers, saying Hanratty's conviction was contrived. Later, however, he withdrew them all. Charles France, Hanratty's friend, who had given evidence about the gun against him in court, hanged himself, leaving a note about the case. But it was not read at the inquest on the grounds that it was not in the public interest. Witnesses then came forward to claim that they had seen Hanratty in Rhyl on the night of the murder.

Books by Louis Blom-Cooper, Paul Foot and Ludovic Kennedy all helped to make Hanratty the greatest *cause célèbre* since Timothy Evans, another none-too-bright man executed for murder. But whereas Evans was condemned by Christie's evil lies, and was posthumously pardoned, Hanratty had virtually condemned himself by changing his alibi in court. And for everyone who claimed he was unjustly hanged, there were others who agreed with Detective-Superintendent Acott that Hanratty was 'one of the worst types of killers in recent years.'

The Mass-Murderer of Hanover

FRITZ HAARMANN

Wild terror, more akin to the Middle Ages than the 20th century, swept the north German town of Hanover in the spring of 1924. In winding alleys beneath the gabled roofs of the old quarter, people whispered that a werewolf was at large, devouring anyone foolish enough to venture out after dark. Some said children were being butchered in cellars. Police doctors were inundated with strange-tasting meat brought in by housewives who feared it was human flesh. The authorities dismissed the alarm as 'mass hysteria'. And they blamed a prank by medical students when children found the first of many human skulls beside the river Leine on 17 May.

The authorities were as wrong as the panic-stricken public. But the truth, when it emerged later that year, was just as macabre as the people's wildest fears. It ended in execution for a 45-year-old mass murderer called Fritz Haarmann, the jailing of his 25-year-old partner in crime – and a national scandal.

Haarmann had been a wandering vagrant, hawker and pilferer for most of his life. He worshipped his mother – an invalid after his birth in Hanover on 25 October, 1879 – and hated his father, a morose, miserly locomotive stoker known to all as Sulky Olle. When Fritz's bitterness spilled into violence, his father tried to get him committed to an asylum. But doctors decided that, though the boy was incurably feeble-minded, there were no grounds to commit him.

He roamed the country, a popular figure with the underworld and the police of many cities. Fellow petty crooks regarded him as fat and stupid, but kind, always ready to offer help, money and advice to those worse off than himself. The police liked him because he always came quietly when arrested, laughing and joking with them. He was always a model prisoner, accepting and even enjoying jail discipline. He served time for picking pockets, petty thieving and indecent behaviour with small children.

In 1918, Haarmann emerged from a five-year sentence for theft and fraud to find post-war Germany in chaos. Law and order had broken down, and profiteers, swindlers and crooks reigned supreme in the anarchy. These were the people Harrmann understood. He returned to Hanover, spending most of his time among the con-men and dubious traders at the straggling markets outside the central railway station. He became obsessed with the people inside the station – refugees from all over Germany, human flotsam without jobs or money, homes or hopes, who cowered round stoves by day, and huddled on platform benches at night.

Haarmann knew he could make a living in this twilight world, but, as he grew more and more acustomed to it, he realized there were other opportunities for him. Among the down-and-outs were many teenage boys, some no more than 12 years old. They had run away from home, often unable to cope with life there once their stern fathers returned from the war after years away. Haarmann turned on his charm with them, listening to their grievances, offering them advice, winning their confidence. In a country where everyone was carefully documented, he had discovered a constant flow of people nobody could trace. They could disappear for ever, and their parents and the police would be none the wiser.

Haarmann took lodgings at 27, Cellarstrasse, and set up in business as a meat-hawker and seller of secondhand clothes. He could haggle with the best of the market traders, and his business soon prospered. Housewives quickly learned that his prices were lower than anyone else's, and that his stock was always plentiful and varied. But he still spent his evenings with the boys at the station, laughing and joking with them, handing round chocolates and cigarettes, greeting hungry, forlorn new arrivals with the cheery offer of a meal and a mattress for the night.

Within weeks, Haarmann was such a familiar face there that welfare workers considered him almost as one of them. And the police decided to use his services, too. They needed spies in the underworld to try to stem the growing crime and corruption, and rewarded their 'narks' by turning a blind eye to their activities, legal and otherwise. Haarmann was delighted to help. Using the intimate knowledge of crooks he had gained over the years, he quickly earned the nickname of 'Detective' by reporting crimes, hiding places and plots. In return, the police did not pry into his business. And they were loathe to inquire too closely in September, 1918, when the parents of 17-year-old Friedel Rothe reported him missing after he was seen with Haarmann in a billiards room. It took the threat of force to persuade the officers to visit Haarmann's rooms, and their search was merely cursory.

Six years later, Haarmann was to brag at his trial: 'When the police examined my room, the head of the boy Friedel was lying wrapped in newspaper behind the oven.' For the truth was that the 'Detective' was not the bluff, genial do-gooder he seemed. The wretched youngsters he befriended were taken to his home for a good meal, often sexually assaulted, then killed in the most savage fashion – a bite at the throat. The bodies were then dismembered, the meat being sold, the skull and bones being disposed of in the river Leine.

That narrow escape in 1918 did not make Haarmann more cautious. If anything he became bolder as the police relied more and more on his information. And in September 1919 he met the accomplice who was to incite him to more murders. Hans Grans was then 20, and himself a runaway from home. Slim, graceful, cynical and emotionless, the librarian's son soon established ascendancy over his social inferior, taunting him with insults and sarcasm. And he began to order the killing of selected victims, often merely because he coveted their clothing.

The two men moved to rooms in Neuestrasse, then into an alley called Rothe Reihe (Red Row), almost on the banks of the Leine. Neighbours noted that a constant stream of young boys went into the apartment, but that none ever seemed to come out. They overheard sounds of chopping and splashing. Occasionally police brought the grief-stricken parents of missing boys to the rooms. They had heard that their sons had last been seen with the 'Detective'. Somehow, they always left satisfied that Haarmann had nothing to do with the disappearances.

One morning, a neighbour met Harrmann on the stairs. As he stopped to gossip and joke with her, a paper covering the bucket he was carrying slipped slightly, and she saw that the bucket was full of blood. But she said nothing to the authorities. After all, Haarmann had to hack carcasses of meat as part of his trade. Another neighbour once heard him chopping in his room, and asked: 'Am I going to get a bit.' He chuckled: 'No, next time.' She also saw a young boy lying very still on Haarmann's bed, but was told: 'Don't wake him, he's asleep.' A customer took a piece of meat bought from Haarmann to the police doctor because she was suspicious of its taste. She was told it was pork.

By 1923, Haarmann had made himself indispensible to the police. Not only was he still informing on criminals, he had set up a detective agency in partnership with a highly-placed police official, and was also recruiting for the Black *Reichswehr*, a secret organization working against French occupation of the Ruhr. He was so sure of police protection that he was taking enormous risks, selling the clothes of victims only a day or two after murdering them. One woman bought a pair of socks from him for her son, and found two spots of blood on them. She threw them away. A man spotted Grans wearing a suit that, days earlier, had belonged to a boy at the railway station.

But pressure was building up on the police. Newspapers had noted that large numbers of youths from all over north Germany had arrived in Hanover, then vanished. One paper claimed that 600 had disappeared in just one year. Hanover was acquiring a sinister reputation. The published fears brought out into the open suspicions many had been prepared to keep to themselves. The discovery of the skull by the river Leine in May 1924 was the final straw.

Now the police had to deal not with the occasional distraught parent, but with outraged public opinion. Another skull was discovered by the river on 29 May – a small skull, about the size of a young boy. Two more were unearthed on 13 June. A police spokesman claimed they could have been swept down-river from Alfeld, where hurried burials were taking place due to a typhus outbreak. But the explanation was not accepted by the frightened public. They believed a monster was preying on their town – and many were convinced that he lived in Rothe Reihe. Faced with a mounting tide of witnesses pointing the finger at Haarmann, the chief of police decided to act.

Haarmann still had powerful friends, impressed by the help he was giving the authorities. So the police chief moved cautiously. He brought in two detectives from Berlin, instructing them to watch Haarmann's movements at the station. On the evening of 22 June, 1924, he approached a boy called Fromm who objected to his attentions. They began to quarrel, then fight, and the detectives moved in to arrest them both.

With Haarmann safe at headquarters, a police squad swooped on his rooms. The walls were splashed with blood, and there were heaps of clothing and personal possessions. Haarmann protested that since he was both a meat trader and a clothes salesman, such findings were not unexpected. Then the mother of a missing boy recognized his coat – being worn by the son of Haarmann's landlady.

The game was up, and Haarmann knew it. He broke down and confessed to several murders, accusing Grans of instigating and assisting in many of them. Grans was immediately arrested. Meanwhile, more and more human remains were being discovered beside the River Leine. Boys playing in a meadow found a sack packed with them on 24 July. When dredgers probed the black ooze of the riverbed, watched by thousands lining the banks, they brought to the surface 500 bones.

Haarmann and Grans were tried at Hanover Assizes on 4 December, accused of killing 27 boys aged between 12 and 18. Haarmann was allowed to interrupt the proceedings almost as he pleased, and his grisly attempts at humour only added to the horror as the full story of his butchery unfolded.

'You're doing fine,' he shouted when the prosecution finished their opening speech. When one witness took his time pondering a question, Haarmann yelled: 'Come on, old chap. You must tell us all you know. We are here to get the truth.' Impatient when a distressed mother broke down while giving evidence about her lost son, the killer asked the judges if he could smoke a cigar – and was granted permission. And one morning, he protested that there were too many women in court, saying: 'This is a case for men to discuss.'

The names of boys were read to him, and he was asked if he had killed them. 'Yes, that might well be,' he said of 13-year-old Ernest Ehrenberg. 'I'm not sure about that one,' he replied about Paul Bronischewski. And he turned angrily on the anguished father of Hermann Wolf when shown a photograph of the boy.

'I should never have looked twice at such an ugly youngster as, according to his photograph, your son must have been,' he sneered. 'You say your boy had not even a shirt to his name and that his socks were tied on to his feet with string. Deuce take it, you should have been ashamed to let him go about like that. There's plenty of rubbish like him around. Think what you're saying man. Such a fellow would have been far beneath my notice.'

Newspaper reporters in court could not disguise their disgust for the killer, or their sympathy for the relatives of his victims. One journalist wrote:

'Nearly 200 witnesses had to appear in the box, mostly parents of the unfortunate youths. There were scenes of painful intensity as a poor father or mother would recognize some fragment or other of the clothing or belongings of their murdered son. Here it was a hand-kerchief, there a pair of braces, and again a greasy coat, soiled almost beyond recognition, that was shown to the relatives and to Haarmann. And with the quivering nostrils of a hound snuffling his prey, as if he were scenting rather than seeing the things displayed, did he admit at once that he knew them.'

Twice a shudder ran through the court. 'How many victims did you kill altogether?' asked the prosecution. Haarmann replied: 'It might be 30, it might be 40. I really can't remember the exact number.' The prosecution asked: 'How did you kill your victims?' Haarmann replied coldly: 'I bit them through their throats.'

Only when Grans's part in the murders was in doubt did Haarmann lose his composure. 'Grans should tell you how shabbily he has treated me,' he shouted. 'I did the murders, for that work he is too young.' He claimed Grans incited him to kill some victims because he had taken a fancy to the boy's trousers or coat. Grans left him alone overnight to do the murder, returning in the morning for the clothes. Once, though, he was too impatient. Haarmann told the court: 'I had just cut up the body when there was a knock at the door. I shoved the body under the bed and opened the door. It was Grans. His first question was, "Where is the suit." I sat down on the bed and buried my face in my hands . . . Grans tried to console me, and said: "Don't let a little thing like a corpse upset you." '

The cold-hearted cynicism of Grans aroused more horror in court than the unsophisticated blundering of Haarmann. The younger man denied every accusation, but there was never any doubt that both would be convicted. Haarmann knew that, and his main concern throughout was that he was not found insane. Early in the trial he shouted: 'Behead me, don't send me to an asylum.' And after two psychiatrists declared him mentally sound, the court decided he should have his wish.

Twelve armed policemen faced the public gallery on the day of judgment, 19 December, 1924, after anonymous threats that Haarmann would be shot in revenge for his monstrous crimes. The courtroom was packed as sentence of death was pronounced on him. Grans was jailed for life, later commuted to 12 years.

Haarmann remained to the end. On the last day he screamed:

'Do you think I enjoy killing people? I was ill for eight days after the first time. Condemn me to death. I only ask for justice. I am not mad. It is true I often get into a state when I do not know what I am doing, but that is not madness. Make it short, make it soon. Deliver me from this life, which is a torment. I will not petition for mercy, nor will I appeal. I want to pass just one more merry evening in my cell, with coffee, cheese and cigars, after which I will curse my father, and go to my execution as if it were a wedding.'

Next morning, Haarmann was beheaded, and the town of Hanover was at last free from the curse of the worst mass-murderer in modern history. No-one will ever know exactly how many teenage boys he and Grans massacred – but one police source guessed that, during their final 16 months, they were killing two every week.

The Vampire of Düsseldorf

PETER KURTEN

He is the king of sexual delinquents . . . he unites nearly all perversions in one person . . . he killed men, women, children and animals, killed anything he found.' Those were the chilling words used to describe Peter Kurten, the Vampire of Düsseldorf, at his trial in 1930. They came not from the judge, nor the prosecution, but from defending counsel, pleading for a verdict of insanity. But Kurten, 47, did not escape the execution his reign of terror so richly deserved, because the court agreed with the verdict of one of the top psychiatrists called to examine the callous killer: brutal sadist Kurten 'was at the same time a clever man and quite a nice one.'

Psychopaths ran in the Kurten family, and young Peter, the fifth child in a family of 13, saw the exploits of one at first hand in his home at Cologne-Mulheim. His father would arrive home drunk, beat the children, and sexually violate his unwilling wife in front of them. He also committed incest with his 13-year-old daughter, and Kurten followed his father's example with her. From the age of nine, he also had another teacher. The local dog catcher initiated him to torturing animals. Kurten was an enthusiastic pupil, and progressed from dogs to sheep, pigs, goats, geese and swans. What excited and aroused him most was the sight of their blood. He frequently cut the heads off swans and drank the blood that spurted out.

Soon Kurten switched his attentions to human victims. As a boy he had drowned two playmates while all three swam around a raft in the Rhine. By the age of 16, he was living with a masochistic woman who enjoyed being beaten and half-strangled. She had a daughter of 16, and all three enjoyed a sordid co-existence, interrupted only when Kurten's attempts at theft and fraud landed him in prison. He was later to claim that the inhumanity and injustice of his treatment in jail led to his blood-soaked career as a killer. In fact prison provided him with another outlet for sadism. He deliberately broke prison rules to gain solitary confinement, where he indulged his erotic reveries.

'I thought of myself causing accidents affecting thousands of people,' he was to recall in court. 'I invented a number of crazy fantasies such as smashing bridges and boring through bridge piers. Then I spun a number of fantasies with regard to bacilli which I might be able to introduce into drinking water and so cause a great calamity. I imagined myself using schools and orphanages for the purpose, where I could carry out murders by giving away chocolate samples containing arsenic. I derived the sort of pleasure from these visions that other people would get from thinking about a naked woman.'

When he was freed from prison, Kurten began to turn his daydreams into nightmare reality. He became an arsonist – 'the sight of the flames delighted me, but above all it was the excitement of the attempts to extinguish the fire and the agitation of those who saw their property being destroyed.' And he began to attack defenceless women and children.

His first attempt at murder was unsuccessful. He admitted leaving a girl for dead after assaulting her during intercourse in Düsseldorf's Grafenburg Woods. But no body was ever found. It was assumed that the girl recovered enough to crawl away, to ashamed or scared to report the incident. Eight-year-old Christine Klein was not so lucky. She was found in bed, raped and with her throat cut. Her uncle was arrested and tried, and though aquitted for lack of evidence, the shame of the charge stuck to him until he died during World War One. Kurten must have enjoyed that. His own trial was shocked by the detailed, fussy, matter-of-fact way he related what had really happened, 17 years earlier.

'It was on 25 May, 1913,' he recalled in the clipped, precise tone that only made his deeds seem more ghastly. 'I had been stealing, specializing in public bars or inns where the owners lived on the floor above. In a room above an inn at Cologne-Mulheim, I discovered a child asleep. Her head was facing the window. I seized it with my left hand and strangled her for about a minute and a half. The child woke up and struggled but lost consciousness.

'I had a small but sharp pocketknife with me and I held the child's head and cut her throat. I heard the blood spurt and drip on the mat beside the bed. . . The whole thing lasted about three minutes, then I locked the door again and went home to Düsseldorf. Next day I went back to Mulheim. There is a cafe opposite the Klein's place and I sat there and drank a glass of beer, and read all about the murder in the papers. People were talking about it all around me. All this amount of horror and indignation did me good.'

Kurten was not prepared to use his sadism on the Kaiser's behalf when war broke out. He deserted a day after call-up, and spent the rest of the hostilities in jail, for that and other minor crimes. Released in 1921, he decided to marry, and chose a prostitute at Altenburg as his bride, overcoming her reluctance by threatening to kill her. He gave up petty crime and went to work in a factory as a moulder. He became an active trade unionist, and a respected pillar of society, quiet, charming, carefully dressed and meticulous about his appearance – even a little vain. Those who knew he was having affairs with other women did not tell his wife. And the women were not prepared to confide that Kurten was a rough lover, who enjoyed beating and half-choking them.

But once Kurten and his wife moved to Düsseldorf in 1925, blood lust again got the better of him. Though his relations with Frau Kurten remained normal, his assaults on his mistresses became more vicious. Soon he was attacking innocent strangers with scissors or knives, aroused by the sight of their blood. As he escaped detection, he stepped up the rate of attacks, varying his style to cover his tracks. By the summer of 1929, the town of Düsseldorf was in the grip of terror. Police had pinned 46 perverted crimes, including four killings, down to someone who seemed to have vampire tendencies. But they had not clues as to the monster's identity.

On the evening of 23 August, two sisters left the throng at the annual fair in the suburb of Flehe to walk home through nearby allotments. Louise Lenzen, 14, and five-year-old Gertrude stopped when a gentle voice sounded behind them. 'Oh dear, I've forgotten to buy cigarettes,' the man said to Louise. 'Look, would you be very kind and go to one of the booths and get some for me? I'll look after the little girl.' Louise took his money and ran back to the fair. Kurten quietly picked up her sister, carried her into the darkness behind a stand of beanpoles, and efficiently slaughtered her, strangling her and cutting her throat with a Bavarian clasp knife. When Louise returned, he pocketed the cigarettes, accepted his change – and did the same to her.

Twelve hours later, a servant girl called Gertrude Schulte was stopped by a man who offered to take her to a fair at nearby Neuss. As they strolled through woods, he attempted to rape her, but she fought him off. He produced a knife, and began stabbing her in a frenzy, piercing her neck, shoulder and back. When he threw her to the ground, the knife snapped, leaving the blade in her back.

Gertrude was lucky – her screams alerted a passer-by, and she was rushed to hospital. But Kurten had escaped again. The newspapers continued to report his exploits with mounting hysteria. In one half hour, the 'Vampire' attacked and wounded a girl of 18, a man of 30 and a woman of 37. Later he bludgeoned serving girls Ida Reuter and Elizabeth Dorrier to death. And on 27 November he slashed five-year-old Gertrude Albermann with a thin blade, inflicting 36 wounds on her tiny body.

Gertrude was the last victim to die, but the attempted murders and vicious attacks continued through the winter and early spring, attracting headlines across Germany. Maria Budlick, a 21-year-old maid, had read the stories while working in Cologne, 30 kilometres away, but when she lost her job, she boarded a train for Düsseldorf, her desperation for employment outweighing any fears about the vampire.

It was 14 May, 1930, when she stepped on to the platform at Düsseldorf, and

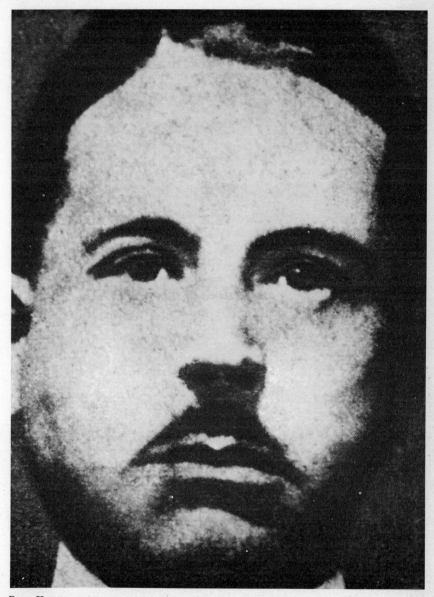

Peter Kurten

was soon approached by a man who offered to show her the way to a girls' hostel. She accompanied him happily through the streets, but when he turned into the trees of Volksgarten Park, she drew back. The man assured her she had nothing to fear, but she refused to be placated. As they argued, another man emerged from the shadows and asked: 'Is everything all right?' Maria's escort left, and she was left alone with her rescuer – Peter Kurten.

Convinced that he had saved her from a fate worse than death, or death itself, Maria agreed to go with him to his home for a meal. Kurten gave her a glass of milk and a ham sandwich, then offered to take her to the hostel. They boarded a tram – but for the second time in less than an hour, poor Maria was being misled. Her rescuer led her straight into Grafenburg Woods, on the northern edge of town, then lunged at her, gripping her throat and attempting to rape her against a tree. Maria struggled, but the man was too strong for her. Then, as she was about to pass out, he let go of her, and asked: 'Do you remember where I live, in case you ever need my help again?" Maria gasped: 'No.' Kurten escorted her out of the woods, and left her.

Maria had remembered where he lived, but surprisingly she did not go to the police. Instead, she wrote about her ordeal to a friend in Cologne. The letter was incorrectly addressed, and opened at the post office to be returned to the sender. An alert official realized the implications of its contents and contacted the authorities. Next day, plain clothes detectives took Maria back to the street she remembered, Mettmannersträsse, and she identified Number 71 as the home of her assailant. She also saw Kurten, but he vanished before she could tip off her police escort.

Kurten had also seen Maria, and realized that the net was closing in on him. He went to the restaurant where his wife worked, and confessed everything to her. He had never felt guilt for his crimes, and even admitting them now did not affect his appetite. He ate not only his own meal, but the one his shocked wife could not touch. On the morning of 24 May, Frau Kurten went to the police, and told them she had arranged to meet her husband outside a certain church at 15.00. Armed officers surrounded the area, and when Kurten arrived four rushed at him, revolvers pointing at his chest. He smiled and offered no resistance, saying: 'There is no need to be afraid.'

In his 15-year career of law-breaking, Jesse James murdered about 10 people and stole about $200,000. He was also one of Quantrill's Raiders who massacred 150 inhabitants of Lawrence, Kansas. He was shot in the back by his cousin, Bob Ford, while fixing a picture on his cabin wall in St Joseph, Missouri, in 1882.

> **Hungarian countess Elizabeth Bathory bathed in the blood of her victims because she believed it preserved her beauty. In the black depths of her castle dungeons at Csejthe, the countess stored well-fed girls ready to have their veins cut open and filtered into pipes that ran into a blood bath. When her blood craving reached a peak, she would nibble one of her victims to a premature death.**
> **Tried for 610 murders, the countess was sentenced to be walled up for life in a room from which all light and sound were excluded. In 1614, she expired after three years of this living death.**

The trial, when it opened in a converted drill-hall at Düsseldorf's police headquarters on 13 April, 1931, was almost a foregone conclusion. Thousands surrounded the building to try to catch a glimpse of the man who had admitted 68 crimes, apart from those for which he had already served time, while being questioned. He was charged with nine murders and seven attempted murders, and the prosecution hardly needed to produce any evidence to gain a conviction – Kurten admitted everything coldly, calmly, and in astonishing detail. Sleek and immaculate, he confessed to being a sex maniac, a rapist, a vampire, a sadist, an arsonist. He gave chapter and verse about his bestiality, his jail fantasies, and how he had strangled, stabbed and clubbed women and children to death. He admitted drinking blood from one woman's cut throat, from a wound on a man's forehead, from the hand of another victim. he described how he had enjoyed reading about Jack the Ripper, and how he had visited a waxworks Chamber of Horrors, and promised himself: 'I'll be here one day.'

A shoulder-high cage had been built round the accused man's stand to prevent him escaping. Behind him were the exhibits – the knives and scissors he had used to kill, the matches he had used to burn property, the spade he had used to bury one woman, the skulls of the innocent strangers he had butchered for the sake of an orgasm. The judge treated him gently, guiding him carefully through the catalogue of appalling crimes. There was no need to be tough, Kurten was as mild-mannered and courteous as his unsuspecting neighbours had always known him. But by the time it came to the prisoner's final speech, even the hardened judge was sickened.

Incredibly, Kurten, who had blamed his childhood and prison for turning him into a killer, now began preaching puritanically about the behaviour of others. He said:

'My actions as I see them today are so terrible and horrible that I do not even make an attempt to excuse them. But one bitter thing remains in my mind. When I think of the two Socialist doctors accused recently of abortions performed on working class mothers who sought their advice, when I think of the 500 murders they have committed, then I cannot help feeling bitter.

The real reason for my conviction is that there comes a time in the life of every criminal when he can go no further, and this spiritual collapse is what I experienced. But I do feel that I must make one statement: some of my victims made things very easy for me. Man-hunting on the part of women today has taken on such forms that . . .'

The judge could stand no more unctuous rhetoric, and angrily banged his desk for silence.

The jury took 90 minutes to find Kurten guilty on all accounts, and he was sentenced to death nine times. On 1 July, 1932, he chose veal, fried potatoes and white wine for the traditional last meal, and enjoyed it so much that he asked for second helpings. At 06.00 next morning he marched to the guillotine in Cologne's Koingelputz prison, and was beheaded after declining the attorney general's offer of a last wish.

But the twisted mind of Kurten had had one final wish. He asked the prison psychiatrist, minutes before he left his cell for that last walk, 'After my head has been chopped off, will I still be able to hear, at least for a moment, the sound of my own blood gushing from the stump of my neck?' As the appalled official sat stunned in silence, Kurten smiled and said: 'That would be the pleasure to end all pleasures.'

Convicted by his Crooked Teeth

THEODORE BUNDY

Law student Theodore Bundy was tall, handsome, charming and well educated, but this gentle, polite young man, with the looks to make girls swoon and the old-fashioned courtesy to appeal to their parents, was consigned to Death Row. The all-American boy Bundy is believed to be one of the worst mass murderers in American history – responsible for the savage rape and killing of 36 young women. Authorities in four states are convinced that beneath his disarming appearance lurked a Jekyll and Hyde. His victims were raped, clubbed, strangled and beaten to death. Investigators found that in every case Bundy had been nearby.

Bundy collected three death sentences in different trials. He was sentenced for the murders of two students in a Tallahassee sorority house in 1978, for the kidnap and murder of a Salt Lake City police chief's 12-year-old daughter, and for the kidnapping and battering of an 18-year-old girl out shopping in Salt Lake City. Yet the college graduate, who has planned to become a lawyer, always maintained his innocence. 'I have never killed, never kidnapped, never desired to injure another human being', he told a court.

The bloody trail of murders which bogged Bundy's footsteps began in 1974, when six strikingly similar and attractive young women vanished in the Seattle area. In January the first girl vanished from her bedroom. The only hint of her fate was a bloodstain on her pillow. Then in March a 19-year-old chemistry student left her dormitory at Evergreen State College for a concert. She was never seen again. A month later the third girl left her college to go to the cinema. She too never returned. In May and June three more girls vanished. No traces have ever been found of them.

All the girls were shapely brunettes. The other common factor was that each had been approached on the beach during the summer by a young, handsome man. He called himself Ted. There were no other clues to the disappearances until some forestry students strolling in the countryside found a jawbone and other bones in a shallow grave.

The discovery of the bones sent shock waves through the community. Detectives made little progress. But they later linked the murders with the disappearance of two more girls. The girls went missing at a picnic park. Three months later their corpses were found 10 miles from the other grave. Again

Drunken gunslinger Jack Slade was notorious for his savage killing of Jules Bene, an old enemy who had once ambushed and shot him. Slade took a slow revenge when they met again. He fastened Bene to a post and, between swigs of whisky, shot at his limbs. Then he blasted off his head and cut off an ear as a key fob.

But it was not the murder of Jules Bene that finished Slade. It was his drunken gun-slinging antics around Virginia City, Montana, whose townsfolk hanged him from the main beam of the saloon in 1864.

His wife soaked the corpse in raw alcohol for the long trip to his native Illinois. But he never made it. Slade's decomposed body ended up in a Mormon cemetary in Salt Lake City.

---

witnesses talked of the mysterious and charming young man called Ted who had been seen before the girls vanished.

Theodore Bundy was never charged with these murders. But he was arrested for the attempted abduction of a 17-year-old girl. He was left alone in a courtroom during a recess and he escaped. He was recaptured but he escaped again. By this time Bundy was awaiting trial for the murders of a Michigan nurse and a policeman's 14-year-old daughter. His escape launched a nationwide hunt by police, who already suspected him of being a mass murderer. But no trace was found of him until seven months later when four students in a sorority house on Florida State University campus were bludgeoned with a broken tree branch. Two of the girls died. After a hunt, Bundy was arrested.

The trial which followed was one of the most sensational in American history. The entire nation followed the proceedings on television, which under Florida law was allowed into the courtroom. The bizarre twists in the case attracted newsmen from around the world.

Bundy was convicted after evidence about the one flaw in his perfect appearance. He had distinctly crooked teeth. And it was those teeth that gave him away.

Evidence from a dental expert proved that bite marks on the body of one of Bundy's victims matched his teeth. As one of the girls lay dying she had been brutally bitten on her breast and buttock. The other dead girl had been battered and strangled – so violently that a police witness said at first he thought she had been decapitated.

When the verdict was announced, Bundy's mother shrieked in anguish and screamed out that he was innocent. But Bundy, who was baptized as a Mormon just before the murder spree began, was described as the 'most vicious criminal in history' by a Utah police captain who investigated some of the murders.

The personality of Bundy remains a mystery. To those who watched him calmly facing the death penalty in courtrooms, it seemed incredible that he could be the same man who battered women to death in frenzied sprees of violence. He was born in a home for unmarried mothers. But after that his background was impecable. He was a Boy Scout and worked as an assistant programmes director at the Seattle Crime Commission, where he battled against white-collar crime. He even helped write a booklet for women on rape prevention.

One person still convinced of his innocence is Carole Boone who married Bundy in a hurried ceremony in a court in Florida just before he was handed his third death sentence. Carole, who has kissed her husband only once, would drive regularly the 150 miles from her home to Talahassee where Bundy waited in a Death Row cell. She knew him before he was arrested and said: 'Ted is not vicious or a savage mass murderer. The charges were the result of snowballing hysteria on the part of law enforcement people looking for a fall guy on whom they could pin all their unsolved crimes. From the beginning, I believed in his innocence. When I looked into the evidence, I was convinced of it'. But the jurors who decided Bundy should die for the murders he committed feared that if he remained alive he might break out of jail and 'do it all a second time'.

The Triangular Chamber of Death

DR MARCEL PETIOT

Few mass killers have cashed in on the chaos of war as profitably as Dr Marcel Petiot. When the guillotine sliced his scheming head from his body on the morning of 26 May, 1946, he had made more than a million pounds from murder. And but for foolish pride, the 49-year-old doctor, might have escaped to enjoy his ill-gotten gains.

The medical profession was a natural choice of career for a man who showed sadistic tendencies even as a boy in his native Auxerre, where he relished cruelty to animals and smaller children. He spent World War One in a casualty clearing station at Dijon, peddling stolen morphia to drug addicts, before entering an asylum, where he studied medicine. By 1921 he had qualified as a doctor, and set up a practice in Villeneuve-sur-Yonne.

Flouting the Hippocratic oath, Petiot quickly prescribed a life of luxury for himself. He overcharged the rich while treating the poor for free. And villagers soon realized that Petiot was the man to see if they wanted drugs or illegal abortions. The mysterious disappearance of his young and pretty housekeeper when she became pregnant, and strange cries of pain from the good doctor's house, caused no more than idle gossip, and Petiot was soon sufficiently well-regarded to be elected Mayor.

But by 1930 life at Villeneuve had become too hot for him. One of his patients, a local shopkeeper, was robbed and killed, and Petiot was suspected, though nothing could be proved. Another patient persisted in accusing the doctor while continuing to visit him for treatment for his rheumatism. When he died suddenly, Petiot wrote 'natural causes' on the death certificate, and headed for bigger things in Paris.

Again his readiness to supply addictive drugs and terminate unwanted pregnancies soon earned him plenty of loyal patients. Quickly his practice at 60 Rue Caumartin became one of the most lucrative in the city. Petiot kept up the pretence of the good citizen – model husband and father, attending church each Sunday. His outward respectability helped him survive a fine for drug offences and the disappearance of a woman who unwisely accused him of turning her daughter into a junkie. Then, in 1940, the Nazi army marched into Paris. And Petiot seized the chance to set up a sinister sideline that satisfied both his passion for profits and his sadistic perversions.

Dr Marcel Petiot, aged 49 in the Seine Assize Court

Gestapo activity had turned the French capital into a city of fear. Jews disappeared to concentration camp gas chambers, able-bodied Frenchmen were rounded up for labour camps, and those left behind soon learned that it did not pay to ask too many questions about friends who vanished. The situation was ideal for what Petiot had in mind.

He bought a disused mansion at 21 Rue Lesueur for half a million franc, then set about modifying it for his purposes. The house included a sound-proof triangular room with no windows and only one door. Petiot installed peepholes, telling the builders the room was for his mental patients. He installed a furnace in the cellar under the garage. Shortly before Christmas, 1941, everything was ready.

Petiot now spread the word that he was in touch with the French Resistance, and could smuggle people hunted by the Gestapo to safety in Spain or Cuba. The desperate refugees who contacted him were told that their escape would be costly, and that they would need innoculations before being allowed into their new lands. Such was their state of fear that they readily agreed, selling up all their possessions to meet the bills, or giving them to Petiot. One of the first customers, a Polish-born tailor, paid two million francs to get himself and his family out of France. One by one, they crept surreptitiously to Rue Lesueur, bared their arms for the necessary injections, and were ushered into the hidden triangular room. None of them left it alive.

When the doctor was satisfied, via his peepholes, that his deadly serum had done its work, he dragged the bodies to the cellar, where he treated them in quicklime – bought in bulk from his brother Maurice at Auxerre – before stuffing them into his grisly furnace. Then he scrupulously noted the details of each transaction – the money, jewellery, furs, gold and silver each victim had handed over.

As word spread, more and more customers queued at Petiot's door – Jews, people who had fallen foul of the Gestapo, rich families who were not prepared to wait until France was free of the Nazi terror. Petiot even dispatched a friend of his, Dr Paul Braumberger, a drug addict whose prostitute companion was appropriated by German troops, making it impossible for her earn the money to satisfy his cravings.

For 18 months, Petiot was able to combine curing patients at Rue Caumartin with killing them at Rue Lesueur. Though his wife noted how tired he was becoming, she never suspected the evil nature of his extra work.

But in the late spring of 1943, Petiot hit a snag. The Gestapo had been puzzled by the disappearance of several Jews they were seeking. When their investigations revealed that all had had links with Petiot they suspected he was what he pretended to be – a Resistance agent smuggling refugees to freedom. They sent a Gestapo man to Petiot, pleading to be sent abroad. Petiot had no reason to

Dr Marcel Petiot's execution

believe he was any different from his usual clients, and promptly killed him.

The Nazis arrested the doctor, and held him for several months before releasing him early in 1944. The suspicion was that Petiot had earned his freedom with one of the most bizarre defences ever – that he was only doing what the Germans were doing, killing Jews and anti-Nazis. However he had achieved it, he returned to his factory of death, and was soon busy burning bodies again.

Now, however, he had no way of treating them before throwing them into the flames. During his enforced absence, his brother Maurice had visited Paris, and called at the Rue Lesueur premises. Family loyalty and loathing for the Germans persuaded him to keep what he found there a grim secret, but he was no longer prepared to act as an accessory to disposing of human flesh, and cut off his supplies of quick lime.

Incinerating untreated remains made the smoke belching from Petiot's chimney even blacker and more acrid, and soon the doctor's neighbours, never happy about the pollution found it intolerable. On 11 March, 1944, the owner of 20 Rue Lesueur called both the police and fire brigade, saying the fumes were a fire danger. Petiot was not in, and a card on the door directed inquiries to his practice in Rue Caumartin. The gendarmes set off there while firemen broke in. They soon located the furnace, but what they found around it horrified them. Dismembered corpses littered the floor. Limbs, heads and torsos were scattered in grisly disarray. The firemen refused to do anything until the police returned.

Forensic experts later pieced together the bones and made a total of 27 human bodies. But when Petiot arrived, he blithely informed the gendarmes that all were Nazi collaborators who had betrayed the French maquis, and deserved the execution he had carried out. Amazingly, the police were prepared to give him at least some benefit of their doubt. Though still under the control of the Germans, they were Frenchmen who hoped the Allies would soon free them from Nazi oppression. They returned to HQ without Petiot.

The doctor was intelligent enough to know that the game was up. Once his story was checked, it would be obvious that he had lied. He fled Paris and for months laid low in the countryside. Meanwhile, senior police officers visited 21 Rue Lesueur, and discovered the cache of treasures, and Petiot's meticulous records. They showed that 63 people had entered the triangular room, never to leave it alive. And it was soon clear that none of them were traitors to France.

Far from being a patriot, Petiot was suspected of being a Gestapo agent. The front-page story of his horrific exploits stunned even a nation accustomed to Nazi atrocities. Yet the doctor declined to take his chance of disappearing in the confusion of the German retreat as the Allied armies reconquered France. He had talked his way out of so many awkward corners that he doubtless thought he could do it again. He wrote to the newspaper *Resistance*, claiming the Nazis had framed him by dumping bodies round the furnace while he was under arrest. Then he had the effrontery to enlist in the Free French forces under a false name.

As life returned to normal after the liberation, police began tidying up the loose ends of law and order. Petiot's case was a priority. Detectives guessed they had not seen the last of him, and they were right. When General de Gaulle led his army in a victory parade down the Champs Elysees, there was Petiot, marching proudly in rank with phoney medals on his chest. He had grown a beard, but he was wanted too badly to escape recognition.

Petiot insisted throughout his 18-month interrogation by a magistrate that he had killed only Germans and collaborators. But when he was brought to trial, the jury were not so gullible. They were shown 47 suitcases packed with more than 1,500 items of clothing, almost all without identity tags. They visited Petiot's triangular room, saw his cellar of death, and heard that he had plundered more than one million pounds from those he butchered.

When the verdict was announced, Petiot could not hear it above the excited babble of the court. He had to ask whether he had been found guilty or not. And when sentenced to death, he screamed: 'I will be avenged.' But he went to the guillotine quietly enough, leaving behind him an ironic epitaph to a blood-soaked life. He asked a companion on that final walk whether he could relieve himself. Permission was refused. Petiot was alleged to have joked: 'When one sets out on a voyage, one takes all one's luggage with one.' It was a luxury he did not allow any of his 63 victims.

The Suicide Murders
ROUSE, TETZNER, SAFFRAN AND KIPNIK

O ver the years, many people have tried to evade their problems and responsibilities by disappearing, but three Europeans devized more fiendish means of vanishing. The men had never met, but within 12 months, each tried similar ways of escaping the mess they had made of their own lives – by taking the lives of complete strangers.

Alfred Arthur Rouse was known to his neighbours in Buxted Road, Finchley, London, as a cheery, chatty, charming chap. He and his wife Lily May had built a comfortable little home on the proceeds of his job as a commercial traveller for a Leicester company. Rouse loved his work. He was obsessed with cars, and had the gift of the gab when it came to selling.

Then, on 6 November, 1930, two plain clothes policemen called on Mrs Rouse. Her husband's Morris Minor car, registration number MU 1468, had been found burnt out in Hardingstone Lane, just off the London road near Northampton. A charred body had been found inside. Would she go with them to Northampton to try to identify some of the few personal effects left undamaged?

Mrs Rouse inspected some braces buckles and items of clothing, and thought they may have belonged to her husband. She was not allowed to see the corpse, which was virtually unidentifiable, but she was satisfied enough to start thinking of the £1,000 life insurance her husband had taken out on himself.

The police, however, were not so sure. Two young cousins, one of them the son of the village policeman at Hardingstone, had reported a strange encounter as they walked home from a 5 November Bonfire Night Party in Northampton. At 02.00, a car had flashed past them bound for London, and as they watched it, they saw a man scramble out of a roadside ditch. He was agitated and breathless, carrying an attache case and wearing a light raincoat, but no hat. As they wondered what he could be doing, they noticed a bright ball of flame 200 yards down Hardingstone Lane. The man said: 'It looks as if someone has had a bonfire.' But he went off in the opposite direction when the boys ran towards the blazing car.

That was enough to arouse police suspicions. What was a respectably-dressed man doing crawling about in a ditch at 02.00? Why did he not share the alarm

Alfred Rouse

Eight-year-old Fanny Adams was abducted while picking blackberries at Alton, Hampshire in 1867. Her dismembered body was found later that day. Her young killer was arrested and subsequently hanged. Sadly for Fanny's memory, the Royal Navy had just been issued with a new and unpalatable variety of canned meat which the sailors jokingly referred to as 'sweet Fanny Adams'. The phrase has since become part of the English language.

of the youngsters, and try to see if he could help fight the fire? They issued a nationwide alert for a man of between 30 and 35, about 2 metres (5ft 10in to 6ft) tall, with a round face and black curly hair. And at 21.20 on 7 November, they found him. Rouse was met by Scotland Yard detectives as he stepped from the Cardiff to London coach. And slowly they pieced together an amazing story of deception and callous cruelty.

Far from being a happily married suburban husband, Rouse was a bigamist. He had discovered that his good looks and amiable chat worked wonders with women, and he began to pick up waitresses and shop assistants on his travels.

In 1920, he made a 14-year-old Edinburgh girl pregnant. The child died after only five weeks, but Rouse persisted in the relationship, posing as a single man, and in 1924 went through a marriage ceremony with her at St Mary's Church, Islington, North London. A second child was born, and Rouse somehow persuaded her to let his real wife look after the boy from time to time in Buxted Road. In 1925, Rouse met a 17-year-old maid servant from Hendon, London, and was soon taking her with him on trips, and promising to marry her when trade picked up. She had a child by him in 1928, and gave birth to a second girl in October 1930 – seven days before he burnt his car. At the same time, a girl in the Monmouthshire village of Gellgaer was lying ill in her parents home. She too was pregnant by Rouse, and believed she was married to him. Rouse had promised her parents he had bought and furnished a house for him and his 'wife' at Kingston, and they would move there when the baby was born.

But the commercial traveller was earning only £10 a week. The new baby and the imminent one only added to his problems, which also included an illegitimate child in Paris and another in England. Rouse decided there was only one thing to do. He had to disappear, and start a new life, unfettered by responsibilities. A few days before the fateful 5 November, he met an unemployed man outside a public house in Whetstone, London. The man told him of his desperate hitch-hiking round the country in search of work, and added: 'I have no relations.' A fiendish idea came to Rouse as he noted that the man was about his own height and build.

On 5 November, Rouse visited the girl who had borne his daughter seven days earlier. She noticed that he seemed pre-occupied, constantly glancing at his watch. He left, muttering about bills he had to pay, and shortly after 20.00 met the unemployed man by arrangement in Whetstone High Road. He had promised to drive him to Leicester in search of a job.

Rouse was a teetotaller, but he brought along a bottle of whisky for his new friend, and the man drank from it liberally. Near St Albans, the inebriate switched off the car lights by mistake, and they were stopped by a policeman, but allowed to drive on after a warning. What happened next was told with chillingly clinical efficiency in a confession Rouse wrote just before his execution.

'He was the sort of man no-one would miss, and I thought he would suit the plan I had in mind,' he wrote. 'He drank the whisky neat from the bottle and was getting quite fuzzled. We talked a lot, but he did not tell me who he actually was. I did not care.

I turned into Hardingstone Lane because it was quiet and near a main road where I could get a lift from a lorry afterwards. I pulled the car up. The man was half-dozing – the effect of the whisky. I gripped him by the throat with my right hand. I pressed his head against the back of the seat. He slid down, his hat falling off. I saw he had a bald patch on the crown of his head.

He just gurgled. I pressed his throat hard. The man did not realize what was happening. I pushed his face back. After making a peculiar noise, the man was silent. I got out of the car, taking my attache case, a can of petrol and a mallet. I walked about eight metres (ten yards) in front of the car and opened the can, using the mallet to do so. I threw the mallet away and made a trail of petrol to the car. Also I poured petrol over the man and loosened the petrol union joint and took the top off the carburettor. I put the petrol can in the back of the car.

I ran to the beginning of the petrol trail and put a match to it. The flame rushed to the car, which caught fire at once. Petrol was leaking from the bottom of the car. That was the petrol I had poured over the man and the petrol that was dripping from the union joint and carburettor. The fire was very quick and the whole thing was a mass of flames in a few seconds. I ran away.'

In fact Rouse had planned the killing flawlessly. The left leg of the unconscious man was doubled up under the leaking union joint, so that the constant drip would send intense heat into the victim's face, making it unrecognizable. The man's right arm was stretched towards the can in the back seat, and soaked to produce another source of flames to the head and shoulders. And though he had tampered with the engine, the damage was consistent with what might be expected in an accidental blaze.

But the calculating killer had not reckoned on meeting two witnesses as he ran away. And it was that which proved his undoing. Knowing he had been seen, he panicked. Instead of escaping to a new life, he hitched a lift home to Finchley in a lorry, arriving at 06.20. He stayed only to change his clothes, then took a coach to Cardiff and Gellygaer. All the way, he unnecessarily told people his car had been stolen, but changed the details each time. To his amazement, the story of the burned-out car was on the front page of every newspaper. People who knew him in Gellygaer kept asking if it was his car. He denied it, and decided to return to London. Waiting for the coach in Cardiff, he again told conflicting tales about how his car had gone missing. He seemed almost relieved to be met at Hammersmith by the police.

But his horrific confession was still many months away. He first claimed that he had picked the man up as a hitch-hiker near St Albans, then lost his way. When the engine started to spit, he stopped to relieve himself, and told the passenger to fill the tank from his petrol can. The man asked for a cigarette. Next thing, Rouse claimed, he turned and saw a ball of flame. He ran back to the car, but could not get near it because of the heat. Then he had 'lost his head' after coming over 'all of a shake', and had fled, feeling vaguely responsible but not knowing what to do.

It was a plausible story, and though Rouse changed certain details in subsequent re-tellings of it, he still arrived at Northampton Assizes with a jaunty, self-assured air on 26 January, 1931. The prosecution, led by Norman Birkett, had a tricky task to prove murder, and Rouse knew it.

Unfortunately for him, his confidence was his undoing. Rouse had been invalided out of World War One with head wounds after a shell exploded close to where he was standing in the trenches at Givenchy, northern France. A medical report on him in September 1918 said: 'The man is easily excited and talkative.' That, as much as the chance meeting in the country lane, was to condemn him to the noose.

When Birkett suggested Rouse had thrown the man into the car carelessly, face down, Rouse was foolish enough to argue that he had more brains than to do that. Another witness, an expert on car fires, noticed that Rouse seemed unperturbed, even amused, while the court discussed whether the carburettor top might have melted or fallen off. Rouse was also too keen to offer technical explanations about what might have happened inside the blazing engine. He was too clever by half.

The most damning evidence was produced by the eminent pathologists Sir Bernard Spilsbury and Dr Eric Shaw. They testified that the victim had been unconscious but alive when the fire began, and that a tiny scrap of unburnt clothing from the crotch of his trousers was soaked in petrol. Other expert witnesses contended that the man could have spilled petrol over himself, but

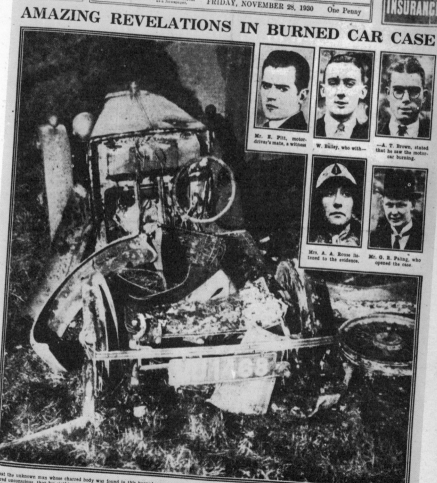

The burned-out car containing Rouse's victim

they did not carry much weight with a jury who looked on appalled at an accused man who coldly discussed leaving his 'good wife' because she never made a fuss of him, inexplicably made no real effort to rescue the man in his car, and, worst of all, never showed the slightest compassion or concern for the unknown wretch who had died.

On 31 January, 1931, Mr Justice Talbot sentenced Alfred Arthur Rouse, one of the most ingenious yet most loathsome murderers in British criminal history, to death. His appeal against sentence was dismissed 23 days later, and on 10 March Rouse was hanged at Bedford.

A week later, Kurt Erich Tetzner, also a young commercial traveller, stepped into the dock at Ratisbon, Germany, accused of burning to death in his car an unknown man with intent to defraud insurance companies by passing the body off as his own.

Tetzner had been in custody for 14 months, having been arrested ten days after his burnt-out car was found on the outskirts of Etterhausen, Bavaria, on 25 November, 1929. The charred body at the wheel was buried in lavish style by a weeping Frau Tetzner, who had identified it as her husband, but police were alerted by insurance companies who stood to pay out nearly £7,500. They watched the widow take two telephone calls at a neighbour's house from a Herr Stranelli in Strasbourg, Alsace, and soon discovered that Stranelli and Tetzner were the same man.

Tetzner was worse than Rouse at explaining his crime. He admitted the insurance fraud, and at first confessed to murdering the passenger. But five months after his arrest, he changed his story, saying the man in the car was a pedestrian he had run over who had died as he took him to hospital.

The court found it inconceivable that anyone would confess to murder to try to cover up a case of manslaughter. And it doubted the second story after Tetzner made another admission. Once he had advertised for a travelling companion, but the man who answered dropped out. The second time, he had attacked his passenger, a motor mechanic called Alois Ortner, with a hammer and a pad of ether, after first giving him money to make himself look respectable by having a shave and buying a collar. But Ortner had proved too strong for him and escaped into a nearby forest. Ortner was called as a prosecution witness, and revealed that he had gone to police after the attack – but they refused to believe his 'fantastic' story.

Tetzner was condemned to death, and the sentence was carried out on 2 May, 1931. Shortly before, the young murderer at last confessed the truth. He had picked up an unknown young man in thin clothes who complained of being cold. Tetzner wrapped a rug around him, trapping his arms, then strangled him with rope. He then crashed the car into a tree, made a petrol trail and set fire to it.

The public prosecutor at Ratisbon referred to Rouse as 'just a pupil of Tetzner.' It is not known whether Rouse had heard of the German case before he hatched his own scheme. But the third man who tried to disappear by substituting another man's body for his own certainly had.

Fritz Saffran was young, good-looking and successful. He had made such a good job of running the Platz Furniture Store in Rastenburg, eastern Prussia, that the owner of the shop, whose daughter he married, felt able to retire early, and leave things to his 30-year-old son-in-law.

Then, on 15 September 1930, an explosion rocked the store, and flames quickly destroyed it. Thirty workers escaped, but one did not. Chief clerk Erich Kipnik claimed Saffran had dashed into the blazing building to try to save the ledgers. Sure enought, firemen sifting the debris found the charred body. It wore the remains of one of Saffran's suits, had two of his rings on its fingers, and his monogrammed watch in an inside pocket.

Saffran had been popular with all his staff and customers, but one employee in particular was inconsolable at his death. It was known that Ella Augustin had been in love with him for years, but that he had publicly refused to respond to her flirting. He was, after all, a happily married man.

Two days after the fire, Ella called at several garages in the town to try to hire a car to take her mother, who was seriously ill, to Konigsberg. The chauffeur who accepted the task was surprised to be asked to arrive at her house at 03.00. He was even more amazed when the ailing mother turned out to be Saffran.

The man drove to the village of Gerdauen; but refused to go further. He had worked for the Platz firm before, and was reluctant to go to the police. But he told a friend about the secret journey, and was arrested – though later cleared – for aiding Saffran's escape. The friend alerted the police, who quickly discovered that all was not what it seemed at the prosperous Platz store. Saffran had burdened the business with huge debts after hire purchase buyers defaulted on payments. He had also raised money fraudulently on fake hire purchase deals and falsified the ledgers. Ella Augustin had helped him do this, and was his secret lover.

Greedy Mongol Tamerlane the Great was feared as much by his own men as by his enemies. After one battle, he built pyramids out of layer upon layer of murdered prisoners' heads. And if anyone dared to tell a joke in his company, they would be instantly killed. He died after a month of gluttony in 1405.

> The seventeenth-century Tsar of Russia, Peter the Great,
> murdered his own son when he remonstrated with him about his
> cruel laws. Anyone who opposed this giant of over 2 metres in
> height suffered a chilling death. His mistress, a Scot named Mrs
> Hamilton, was unfaithful to him – so he pickled her head and
> placed it beside his bed.

She was arrested, and tried to smuggle a note out to Saffran. It told the police that he was staying with one of her relatives in Berlin. Saffran somehow learned that police in the German capital were looking for him. Seven weeks after his getaway he stole the relative's identity papers, took a local train to the suburb of Spandau, and boarded the 01.00 train to Hamburg, where he hoped to get a ship to Brazil. But a fluke thwarted his clever plans. The rail official at Spandau had lived in Rastenburg several years earlier, and recognized the fugitive. Police were waiting when the train pulled into Wittenburg, the next station down the line.

Dental records helped detectives identify the body in the Platz store as Friedrich Dahl, 25, a dairyman from Wermsdorf, near Konigsberg. And on 23 March, 1931, Saffran and Kipnik, arrested when he was implicated in the conspiracy, went on trial at Bartenstein charged with Dahl's murder, attempted murder, arson, forgery, bribery and insurance frauds. Ella Augustin was accused of incitement to murder and complicity in frauds.

It quickly became clear that all three were more than anxious to blame each other for the murder. And what emerged was a chilling story of cold, calculated killing. Ella claimed that Saffran started it, brandishing a newspaper and saying: 'Have you read the report about this man Tetzner? That is how I will do our job too.'

Saffran claimed he took out an insurance policy for £7,000 so his wife would be well provided for. It was his intention to commit suicide, but Ella argued him out of it. Kipnik then suggested securing a body and burning it. They considered digging up a corpse from a grave, but dismissed the idea as impractical for their purposes.

The court was hushed as Saffran continued: 'We established a murder camp in the Nikolai Forest. The girl stayed there while Kipnik and I, each in his own car, roved the countryside for miles around, looking for a likely victim, then reported to the camp at evening. After a while we all three began to go out on these manhunts together.'

Several countrymen had lucky escapes. Once, near the village of Sorquitten, a man accepted a lift. Saffran said he speeded up, then jammed on the brakes, and Kipnik was supposed to smash the victim's skull as it jolted back. But Ella lost her nerve, clutched Kipnik's arm, and the man got away.

Kipnik claimed that, on another occasion, they picked up a pedestrian and were about to kill him when he revealed that he had six children. Sometimes they hid in woods or behind hedges, waiting for a likely victim to come along. The search went on night after night. Finally, on 12 September, 1930, Kipnik and Saffran met a man near Luisenhof just about midnight. It was Dahl.

Both men accused the other of firing the fatal three shots into his head, and both made exaggerated claims of contrition when the victim's widow took the stand. The public prosecutor had to tell them sternly to stop play-acting. But both continued to speak in terms more suited to a playhouse than a courtroom. 'Gentlemen of the jury, think of my terrible position,' Saffran pleaded, arms outstretched. 'I was leading a double life. At home I had to appear cheerful and contented while my heart was breaking. At night I was forced to go out hunting for men to murder.' Later Kipnik shouted: 'Saffran has ruined my life. I place my fate in the hands of the court. I wish I could prove to them that I am really a decent man.'

The jury believed neither story, and both men were sentenced to death. Accomplice Ella was jailed for five years. But Saffran and Kipnik were luckier than Rouse and Tetzner. The Prussian government commuted their sentences to life imprisonment. Many Germans wondered why two such callous killers should be spared the fate they had so cold-bloodedly meted out to an innocent stranger.

Bunkum With a Capital B

The most infamous doctors in the annals of crime were generally cunning poisoners. Dr Ruxton's case was different. It is true that he used his medical knowledge to a gruesome degree in trying to cover up his atrocity. But all the facts indicate that the murder itself was an impulse killing accomplished in a state of high emotion. No science or stealth contributed to the initial act – his was a crime of passion.

He was born in Bombay as Bukhtyar Rustamji Ratanji Hakim and qualified in his native country. Moving to England, he was made a Bachelor of Medicine in London. After further studies at Edinburgh he took up a practice in Lancaster in 1930. It was at about that time that he changed his name by deed poll to that of Dr Buck Ruxton.

With him to London came Isabella Van Ess, a married woman from Edinburgh. Her husband divorced her when she followed the doctor down. And although Isabella never married Dr Ruxton she lived with him as his wife. She also bore him three children, and was known to everyone simply as Mrs Ruxton.

They lived with the children at No. 2 Dalton Square, Lancaster. The doctor was highly regarded in his profession and well liked by all of his patients. This was despite the fact that the doctor and his 'wife' had an intensely emotional relationship. The couple quarrelled incessantly and often came to blows. But they always made up afterwards. At the trial, patients were to remember how Mrs Ruxton would rush into her husband's surgery and urgently embrace him to achieve a reconciliation.

The rows, though, were more than mere tiffs. Ruxton commonly threatened his wife and once held a knife to her throat. On two separate occasions the police were called in, but Mrs Ruxton never pressed charges. On the whole, she seems to have given as good as she got. 'We were the kind of people who could not live with each other and could not live without each other', the doctor was to admit.

Once, Mrs Ruxton attempted suicide to try and escape from the bonds that tied them together. And in 1934 she fled to her sister in Edinburgh intending a final breach. Ruxton, however, followed her and persuaded her to come back to him and to their children.

The root of the problem appears to have been Ruxton's obsessive jealousy. Constantly he accused his wife of infidelity, complaining on one occasion that she behaved like a common prostitute. His morbid suspicions were entirely without foundation, but jealousy feeds on chance happening and trifling coincidence. Things came to a head in autumn 1935, when Ruxton persuaded

TWENTIETH CENTURY KILLERS 171

himself that she was having an affair with a young town clerk named Robert Edmondson.

On 7 September, the Edmondson family drove up to Edinburgh. Their party included Robert, his sister and parents. And they agreed to take Mrs Ruxton up too for a visit to her native city.

Seething with suspicion, Ruxton abandoned his surgery and followed them in a hired car. He discovered that his wife was staying in the same hotel as the family, rather than with her sister as planned. It was for a perfectly innocent reason, but back in Lancaster, Ruxton was to rant for days at his wife about her supposed liaison.

On 14 September, the following weekend, Mrs Ruxton made another blameless excursion. Taking the doctor's Hillman, she drove to Blackpool as she did once every year to see the illuminations with her sisters. She left the resort at 23.30 that night, intending to go back the next day. But she never did return to Blackpool. In fact, having driven back to Dalton Square in the car, she never went anywhere again. Not in one piece, that is.

It is known that she reached home, because Ruxton was using the Hillman the next day and in the period that followed. It is known too that the doctor was in the house with his three children and the housemaid, Mary Rogerson. The children were all under five; Mary Rogerson was aged 20. But she could give no account of what transpired that night, for Mary Rogerson disappeared with Mrs Ruxton. The next time anyone but the doctor saw the two women they were barely identifiable: no more than dismembered chunks of bone, tissue and skin all wrapped up in bloodsoaked packages.

The story emerged at the trial. It has to be assumed that Ruxton was waiting in a mood of frenzied suspicion. There was yet another row which this time reached its climax in bloody murder. Ruxton killed his wife with a sharp-bladed instrument, and Mary Rogerson no doubt saw everything. She had to die too – and afterwards began the grisly business of destroying the evidence.

From what is known of Ruxton's character, anguish, remorse – and concern for his children – must have been coursing through his veins. But he set to work like a Trojan on the bodies of the two women and the welter of blood everywhere. Probably he worked all night while the children slept, and still there was much to be done.

One of the family's three charladies, Mrs Oxley, was due to arrive at 07.00 on Sunday morning. At 06.30, as she was preparing to leave her home, Dr Ruxton appeared on her doorstep. It was the astonished Mr Oxley who opened the door, with his wife standing not far behind him. Both heard what Ruxton said quite clearly: 'Tell Mrs Oxley not to trouble to come down this morning. Mrs Ruxton and Mary have gone away on a holiday to Edinburgh and I am taking the children to Morecambe. But tell her to come tomorrow.'

The 'murder ravine' where the bundles of human remains were found

At the trial, Ruxton was to deny that he had ever been to the Oxleys' house.

Returning home, Ruxton made the children's breakfast. He received the Sunday papers and milk, delivery women noting that he seemed to be shielding an injured hand. On a brief excursion in the Hillman he bought a full tank of petrol and two spare gallons besides.

Nursing his wounded hand, Ruxton was busy all Sunday. A woman patient turned up at Dalton Square with a child needing treatment. Ruxton postponed the appointment, saying that he was busy taking up carpets because decorators were due the next morning. At midday, he asked a neighbour to look after his children for the afternoon, saying that his wife had gone with Mary to Scotland and that he had cut his hand opening a tin of fruit at breakfast.

That afternoon he toiled undisturbed at the house until it was in a more or less presentable state. Then, at 16.30, he called on a friend and patient, Mrs Hampshire, to ask if she would help him get the house ready for the decorators. It was in a strange condition when she arrived. The carpets on stairs and landing had been taken up, and straw was scattered around. It even bristled out from under the two main bedroom doors – which were locked and remained so all evening.

In one room was a bloodstained suit; in the backyard were bloodstained carpets. Ruxton asked if she would be kind enough to clean the bath. It was filthy, with a grubby yellow stain extending high around the inside of the tub.

At the trial, Ruxton was to claim that the blood marks all derived from the severely gashed wound to his hand. But there was an awful lot of it about and, daunted by the size of the task, Mrs Hampshire asked if she could get her husband to help. Ruxton agreed, and the business of cleaning up went on until 21.30. As a reward for their labours, Ruxton offered the pair the stained suit and carpets, which they took with them when they left.

Presumably, the bodies were in the two locked bedrooms. No doubt the doctor was not idle that night. And he must have had nagging fears about the stained articles he had given the Hampshires, for first thing on Monday morning he went round to their house and asked for the suit back. He stood there, dishevelled and unshaven, explaining that he wanted to send it to the cleaner's. Mrs Hampshire insisted that she was quite happy to take it for cleaning herself. Ruxton then demanded that she take the name-tag from it, claiming that it would be improper for her husband to go around wearing a suit with another man's name in it. She duly cut it off. 'Burn it now', he demanded, and she tossed the tag onto her fire.

Afterwards, she looked at the suit and found the waistcoat so badly stained that she also put that on the flames. As for the carpets, she was to testify: 'The amount of blood on the third carpet was terrible. It was still damp where the blood was, and it had not been out in the rain. I laid the carpet in the backyard and threw about 20 or 30 buckets of water on it to try to wash the blood off, and the colour of the water that came off was like blood. I threw it on the line and left it to dry, and when it was washday I had another go at it with the yard brush and water, and still could not get the congealed blood off.'

In the week that followed, the doctor kept fires going night and day in his own backyard. He called in the decorators. And when the charladies complained of peculiar smells about the house he replied by spraying Eau de Cologne around.

To neighbours, Ruxton gave varied and inconsistent accounts about why Mrs Ruxton and Mary were away. To one he confided, sobbing and agitated, that the pair had gone to London, where his wife had eloped with another man. But Mary's parents, the Rogersons, were not easily convinced. Eventually, Ruxton told them that their daughter had been got pregnant and that this accounted for her going away. Mr Rogerson was undeterred. He threatened to ask the police to find his daughter.

At some stage (probably Thursday 19 September) Ruxton must have driven up to Scotland. For ten days later, exactly two weeks after the women vanished, the first grisly package was discovered.

A woman found it by a bridge near Moffat, off the Carlisle-Edinburgh road. She saw what seemed to be a human arm protruding from a wrapped bundle at the water's edge. Horrified, she called her brother who in turn summoned the police. The constable found four bundles: 'a blouse containing two upper arms and four pieces of flesh; a pillowslip enclosing two arm bones, two thigh bones, two lower leg bones, and nine pieces of flesh; part of a cotton sheet containing 17 pieces of flesh; and another piece of sheet containing the chest portion of a human trunk and the lower portions of two legs.'

More parcels were to turn up in due course. The police determined that pieces from two separate bodies had been jumbled up in the packages together. But certain distinguishing characteristics had been removed: some of the teeth, eyes and finger ends (presumably to prevent fingerprint identification). In fact, during the early investigation, the surgical removal of various organs made it impossible to discover the sex of the victims. The police began by announcing that they believed the bodies to be those of a man and a woman.

Reading this news in his daily paper seems to have given Ruxton some rare moments of good humour. In jovial mood, he told one of the charladies, 'So you see, Mrs Oxley, it is a man and a woman, it is not our two.' On another occasion: 'Thank goodness the other one in the Moffat case was a man and not a woman' – or people would be saying that he had murdered his wife and Mary.

But the police had already connected the Moffat bodies with the doctor's home town. One of the bundles had been wrapped in a copy of the *Sunday Graphic* dated 15 September (the murder morning). It happened to be a special edition sold only in Morecambe and Lancaster.

On 9 October, the Rogersons reported their daughter a missing person. On that day too, Ruxton asked Mrs Hampshire what she had done about the suit: 'Do something about it', he insisted. 'Get it out of the way. Burn it!' On 14 October, the doctor was taken into custody and questioned at length. In the small hours of the next day he was charged with Mary's murder. Cautioned, he protested, 'Most emphatically not, of course not. The furthest thing from my mind. What motive and why? What are you talking?' Some days later he was also charged with the murder of his wife, and it was on this indictment that he was to stand trial at the Manchester Assizes.

Precisely identifying the two bodies remained problematic for the authorities. The affair was to become something of a textbook case in medico-criminal history. A team of pathologists and anatomists fitted together their grim jigsaw of remains, proving that the age and size of the missing women roughly matched those of Bodies I and II. But key features had been removed. For example, Mrs Ruxton had prominent teeth and these had been withdrawn. Miss Rogerson had a squint – the eyes had been taken from their sockets. Nevertheless, it did prove possible to identify Mary's body by fingerprints. And Mrs Ruxton was identified when a photograph superimposed on Head II matched exactly.

It was proved that the doctor had been delivered the local edition of the *Sunday Graphic* for 15 September. Moreover, the linen sheet in which one bundle was wrapped was the partner of a single sheet left on Mrs Ruxton's bed.

The doctor made a miserable impression in the witness box. He vehemently denied the testimony of his charladies and his neighbours, claiming for example that he never visited the Oxleys; that he never asked Mrs Hampshire to burn the suit. His own account of his movements was deeply implausible and his manner both pitiable and arrogant. Sometimes he sobbed and became hysterical; sometimes he waxed bombastic. Once, taxed with murdering his wife and disposing of the witness, he replied, 'That is absolute bunkum with a capital B'.

A fit verdict on his own hopeless attempts to clear himself. Ruxton was found guilty, and when an appeal failed he was hanged at Strangeways Prison. The date was 12 May 1936. Soon afterwards, his own terse confession was published, a note penned at the time of his arrest:

I killed Mrs Ruxton in a fit of temper because
I thought she had been with a man. I was Mad at the time.
Mary Rogerson was present at the time. I had to kill her.

It had been one of those cases that haunt the public imagination, and in the streets and playgrounds the children chanted their own summary in rhyme:

Red stains on the carpet, red stains on the knife,
For Doctor Buck Ruxton had murdered his wife.
The maidservant saw it and threatened to tell,
So Doctor Buck Ruxton he killed her as well.

Bad But Not Mad

PETER MANUEL

Sentencing Peter Thomas Anthony Manuel to death at Glasgow in May, 1958, the judge Lord Cameron said: 'A man may be very bad without being mad.' Manual, who callously killed at least nine people, certainly qualified as very bad. But does a sane man pick victims at random, murder for no apparent reason, attempt to extort money from a man he has made a widower, then eagerly offer the evidence that will lead him to the gallows?

Manuel was certainly no fool. Halfway through his trial, he dismissed his lawyers and conducted his own defence so well that Lord Cameron congratulated him on his peformance. He used legal knowledge studied during his frequent prison sentences for burglary, theft, indecent assault, rape and violence. But he forgot one vital fact: in Scotland, a multi-murderer is charged with every killing. In England, on the other hand, he would have been charged with only one of them, on the grounds that evidence of other crimes might prejudice a jury unfairly.

Manuel's astonishing record as a killer reads like that of a gangster in Chicago, and he would have been proud of the comparison. He was, in fact, born in America. His parents left Scotland for New York in the 1920s, and Peter was born there in 1927. But the Depression forced them back to Britain, and their misfit son was soon in trouble. By the time he was 16, a senior probation officer said he had the worst record he had ever known in a boy. In January 1956, Manuel added murder to that record.

Anne Kneilands was just 17 years old. She was waiting for her boyfriend in an East Kilbride street when Manuel met her. He had rugged, Teddy Boy good looks, and she agreed to go to a nearby cafe with him. But as he walked her home later, he suddenly dragged her into a wood, and smashed her to death, beating her skull with a piece of iron.

Police were baffled by the seemingly motiveless attack. They interviewed all the possible suspects on their books, including Manuel, but put the scratches on his face down to Hogmanay excesses. Manuel had had enough police interviews in his life to know exactly what to say.

During that summer Manuel, the rebel without a cause, decided he needed a gun. His criminal ego was growing. He had killed once and got away with it. He could do it again.

Peter Manuel

Isabelle Cooke, murdered in January, 1958

On 16 September, 1956, he and two other men and a woman went on a robbery expedition to the wealthy area of High Burnside, a few miles south of Glasgow. They plundered one empty house, and even started a drinking party there. Manuel pointed out another home nearby, but the others were reluctant to stage a second break-in. Manuel went alone.

Getting in on the ground floor, he went straight upstairs, and saw two women asleep in one room. He opened another bedroom door, and saw 16-year-old Vivienne Watt. She was awake, and sat up in fear when she spotted him. Manuel bounded across the room, knocked her out and tied her up. Then he returned to the other room. Mrs Marion Watt, a semi-invalid and Vivienne's mother, was still asleep. So was her sister, Mrs Margaret Brown. Manuel calmly drew his gun and shot them both at close range. Then he walked back to Vivienne, who had come round and was struggling with her bonds. Holding her roughly down on the bed, he shot her through the left eye.

Manuel interfered with the night-dresses of all three women but, again, did not touch them. Expert witnesses later declared that he got sexual satisfaction from killing without the need for contact. It was 03.00 when he rejoined his pals in the first house, and about 05.00 when they went back to Glasgow.

But Manuel's shot had not killed Vivienne instantly. Her body was still warm when the family's daily help arrived next morning. And if that gave Manuel added satisfaction, the next development delighted his twisted mind. Police arrested Mrs Watt's husband, William, and accused him of the three murders.

Mr Watt, a baker, had been staying at a hotel in Lochgilphead, Argyll, 80 miles away, on the night of the killings. Witnesses had seen him there at midnight and 08.00. But police proved it was possible for him to have driven to his home and back comfortably in those eight hours. And they had witnesses who swore they had seen Mr Watt in his car on the Renfrew Ferry at 03.00.

The unfortunate man spent two months in prison before he was set free. The police could find no reason why a prosperous, loving father would kill his happy family. But Mr Watt's ordeal was not over. For Peter Manuel, who had equally little reason for killing his loved ones, now tried to extort money from the bereaved man. First he told Watt's solicitor he could name the Burnside murderer for a price. Then he met Mr Watt, and offered to remove lingering suspicions by killing the Burnside murderer, and making it look like suicide. It would only cost £120. The baker declined.

Manuel was playing with fire, but amazingly he got away with it. And he was also continuing to kill. On 8 December, 1957, he took a train to Newcastle upon Tyne, south of the border. He then took a taxi and ordered Sidney Dunn, the driver, to a deserted moorland road near Edmondbyers, then shot and stabbed him. Just after Christmas, he met 17-year-old Isabelle Cooke on the outskirts of Glasgow, dragged her into a field, tore off most of her clothes, and strangled her.

He then buried the girl he had never seen before in a shallow grave.

While the rest of Scotland was sleeping off Hogmanay, Manuel broke into the Glasgow bungalow of Peter Smart on New Year's Day, 1958. He found £25 in a wallet, and could have left undetected because Mr Smart, his wife Doris and their son Michael had not heard a thing. Instead, Manuel went into their bedrooms and shot all three dead. Then he calmly fed two tins of salmon to the family cat.

But at last Manuel had made a mistake. Under routine surveillance as he was after every major crime, he was seen passing some new blue £5 notes – notes of the type Peter Smart had drawn from the bank before his death. The home Manuel shared with his parents was searched, and after discovering house-breaking equipment, the police arrested both Manuel and his father. Manuel then agreed to make a statement on condition his father was released.

What he told them was an emotionless, detailed story of his murders. The cold-blooded confession stunned hardened officers, who reported that, when he led them to Isabelle Cooke's grave, he said almost light-heartedly: 'This is the place. In fact, I think I'm standing on her now.'

Manuel craved the limelight, and longed to be feared as a big man. But neither the police, nor the court, were awed by his exploits. After listening to 250 witnesses and a three-hour closing speech from Manuel himself, the jury found him guilty of seven of the eight murders with which he was charged – the Newcastle killing was outside Scottish jurisdiction, and the killing of Anne Kneilands was not proven for lack of evidence.

Peter Manuel, a particularly vicious and wanton murderer, was hanged at Glasgow's Barlinnie Prison on 11 July, 1958.

The Case of the Lethal 'Cuppa'

GRAHAM YOUNG

He was the most charming and efficient tea boy. His coffee was good, too. But a price had to be paid for it. It cost two people their lives. In April 1971, 23-year-old Londoner Graham Young, who was on a government training course at Slough, Berkshire, answered a 'help wanted' advertisment in a local paper. It said that John Hadland, manufacturers of specialist, highspeed optical and photographic instruments, needed a storeman at their small factory in the Hertfordshire village of Bovingdon.

Young said on his application form that he had 'previously studied chemistry, organic and inorganic, pharmacology and toxicology over the past 10 years' and had 'some knowledge of chemicals'.

He told the managing director, Mr Godfrey Foster, that before going to the training centre he had a nervous breakdown after his mother's death and had had mental treatment. Mr Foster was sent the report of a psychiatrist who had treated Young. It said that Young had made 'an extremely full recovery' from a 'deep-going personality disorder' and would 'do extremely well training as a storekeeper'. It also said Young was of above-average intelligence and 'would fit in well and not draw any attention to himself in any community'.

The report was hopelessly wrong on all counts – as Young's workmates were to find out. They did their best to make him feel at home, and he was befriended in particular by the head storeman, Bob Egle, 59, Frederick Biggs, 61, head of the works-in-progress department, and storeman-driver Ronald Hewitt, 41. Rob and Frederick would often lend him cigarettes and money, and Young offered to get tea and coffee for everybody who was kind to him.

Then a strange illness which was nicknamed the 'Bovingdon Bug' began to hit the staff at Hadland's. About 70 members of the staff went down with the illness. Symptoms included diarrhoea, stomach pains, loss of hair and numbness in the legs. Some said their tea tasted bitter, and a medical team was called in to find out if the chemicals used at the factory were responsible. The 'bug' killed two members of the staff – the kindly Bob Egle and Frederick Biggs. Bob died first. He became ill less than a month after Young joined the firm. His condition deteriorated rapidly and he was admitted to hospital. His heart

Above: Broadmore where Young was sent as a 14-year-old schoolboy

Left: Graham Young, aged 24

stopped twice while he was in intensive care unit and he died, paralyzed, on 7 July. Young appeared to be very concerned at Egle's death and attended the funeral. Then, in September 1972, Frederick was taken ill with stomach pains and vomiting. He died three weeks later in a London hospital.

When he heard about it Young is reported to have said: 'Poor old Fred. I wonder what went wrong? He shouldn't have died. I was very fond of old Fred.'

With Biggs' death, panic set in at the factory and several employees threatened to resign. Iain Anderson, the firm's medical officer, became suspicious when Young boasted about his knowledge of medicine and poisons. Detective Chief Inspector John Kirkland, of Hemel Hempstead police, was called in and asked Scotland Yard to check Young's background. When the answer came back, Young was arrested on suspicion of murder.

Police found that his bedsitter was full of bottles containing various chemicals and poisons, and the walls plastered with photographs of his heroes – Hitler and other Nazi leaders. A bottle of thallium, a deadly poison, tasteless and odourless, was found on Young when he was arrested.

Young went on trial at St Albans in July 1972. It took the jury less than an hour to find him guilty of two murders, two attempted murders and two charges of administering poison.

He was jailed for life and placed in a top security hospital. But it was only there that his background came to light. The hospital in which he had been treated for his breakdown turned out to be Broadmoor. In 1962 he had pleaded guilty at the Old Bailey to poisoning his father, his sister and a friend. Young was, in fact, a compulsive poisoner before he was 15.

Mr Justice Melford Stevenson had committed Young to Broadmoor with a recommendation that he should not be released for 15 years. He was discharged nine years later as having made 'an extremely full recovery', and the result was that two kindly innocent men died.

Chapter three

TYRANTS AND DESPOTS

The world over has seen its fair share of tyrants – they come and go with seeming rapidity, but nonetheless leave behind their own particular trademark – a régime of incredible cruelty and fear. Remember Idi Amin and Papa Doc, Adolf Hitler and Al Capone. These are just a few of the names inextricably linked with terror

Idi Amin

The dimming of the street lights on the warm, tropical nights in Kampala was always an accurate barometer of the morale of the people of Uganda.

Privileged visitors, arms salesmen and foreign diplomats in the two showpiece hotels would grumble loudly when the cocktail bars were plunged into darkness and the elevators jammed between floors.

But the uncomplaining residents of Kampala would leave the unlit cinemas and cheap little coffee shops in fearful silence to go home and spend a sleepless night behind barricaded doors.

Fitful blackouts in the power supply were a sign that Uganda's President Idi Amin had just completed another busy day of butchery. The drop in the voltage usually meant only one thing . . .

That the hydro-electric generators at Owen Falls Dam, 40 miles west of Kampala, were once again clogged with rotting corpses.

Despite the constant boat patrols on Lake Victoria, the source of the waters of the Nile, the maintenance engineers couldn't hope to spot every dead body swept by the currents towards their filter grids. They had allies helping them to scavenge the lake clear of the harvest of murder victims: the teeming colonies of crocodiles. But even these voracious reptiles became bloated and lazy. The pickings were too rich for them.

Time after time the generators had to be shut down and the water inlets cleared of that day's toll of death, usually 40 or 50 bodies in a 24-hour period.

In eight years of ruling his country in a torrent of blood and terror, Idi Amin had 500,000 of his fellow Ugandans ruthlessly and systematically butchered. He ordered the grisly mutilation of one of his own wives. He killed crusading clergymen, nosy journalists, his own diplomats and a helpless, frail elderly hijack hostage. He even tasted the flesh of some of his victims in cannibal ritual.

He killed political opponents, real and imagined, to stay in power. And he killed countless ordinary men and women for profit, sometimes for the sake of a few hundred pounds.

He personally supervised the actions of Uganda's 'State Research Bureau', an organisation which was a cross between the Gestapo and Murder Incorporated, dealing in state-sponsored torture, contract killing, drug running and currency smuggling.

For almost a hundred years, the fertile land of Uganda had been part of the

British Empire, 'The Pearl of Africa' according to its colonial administrators. Spread over the hills and valleys of a high plateau, its gentle climate makes it a pleasant garden nudging the Equator. It had enormous strategic value but when the 'wind of change' blew through Africa, the pressure for independence for Uganda became irresistible.

An astute lawyer and professional politician, Milton Obote became the first Prime minister when he triumphed in the hastily organized elections in 1962. His first priority was to forge some sort of unity among the 14 million Ugandans who owed more allegiance to their tribal chiefs than to any government in Kampala.

The ruling edicts of some of the chiefs of the 40 different tribes of Uganda often seemed to carry more authority than the decisions of any ballot-box Government. Mindful of this, Obote, a member of the minority Langi tribe, appointed the powerful ruler of the Buganda tribe, King Freddy, as President of Uganda. The Buganda tribe, largely Anglicized by colonial commissioners and missionaries, were the largest single tribal group. They considered themselves an elite.

But in placating them, Milton Obote earned himself the growing distrust of all the other tribes. Shortly after independence, however, he began slowly to reduce the powers of King Freddy.

By 1966 Buganda tribesmen were agitating more and more violently for Obote's overthrow. He needed to pit some military muscle against them and chose the deputy commander of the army, Idi Amin.

Amin had all the qualifications. He was an outsider, a Kakwa tribesman from the furthest flung province of Uganda, bordering Sudan. He was a Moslem who spoke virtually no English and was only semi-literate. He wouldn't be loath to dish out some rough justice to the Bugandans.

A former sergeant in the King's African Rifles, Amin was the ex-heavyweight-boxing champion of Uganda, a hulk of a man who, at six feet four inches tall and weighing more than twenty stone, easily dominated his fellow Ugandan Army staff officers.

His British commanding officer before independence had enthusiastically earmarked Amin as 'a tremendous chap to have around.' And though he was tough and swaggering, he was slow-witted and had never shown even the slightest tendency to try to grasp the complexities of politics.

Amin responded swiftly and energetically to the task the Prime Minister had given him. Using a 122mm gun mounted on his personal Jeep, he blew gaping holes in King Freddie's Palace. The Bugandan leader, warned of the danger just before the attack, fled into hiding and eventually made his way to Britain where he died in lonely exile.

For the next four years, Idi Amin was the Prime Minister's trusted strong arm man. Milton Obote was calm and relaxed when he flew off to Singapore in January 1971 to attend a Commonwealth Conference. He was about to fly home to Uganda when he heard the news on the radio . . . Idi Amin had just mobilized the Army and declared himself the country's new ruler.

The overgrown village bully turned military chief had decided that if he was to do the dirty work in Uganda he might just as well install himself as its supreme authority.

Milton Obote went into exile having learned an embarrassing political lesson. For the people of Uganda, cautiously celebrating his overthrow, the experience was to be painful to the point of torture and death.

Amin's first move was to pacify tribal enemies and buy valuable breathing space. He persuaded Buganda leaders that he himself had actually tipped off King Freddy and given him time to flee to safety. He arranged for the release of many political prisoners detained by Obote and had the body of the dead tribal King flown back from Britain for a ceremonial burial.

Amin was deeply affected by the ritual outpouring and lavish expense of the Buganda tribesmen at the burial ceremony. The experience was to be put to hideous use later.

Amin then moved against the most potent potential threat to his new power – the officers of the Ugandan Army.

He announced a new programme of army re-structuring and began by ordering 36 senior officers, Langi and Acholi tribesmen, to report to Makindye Prison for training in internal security. Disgruntled, but seduced by the thought of forming part of a government of military men instead of politicians, the officers arrived at Makindye. They were locked in cells and bayonetted to death.

The former army chief-of-staff, Brigadier Suleiman Hussein, was arrested and taken to yet another prison where he was beaten to death with rifle butts. His head was severed and taken to Amin's new palatial home in Kampala where the president preserved it in the freezer compartment of his refrigerator.

In two widely separated army barracks, at Mbarara and Jinja, the elite of the officer corps were lined up on the parade ground to take a salute from an armoured column. The tanks swept across the square, swung into line abreast formation and crushed most of the officers to death. Those left alive were used for target practice by riflemen. At another barracks, the remaining staff officers were herded into a briefing room for a lecture by Amin. As they saw his gleaming black Mercedes sweep into the square, the doors were locked from outside and grenades were lobbed through the windows.

Within five months Amin had killed most of the trained professional officers in his army. Yet the news was kept secret from the Ugandan people, who were simply told that a few disloyal officers had been court-martialled and executed. To make up the gaps in the ranks, Amin promoted fellow Kakwa tribesmen. Cooks and drivers, mess orderlies and wireless operators became majors and colonels overnight.

Idi Amin, one-time Life President of Uganda

But the word of the massacres had filtered out to two inquiring Americans, Nicholas Stroh, son of a wealthy Detroit brewer and a former writer for the *Philadelphia Bulletin* newspaper, was working as a freelance journalist in Africa. He joined forces with another American, Robert Siedle, a sociologist at Makere University in Kampala, to start asking questions about the army massacres.

At Mbarara barracks they were granted an interview with the new commander, Major Juma Aiga, a former taxi driver who had won an instant army commission. When their persistent questioning became too much, Major Aiga telephoned President Amin. His reply was terse: 'Kill them'.

Both men were gunned down on the spot and a few days later Aiga was openly driving around Kampala in Stroh's Volkswagen car. When the American Embassy demanded an investigation into the disappearance of the two men, they got nowhere.

As Amin went off on his first foreign trip as a head of government, he had already broken the backbone of the Ugandan Army. He was all-powerful, but he returned from his journeys to Israel and Britain empty-handed. His outright demands to both countries for millions of pounds in cash donations were refused. And the word went round the tight community of international diplomacy that the new president was not just a stupid, arrogant man. He was mad and dangerous.

Within a year Uganda was bankrupt. Amin's reaction was to order the Bank of Uganda to print millions of worthless banknotes to pump into the economy. All that remained of the reserves of U.S. dollars and sterling were made available for his personal use.

In Kampala the price of a bar of soap rose to £6, two weeks' wages for the average worker on the coffee plantations which were among the country's few sources of income.

Temporary salvation was offered by one other extravagant dictator, Libya's Colonel Ghadaffi. The price was one Amin was only too happy to pay for their newly formed alliance. As Libyan money poured into Kampala to keep the country barely afloat, Amin kept his side of the bargain. He ranted and raved against the State of Israel and kicked out the small group of skilled Israeli engineers employed on the construction projects which formed Israel's limited aid to Uganda.

Angered and hurt, the Israelis pulled out with their bulldozers and a meticulous mass of paperwork and blueprints. The documents included one slim volume which was later to help make history – the plans of Israel's last gift to Uganda, the new passenger terminal, control tower and runway layout of Entebbe Airport.

Amin, anxious to prove to Ghadaffi that he was a worthy protégé, opened an office in Kampala for the Palestine Liberation Organization with full diplomatic status. He capped it by pronouncing his admiration for his political hero, Adolf Hitler. As Amin drew up plans for a memorial to Hitler in the centre of Kampala, the world began to realize that some awful disaster was beginning to unfold.

They didn't have long to wait.

The Libyan money was barely propping up Uganda, and now Amin had hundreds of his chosen henchmen on the payroll of his new police force, The State Research Bureau. He bought their loyalty with lavish gifts of money and expensive cars, luxuries like video tape recorders and whisky and clothes imported from London and Paris.

One hot August night in 1972, dinner guests at Amin's palace, State House in Entebbe, were shocked and revolted when he left the table and returned from the kitchen with the frost-encrusted head of Brigadier Hussein from the freezer. In a ranting fit of rage Amin screamed abuse at the severed head, heaving cutlery at it, then ordered his guests to leave.

Two nights later he turned up unexpectedly in eastern Uganda and announced that God had appeared to him and told him that Uganda's population of 50,000 Asians, mainly tradesmen and merchants, doctors and nurses, were causing all Uganda's economic problems. He ordered them to leave the country within 90 days.

For the next three months Amin's voice could be heard on Uganda radio, making a daily count down to his deadline. Although most of the Asians had lived in Uganda for generations, forming the backbone of the nation's commerce, they fled in terror leaving behind their homes, offices, shops and plantations.

In November that year, Amin gave away the choice businesses to his friends and cronies. Pharmacies and surgeries were handed over to motor mechanics from the State Research Bureau, textile warehouses were given to Research Bureau telephone operators and army corporals. Within weeks the shops were deserted, their stocks sold and the shelves never filled again . . . and the men of the State Research Bureau wanted to be paid again.

With no money or property left to meet their demands, Amin gave them the only asset he had left, the lives of his fellow Ugandans.

It was the most bestial mass murder contract in history. Amin gave his bureau torturers the licence to kill for profit.

He knew the tradition of Ugandans, their deep reverence for the last remains of dead relatives and how they will spend every last Ugandan shilling of their money and part with anything of value to recover the body of a loved one for burial. In many of the tribes 'body finders' will earn their rewards by tracking through the bush to find the body of some father or son who has died in some remote cattle grazing area or drowned in the fast flowing waters of the Nile. The State Research Bureau became the killers – and the body finders.

Cruising through the street of Kampala in their imported cars, wearing their 'uniform' of gaudy silk shirts and bell bottom trousers, they openly arrested ordinary townspeople. And at their headquarters, only a few hundred yards from Amin's palatial home, they ruthlessly butchered their victims.

As the corpses piled up in the basement cells of the three storey building, other Research Bureau jailers were despatched to tell grieving families that their loved ones had disappeared after being arrested and were feared dead. For a body finding fee of £150, or every last possession the family owned, the State Research murderers drove the widows and weeping sons and daughters to a lush forest on the outskirts of Kampala.

Almost every gulley and bush concealed a dead body. Many nights as many as a hundred families made the grisly trip. The bodies not reclaimed were thrown into Lake Victoria, useless assets written off as a 'business' loss until they floated through the sluced gates of the Owens Falls Dam and the hydro-electric generators.

But the executions by firing squads at the Research Bureau became a problem. The neighbouring French Embassy staff complained directly to Amin about the constant gunfire throughout the night. Amin, sinking deeper and deeper into depravity, discussed a solution with the head of the Bureau, Lieutenant Isaac Malyamungu.

Malyamungu, a gatekeeper at a textile factory before Amin made him a government official, was a notoriously sadistic killer. Before executing the mayor of the provincial town of Masaka, he had paraded the badly mutilated man through the streets carrying his own amputated genitals in his hands. Now he and Amin calmly came up with the answer to the problem of maintaining the horrendous flow of lucrative killings without the disturbing, continuous rattle of gunfire. The murder victim would be kept alone in the basement, while another prisoner was offered the promise of reprieve if he would batter the solitary man to death with a 16lb sledgehammer.

Terrified and pleading for their lives, few prisoners were brave enough to refuse the offer. But once they had carried out their sickening task, the roles were changed. The unwilling executioner, usually sobbing and demented, would be left alone. He would become the solitary man, while in the cell next door another Ugandan was being given the sledgehammer and the heartless promise of life if he would repeat the procedure.

Even as the death toll rose, Amin still found time to indulge in personal episodes of unbelievable horror.

In March 1974 he went through a simple Moslem ritual to divorce three of his four wives. He accused them of meddling in his affairs and ordered them out of his home. Three months later one of the young ex-wives, Kay Amin, died in an apartment in Kampala as the result of a clumsy abortion attempt. She had been four months pregnant. Amin, in a state of fury, rushed to the mortuary to see her body. A few minutes later, quiet and unemotional, he gave a series of orders to the hospital surgeons and then left.

Two hours later he returned and satisfied himself that his orders had been carried out. Then he strode into the hospital morgue with his most junior wife, Sarah, and six-year-old Aliga Amin, the young son of Kay.

'Pay close attention to what you see,' he roared at them. 'Kay was a wicked woman, now look at what has become of her.'

Kay Amin's mutilated torso lay on the operating table. Her head and all her limbs had been amputated. Now her head had been reversed and sewn back on face down on her torso. Her legs had been neatly sutured on to her shoulders and her arms attached firmly to her bloodstained pelvis.

The swaggering arrogance of Idi Amin came to an end on 4 July 1976 although his brutality was to continue for almost another three years.

On 28 June an Air France airliner hijacked by a team of Palestinians arrived at Entebbe Airport. The plane had been en route from Tel Aviv to Paris when it had been commandeered shortly after a stop-over in Athens. It carried some 300 passengers.

In the heart of an African country governed by a Hitler-worshipper, far from any hope of rescue, the Palestinians confidently drew up their demands while Amin looked on, gloating and basking in the world limelight.

Amin helped to draft the blackmail demand that all the passengers would be killed in 48 hours if 53 Palestinian prisoners in jail in Israel and Europe were not released. As international tension mounted, the deadline was extended until the early hours of July 4, and passengers who were not Jewish were allowed to go.

Two days before the deadline, as the terrified hostages were huddled in the passenger terminal, one elderly Londoner, Dora Bloch, who held dual British-Israeli nationality, choked on a piece of food and was driven 20 miles from the airport to hospital in Kampala.

But as Idi Amin was being seen world-wide on television, badgering the hostages in the passenger lounge, the Israeli engineers in Tel Aviv unlocked a filing cabinet and began to pore over the vital blueprints of the airport they had helped to build.

Up and down the east coast of Africa an incredible international humanitarian conspiracy began to take shape. Shortly after midnight on 3 July, a task force of Israeli Air Force planes filled with commandoes came swooping over Lake Victoria. In silent co-operation they had been allowed to refuel and fly through the radar screens of Kenya, Uganda's neighbour.

The Israeli planes, guided by their own blueprints, landed swiftly and taxied to the precise spot in the terminal buildings where the hostages were being held. In less than an hour they took off again with the rescued hostages, leaving behind 20 of Idi Amin's troops dead and the seven hijackers killed on the spot. They also took with them the bodies of two of their own men caught in the crossfire.

But elderly Dora Bloch remained behind in hospital in Kampala, frail and barely able to breathe. Amin decided to vent his fury on her.

Sixteen hours after the Entebbe rescue mission, British High Commissioner Peter Chandley was allowed to visit Mrs Bloch. He tried to reassure the frightened woman and left the hospital briefly to prepare some food for her.

Shortly after he left, two State Research Bureau officials crashed through the doors of the hospital ward. They pistol-whipped the frail widow and dragged her down three flights of steps. Half an hour later they dumped her bullet-riddled body in a field on the outskirts of Kampala.

When the High Commissioner returned to the hospital, Amin simply announced that Mrs Bloch had gone the day before, returned to the airport under escort before the Entebbe Raid.

Idi Amin's last desperate mad gamble to hold the reins of power collapsed in April 1979. To scare the Ugandan people into submission, he claimed that the country was threatened by bloody invasion from its southern neighbour, Tanzania.

To give substance to his fantasies, he ordered small contingents of his troops across the Tanzanian border on raids against the 'invaders'. Such provocation was too much for Tanzanian President Julius Nyrere. His soldiers repelled the attacks and then drove deep into Uganda. They were welcomed with open arms by the long-suffering Ugandans as they advanced swiftly towards Kampala.

In one final broadcast, Idi Amin urged his troops to join him in a last stand at the town of Jinja, near the Owens Falls Dam. The soldiers didn't turn up. But then neither did Idi Amin. He had fled in his personal aircraft to the safety of Libya to seek sanctuary with his ally, Colonel Ghadaffi.

Five years after his overthrow, Idi Amin was still safely living in luxury in a private suite of an hotel in Saudi Arabia, the guest of the Moslem royal rulers of that country.

He would still rant about his return to Uganda and his self-appointed role in international politics. But this time no one was listening.

Prime Minister Milton Obote was back in power in Kampala. The country still suffered the ravages of the long years of Amin's tyranny. But the power supply flowed smoothly from the Owens Falls Dam hydro-electric generators, and the crocodiles in Lake Victoria had only the birds' nests in the swamps to prey on for a decent meal.

Papa Doc

Many tyrants have held power over nations by preying on simple human emotions, like fear of invasion by hostile neighbours or by nationalistic pride in conquest over weaker countries. Others have kept themselves in government by rigged elections or by armed suppression of their own downtrodden populations.

But only one modern dictator has ever managed to keep his people enslaved by a grisly combination of machine-gun and mysticism, by the force of a vicious police state and an unholy alliance with the Devil himself and his legions of demons and ghosts, vampires and zombies.

In the era that saw astronauts land on the moon and orbiting laboratories in space, President 'Papa Doc' Duvalier still ruled the republic of Haiti by bullets and black magic, by real live bogeymen who carried very real automatic pistols and by a supernatural 'police force' of living skeletons raised from the dead. Millions of Haitians who suffered the terrors of his 15 years of brutal dictatorship are convinced that he still reigns from beyond the grave, controlling his country's destiny from within the gates of Hell.

The bitter irony of the plight of the 5 million inhabitants of Haiti is that their struggling nation was once hailed as the most progressive in the Caribbean, a proud democracy which showed the way for other countries to free themselves from exploiters and foreign rule.

Haiti shares the island of Hispaniola with the Dominican Republic, and its lush and rolling sub-tropical forests were one of the wondrous sights of the New World for explorer Christopher Columbus when his ship foundered and was wrecked there in December 1492. It was an inauspicious start for a new nation. And over the centuries the people of that island have paid a terrible price for its accidental introduction to the adventurers from the Old World.

By the end of the 16th century most of the original population of Arawak Indians had been wiped out. Many fell victim to newly introduced European diseases. The survivors were literally worked to death on the plantations of their new Spanish masters. When the Spaniards moved on, there was little left to plunder for the next occupants, the rapacious pirates who used Hispaniola as their base for marauding, murder and looting. The buccaneers who controlled the whole western part of the island renamed their territory by its original Indian name – Haiti.

They were soon ousted by a new set of colonial rulers, the French, who revived the plantation system and peopled Haiti with black slaves captured on the west coast of Africa and packed into stinking hulks for the voyage to their new 'home'. The wretched slaves brought with them only two possessions – hatred of their new oppressors and their age-old belief in African witchcraft and demons. The first of these two emotions was to lead to uprisings so passionate and violent that even the all-conquering Emperor Napoleon eventually had to concede defeat in 1804 and Haiti, with its short history of bloodshed and superstition, became the first independent black-governed republic in the world.

Over the years this unhappy land lurched from one incompetent or greedy regime to another. From 1915 to 1934 it was occupied by US Marines. There followed a string of provincial presidents, mostly, mulatto descendants of mixed French-negro marriages, each being toppled in the midst of scandal and crisis which only made the already poverty-stricken population more miserable.

But in 1957 a popular new president emerged: François Duvalier, known to his friends and foes alike as 'Papa Doc'. Duvalier was a trained doctor, working on a US medical aid scheme before he turned to politics. Since they provided almost the only source of income for Haiti, the Americans were pleased to see a modern man of medicine as the new ruler. But the black peasants who formed 95 per cent of the population welcomed him for a totally different reason.

To them Duvalier was not so much a doctor, more a medicine man and a pure descendant of African slaves. They were enthralled by his open boast that he was a skilled witch doctor with experience in the dark practices of their voodoo religion, a mixture of French-inspired Christianity and ancient African superstitions. Papa Doc promised that by witchcraft and black magic ritual he would summon the Devil himself to share his power with all the voodoo worshippers of Haiti. On a more practical note, to placate the more educated political opposition, he vowed that the millions of dollars in American aid would be used to raise living standards. At that time, only 10 per cent of the population were literate, the national income averaged £1 a week, and most Haitians died of malnutrition and disease by the age of 35.

Within a few years of gaining control, Papa Doc made it plain he would share his power with no-one. Most of the finance from the United States was funnelled into his own private bank accounts while he lived in seclusion in his palatial presidential mansion. In 1961 he declared himself president for life and ordered the ill-disciplined Haitian Army to murder scores of political opponents. Their bodies were strung up on lamp posts around the capital, Port-au-Prince, with bloody voodoo symbols engraved on their corpses.

They had been killed, Papa Doc warned, by the forces of 'Baron Samedi', the avenging zombie of witchcraft. Baron Samedi, a hellish figure dressed in a black hat and a suit of mourning, was a voodoo demon, a soul raised from the dead to prowl the earth and carry out the wishes of the Devil.

To ensure that his own Army was in fear of him, Duvalier raised a secret police force, the Ton Ton Macoute – voodoo bogeymen who swore allegiance to him as the supreme witch doctor. The 10,000 members of the Ton Ton were given the task of killing hundreds of Army officers who were threatening rebellion against the bloodthirsty tyrant. In return they were given free rein to terrorise the countryside, looting and stealing from the starving peasants, carrying out murders which were always staged to bear the hallmarks of terrifying religious ritual.

The savagery of Papa Doc and his declaration of the grotesque cult of voodoo as Haiti's official national religion looked certain to prove his downfall. In the United States, recently elected President John F. Kennedy reacted with fury and indignation. Reflecting the civilised world's revulsion with Pap Doc's depravity, Kennedy announced that American aid to Haiti would cease as long as the Devil-worshipper was in power. It was thought to be only a matter of time before the pangs of hunger of the Haitians overcame their fear of demons and zombies. As the rumblings of discontent grew, even the gunmen of the Ton Ton Macoute were hard pressed to silence the increasing number of voices raised in anger against Duvalier.

For Papa Doc there was only one source of help to which he could turn. With power slowly beginning to slip from his grasp, he announced that he had performed a nightmarish voodoo ceremony to raise the Devil from Hell to put a curse on the American President. Six weeks later, John F. Kennedy died of an assassin's bullets in Dallas.

In Haiti the news was greeted with stunned despair. Nothing could shake the belief of terrified Haitians that the trigger of the assassin's gun had been pulled by the bony finger of the grinning zombie, Baron Samedi. Now Duvalier found new ways to bleed his people dry – literally. Still grasping for American dollars, he used the Ton Ton Macoute to round up thousands of Haitians daily and march them to medical centres in the capital, Port-au-Prince. There, each was given a week's wages of £1 in exchange for a litre of blood. The blood was flown to America and sold for transfusion at £12 a litre.

Papa Doc continued to rule supreme in Haiti. Any challenge to his power was met swiftly by the murder squads of the Ton Ton Macoute. In 1971, dying of diabetes and heart disease, he altered the constitution of Haiti to allow his podgy playboy son Jean-Claude, known as Baby Doc, to assume the mantle of power . . . Papa Doc had been president for life. Now he was trying to ensure that his devilish dynasty survived even in death.

Josef Stalin

Bolshevik bullets finally ended 400 years of repressive rule by Russia's Tsars. Nicholas II, gunned down with his haemophilic son Alexei in the cellar of a house in Ekaterinburg in July 1918, had fought to the last against what he called the 'senseless dream' of the people having a say in how their lives were governed. Bolstered in his belief in absolute autocracy by the sinister 'mad monk' Rasputin, he allowed ruthless henchmen to try to silence with savagery the growing clamour for basic human rights.

Chief of police Vyacheslav von Plehve mounted pogroms in Kishiniov and Gomel to 'drown the revolution in Jewish blood.' Minister of the Interior Peter Stolypin executed so many people for political offences – 5,000 in less than two years – that the gallows were nicknamed Stolypin's Necktie. And on Bloody Sunday, 22 January 1905, when riflemen and Cossack horsemen killed 150 defenceless men, women and children and injured a thousand more by brutally attacking a peaceful protest march to the St Petersburg Winter Palace, the Tsar's only question was: 'Have they killed enough?'

But there was by then no way that the revolution could be prevented. All it needed was a catalyst . . . and that came with the carnage of World War One, in which Russia lost vast tracts of land and 4 million men.

By 1916 abysmal leadership and terrible suffering had sapped the army's strength. And a year later, when soldiers and sailors garrisoned near St Petersburg sided with the strikers protesting at food shortages, inflation and corruption, the Tsar was forced to abdicate. The dreaded Ochrana, the secret police who maintained his reign of terror, were disbanded. Land confiscated from the rich was given to the peasants. Workers were promised an eight-hour day. Genuinely free elections were called. To the suddenly unsuppressed masses, Utopia seemed theirs.

But the revolutionaries had inherited a bitter legacy. In maintaining power at all costs, the Tsars had neglected the nation's interests. Revolutionaries like Lenin, returning from exile, knew from first-hand experience in Europe how backward the country was. 'Our task,' Lenin told his Politburo colleagues, 'is to take the lead of the exhausted masses who are wearily seeking a way out and lead them along the true path, along the path of labour discipline . . .'

But Lenin died in 1924, having taken only a few steps along that path. And his successor was to turn the democratic dream into a blood-soaked nightmare of tyranny on a scale that even the most sadistic Tsars never contemplated. In just

30 years of power, Josef Stalin killed more people than the Tsars had accounted for in four centuries. He turned a popular revolution based on ideals of freedom and equality into a totalitarian dictatorship maintained solely by terror. Although in the process he turned the Soviet Union into one of the world's two great super-powers, and extended its empire far beyond the boundaries established by the Tsars, even the communists who succeeded him denounced his monstrous excesses.

The dying Lenin had warned the communist Central Committee against Stalin, the shoemaker's son who had robbed banks in his native Georgia to raise funds for the Bolshevik cause, and rose to become party General Secretary in 1922. Lenin urged his colleagues to find someone 'more tolerant, more loyal, more polite, more considerate, less capricious,' and added: 'Comrade Stalin has concentrated boundless authority in his hands and I am not sure whether he will always be capable of using that authority with sufficient caution . . .' The party hierarchy did what they could, appointing Comrades Zinoviev and Kamenev to share leadership with Stalin. But already he was too powerful to be shackled. Adroit manoeuvring of the Politburo power blocs enabled him to demote, expel, even exile all potential rivals. By 1928 he was undisputed master of Moscow. Nikolai Bukhanin, one of Lenin's closest aides, confided to a friend when he was ousted: 'Stalin is a Genghis Khan who will kill us all.' It was a chillingly accurate prediction.

Stalin decided to accelerate Russian development. Huge new coal, iron and steel complexes were built all over Russia at a tremendous cost in human life. One of the American engineers called in as a consultant said: 'I would wager that Russia's battle of ferrous metallurgy alone involved more casualties than the Battle of the Marne.'

The programme was partly financed by swingeing taxes on richer peasants, the kulaks, who had been allowed by Lenin to sell surplus food to ease shortages. Dogmatic Stalin allowed no such 'deviations.' Soon the kulaks lost not only the

---

Walter Krivitsky was Stalin's military intelligence chief in Western Europe until he defected to escape a purge in 1936. He told a British interrogator: 'If you ever hear I have committed suicide, don't believe it. I will have been murdered.' In February 1941 his body was found in a hotel room in Washington DC. An inquest studied farewell notes before deciding that bullet wounds to his head were self-inflicted. But Krivitsky's widow Tania said of the notes: 'The writing is Walter's but the words are not.'

right to sell but their land and livestock. Stalin announced the elimination of the kulaks as a class. Millions were ordered to join vast state-run collective farms. Millions more were herded to towns to become forced labour in the new state-owned factories. Others disappeared into the growing network of 'corrective labour camps', the harsh 'Gulags' much later exposed by writer Alexander Solzhenitsyn. More than 25 million were forcibly evicted. More than three million were killed.

Stalin – the revolutionary name meant 'Man of Steel' – imposed his Marxist will on all walks of life. The party and government bureaucracies were purged of 'unreliable' workers – 164,000 Moscow civil servants were kicked out in 18 months. Church publications were suppressed, church buildings confiscated and the leaders exiled or jailed. Local nationalism in satellite states was dismissed as another 'deviation' and ruthlessly eradicated. Writers were subjected to intense censorship to ensure they wrote only work to inspire the proletariat. 'Where else do they kill people for writing poetry?' one artist asked plaintively. The grip of the secret police, the OGPU, tightened over everyone. Internal passports were re-introduced to make keeping track of people easier. Often alleged enemies of the state were quietly liquidated without troubling the courts. After all, the OGPU were working for a man who said: 'The death of a man is a tragedy; the death of a thousand is a statistic.'

Statistically the first five-year plan was a success. By 1935 industrial production was four times greater than in 1913. But progress had been bought at staggering cost. Results of a census in 1937 were so appalling they were suppressed. Two years later experts estimated that Russia's population was an astounding 20 million short of what it should have been. Emigration and famine

Stalin set up a special overseas sabotage and murder squad within his secret service in January 1946. Its first chief, war hero Pavl Anatolevich Sudoplatov, gave one officer – who later defected – this advice on recruiting killers: 'Go search for people who are hurt by fate or nature – the ugly, those suffering from an inferiority complex, craving power and influence but defeated by unfavourable circumstances. The sense of belonging to an influential, powerful organization will give them a feeling of superiority over the handsome and prosperous people around them and for the first time in their lives they will experience a sense of importance. It is sad and humanly shallow but we are obliged to profit from it.'

were factors. But Stalin's purges and the breakneck pace of industrialization accounted for many millions more. Historian E.H. Carr wrote: 'Seldom perhaps in history has so monstrous a price been paid for so monumental an achievement.'

In November 1932 Stalin's wife Nadezhda Alliluevna committed suicide with a revolver. At one time she had helped Stalin, telling him secrets learned from her job as a confidential code clerk in Lenin's private office. Now she was appalled at his increasingly brutal nature. He had become a foul-mouthed drunkard prone to violent rages, abusing underlings and indulging in debauched delights to test their loyalty. On one occasion he rolled five slim tubes of paper and stuck them on his secretary's fingers. Then he lit each like a candle and grinned as the man writhed in agony, not daring to remove them. Nadezhda's death removed one of the few remaining checks on Stalin's absolute authority. Their daughter Svêtlana said later: 'It deprived his soul of the last vestiges of human warmth.'

Then, in December 1934, a young communist shot dead party secretary Sergei Kirov in St Petersburg – which had been renamed Leningrad. Stalin instantly ordered the security services to speed up cases against people accused of executing or preparing to execute acts of terror. And he told courts to carry out death sentences immediately, since the government would no longer consider petitions for possible pardons. The ruling, as Nikita Khruschev later said, was 'the basis for mass acts of abuse against socialist legality.'

Stalin now began moving against old revolutionary colleagues. Zinoviev, Kamenev, Bukhanin and OGPU chief Yahoda were just four of the prominent communists accused of conspiring against the state in a series of show trials which lasted from 1936 to 1938. Astonishingly, they all pleaded guilty, perhaps through loyalty to the revolution, but more probably because they had been broken by torture and warned that their families would suffer if they caused a stir. By 1939, of the 139-strong Central Committee, 98 had been shot, and every member of Lenin's Politburo except Stalin himself and Trotsky, exiled in 1929, had been condemned by the courts.

New massive purges began throughout society. The Red Army leadership was more than halved. Naval top brass was devastated. The Communist Party rank and file was cleansed of intellectual idealists who put principles before the new politics of power, privilege and practicalities. Ruthless sycophants took their places, men with whom Stalin felt more secure. The secret police were shaken up and renamed the NKVD, under the notorious Beria. Even secret agents abroad, including spies who recruited and controlled English traitors Philby, Blunt and Burgess, were summoned back to Moscow and eliminated. Stalin, who knew more than most about conspiracy, saw plots everywhere. Others had to die because they knew too much about his previous misdeeds.

More than 500,000 people were summarily shot. Millions more were tortured and incarcerated. Even President Kalinin's wife spent seven years in a prison camp to guarantee her husband's behaviour.

The purges suddenly ceased in 1939. With the promise of a new, liberal constitution, people began to breathe more easily. But their relief was short-lived, for World War Two was about to begin . . .

To the war-weary nations allied against the Nazis, Soviet Marshal Stalin was avuncular Uncle Joe, a hero helping America and Britain end the evil of Hitler. Winston Churchill posed for photographs with him at the Yalta summit, and told journalists Stalin's life was 'precious to the hopes and hearts of us all.' He added: 'I walk through this world with greater courage when I find myself in a relation of friendship and intimacy with this great man.' It was not a sentiment shared by many of the millions who entered the war under Stalin, or the peoples he subjected during the hostilities. For Stalin's smiles at Yalta concealed a cruel and calculating nature prepared to condone and commit war crimes at least as evil as those of the enemy, and an ambition which was already bent on betraying the leaders who sang his praises.

Stalin had already betrayed the Allies once when, in August 1939, he had signed a non-aggression pact with Hitler. It was a cynical deal between a man who secretly planned to murder 30 million Slavs and a man who was already well on his way to doing so. Under its terms, the NKVD and the Gestapo compared notes on dissident refugees. Jewish prisoners in Soviet Gulags were swapped for concentration camp inmates Stalin wanted to get his hands on. Germany was allowed to use Murmansk as a submarine base and Russia supplied the Nazis with vital war materials. Most importantly for Stalin, he was given a free hand in certain areas to extend his reign of terror.

The Red Army marched into the Balkan states, ostensibly to preserve their neutrality. When Finland refused to hand over strategically useful land and islands, Stalin invaded to force the transfer at gunpoint. But it was Poland, a traditional enemy of Russia for centuries, which was most callously abused. The two dictators had drawn a line down the middle of the independent state. When Hitler invaded from the west, forcing Britain and France to declare war, Stalin's troops went in from the east, taking cruel advantage of Polish preoccupation with the Nazi attack. More than a quarter of a million Polish officers and men were captured – and 14,000 were never seen alive again.

In all the captured countries, the sinister NKVD arrived soon after the army had established control. They eliminated political and cultural leaders who might stand in the way of Stalin's planned Russification of the different nationalities. Millions were transported to the remote wastelands of Russia. Others were simply shot. As were Russians returned from captivity by the Finns. Stalin had no time for Soviet soldiers who failed him.

The fate of some of the missing Poles was revealed in 1943. The bodies of 4,000 officers were unearthed in shallow graves beneath a grove of young conifers at Katyn, near Smolensk. Most had their hands tied behind their backs and bullet wounds in the back of their necks. A few had smashed skulls. Some had straw or sawdust stuffed in their mouths, to kill them while saving ammunition. What happened to the remaining 10,000 who vanished has never been conclusively established, but some experts suspect they were loaded on barges and drowned in the White Sea by the NKVD. The missing included 800 doctors and 12 university professors.

Stalin was able to indulge himself in such blood-letting against his own and other peoples because he trusted Hitler. But by late 1940, the Führer was the master of mainland Europe, and able to prepare for the move he had planned all along: Operation Barbarossa, the invasion of Russia.

When Hitler's troops crossed the border at dawn on 22 June, 1941, Stalin was stunned. For 11 days he did nothing as the Red Army, weakened by purges and assured by their leader that invasion was impossible, fell back in disarray. But Stalin was eventually stung into action, when it became clear that many of his subjects were not resisting the Nazis, but welcoming them as liberators.

Long-silent church bells rang out in occupied towns as a religious people, denied the right to worship for years, joyously assembled for services. Civilians began hoping for the freedoms promised in 1917. Even the Jews, victims of Stalin's anti-semitism, responded willingly to Nazi posters asking them to register with the invaders. Nobody dreamed that Hitler could be as murderous a master as Stalin. Disillusioned Russian troops surrendered in droves. In less than six months, the invading army of just over 3 million captured nearly 4 million of the Red Army.

But Hitler and his army threw away their chances of capitalizing on Russian misery. Freed towns were soon appalled by the cruelty of the occupying forces. Hitler himself refused to allow nearly 800,000 Russian volunteers to fight for him

---

Stalin was a sadist. He liked to watch interrogations of political suspects by his secret police, and is quoted as ordering them to 'beat, beat and beat again until they come crawling to you on their bellies with confessions in their teeth.' Some historians attribute such brutality to the savage beatings he took from his father, a Georgian shoemaker who drank heavily. A childhood attack of smallpox, which left Stalin pockmarked for life, also contributed to his bitter inferiority complex.

against Stalin under rebel general Alexander Vlasov. And when Stalin appealed over the radio to 'his friends' the Russian people, they rose heroically to throw off the Nazi yoke.

Yet while his troops were battling back with courage, and Stalin was appealing to the Allies to send him battalions of reinforcements or to invade Europe to open a second front, the NKVD were waging war on the Russian people. Fearful of anyone who might try to topple him for his earlier savagery or for his military mistakes, Stalin launched yet another great purge. Army officers were killed by the hundred. Gulag inmates were slaughtered by the thousand. Potential 'enemies of the people' were massacred in every area that might fall into German hands. In his book *Stalin's Secret War*, Count Nikolai Tolstoy wrote: 'At Lvov, as the Soviet 4th Army battled against odds to save the city, the NKVD was working for a week with machine guns, grenades and high explosives in its frantic effort to liquidate thousands of Ukrainian prisoners. Thousands more were being transferred east under heavy armed guard.'

The Germans knew how Stalin dealt with Ukrainians. They had uncovered a mass grave of 9,000 bodies, clinically laid head to toe to save space, in the Ukrainian town of Vinnitsa, population 70,000. Again, most had their hands bound and bullet wounds in the back of the neck. Nazi propaganda chief Joseph Goebbels was making a rare excursion into truth when he said: 'If the Germans lay down their arms, the whole of eastern and south-eastern Europe, together with the Reich, would come under Russian occupation. Behind an iron screen, mass butcheries of people would begin, and all that would remain would be a crude automaton, a dull fermenting mass of millions of proletarians and despairing slave animals knowing nothing of the outside world.'

Slowly the Red Army pushed back the Germans and began pursuing them beyond Russia's borders. At their Yalta summit, the Allied leaders had agreed how to divide the spoils, once Hitler was forced into unconditional surrender. American forces held back to allow Stalin's troops to take Prague. In Poland, the Russians roused the Warsaw resistance via radio to attack their German oppressors and help the liberating army. Then the advance was halted for several days, giving Nazis time to kill as many Poles as possible.

By the end of the war, Stalin had added parts of Finland, Romania and Czechoslovakia, half of Poland and East Prussia, and most of the Baltic States to the Soviet Union. He had also established sympathetic buffer states in the rest of Czechoslovakia, Hungary, Bulgaria and Romania. And by entering the fighting against Japan after America dropped its A-bombs, he legitimized his annexation of the Kurile Islands, Sakhalin Island and parts of Mongolia. His sinister rule now stretched from the South China Sea to the River Elbe in Germany. And, just as Goebbels predicted, mass butchery began behind heavily policed borders.

Stalin in 1949

Beria's NKVD took savage revenge on anyone suspected of collaborating with the Nazis. Whole peoples from outlying areas – the Crimean Tatars, Kalmyks, Karachi-Balkars, Chechens – were transported to starvation in Siberia and Central Asia. Russian soldiers, returning either from captivity or victorious invasion, were thoroughly vetted. Those impressed by what they had seen in the West were shot or incarcerated. Stalin could not allow anyone to spread the word that the capitalist masses actually enjoyed a better standard of living than his Soviet proletariat. Even heroes suffered. Author Alexander Solzhenitsyn, twice decorated for bravery as an artillery officer, vanished into a Gulag for 8 years for 'insulting Stalin.' In the new satellite countries, loyal

Marxist-Leninists were executed or jailed after show trials and the communist parties purged of anyone not proved to be a committed Stalinist.

But the most terrible retribution leaked out only years later. At Yalta, Western leaders agreed to return to Stalin not just prisoners of war, but all refugees from his iron rule. The list ranged from Soviet citizens and soldiers who had tried to fight for Hitler to White Russians who had fled after the civil war ended in 1921. More than three million desperate escapees were in Western hands in 1945. By 1948 almost all had been forcibly repatriated. Britain alone sent 30,000. At Scarisbrook camp on Merseyside, one man hanged himself rather than fall into Stalin's clutches. Another cut his throat as he was led towards a ship on Liverpool dockside. In Rimini, Italy, British soldiers forced reluctant returnees to board trains at gunpoint. One man beat his brains out with a stone. Another was shot by troops as he tried to break free.

Back in the USSR, thousands of the helpless hostages were marched straight off boats and trains into makeshift execution yards. At ports on the north coast and in the Crimea, Soviet air force planes flew low to try to drown the sound of shooting. Those who escaped the quayside massacres were bundled into closed trains for a lingering death in the Gulags.

If Western governments hoped such sacrifices would satisfy Stalin, they were in for a shock. Instead of planning for peace, he ordered exhausted Russia into massive rearmament. Iron and steel production was trebled. Coal and oil targets were doubled. Hundreds of captured German scientists and technicians were forced to try to bridge the technology gap between the USSR and the West. The growing army of Moscow moles abroad was ordered to steal the secrets of the A-bomb. And the Soviet communist party was purged of anyone who refused to toe the hard-line Stalinist policy of cold war.

But the man hell-bent on imposing his brand of Soviet slavery on free nations was now a prisoner of his own terror. Otto Kuusinen, a Finn who knew Stalin better than most, said: 'The more ruthless and cold-blooded he became, the more he lived in an almost insane fear of his life.' Stalin's daughter Svetlana described her father as being 'as bitter as he could be against the whole world. He saw enemies everywhere. It had reached the point of being pathological, of persecution mania.'

Even in the Kremlin, Stalin wore a special bullet-proof vest. Tunnels were dug to link his office with other government buildings. Moscow's underground railway was secretly extended to his villa at Kuntsevo. When forced to appear above ground, Stalin used only an armour-plated car with bullet-proof windows 3 inches thick. NKVD squads checked out every route, and lined the roads when their leader drove past. All Stalin's food came from farms run by the NKVD. It was analyzed by a special team of doctors, served by bodyguards posing as waiters, and always tested for poison by companions before Stalin took a mouthful. His tea had to come from specially sealed packs which were used just once, the rest being thrown away. When the woman who always prepared his tea was spotted taking leaves from a pack with a broken seal, she was thrown into Lubianka prison.

But even a man as powerful as Stalin could not cheat death for ever. On 5 March, 1953, he collapsed with a cerebral haemorrhage, aged 73, apparently in a fury because some of the Politburo opposed his plans to transport thousands of Soviet Jews to wasteland near the Chinese border. According to Czech defector Karel Kaplan, he had even more sinister plans in mind. Kaplan, who fled to the West in 1976, reported that in 1951 Stalin told leaders of the East European satellite states to prepare for all-out war to occupy Western Europe 'in three or four years at the most.'

Stalin had taken Russia from the wooden plough to the nuclear age in 30 years. He had caught up with the advanced countries who had spent centuries making the transition. But in the process, the lives of more than 20 million Soviet citizens had been sacrified. Another 14 million were still in Gulag camps when he died. Count Nikolai Tolstoy wrote that, in a nation of 200 million people, 'scarcely a family had been untouched by tragedy.' It was too much even for the stomachs of those who succeeded Stalin as Soviet leaders.

The NKVD apparatus of fear, which had mushroomed to $1\frac{1}{2}$ million men and women, was slimmed down and renamed the KGB. Beria and other powerful aides were shot within months of their patron's death. In 1956 Nikita Khruschev accused the man for whom he had once worked of unjustified harshness against 'punished peoples' and Russians captured by the Nazis. He also attacked Stalin for killing 'many thousands of honest and innocent communists.' And he added: 'Arbitrary behaviour by one person encouraged and permitted arbitrariness in others. Mass arrests and deportations of many thousands of people, execution without trial and without normal investigation created conditions of insecurity, fear and even desperation.'

Slowly Stalin slipped from public adulation in Russia as revelations about the means he used overshadowed the ends he achieved. In 1961 his remains were removed from the Red Square mausoleum and buried outside the Kremlin walls. His entry in Soviet encyclopaedias shrank. In 1977 his name vanished from the national anthem, though Lenin's stayed. But the most telling blow was a name change which symbolized the passing of two of the world's most repressive regimes. The Volga town of Tsaritsyn was retitled Stalingrad in honour of Stalin's gallant defence of it during the Russian civil war. Within a few years of his death, it became known as Volgograd.

Pol Pot

He has a broad, chubby face with sparkling, grandfatherly eyes and thick lips which split into a toothy, genial grin. He looks slightly comical, an impression not dispelled by his peculiar name, Pol Pot. But there is nothing funny about Pol Pot . . . he is a tyrannical fanatic responsible for the coldly calculated extermination of three million people.

Pol Pot spent just four years on the world stage, as the shadowy leader of Kampuchea (formerly Cambodia) after the overthrow of President Lon Nol in 1975. Yet in that short period he virtually destroyed a nation – all for the sake of an unworkable creed that he imposed unyieldingly on a starving and terrorized population. Under his rule, a once-beautiful country became known as 'The Land of the Walking Dead'.

Little is known of Pol Pot's background, and what is known could easily have been the invention of his propaganda machine. It is said that he was brought up in a peasant community in Cambodia's Kampong Thom province and was educated at a Buddhist temple where, for two years, he was a monk. In the 1950s he won a scholarship to study electronics in Paris where, like so many other students at the time, he found it fashionable to espouse left-wing causes.

Also in Paris in the 1950s was another left-wing Cambodian student, Khieu Samphan, who used his political science courses to formulate an extraordinary philosophy of rural revolution. His theory was that to rid itself of the vestiges of colonial rule and to avoid capitalist exploitation, Cambodia must regress to a peasant economy – without towns, without industry, without currency, without education.

It is unlikely that Pol Pot and Khieu Samphan ever met in Paris. But back among the Khmer people of Cambodia, they teamed up and set about making Khieu's crackpot creed come true, using as their instrument the newly-formed and Chinese-backed Communist Party of Kampuchea.

After a decade of political intrigue and rural guerrilla warfare, in 1975 the communists finally overthrew President Lon Nol and became masters of the capital, Phnom Penh. By now the party was known as the Khmer Rouge. Khieu Samphan became its figurehead. But the real power lay in the hands of the former peasant from the provinces, Prime Minister Pol Pot. And he immediately put political daydreams into horrific, brutal, uncompromising reality.

The capital was emptied. As many as three million of its citizens were stripped of all they possessed and were ordered out of their homes. Irrespective of whether they were old, sick, pregnant, crippled, newly born or dying, they were marched into the countryside and herded into vast communes of as many as 10,000. No town was left inhabited. Even villages were emptied of their people. Everybody had to work in the fields.

Of course, not everyone could. The aged and the ill died of exhaustion. The young died of starvation. And the crippled and the lame were clubbed to death.

Living in malaria-ridden swamps, with no proper shelter or sanitation, the new 'peasants' were frogmarched into the paddy fields to work a minimum of eleven hours a day. They were fed a daily bowl of gruel and a morsel of dried fish. They worked nine days on and one day off . . . but that tenth day of rest was taken up with political indoctrination. Children began their working lives at the age of seven.

Not only did the Khmer Rouge abolish towns and communities, they abolished families, husbands and wives being split up and placed in different co-operatives. They also abolished personal property, apart from the one sleeping mat and one pair of black overalls handed out no more than once a year. Since there was no property and no trade, there was no need for money, so they abolished that too.

Because there was no education apart from political indoctrination, Pol Pot abolished the schools and colleges. All books were burned. With education thereby shown to be non-essential, he abolished the educated classes – and had them murdered by the tens of thousands. Also eliminated, by bayonet or pickaxe, were priests, political reactionaries, prison inmates and the defeated soldiers of ex-president Lon Nol.

Anyone who complained, or even questioned the system, would be instantly executed by clubbing. Special offenders, like those starving peasants found cannibalizing dead bodies, would be buried up to their heads in the ground and left to die. Their heads would then be cut off and stuck on stakes as a warning to others.

The extermination continued for four years, with no hope of help from the outside world. Refugees reaching neighbouring countries told stories of horrors that were unbelievable. Yet, with no diplomatic ties, no travel, not even a postal service, the renamed nation of Kampuchea was an impenetrable armed camp seemingly set on the genocide of its own people.

The world's repugnance was unheeded; protest appeared futile. In March 1978, Britain reported Kampuchea to the United Nations Commission On Human Rights. The Khmer Rouge's embassy in Peking issued an hysterical response, saying: 'The British imperialists have no right to speak of the rights of man. The world knows well their barbarous and abject nature. Britain's leaders are living in opulence on top of a pile of rotting corpses while the proletariat have only the right to be unemployed, to steal and to become prostitutes.' There was

A grim scene in the Museum of Genocidal Crime outside Phnom Penh

little chance of a reasoned debate . . . and indeed Pol Pot's ministers sent their regrets that they could find no one with the time to spare to attend the United Nations human rights hearings.

Predictably, it was military might, not moral right, that brought the overthrow of Pol Pot and his murderous henchmen. Vietnam signed a pact with Kampuchea's only ally, China, and in 1978 Vietnamese forces which had been skirmishing with the Khmer Rouge for years launched a full-scale invasion. The Chinese did not step in to aid Pol Pot, and in January 1979 his regime fell to the invading Vietnamese. So swift was his overthrow that the chubby little despot had to flee from Phnom Penh in a white Mercedes limousine only two hours before the first of Hanoi's troops arrived.

Pol Pot fought on from his power base among his dedicated followers in the countryside. He formed the Khmer People's National Liberation Front and announced a hypocritical manifesto promising political and religious freedom. Khieu Samphan remained titular head of the Khmer Rouge. In a rare interview with foreign journalists in 1980, he said the mistakes made by his regime were mainly in implementation of policy. For instance, he said, over-zealous commune leaders had often forgotten to give workers their one day off in ten. And as for the massacres, he said: 'To talk about systematic murder is odious. If we had really killed at that rate, we would have no one to fight the Vietnamese.'

No one will ever know the truth about how many Khmers died of disease, starvation, neglect, brutalization, murder or massacre. But in June 1979, Foreign Minister Ieng Sary admitted to three million deaths since the Khmer Rouge came to power. As there were only eight million Khmers in the pre-revolutionary census, it was pointed out by journalists that this did not seem a good record for a four-year-old government. The Minister was apologetic. He had an explanation, he said. The orders from Pol Pot had been 'misunderstood.' The massacres had, he said, been 'a mistake'.

'Emperor' Bokassa

For a brief period just before the 'coronation' of self-styled Emperor Jean Bedel Bokassa it seemed as if some glimmer of humanity might be creeping into his tyrannical madness. Important diplomats and influential international businessmen from many parts of the world were preparing to attend his spectacular enthronement ceremony in Bangui, capital of the land-locked Central African Republic, the sprawling former French colony in the heart of the continent.

At the beginning of December 1977, as rehearsals began for the great event, Bokassa had locked himself away in his palace 50 miles outside the capital watching endless re-runs of a film which had been specially flown to him from London. The film showed the majesty and splendour of the Coronation of Britain's Queen Elizabeth. Bokassa, a violent, squat, ugly little man, seemed to be genuinely moved by the scenes of the splendid pageantry and the spontaneous, heart-felt joy and devotion of the Queen's loyal subjects.

His own coronation, he decided, would be a similarly historic occasion. Even if he couldn't hope to win the hearts of the people he ruled, at least his guests couldn't fail to be impressed. Apparently on a whim, he ordered the governor of Bangui Prison to select a dozen prisoners for more humane treatment. They were to be moved to less cramped cells, given better food than the other inmates and allowed some fresh air in the prison yard. Some prison guards even talked excitedly of a partial amnesty to celebrate the coronation. The prisoners, Bokassa promised, wouldn't be in jail much longer.

Then Bokassa busied himself again supervising the last-minute preparations for the ceremony. The Government of France, headed by his frequent holiday guest, President Valéry Giscard D'Estaing, had generously provided him with credit of £1 million to buy a fleet of Mercedes limousines' for his guests and to equip their ceremonial escort with 200 new BMW motorcycles.

It mattered little to the 58-year-old dictator that his country ranked as one of the poorest in the world, with barely ten per cent of the two million population able to read and write and more than a quarter of their children dying of disease and malnutrition before they reached their first birthday.

He planned to spend £10 million in a 48-hour spectacular binge, a regal extravaganza to rival the coronation of his 'hero', the Emperor Napoleon. President Bokassa himself would assume the title Emperor Bokassa and his bankrupt country would be grandly re-named The Central African Empire.

Many political leaders had no stomach for his lunacy and returned their gold-lettered invitation cards with scant apologies for their absence. Even the formally polite British Foreign Office were blunt and rude when they refused to attend. American President Jimmy Carter, outraged by Bokassa's insane claim to Napoleonic grandeur, promptly responded by cutting off all aid to the country.

Bokassa was unrepentant. His rag-tag army formed most of the unenthusiastic onlookers at the triumphal parade through Bangui where the new Emperor would ride in a gilded carriage drawn by eight white horses along the city's only two miles of paved road.

The coronation went ahead with all the panoply of crowns and ermine robes in the sweltering African heat, and the guests were treated to a mouth-watering imperial banquet in Bokassa's palace at Berengo.

Protected by screens of bullet-proof glass in a landscaped garden amid fountains and ornate ivory carvings, they were pampered by uniformed servants who brought them elaborately cooked delicacies served on gold and white porcelain dishes specially imported from the workshops of the master designer, Berardaud of Limoges.

Some of the French and African diplomats, and the Italian and German businessmen, seemed ill at ease in the absurd splendour of their bizarre surroundings. They would have felt distinctly more queasy if they had realized the origins of some of the tastiest morsels served up to them on the Limoges porcelain.

Bokassa had kept his promise to the prison governor. The inmates who had been given food, fresh air and exercise had found their new privileges short-lived. As soon as they had been restored to near normal health, they had been killed, expertly butchered and served up to the unsuspecting guests at Bokassa's celebration feast.

His obsession with the trappings of the power and grace of the age of Napoleon were flattering to many of his French VIP visitors. At least most of them found his mania for all things French to be understandable. His character had been moulded by his long years as a soldier in the French colonial army, where all new

The Coronation of Emperor Bokassa, 28 December, 1977

recruits were thoroughly indoctrinated in the glories of French history and the awesome achievements of its finest soldier, Napoleon Bonaparte.

In 1960, when the French gave independence to the republic, an area almost as large as France itself, most of them were glad to be rid of the task of governing its vast, arid waste. There was some embarassed amusement in 1966 when Colonel Bokassa seized power in a coup from the Republic's civilian government and began to boast of his devotion to France. He swore undying loyalty to French President Charles De Gaulle, whom he lovingly called 'Papa'. The French Government responded with generous aid in return for some minor business concessions and a military foothold in a strategic part of Africa.

In 1975, the new French President Valéry Giscard D'Estaing took advantage of Bokassa's welcome to make several big-game hunting trips to his private game reserve, an area covering most of the eastern half of the country.

There were reports that Bokassa was never slow to shower his visitors with lavish gifts, including fistfuls of diamonds, one of his country's few precious resources, which should have gone to help alleviate the crushing poverty of its people.

By the time Bokassa was in the full grip of his 'imperial' mania, the soaring price of oil had made the country's only other asset, uranium deposits, look like a promising commercial prospect for French developers. Wary of growing evidence of Bokassa's brutality, the French uneasily indulged his regal fantasies while keeping a discreet eye on his appetite for power and showmanship. Within two years of the ludicrous coronation, he had become more than a posturing embarrassment to Paris. He was a bloodthirsty, dangerous liability.

Apparently determined to transform his dusty capital city into a model of French 'provincial' fashion, Bokassa ordered the barefoot schoolchildren of Bangui's only high school to buy expensively tailored school uniforms to be worn at all lessons. Their parents could hardly afford to buy the text books their children needed if they were to have even a basic education. And it hadn't passed unnoticed that the Emperor owned the only clothing factory which produced the school uniforms. It was yet another impossible order from the Emperor which they couldn't obey even if they wanted to. No one foresaw the consequences.

President Bokassa, who had seen his demands for national opera, ballet and art societies dismissed by his weary people, had at one time seemingly grown accustomed to being ignored. But *Emperor* Bokassa, the Napoleon-worshipper, expected every order to be carried out without question.

Two hundred ragged schoolchildren were rounded up by the 'Imperial Guard'. Bokassa gathered them in the yard of Bangui Prison, swaggering among them with his gold-topped cane, bullying the overawed, frightened pupils. 'You will not need school uniforms as long as you stay in prison,' the Emperor screamed at them. Under the threatening guns of the guards, the children were herded into the already overcrowded cells.

Over the next few weeks the killings began. One by one the children were led from the cells for 'school uniform inspection' . . . and mercilessly beaten to death.

News of the mass murders finally reached the disbelieving ears of officials of the French Embassy in Bangui. At first they couldn't bring themselves to accept the evidence. But witness after witness from the prison repeated the same story. And Paris finally woke up to the fact that Jean Bedel Bokassa was more than a comic opera Emperor with his crown and robes and sceptre. He was a monster.

For the honour of France, for the sake of common decency, the Emperor had to go.

The opportunity came a month later when the demented Emperor left Bangui for a visit to another dictator, Colonel Ghadaffi of Libya. As Bokassa stepped off his plane in Tripoli, he learned a lesson in the true French art of power politics and military muscle which would have delighted his long dead hero Napoleon.

At his home in Paris where he had lived since being ousted by Bokassa, African politician David Dacko was roughly shaken awake by French Secret Service agents and given a prepared speech to rehearse and memorize before being bundled into a waiting car. Ten hours later he stumbled from a French military jet at Bangui and asked the French Foreign Legion troops who landed immediately after him to help him to a 'spontaneous' humanitarian overthrow of the evil Bokassa.

Within 24 hours the 'Empire' was effectively back under French control. The deposed Emperor went into exile from Libya to the Ivory Coast in West Africa and then to a run-down château in an unfashionable Paris suburb.

The hardened Legionnaires who searched the grounds of the prison had the grim task of uncovering the mass grave which held the bodies of the dead schoolchildren.

Later, when they stormed the Emperor's Napoleonic palace, they found the bones of another 37 children lying on the tiled floor of the Olympic standard swimming pool. Lounging by the poolside were the predators who had enjoyed the grisly feast, Bokassa's four pet crocodiles. And in the cold storage rooms of the palace kitchens, they found the half-eaten remains of another dozen unnamed victims who had been served up at the Emperor's dining table only the week before.

As the uniform-obsessed Emperor began a new career in exile as a supplier of khaki safari suits to African tourist boutiques, President Giscard D'Estaing announced in Paris that he had sent a personal cheque for £10,000, the value of the diamonds given to him as gifts, to a charity school for children in Bangui.

Attila the Hun

Mass slaughter, rape and pillage were an integral part of life for most of northern Europe for centuries. Though the Greeks and Romans established the Mediterranean as the cradle of civilization, it was constantly rocked by murderous incursions from barbarian hordes to the north. Greek historian Herodotus, born in 484 BC, described savage Scythians north of the Black Sea who skinned opponents to make coats, sawed off the top of their skulls to make drinking cups and drank the blood of their victims. Wild Goths swept south from Sweden, and in AD 410 sacked Rome in a six-day orgy of rape and killing. Vicious Vandals reached the city less than 50 years later after storming through Germany, Gaul, Spain and North Africa, leaving death and destruction in their wake. Saxons, Franks and Vikings were other warlike and unmerciful raiders. But of all the brutal barbarians who terrorized Europe, none struck greater fear in men's hearts than a tribe whose roots were in the harsh steppes of Mongolia.

The Huns were wild horsemen driven out of their homeland by the Chinese in the second century AD. They rode west, conquering and cold-bloodedly massacring any tribe that stood in their way. Eventually they settled north of the river Danube, between the Volga and the Don, and established uneasy detente with neighbouring Romans, even helping the legions subdue troublesome tribes. Rome paid the Huns' King Ruas an annual tribute of 350 pounds of gold, but in return took hostages as a guarantee of good behaviour. The king's nephew, Attila, born in AD 406, spent part of his youth as a hostage in Italy. It was invaluable experience for a leader whose bloodthirsty campaigns were to earn him the title 'Scourge Of God'. Attila the Hun was 27 when King Ruas died. At first he ruled jointly with his brother Bleda, strengthening the kingdom by defeating Teutonic tribes like the Ostrogoths and Gepidae. By AD 444 he had complete control of the territory known today as Hungary and Romania. And he was absolute ruler after having his brother murdered. Now his ruthless ambition was ready to take on the Romans. The plaintive plea of a damsel in distress gave him the pretext for war.

Honoria, sister of Roman emperor Valentinian III, caused a scandal by having an affair with a court chamberlain and getting pregnant. Valentinian had her sent off to Constantinople, where she lived with religious relatives virtually a prisoner. Frustrated and bored, she smuggled her ring together with a message for help to Attila at his camp near Budapest, offering herself as his

**Attila, King
of the Huns**

bride if he rescued her. The Hun chieftain already had as many wives as he needed, but he made the most of the request. He asked Valentinian for Honoria's hand – and half the Roman Empire as dowry. Rejected, he unleashed a furious onslaught.

His hordes swept south, through Macedonia – now mostly part of Greece – to the gates of Constantinople in AD 447. The Romans bought him off, increasing their yearly tribute to 2,100 pounds of gold, and paying a heavy indemnity for withdrawal. Attila went home with his booty, but four years later he led a vast army of Huns, Franks and Vandals across the Rhine into Gaul.

Town after town was ravaged and razed, but as the unscrupulous barbarians were about to storm the city of Orléans, the city was saved by the arrival of Roman legions allied to an army of Visigoths. Attila withdrew to the plains near Châlons-sur-Marne and prepared for battle. It lasted all day, with appalling carnage on both sides. One eye-witness later described the hand-to-hand fighting as 'ruthless, immense, obstinate.' The Visigoth king was just one of the thousands slaughtered. But Attila was forced to retreat back beyond the Rhine. Historians describe the battle as one of the most crucial ever. Had the Romans not won, they say, Europeans might today have slant-eyed, Mongol-like features.

Attila was bloodied but unbowed. A year later his men again swarmed south into Italy. Aquileia, the major city in the province of Venetia, was completely destroyed after appalling atrocities against its inhabitants. The Hun hordes swept on to the Adriatic sea, slaughtering the civilians of Concordia, Altinum and Padua before burning their properties. Frightened refugees fled to the islands and lagoons where horsemen could not follow. There they established the city we know as Venice.

The power-crazed heathen turned his army towards the Lombardy plain and Milan, plundering and pillaging until northern Italy was devastated. As Rome itself was threatened, Pope Leo I courageously left the Vatican for a personal interview with the irresistible invader. Attila, his fury subdued by such a bold move, agreed to lead his men home, though he talked menacingly of returning if Honoria's wrongs were not righted.

But there were to be no more atrocities from the most ruthless despot the world had then known. On 15 March, AD 453, he hosted a gigantic banquet to celebrate the taking of yet another wife, the beautiful virgin Ildico. That night, as he tried to consummate the marriage, an artery burst, and bloodthirsty Attila bled to death.

> **History has hailed Peter the Great as the Tsar who civilized Russia by introducing European customs and by fostering trade. In fact, he could be just as barbarous as Ivan the Terrible. When troops mutinied in Moscow in 1698, Peter personally supervised bloody reprisals which left 1,200 of them dead. For two months, men were flogged, broken on the rack or roasted slowly over flames. Peter was seen wielding an executioner's axe with relish. And he insisted that mutilated bodies be left on display for months as a warning to others.**

Genghis Khan

Nearly 800 years after Attila's demise, Europe was reeling from the onslaught of another Mongol conqueror whose callous cunning and cruelty have never been matched. He was born in 1162 and named Temuchin after a tribal chief his father Yesukai had just defeated. At the age of 13 Yesukai's death in an ambush plunged the boy into the terror and treachery of tribal infighting. But he proved equal to every challenge. He cold-bloodedly killed one of his brothers in a dispute over a fish. He slaughtered every man, woman and child in a tribe of nomads who dared to kidnap his wife. And though rivals battled bitterly – one boiled 70 of his followers alive in cooking pots – by the spring of 1206 Temuchin was powerful enough to impose his power on all the Mongol tribes. He summoned leaders of dozens of warring factions to a conference on the banks of the river Onon and proclaimed himself their chief. He also took a new name – Genghis Khan, which meant perfect warrior.

China was first to feel his wrath. The Kin Tartars ruled the northern half of the country, and had been glad to accept when Genghis offered them some of his troops to suppress troublemakers. In 1211 that move rebounded on them. The troops had gained a comprehensive knowledge of the land inside the Great Wall, and even subverted sentries at some of the gates. The Mongol armies poured south, besieging and sacking cities, trampling and burning crops. By 1214 Genghis Khan controlled almost all the country north of the Yellow River. He offered the Kin emperor peace, adding: 'It will be necessary that you distribute largess to my officers and men to appease their fierce hostility.' Two royal princesses, 500 young men and girls, 3,000 horses and a herd of rare white camels were among the prizes the Mongol armies carried home. But within a year they were back, ruthlessly besieging the few cities that had survived the previous invasion.

Genghis Khan's empire was soon secure, ruled by a regime of fear which meant instant death to any rebel. The savage warlord now looked to the west and his neighbours the Khwarizms. Their vast territories stretched from the Ganges to the Tigris, and included present-day Turkistan, Iran and northern India. Genghis sent envoys to Shah Mohammed, promising peace and proposing trade. The reply seemed favourable. But when the first caravan of 100 Mongol traders arrived in the border town of Otrar, governor Inaljuk had them all massacred as spies. Furious Genghis sent more envoys, demanding the governor's extradition. Mohammed beheaded their leader and sent the rest home minus their beards. The insult was to cost the Shah his kingdom – and bring unprecedented horror to Europe's door.

More than 400,000 Khwarizm troops were strung along the Syr Daria river to repel the invasion, but they were like lambs to the slaughter when the Mongol armies struck in a three-pronged attack. One army attacked in the south, threatening the strategic cities of Bukhara and Samarkand. Two others crossed the mountains to the north and besieged Otrar. A bitter battle ended with the errant governor being executed as painfully as possible – molten metal was poured into his eyes and ears. Then, while one army turned south to link with the first near Bukhara, 40,000 men led by Genghis Khan vanished into the vast Kizylkum desert. They re-emerged behind Bukhara and behind the enemies' lines. The Shah fled as the city suffered the Mongol victory rites. Its mercenary defenders were slaughtered, and the civilians ordered outside what was left of the walls to allow uninterrupted looting. Then the women were raped in front of their families, craftsmen were taken as slaves and the remaining residents put to the sword.

The terror-struck Khwarizms had no answer to the Mongols' devastating military efficiency. Their infantry was helpless against hordes of horsemen who unleashed waves of arrows which decimated defenders, then moved in to finish them off ruthlessly with their curved sabres and lances. If a city or a pass seemed too secure, the Mongols would appear to retreat, then turn and scatter their pursuers with savage ferocity. As they moved further into Khwarizm territory, they herded crowds of captives in front of them as a human shield. Giant catapults, manned by up to 100 Mongol warriors, hurled rocks at city walls. Other defences were breached by means of a weapon unknown to the West, gunpowder.

Towns which opened their gates to the invaders were spared. Those that fought, like Samarkand, were not. The Mongols arrived in May 1220 to find a garrison of 50,000 men well dug in. When the attackers pretended to flee, the defenders poured after them and were cut to ribbons. When half the mercenaries deserted to Genghis Khan, the civilians surrendered, leaving soldiers besieged in the citadel. They were starved out and killed – then the turncoat mercenaries were massacred for treachery. Nearly 30,000 civilians were herded away to form a living shield at the next siege.

At Urgenj, the Mongols slaughtered every man and took the women and children as slaves before breaching dykes to flood the burning ruins. In Termez every body was cut open after Genghis discovered that one old woman had swallowed some pearls. At Nisa, Genghis's son Tulé had all the inhabitants' hands tied behind their backs, then watched them die in a hail of arrows. At Merv the poor were beheaded while the rich were savagely tortured to reveal the whereabouts of their treasures. When Nishapur surrendered, the severed heads of the residents were arranged in three gruesome pyramids of men, women and children.

Shah Mohammed had been broken by the speed and savagery with which his empire had been destroyed. He fled to a village on the Caspian Sea, and died of pleurisy. Genghis pursued his son and successor, Jelaleddin, south through Afghanistan, slaughtering hundreds of thousands of innocent civilians as he went. When his quarry took refuge with the Sultan of Delhi, the Mongols ravaged Lahore, Peshawar and Melikpur before turning north west again. News had reached Genghis that the people of Herat, spared after surrendering without a fight, had deposed the governor he installed. A six-month siege by 80,000 men ended the rebellion. Then a week of unbridled murder meted out the punishment. Thousands of corpses lay in the rubble of the city when Genghis at last headed for home. He had unfinished business with the Tangut tribe, who had declined to send troops to aid his Khwarizm campaign. He vowed to exterminate them all.

But age and weakness following a hunting accident were finally to achieve what no foe could manage. Genghis Khan was besieging the Tangut capital of Ninghsia in August 1227, when he fell ill and died, aged 65. His will named his son Ogotai as successor, but the warlord's aides decided that the death must remain secret until Ogotai was safely in command. The final victims of the man described by one historian as the 'mightiest and most bloodthirsty conqueror of all time' were the innocent souls who accidentally spotted the funeral procession as it headed for the burial ground in the valley of Kilien. Without exception, they were put to the sword.

Genghis Khan left an empire stretching from the China Sea to the Persian Gulf. But trembling neighbours who hoped his death would spare them further conquest were sadly mistaken. For the mighty Mongol had fathered a dynasty of ruthless rulers almost as callous and cruel. And they had their own territorial ambitions to extend their legacy.

Genghis's successor, Ogotai, spent his first years in power consolidating his grip on China and extending his empire in Korea. Then his avaricious eyes strayed westward again. The Mongol warriors surged through central Asia, laying waste to the cities of Tiflis and Ryazan, in Georgia, and massacring the

---

Not all deaths ordered by Genghis Khan were gory. Once he defeated another tribe led by a childhood friend. He offered to spare his life, but the rival insisted on execution. So Genghis decided to kill him without spilling blood. He was wrapped in a carpet and kicked to death.

inhabitants. Moscow, then an insignificant wooden township, was quickly taken. At Koselsk, revenge for an earlier reversal resulted in such a carnival of death that the laughing invaders renamed the town Mobalig, 'city of woe'. Finally Kiev, known as 'the mother of cities', was battered into submission. The residents were slaughtered and the buildings razed.

Now the Mongol army split. One of Genghis Khan's old lieutenants, Subatai, led a three-pronged assault on Hungary, aiming to rendezvous with the rest of the army at the Danube. But first the armies of Poland, Germany and Bohemia had to be prevented from coming to the aid of Hungary's fearsome Magyars. The rest of the invasion force swarmed into Poland, moving at a pace which staggered generals accustomed to slow-moving traditional battle strategy. The Poles were routed at Szydlow and the Germans at Liegnitz. The Bohemians beat a hasty retreat. In less than a month the Mongols had covered 400 miles, won two decisive battles, captured four major cities and cleared the way to the main objective – Hungary.

Hungarian King Bela IV had massed his men to meet Subatai at the Danube. But the Mongol commander declined to fight on ground which did not suit his horsemen. He began a calculated retreat to the Sajo river, and for six days the Hungarians followed, being lured further from their stronghold and reinforcements. Then Subatai turned for a savage dawn attack. Most of Bela's army was still asleep. By mid-day, more than 70,000 Magyars had been massacred. 'They fell to the left and right like leaves in winter,' wrote one chronicler. 'The roads for two days' journey from the field of battle were strewn with corpses as the rest tried to flee.'

Subatai stormed Budapest while part of his force chased King Bela to the Adriatic coast, burning and destroying everything in their path. On Christmas Day 1241 he led his forces across the iced-up Danube and took the city of Esztergom. But as Europe waited in trepidation for the next move, the Mongols again turned back. News had reached them that Ogotai was dead, and a bitter battle for succession was likely. No one wanted to miss it.

It was ten years before Genghis Khan's grandson Mangu, son of the tyrant Tulé, emerged as undisputed Mongol leader. Unrest in Persia, fostered by the Ismailites, prompted him to send his brother Halagu to the Middle East to storm the strongholds of a sinister sect known as the Assassins. Halagu rode on to Baghdad, then the major city in the region. After resisting for a month, the city

---

Genghis Khan gave the Mongols their first written laws, the Great Jasagh. Refusing to work, urinating in running water and gluttony all received the same sentence – death.

surrendered in February 1258. Halagu's marauders massacred everybody inside, trampling the sultan to death under horses. They set fire to the city, then turned towards Syria. Aleppo was sacked, Damascus surrendered, and Halagu was about to attack Jerusalem when, once again, a single death prevented thousands. The news was received that Mangu had died, and the hordes rode home.

Mangu's brother was Kubla Khan, celebrated in Coleridge's verse. Alone amongst the family, he treated captives humanely and banned indiscriminate massacres. For 34 years he concentrated on conquests in the East, in southern China, Tibet and Vietnam. He even tried to invade Japan without success. And after his death, the empire fell apart as his heirs squabbled. Even the Chinese cast off the Mongol yoke as the Ming Dynasty forced the wild warriors back to their Mongolian homeland.

Tamerlane the Great

The world had not heard the last of the merciless Mongols. In 1336 a boy called Timur was born at Kesh, near Samarkand. He was the great-great-grandson of Genghis Khan and conceived the desperate dream of rebuilding his forefather's empire, by then divided into a multitude of smaller principalities. Locals nicknamed him Timur i Leng, or Timur the Lame, because of a disability which made him limp. But the world remembers him as Tamerlane the Great, a wicked warmonger with a savage sadistic streak.

At 33 he usurped the Transoxian throne at Samarkand and gained the power base he needed for his conquests. Superb military management earned him mastery of Persia, Turkistan, the Ukraine, the Crimea, Georgia, Mesopotamia and Armenia. Governors who appealed to him for help frequently found themselves betrayed once he had restored their realms. He dethroned a rival khan to occupy Russia, then over-ran India, leaving a trail of carnage all the way to Delhi, where he reduced the city to rubble and massacred 100,000 inhabitants.

Like his ancestors, Tamerlane, tall with a huge head and white-haired from childhood, found that fear was no way to establish allegiance among the peoples he conquered. Revolts in the growing empire were frequent, but repressed ruthlessly. Whole cities were destroyed out of spite and their populations slaughtered. Massive towers or pyramids of skulls were constructed for the emperor's enjoyment. Twice he had thousands of opponents bricked up alive for agonising slow suffocation and starvation. Another time he hurled all his prisoners to their deaths over a cliff.

After his Indian campaign, Tamerlane stormed into Syria to settle old scores with leaders who refused to help in his earlier wars. Aleppo was seized and sacked and Damascus occupied in 1400. Baghdad, still smarting from Halagu's atrocities a century earlier, was devastated again by fire, and 20,000 people put to the sword. In 1402 Tamerlane unleashed his wrath on Anatolia – now Turkey – and beheaded 5,000 Ottoman fighters after one siege. Their sultan was killed in captivity in a barbarous iron cage.

The nightmare return to the depravity of an earlier age ended only with Tamerlane's death. His hordes were on their way to attack China when, in January, 1405, he fell ill while camping on the Syr Daria river and died. By a bizarre twist of fate, it happened at Otrar – the town whose governor had unwittingly sparked off the fury of the Mongols under Genghis Khan nearly 200 years earlier when he executed 100 traders. Millions had since paid the Mongols' bloody price for that rash act.

Ivan the Terrible

In July 1662, a mob of 5,000 angry Russians marched to the palace of Tsar Alexis in the suburbs of Moscow. Poor harvests and a long war with Poland had exhausted their patience over harsh taxation, currency devaluation and corrupt officialdom, and they extracted a promise from the Tsar that he would act on their grievances. But his solution to the problems was not what they had in mind. According to historian V.O. Klyuchevsky, 'Tsar Alexis called on the streltsy (musketeers who formed the Tsar's bodyguard) and his courtiers for assistance, and an indiscriminate slaughter ensued, followed by tortures and executions. Hundreds were drowned in the River Moskva and whole families were exiled permanently to Siberia.'

Alexis was pious and artistically-minded. He tried to leave government to ministers. But he had been born into a succession of Tsars who inherited absolute rule from the Mongols – and were equally merciless about maintaining it. Any challenge to their authority was met by torture, exile and execution. The loyalty of a few select aristocrats was bought with land and honours. The peasants – 90 per cent of the population – were shackled in medieval-style serfdom; denied education, the right to change jobs, even the right to choose their own marital partners. And if they grew restless about their lot, soldiers and a secret army of informers soon brought them back into line with bloodshed. For four centuries, the Tsars ruled Russia by fear. And few rulers inspired more fear than Ivan the Terrible.

Ivan, born in August 1530, was an orphan by the age of eight. His father Vasily, Grand Duke of Moscow, died when he was three. Five years later his mother Elena, who acted as Regent, was poisoned. After that, Ivan was to claim that he received 'no human care from any quarter.' Vicious power battles between leading families marked his early years. Ivan was used as a pawn by rival factions wrestling for control, only to lose it, in a succession of bloodbaths. He watched one of his uncles carried off to death by a Moscow mob in one uprising. But he quickly learned how to fight back. He was just 13 when he ordered his first assassination. Then he threw the body of his victim, a troublesome Shuisky prince, to his dogs.

In 1547, Ivan had himself crowned Tsar and, at a parade of the nation's most beautiful and eligible virgins, he selected himself a bride – 15-year-old Anastasia. She produced six children for him, but only two were still alive when she died in 1560. Their deaths, plus the loss of his wife's calming influence and the trauma of his childhood, may all have played a part in the horrors that followed.

First Ivan banished his closest advisers, his personal priest Father Silvestr, and nobleman Alexei Adashev, accusing them of plotting to kill Anastasia. Then he left Moscow for virtual monastic seclusion in the provinces. All sections of the community begged him to return, fearing a power vacuum. Ivan agreed – but only if he was allowed to govern without any interference. When his terms were accepted, he split the nation into two vast sections. In one, he was absolute master. The rest of the country was to be governed for him by bureaucrats.

Now Ivan unleashed unprecedented terror on his people, using the sinister oprichniki. They were black-cloaked riders on black horses, whose saddles carried the symbols of a broom and a dog's head. With unbridled fury, they slaughtered anyone suspected of opposition to Ivan, and settled many of his old scores from the turmoil of his teenage days. More than 4,000 aristocrats were purged. The Staritsky family, relatives of Ivan but potential rivals for power, were wiped out. When Metropolitan Philip, leader of the Orthodox Church in Moscow, condemned the oprichnikis' attacks and refused to bless the Tsar, the ruthless riders tracked him down and savagely executed him.

Ivan himself often took part in their orgies of rape, torture and death. And his rage really ran wild when an informant told him civic leaders of Novgorod, then Russia's second city, were planning rebellion. Without bothering to check the allegation, which was almost certainly untrue, Ivan led his oprichniki north, pillaging and plundering aristocratic homes, monasteries and churches within 50 miles of the city. Having laid waste to the fields that fed Novgorod, he then built a wooden wall around the metropolis to prevent anyone fleeing. And for five weeks, he watched, or took part in, wholesale slaughter.

Husbands and wives were forced to watch as their partners – and sometimes their children – were tortured. Many women were roasted alive on revolving spears. Other killings were treated almost as sport. One German mercenary wrote: 'Mounting a horse and brandishing a spear, he (Ivan) charged in and ran people through while his son watched the entertainment . . .'

Though Soviet scholars have claimed recently that no more than 2,000 people died, Western historians put the total toll in the annihilation of Novgorod at over 60,000. And Ivan's sadistic savagery there, and at Pskov, also suspected of plotting, certainly had an effect on later opponents. When he invaded neighbouring Livonia, one beseiged garrison blew themselves up rather than fall into his cruel clutches.

In 1572 Ivan suddenly disbanded the oprichniki and banned all mention of them. Throughout his life, his sadism alternated with periods of manic religious depression, when he would publicly confess his sins and don sackcloth. So perhaps genuine shame ended the six-year reign of terror. Perhaps an attack on Russia from the south by Turks forced him to call off internal vendettas. Or perhaps his assassins had eliminated almost everyone Ivan wanted out of the way.

Ivan got away with his ruthless rule because he had the support of the Orthodox Church. Western Europe was undergoing the religious crisis of the Reformation, and Orthodox leaders were terrified of free-thinking Protestant-ism which would weaken their hold on the unthinking masses. In exchange for a hard line on all religious dissent, including burning for 'heresy', the Church backed the Tsar and became an effective propaganda machine on his behalf. When peasant revolts were crushed with total brutality, the causes and the consequences were never attributed to Ivan. They were blamed on the corruption or excessive zeal of those who worked for him.

For a few Russians, Ivan was not so terrible. They were the people granted lands and power in the territories the Tsar added to his empire, north of the Black Sea and in Siberia. But the wars that won them, and campaigns which won nothing, forced an ever-increasing tax burden on Russian landowners and their peasants. And by the end of Ivan's reign, English ambassador Giles Fletcher was reporting to London: 'The desperate state of things at home maketh the people for the most part to wish for some foreign invasion, which they suppose to be the only means to rid them of the heavy yoke of his tyrannous government.'

In fact there was another way – Ivan's death. It came in March 1584, three years after he killed his son and heir Ivan with a spear during a quarrel. A life of licentiousness – six more wives and innumerable mistresses – had left the Tsar riddled with disease. As British trader Sir Jerome Horsey put it: 'The emperor began grievously to swell in his cods, with which he had most horribly offended above 50 years, boasting of a thousand virgins he had deflowered and thousands of children of his begetting destroyed.' Ivan collapsed and died as he prepared to play a game of chess.

Yet even his departure did not spare Russia agony. His heir's death left Ivan's imbecilic son Theodore as successor and he soon proved hopelessly unable to govern. The country was plunged into 30 years of chaos, which included occupation by the armies of both Poland and Sweden, before the Romanovs – relatives of Ivan's wife Anastasia – were able to reimpose the authority of the Tsars.

Historians still dispute whether Tsarist Russia's most bloodthirsty tyrant was consciously bad or completely mad. Some seek excuses in his traumatic childhood. Others blame a painful spinal defect for his excesses. It was nearly 350 years before Ivan the Terrible found sympathetic consideration from someone who believed his oprichniki had played a 'progressive role', someone who claimed his only mistake was not taking his purges further. That sympathiser was Josef Stalin. And as the earlier chapter on Stalin shows, he did not make the same 'mistake'.

The Ottoman Sultans

Turkey was known as the sick man of Europe throughout the 19th Century. Crisis followed crisis – one culminated in the bloody Crimea War – as the continent's super-powers bolstered the weak and crumbling regime of the once-great Ottoman Sultans to prevent rivals like Russia from seizing Constantinople and threatening trade routes. Then the outraged western world learned that Turkey was even sicker than they feared – but in a very different sense.

Like the Mongols before them, early Ottoman armies conquered mercilessly. Massacres of captives were commonplace, an accepted aspect of warfare. And by 1588 – the year Spain's Armada was routed by England – the Sultans ruled an empire which circled most of the Mediterranean. It stretched from the Red

Sea port of Aden to Budapest and Belgrade, from the Crimea north of the Black Sea to Algeria. Huge chunks of present-day Hungary, Poland and Russia shared the same masters as the people of Greece, Egypt, Tunisia, Libya, Lebanon, Syria, Israel, Yugoslavia, Romania and Bulgaria. Any revolts among the 30 million subjects were ruthlessly suppressed.

But the absolute power of the Sultans not only corrupted them, it blinded them to the changing world outside their realms. In 1876 a rebellion in Bulgaria was repressed with traditional carnage. Ottoman troops ran amok in an orgy of killing, and more than 12,000 men, women and children were slaughtered. But by then the western world had newspapers, and millions were appalled to realise that medieval-style tyranny still went on in the 'modern' age. Historians were to discover that such tyranny had run virtually unchecked for 350 years – and would carry on well into the 20th Century.

The sinister Sultans had more reason than most absolute rulers to be paranoid about plots. A strong tradition of strangulation by deaf mutes, using silk bowstrings, existed inside the walls of their Grand Seraglio palace. Mahomet the Conqueror (1431–81) formulated a law by which his successors as Sultan had 'the right to execute their brothers to ensure the peace of the world.' It was designed to stop disputes over succession. But when Mahomet III took the throne in 1595, his father Murad III's prowess in the harem meant he had to murder 19 brothers, all aged under 11, and throw seven pregnant concubines into the Bosporus tied up in sacks.

Thereafter, close male relatives of the incoming Sultan were locked up in a windowless building within the Grand Seraglio complex until the Sultan's death called them to the throne. Cut off from the outside world, with only deaf mutes and sterilized concubines for company, many were completely deranged when they came to power, sometimes after more than 30 years incarceration. It was 1789 before the practice was abolished – and by then, madness was in the blood of the Ottoman dictators.

Suleiman the Magnificent, who ruled from 1520 to 1566, is regarded by most historians as the last great Sultan. In 1526 he seized more of Hungary, massacring 200,000 – 2,000 were killed for his enjoyment as he watched from a throne – and taking 100,000 slaves back to Constantinople. Three years later, when Vienna stubbornly refused to surrender, he scoured the surrounding countryside and selected the most nubile girls for Turkey's harems. Then he threw hundreds of unwanted peasants on a gigantic fire in view of the city walls. Such 'sanity' in the name of military strength was succeeded by a dynasty of Sultans who were weak, debauched, indecisive or insane – or sometimes all four.

Suleiman's son Selim II was a drunkard, despite the proscription of alcohol by the Koran, and decided to wrest Cyprus, source of his favourite wine, from its Venetian rulers. His soldiers sacked Nicosia, slaughtering 30,000. When the key fortress of Famagusta fell after a two-year siege, the Turks promised to spare the heroic garrison – then killed them all. Their commander was flayed alive, then paraded in front of the Turkish troops, his body stuffed with straw. Venice, Spain and Austria retaliated with the humiliating naval triumph of Lepanto, at which 50,000 Turks died. But the Ottomans still held Cyprus when, in 1574, Selim lost his footing climbing into his bath after a drinking session, and died from a fractured skull.

His son, Mahomet III, the man who killed his 19 young brothers, was a man with a fiery temper who enjoyed the sight of women's breasts being scorched off with hot irons. Osman II, who ruled for less than a year before his 1618 murder, enjoyed archery – but only if his targets were live prisoners-of-war or page boys. And while these two, and a string of insignificant Sultans, indulged themselves, the empire began to fall to pieces. Neglect and oppression ravaged the countryside, with tax income tumbling as famine laid waste to whole areas. The rigid disciplines which had made the Ottoman empire strong were also disintegrating.

Murad IV, a savage, dark-eyed giant, tried to reimpose them when he took over in 1623. After the Janissaries, the Sultan's special army, forced him to sack the chief minister and 16 other officials, he later revenged himself for their impudence by having more than 500 of their leaders strangled in their barracks. Then he set about the rest of the nation, as author Noel Barber records in his excellent book, *Lords Of The Golden Horn*.

'Murad quickly found a simple panacea for the ills of the country,' writes Barber. 'He cut off the head of any man who came under the slightest suspicion. In 1637 he executed 25,000 subjects in the name of justice, many by his own hand. He executed the Grand Mufti because he was dissatisfied with the state of the roads. He beheaded his chief musician for playing a Persian air. He liked to patrol the taverns at night and if he caught anyone smoking he declared himself and executed the offender on the spot. When he caught one of his gardeners and his wife smoking, he had their legs amputated and exhibited them in public while they bled to death.'

A Venetian who added a room to the top of his house was hanged because Murad thought he had done it to spy on the Sultan's harem. A Frenchman who arranged a date with a Turkish girl was impaled. And, according to Barber, Murad 'spent hours . . . exercising the royal prerogative of taking ten innocent lives a day as he practised his powers with the arquebus on passers-by who were too near the palace walls. On one occasion he drowned a party of women when he chanced to come across them in a meadow and took exception to the noise they were making. He ordered the batteries to open fire and sink a boatload of women on the Bosporous when their craft came too near the Seraglio walls . . .'

Murad's atrocities were not confined to home. In 1638 he led his troops to the Persian capital, Baghdad. After a six-week siege, during which he sliced in half the head of a Persian champion in single-handed combat, he ordered the massacre of the defending garrison of 30,000. When an accidental ammunition explosion killed some Turkish troops, Murad slaughtered 30,000 men, women and children.

But Murad was the last of the all-conquering Ottoman despots. His son Ibrahim's most notable conquest was deflowering the virgin daughter of the Grand Mufti, Turkey's highest religious leader. Then, when one concubine from his harem was seduced by an outsider, he had all 280 girls tied in weighted sacks and thrown into the Bosporus. Even Constantinople, which could forgive its Sultans almost anything, could not condone that. The Grand Mufti took revenge by organising a coup which toppled Ibrahim, then had him, his mother and his favourite lover strangled.

The Ottoman armies had long lost their invincible reputation. In 1683 an alliance of European forces crushed another attempt to take Vienna. In 1790 the Russian forces of Catherine the Great took Ismail, 40 miles north of the Black Sea, and dropped the corpses of 34,000 fallen Turks into the Danube through holes in the ice. In 1827, a six-year war, with massacres on both sides, ended with the Greeks winning independence. Egypt achieved a large measure of self-government.

The Ottoman empire was in steady decline. Elsewhere in the world, such events as the French Revolution, the American Constitution, with its declaration of rights, the Industrial Revolution, a more general right to vote and the introduction of newspapers had all helped foster an awareness of human rights which forced governments to act more humanely. But in 1876, the Ottoman Sultan showed just how far behind the tide of civilization his country had fallen.

In that year, the Bulgarians, who had been part of the Ottoman empire for nearly 500 years, revolted – and Sultan Abdul Aziz unleashed the bloodlust of unpaid troops who were rewarded only by what they could loot. Within days 12,000 men, women and children were dead and 60 villages burned to the ground. The Sultan gave the commander of the troops a medal.

The carnage in the town of Batak was witnessed by American journalist J. A. MacGahan and, when his report appeared in the *Daily News*, the stunned world had its first eye-witness account of an Ottoman atrocity. 'On every side as we entered the town were the skulls and skeletons of women and children,' he wrote. 'We entered the churchyard. The sight was more dreadful. The whole churchyard for three feet deep was festering with dead bodies partly covered. Hands, legs, arms and heads projected in ghastly confusion . . . I never imagined anything so fearful. There were three thousand bodies in the churchyard and the church. In the school 200 women and children had been burnt alive . . . no crime invented by Turkish ferocity was left uncommitted.'

Western governments at first refused to accept the reports, labelling them 'picturesque journalism.' But when Britain sent an investigator from the Constantinople embassy, he told Whitehall the troops had perpetrated 'perhaps the most heinous crime that has stained the history of the present century.' Ex-Prime Minister William Gladstone issued a pamphlet describing the Turks as 'the great anti-human specimen of humanity.' The storm of worldwide protest caused a coup which installed Abdul Aziz's drunken nephew Murad as Sultan. His reign lasted three months, until he was declared insane, and his brother Abdul Hamid II took over.

Abdul was so paranoid about possible plots that he built an entire village, designed only for his safety. Behind the barricades he kept loaded pistols in every room – two hung beside his bath – and constructed glass cupboards which, when opened, blasted the room with bullets from remote-controlled guns. He personally shot dead a gardener and a slave girl whose sudden movements alarmed him. He countered the growing revolt of the Young Turks with a network of spies and a torture chamber under a cruel executioner who delighted in slowly drowning broken men.

But his most astonishing act was to order the monstrous slaughter of the Armenians, a minority race whose homeland was in the north-east of the dwindling empire, close to the Russian border. He regarded the business-minded Armenians much as Hitler later regarded the Jews. First he banned the word 'Armenian' from newspapers and school books. Then he told Moslems they could seize Armenian goods – and kill the owners if they resisted.

Clearly, Abdul had learned nothing from the 1876 atrocities. And his massacres were far worse. It was cold-blooded, premeditated genocide. For days a bugle at dawn and dusk called the faithful to murder. Nearly 100,000 Armenians were killed. And Westerners witnessed the terror in Trebizond, where every Christian house was plundered before the owners were ritually slaughtered, their throats cut as if they were sheep. Those who jumped into the river to flee were caught and drowned by Moslem boatmen. At Urfa 3,000 men, women and children were roasted alive in the cathedral after seeking sanctuary. Sultan Abdul noted every detail as his spies sent detailed reports.

If the Sultan hoped to curry favour with his people, using racial prejudice to blind them to the economic ruin of his empire, he was sadly mistaken. Many Moslems felt only shame, labelling him Abdul the Damned. And this time, it was not only Europe that was outraged. Two Armenian professors at an American missionary school were arrested, taken in chains for trial for printing seditious leaflets, and sentenced to die. America was scandalized. Finally, when 7,000 Armenians were slaughtered in Constantinople in reprisal for a band raid carried out by 20, every European power signed an open telegram to the Sultan. If the massacres did not end at once, it read, the Sultan's throne and his dynasty would be imperilled.

Sultan Abdul Hamid survived to celebrate his Silver Jubilee as the new century dawned. But he was now an obsolete leftover from another age. And in 1908, the Young Turks – whose numbers and influence had been growing, first in exile, then in Turkey – seized power. The Sultan was exiled to Salonika and his brother, a stooge figurehead, installed as constitutional monarch. Sacks of gold and precious gems, a fortune in foreign bank accounts and shares in international companies were discovered at Abdul's palace, all obtained with money milked from the Turkish treasury.

The repressive rule of the Ottomans had finally ended. But if Turks and the West thought they had seen the end of evil and tyranny, they were in for a shock. For in 1915, Enver Bey, one of the three Young Turk leaders, ordered a new massacre of Armenians, even more ruthless than that of the Sultan. Using the

Abdul Hamid II, overthrown by the Young Turks in 1908

excuse that some Armenians had collaborated with the Russians during World
War I battles – Turkey fought on the Kaiser's side – he made his brother-in-law
Djevet Bey governor of the region, with orders to exterminate the Christians.

The inhabitants of more than 80 villages were rounded up and shot.
Thousands of women were raped. Men were tortured, often by having
horseshoes nailed to their feet. One official admitted he 'delved into the records
of the Spanish Inquisition and adopted all the suggestions found there.' More
than 18,000 Armenians were sent on a forced march of exile across the Syrian

desert to Aleppo. Then Kurdish rebels were encouraged to attack them. Only 150 women and children reached Aleppo, 70 days after setting out.

The official British report on the atrocities, presented to Parliament, estimated that, of two million Armenians in Turkey in 1915, a third died and another third fled to Russia. The American Ambassador in Constantinople asked Enver Bey to condemn his underlings for the outrages. To his astonishment, the callous leader accepted responsibility for everything that had taken place. His co-leader, Talaat Bey, said it was unwise to punish only those Armenians who had actually helped the Russians 'since those who are innocent today might be guilty tomorrow.' And he had the audacity to ask the American Ambassador for a full list of Armenians covered by U.S. insurance companies. As their relatives were probably dead, he said, life assurance payments should go to the government.

Enver, Talaat and Djevet fled in November 1918, denounced for choosing the wrong side in a war which cost Turkey half a million battle casualties and for profiteering in food at a time of famine. The victorious allies took control in Constantinople. The empire was now smashed, and Turkey pushed back almost to its present borders. But to head off feared Italian territorial ambitions, the allies allowed the Greeks to occupy the port of Smyrna. Revenge for centuries of repression resulted in massacres of Turks – and fuelled the fury that, in atoning for wrongdoing, would make Turkey once again an international outcast.

Patriot Mustafa Kemal was the focus for Turkish anger at the allied occupation, and the loss of Smyrna. Though he was courtmartialled and sentenced to death in his absence, his support grew, and the allies were unable to control his rebel forces. Finally the Greeks offered their army to restore order. In 1920 their campaign pressed the Turks back. But in August 1921, Mustafa's men won a three-week battle along a 60-mile front at Sakkaria river. The Greeks fled towards the coast. The following year, reinforced by arms from France, Italy and Russia, the Turks again routed their most bitter foes, forcing them back to Smyrna. In September, Mustafa arrived in triumph at the port, and decreed that any Turkish soldier who molested civilians would be killed.

Peter the Great set up the first efficient secret police force in Russia and ruled by fear through a network of spies. He financed his almost constant wars by seizing Church assets and introducing bizarre taxes on beards, bee-keeping, coffins, clothes and foodstuffs. By the end of his reign, the peasants who made up 90 per cent of Russia's population were far worse off than when he came to power.

But within hours, the Greek Patriarch had been torn to pieces by a Turkish mob, under the eyes of the town's new commander. Mass looting, raping and killing began, Turkish troops methodically moving from house to house in the Greek and Armenian areas in the north of the town. 'By evening dead bodies were lying all over the streets,' said one American witness. Worse was to come. On Wednesday 13 September, Westerners saw squads of Turkish soldiers setting fire to houses in the Armenian quarter using petroleum. The wind spread the flames northwards, and thousands of flimsy homes were engulfed. Five hundred people perished in a church set ablaze deliberately. The reek of burning flesh filled the air. Tens of thousands fled to the waterfront, pursued by a rapidly growing wall of fire. In the bay lay warships from Britain, America, Italy and France. They were there to protect their nationals – but they had strict orders to maintain neutrality in the war between Greek and Turk. The sailors watched in horror as the inferno changed the colour of the sea and silhouetted the throng of helpless refugees on the wharfs. Then, at midnight, they heard what one described as 'the most awful scream one could ever imagine.'

Humanity over-rode orders next morning, when a massive rescue attempt began. Mustafa Kemal had said as he watched the fire: 'It is a sign that Turkey is purged of the traitors, the Christians, and of the foreigners, and that Turkey is for the Turks.' Three days after the blaze began, he announced that all Greek and Armenian men aged between 15 and 50 were to be deported inland in labour gangs. Women and children had to be out of Smyrna by 30 September or they too would be rounded up. He was later persuaded to extend the deadline by six days. Military and merchant ships performed a miracle, ferrying nearly 250,000 people to safety. No-one has ever been able to say how many corpses were left behind, though most estimates start at 100,000.

Mustafa Kemal always maintained that the Greeks and Armenians started the great fire of Smyrna. But a report for the American State Department said all the evidence pointed to an attempt by the Turks to hide evidence of 'sack, massacre and raping that had been going on for four days.'

Mustafa, oddly, later changed his name to Kamal Atatürk and instigated massive reforms throughout the government and society which finally dragged Turkey into the 20th Century. The last vestiges of the scourge of the Ottomans were buried forever.

Caligula

There was relief and rejoicing in Rome in AD 37 when 25-year-old Gaius Caesar succeeded to the title of Emperor from the elderly tyrant Tiberius. Tiberius, who had spent brooding years of self-imposed exile on the island of Capri, had become feared and despised because of the cruel executions of his critics in the Roman army.

But it seemed as if the embittered old emperor might have done some sort of penance by appointing Gaius Caesar as his successor. The young man was a great-grandson of Augustus and son of the soldier Germanicus, one of the unsullied military heroes of the Roman Empire.

As a baby, Gaius had often been taken by his father on Roman army campaigns and the legionaires who doted on the child adopted him as a lucky mascot. They dressed him in a tiny uniform complete with hand-crafted boots, called caligae. And they gave him the fond nickname 'Caligula' – little boots. In four brief years that nickname was to strike terror into the hearts of the citizens of Rome and even the old soldiers who helped to rear him.

Caligula had a wild streak of youthful extravagance and an appetite for sexual adventuring. But if his elders thought he would grow out of such excesses as he adopted the mature responsibilities of Emperor, they were mistaken. His youthful excesses masked a depraved insanity which only surfaced when he began to revel in the full power of his new office.

The first six months of Caligula's reign were a spectacular 'honeymoon' period for the citizens of Rome. He quickly won their affection by giving away most of the treasury of Tiberius in generous tax rebates and cash bonuses for the soldiers of the garrison in Rome. And he paid small fortunes to the soldiers he trusted most – the broad-shouldered German mercenaries who made up his personal bodyguard.

With reckless disregard for the worried senators who warned him he would bankrupt himself and the office of Emperor, he began to lavish unheard-of expense on the blood-letting rituals of the circuses in the Roman amphitheatres.

From all parts of the Empire, a sinister menagerie of lions, panthers, elephants and bears were captured in the forests and deserts to be brought to Rome and bloodily butchered in staged 'hunts' in the arenas, to the delight of the spectators.

Prize money for gladiators and charioteers was doubled and trebled to encourage them to fight each other to the death at the circuses. The shows were breathtaking extravaganzas, wildly acclaimed by their audiences – and they made Caligula an Emperor to be admired and applauded.

The popularity of the circuses also helped his subjects turn a blind eye to the fact that Caligula had made his three sisters leave their husbands and move into his palace in Rome to share his bed. And it helped to stifle any misgivings about reports that the fun-loving young Emperor spent many nights wandering the city with his guards, indulging in orgies with the prostitutes before burning their brothels to the ground.

In AD 38, with his reign only a year old, Caligula was still a popular Emperor when he fell ill with a fever. The circuses suddenly stopped.

Sympathetic Romans gathered in their thousands day and night outside his palace. All traffic of chariots and handcarts, and the noise of music and trade in the street were banned within half a mile of the palace, while the citizens prayed for Caligula's recovery.

For a month he hovered between life and death. Then the fever broke. The Emperor awoke weakened but growing stronger every day. But he had gone stark, raving mad.

Calling his friends and family around him, he confided: 'I wasn't really ill, I was just being reborn as a God!'

And with just enough money left at his disposal, Caligula celebrated with a programme of circuses which surpassed all his previous spectaculars. He was determined that everyone should enjoy themselves as much as he did. Trade and commerce almost ground to a halt as Caligula declared day after day a public holiday so that none of the citizens might have an excuse for not attending the circuses.

The constant bloody carnival soon took its toll. For the Romans, it was too much of a good thing. And for Caligula's purse, it was an expense he could no longer support. With most of his money gone in spendthrift celebration, even the Emperor felt the pinch of the expense of fresh meat to feed the lions being prepared for their daily battle with gladiators – who were themselves deserting the circus because of the falling prize money.

And when one mediocre circus featured mangy, underfed lions and paunchy, middle-aged gladiators lured from retirement, it was unacceptable to the crowds, who demanded more and more excitement each time. They rose in the 30,000 seat amphitheatre and actually booed the Emperor.

The mad Caligula reacted swiftly. The ringleaders who had led the jeering were seized by his guards and dragged away to the cellars under the arena. There their tongues were cut out and, choking on their own blood, they were forced into the arena to do battle with the wild animals.

The Roman crowd, used to seeing trained professional 'huntsmen' kill the lions, were stunned into silence by the sight of their fellow citizens being made to

The victims who suffered most from the sexual depravity of
the Emperor Caligula were members of his own family. It
is likely that his own grandmother, who was besotted by
him as a boy, introduced him to sex. As a 13-year-old, he
began to have an incestuous affair with his sister Drusilla,
who was one year older than him. When he became
emperor he forced his two other sisters, Agrippinilla and
Lesbia, to divorce their husbands and to share his bed with
him. But it was Drusilla who paid the ultimate price. When
she became pregnant, the emperor believed that she was
going to give birth to his child and that the baby of their
incestuous union would be endowed with God-like powers.
Drusilla died in one night of bloody butchery, when
Caligula disembowelled her to pluck the unborn baby from
her womb. The emperor announced that his beloved sister
had died of a crippling disease and her body was hastily
bound in a tight shroud and buried before any mourner
could see the bestial wounds and dismemberment he had
inflicted on her.

face the beasts. But Caligula enjoyed the scene immensely, whooping and
clapping until the last of the insolent hecklers had been killed and dragged back
to the cages by the emaciated lions.

As he left the arena with a mad glint in his eye, he told the Captain of the
Guard wistfully: 'I only wish all of Rome had just one neck so I could cut off all
their heads with one blow.'

Caligula had cowed even the bloodthirsty Romans into shocked submission.
Still he needed more money to stage even more circuses and to keep paying his
army for their shaken loyalty. And mad though he was, he knew that nothing
would bring the wrath of his disenchanted subjects down on him quicker than a
hefty increase in their taxes.

At least he had solved the problem of the food bill for the lions. From then on,
the common criminals of Rome's jails were transported to the amphitheatres at
night and fed to the lions. He began to ease his other financial problems with a
series of trumped-up treason charges against some of the capital's wealthiest
citizens. Their vast estates and fortunes were seized as fines and punishment, and
the paid informers who gave perjured evidence against them were rewarded
with a few gold coins.

With all of Rome turning against him, the Emperor seemed to see some sense at last and turned to the time-honoured way of raising cash – plundering the captive peoples of France and Spain.

He reserved the last of his Imperial revenues for one bizarre display in the Bay of Naples, where he moored 4,000 boats in a floating causeway – to give the lie to a prediction by a soothsayer who had told him as a boy that he had as much chance of becoming Emperor as crossing the bay and keeping his feet dry.

Caligula galloped across a wooden road of ships laid with turf, flanked with artificial gardens and mock taverns, to loot the city of Puteoli. Caligula then returned to Rome happy that he had proved the soothsayer wrong.

That night a storm wrecked almost half the ships still riding at anchor, and Caligula swore he would take his revenge on Neptune, the God of the Sea. The loss of the ships hasn't dampened his spirits enough to prevent him throwing a party for his favourite horse Incitatus, 'the swift', and presenting the animal with more classical paintings to join the collection already hanging on the walls of its marble bedroom. And Incitatus was 'promoted' from Senator to Consul of the Roman Empire.

Broke and desperate to recoup the cost of his Bay of Naples escapade, Caligula threw all caution to the wind. His guards rounded up ordinary citizens in the street and forced them to contribute every coin in their purses to the Emperor's treasury. Holding back a single coin could mean instant death.

When his loyal guards explained that they had even managed to rob the city's prostitutes of their meagre earnings, Caligula hit on his most obscene idea for raising even more revenue. At a family meeting in his palace, he raged at his sisters Agrippinilla and Lesbia: 'Everyone else in Rome has to work to support me, but I never see any money from you. Now it's your turn to work.'

By imperial decree, Caligula announced that his palace was to be opened as a brothel, with his sisters as prostitutes. Eminent senators were ordered to turn up at the enforced sex orgies and pay an entrance fee of 1,000 gold pieces. To the shame of the most noble men of the Senate, they were then summoned to return

---

Rome's enemies were equally capable of cunning cruelty. Mithridates was king of Pontus, a state on the Black Sea, now part of Turkey, for 59 years from 124 BC. In a surprise attack, he seized Syria and part of Asia Minor, taking thousands of Romans captive. Then he secretly instructed his generals to arrange a day of massacre. When the date arrived, 100,000 Roman men, woman and children were dragged out on the streets from their homes and slaughtered without mercy.

to another series of orgies and to bring their wives and daughters as prostitutes to join Caligula's sisters.

When Rome had been bled almost dry, Caligula decided to look further afield and, to the relief of his countrymen, set out to plunder his way through the captured provinces of France and Germany. He sent word ahead to the military garrison commanders and provincial governors in France that he wanted all the richest men in their areas to be assembled in Lyons to meet him. Nervously the Roman administrators complied, fearing that Caligula might rob and kill the

---

The young Emperor Nero never looked like being a threat to his fellow Romans when he succeeded to the supreme title at the age of 17 on the death of his stepfather Claudius. A foppish, bloated young poet who also fancied himself to be a talented musician and gifted architect, he showed no inclination to follow his predecessors as a warrior and great general. In the 13 years of his reign, he liked to pick on imagined enemies he could easily crush.

In 64 AD, when Rome was devastated by a fire which burned for a week. It was rumoured that Nero had started the blaze himself to rebuild the city and practise his amateurish architectural skill. But, far from accepting any blame, Nero found the perfect scapegoat for the blaze. The Christian religion was claiming a growing number of converts in Rome and Nero delighted in dreaming up cruel and bizarre new tortures for them. Instead of 'noble' gladiatorial contests in the circuses, he fed Christians to the lions. The wide roads leading to the arenas were lined with crucified Christians, coated in tar and set alight to form avenues of glowing torches to lead the audiences to the spectacle.

The citizens of Rome revelled in such delights. It helped them overlook the fact that Nero had murdered his own mother and his wife. But they drew the line when they discovered that he had castrated a slave and 'married' him to live as man and wife. When he heard he had been declared a public enemy and ordered to be flogged to death, the whimpering emperor clumsily committed suicide by slitting his own throat. His conceited dying words: 'This is a terrible loss to the world of art.'

French noblemen and provoke another Gallic uprising. But the tortured mind of the Emperor had produced an outrageous compromise. The rich merchants were being offered the bargain of a lifetime, a chance to buy some of the 'treasures' of Caligula's palace at knock-down prices.

So began the weirdest 'auction' any of them had ever witnessed. Caligula himself did the bidding on behalf of his captive buyers, bidding merchant against merchant until he was satisfied he had taken every piece of gold from them. When his sales assistants, the Imperial Guard, passed out the merchandise to the baffled bidders, the French merchants found they had unwittingly paid thousands of pieces of gold for packages of cloth which contained only old sandals and mouldy pieces of cheese.

With another small fortune in running expenses, Caligula set off for the Rhine, vowing to exterminate his German enemies. In one small skirmish, his legions captured about 1,000 prisoners. Caligula picked out only 300 men from the dishevelled ranks and ordered the remainder to be lined up against a cliff, with a bald man at each end. Satisfied he had enough prisoners for a swaggering triumphal entry to Rome, he ordered his Legions: 'Kill every man from bald head to bald head.'

Then he set off for his last great 'battle'. Camping outside the port of Boulogne, he ordered his dispirited and nervous army to line up on the beaches. Roman archers formed ranks at the water's edge. Huge catapults and slings were dragged on to the sand dunes to support the infantrymen; massed troops of cavalry waited on the flanks. All eyes were set on the horizon, watching disbelievingly for the appearance of some distant enemy.

Then Caligula rode with imperial majesty into the shallow water. With blood-curdling oaths, he unsheathed his sword and swore revenge on the sea god Neptune who had wrecked his ships in the Bay of Naples. The soldiers watched in silence as Caligula slashed at the foam with his sword. Then he ordered the catapults to be fired into the sea. The infantry charged, trampling the waves. The archers shot their arrows at the breakers. The shallow waters were pierced with spears and the cavalry rode in and out of the surf, stabbing the seawater with their swords.

'Now for the plunder', shouted an overjoyed Caligula. And each man had to begin looting the sea – gathering piles of sea shells in their helmets.

It was too much. The mighty Roman army had been reduced to clowning for their insane Emperor.

As Caligula began the long march home, the long-overdue conspiracy to rid the empire of the bestial lunatic quickly gathered strength. When Caligula entered Rome, bringing the straggling German prisoners and a handful of Britons he had captured from a trading boat in Bologne, together with tons of sea shells, the Senate was seething and the Army close to revolt.

For the next month they plotted. They let the mad Emperor rant and rave and award himself great honours for his 'victories'. Caligula drew up plans for all the statues of the Gods in Rome to be beheaded and replaced with an image of his own head. He danced through his palace in silken women's clothes and carried on blatant love affairs with young men he selected to be his bed partners.

But his days were numbered.

There was no mass uprising to overthrow him, just the sudden anger of one old soldier who had reached the end of his tether.

To Cassius Chaerea, colonel of the Imperial Guard, was given the most menial task of tax collecting. As an honourable soldier, he was sworn to give total obedience to his Emperor, no matter what the provocation. But when Cassius was ordered to torture a young girl falsely accused of treachery, he broke down and wept at the girl's pain and innocent anguish. Word of the veteran soldier's tears reached Caligula and the Emperor began to taunt him with shouts of 'cry-baby'.

To make sure all of the Guard knew of his insults, he teased Cassius mercilessly each day when he issued the new password for the Guard. Cassius was given the password personally by Caligula and had to repeat it in turn to each of his junior officers. The passwords had always been stern military slogans like 'victory' and 'no surrender'. Cassius had to repeat a new series given to him by the mocking Emperor, slogans like 'perfume and powder' and 'kiss me soldier'.

Cassius's sense of honour finally outweighed loyalty to a madman. In January AD 41, he waited in the covered walkway which separated Caligula's palace from his private theatre and sent in word to the Emperor who was watching rehearsals for a new play a troupe of young Greek dancing boys had arrived to perform for him. The perverted Emperor couldn't wait to meet the youngsters. He abandoned the audience and, as he hurried along the passageway, the old soldier Cassius stepped forward.

'I need the password for today, Emperor,' he told Caligula.

'Oh, yes,' said the leering Emperor. 'Let me see now. I think the password for today should be "old man's petticoat".'

It was to be his last insult. Cassius drew his sword and smashed Caligula to the ground.

With ten thrusts of the sword, from the skull to the groin, he ended the rule of the Divine Emperor Caligula. Seconds later he strode into the theatre and told the audience: 'The show is over, the Emperor is dead.'

There was a stunned silence. Then a roar of applause louder and more joyous than any heard during four years of depraved circuses and orgies of the wicked reign of Emperor Caligula.

Vlad the Impaler

If Dracula ever walked the earth as a creature of flesh and blood rather than a figure of fiction, then the person who deserved that terrible title was Vlad Tepes. But the legend of Count Dracula is a fairy-tale compared with the catalogue of terror, torture and sheer blood lust that marked the violent life of Tepes – otherwise known as Vlad the Impaler.

Vlad Tepes ruled over Walachia, now part of Romania, between 1456 and 1476. His father had been given the title 'Dracul' (meaning Dragon) because that creature was the emblem on his shield. His son, Vlad the Fifth, gave the title a new meaning by his habit of drinking the blood of his victims, of whom there was no shortage of supply. And his ingenuity in devising ever more horrible forms of death for his enemies was awesome.

On one occasion, he sat down to dinner surrounded by a large number of slowly dying victims. When one of his guests, sickened by the stench and the screams, made the mistake of complaining, Vlad had him impaled 'so that he could be above the smell'.

Twelve years of his reign were spent imprisoned in Hungary where, denied the pleasure of human victims, he pursued his solitary hours in the torture of animals.

Yet Vlad the Fifth was a hero in his own country, a brilliant general who ferociously set about putting an end to decades of internal strife and who then turned his attentions towards the Turks whose territorial ambitions were a perpetual threat to his borders. When the Turks sued for peace, Vlad summoned their envoys before him and had their hats and coats nailed to their bodies, using short nails to prolong their agonies.

Hungarian company director Sylvestre Matushka was tried in 1932 for causing the deaths of 22 people for his sexual gratification. He gained pleasure from witnessing catastrophe on a grand scale and sated his lust in a most extraordinary way. In August 1931 he set off an explosion that derailed an express train near Berlin, injuring 16 people. A month later he repeated the crime, blowing apart a Budapest-Vienna express and killing 22. He was apprehended while attempting a third explosion and jailed for life.

Impaling his victims on stakes was Vlad's favoured method of execution. He once triumphantly impaled 20,000 of his enemies. On another occasion, he partook of a hearty breakfast in a field of impaled peasants. He generally insisted that the stakes be made not too sharp – so that his victims would suffer more.

But there were other ways of avenging himself on those who offended him. A group of protesting peasants were invited to a feast at one of his homes, which was then locked and set on fire. He put down one rebellion by making it known that the bodies of plotters would be fed to the crabs, and the crabs then force-fed to their families – a threat he gleefully carried out. He also forced wives to eat the roasted bodies of their husbands and made parents cannibalize their children.

Vlad's excesses were not simply due to a cruel nature. He was a sadist who gained a perverted pleasure from his deeds and whose habit of drinking his victims' blood made him the model for the Dracula myth.

Vlad the Impaler's terrible rule came to an end in 1476 when he was killed in battle against the Turks – although it is believed that the blow that felled him came from one of his own lieutenants.

Gilles de Rais

While Vlad the Fifth was gaining infamy for his barbarity, a noble contemporary of his was gaining glory at the other end of Europe. Gilles de Rais (or de Retz) was a Marshal of France, one of the richest and bravest noblemen in the land, cultured, sophisticated and pious. His main claim to fame was that he fought alongside Joan of Arc. But his claim to infamy is in many ways more horrific than even Vlad's . . . for de Rais secretly tortured and killed hundreds of children to satisfy his craving for the shedding of blood.

Born in 1404, de Rais married into an equally noble family at the age of 16. He owned five vast estates, had a private chapel that required the attendance of 30 canons and was so esteemed in the eyes of the court that he was appointed to the post of Marshal so that he could personally crown King Charles VII of France. Of proud and muscular bearing, he was a brilliant warrior, being instrumental in securing Charles's victories over the English. He rode alongside Joan of Arc and was followed by a personal retinue of 200 knights.

Yet for all those glittering prizes, de Rais maintained a sick and savage secret. He was guilty of what a contemporary described as 'that which the most monstrously depraved imagination could never have conceived.'

He is said to have sadistically tortured and murdered between 140 and 800 children. Obsessed with the letting of blood, he would order his servants to stab his young victims in their jugular vein so that the blood would spurt over him. He was alleged to have sat on one dying boy while drinking his blood.

Ten years after Joan of Arc's trial for heresy, de Rais was charged with the same offence after he attacked a priest. Haughtily refuting that accusation, he was then charged with murder. In the words of his ecclesiastical accusers, he was a 'heretic, sorcerer, sodomite, invocator of evil spirits, diviner, killer of innocents, apostate from the faith, idolator.'

There was good reason for the Church to have fabricated the case against de Rais. He was a secular challenge to their power over the king and his court, and if found guilty the Church stood to seize his lands. No effort was spared in preparing the most damning case: de Rais's servants were tortured until adequate evidence was given against their master.

De Rais himself was probably not tortured. Yet he made a full and ready confession – not only to the murder of 140 children, of which he was charged, but to the murder of 'at least 800.'

Two rational reasons were given for this slaughter. The first was the influence on him of a book, an illustrated copy of *Lives of the Caesars* by Suetonius, which included graphic descriptions of the mad Emperor Caligula's sadistic excesses. The second was the approach of an Italian alchemist, Francisco Prelati, who promised the secret of turning iron into gold by black magic rites and sacrifices. But the real reason for the mass killings de Rais perpetrated could only have been what we now know as paedophilia and sadism – both carried out on a scale probably unequalled before or since.

Predictably, de Rais was found guilty and in a show of public contrition and humility begged forgiveness from the parents of the children he admitted slaughtering. Like Joan of Arc before him, he was sentenced to death by fire. But as an act of 'mercy' for not recanting his confession, he was first garrotted to death before being thrown on the flames on 26 October, 1440.

> A mass murderer who was never caught, and whose reign of terror ended as suddenly and mysteriously as it had begun, stalked the streets of Cleveland, Ohio, between 1935 and 1938. Known as 'The Mad Butcher of Kingsbury Run,' he killed more than 12 men and women, chopping up the bodies into small pieces and leaving them in neat piles in alleys and on wasteland. Sometimes the victims, usually vagrants, would have parts of other corpses mixed in to the grisly pie. Few of the victims' heads were ever found – and the identity of the killer remains a mystery.

The Borgias

It was a city where the brazenly licentious indulged in perverse orgies and incestuous relationships. Where ambitious and greedy men grabbed power and personal fortune by bribery and extortion. And where anyone who stood in their way was ruthlessly eliminated. Yet the city where all this happened was not the hub of a barbarian empire. This citadel of sin was the Vatican City in Rome. And the evil masterminds putting vice before virtue, riches before religion and power before piety were the Pope, Alexander VI, alias Rodrigo Borgia, and his illegitimate son Cesare.

For centuries, the Catholic Church was the only Christian faith in Europe. But its monopoly on salvation brought corruption. It sanctioned merciless killing in crusades against so-called heathen-races who worshipped other gods. It exterminated as heretics all who dared question its edicts about the world and life. And it amassed immense wealth by charging a high price for forgiveness of sins. By the 15th Century, the Pope was not only a religious leader, but a powerful political force. Secular rulers in the confusing cluster of small states that made up the Italian peninsula competed for his favours and support – and his requests, backed by the threat of excommunication if they were refused, were compelling even for the strongest kings and princes.

Rodrigo Borgia was well grounded in the intrigues and intricacies of the Holy See long before he assumed its highest office. In April 1455, his mother's brother became Pope Calixtus III. Rodrigo, born 24 years earlier at Xativa, near Valencia in Spain, was immediately made a bishop, and quickly progressed up the Catholic hierarchy, to cardinal and vice-chancellor. He served in the Curia under five Popes.

But behind the facade of faith, hope and chastity, Rodrigo was busy seducing as many young virgins as he could lay his hands on. A highly sexed, handsome charmer, he could not resist the temptations of the flesh and one of his brazen open-air orgies earned him a reprimand from the Pope. In 1470 he began a torrid romance with a 28-year-old beauty, Vanozza dei Catanei. She bore him three sons, Giovanni (1474), Cesare (1476) and Goffredo (1481) and a daughter, Lucrezia (1480) before he tired of her and fell for the charms of the 16-year-old Giulia Farnese. For appearance's sake, he had Giulia betrothed to his young nephew – but he forbade the boy to consummate the marriage.

When Pope Innocent VIII died in 1492, Rodrigo was one of three contenders to become Pontiff. On the first poll, the electoral college of cardinals voted for

Cesare Borgia, Renaissance tyrant

Giuliano della Rovere, the successor nominated by Innocent. But Borgia began handing out huge bribes and promised delegates luxurious palaces and lucrative posts if he was chosen. On 10 August he duly became Pope, taking the name Alexander VI.

Instantly he showered his illegitimate children with riches. Cesare, aged just 16, was appointed Archbishop of Valencia. A year later he became a cardinal. But the titles meant little to the ambitious teenager. He was furious that his older brother had been given command of the Papal army. Cesare rode disdainfully round Rome, fully armed, with a succession of shapely mistresses at his side. He canoodled outrageously in public with his sister Lucrezia. And he rivalled his father's scandalous sexual exploits. When Sanchia, promiscuous teenage daughter of the King of Naples, arrived at the Vatican as a prospective bride for Goffredo Borgia, both the Pope and Cesare made a rigorous check on her credentials between the sheets of their own beds.

One of Cesare Borgia's few admirers was a man whose
name later became synonymous with evil cunning: Niccolo
Machiavelli. When the Papal army threatened Florence,
Machiavelli, a city official, was sent to gauge Cesare's
intentions. Borgia demanded gold in return for not
attacking Florence. Machiavelli stalled while accompanying
the army on conquests of other cities. He studied Cesare's
ruthless methods, and used them as the basis for his book
The Prince.

Its cynical dictates made survival of the state an end which
justified any means. 'A prudent ruler ought not to keep
faith when doing so would be against his interests,'
Machiavelli wrote. Using force was justified if the rule of
law proved insufficient, and governors were urged to give
'no consideration to either justice or injustice, to kindness
or cruelty or to actions being praiseworthy or ignominious.'
But Machiavelli was not an innovator advocating calculated
corruption. He was a patriot who despaired because the
squabbling states of Italy were too fragmented to stop
France and Spain dominating the Italian peninsula. In
Cesare Borgia he saw a man strong and unscrupulous
enough to forge those states into a united nation. When
Cesare lost power, Machiavelli passed on his hard-hearted
philosophy in the hope that a later warrior would achieve
the dream. And as a contemporary noted, Machiavelli's
work contained little that was new. Though pious people
thought him heretical and good people branded him
wicked, the chronicler wrote: 'To the evil ones, he was
merely too knowledgable in their ways.'

Rodrigo's reign began in embarrassing fashion. When King Ferrante of
Naples died, the new Pope recognized the king's son Alphonso, father of saucy
Sanchia, as successor. But the French King, Charles VIII, thought he had a
better claim – and invaded Rome to prove it. Rodrigo grovelled and agreed to
let Charles take Cesare along as a hostage on his journey south to the Naples
coronation. But Cesare slipped away during the trip, returned to Rome and
helped his father form an anti-French alliance with the rulers of Spain, Milan
and Venice. Charles, afraid of being cut off from his homeland, scurried back to
France and Alphonso was reinstated.

The Borgias then set about punishing those who had helped Charles to humiliate them. Cesare seized some Swiss mercenaries who had broken into his mother's home during the French occupation of Rome, and tortured them unmercifully. Rodrigo ordered the people of Florence to arrest and torture Girolamo Savonarola, a puritan monk who had denounced corruption in the Church and had welcomed Charles as a redeemer arrived to restore Catholicism's old values. The Florentines responded with enthusiasm, because the killjoy cleric had forced them to abandon their carefree carnivals. He was stretched on the rack 14 times in one day during weeks of persecution before being publicly hanged. His body was then burned.

The Pope sent his son Giovanni off with the army to attack the fortresses of the Orsini family, who had also collaborated with the French. But he proved a hopeless general and returned to Rome in disgrace early in 1497 after losing a battle against the foes he was supposed to punish. Months later, on 14 June, he dined with his mother and brother Cesare. The two men left separately on horseback. Next morning Giovanni's body was dragged from the river Tiber. He had been stabbed nine times.

Giovanni's assassin was never caught, and officially the murder remained a mystery. But wagging tongues noted that one man gained more from the death than most – younger brother Cesare. It meant he could give up the religious positions he held so reluctantly and become the Pope's political and military strong man. That was good news for the Pope, too. Rodrigo could send Cesare away from Rome on business and quell the growing clamour of scandalized gossip. The cardinal's sexual proclivities – he found young boys as alluring as girls, and was far from discreet about his flings with either sex – were the talk of the town. Most embarrassing was his continuing affair with his own sister, Lucrezia. She was placed in a convent when her first husband fled for fear of Cesare's jealous rages. But six months later, after visits from Cesare and his father, she became pregnant. The baby boy was later taken to the Vatican and made heir to the Borgia fortune.

Cesare's new duties took him first to Naples, then to France. The new French king, Louis XII, wanted to annul his marriage and wed his mistress. Rodrigo agreed. In return, Cesare was made Duke of Valentinois and given a bride, the 16-year-old sister of the King of Navarre. More importantly, he was offered French armed help to subdue rebellious nobles in northern Italy and carve out a kingdom for himself in Romagna, south of Venice. The joint invasion began in 1499.

Cesare proved as cunning and unscrupulous in war as he had proved in love. When he crushed the forces of Caterina Sforza and captured her castle at Forli, he insisted that she also surrender her body to him. He wrote a gloating description of their love-making to his father in Rome before confining her in a convent. He took the town of Faenza after stubborn resistance by a population devoted to their 18-year-old master, Astorre Manfredi. The teenager agreed to surrender only after he was promised that his life would be spared. But Cesare sent him to Rome and had him horribly tortured, then killed.

Friends and allies of Cesare had as much to fear from him as from their foes. He betrayed the trust of the Duke of Urbino, marching his men past the city, then doubling back to launch a surprise attack. He appointed a ruthless governor to rule his new lands in Romagna – but when protests about the man's cruelty became impossible to ignore, he had him hacked in two and left on display in Sesena town square. Soon even some of Cesare's lieutenants were alienated by the reign of terror imposed by their morose, unsympathetic leader. Afraid that he might reclaim estates he had given them, they began plotting against him with princes he had deposed. Cesare learned of the conspiracy and lured some of the unsuspecting plotters to a banquet at the town of Senigallia. When they arrived, unarmed, they were seized. Two were instantly strangled.

Cesare's costly campaigns were funded by the Pope. Rodrigo sold cardinal's hats to wealthy aspirants, some of whom died mysteriously only months later leaving their estates to the Vatican. He declared the year 1500 a Jubilee, which meant pilgrims prepared to pay would receive total absolution for their trespasses. As an added inducement, he announced the unveiling of a 'secret holy door' in St Peter's which was only ever revealed once every 100 years. Grateful and gullible sinners paid handsomely for the rare privilege of viewing the door, which had been cut in the wall shortly before their arrival.

Rome's death rate rose every time Cesare returned from his territorial conquests. He answered insults, real or imagined, with murder. Many of his homosexual partners were also found poisoned, or dragged from the Tiber with fatal knife wounds. The Venetian ambassador wrote: 'Every night four or five murdered men are discovered – bishops, prelates and others – so that all Rome is trembling for fear of being destroyed by the Duke· Cesare.' Then, in 1500, Cesare's fiery passion for sister Lucrezia led to a sensational killing.

Rodrigo had quietly annulled his daughter's first marriage after her husband fled Cesare's jealousy. And in the wake of the scandal over Lucrezia's baby, the Pope had rushed her to the altar with Alphonse, Duke of Bisceglie and the brother of Sanchia. Sadly, Lucrezia had genuinely fallen in love with him. That infuriated Cesare, who still prefered his sister's embraces to those of his wife.

In July 1500, Alphonse was walking across St Peter's Square after sharing supper with the Pope when a gang of thugs disguised as pilgrims attacked him with knives. He survived, though seriously wounded, and was given a room near the Pope's quarters to ensure his future safety. Lucrezia nursed him devotedly. But one night, having left his bedside briefly, she returned to find him dead. Amazingly, Cesare confessed to strangling him, saying the Duke had earlier tried to murder him with a crossbow. But no action was taken. And in less than two weeks Cesare was again forcing his attentions on his grief-stricken sister. Their incestuous liaison continued until Rodrigo arranged another match for Lucrezia, with the Duke of Ferraro's son. On their last night together before she left for the nuptials, Cesare arranged a special treat in his Vatican rooms – 50 local socialites rolled naked on the floor, scrambling for hot roasted chestnuts tossed to them by the illicit lovers.

But the debauched days of the unholy Borgia alliance were numbered. In August 1503, Rodrigo and Cesare both fell ill with malaria after attending a party thrown by a cardinal in a vineyard just outside Rome. Within a week the 72-year-old Pope was dead. And Cesare, who knew that all his power derived from his father's protection, was too weak to look after his own interests.

For a while he had reason to hope that he could still maintain power. Rodrigo's successor as Pope was an ineffectual old man who bore no grudge against Cesare. But he died just one month after taking office. Unluckily for Cesare, the old man's successor was Giuliano della Rovere, who still resented his defeat by Rodrigo in the election of 1492.

Cesare was arrested and forced to relinquish his Romagna kingdom. He left Rome for Naples, then under Spanish rule, hoping to be allowed to build a new power base. Instead he was again arrested, for disturbing the peace of Italy, and taken to Spain where he spent two years in jail. In 1506 he escaped and sought sanctuary with his brother-in-law, the King of Navarre. But, on 12 March, 1507, he was wounded leading a siege of the town of Viana during a territorial dispute with Spain. His captors showed him as much mercy as he had shown his own victims – they stripped him naked and left him to die of thirst.

The Conquistadores

Christian fervour reigned in Catholic Spain in the 16th Century. The dreaded Inquisition spread its bloody tyranny, the entire Dutch people were excommunicated and an invasion armada was sent· to convert Protestant England. But missionary mania was not confined to Europe. When explorers sailed home with news of distant lands across the Atlantic full of strange peoples and untold riches, armed expeditions set out to claim them for

King and Pope. Natives of the Caribbean, Mexico and Central America were conquered and tamed in the name of Christ. Then the discovery of the Pacific Ocean opened up fresh horizons.

In 1527 a Spanish galleon investigating the new sea captured a balsa raft crammed with beautiful gold and silver objects studded with precious gems. The natives crewing the raft were the first clue to an unexpected and extraordinary civilization which had prospered in total isolation from the known world – the Incas. And the cargo they carried was enough to condemn their well-ordered empire to destruction. For although Spanish conquistadores, led by Francisco Pizarro, justified their invasion as a crusade for God and the Bible, they committed every sin in the book in pursuit of their real aim – treasure.

Pizarro, illegitimate son of a soldier from Trujillo, had spent 30 years in the new world subjugating 'savages'. Though an important member of Panama's Spanish community, he had not yet found the crock of gold that would make his fortune. With seizure of the Inca raft, he saw his chance. He obtained royal permission to explore and conquer Peru. Dominican monk Friar Vicente de Valverde was to go with him as 'protector' of the Indians.

The expedition left Panama in December 1530. Pizarro established a coastal base, killing the local chief to intimidate nearby natives, then moved inland with 168 soldiers, 62 on horses. He could not have arrived at a better time for Spain. Disease had ravaged the Inca court, killing the Inca himself, Huayna-Capac, and his heir. Two more of his sons, Huascar and Atahualpa, had begun a civil war for control of the empire, which stretched 3,000 miles through Chile, Bolivia, Ecuador and south Colombia as well as Peru. The conquistadores found towns in ruins and Indian corpses dangling from trees as they pressed up into the mountains.

Atahualpa, who commanded the area of Peru where the Spanish had landed, was none too pleased when his scouts reported that the strangers were pillaging the countryside as they advanced. But he sent the conquistadores gifts and invited them to meet him at Cajamarca. His army was camped beyond the town, and Atahualpa told Pizarro's envoys he would visit their leader in the town's central square next day. But when he arrived, carried on a litter by 80 men and surrounded by thousands of unarmed natives, the conquistadores stayed hidden in the buildings around the square. Friar Valverde emerged with an interpreter, carrying a cross and a Bible, and began explaining his religion to the baffled chief. Then he handed Atahualpa the book. But the Incas did not understand writing. They worshipped the sun, and claimed their images of it spoke to them. When the pages of the Bible did not speak, Atahualpa threw the book to the ground. The furious priest screamed for the insult to be avenged – and Pizarro unleashed a brutal and carefully planned ambush.

'The Spaniards began to fire their muskets and charged upon the Indians with horses, killing them like ants,' Inca nobleman Huaman Poma told chroniclers. 'At the sound of the explosions and the jingle of bells on the horses' harnesses, the shock of arms and the whole amazing novelty of the attackers' appearance, the Indians were terror-stricken. The pressure of their numbers caused the walls of the square to crumble and fall. They were desperate to escape from being trampled by horses and in their headlong flight a lot of them were crushed to death. So many Indians were killed that it was impractical to count them.' After two hours of horrific slaughter, nearly 7,000 natives were dead and thousands more maimed by sword slashes. All 80 carriers of Atahualpa were massacred, but he himself was spared. Pizarro needed him alive as insurance for the invaders' safety until reinforcements arrived.

The captive Inca noted the conquistadores' glee as they ravaged his camp for treasure, and made a shrewd offer. He would buy his freedom by filling a room 22 feet (6.7m) long by 17 feet (5.1m) wide with treasure, to a depth of 8ft (2.4m). He would fill it once with gold and twice with silver. Pizarro accepted, promising to restore Atahualpa to his stronghold at Quito as long as he instigated no plots against the Spanish. The Inca told the invaders where to find his temples and directed a scouting party to his capital, Cuzco. It returned with 285 llamas loaded with gold and silver stripped from palaces, tombs and holy places. Other treasure trains poured in from all over the empire. Pizarro crushed jars, jugs and sculptures so the room would hold more. Then he set up furnaces to melt all the precious metals into bars. There were six tons (6,096kg) of 22 carat gold and 12 tons (12,192kg) of silver, a total then worth nearly £3 million.

Atahualpa, confident of release, had secretly continued his civil war, having his troops kill Huascar and two of his half-brothers. But all he was doing was playing into Pizarro's hands by weakening the empire's chances of ever repelling the invaders. Pizarro had no intention of letting the Inca go. Now he had Atahualpa's treasure, he planned to march on to Cuzco with recently arrived reinforcements, and could not afford to take the native leader along as a magnet for possible attacks. Rumours of an approaching Inca army, out to rescue their chief, were the excuse Pizarro needed. He sent out search parties to check the reports. But before they returned, Atahualpa was dead. Condemned without trial for treason, he was tied to a stake on 26 July, 1533, and told he would be burned alive unless he became a Christian. He agreed to be converted, taking the name Francisco in honour of Pizarro. Then he was garrotted.

The death caused a furore in Spain and its other colonies. In Madrid the King was angry that a fellow royal had been illegally executed. The governor of Panama said Atahualpa had 'done no harm to any Spaniard'. But Pizarro survived the storm. He reasoned, rightly, that the crown's one-fifth share of all booty would calm humanitarian qualms.

The march to Cuzco started uneventfully. The invaders were going through

Francisco Pizarro

Huascar country, and locals welcomed the death of Atahualpa. They were trusting, gentle people – their homes did not have doors, let alone locks – and were in awe of the magnificent appearance of the newcomers. Having never seen horses before, some thought mount and rider were one being. Others believed the armour-plated conquistadores, white-faced and wearing strange beards, heralded the return of their sun god Viracocha. They were to pay for their naïveté by losing their wealth, their land, their women, their religion – and, for thousands, their lives.

The first armed opposition to Pizarro's men came 17 months after he landed in Peru. Troops loyal to Atahualpa attacked at Jauja, 250 miles north of Cuzco. But they were trying to fight cavalry armed with pistols, lances and steel swords using only clubs, bronze axes and stone slingshots. The native forces were routed by charging horses and mercilessly pursued and cut down as they fled. When the futile ambushes continued, Pizarro burned captive commander Chulcuchima alive, accusing him of inspiring the raids. The Inca general defiantly refused to spare himself agony by becoming a Christian.

The town of Cuzco welcomed the Spanish as liberators. And Huascar's son Manco welcomed them most. He was ready to collaborate if they made him Inca. Pizarro willingly installed him, then organized systematic looting of the empire's richest city. Temple walls, priceless statues, jewels and vases buried with the dead, even a unique artificial garden of intricate golden plants, were melted down. A young priest who watched with horror wrote: 'Their only concern was to collect gold and silver to make themselves rich . . . What was being destroyed was more perfect than anything they enjoyed or possessed.' But clerical concern at the abuse of a peaceful people in the Church's name could not stop it. As the governor of Panama reported to the King: 'The greed of Spaniards of all classes is so great as to be insatiable. The more the native chiefs give, the more the Spaniards kill or torture them to give more.'

Reports of the riches available in the Inca land sparked off a gold rush in other colonies. In Puerto Rico, the governor banned anyone leaving. When he caught a boatload of would-be treasure-hunters, he flogged them and cut off their feet. But still new adventurers reached Peru, committing atrocities in the race to get rich quickly.

Pedro de Alvarado marched into northern Peru, chaining up hundreds of native porters from the tropical coastal areas and watching them die cruelly in the icy Andes. Men, women and children were killed as towns were sacked, and local chieftains were hanged, burned or thrown to dogs when, under torture, they refused to divulge the whereabouts of treasure. Sebastian de Benalcazar burned the feet of chiefs to force them to reveal treasure troves. In one village, where all the men had fled to join Inca armies, he massacred the remaining women and children because there were not enough riches to satisfy his cravings. It was 'cruelty unworthy of a Castillian', according to the official chronicler of the Peruvian conquest. Other Spaniards buried native chiefs up to their waists in pits to try to force them to give away the hiding places of gold. When they would not – or could not – they were flogged, then buried up to their necks before being killed.

Reports of cruelty flooded into Cuzco, angering the Inca Manco. He also had personal reasons to regret collaborating with the Spanish. The town was in the control of Pizzaros's brothers, Juan, Hernando and Gonzalo, after Francisco left for the coast to found the new city of Lima. The Inca was continually pestered to reveal more treasure caches. His mother and sisters were raped. Then Gonzalo stole his wife. Such humiliation of himself and his people was more than the proud prince could stand. He and his elders decided to rebel. In 1535 he slipped out of the town at night, but was recaptured by horsemen and returned in chains. Spaniards urinated on him and tortured him, burning his eyelashes with a candle. But a year later he successfully escaped, determined to make the invaders pay for treating him so disgustingly.

Manco had secretly mobilized a vast native army, and began deploying it with devastating effect. He lured Cuzco's cavalry to nearby Calca, allowing them to seize a treasure train. While they counted their plunder, thousands of natives surrounded Cuzco, diverting irrigation canals to flood fields, making them impossible for horses to operate on. It was the start of a four-month siege. Three squads of Spaniards marching to the rescue were wiped out by native ambushers, who hurled giant boulders down deep gorges to knock them off tortuous mountain paths. Spaniards in Jauja were all killed in a dawn raid. But the conquistadores hit back with subterfuge and savagery to quell the rebellion.

Four shaved off their beards and blacked their faces to appear like Indians. Then, with the help of a native traitor, they got into an inaccessible fortress and opened the gates for colleagues to run amok. Hundreds of Indians leapt to their deaths off cliffs to escape Spanish swords. Morgovejo de Quinones, riding to relieve Cuzco, decided to avenge the death of 5 Spanish travellers by herding 24 chiefs and elders of a nearby town into a thatched building, then setting light to it and burning them alive. When the encircled horsemen in Cuzco broke out to attack a native fortress – Juan Pizarro was killed by a sling stone in the raid – so many Indians leapt from the battlements that the last to jump were cheated of death because the bodies piled beneath them broke their fall. More than 1,500 natives still in the fort were put to the sword. Conquistadores led by Gonzalo Pizarro surprised an indian army and massacred the men. Those who plunged into a lake to try to escape were pursued by horsemen and 'speared like fish.'

Horror and mutilation were deliberately used by the Spanish to demoralize their foes. Hernando Pizarro ordered that all women caught near battlefields were to be killed. They were the Inca soldiers' wives and mistresses. When brother Gonzalo captured 200 Indian fighters, he paraded them in the square at Cuzco and sliced off all their right hands. Then he sent them back to their comrades as 'a dreadful warning.' Later male captives had their noses cut off. Women who escaped death had their breasts chopped. In the Huaylas area, Francisco de Chaves instituted a three-month reign of terror. Homes and fields were destroyed, men and women burned or impaled, and 600 children aged under three were slaughtered.

The final blow to Manco's hopes came when an army led by his commander Quizo tried to take Francisco Pizarro's capital, Lima. Cavalry devastated the foot soldiers as they advanced across the coastal plain, and the horsemen massacred survivors of the charge as they fled towards safety in the mountains. Quizo and 40 fellow generals were among the dead.

Manco now realized he could not save Peru from the Spanish. More than 20,000 of his people had died trying. He retreated to Vilcabamba, a desolate valley screened by misty crags, and escaped his pursuers by hiding with forest Indians. But the Spaniards caught his wife, Cura Ocllo. And Francisco Pizarro took out his anger on her. Pizarro had proved during the siege of Lima that he had no qualms about killing women. Atahualpa's sister Azarpay was his prisoner there. He suspected her of encouraging the native attackers and had her garrotted. He had an even worse fate in mind for Cura Ocllo.

The poor woman only escaped rape at the hands of her escort soldiers by smearing herself with excrement. When she reached Cuzco, where Pizarro was waiting for news of the pursuit of the Inca, she was stripped naked, tied to a stake and savagely beaten. Finally she was killed by arrow shots. Her battered body was loaded into a basket and floated on a river which flowed into Vilcabamba, so the Inca could see the fate of his spouse. It was yet another horror to appal decent-minded Spaniards. One called it 'an act totally unworthy of a sane Christian gentleman.' Sadly, such acts were becoming all too common in the conquest of Peru.

But Pizarro's days were numbered. The lure of gold had led Spaniards to fight each other. Hernando Pizarro was recalled to Spain and jailed for garrotting without trial Diego de Almagro, one of the first conquistadores, who had rebelled for a bigger share of the booty. On 26 June, 1541, Almagro's followers took revenge. Twenty of them stormed Francisco Pizarro's Lima palace and stabbed him to death. Another victim of the raid was the cruel child-killer Francisco de Chaves. Friar Vicente de Valverde, the man who had helped dupe Atahualpa, panicked at the death of his patron Pizarro and took ship for Panama. On an island off Peru, he was captured by cannibals and eaten.

Pizarro had succeeded in his quest. Contemporaries praised him for acquiring more gold and silver than any other commander the world had seen. But the religious cause which justified his exploits played little part in his epitaph. His achievements were best summed up in the coat of arms awarded him by the King of Spain when he made him a marquis. It showed seven native chiefs with chains round their necks, and a shackled Atahualpa, his hands delving into two treasure chests.

Pizarro's passing did not end the suffering his invasion inflicted on Peru. And deaths resisting his takeover accounted for just a fraction of the estimated five million drop in the empire's native population between 1530 and the end of the century. The other reasons were spelled out damningly in John Hemming's authoritative book, *The Conquest Of The Incas*. They were:

Disease: Peruvians had no immunity to European ailments such as smallpox, measles, the plague. Epidemics raged uncontrollably. The town of Quito lost 30,000 in just one.

Neglect: Preoccupied by gold and silver, the Spaniards failed to maintain precious irrigation canals, agricultural terraces, roads and bridges. Where the Incas filled communal storehouses for times of hardship, the Spanish merely looted them.

Hunger: Apart from taking the natives' precious metals, the conquistadores and their successors seized, slaughtered and sold at ridiculously cheap prices their herds of llama. Harvests were also grabbed for cheap sale.

Exploitation: Francisco Pizarro had divided the nation into vast estates. Natives living on them had to provide annual tribute – gold, silver, livestock, grain, potatoes, eggs, salt, timber, utensils, clothing – whether the land provided them or not. Get-rich-quick landlords increased their demands until many natives worked all year just to provide the tribute, with no time or energy to look after their families. Many became wandering vagabonds to escape impossible obligations.

Plantations: Indians from the snowbound Andes were herded down to humid forests to harvest lucrative crops of coca, the plant that provides cocaine. They died in their thousands from heat and coca-related diseases.

Expeditions: Greedy Spaniards followed up every rumour of another rich El Dorado, however remote the gold was said to be. Hundreds of natives were chained to act as porters. They died like flies from exhaustion, exposure or abuse.

Forced labour: Giant silver and mercury mines were set up by the Spanish, and natives from catchment areas up to 600 miles wide were forced to work them. Conscripts chipped at narrow, unsafe faces for six days at a stretch, sleeping in the fetid air of the galleries, full of acrid smoke from tallow candles which were the only lighting. Toxic gases containing arsenic added to the toll of exhaustion, heat and bad diet in the mercury mines. A monk, Domingo de Santo Tomas, called the mines 'the mouth of hell, into which a great mass of people enter every year, and are sacrificed by the greed of the Spaniards to their god.' But the carnage was too profitable to stop. The royal fifth of the annual output at the Potosi silver mine alone came to $4\frac{1}{2}$ tons (4,550kg).

Yet according to John Hemming, none of these evils was the biggest killer. The main cause of death, he says, was 'profound culture shock.' The Inca people had lived without money in a benevolent welfare state which cared for them. Now, after decades of fighting, they were expected to work for cash wages by a government which cared nothing for them. Hemming quotes an Inca elder as saying: 'The Indians, seeing themselves dispossessed and robbed, allow themselves to die and do not apply themselves to anything as they did in Inca times.' They lost the will to live – and recreate. The birth rate fell as dramatically as the death toll rose.

The Madrid government tried to impose liberal laws, but the settlers rebelled – once led by Gonzalo Pizarro – insisting it was their right to exploit the land they had won as they thought fit. Rather than risk losing the flow of New World riches, the King made concessions. The exploitation went on.

The final nails in the coffin of the Inca empire were driven in by Francisco de

Toledo, who arrived as Viceroy in 1569. In two years, $1\frac{1}{2}$ million natives from isolated farms and villages were forcibly uprooted and settled in towns where they were easier to convert and control. Then the Church began a drive against native religions, seizing leaders, smashing relics and rooting out rites. And the last Inca king was captured and killed.

The murder of a Spanish messenger, trying to deliver letters to the new Inca, Tupac Amaru, was the excuse Toledo needed to invade Vilcabamba, the mysterious last refuge of the Peruvian royal family. Native sticks and stones were no match for the cannons and muskets of the 250-strong Spanish force. The Inca and his generals were caught as they tried to flee through the forests, and dragged to Cuzco in chains. Tupac Amaru was accused of ruling a heathen state which allowed heathen practices and raided Spanish Peru. He was also charged with specific murders, including that of the messenger. Despite pleas for mercy from all over Peru, and despite an astonishing public admission that the Inca religion of sun worship was a sham, Tupac Amaru was beheaded in front of vast, emotional crowds. It was almost 40 years to the day since the death of his great-uncle Atahualpa.

Toledo wanted to rid Peru of all Inca influence. He married princesses to Spaniards against the girls' wills, and sentenced several relatives of Tupac Amaru to Mexican exile – a decision over-ruled by Madrid. But all his efforts were in vain. Over 200 years later, when Peruvians successfully fought for independence from Spain, one of their heroes was Jose Gabriel Condorcanqui Tupac Amaru – great-great-great-grandson of the last Inca.

The Richardson Gang: Scourge of South London

If the Krays were infamous for meting out instant vengeance, the rival Richardson gang, based on the south side of the Thames, were the masters of the slower punishment. They vied with the Krays for the reputation of being the most monstrous merchants of terror in London. Known as the 'torture gang', their speciality was pinning their enemies to the floor with six-inch (15 cm) nails and removing their toes with bolt cutters.

The gang's leader was Charles Richardson, born in Camberwell in 1934. He and his younger brother Eddie turned to crime after their father left home –

leaving the family without any source of income – while the children were still schoolboys.

From petty theft, the brothers slowly built up a thriving string of businesses – some legitimate, others not – throughout south London. Charles specialized in scrap metal but he also ran furniture and fancy goods firms. Eddie operated fruit machines and a wholesale chemists' supplier.

On their own, these companies would have made the brothers comfortably well off, although not rich. But largely they were no more than fronts for the other and more profitable sides of their business – fraud, theft and receiving stolen goods.

Eddie's fruit machine business, for instance, was more successful than most in the same line. The reason was simple – if a pub or club owner was offered one of Eddie's machines, he would be wise to accept. If not, he knew his premises would be broken into, and vandalized, or quite openly smashed up, by 'heavies' in broad daylight.

The Richardsons' most masterful money-making strokes, however, involved what were known as 'long firms'. A company would be set up under a Richardson nominee and begin trading perfectly legitimately. Goods would be ordered from suppliers and paid for promptly, so creating good credit ratings. After a few months' operation, massive orders would be placed on credit with all the suppliers. The goods would be quickly sold, the Richardsons would pocket the money, and the company would seemingly evaporate into thin air.

Charles was once arrested for receiving stolen goods, but police had to drop the charge for lack of evidence. They kept a careful watch on the gang's activities, however, and in 1965 they got an insight into the full horrors of the Richardsons' methods for keeping order and repaying old scores.

In July of that year one of the gang's victims walked into a South London police station and related a horrific story of how he had been tortured by the gang after a kangaroo court had found him guilty of disloyalty. Finally, he had been forced to mop up his own blood from the floor.

The trials and torture sessions were, police discovered, the sadistic speciality of Eddie. Sick with fear, the victims would be hauled in by gang members and tried before Eddie and the others in a mock court. Then the punishments were meted out – anything from beatings to more fearsome forms of torture. Men were whipped, burned with cigarettes, had their teeth pulled out with pliers, were nailed to the floor, had their toes removed by bolt cutters or leaped in agony from the effects of an electric shock machine. Afterwards if the victims were too badly injured they would be taken to a struck-off doctor for emergency treatment.

In 1966 the police decided they had enough evidence to act. The clincher was the murder trial of a man accused of killing a South African mining speculator to whom Charles Richardson was said to have entrusted a considerable sum of money which had never been returned. There were also stories about Charles being involved with the South African secret service, BOSS – and even talk of an attempt to bug the telephone of Prime Minister Harold Wilson.

Eddie was by now already inside jail, serving five years for affray. In July 1966 police mopped up the rest of the gang in a series of raids throughout south-east London.

It was not until April 1967 that the Old Bailey trial began, with charges of fraud, extortion, assaults and grievous bodily harm. Despite an attempt to bribe a juror, the Richardsons were found guilty after 46 days of evidence. Eddie had another ten years added to his existing sentence. Charles was jailed for 25 years for grievous bodily harm, demanding money with menaces and robbery with violence.

The judge, Mr Justice Lawton, told him: 'You terrorized those who crossed your path in a way that was vicious, sadistic and a disgrace to society . . . One is ashamed to think one lives in a society that contains men like you. You must be prevented from committing further crime. It must be made clear that all those who set themselves up as gang leaders will be struck down, as you have been struck down.'

Like the Kray brothers, Charles Richardson was later to issue an apologia for his crimes. He said: 'The men I was involved with were professional swindlers. I was only trying to get my own money back. I feel sick about the way I have been portrayed. I'm a scapegoat. I got 25 years for grievous bodily harm and not one of them need an aspirin.'

He told the London *Sunday Times* in 1983 that his links with South Africa and the shadowy BOSS organization had been an embarrassment to the British

---

Pride swelled in Jimmy Eppolito's chest as he posed for a photograph beside U.S. President Jimmy Carter's wife Rosalynn. But when Eppolito later flaunted the picture, his underworld bosses were far from amused. They sentenced him to death for 'showboating' – attracting unwanted publicity to the Mafia.

Eppolito, 34, who worked for Carlo Gambino's New York crime family as well as helping out the Carters' favourite children's charity in his spare time, was lured to a non-existent business appointment in March 1980. As he and his 64-year-old father waited in their car, they were machine-gunned to death by unknown assailants.

government. 'I was a pawn,' he said. 'The bigger a criminal the British made me out to be, the more leverage they could apply on the South Africans for having used me. Most business is pressure and blackmail, isn't it?

'I never tapped Harold Wilson's phone – it could have been done but it wasn't. But people here got very upset about that. They wanted to get rid of me for as long as possible.'

A vociferous campaign for his early release was launched by Charles Richardson's loyal family and friends, backed by parole board reports stating that he was no longer a danger to society. They fell on deaf ears.

In 1980 he walked out of an open prison and went on the run for nearly a year, supposedly to publicize his claims for freedom. He even dressed up as Father Christmas and handed out presents at a children's party. On his return to prison, he was allowed a day release to work with the handicapped. In 1983, anticipating his early release within a year or two, he was allowed home for a long, quiet weekend to prepare himself for life again on the outside.

A preview of the lifestyle befitting one of the biggest ex-crooks in London was revealed when he was collected at the gates of Coldingley Open Prison, Berkshire, by Rolls-Royce. He was driven home for a family reunion, then took his relatives – including his freed brother Eddie – to a champagne lunch.

In the following days the festivities continued at a nightclub and a public house. At the Sidmouth Arms, off the Old Kent Road in the Richardsons' old stamping ground, 350 people thronged the bars and lounges to pay their respects to Charles.

'Look around you,' he told reporters. 'I love these people and they love me. I get 200 Christmas cards a year in jail. That's what a bad man I am.'

Charles Richardson was finally freed from prison in July 1984.

Catherine the Great

'**S**he is romantic, ardent and passionate. She has a bright glassy hypnotic look like that of a wild animal. She has a big forehead and unless I am mistaken, a long and terrifying future marked upon it. She is thoughtful and friendly and yet when she approaches me I automatically back away. She frightens me.'

So wrote the Chevalier D'Eon, secret agent and wily observer at the Russian Court in 1756. The woman he was writing about became Catherine the Great, Empress of Russia and, to this day, one of the most remarkable women ever to sit on a throne.

D'Eon summed up her complexity. She was no tyrant, yet she demanded blind obedience. She thought only of making Russia great, yet treated the wretched serfs as scarcely human. She could never be directly accused of murder, yet the assassinations of Tzar Ivan VI and her husband, Peter III, undoubtedly left blood on her hands. She remained a virgin until she was 23, then for the rest of her life hardly ever went to bed without a lover.

Strangely enough, Catherine had not a drop of Russian blood in her veins. She was German.

Her given name was Sophie Augusta Frederica of Anhalt-Zerbst and she was born at Stettin, Pomerania, in April 1729. Her father was Prince Christian Augustus, an impoverished royal who had been given the post of Commandant at Stettin. Her mother, related to the great ducal house of Holstein, was a discontented woman who considered she was living a dull, provincial life, unworthy of her status and talents. She had no real affection for her daughter. But in spite of her father's lack of money and her mother, Princess Johanna's coldness, the young Sophie had a normal childhood.

Life changed dramatically when she reached the age of 15. Mysterious comings and goings, letters with imperial seals and her mother's excitement were all for one reason. She had been chosen as a possible bride for the Grand Duke Peter of Russia. Frederick of Prussia had probably suggested her because her humble place in the list of German princesses was thought more likely to make her grateful for the honour and therefore, easy to manipulate.

Summoned to the Russian Imperial Court by the Empress Elizabeth, mother and daughter set off with a scarcely adequate wardrobe, the Prince refusing to spend money on fancy clothes. They were received with great splendour. Princess Sophie nearly fainted when the Empress aproached her, looking like a goddess in silver watered silk and diamonds. This beautiful, imposing woman known only too well for her vanity and cruelty, examined her coolly and liked what she saw. Princess Sophie, with her beautiful pale skin, long dark hair, blue eyes and natural grace could be the right choice. After days of further scrutiny, during which she felt like a piece of merchandise, she was accepted as the Grand Duke's bride.

When she first saw him, she was appalled. Twisted and deformed with an ugly, thick lipped face, he behaved like a whimpering child one minute and a drunken sadist the next. But what mattered was her destiny. She took the name Catherine on 28 June 1744, the day of her conversion to the Orthodox faith and the following day became engaged. The Grand Duke was not much older than her. They sometimes found enough in common to keep each other company and play games in the palace corridors. But as the days went by a growing mutual dislike became obvious. It was decided to bring forward the day of the wedding.

They were married in Byzantine splendour, both dressed in cloth of silver and smothered in jewels. That night, after a great dinner and ball, he fell into bed brutishly drunk. Catherine did not know whether to be angry or relieved. On following nights he often took his toy soldiers to bed and played with them on the counterpane. It was obvious to everyone that the marriage was a failure.

The Grand Duke, pitifully aware of his own ugliness, took a perverse pleasure in rousing Catherine's disgust. He was impotent by night and repulsive by day; terrified of the Empress and irritated by his wife's devotion to her duties. She had almost made herself ill by spending long hours learning the Russian language and Orthodox rites.

After eight years of marriage, Catherine was still a virgin. She was desperate for love. One day she decided to flirt with one of the chamberlains at her Court whose name she discovered was Serge Saltykov. He was attractive to women and knew it. Although married to one of the Empress's ladies-in-waiting he had travelled and learned sophisticated manners and habits. Catherine, whose appetite for beautiful young men became a mania, was bowled over. Before long they were lovers. Nobody seemed to mind. The Grand Duke had his whores and the Empress turned a blind eye for state reasons. There was still no heir.

In 1754 Catherine became pregnant and when she gave birth to a baby son he was called the Grand Duke Paul. Saltykov was advised to travel for the sake of his health and the Empress whisked the child away to bring him up herself. Catherine was heartbroken, but made up her mind never to be hurt by a man again. When she returned to court, the steel in her nature had begun to show.

'My misfortune is that my heart cannot be happy even for an hour without love' she was to write later. Fortunately for her there now appeared a romantic young Pole, Count Stanislas Poniatowsky. He was not as handsome as Saltykov but had a cultivated mind and great sensitivity. Catherine yearned for him. Once she fixed her eyes on a man, he was as good as lost. Though nervous at first, Poniatowsky agreed to disguise himself as a tailor or musician to gain access to the Grand Duchess' apartment. He was caught slipping out one morning and dragged before the Grand Duke. 'Confide in me,' said Peter smoothly, 'and it can all be arranged.' He was indifferent to his wife's amours, but liked to know what was going on. It was a dangerous moment. The Grand Duke was terrifyingly unpredictable and could have run him through with a sword. As it turned out, Peter fetched his mistress and the four of them played a game of cards.

Poniatowsky became a pawn in an intricate game of diplomacy that was being played in St Petersburg and in the end he was driven from Russia.

Years later Catherine broke his spirit by a callous political manoeuvre, making him King of Poland one day and forcing him to abdicate the next. The humiliation killed him.

Swift on the heels of the Pole came one of the most important and useful men in her life.

Gregory Orlov was a magnificent Tartar, one of five brothers, all noted for their looks and their strength. He was only moderately intelligent and had no deep conversation to offer her, but he had marvellous sensuality and made her feel alive. Politically he was a brilliant choice. The whole Orlov clan was proud of having one of themselves chosen to be the Grand Duchess' lover and they vowed undying life-long loyalty, raising support among their fellow officers. Having the army behind her was to be vitally important.

On Christmas Day 1761 the Empress Elizabeth died and suddenly the ugly, debauched nephew she had terrorised was Peter III, Tzar of all the Russians. He went wild with his newly attained power. He mocked Elizabeth's coffin, refused to wear mourning and played the fool in her funeral procession. Catherine, to give a good impression, wore black from head to foot and kept vigil by the embalmed body of the woman she had hated.

Once again she was pregnant, this time by Orlov. When her baby son was born, he was sent out to foster parents. Peter, who had made threats to crush the wife who was ice cold to him, shouted across the table at a banquet: 'God knows where she gets her children from, but at least I know they are not mine!'

That sealed his fate. From that time on Catherine began to scheme against him and to await his downfall. He dug his own grave. Mad with power he made enemies on every side, mocking the Orthodox religion and courting his great Hero, Frederick the Great, who had beaten Russia to her knees.

The coup d'etat which made Catherine the ruling Empress came so swiftly that people scarcely had time to realize what had happened. It took place dramatically, by night, with the Orlov brothers predominant and the army solidly behind her. Next day, Sunday 30 June 1762 she made a triumphal entry into St Petersburg, with all the bells ringing.

It had been bloodless and swift. She took power at the head of 20,000 soldiers, dressed in officer's uniform, and all the important factions submitted to her.

Peter, green with fear and whimpering like a child had been bundled off his throne and into a carriage to be imprisoned in the fortress of Schlusselburg, a place long associated with torture and misery and which he dreaded. He pleaded with Catherine to let him keep his mistress, his dog, his negro and his violin. She wrote sardonically 'Fearing scandal, I only granted him the last

Catherine the Great

three.' There was nothing but hatred left in their feelings for each other.

Only three weeks after he had been deposed, Peter was dead. Catherine always maintained he had died from apoplexy, but this was not true. It was known that he did not die of natural causes but from violence. The full story of his death has never been told but at the time it was universally believed that he had been poisoned by a glass of burgundy then, when that did not work fast enough, strangled with a table napkin by one of the Orlov brothers. Catherine swore she had nothing to do with it, but she was not believed. Feeble though he was, as long as he remained alive he had been a threat.

Another threat, infinitely more pathetic, was removed very soon after. Catherine had been to visit a prisoner in his cell. He was a young man of 22 with a thin white face and wild eyes whose mind had slowly atrophied in isolation. He was called Prisoner Number 1 but he was in fact the rightful ruler of Russia, Tzar Ivan VI. Shut away since he was six years old by the Empress Elizabeth, he knew nothing of the world but damp prison walls and iron bars. As Catherine stood before him he mumbled his claims over and over again. The fact that he should have been Emperor was the only thing he could remember. She stared at him with cold eyes, then left.

Her orders were that the guard on him was to be doubled and he was to be killed outright if any attempt was made to rescue him. She knew she had enemies and sure enough certain groups began to talk of restoring the martyr to his rightful place and getting rid of the German woman. One night, Ivan was stabbed to death by a hot-headed lieutenant called Basil Morovitch. But Morovitch had not acted alone and again the rumours started. Was he merely an agent for Catherine?

Only one rival remained – her own son. She loved the Grand Duke Paul in her way but had him brought up to be submissive. After he asked why his 'father' had been killed she made sure he remained a nonentity.

Her whole aim was to raise the power and might of Russia over all other empires and to expand her frontiers as far as possible. She had a rock-like will when it came to achieving her ends. She claimed to hold liberal views but did nothing to change the barbaric, cruel and miserable life endured by the millions of human beings called serfs. She handed them out by the thousand to reward the architects of her coup d'etat. Serfs had no more rights than defenceless animals and were often valued at less: In Catherine's Russia a pedigree dog was worth 2,000 roubles but you could get a male serf for 300 roubles and a young peasant girl cost less than one hundred.

Catherine never forgot what the Orlovs had done for her. Gregory and his brothers, over a period of ten years, received seven million roubles as tokens of her gratitude. This did not include gifts of palaces and jewels. On their estates they were absolute lords of 45,000 serfs.

Gregory Orlov remained her great love and she allowed him to behave with such familiarity that people began to resent his influence on her. He wore a miniature of her, studded with diamonds, as a mark of her special favour and soon became so aware of his power that he was no longer satisfied with his role as lover. He tried to persuade Catherine to marry him so that he could be consort. When he received her refusal with a show of haughty bad temper she began to see that it was time for him to go. She conferred on him the title of Prince then sent him off on his travels. He dazzled Europe with a succession of magnificent uniforms but caused one wit to remark 'He is like an ever boiling pan of water which never cooks anything.' On his return the Empress gave him a marble palace and he presented her with an enormous blue Persian diamond, the 'Nadir-Shah' which became known as the Orlov diamond.

She was glad to see him and put up with his behaviour because he had such a special place in her life. But there was already another lover in her bed, a dark, good looking young man called Vasilchikov. The shock brought him to his senses but it was too late.

Waiting in the wings was the most famous of all Catherine's lovers, the great Prince Potemkin. She was 45 when he stormed her emotions, causing her to write him scorching letters confessing her greed for him. 'Every cell in my body reaches towards you, oh, barbarian! .... Thank you for yesterday's feast.' Yet it was power not love that Potemkin was seeking and it was her mind that he valued. Between kisses they would discuss affairs of state and gradually Catherine began to see that he was more than a lover to her. He was indispensible and worked with her to further her ambition and all the great schemes she had for Russia. When she heard he had died, she fainted.

At a time of life when her ardour should have been on the wane Catherine started on a string of young lovers whose only qualifications were beauty of face and form. She adored young men, even the most humble. The money Catherine lavished on her favourites is almost without parallel. In cash alone, forgetting all the lavish presents and houses she dispensed, she cost Russia one hundred million roubles. Potemkin had 50 million of this sum but at least he gave Russia the Crimea, the Caucasus and the Black Sea!

Potemkin's death was such a terrible blow to Catherine that she never wholly recovered. Her last favourite was a brilliant, handsome courtier called Plato Zubov, who soon began to show a taste for insolence and intrigue. He was forty years her junior, and though she was never to know it, he was to strike the first blow in the murder of her son after he ascended the throne.

Her end came suddenly, as the snow fell on St Petersburg. She suffered a stroke, from which she never recovered and died in her bed on 7 November 1796.

Queen Christina of Sweden

Through the Monaldesco affair the whole world came to know that Christina of Sweden meant what she said when she cried: 'I never forgive'. This strange queen who dressed as a man, despised women, and after abandoning her throne spent a lifetime storming about Europe, shocked even the most worldly by her part in the cold blooded murder.

It took place while she was staying at Fontainbleau in France, an unwelcome and uninvited guest as far as the French government was concerned. With her were two of her Italian courtiers, Count Santinelli, her captain of the guard, and the Marquis Monaldesco, her chief equerry. The two men loathed each other. They were constantly plotting and scheming to see which of them could find greater favour with the queen. Santinelli had cheated and swindled her over her property in Rome and the Marquis, seeking to incriminate him, forged a series of letters in his hand including, for good measure, insinuations about her relationship with a Cardinal in Rome and her ambition to take the throne of Naples.

The whole thing went desperately wrong for Monaldesco. Christina, always in the habit of opening other people's letters, recognized his hand through the forgery and came to the conclusion that it was he who was betraying her. She summoned him to her room and asked him what he would consider a fitting punishment for a traitor. 'Death', said Monaldesco, thinking she was convinced of Santinelli's guilt. 'Good', said the Queen. 'Remember what you have said. For my part, let me tell you, I never forgive.'

The climax to the terrible affair came on 10 November 1657 when the Queen summoned him to the *Galerie de Cerfs* at Fontainbleau. She had also summoned Father Lebel, prior of the nearby Mathurin Monastery and told him to read the letters. Monaldesco had a sudden premonition of what was to happen, but it was too late. The doors were guarded by soldiers and the Queen, dressed in black and toying with an ebony cane talked of trivial matters for a while as though playing for time. Suddenly Santinelli and two guards strode into the room, bared daggers in their hands.

Trembling, Monaldesco threw himself on his knees and begged for her pardon, confessing the forgery was in his hand. He pleaded with her to listen, to let him tell the whole story. She turned to the prior and said 'prepare his soul for death' then left the gallery.

Lebel followed her asking her to have mercy. Serene and unmoved she replied that after the treachery this man had shown towards her he could not have mercy. Even the rogue Santinelli went down on his knees and begged her to change her mind, to let the case come before the Royal Courts. Christina merely urged him to make haste.

Monaldesco died a terrible death. He had put on armour underneath his ordinary clothing and his executioners found it hard to kill him. He took 15 minutes to die and his screams must have reached her ears. She salved her conscience by sending money to the local convent to have prayers said for the repose of his soul.

To her enemies the affair offered proof of what they considered her arrogance and lack of humanity. They thought that far from being executed for political treachery Monaldesco had probably come into possession of some delicate personal secrets which she preferred not to be known.

Queen Christina was an extraordinary woman whose whole life was an enigma. She amazed everybody by her learning, the brilliance of her mind and the vivacity of her conversation. She also worried them by her odd sexuality, her meddling in politics and her lack of feeling for people generally. She always preferred the company of men and was awkward in feminine pursuits. When young she thought nothing of hunting reindeer in snow and biting cold for ten hours at a time, galloping at such a crazy speed that no one could keep up with her. Whenever she could she dressed in men's clothing. Her sexual leanings were not straightforward. Although she fell deeply in love with one of her ladies-in-waiting as a young woman, the other great loves of her life were all men.

Christina gave up the throne of Sweden because she had become bored with the plain, Protestant life and bored with being queen. She also refused to marry. For the rest of her life she went flinging and swaggering about Europe, creating such problems that men went pale when they saw her coming.

When she was born on 8 December 1626 she was so hairy and cried with such a deep voice that everyone told her father, the great King Gustavus Adolphus, that he had a son. The mistake caused great embarrassment but Gustavus was typically good natured about it and said 'The little thing will grow up to be clever. She has already fooled us all.'

He was killed in battle in 1632 when she was six and five regents took over until she reached her majority. They kept her away from her mother's melancholy influence as much as possible. After Gustave's death, Queen Marie lived in a room hung with black in which candles burned night and day. She kept a shroud by her side and Gustave's heart, encased in gold, above her bed. As a result, Christina received a somewhat masculine education, directed almost exclusively by men.

Queen Christina of Sweden

On her 18th birthday she took the oath as King of Sweden as it was not considered suitable to have the first woman to sit upon the throne called merely Queen. For ten years Christina handled politics vigorously and well. Europe was agog at this extraordinary girl whose statesmanship was remarkably mature, whose thirst for knowledge had become a mania and who was so unorthodox. It seemed she only required four hours sleep a night, spent the minumum time on her appearance, preferring Hungarian riding clothes of masculine cut and had declared her love for a woman.

Her great passion was for the beautiful Ebba Sparre, a lady-in-waiting. The girl was already betrothed to the Count Jacob de la Gardie and Christina tried in every way to take her away from him. The Queen's intensity must have frightened her and she had no intention of turning down a splendid offer of marriage to become an old maid. She married the Count while Christina suffered agonies of jealousy. Typically, she never forgave him.

But Christina was never predictable. Just as everyone had made up their minds she was lesbian she took as her favourite the brilliant, French oriented brother of this same Count, and it was obvious she fell deeply in love with him. In the eyes of the world he was her lover but eventually she loaded him with honours and sent him away, perhaps because she was aware of the ambiguity of her sexual nature.

Christina had become bored with Protestant Sweden. She began to regard the teachings of Luther and Calvin as 'moth-eaten' and called her Prime Minister an 'Old Goth'. She wanted to strengthen Sweden's alliance with France, a move which her ministers regarded as a sin against the Protestant cause. She admired French culture and the French way of living and had already enlivened the court with considerable style. She came under the influence of four foreign *bon viveurs* who were only too ready to help her change and life became all festivals and ceremonials, ballets and masquerades. She began to neglect the affairs of state to such an extent that sometimes she would let a month go by without seeing her ministers. What they did not know was that one of her friends, the elegant Spanish Ambassador, Don Antonio Pimentel, had already brought numerous Jesuit priests to Stockholm in disguise and that she was on the verge of conversion.

Christina had two shocks ready for her government. First, she refused to marry. She told them 'Marriage would entail many things to which I cannot become accustomed and I really cannot say when I shall overcome this inhibition. . . .' Then she told them she intended to abdicate and suggested the throne should be offered to her cousin, Prince Charles Gustavus, who would be better able to secure the succession. Their reaction, and that of her people, was as though she had committed high treason. Who would have believed this of the daughter of the great King Gustavus!

She greeted the day of her abdication with relief. There was a rather ludicrous little ceremony in which she had to put on her crown, her blue velvet coronation robe and her insignia then have them stripped from her. No one dared touch the crown and she had to take it off herself. The coronation of Charles x took place the same day.

Seeming to care little for the chaos, anxiety and disappointment she left behind she dressed in male clothes, took the name Count Dohna and set off for Denmark, promising she would return, though she had no intention of doing so. The new King found his palace in Stockholm so emptied of furniture and carpets that he had difficulty finding somewhere to sleep. Christina had shipped them off to Rome, where she intended to bask in the approval of the Pope.

On 23 December 1654 Christina made a triumphal entry into Brussels where she declared herself a Catholic. Those who knew her doubted her motives and thought she made the change because she liked the colour and pageantry. People crowded round to catch a glimpse of her. They saw a woman of medium height dressed in a strange mixture of clothes with a ribbon tied carelessly round her unruly hair. Her face was rather sallow and her features strong, her nose being somewhat aquiline. She rode like a man.

She enjoyed herself in Brussels with one long round of festivities, but her reputation for unconventional behaviour became so widespread that the government in Sweden threatened to stop her income. The scandal sheets accused her of every kind of sexual irregularity. She was called the 'Queen of Sodom'.

The Pope, Alexander VII sent word that he would receive her in Rome just before Christmas in 1655. It was the moment she had been waiting for. Dressed magnificently for once, but riding her horse astride like a man, she made her way towards the Vatican through streets festooned with flowers, triumphal arches and flags. Fanfares and salvos greeted her all the way along the route. Then she walked in a brilliant procession to where the Pope waited to give her the sacrament of confirmation. She was the sensation of Rome.

But if the Pope thought he had gained a model convert he was soon to be disillusioned. She had had her fill of piety and had other things to do. Humility was never one of her virtues and it did not suit her to be openly humble as His Holiness wished. She made fun of the relics and jabbered away to her companions during mass. Being informed of this the Pope sent her a rosary and begged her to tell her beads while in church. She answered bluntly that she had no intention of being a mumbling Catholic.

Worse was to come. She won over two of his cardinals by her brilliant talk. One of them, Cardinal Colonna, became so involved that he fell in love with her and the exasperated Pope had to send him away from Rome to avoid a public scandal. The other was Cardinal Azzolino, whom she undoubtedly loved and who became a devoted friend to her, though no one is sure of the relationship.

Though she made fun of Italian tastes and manners, the intellectuals gathered around her and she pleased them by inaugurating an Academy of Moral Science and Literature. She began to concern herself with politics with the most unfortunate results and Alexander began to wish his guest would go. She too had become tired of being under the eye of Rome.

She decided to leave for a time but was obliged to sell horses, carriages and jewellery to get herself to Paris. It was worth it. The French gave her a state reception watched by 200,000 people. She rode into the city astride her charger wearing a hat trimmed with sable plumes and a tunic heavily trimmed with gold and silver lace. She was escorted by 16,000 men of the Paris militia and 10,000 horses.

People were rather surprised at the coolness with which she accepted this display in her honour. 'Providence arranged that I should be born surrounded on every hand with laurels and palms....' she explained sanctimoniously. 'All Sweden went on its knees and worshipped me in my cradle'. She was not liked by the ladies of the Court but impressed the men by her intellectual brilliance and mastery of languages.

She stayed at Fontainebleau and it was then that the Monaldesco execution took place. The French were appalled at what they described as a medieval barbarity. She had to wait several months for the affair to blow over before she could return to Paris. Cardinal Mazarin, her host, gave her to understand that the sooner she went, the better, and she set out once more for Rome.

Her reception in Rome was very unfriendly. Only the devoted Cardinal Azzolino who had written to her regularly while she was away, seemed delighted to see her. The Pope wanted nothing to do with her and complained to the Venetian Ambassador that she was a barbarian. He neither replied to her letter informing him of her arrival or received her at his summer palace. He was furious with her and suggested she took residence outside Papal See. But he did grant her an annuity and appointed Azzolini to look after her financial affairs.

As the years passed Christina began to be plagued with regrets. She no longer seemed to have any place in the world. Her position was too humble for her liking. It was at about this time she heard that a woman called Gyldener who was the same age as herself and strongly resembled her had been passing herself off as Queen Christina in Sweden. Several months elapsed before her real identity was discovered. Full of rage the exiled Queen sent word to King Charles to have the wretched woman put to death. The

King decided to be more merciful and put her in prison for a month on a diet of bread and water.

Christina now began to meddle in European politics and at one point even suggested a new crusade to unite all Christian countries against the Turks, saying that modern Turkey must be completely destroyed. Nobody took much notice of her.

She seized upon another ambition: to rule another European country so that her name would mean something again in the councils of the world. The throne of Naples was vacant and she wanted to be queen. First, however, she wanted to drive the Spaniards out of Sicily and asked France to help her. But France would not commit herself to Christina in any way.

Then, in February 1660 another throne became empty, the one she had once abdicated so joyfully. Charles X had died suddenly leaving as his heir a five-year-old child. Christina made up her mind to go to Sweden. When she got as far as Hamburg the Swedes sent her a letter more or less asking her to go away, but she ignored it. For one thing she wanted to find out what would happen to the already desperate state of her finances. She also wanted to revive her image as a great queen and possibly spy out the land for the future. In Stockholm she was received with due respect and even given her apartments in the royal palace. But her hosts were wary. They were afraid that she was beginning to regret her abdication and would take this opportunity to make a claim to the throne. They allowed her to retire to one of her estates for a time where she ordered mass to be said regularly, then, after a decent interval the government hinted that it was high time she left.

The remaining years were spent wandering about the world, often dishevelled, and as she grew older any charm she once had disappeared under a layer of fat. Her eyes, too, took on a steely, hard look and she was inclined to make extraordinary statements like 'to attack me is to attack the sun.'

She returned to Rome at last and lived for a while in a villa where the Garibaldi Monument now stands. Her relationship with Cardinal Azzolino had become more and more remote. She swore she would love him to the end but he was in line for the papal crown and had to watch his reputation.

There was one more throne she had her eye on; that of Poland. But the Poles, thinking over her reputation, her life as a man-woman and her material dependence on the Pope, declined her offer. They chose the Duke of Lithuania instead and sternly reminded her of Monaldesco's assassination.

Her last years in Rome were full of cultural activity and she gathered a loyal circle around her. In February 1689 her health began to waver. She contracted a lung disease. The Pope gave her his absolution and promised to visit her in person but before he could do so she died, on 19 April, with Azzolino by her side.

Hitler:
the Making Of A Monster

There was nothing to set the young Adolf Hitler apart from his schoolmates. He was a studious lad, his report cards showing regular columns of A grades. He was seldom absent, his stern father saw to that. If his teachers had any criticism of his work, it was that his mind tended easily to wander. He could not concentrate for long on a single subject. He was a bit of a dreamer.

In later years, a glorious legend would be carefully fabricated about young Adolf's schooldays in Austria. That he was a born leader whom his classmates followed instinctively. That, as well as extraordinary artistic gifts, he was also possessed of a formidable political understanding. And that at the age of 11, he gained an 'insight into the meaning of history'. All bunkum, of course. The true character of Adolf Hitler was subordinated to the Nazis' needs to make a myth, a superman and a master race. And buried so well that today psychiatrists can only guess at the boy's mental and emotional state.

Yet, at the turn of the century, *someone* should have had an inkling that there was something a little different about the blue-eyed, dark-haired, impish youngster with the intense gaze who sat scribbling at a desk in a drab secondary school in the Austrian town of Linz. Someone should have seen into the dark depths of his young mind when the pattern of his future – and therefore the future of the entire world – was being settled.

That very someone could have prevented the making of a monster, and he failed. That man was his father.

Alois Hitler was a customs official in the Austrian town of Braunau-am-Inn, close to the border with Bavaria. He was a stern man and the young Adolf had little affection for him. Alois had risen from the most modest background to a position of lower-middle-class respectability, adopting along the way a severe conservatism, a self-conscious caution and a strict, pedantic, pompous attitude towards his job and his family. He felt that he had a great deal to be proud of and even his long suffering colleagues had to admit that he had achieved much in life.

Alois Hitler's father had been a poor country miller who had apprenticed his son to a cobbler while still a child. Alois married young but details of his first wife are scant. His second wife, Franziska Matzelberger, bore two children before dying of consumption. He married for a third time but tragedy still dogged him.

Hitler in one of a series of photographs he had taken in 1925 to perfect his oratorical manner

Klara Hitler produced two children who died in infancy. A third child, a son, was born at Braunau at 18.30 pm on 20 April, 1889, and survived. He was given the name Adolf.

There were to be two further children. Another son, Edmund, died at the age of six, causing an early trauma in the elder brother Adolf's life. Then came a sister, Paula, who survived.

Apart from the death of his brother, there was a further detail of family history that was to plague Adolf Hitler throughout his life. It was that his father had been born out of wedlock. This resulted in the wholly erroneous claim, loudly proclaimed by political opponents in the 1930s and by the Allies during World War Two, that Adolf himself was illegitimate and that his real name was Schicklgruber. The stigma stuck despite the fact that Hitler's father's birth had subsequently been legitimized by the marriage of Hitler's grandfather to the unmarried mother, Maria Schicklgruber.

There is believed to have been conflict between Adolf Hitler and his father Alois throughout the boy's schooldays. Faithfully protective of his mother, Adolf found his father a boorish brute. There were stories of young Adolf having to support his drunken father home from late-night drinking houses and of having to watch his mother being verbally abused by her husband. There is some doubt about these tales but there is every indication that, while adopting many of his father's middle-class prejudices, Adolf nevertheless detested the man. And in return, Alois Hitler, the one man whose behaviour could have changed the boy's character, showed no interest in his dreaming son's high-flown aspirations.

Adolf was 14 when his father died and the family moved to Linz where Klara managed to keep herself and the two children on a government pension. It was here that Hitler decided that his future lay as an artist. The fact that his talent was slight did not dissuade him and in 1907, at the age of 18, he travelled to Vienna to pursue his calling.

It is here again that fact and fiction diverge. According to the Nazis' rewriting of the history books and Hitler's own romanticized version of events, Adolf struggled in poverty, living the life of a typical garret-dwelling artist while, in pavement cafés, he pursued a soul-deep search for a political philosophy that would lead him to his destiny.

What Hitler was doing in Vienna was somewhat less romantic. Having quarrelled fiercely with his mother, who wanted him to pursue his studies, the pampered Hitler persuaded her to give him a generous allowance. He then approached the Vienna Academy of Art which, after viewing his test drawings, firmly rejected his application to become a student. At his second attempt a year later, he was not even offered a test for entry. He had no greater luck at the Academy of Architecture, where he was told that he had not completed to an adequate level his studies back at Linz.

The vision of himself at this time of his life later presented by Hitler soon became even more ludicrously divorced from reality when just before Christmas 1908 his mother died. Adolf was genuinely distraught but her demise did mean that he could pursue his sojourn in the cloud-cuckoo-land he had created for himself with even greater ease. He was provided with a healthy inheritance, including the proceeds of the sale of Klara's house in Linz. On top of this, he claimed part of his mother's continued pension on the basis that he was still a full-time student – an act which was no less than fraud.

Hitler now spent his time lounging around cafés and joining in any and every discussion on politics and philosophy. There would also be visits to the opera, an occasional water-colour, the writing of a never-to-be-performed play. But most of the time his life was idle and unproductive as he used up the money that his late father had spent all his life amassing.

At this stage in his life, he still did not have a single close friend. And despite stories of an assault on an artist's model and of his contracting syphilis from a prostitute, there is no indication of an interest in women. The well-known syndrome of bullying father and cossetting mother may have produced an oedipus complex making it difficult for him to form such relationships.

What he was acquiring, however, was a fierce, fiery unremitting hatred of the Jewish people. In classic style, the self-blame that should have been brought to bear on his own failures was transferred to another 'guilty' party. The Jews were an easy target in the early years of the twentieth century as more and more of their peasant communities in Russia and eastern Europe were driven west by the pogroms being conducted against them. Hitler encountered these dispossessed people in his early, jobless days and, like others before and since, blamed the immigrant minority for taking work away from the 'more deserving' majority. Other traits that characterized his later life revealed themselves at this time . . . his inability to establish ordinary human relationships, his hatred of the establishment and his sudden, passionate, ranting outbursts. He was beginning to live in a fantasy world to evade the reality of his own failure.

In 1912 Hitler's inheritance ran out and he took a job on a building site, returning at night to a malodorous doss-house. For a few months his lifestyle really did match the accounts later given to an adoring nation. But not for long.

Adolf Hitler was later to relate how he made up his mind to live in the Fatherland, the heart of the German peoples, of whom the Austrians were no more than a provincial part. True, in 1913 he moved to Munich – but not for the reason he gave. The cross-border flit was to avoid his conscription into the

---

Only one member of Hitler's family survived to see his rise to power: his younger sister Paula. But there were those among his less immediate relatives with whom he remained close.

One of these was his half-sister Angela, the daughter of Adolf's father, Alois, by his second wife. In 1939 Hitler rented a country home at Berchtesgaden in the majestic Bavarian Alps and asked Angela to run it for him as housekeeper.

She agreed and moved in with her own daughter, Angelika, who was addressed by her Uncle Adolf as 'Geli'. He became deeply infatuated with her and clumsily pursued her, although – it is assumed – without his feelings being fully reciprocated. It will never be known to what degree and with what success Hitler pressed his suit . . . but Geli was to commit suicide under the pressure.

Adolf Hitler and Rudolph Hoess, outside Hitler's Bavarian retreat

Austrian Imperial Army. When the Munich police caught up with him and handed him over to the Austrian authorities, he sent a letter to Vienna pleading that he be excused military service. It was an unnecessary humiliation as he was shortly afterwards rejected on medical grounds.

In 1914, the events that led to World War One set off the slow time-bomb that exploded into World War Two. Through those first hostilities, Hitler, the 25-year-old failed artist, realized that he really could become a German hero. He decided that action, not words, would be his way.

Though still an Austrian citizen, he succeeded, through a personal petition to the Kaiser, in joining a Bavarian infantry regiment. Sent to the front, he was employed in what was considered the most dangerous job in the trenches – as a company runner, forever exposed to the machine-guns, shrapnel and sniper-fire from across no-man's-land. His valour was redoubtable and he soon gained a Mercury-like reputation as a man immune to enemy bullets. He was decorated twice, the second time with the Iron Cross, first class.

Corporal Hitler avoided bullets but he was unable to escape the greatest horror of that war, mustard gas. It was while he was recovering, half-blinded, in hospital that news of Germany's capitulation came through. Like most of the rank and file of the German army, Hitler believed the armistice to be an act of treason on the part of the politicians and blamed it on a communist and Jewish conspiracy. Still in the army, though certified disabled through gas poisoning, he returned to Munich and became card-carrying member number five of the newly formed German Workers Party. He attended meetings, became elected to its executive, quit the army and threw himself into the task of recruiting members. He changed the party's title to the National Socialist German Workers' Party – Nazis for short. He adopted the swastika armband and discovered his gift for oratory. He found he could manipulate the minds of the masses.

The machinations that led Hitler to final and supreme power are well documented. There was no steady rise to his eventual position as Führer; his political and brutal struggle was one of Machiavellian successes and sudden disappointments. During one reversal, when he was languishing in Landsberg Prison for his part in the bungled 1923 putsch to overthrow the Bavarian government, he wrote the major part of his book *Mein Kampf* (My Struggle) outlining his vision of the future of Germany. This and his other pronouncements gave a clear warning to the races that were to suffer most to avenge the insults, real or imagined, visited on the Fatherland at their hands.

It was a ranting, sometimes unreadable, diatribe against Jews, Slavs, communists, pacifists, gipsies, the mentally ill, the 'subversive' and the 'inferior'. Because of this doctrine of hate, not one life in Europe or throughout most of the world would remain unchanged. The dreaming artist who had no friends, whom no one loved, whose work was derided, who was shunned even by his own father, wrote:

'What we must fight for is to safeguard the existence and reproduction of our race and our people, the sustenance of our children and the purity of our blood, the freedom and independence of the Fatherland, so that our people may mature for the fulfilment of the mission allotted it by the Creator of the universe.'

It was a creed that was to destroy Germany, sentence eastern Europe to the Russian yoke, cause civilian suffering on a scale never before known, and leave many millions dead.

SS Bloodbath In The Ghettoes

When Hitler's evil genius dreamed up the genocide of the Jews as his 'Final Solution' for the Jewish 'problem', he could have wished for no more willing, obedient and ruthless lieutenants than Heinrich Himmler and Reinhard Heydrich. With cold-blooded relish, they became the most methodical mass murderers of all time, forever seeking 'improvements' in their machinery for massacring an entire race. And they logged their lethal efficiency with the pride of obsequious civil servants.

Himmler's big regret was having been too young to fight in World War One. The Munich schoolteacher's son, born in October 1900, idolized the veterans returning from the front and shared their conviction that their efforts had been foiled by traitors at home. Jews, Freemasons, Bolsheviks, Slavs and Poles were all scapegoats for the right-wing radicals whose para-military retribution squads flourished under the weak Weimar administration. The young Himmler was carried along with the anti-semitic tide, and saw nothing wrong in the motto that it was better to kill a few innocent people than let one guilty party escape.

He was far from the Nazi ideal of a strong blond Aryan superman. A weak stomach barred him from the traditional Bavarian drinking duels and an attack of paratyphoid in his teens had ruled out strenuous physical work. But his orderly mind and diligent clerical skills made him useful to the organizations springing up in the effort to build a new Germany. He became an invaluable administrator and an effective propagandist.

Himmler was also Hitler's most slavishly sycophantic follower. As the future Führer emerged from political infighting as the strongman of the right, Himmler praised him as the German Messiah, 'the greatest genius of all time.' But it was 1927 before Hitler rewarded 'Loyal Heinrich' with more than a mundane task. Worried that many men in his para-military *Sturmabteilung* (SA) were more loyal to their brigade leaders than to him, he set up the rival *Schutzstaffel* (SS) and made Himmler its deputy leader, with orders that his instructions were to be obeyed without question.

At first Himmler had only 280 men to command. But he was shrewd and patient. Slowly he compiled dossiers on enemies of Hitler, real or imagined, and built up his leader's trust by regularly telling him of assassination plots, actual or invented. After two years he became SS chief. But he was still bogged down in Bavaria while the action was switching to Berlin and the North. Then luck presented him the accomplice he needed to achieve his ambitions.

Reinhard Heydrich was also a teacher's son, born at Halle in the Teutoburg Forest in 1904. At the age of 18 he joined the navy. Tall, blond and handsome, he was an expert on the ski slopes and a fine fencer, and a delicate violinist who shared weekends of croquet and chamber music at the home of cultured Admiral Canaris. But at 26 he impregnated the daughter of an influential industrialist and refused to marry her, declaring that any woman who made love before wedlock was not a worthy wife. The navy gave him a dishonourable discharge for 'impropriety', but he was not jobless for long. In October 1931 Himmler appointed him to his personal staff. Heydrich's quick brain and imaginative cruelty, allied to Himmler's plodding thoroughness, produced a deadly double act that would become the most feared combination in Germany.

Hitler's election as Chancellor in January 1933 opened the door to unprecedented power for the SS. Within three months, Himmler set up the first concentration camp, at Dachau, and crammed it with Bavarian communists and other anti-Nazis. Heydrich formed the *Sicherheitsdienst* (SD), a counter-espionage corps, to tighten the net around potential opponents. Its targets included Admiral Canaris, rightly suspected by Heydrich of clandestine contact with the British as war approached. By 1934 Himmler controlled the police of almost every German state. That April he also took over the Gestapo, the secret police network founded by Göring. Heydrich was second-in-command. Two months later, the two organized their first massacre.

Hitler's distrust of the SA had been carefully nurtured by the SS chiefs. Now Himmler and Heydrich stepped up their warnings that an SA coup was imminent. As the damning revelations piled up, angry Hitler summoned SA leaders to a meeting at Bad Wiesse, Bavaria. They were marched off to jail and shot. SA supremo Ernst Röhm had been Himmler's patron 12 years earlier, arranging for him to join a para-military unit. Himmler had been his flag-bearer in the abortive Munich *putsch* of 1923. But now he had no qualms about ordering the death of his former leader. The Bad Wiesse killings were the signal for the SS to run amok throughout Germany, liquidating prominent politicians on lists meticulously prepared by Himmler and Heydrich. Hitler told the Reichstag that 79 died on the so-called 'Night of the Long Knives'. Most historians put the total of victims at over 500.

Hitler now declared the SS his executive arm, completely independent within the Nazi Party. And in May 1935, in an astonishing ruling, the Prussian High Court decreed that actions of the Gestapo could not be contested in court if the secret police were carrying out the will of the leadership. Himmler and Heydrich were now beyond all criticism except that of the Führer. The SS was the spearhead of Himmler's drive for racial purity. Applicants had to prove there had been no Jewish blood in their family since 1800. For officers the date was 1750. The SS leadership had to approve marriage between true Aryan types, who were rewarded with gifts for every child. SS men who preferred to remain single took advantage of the *Lebensborn* – a system which enabled them to father children by attractive, racially pure German girls. Most SS personnel were country peasants, for Himmler had a maniacal belief that towns were evil and controlled by Jews. 'Cowards are born in towns,' he once said. 'Heroes are born in the country.' But the job Himmler had in mind for his troops was hardly one for heroes.

In October 1938, 17,000 Polish Jews living in Germany were stripped of their citizenship by the Polish government. Days later, the SS told them that Germany did not want them either. Heydrich organised a massive round-up, and the Jews were taken by truck and train to the Polish border, and dumped in no-man's-land between the two frontiers. The 17-year-old son of one of the victims was in Paris when he heard of the savage treatment. He went to the German embassy, intent on shooting the ambassador. Instead he killed a minor envoy, and was instantly arrested.

Here was a chance Heydrich could not miss. He wrote to every German police chief warning that anti-Jewish demonstrators 'are to be expected' on the night of 9 November, and instructed the officers to inform local political organizers of the rules of the game. No German life or property was to be endangered. And 'synagogues may only be set on fire if there is no danger of fire spreading to adjoining properties.' He added: 'Houses of Jews may only be destroyed, not plundered.'

The 'spontaneous' demonstrations that followed left 35 people dead, nearly 180 synagogues destroyed and 7,500 businesses wrecked. Insurers estimated the damage at more than £3 million. *Kristallnacht* – so called for the amount of glass

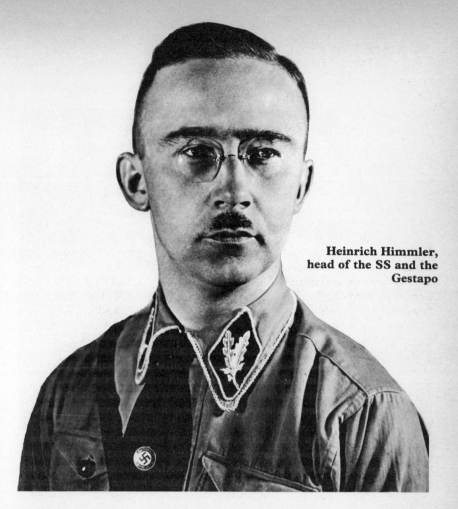

**Heinrich Himmler,
head of the SS and the
Gestapo**

smashed – was a clear warning to the Jews of Europe. Those who were able to fled to more friendly countries. Those who could not faced far worse atrocities in the near future.

Before the Nazi invasion of Poland on 1 September, 1939, Hitler warned his army generals: 'Things will happen which will not be to your taste. But you should not interfere. Restrict yourself to your military duties.' It was an order Wehrmacht officers, ingrained with a traditional sense of fair play in war, were to find hard to obey. For it was in Poland, the Baltic states and Russia that the full horror of Hitler's policies, ruthlessly implemented by Himmler and Heydrich, was to be revealed.

The SS had paved the way for war by helping Hitler purge his High Command of waverers. Many generals felt the Führer's timetable of invasions too demanding and too dangerous. Some were unwise enough to ask for postponements. Himmler and Heydrich gave Hitler rigged evidence that

Reinhard Heydrich, the 'brains' behind the concentration camps

enabled him to dismiss and replace the 'faint hearts' with men more ready to follow orders blindly. Heydrich then devised a cunning way to check on the loyalty of all Nazi leaders. He set up an exclusive Berlin brothel, Madame Kitty's, and staffed it with the most attractive call-girls in the country. But each bedroom was wired with microphones, and all careless pillow talk was taped.

Heydrich was also the brains behind one of the SS's most lucrative money-spinning schemes. After the 1938 union with Austria – the SS prepared for it by assassinating Austrian Chancellor Engelbert Dollfuss – an Office of Jewish Emigration opened in Vienna. For extortionate sums, Jews could buy exit visas rather than risk death or incarceration in concentration camps. By the end of 1939, 60 per cent of Austrian Jews had sold everything to the SS and fled. A second Office in Prague after the occupation of Czechoslovakia proved equally profitable.

And it was Heydrich who came up with the propaganda ploy to 'justify' invasion of Poland. On the evening of 31 August, a German radio station in the border town of Gleiwitz was attacked by Polish soldiers. They soon withdrew, leaving the area strewn with Polish and German bodies. Next day, as Nazi tanks rolled into Poland, German newspapers justified the move as retaliation for provocation. But the Polish soldiers had been SS men in disguise. And the corpses were inmates from concentration camps, dumped from trucks during the charade.

Within days of the invasion, the Wehrmacht knew that Hitler's warnings had been no joke. SS men were discovered shooting 50 Jews in a synagogue and arrested. Himmler instantly ordered their release. The generals had been told men, women and children would be killed without mercy. At the time it seemed impossible. Now it appeared all too probable. They pleaded for the slaughter to be delayed until the army withdrew once conquest was complete. They feared the world would blame them for any atrocities. But Himmler and Heydrich refused to compromise on the Führer's orders. They began herding Jews behind the high walls and barbed wire of 55 city ghettoes. And Himmler started his duties as head of the Reich's Commissariat for the Strengthening of German Nationhood.

The people of the conquered North were to be evicted to provide land for Germans to farm. In Nazi parlance, this was 'population exchange'. But the euphemism hid a multitude of sins. Himmler spoke of killing 30 million Slavs during the Russian invasion. And of the first year in Poland he said: 'We had to drag away hundreds of thousands of people. We had to have the toughness to shoot thousands of leading Poles, otherwise revenge would have been taken on us later.'

Mass murder was soon second nature to the SS. Nearly 45,000 Jews died in the Polish ghettoes in 1941 alone after Himmler reduced rations to starvation level. On the Russian front, appalled Wehrmacht officers watched units of the military Waffen-SS send hundreds of bullet-riddled bodies tumbling into blood-soaked mass graves. At the war trials in Nuremburg, one SS leader estimated that his squads liquidated 90,000 men, women and children in that way in 12 months. Ironically, the practice decreased after Himmler witnessed the machine-gunning of 100 helpless captives at Minsk. The man who condemned millions with each stroke of his pen retched at the sight. In future, he ordered, victims were to be eliminated in mobile gas coaches.

Meanwhile, Heydrich had been appointed Reich Protector for Bohemia and Moravia. Within weeks he was known as the Butcher of Prague, as the Gestapo ruthlessly destroyed Czech resistance movements. The Czech premier was condemned to death after a bogus trial. But Czechoslovakian agents were the link between London and a vital spy in the Nazi-hierarchy, code-named Franta. Heydrich was getting too close to unmasking him. British intelligence chiefs and the Czech government in exile agreed that Heydrich was too dangerous to live, and parachuted two assassins into the country.

Jan Kubis and Josef Gabcik set their ambush for a hairpin bend on the road that took Heydrich from his country villa to his office in Prague's Hradcany Palace. As the SS chief's Mercedes slowed to negotiate it on 27 May, 1942, Gabcik stepped into the road and raised his sten-gun. The trigger jammed. As the car halted, Kubis threw a grenade. Heydrich leapt from the car wielding his revolver. Then he staggered and fell. After a nine-day battle for life, he died in hospital. The SS and Gestapo made 10,000 arrests. But the most brutal reprisal was on the village of Lidice. It was burned to the ground, and all 1,300 male inhabitants were shot.

Himmler was left alone to carry through Hitler's ghastly plans for German supremacy.

'Final Solution' Of The Exterminators

Street shootings, starvation in the ghettoes, gassing in rail coaches . . . this was how Jews, communists and other 'undesirables' died by the hundreds of thousands in the 1930s. But still this unprecedented genocide was not fast enough for the coldly efficient masters of the SS. So the concentration camps, established years before to house political prisoners, were turned into extermination camps. Gas chambers and cremation ovens were added. And, to meet demand, new 'purpose-built' camps were erected.

There were 16 extermination camps throughout the Reich but the busiest were in Poland, at Auschwitz and Treblinka. And their sinister efficiency was a tribute to the untiring efforts of Adolf Eichmann.

Born in the Rhineland in 1906 and brought up in Austria, Eichmann was an unemployed travelling salesman before joining the SS as a 'researcher', studying the 'evils' of Freemasonry. When Reinhard Heydrich opened the Offices Of Jewish Emigration, Eichmann found his niche. By streamlining the bureaucracy, he dealt with more applications than ever before – and thereby raked even more money into the SS coffers. He was so successful in Vienna and Prague that, when Poland was invaded, Eichmann was called to Berlin and appointed chief of the Reich Centre for Jewish Emigration.

But in August 1941 Heydrich told him that the days of milking escaping Jews was over. From now on, the policy was their total extermination.

Eichmann was put in charge of transporting Jews from all over Europe to the death camps. It was his responsibility to round them up and provide the special trains to take them to eternity. Nobody minded much if some died on the way in the over-crowded cattle trucks. Once a train returning to France from Auschwitz was found to contain the bodies of 25 children aged from two to four. Guards at the camp had not bothered to unload the tiny corpses.

Eichmann's hideous success became horrifyingly clear at the Nuremburg trials. Rudolf Hoess was commandant at Auschwitz from August 1941 to December 1943. Under cross-examination, he estimated that 2,500,000 men, women and children died in the gas chambers at that time, and a further 500,000 from starvation or disease. Jews were sent to him from Germany, Holland, France, Belgium, Hungary, Czechoslovakia and Greece as well as Poland. More than 400,000 Hungarian Jews were liquidated in the summer of 1944 alone, he said.

Then Hoess clinically drew macabre comparisons between his camp and Treblinka, which dealt mostly with inmates of the Warsaw Ghetto. 'They used monoxide gas, which I considered not particularly effective,' he said. 'I decided to use Zyklon-B, a crystallized prussic acid . . . A further improvement we introduced was that we built gas chambers which could take 2,000 people at once, while the ten chambers at Treblinka only had a capacity of 200 each.' The Zyklon-B chambers were Eichmann's brainchild, after a painstaking study of the alternatives. They speeded up the business of extermination, enabling 24,000 Jews a day to be eliminated and cremated. The air at Auschwitz was constantly full of the nauseating stench of burning bodies.

The SS exploited every aspect of genocide. Gold rings were ripped from the fingers of corpses, and gold teeth torn out. Bones were ground down for fertiliser. In 1942 all camp commandants received a stunning directive from SS economics chief Oswald Pohl: 'Human hair must be collected. Women's hair can be used in the manufacture of socks for U-boat personnel and for employees of the State railways . . . As to men's hair, it is only of use to us if it has a length of at least 20 millimetres.'

Crude medical experiments were carried out on captive 'guinea pigs' before execution. Sterilizations without anaesthetic, injections to test new drugs and bizarre tests of human resistance to pain, heat and cold were all encouraged. Some patients did not survive for the gas chambers. Yet in the midst of death, Himmler was concerned about life. He took particular interest in a herb garden just yards from the Auschwitz slaughter houses. He was anxious to help Germans revert to natural foods and remedies.

Utter disregard for human life coupled with concern for seeming trivialities seem the hallmarks of madmen. Yet the most guilty Nazis knew full well that what they were doing was evil and wrong. Eichmann, in particular, always took great care to cover his tracks. And as the Allied armies closed in on Germany, SS leaders destroyed their carefully compiled dossiers on who had died where. The world might not understand . . .

After July 1944, when Hitler survived a bomb attack by army chief Count Claus von Stauffenberg, Himmler's power was further boosted. In addition to his SS, police and Gestapo responsibilities, he was given command of the vast Reserve Army. Paranoid Hitler could no longer trust a military man with the job.

Himmler knew it was already too late to save Germany. The Allies were consolidating after their D-Day landings, and he was soon trying to save his skin by offering secret peace initiatives to them behind the Führer's back. But that did not stop his brutality. Field marshals and generals convicted of complicity in Stauffenberg's plot were hanged in agony on piano wire strung from butcher's hooks. Would-be deserters from the Reserve Army were warned to remember their families' well-being. They could see the corpses of deserters hanging from trees, with placards pinned to their chests which read: 'I left my unit without permission.'

Even after Hitler's suicide, as the Allies closed in on Berlin, Himmler believed he had a future as a German leader. Only after the Führer's successor, Grand Admiral Dönitz, dismissed him from all his posts as 'politically questionable' did he go to ground. With false papers in the name of Heinrich Hitzinger, and without his glasses and moustache, he tried to lose himself in the huge crowds of refugees and soldiers heading for home in the chaos of beaten Germany. But his civil service mentality gave him away. He joined a long queue shuffling across a narrow bridge at Meinstedt under the casual scrutiny of British soldiers – and was the only man in the line to volunteer his papers. He was instantly suspected and arrested, though not then recognized.

In prison he confessed his real identity and demanded to be taken to Field Marshal Montgomery. The request was declined. His captors had found one cyanide suicide pill in his clothing, but another was hidden in a dental cavity. As British intelligence men arrived to interrogate him, he chewed on it. On 26 May, 1945, his body was taken to the woods near Lüneburg and buried without ceremony in an unmarked grave. Only the burial detail of five knew where the second most sinister man in the Reich ended his days.

Adolf Eichmann was also arrested in May 1945 – but he was not recognised. When American soldiers stopped him, he was disguised as a Luftwaffe pilot, and the Allies were not too interested in ordinary airmen. Eichmann took advantage of the confusion to slip away and vanish.

It was 1957 before Israeli agents hunting the monster who supervised the murder of six million Jews received their first real lead to his whereabouts. The German secret service passed on a report from a former inmate of Dachau who had emigrated to Argentina after the war. A schoolmate of his daughter had been making violently anti-semitic statements. His name was Nikolaus Klement. And from the girl's description of the schoolboy's father, the man was convinced he was Eichmann.

The name Klement rang bells in Tel Aviv. Israeli agents had traced the escape routes of 30 high-ranking Nazis via Spain and Italy. One had headed for Latin America on refugee papers issued by Vatican authorities. His name was Ricardo Clementi. Now the Germans had passed on an address for the Klement family – 4261 Chacabuco Street, Olivos, Buenos Aires.

After delicate negotiations with the Argentinian government, Israeli agents were given permission to put Klement under surveillance. Long-range photographs were sent back to Tel Aviv and shown to death camp survivors, but none could positively identify the man as Eichmann, and the Israelis dared not make a move without irrefutable proof. Seizing the wrong man would make them an international laughing stock.

Adolf Eichmann at his trial in Jerusalem, 1961

Then a bunch of flowers gave the game away. Klement bought them on 21 March, 1960, as he left work at the Mercedes Benz factory in the Suarez suburb of Buenos Aires. He was still carrying them when he got off the bus outside his Olivos home. It was enough to finally convince the watchers. They knew 21 March was the Eichmanns' wedding anniversary.

Israeli intelligence chiefs gave the go-ahead for what was later described as one of the world's best-organized kidnappings. Simply killing Eichmann would not have been enough. Ace Nazi hunter Simon Wiesenthal had said, 'If you kill him, the world will never learn what he did. There must be an accounting, a record for history.' On 11 May, Klement was bundled into a car as he got off the bus and driven to a safe house. He was stripped and examined for distinguishing marks. The appendicitis scar, the scar above the left eyebrow, and the SS blood group tattooed under the left armpit all proved he was Eichmann.

He was drugged and driven to Buenos Aires airport, his captors posing as nurses and relatives. Forged papers declared him to be an Israeli car crash victim, fit enough to travel but not to be disturbed. He was waved through to an El-Al jet which had brought Israeli politicians to help celebrate the 150th anniversary of Argentina's independence. Within 24 hours the man the Jews hated most was in Tel Aviv.

His trial began on 12 December, 1961. The 15 charges included deporting and causing the deaths of millions of Jews, being party to the murder of thousands of gipsies, and being party to the murder of 91 children. Eichmann claimed that, by streamlining Jewish emigration in the early years of his SS career, he was only doing what Zionists proposed – sending Jews out of Europe to find a new homeland. He said he tried to organize Jewish settlements in Poland and even Madagascar, but was thwarted by others in the Nazi hierarchy. When told in 1941 that the Führer had ordered extermination of the Jews, 'I lost all joy in my work, all initiative, all interest.' Thereafter he simply did his duty and carried out orders.

The Israelis were scrupulous in ensuring a fair trial, and the full procedure of appeals. But at 11.53 pm on 31 May, 1962, Adolf Eichmann was hanged at Ramleh Prison, outside Tel Aviv. His defence cut no ice with a people who knew that, when Himmler tried to stop the activity of extermination camps as the end of the war loomed, Eichmann protested violently. They preferred to believe the words of Dieter Wisliceny, executed in Czechoslovakia for war crimes as one of Eichmann's lieutenants. 'He told me in 1944 that he did not care what happened if Germany lost the war,' Wisliceny said. 'He said he would leap into his grave laughing because the feeling that he had five million Jews on his conscience only filled his heart with gladness.'

Klaus Barbie, The Butcher of Lyons

Wartime occupied France was a place without sanctuary for those in fear of the Nazis. The German armies occupied the north. In the south the puppet government of Marshal Philippe Pétain did the Nazis' dirty work for them with an unseemly willingness. And everywhere the SS and the Gestapo ruled by terror.

In greatest fear were the Jews, who knew that unless their identities could be disguised they would end up in transports heading eastward to the terrible death camps like Auschwitz, Mauthausen and Ravensbruck. In the southern part of France, where arrest seemed less imminent, many persecuted families sent their children off to homes in the country, surreptitiously set up as refuges for Jewish infants.

France was dotted with such homes, and generally the local German commanders turned a blind eye to this slight lapse in the otherwise rigid pursuance of the Final Solution to eradicate the Jewish race. But one SS leader thought differently. He was Klaus Barbie, the 'Butcher of Lyons'.

Barbie discovered that a refuge for Jewish children had been established in a large drab, grey house in the centre of the village of Izieu, high in the hills close to France's border with Switzerland. Early in the morning of 6 April 1944 Barbie sent a number of trucks up the steep winding road to the village. Soldiers ordered the children and staff out of the home and into the trucks and they were driven away.

On the night of the raid on the children's home, Klaus Barbie sent a telex message to the Gestapo headquarters in Paris detailing his latest achievement. It read:

'In the early hours of this morning the Jewish children's home, Colonie Enfant, at Izieu was raided. In total 41 children aged from three to 13 were taken. Furthermore, the entire Jewish staff of 10, five of them females, were arrested. Cash and other assets were not taken. Transportation to Drancy follows tomorrow. – Barbie.'

Drancy was the 'holding camp' in a Paris suburb, from where two months later the children were transported by cattle train to the most notorious death camp of all, Auschwitz.

Not one of the children survived the gas chambers.

Today on the wall of the grey old house in Izieu there is a plaque bearing the names of all 41 children. It was put there after the war, to remind the people of the region of the blackest period in their history . . . Of the valour of the resistance fighters, of the shame of the collaborators who made the Nazis' task so easy, of the terror reign of the SS and Gestapo, and above all of the horrors perpetrated in the name of Hitler by one of his most ardent henchmen, Klaus Barbie.

Thirty-nine years after the capture of the innocents, memories of Barbie's infamy came flooding back. In February 1983 he was expelled from Bolivia and flown to France to stand trial for crimes against humanity. He was placed in a special wing of St Joseph's prison, Lyons, while prosecutors sifted through a mountain of evidence to build a damning case against him.

The files reveal a youthful fanaticism that helped build the 'perfect' Nazi. Klaus Barbie was born on 25 October 1913 at Bad Godesberg, near Bonn. He was illegitimate, though his parents later married. He joined the Hitler Youth and at 22 volunteered for the SS (*Schutzstaffell*, or Protection Squads) and he was posted to Dortmund to work in the SS's own elite security branch. There he met Regina Willms and they became engaged. Their marriage was conducted with full SS guard of honour in Berlin in 1940. Two years later, promoted to Obersturmführer, he was sent to Lyons as head of the Gestapo in the city.

He quickly discovered that his task of 'cleansing' the region of Jews and subversives was far simpler than he had imagined. Collaborators and informers abounded, ready to turn on their own countrymen to win favour, reward and acclaim from their new masters.

Marshal Pétain's puppet government ensured that no more German troops than absolutely necessary were occupied controlling the country. Indeed, the French often enforced law and order more harshly than the Germans. They rounded up Jews for deportation even before being ordered to by the Nazis. Still more thorough in their new duties were French paramilitary units called the

Death's Head Units of the Waffen-SS fought alongside the regular German army in France – and sickened battle-hardened soldiers by their butchery. Near Bailleul in May 1940, British forces defending La Bassée canal ran up the white flag after fighting bravely though outnumbered. As they walked towards the enemy, arms above their heads, SS company commander Lieutenant Fritz Knoechlein ordered his men to mow them down. Dead and wounded were then dumped in a nearby farmyard. But one man survived, and testified when Knoechlein was brought to trial after the war.

> **Architect Albert Speer was Hitler's Minister for War Production from 1942 to 1944, and historians believe his success in stepping up the supply of tanks, planes and armaments delayed peace by two years. But Speer realized the folly of his slavish devotion to the Führer when he became aware of the atrocities Hitler condoned. He complained that Himmler's brutal SS killers were robbing him of 40,000 foreign workers a month in 1944, and even considered a nerve gas attack on Hitler's bunker to end the evil of the Third Reich. He was the only defendant to plead guilty at the Nuremburg war crimes trials, and served 20 years in Spandau Prison, Berlin, before release in 1966.**

Milice who carried out many executions at their masters' behest.

Barbie's headquarters were in Lyons' Ecole Santé Militaire where he installed torture chambers equipped with whips, chains, spiked coshes, electric-shock boxes and welders' torches.

In an astonishing book about the Butcher of Lyons (entitled *Klaus Barbie – His Life And Career*), author John Beattie uncovered some of his horrifying practices.

Barbie installed twin baths at his headquarters, one filled with near-boiling water, the other with ice-cold water. Prisoners would be ducked in them alternately until they submitted.

Women were stripped, tied down and covered in raw meat. Then Barbie's German shepherd dogs would be set loose on them. Other tortures involved acid injections, burning by blow torch or being wired up for electric shock treatment.

Author John Beattie traced Barbie's old interpreter, Gottlieb Fuchs, who spoke of the interrogation of a young Jewish boy and girl who adamantly refused to divulge the whereabouts of the rest of their family. In a rage, Barbie picked them up one at a time and smashed their heads against the cell wall.

Fuchs revealed that on another occasion Barbie's over-abundance of zeal lost the Nazis a valuable prisoner. General de Gaulle's top resistance organizer in France, Jean Moulin, was betrayed and captured with eight comrades at a secret meeting in Lyons in June 1942. He was tortured until he passed out and was then dragged by his feet down several flights of stone stairs until his head was battered beyond recognition. He was sent to Germany for further interrogation but died of his injuries.

Barbie's greatest mistake, however, was employing Fuchs as his interpreter. He was a double agent, working for the allies and feeding information gleaned from Barbie to the Swiss secret service across the border.

Within three months of D-Day, the allies were on the outskirts of Lyons. By then, Barbie's sadistic excesses had reached extraordinary proportions. He would conduct torture sessions seated with a naked woman on his knee, getting a perverted pleasure out of his victims' agonies.

After a café popular with German officers was damaged he took revenge. Barbie ordered a Gestapo raid; five innocent young men were hauled out of the café and shot dead in the street.

He once called local gendarmes to his headquarters to clear out a cellar. They found it piled with the corpses of young men, all machine-gunned, their blood lying deep on the floor.

He took 110 men and women from Montluc prison and had them driven to the village of St Genis-Laval. There, in an upstairs room of an old fort, they were machine-gunned to death until their blood literally ran through the ceiling.

Allied troops entered Lyons on 3 September 1944, but by then Barbie had fled. The Butcher had ruled the city by fear for just 657 days. In that time he had organized the executions of more than 4,000 people, including many collaborators who could have borne witness to his crimes.

Barbie laid low at the end of the war, earning a living in Frankfurt from the black-market. He kept in close touch with other ex-SS men, whose tip-offs saved him from capture on at least one occasion. He thought his luck had run out in August 1946, however, when he was arrested by Americans and driven towards their base in the back of a Jeep. He leaped out of the vehicle which, in the ensuing confusion, crashed into a tree. Barbie was once again a free man.

> **Sadistic doctor Marcel Petiot cashed in on desperation in the chaos of Nazi-occupied Paris. He told rich Jews and others wishing to flee Gestapo persecution that he could smuggle them out to Spain and Cuba for a price. But when they arrived at his mansion in Rue Lesueur laden with money, jewellery, furs, gold and silver, he gave them a lethal injection, then watched through specially drilled peepholes as they died in a windowless triangular room. Once he was pulled in by the Gestapo, puzzled by the disappearance of Jews destined for the death camps. But he was freed, presumably because he convinced the Nazis he was saving them time and effort. Only after the Allies freed France was Petiot arrested. His meticulous records showed that 63 people perished in the triangular room – and that their payments made Petiot a millionaire. He died on the guillotine on 26 May 1946.**

John Beattie asserts that Barbie spent a period after the war working first for British Intelligence and then the Americans, feeding them information about undercover Communist groups. He lived under the name Klaus Altmann in the Bavarian town of Augsburg until 1951 when he, his wife Regina and their two children set sail for South America from the Italian port of Genoa.

They settled in the Bolivian capital, La Paz, where Barbie became a respected businessman, owner of a saw mill and friend of politicians. He was even able to travel abroad on business trips with impunity.

The good life for Klaus Barbie ended in the 'eighties. His son died in a hang-gliding accident and his wife died of cancer. Shortly afterwards a new, more liberal president, Siles Zuazo, came to power, vowing to rid his country of Nazis.

France's constant pressure on the Bolivians to extradite the Butcher bore fruit on 4 February 1983, when Barbie was arrested and told he was to be sent abroad. He was driven to La Paz airport and put on an unmarked transport plane. Barbie was unruffled – until the crew of the plane revealed themselves as French officers. The Butcher of Lyons was on his way to jail in the city where he had imprisoned, maimed and murdered so many innocent people.

Marat and Robespierre: evil in the name of Liberty

Hailing the almost-bloodless start of the French Revolution, Honoré Gabriel Riqueti, Comte de Mirabeau, said in May 1789: 'History has too often recounted the actions of nothing more than wild animals . . . Now we are given hope that we are beginning the history of man.' But, within five years, that hope had been wiped out by one of the world's worst outbreaks of mass murder. Frenchmen freed by negotiation from almost-feudal tyranny turned into brutal, barbaric beasts on the pretext of achieving liberty, equality and fraternity. And the most poignant epitaph for Mirabeau's dream was the anguished cry of a fallen revolutionary as she was led to the guillotine: 'Oh liberty, what crimes are committed in your name.'

The Revolution erupted when public patience with the King's absolute power to impose taxes and laws ran out. Louis XVI and the privileged nobility were forced to make concessions to democracy and individual freedom. But each concession merely made the increasingly strong citizens greedy for more. 'The difficulty is not to make a revolution go, it is to hold it in check,' said Mirabeau shortly before his death in 1791. For as the people realized they had the power of life or death, negotiation was abandoned for naked force. After the storming of the Bastille, symbol of the old regime's authority, revolutionaries advocating cautious progress were drowned by the clamour of radical factions urging war on France's neighbours and dissidents at home. Then a more sinister voice demanded massacres.

Jean-Paul Marat was not even French – his father came from Sardinia, his mother was Swiss. But when the Revolution began, he abandoned his career as a scientist and doctor to become one of Paris's most vitriolic pamphleteers. His early extremism was unpopular, and several times he was forced into hiding. Once, when he took refuge in the city sewers, he contracted a painful and unpleasant skin disease, which added to his bitter persecution complex. But as the mob became increasingly impatient with a Revolution which seemed to be doing nothing to reduce raging inflation and food shortages, and with leaders who were prevaricating over the fate of Louis and his hated Austrian wife Marie Antoinette, Marat's messages began to find a receptive audience. And he spoke with chilling clarity. 'In order to ensure public tranquility,' he wrote, '200,000 heads must be cut off.'

On 10 August, 1791, an armed procession of 20,000 Parisians marched towards the royal residence, the Tuileries. The King and Queen, and their two children, were smuggled out by elected representatives and taken to the National Assembly building for protection. The Palace's Swiss Guards held the mob at bay until their ammunition ran out. They surrendered – but the mob was in no mood for mercy. More than 500 soldiers were slaughtered with pikes, bayonets, swords and clubs. Another 60 were massacred as they were marched away as captives. Palace staff, even cooks, maids and the royal children's tutor, were slashed to pieces as the Parisians ran riot. Bodies were strewn in rooms and on staircases. The grounds were littered with corpses. And onlookers were sickened to see children playing with decapitated heads. Women, 'lost to all sense of shame, were committing the most indecent mutilations on the dead bodies, from which they tore pieces of flesh and carried them off in triumph.'

The hideous orgy of blood lust instantly brought fears of a backlash from royalists or counter-revolutionaries. Marat had the answer. Many opponents of the Revolution were already packed in the jails of Paris, and might break out to seek revenge. 'Let the blood of the traitors flow,' wrote Marat. 'That is the only way to save the country.' Hysteria was whipped up by pamphlets warning of a plot to assassinate all good citizens in their beds. In September, the good citizens took steps to make that impossible.

A party of priests who had refused to take a new vow severing their allegiance to Rome were being escorted to prison in six carriages. A mob ambushed them, plunging swords through the carriage windows to wound and mutilate indiscriminately. Then, at the gates of the jail, another mob was waiting. When the convoy arrived, and the priests tried to dash inside for safety, they were slaughtered. Soon afterwards, a bunch of thugs burst into a convent where 150 more priests were being held, along with an archbishop. He was stabbed first. Then the others were killed in pairs, their bodies thrown down a well.

Over the next week, gangs broke into jails, prison hospitals and mental asylums all over Paris, massacring inmates with swords, axes and iron bars. Only prisons for prostitutes and debtors were spared. Women were on hand with food and drink for the executioners. Drunken killers held mock trials for some of the victims. One woman awaiting trial for mutilating her lover had her breasts cut off and her feet nailed to the floor before being burned alive. Marie Thérèse de Savoie-Carignan, Princesse de Lamballe, a friend of Marie Antoinette, was stripped and raped. Then her body was ripped to pieces. A leg was stuffed into a cannon, her head was stuck on a pole, and her heart cut out, roasted and eaten.

Ghastly scenes of grisly glee were reported as the piles of corpses built up. Drunken women sat watching the debauched death-dealers, laughing and applauding at each new depravity. Some pinned cut-off ears to their skirts as gruesome souvenirs. Others drank aristocratic blood handed round by the killers, or dipped bread in it. Men sat on bloodied bodies, smoking and joking while they rested from their labours. In six days, during which the gutters ran red, half the prison population, nearly 1,200 people, were murdered. And those who took a day off work to join the extermination squads were paid compensation for lost wages by delighted leaders of the Paris Commune.

The excesses appalled many of the most radical revolutionaries. But Marat was unrepentant. He signed a letter sent by the Commune to its counterparts in provincial towns, explaining that the 'act of justice' was 'indispensable in order to restrain by intimidation the thousands of traitors hidden within our walls.' And the letter went on: 'We do not doubt that the whole nation will be anxious to adopt this most necessary method of public security; and that all Frenchmen will exclaim, with the people of Paris, "We are marching against the foe, but we will not leave these brigands behind us to cut the throats of our children and wives."' Republicans in many towns took that as their cue to match the capital's atrocities by massacring the inmates of their own jails.

In January 1793, the Revolution reached the point of no return. The elected national assembly, now called the Convention, unanimously condemned Louis XVI to death for trying to 're-establish tyranny on the ruins of liberty.' He was executed in the Place de la Révolution, formerly the Place de Louis XV. Within weeks, every major country in Europe had declared war on France, and civil

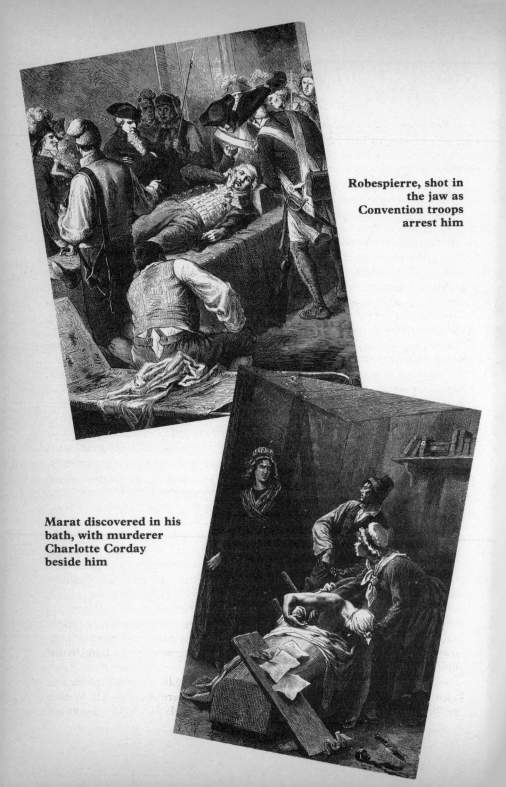

Robespierre, shot in
the jaw as
Convention troops
arrest him

Marat discovered in his
bath, with murderer
Charlotte Corday
beside him

war raged as peasants resisted compulsory call-up to the armed forces.

Minister of Justice Charles Danton set up a Revolutionary Tribunal to try to maintain order and avoid atrocities like the September massacres. 'Let us be terrible to prevent the people from being terrible,' he thundered. But Convention moderates believed the people would stay terrible as long as Marat was free to incite them. They ordered he be tried by the Tribunal. To their consternation, he was cleared. Carried back to the parliament in triumph by the mob, he forced through a decree ordering the arrest of 22 of his accusers.

Marat did not savour his victory for long. On 13 July, 1793, he was at home, wrapped in towels in a copper bath to ease the pain of his skin affliction, when a young girl arrived, claiming to know of moderates who were plotting an anti-leftist coup against Marat's party. 'They will all soon be guillotined,' Marat assured her as he jotted down the names. But the girl, Charlotte Corday, was not what she seemed. She suddenly drew a knife from her cleavage and stabbed Marat. He fell dying as aides manhandled Charlotte to the ground. She seemed oblivious to their blows. 'The deed is done,' she shouted. 'The monster is dead.'

But once again the moderates had miscalculated. Marat the monster became the mob's martyr. All over France, streets and squares were named after him. More than 30 towns changed their name to his. And his death did not divert the Revolution from the path of blood. For an even more evil man had taken over leadership of the lethal extremists, a man prepared to sacrifice even the parents of his godson at the altar of his ambitions.

Maximilien Robespierre, a cold, humourless barrister from Arras, was despised by many of his fellow revolutionaries for his fastidious appearance and his squeamishness at the sight of bloodshed. Yet by 1793 the dapper lawyer who shunned public executions because they corrupted the human soul was the most feared man in France. And he used his power, as chief of the ironically named Committee of Public Safety, to institute one of the most cruel reigns of terror in history.

Robespierre's committee directed the Revolutionary Tribunal in eradicating enemies of the republic. France was still in danger of invasion by its European neighbours, and Robespierre could justify early severity on those grounds. He ruled that all foreign nationals not living in France on 14 July, 1789 – the day the Bastille was stormed – should be arrested. And he executed the most famous foreigner on French soil – Austrian-born Queen Marie Antoinette. Charges against her included conspiracy with her brother, the Austrian Emperor, and incest with her son. Though she denied them all, she followed her husband to the guillotine on 16 October, 1793.

Soon the dreaded tumbrils were speeding almost daily to the scaffold in the Place de la Révolution bringing new victims. Pierre Vergniand, former president of the Revolutionary parliament, had warned: 'It is to be feared that the Revolution, like Saturn, will end up by devouring its own children.' Now his prophecy was coming true. He was among 20 moderates accused and condemned to death at a show trial. One stabbed himself to death in the courtroom with a concealed dagger – but his lifeless body accompanied his luckless colleagues for ritual decapitation next day.

More than 3,000 Parisians followed them to the blade. They included former royal mistress Madame Du Barry, accused of mourning the executed king while she was in London; a general who 'surrounded himself with aristocratic officers and never had good republicans at his table'; an innkeeper who 'furnished to the defenders of the country sour wine injurious to health'; a gambler who insulted patriots during a card game dispute; and a man who rashly shouted 'Vive le Roi' after a court jailed him for 12 years for another offence. Author Christopher Hibbert, in his authoritative book *The French Revolution*, says alleged speculators and hoarders died for 'starving the people' and one man paid the penalty 'for not giving his testimony properly.'

Vast crowds watched the executions, eating, drinking and laying bets on the order in which each batch of victims would lose their heads. English writer William Hazlitt reported: 'The shrieks of death were blended with the yell of the assassin and the laughter of buffoons. Whole families were led to the scaffold for no other crime than their relationship; sisters for shedding tears over the death of their brothers; wives for lamenting the fate of their husbands; innocent peasant girls for dancing with Prussian soldiers; and a woman giving suck . . . for merely saying, as a group were being conducted to slaughter, "Here is much blood shed for a trifling cause."'

The Place de la Révolution guillotine was so busy that, according to author Hibbert, people living in nearby Rue Saint-Honoré – ironically the street where Robespierre had lodgings – complained that the smell of stale blood from the stones was a health hazard and lowered the value of their houses.

Outside Paris, the vicious purges were even worse. 'The whole country seemed one vast conflagration of revolt and vengeance,' wrote Hazlitt. More than 14,000 people died as sadists and butchers in positions of office in the provinces made the most of Robespierre's instructions. Others killed to keep up with them, afraid they might be labelled weak or counter-revolutionaries. At Lyons, the Committee of Public Safety mowed down 300 convicted prisoners with a cannon. At Bordeaux a woman who wept when her husband was guillotined was forced to sit beneath the blade while his blood dripped on to her. Then she too was beheaded.

At Nantes, Jean-Baptiste Carrier was busy earning himself immortality as one of the worst brutes in the annals of infamy. Mass-killer Carrier, a lawyer like Robespierre, found the guillotine too slow for his taste. He packed victims into barges, towed them to the middle of the river Loire, then drowned them. Some couples were stripped naked and strapped together, face to face. Men waited with hatchets on the shore, to make sure no one got away. More than 2,000 people died in the river. Ships setting sail brought corpses up with their anchors, and the water became so polluted that catching fish in it was banned.

Carrier was also a child-killer. The guillotine was unsatisfactory – tiny heads were chopped in half because the necks made too small a target for the blade. And one executioner collapsed and died from the trauma of beheading four little sisters. So Carrier had 500 children taken to fields outside the town, where they were shot and cudgelled to death. But disease cheated the butcher of some of his prey. An epidemic swept through his overcrowded prisons, killing 3,000 inmates.

Millions of Frenchmen lived in terror of the midnight knock on the door that spelt arrest. Robespierre's spies were everywhere, and his assistants ensured that the pace of persecution never slackened. 'Liberty must prevail at any price,' declared Louis de Saint-Just, nicknamed Robespierre's Angel of Death. 'We must rule by iron those who cannot be ruled by justice,' he ordered. 'You must punish not merely traitors, but the indifferent as well.'

Early in 1794 Robespierre arrested more than 20 Convention members suspected of being critical of the way their Revolution was going. One of them was Camille Desmoulins. Robespierre was godfather to his son, but that made no difference. Desmoulins had said: 'Love of country cannot exist when there is neither pity nor love for one's fellow countrymen, but only a soul dried up and withered by self-adulation.' He named no names, but everyone knew who his target was. Saint-Just hit back: 'A man is guilty of a crime against the republic when he takes pity on prisoners. He is guilty because he has no desire for virtue.' Desmoulins died – and so did his 23-year-old widow, because she appealed to Robespierre for mercy.

Danton, too, was among this consignment of children of the Revolution to be devoured. Robespierre had decided that the notorious womanizer could never be a fit champion of freedom. Danton confided to friends that he would not fight his accuser, because 'far too much blood has been shed already.' He added: 'I had the Revolutionary Tribunal set up. I pray to God and men to forgive me for it.'

With his main potential rivals purged, Robespierre again stepped up the slaughter. The Committee of Public Safety decreed that death was henceforth the only sentence it would impose. Defence lawyers, witnesses and preliminary investigations were all banned, and an official said: 'For a citizen to become suspect, it is now sufficient that rumour accuses him.' Hundreds more aristocrats were executed – 1,300 in Paris in one month alone. 'At the point we are now, if we stop too soon we will die,' Robespierre told the Convention. 'Freedom will be extinguished tomorrow.'

But in the Convention, more and more delegates shared Danton's belated repugnance at the killings – and, at last, summoned the courage to resist Robespierre. For 24 hours the Convention was split, with both sides drawing up indictments to arrest their opponents. Finally, the vote went against Robespierre, Saint-Just and 18 of their closest associates. But in the confusion, troops detailed to escort Robespierre to jail proved loyal to him, and installed him in a safe house. The Convention summoned more soldiers to recapture him. When they burst in, a shot smashed Robespierre's jaw. Next day, 28 July, 1794, he was in agony as the Revolutionary Tribunal he had used so lethally sentenced him and his aides to death. Hours later, the tumbrils took all the arrested men to the guillotine, pausing momentarily outside Robespierre's lodgings while a boy smeared blood from a butcher's shop on the door. Robespierre was the last to die. When his turn came, a woman screamed at him: 'You monster spewed out of hell, go down to your grave burdened with the curses of the wives and mothers of France.'

The new Revolutionary regime revenged itself on Robespierre's followers. Many were executed after trials – Carrier was guillotined on 16 November – and hundreds more were lynched in jails all over the country. The people's revolution was at last over.

The French had paid a bloody price for allowing the likes of Marat and Robespierre to lead them towards their dream of liberty, equality and fraternity.

Rev. Jim Jones

It is just possible that the Reverend Jim Jones set out to be a loving religious leader who would champion the cause of the poor and the oppressed.

Certainly, thousands of sincere worshippers, inspired by his message of brotherhood and justice, flocked to join his faithful congregation. Politicians and civic leaders hailed Jones as a selfless, tireless worker whose personal sacrifices pointed the way towards building a better society for millions in the United States.

But somewhere along the line, it all went grotesquely wrong.

Jones changed from Good Shepherd to tyrant, from benign pastor to brutal torturer. In the end he led nearly 1,000 of his followers into a nightmare in a tropical jungle in South America with the promise of building them a paradise on earth. And when concerned relatives began to plead for an investigation into the plight of the faithful in the jungle settlement of Jonestown, he had the inquiring visitors assassinated to stop them telling the outside world the truth about the living hell he had created in the name of social progress and humanity.

As his religious empire came crashing down under the weight of the terrible suffering he had inflicted on his own followers, he ordered them to commit mass suicide.

Chanting and singing his praises, elderly women and young couples cheerfully drank the deadly arsenic potion of 'holy water' he offered them. Loving parents fed their children a sweet mixture of poison and lemonade. And for those whose nerve failed them, the elders of Jones's church were ready to slit their throats or put a .38 bullet in their heads. The whole congregation died.

Jim Warren Jones was born on 13 May, 1931 in the small farming town of Lynn, Indiana, and he was doomed to grow up a lonely child. His father was a World War One veteran who suffered a disabling lung disease and who could only contribute a meagre Government pension towards the support of his family. Embittered and partly crippled, he reserved most of his strength for the fiery rallies of his favourite political cause, the racist Klu Klux Klan.

Jones's mother, Lynetta, was forced to take a factory job to make ends meet. As an adult, Jones was to claim that she was a full-blooded Cherokee Indian. Certainly he took his dark complexion and handsome features from her. And it was obvious from an early age he felt compelled to spread a different message from that of his father's racial hatred. Only an average student at school, he showed an unusual zeal for Bible studies. While his schoolmates demonstrated their energy on the football field, the Jones boy would stand on the porch of the family's run-down home and preach sermons at passers-by.

In 1949, at the age of 18, he took a part-time job as a hospital porter in nearby Richmond to support himself through religious studies at Indiana University. He also married hospital nurse Marceline Baldwin, four years his senior. The following year, although not yet an ordained minister, he became a pastor at a church in Indianapolis and helped to run its racially integrated youth centre.

For the next ten years, Jones suffered abuse at the hands of Indiana's racial bigots. Even the more conservative members of the church where he served protested about his plans to welcome black worshippers into their midst. Eventually Jones quit, but not before he had learned a valuable lesson about human behaviour. Members of the congregation who had only been lukewarm about their young pastor had closed ranks and rallied round him when Jones was attacked by outsiders. The message was clear: even people who don't enthusiastically share each other's beliefs can become loyally bound together if they feel threatened by a common enemy.

With money from his followers he eventually bought his own church, grandly named The People's Temple, in a run-down part of Indianapolis which had changed from a poor white area to a black ghetto. He preached racial integration and equality, not because it was fashionable, but because he honestly believed in it.

He and his wife adopted seven children, black, white and Asian. Boasting of his mother's Cherokee blood, he called himself 'biracial'.

Now that his new parish was to consist mainly of black churchgoers, he set out to study the style and technique of black preachers who commanded rapturous devotion from their flocks. And in Philadelphia he watched one black preacher who held his congregation absolutely spellbound. Father Divine was a hellfire-and-damnation orator, faith healer and showman who lived a life of luxury on the offerings of totally trusting followers who even believed his claims to be able to raise the dead. Jones was enthralled – and decided to test the level of allegiance of his own churchgoers.

Overnight the campaign of racist abuse against him mysteriously reached a sinister climax. He claimed he had been concussed when a Klan member smashed a bottle in his face on his doorstep. A stick of dynamite thrown into his garden caused a tremendous explosion but no damage or injuries. Newspaper reports, based mainly on information supplied by Jones himself, told of how he bravely stood up to the threats against himself and his family.

In recognition of his courageous stand, the mayor of Indianapolis appointed Jones to a £3,000-a-year job on the city's Human Rights Commission. And his congregation, feeling their young pastor to be beleaguered, gave him their unswerving devotion. Jones decided the time had come to weld the congregation even more tightly together with a common fear that was more terrifying than the threat of racism.

In 1960, when the country was going through 'nuclear war fever', millions of worried Americans built backyard nuclear fallout shelters. A popular magazine ran a tongue-in-cheek article, claiming to be a scientific survey of the 'ten safest places to live in the event of nuclear war'. Jones seized on the idea as a perfect trial of how thoroughly he could rule the lives of his followers. Two of the safest 'bolt-holes' from nuclear destruction were reported by the magazine to be Belo Horizonte in Brazil and the rural backwoods of Ukiah in California, 120 miles north of San Francisco.

The Rev. Jones suddenly announced to his church members that he had experienced 'a personal vision of the nuclear holocaust' and he told them they should be prepared to follow him to distant pastures to escape. Leaving abruptly with his family, at church expense, for a visit to Brazil, he ordered them to be ready to sell up their homes and withdraw their savings from their banks.

Jones returned from his South American trip unimpressed by Brazil but

The Rev. Jim Jones

curiously interested in the prospects of the tiny, newly independent country of Guyana where he had stopped over for a few days. The former British colony, now a left-wing socialist republic, fulfilled many of his dreams of social justice, he told his congregation. As an afterthought he added that his terrible premonition of the nuclear holocaust had receded for the time being.

Emboldened and flattered by the number of devotees who had already put their homes up for sale just because of his 'premonition', Jones decided the option of fleeing from civilization should be held for a future emergency. If they believed in him enough to let his fantasies rule their lives, he reckoned, they would believe in just about anything he told them. Now was the ideal time to launch himself into the lucrative faith-healing market.

The healing services were spectacular, profitable and fraudulent. In a religious frenzy, Jones would pass among the 'sick' and 'crippled' newcomers to his church, laying his hands on them. Selected patients would then leap joyously to their feet saying their injuries and diseases had been totally cured.

But when Jones's inner circle of church officials began to claim that he had raised forty followers from the dead, newspapers and the State Board of Psychology began to take a close interest.

The time had come to make a quick move before the press and local authorities began to pry too deeply. The ideal bolt-hole proved to be in California's Redwood Valley, near Ukiah, one of the so-called 'nuclear safe zones'.

California of the mid-sixties provided the perfect camouflage for the People's Temple. The arrival of three hundred religious enthusiasts preaching love and peace blended in neatly with a culture which had more than its fair share of 'flower children', 'peaceniks' and hippy communes.

For his so-called People's Temple to grow and flourish it only remained for Jones to convert the two potential troublemakers, civic busybodies and the press, into allies. He succeeded almost overnight. Temple members who became hard-working shop assistants and farm labourers were always the first to volunteer to work long unpaid hours organizing local charities. The church-goers acted as foster parents to take in scores of problem children from orphanages. Jones himself wooed local politicians until he was elected as foreman of the county grand jury and a director of free legal aid services.

Jones now had hundreds of supporters whose regard for him had been cleverly nurtured from respect to allegiance, from devotion to mindless blind loyalty. One shortcut for him to bring about social justice, he explained to them, was to work tirelessly in elections and canvassing to get him more political power – and to hand over most of their earnings to him.

With the dollars pouring in and the People's Temple a respectable state-registered, tax-exempt, religious organization with the worthiest ideals, he was ready for the big-time.

Jones and his flock left the backwoods for the bright lights of San Francisco. Their reputation as an industrious band of do-gooders quickly followed them as Jones set up a new Temple in downtown San Francisco. The membership swelled to 7,500.

City officials, impressed by Jones's boundless energy and his flair for organization, soon turned over to him part of their welfare programme and his Temple took over the task of dispensing thousands of free hot meals in their dining hall every day. No one realized that among the grateful recipients of the meals were many of Jones's own followers who had handed over to him their wages, their savings and even their social security payments.

In 1976 a naïve local political worker who feared an embarrassingly small turnout at a meeting for Rosalynn Carter, wife of presidential candidate Jimmy, asked Jones for help to swell the numbers at the election rally. Jones packed the hall with his supporters and received a standing ovation from the crowd. The next day the papers ran his photograph with Rosalynn Carter and when Jimmy was duly elected, Jones received an invitation to the presidential inauguration in Washington.

In the eyes of the local community he was a pillar of respectability. He openly boasted about funnelling hundreds of thousands of dollars from his Temple funds to South America to aid starving children in Guyana.

But the first defectors from his Temple began to tell a different story. They spoke of Jones's long tirades about sex during his sermons and how he demanded that happily married couples should be forced to divorce each other and remarry partners he had chosen for them among his inner circle of church elders.

They revealed how Jones insisted that, as their spiritual leader, he had the right to have sex with any woman or girl in the congregation and how he forced them to submit to his sexual demands.

They gave details of how browbeaten Temple members were made to confess publicly to imagined sins of homosexuality. And they revealed how young children were cruelly beaten on a platform in the Temple by Jones to 'make them show respect'. Young girls were made to take part in 'boxing matches', outnumbered by teams of bigger, stronger opponents who knocked them senseless. Other children vanished into a private room to meet 'the blue-eyed monster'. No sounds of beatings came from the room, only the screams of the young victims and the crackling noise of an electric cattle prod which sent surges of high voltage electricity through their bodies.

And all the time, hundreds of thousands of dollars poured into the Temple funds.

Many San Francisco newspapers had been the proud winners of hefty cash bonuses from Jones through his Temple awards for 'outstanding journalistic contributions to peace and public enlightenment'. Even the local police department had benefitted from his generous donations to the widows and orphans of officers killed in the line of duty.

There was a deep sense of disappointment in the highest circles, even up to the level of President Carter in the White House, that Jones the civic hero might just be a vicious crackpot.

As the bubble began to burst, Jones put into action his escape plan. The millions of dollars he had salted away in Guyana had already been put to use buying a lease on 20,000 acres of jungle and swamp near Port Kaituma on the country's Caribbean coast. A pavilion had been built as headquarters of 'Jonestown' and dormitories were ready for a thousand followers to join Jones in setting up a 'new, just, socialist society'.

Amazingly, a thousand loyal volunteers did go with him to Jonestown in November 1977 and San Francisco's politicians breathed a sigh of relief that a growing scandal had removed itself 2,000 miles from their doorstep. But they reckoned without the tenacity of one tough, independently-minded Congressman who wasn't prepared to leave the scandal uncovered.

Fifty-three-year-old Leo Ryan was a politician who believed in confronting problems first-hand. He had left the comfort and safety of his plush Congress office to spend time in the solitary confinement cell of Folsom Prison, California's toughest maximum security jail, to see for himself the treatment of prisoners. And he had worked undercover as a teacher in ghetto schools to expose failures in the education system.

When worried constituents told him they feared many of their loved ones – husbands and wives, sons and daughters – had discovered the truth about Jones in Guyana but were held there against their will, Ryan pressured the U.S. State Department to force a reluctant Guyanese government to allow him to fly to Jonestown to speak to Temple members himself.

Accompanied by a group of newspaper and television reporters, he arrived by chartered plane at the settlement on 17 November 1978 and walked straight into the lion's den. Jones himself was holding court in Jonestown's central pavilion. Locked away in a strongroom at the rear were 1,000 American passports which he had taken from his followers. Armed guards patrolled the outskirts of the remote settlement – 'to keep away bandits', Jones explained to the Congressman. Settlement pioneers were gaunt and hungry but most of them appeared to be still fanatically devoted to Jones.

Ryan was characteristically blunt. Addressing a meeting of the worshippers, under the gaze of the Jonestown armed guards, he explained: 'I am sure there are some of you who think this is the best thing that has ever happened to you in your lives.' He was drowned in a crescendo of shouting and cheering. 'But I promise if any of you want to leave you can come with me under my personal guarantee of protection.'

There was sullen silence.

Jones was seething. Any defectors who left with the Congressman would tell the truth about Jonestown as soon as they were away from the power of his evil spell. The façade cracked a little when one volunteer stepped forward.

That night Ryan was allowed to stay in Jonestown to talk to the settlers. The party of journalists was sent packing, to stay in Port Kaituma, six miles away. When they got there, TV reporter Don Harris reached into his pocket for a note which had been secretly thrust into his hand in Jonestown. It bore four names and the plaintive cry for help: 'Please, please get us out of here before Jones kills us'.

The following day when the journalists returned, Ryan was waiting for them with 20 terrified worshippers who wanted to leave. One by one Jones hugged them as they lined up to ride in an earth-moving truck through the jungle to the airstrip. But there were too many of them for the small plane to carry in one trip and Ryan bravely volunteered to stay behind until the plane could make a second journey.

Then there was a scuffle and a spurt of blood, followed by a grisly cheer. One of Jones's elders had pulled a knife and accidentally slashed himself as he tried to stab Ryan. The journalists pulled the blood-stained Congressman aboard the truck and roared away towards the airfield. They were still trembling beside the runway, briefing the pilot, when a tractor drove through the undergrowth on to

---

For centuries, European knights launched crusades in the name of God against the 'heathen' Turks occuping the Holy Land. But the murderous missionaries were out to kill rather than convert. The most bloodthirsty expedition was led by Godfrey of Bouillon, in response to pleas from Pope Urban II, who alleged Christians in the Middle East were being persecuted by the Turks. Godfrey's forces besieged the Syrian city of Antioch for seven months in 1097. When the inhabitants finally surrendered, every Turk within the walls was slaughtered. The evangelical army then marched on Jerusalem. Huge siege towers enabled the soldiers to swarm over the battlements and begin another orgy of death. Jews who sought sanctuary in their synagogue were burned alive. Historian Salomon Reinach wrote: 'It is said that 70,000 persons were put to death in less than a week to attest the superior morality of the Christian faith!'

The dead of Jonestown lie strewn around a vat of the poisoned drink

the concrete. A volley of shots rang out from the men on the tractor. Ryan was killed instantly, his face blown off. Don Harris, the TV reporter, died as he took the full force of a blast from an automatic rifle. His cameraman was killed as he filmed the scene. A young photographer from the *San Francisco Examiner* was slain in a hail of bullets.

To add to the horror, one of the Jonestown 'defectors' suddenly pulled a gun from his shirt and began pumping bullets at the pilot. It was carnage.

At the settlement, the Reverend Jim Warren Jones called his loving congregation around him for the last time. 'I warned you this would happen,' he told them sobbing. 'We were too good for this world. Now come with me and I will take you to a better place.'

There was some crying and praying as the elders of the People's Temple struggled from the pavilion carrying huge vats of poison laced with Kool-Aid soft drink. Gospel singing began as the mesmerized followers queued up to drink the cups of death.

The babes in arms died first, the poison squirted into their helpless mouths with syringes. Then the children, then their parents.

When Guyanese troops arrived the next day, they found the corpses of entire families with their arms locked around each other in a last loving embrace.

Jones himself lay sprawled with a bullet in his brain. The People's Temple had held its last prayer meeting.

One devotee had left behind a suicide note addressed to Jim Jones. It said: 'Dad, I can see no way out, I agree with your decision. Without you the world may not make it to Communism. I am more than tired of this wretched, merciless planet and the hell it holds for so many masses of beautiful people. Thank you for the only life I've known.'

Congressman Leo Ryan had a more fitting epitaph for Jones. Just before he died in the airstrip massacre, he was interviewed by the television crew. His last words faithfully preserved on their tape recorder, found under the pile of bodies, were: 'Jim Jones talks a lot about love, brotherhood and humanity and his faith and the power of religion. But never once did I hear him mention God.'

Chapter four

DEADLIER THAN THE MALE

The female gender of most species, it has been said, is often more
deadly and venomous than the male. There is a certain type of
wickedness that only women can dispense. They are past mistresses
at the art of cunning and deceit, they can manipulate with genius.
But whether as tyrants or killers, deadly women hold
an intriguing fascination.

Amelia Dyer

Her name was used, like that of the bogeyman, to scare young children into being good. If you don't behave, Victorian parents would say, you'll go and stay with Amelia Dyer. And everyone knew what that meant. It meant you didn't come back.

Amelia Dyer was a 'baby farmer' who, when finally charged with her appalling crimes, was discovered to be a monster who had been quietly killing off unwanted infants for a period of about 20 years.

She was originally a Bristol woman who had been born, brought up and married in that city. Short and squat, with a well-scrubbed look, her hair dragged into a bun at the back of her head, she belonged to the Salvation Army and went out at weekends to sing hymns on draughty street corners. Her husband worked in a vinegar factory.

When the Dyers split up, about the year 1875, she found it necessary to earn money to keep herself and her daughter, Polly. Rather than take in washing, she became the local midwife, occasionally fostering those she brought into the world. But, she discovered, far more lucrative than midwifery or casually looking after children for whom she might, or might not, get paid, was the business of baby farming. This was a practice that sprang up towards the end of the last century. It was considered illegal, but thrived nevertheless. Mothers with unwanted or inconvenient infants farmed them out to working-class women sometimes for a few months, sometimes for years. The women were suitably paid at the start, then left alone to get on with the job. Sometimes, the real mother never came back.

Amelia Dyer realized she could earn a reasonable living if she was clever about it. The more babies she 'farmed' the more money she would earn. Her problem would be, how to accomodate them all, how to make room.....

She started a baby farm at her cottage in the village of Long Ashton, south west of Bristol, but eventually she was discovered and jailed for six weeks. After that she fell on bad times, was taken into the workhouse at Barton Regis and did not leave again until June 1895.

She left the workhouse with an old crone called Granny Smith and the pair of them went to live in Cardiff with Amelia's daughter, Polly, now married. It must have been a wretched household. Polly's husband, Arthur, was unemployed; they had a baby that died of convulsions, and there was no money.

Soon it became necessary to get out of the way of creditors and the police so the entire household packed up its belongings on an old cart and took to the road. They came eventually to the village of Caversham, outside Reading and took a cottage there in Piggott's Road.

Amelia Dyer decided to go back to her old business, using a false name. She inserted an advertisement in the local paper: 'Couple having no child would like the care of one or would adopt one. Terms £10' and made it known by word of mouth that the house was open for boarders.

First to arrive was the ten-month-old baby daughter of a barmaid, then came a nine-year-old boy, Willie Thornton, followed by another baby and a girl of four. Amelia was also paid £10 by a woman called Eleanor Marmon, who asked her to take care of her illegitimate daughter, Doris. A baby boy, Harry Simmons, was received from a lady whose maid had given birth to him, then disappeared.

Amelia took them all into her loving care. But on 30 March 1896 bargemen working on the river Thames near Reading fished a brown paper parcel out of the water. To their horror they found it contained the body of a baby girl, strangled with tape, and a brick used to weigh her down. Then on 2 April two more parcels, this time in a carpet bag, were dragged out of the water. They contained the tiny bodies of Doris Marmon and Harry Simmons, who had also been strangled with tape.

The police made a discovery that led them straight to the murderer. On one of the pieces of brown paper they could just decipher the address 'Mrs Thomas, Piggott's Road, Lower Caversham'. Two days later, having identified Mrs Thomas as Amelia Dyer, they arrested her.

There was pandemonium when she was taken to the police station. First she tried to kill herself with a pair of scissors then, that having failed she tried to throttle herself with a bootlace. Both her daughter, Polly, and her son-in-law, Arthur, were also taken in.

Police continued dragging the river and found four more of Amelia Dyer's tiny victims, bringing the number to seven. She never revealed how many she had killed altogether but it was known that at the time of her arrest she was still taking payment for infants long dead. She said, without emotion 'you'll recognize mine by the tape.'

While in prison she did try to save her daughter and son-in-law and clear them from suspicion by writing a letter to the Superintendant of Police. 'I do most solemnly swear that neither of them had anything to do with it' she wrote. 'They never knew I contemplated doing such a wicked thing until too late.' As it happened, Polly, the daughter she loved, became chief witness for the prosecution, giving evidence against her mother both at the magistrates hearing and later at the Old Bailey.

Amelia Dyer was charged with the murder of Doris Marmon and tried before Mr Justice Hawkins on 21 and 22 May 1896. Polly described how her mother had turned up at her home in Willesden carrying a ham and a carpet bag and holding the baby girl, Doris Marmon, whom she said she was looking after temporarily for a neighbour. It was cold and Polly sat her mother down by the fire in the kitchen while she went out to fetch more coal. When she came back, the baby had disappeared, and her mother was pushing the battered old carpet bag under the sofa. That night she insisted on sleeping on the sofa. By next morning Harold Simmons, a baby Polly was minding for her mother, had also disappeared. She was puzzled, but didn't know what to do. Later that day, the Palmers took her to Paddington station to catch the Reading train. While she went to buy some cakes to eat on the journey, her son-in-law held the carpet bag, remarking on how heavy it was. It was of course the same carpet bag she later dumped in the Thames with the two tiny strangled corpses huddled inside.

Her defence lawyer, a Mr Kapadia, accepted that she was guilty – she had in fact never denied her actions – but that she was insane. There was much argument and contention over this point, but the jury took just five minutes to find her 'Guilty' but 'Not insane.' For had she not kept a careful list of those she fostered and an even more careful list of the money paid to her, often long after the babies were dead.

She was hanged at Newgate Prison on 10 June 1896 leaving a letter stating 'What was done I did do myself' and regretting the trouble she had brought on her daughter.

But Amelia Dyer's trial achieved something. It brought about a sharp decline in the practice of baby farming. For who knew whether there might be another Mrs Dyer, waiting to earn an honest £10?

Frances Howard

As a family the Howards were a violent crowd, full of valour in wartime, full of passion in peace. But few of them had as little respect for human life as the bewitching Frances, one of the great beauties at the court of James I.

Their lineage was ancient and powerful, dating back to William the Conqueror and Lord Howard of Effingham who improved their image by defeating the Armada in 1588. But throughout history they had also been famous for a record of intrigue and plotting, violent temper and greed that made all men wary of them. They had managed to stay in power and royal favour by sheer skill.

Frances was the daughter of Lord Thomas Howard, created Earl of Suffolk when James I came to the throne in 1603. He was an unscrupulous man whose career ended in disgrace when he was accused of gross embezzlement of public funds. Her mother was no less greedy. She was born and brought up at the family's country seat at Audley End, near Saffron Walden and for a time her charm and sweet face hid her true character. It was her father's uncle, the Earl of Northampton, who detected the embryo of something evil and, with devilish cunning began to wield a sinister influence over her.

She was married at fifteen to Robert Devereux, Earl of Essex, but the young couple were separated almost at once as the King, who had taken the handsome boy under his wing, insisted that Robert return to Oxford to finish his degree, then join the army abroad.

This left Frances free to practice her powers of seduction at Court as Countess of Essex, and she used them to great advantage. Her first affair was with the Prince of Wales but his attractions paled to nothing once she set eyes on the King's favourite, the darkly handsome Robert Carr, Viscount Rochester, a Scot who had come to England on the accession of James I.

Lord Northampton, aware of her passion and thinking to further his own interests, brought them together. Though Rochester was at first wary of becoming involved because of the King's affection for the absent Devereux, he soon succumbed to the advances of this most seductive woman.

He insisted their intrigue must be carried on away from the eyes of the Court. But he had one disadvantage. He was not an educated man and had no skill in writing love letters. He realized he needed an accomplice, a go-between who would also write the letters for him. The man he chose was Thomas Overbury, son of Sir Nicholas Overbury of Bourton on the Hill in Gloucestershire. Rochester had first met him in Edinburgh when he himself was page to the Earl of Dunbar. They became inseparable friends and travelled south together to join James's Court. The arrangement was successful and for a time the lovers had no cause for alarm.

The first cloud came on their horizon with the return of Essex, who was eager to sample the joys of married life with his beautiful, 18-year-old wife. At first she pretended to be timid. When he became more pressing she was frigid. Though they occupied the same bed and the same room she would not yield. She cared only for Rochester and any other man repulsed her. Desperately, the Earl asked her father 'to remind his daughter of her obedience as a wife'. But a father can do little in such circumstances. The stalemate lasted until

Essex was struck down with smallpox and was too ill to bother about his wife.

This gave Frances time to scheme. She had two objects: to kill her husband's natural desire for her and to inflame Rochester's passion still further. She decided the only effective course would be through witchcraft. She was given, in utter secrecy, the address of a Mrs Anne Turner, widow of a doctor of physic in London who apparantly worked hand in glove with the sinister and infamous Dr Simon Forman. At night she paid a visit to their 'surgery' and was prescribed evil looking potions and powders which were guaranteed to be effective.

When Essex recovered his health and strength and began to act like a normal husband she started to administer her poison. After a few doses he should have been utterly debilitated, but there was no effect. However strong she made the potion, he remained lusty, hale and hearty. Sending a note to Mrs Turner, with instructions to burn it after she had read it (the instructions were never carried out) she begged frantically for a more effective remedy. She wrote the damning words 'I cannot be happy as long as this man liveth'. She had also, it emerged later, consulted a Norfolk witch called Mary Woods who swore she had received a diamond ring and a promise of £1,000 if she could produce a poison that would dispatch Essex within three or four days.

At court Rochester was now at the height of his power, and Frances watched jealously as he moved freely among the beautiful women who sought his favour. She was even more incensed as she realized that her lover was anxious not to jeopardise his favourable position by associating too openly with her. She resorted again to spells and potions and even took part in black magic ceremonies. The repulsive Dr Forman made wax figures of Frances and Rochester in the act of love.

Whatever the reason, Rochester seemed to be drawn more and more towards her, eventually declaring he could not live without her. The lovers met whenever they could either at Mrs Turner's lodgings in Hammersmith or at a house in Hounslow which Frances had bought specially for the purpose. Their meetings were known to only one other person and that was Thomas Overbury, who had now been knighted for his loyalty, Rochester having told the King what a staunch friend he was.

Overbury did not like what was happening. He did not like Frances. He saw her as a vicious woman whose evil practices would bring down his friend. When he heard that she was determined to seek a divorce from her husband in order to marry Rochester he could hold his tongue no longer. 'If you do marry that filthy, base woman you will utterly ruin your honour and yourself; you shall never do it by my advice or consent' he blurted out to the man he loved and admired more than any other. But Rochester was blinded by his infatuation and the relationship between the two men was never the same.

Frances Howard

Frances heard what had happened, heard that Overbury was talking about her openly at court and with hatred vowed she would destroy him. The King had already shown some sympathy for her divorce. If he discovered she was not the virtuous woman he thought, he might change his mind. From that moment Overbury's death was certain.

She turned to her old mentor, Lord Northampton for help. He was jealous of Rochester's influence as the King's favourite and was only too anxious to work against him, whatever the reason. Together they set out to poison Rochester's mind against his friend, making great capital out of their insinuation that Overbury was plotting to step into his shoes and was already being shown great favour by the King.

Poison was also poured into the royal ear so that when Overbury refused James's offer to send him as Ambassador to the Low Countries, the King suspected him of ulterior motives and sent him to the Tower for 'a matter of high contempt'.

Frances was going to make sure he never came out alive. She paid an agent called Weston to work for her, and managed to get him a position in the Tower, eventually arranging for him to become personal assistant to the wretched Overbury. It would be his task to administer the poison to the prisoner's food, making sure that nothing was left on the plate as evidence.

The first attempt to poison Sir Thomas failed because Weston was caught red handed by Sir Gervase Elwes, Lieutenant of the Tower. After some thought Elwes decided to keep silent. For all he knew Weston might be acting on instructions from the highest level and he did not want to make life difficult for himself. But he was a humane man and did not intend to let Overbury be poisoned if he could help it. He must have intercepted most of the jellies and tarts, cold meats and sauces that Frances sent in for him. They contained so much poison that had he eaten them he would have had enough in his system to kill 20 men. Frances had paid Mrs Turner and an apothecary, James Franklin, to supply her with seven different poisons. That none of them had worked seemed unexplicable, unless she was being cheated. When a rumour began to circulate that Overbury was due to be released from the Tower, she got rid of the useless Weston. She took an immense risk. With Northumberland, she contacted a young man called William Reeve, assistant to Dr Paul de Lobell, the French physician who was attending prisoners in the Tower. For £20 reward Reeve stole from his master a solution of mercury sublimate. It was given to Sir Thomas Overbury as a medicine. He swallowed it without any suspicion and died in agony.

Frances had already petitioned for divorce from the Earl of Essex and on 16 May 1613 a commission was at last appointed to examine her claim that her marriage was null and void, because her husband was impotent. Essex denied this emphatically and people were inclined to believe his side of the story. However, after some interference on the part of the King, who found the whole thing distasteful, nullity was declared. The pair of them were free to start again. Essex had no idea at the time how lucky he had been to escape with his life.

The marriage between Rochester, now created Earl of Somerset and Frances Essex took place towards the end of that year, the bride radiant in white with her long fair hair flowing loosely down her back as a symbol of purity and innocence. The whole court attended with the King and Queen and a great deal of money was spent on the occasion.

Rochester still had no idea that he had married a murderess.

But if Frances thought she could now settle down happily with the man who had obsessed her and dominated her passions and emotions, she was mistaken. For very soon after the wedding her health seemed poor. She was nervous and curiously ill-tempered for a new bride. No wonder. All her accomplices were starting to blackmail her. She now lived in dread that she would be found out.

Somerset himself seemed to be out of favour with the King, who had grown rather tired of his favourites's overbearing manner and was tending to prefer George Villiers, who was to become Duke of Buckingham. There was nothing he could do to stop Villier's rapid advancement and his enemies scented blood.

In the autumn of 1615 when Frances had been married for two years William Reeve, who had given Sir Thomas Overbury the fatal dose of poison, fell dangerously ill and began worrying about the fate of his immortal soul. He unburdened himself of his guilty secret and recovered.

The facts were eventually laid before the King who gave orders that justice must be done. Somerset and his Countess were told not to leave their apartments until a preliminary hearing had been held. Gradually the whole story came out, and both of them were arrested on a charge of murder.

From the beginning Somerset protested that he knew nothing of the murder of his friend and stood firm in his denial right to the end. He was sentenced to death but there was a general wish that the King should spare his life and at the twelfth hour he was granted a pardon. On the other hand, feeling ran high against the Countess and at one stage it was thought likely that she would have to submit to the death penalty pronounced in court. The King granted her a pardon, on the grounds that her family had done the country so much good service and that she had sworn to be truly penitent. But there were demonstrations against her in the streets and one day a mob attacked a coach in which the Queen was travelling with a young friend. They had made the mistake of thinking it was 'that vile woman' and her mother.

Robert Devereux, Earl of Essex

Both Frances and Somerset were imprisoned in the Tower. She pleaded with the lieutenant not to put her in the room where Overbury had died. They stayed there until January 1621 when the King allowed them to go to Grey's Court in Oxfordshire where Lord Wallingford, brother-in-law of Frances, had offered them accommodation. The only condition was they were never to leave. They were under house arrest for the rest of their lives.

The punishment was worse than anybody could have dreamed. Somerset loathed the woman who had brought about his downfall and disgrace, turned him against his friend and then had that friend cruelly murdered. He hardly ever spoke to her again. Day in, day out they were forced together in an intimacy that was sheer torture. And when Frances died from a terrible wasting disease in August 1632 the last thing she saw was the contempt in his eyes.

Belle Gunness

There was only one name they could give to Mrs Belle Gunness and that was 'The female Bluebeard'. How else could you described a woman who had coldly and systematically murdered at least 100 people?

To her neighbours she had seemed pleasant enough. She was a widow and ran a small but successful farm in the green hills of La Porte County, Indiana, USA. There was something a bit foreign about her and perhaps she was a bit flighty but that did not mean to say she was not hard working and respectable.

They were terribly shocked when they heard one morning in April 1908 that there had been a terrible fire at the Gunness farm during the night and the comely widow and her three young children had been burned to death in the flames.

But they were even more shocked when the police arrived and started digging up the farmstead and excavating the fields, finding graves and corpses everywhere they looked.

The truth might not have come out for years but someone remembered that a farm hand named Lamphere, who had worked for Mrs Gunness for years, had left the farm suddenly a day or so before the fire. He was thought to have had some grievance against her and would mutter threats when he had had too many beers in the local bar.

Following up this clue the police managed to track down Lamphere and subjected him to continual and intense questioning. He broke down under it and confessed that he had killed his employer and her children with an axe while they slept and had set fire to the farmhouse to destroy the evidence of what he had done.

Why did he do it? 'I had to' he exclaimed. 'If I hadn't killed her, she would have killed me. I knew too much'.

'Knew too much? How do you mean?' asked the policeman in charge of the case.

'The woman was a murderess. She killed people they way you and me would kill rabbits.'

Hardly able to believe what he was hearing, the policeman asked softly 'How did she kill them?'

'With an axe, after she'd chloroformed them' groaned Lamphere. 'She buried them on the farm.'

For weeks following his confession, the Gunness farm was full of grim faced men, digging. Bodies of men, women and children were found neatly interred, mostly in separate graves, but sometimes two buried together. Beneath the cement floor of the farmhouse they found a deep pit full of human bones. Belle Gunness must have been at work for years, filling her own private cemetery.

Eventually the whole story was pieced together and it chilled the blood of even those used to dealing with murder. The scale of her wickedness was beyond anything they had come across.

She was Norwegian by birth and had emigrated to America as a girl. While still in her teens she had met and married a Swede called Albert Sorenson. She poisoned him in 1900 after having insured him for a tidy sum.

With this money she bought the farm in Indiana, and thinking she needed a man about the place to do the heavy work, married Joe Gunness. There was some evidence that she was already deeply involved with a murderer named Hoch whose speciality was advertising for wives then killing them off for their money. Some of these unfortunate women were sent to stay with Mrs Gunness and never heard of again. Her husband must have tumbled onto her secret and was killed with an axe one night to make sure he didn't talk. The man Hoch was arrested and executed and she decided from that time she would operate on her own.

The only difference was, she advertised for husbands.

She inserted the same notice in small provincial papers all over the United States. It read as follows:

'PERSONAL – Comely widow, who owns large farm in one of the finest districts of La Porte County, Indiana, desires to make the acquaintance of a gentleman unusually well provided, with a view to joining fortunes. No replies by letter will be considered unless the sender is willing to follow an answer with a personal visit.'

Whether they were attracted by the thought of the comely widow or by her fortune makes no difference. Gentlemen replied to her advertisements with alacrity – scores of them. She could pick and choose her victims, telling them to bring substantial sums of ready cash with them when they came to inspect the farm, just so that she could be sure of their good faith.

One by one they fell into her trap. The prospective husband would be received with open arms, shown round the farm, then, when he had eaten a huge farmhouse supper he would be shown into her guest room. It was really a death cell. The bed was comfortable enough but the thick oak door was fastened with a spring lock, the windows had iron bars and the walls were of double thickness, the cavity packed with sawdust, making the room completely sound proof. First there would be the chloroform, then she would kill with an axe. She had got the routine down to a fine art.

She had the skill of a siren when it came to those who did not respond quickly enough to her initial overture. This is a letter which was sent to a man called Andrew Helgelein in December 1907:

'To the dearest friend in all the world – I know you have now only to come to me and be my own. The king will be no happier than you when you get here. As for the queen, her joy will be small when compared with mine. You will love my farm, sweetheart. In all La Porte County, there's none will compare with it. It is on a nice green slope near two lakes. When I hear your name mentioned, my heart beats in wild rapture for you. My Andrew, I love you!'

At the bottom of the page she had scrawled 'Be sure and bring the three thousand dollars you are going to invest in the farm with you and, for safety's sake, sew them up in your clothes, dearest.'

Andrew Helgelein visited Mrs Gunness. He was seen by some neighbours as she drove him in her pony and trap towards the farm. But he never came out again.

As her lust for money and possessions grew, she killed more frequently. Sometimes whole families were wiped out. It had always been presumed they had left the district hurriedly until they were discovered in their graves. Something of the sort happened on Christmas Day 1906. Mrs Gunness invited two married women she knew who wore particularly fine jewels. She told them to bring their husbands along to the farm and help a lonely widow celebrate the festive season. As she had anticipated, they came wearing all their best trinkets. By Boxing Day not one of them was left alive and all four were identified when they were found by the police.

Exactly how many people she murdered was never known. The authorities could only make estimates with the help of the imprisoned Lamphere, who had made a long confession. He said she had carried on her foul trade for roughly five years and that she averaged three victims a month. His estimate was thought to be exaggerated. Still, even allowing for that, the police found that by adding on the victims of other murders she was known to have committed outside the farm, the total must be well over one hundred.

Why did no one suspect her before? It appears there had been inquiries about some of the men who disappeared after visiting her at the farm and Andrew Helgelein's brother was about to start an investigation at the time of the fire.

But after all, she seemed such a nice women and the farm was so well run. No one accused her and if a farmhand called Lamphere had not set fire to the place, she might have gone on for years.

Chicago May

Her real name was Mary Vivienne Churchill. She wafted through the foyers of the world's great hotels in *crêpe de chine* and pearls, a vision of loveliness with her spun gold hair, green eyes and white satin skin. Men were captivated by her, willingly became entangled with her, only to find that one morning when they awoke she had turned on them with the venom of a rattlesnake, demanding more money than they dared to think of.

She was known to the police as Chicago May, a leading member of the underworld and one of the most vicious blackmailers of modern times. Her one object in life was to make as much money as possible and, using the bedroom as her centre of operations, she bled her victims white.

Born in Ireland, the daughter of respectable, well-off parents, she was thought to have 'a bit of a devil' in her as a child, but nothing to worry about. By the age of 16 she had turned into a beauty and began to show her true colours. With cool calculation, she threw herself at the son of a leading Irish family, seduced him, then threatened to tell his parents if he didn't pay her handsomely to keep her mouth shut. The young man paid up, but she told them nevertheless. To get rid of her they gave in to her demands: a thousand pounds and a passage to America.

It was 1912, still a decade before Al Capone, but the underworld was bristling with gangsters, hoodlums and big time grafters. May dressed herself in the height of fashion and headed straight for Chicago. Before she was 20 she had been accepted into the fraternity as a high class operator.

Her victims were mostly very rich men in their fifties or sixties, tycoons, heads of industry, public figures and bored husbands all on the look out for a beautiful woman to flatter them and on whom they could spend their hard earned money. Her technique was simple. She would use her considerable charm to enslave some hapless male, modestly accept his homage of jewellery and cash, then allow herself to be seduced. Before he knew what was happening incriminating photographs had been produced, threats made and his reputation put up for sale.

As a result of these tactics Chicago May could soon afford a splendid house with servants, her own personal bodyguard and a film star wardrobe. Then, at the height of her success, she met the criminal Eddie Guerin, a tough, unscrupulous bank robber with flinty blue eyes and a chilling presence. They seemed made for each other. They became lovers and he dominated the rest of her life. Eddie had no squeamish feelings about May sleeping with rich men. That was business. But if she showed any sign of being attracted to someone nearer her own age, he turned very nasty indeed.

Her reign in Chicago lasted for about four years during which time she was estimated to have gained over half a million dollars by blackmail. Her victims' lives were never the same again, even after they had paid their dues. The head of one huge steel combine went straight to the police, only to find that the high ranking officer to whom he complained was already in her pay. Another threatened to shoot her but was frightened off by her henchmen. One younger man she had seduced then bled to the point of ruin, killed himself.

Just when she was at the height of her career in Chicago, the Press decided to run a series of exposure articles that would involve not only some very distinguished citizens but also her part in their corrupt goings on. She was told to quit before something unpleasant happened to her.

May felt that what she had done in Chicago she could do anywhere else. She packed up her sables and headed for New York. Eddie followed in a very short time. But as she drifted round the luxury hotels, planning her campaign, she began to have an unpleasant feeling that things were not going to work out. The social scene in New York was entirely different. She had no contacts. And the top criminals, sensing that she spelled trouble, didn't want to know her. The police, having been warned by their colleagues in Chicago hinted that they had enough evidence to put her away for a long stretch. It was all going wrong. May decided there was only one thing to do. She had to return to Europe.

She started her tour of the major European cities in high style. Booking herself into the most expensive and fashionable hotels she performed her old routine and, for a year or two, tasted something of her old success. In Berlin she managed to separate a great industrialist from a quarter of a million marks. In Vienna she compromised a prince of a royal house and the family paid a huge sum to get her out of their lives. It was the sort of thing she thrived on.

Eventually she crossed the Channel to London, booked into a luxury hotel and prepared to start work. London was not as easy as she had expected. The British male, she found, was far more reticent, more suspicious than his counterpart in America or on the Continent. She made a few minor conquests but had to admit to herself that she had failed. Was it anything to do with the fact that too many late nights and too much brandy had coarsened her skin, left pouches under her eyes and added an inch or two to her exquisite figure?

With great relief she heard that her old lover Eddie Guerin had arrived in Paris and wanted her to join him. She found him staying in seedy lodgings in Montmartre, planning the biggest job of his criminal life. He was going to break into the strong room of the American Express Company. After that, he promised her, they could both retire.

The night that Eddie and his gang blew the safes and brought out nearly half a million dollars in American currency, May was standing on a street corner, playing the uncharacteristic role of look out. She wouldn't have done it for any other man. The money had to be moved out of the country without delay. Every minute counted. The gang split up and began swiftly to put their plan into operation. But they were not quick enough. An informer gave the French police two names: Eddie and Chicago May. They were picked up as they were packing their suitcases with dollars.

Eddie knew he was finished but when May denied she had taken any part in the raid he backed her up. The French police were pretty sure she had been an accomplice but they let her go, content that they had managed to capture one of the most dangerous bank robbers in the world. But May loved Eddie. Though she had managed to escape to London she couldn't bear to think she might not see him for years. She returned to Paris to see him in prison before his trial and this time the French authorities pounced. She was sentenced to five years imprisonment for her part in the robbery. She nearly collapsed when she heard that Eddie had been sent to the dreaded French penal colony on Devil's Island for life.

When she came out of prison she had to face the fact that her beauty was fading fast. The sort of life she had led was etched on her face. Back in London she set up her own organisation: the Northumberland Avenue Gang. She was deep into blackmail again but this time using prostitutes. It was a lucrative but dangerous racket and, to her cost, May found that the police in London were not, on the whole, open to corruption. When the law caught up with the Northumberland Avenue Gang many of its members were arrested but May managed to slip through a back door and lie low.

Next time she surfaced, it was in another trade. With her looks no longer what they were and her gang dispersed she decided to give up blackmail. With the money she had saved she opened a plush opium den only a stone's throw from Picadilly Circus. It became a 'must' for young male tourists who wanted to see the *real* London and soon she added a brothel as an extra attraction. As Gerald Sparrow writes in his account of her life: 'The whole thing was filthy, unsavoury and weird and attracted the dregs of humanity.'

One morning May heard a sharp knock on her front door and opened it to find Eddie Guerin standing there. The shock was almost too much for her. He had escaped from Devil's Island – in one of the greatest prison breaks ever made – and had come to find her. She still loved him but she knew how much she had changed and wondered if she could hold him.

For the first six months they were happy enough together then May started to notice any attention Eddie gave to younger women. Soon she was jealous of every female he looked at. There were violent scenes and Eddie's eyes became colder and colder. One day he vanished as suddenly as he had appeared. He had taken with him an eighteen-year-old girl who was working for her.

When May realised what had happened she went beserk. In her fury and jealousy she only knew she had to destroy him. She hired a young professional gunman and became obsessed with hunting him down. The terrible confrontation came one afternoon in a street in Bloomsbury. As soon as May saw Eddie with his girl friend she rushed at him with a knife, but the gunman shot him before she could use it. They left him sprawled on the pavement in a pool of blood with the girl sobbing over his body.

By some miracle Eddie Guerin did not die. He lost several pints of blood but the doctors pulled him through and he went on living. Chicago May was arrested in 1926 and charged with attempted murder, along with her hired gun. There was no trace left of her golden haired beauty. She sat huddled in the dock like an old woman and when they sentenced her to fifteen years she turned and left the court without saying a word.

Tzu-hsi – The Dragon Empress

The hatred and cruelty of one woman, Tzu-hsi, Dragon Empress of China, came to a terrifying climax in the celestial city of Peking one hot summer's day in 1900.

At the height of the Boxer rebellion – that great upsurgence of Chinese against foreigners and Christians – the French cathedral was burned to the ground killing hundreds of men, women and children. She watched the blaze from a nearby hill. Her order for a ceasefire in the bombardment came, not from mercy, but because her head ached.

While the red turbaned hooligans she championed rampaged around the city yelling 'Burn, burn, burn, Kill, kill, kill' she was engaged in painting delicate designs of bamboo on silk or arranging exquisite water picnics on the palace lake. While Christians were massacred, thousands of Chinese converts among them, she tended her four-inch-long finger nails, shielded with jade, and tottered round her gardens in jewel-encrusted shoes.

'Let no one escape,' she had ordered 'so that my Empire may be purged. . . .' Her soldiers were offered money for the heads of Europeans. Yet many of those who barricaded themselves in the British Legation and staunchly held out until rescue, remembered taking tea with her and being charmed, especially when she confided that she had a great admiration for Queen Victoria and kept a photograph of her beside her bed.

This extraordinary, complex woman, who controlled the destiny of 400 million people for nearly 50 years, believed herself to be the cleverest woman in the world. But eventually her feudal outlook, her conviction that China was the centre of the world and that all foreigners were barbarians, brought about the end of the great Ch'ing dynasty. Her death in 1908 opened the floodgates to change.

Though she stood only five feet tall her appearance was often dramatised, especially in her youth, by mask like make-up and magnificent garments jewelled and fantastically embroidered in brilliant colours. Her raven black hair was never cut. She took great care of her appearance and her health, eating vast amounts of milk curdled with rennet but only small amounts of other foods, always of the finest quality.

She was the daughter of a minor Manchu mandarin. Born in November 1835 her destiny, according to the structure of the society she lived in, was to become a concubine. She was sent to the Imperial court at the age of 16 and a contemporary description of her, given in Marina Warner's biography of the Dragon Empress, is enchanting. Like all Manchu girls she whitened her face and rouged two spots of high colour on her cheeks. Her bottom lip was painted in a scarlet cherry drop. Sometimes she added blue to her eyelids and outlined her eyes with khol. Above this mask-like visage her hair was gathered up from the nape of the neck into an enormous, weighty decoration of jewels, shaped like flowers and insects, which fanned out on either side and hung down with tassels of pearls. She wore the Manchu costume of tunic and trousers in vivid silk and her shoes had a central high wedge hung with pearls and encrusted with jewels.

But she was only one of 3,000 concubines and 3,000 eunuchs whose lives were dedicated to the dissolute 20-year-old Emperor, Hsien-Feng. She was of the fifth and lowest rank and it was quite likely that she would never even meet him, but would spend her days as an exalted servant. Given the name Imperial Concubine Yi she set out to make what she could of her position. The palace had a fine library and as, unlike most girls, she had learned to read and write, she took every advantage of the books and scholarly tutors now available to her. She also befriended and flattered the 15-year-old concubine of higher ancestry who had been chosen to be Hsien-Feng's wife.

After three years her cunning was rewarded. The Empress proved barren and one night she was sent for to share the Emperor's bed. Nine months later, in April 1856, she gave birth to a son, his Imperial Majesty's only male child.

Her status was immediately enhanced. The powerful eunuchs, who infiltrated and dominated court life with their intrigue and malicious gossip, sensed a new star rising and gathered round her. Tzu-hsi never underestimated their influence and enjoyed their silken subservience. Hsien-Feng was amazed at his new concubine's grasp of affairs and her dynamic energy and in the end found it easier to let her take part in politics and run things for him. Effeminate, weak and ill he seemed unable to cope with the terrible wars launched by the Taiping rebels in the north. When these troubles were added to by an invasion of North China by joint forces of England and France, it was the last straw.

To escape the advancing 'foreign devils' the royal court fled from Peking to Jehol, away in the mountains. Signs of a shift in power came with a special decree from the royal palace ordering the decapitation of all prisoners as a warning to the 'bandits' who had dared to invade the Forbidden City. The voice that gave that order was not the Emperor's but that of the Concubine Yi.

Blood flowed in Peking but Hsien-Feng's brother, the statesmanlike Prince Kung, was wise enough to realize that the killing of Europeans could not go on. China's only hope lay in submission. He ignored further imperial decrees and made a peace treaty with the French and English.

The Emperor was to return to his capital in the spring of 1861 but before the winter storms had ceased, he was dead. His Empress and Tzu-hsi became regents. At the first sign of good weather they set out on the long, stony road from Jehol to Peking, taking the child Emperor with them. They had been warned of a plot by conspiritors who wanted to seize power and who planned to kill the two regents and leave their bodies for the vultures. The royal route over the wild mountain passes was changed at the last minute.

All eyes were on Tzu-hsi as she made a triumphal entry into Peking with her son, borne shoulder high on a yellow throne through streets hung with yellow banners and strewn with yellow sand.

This was the point at which she had to decide who were her friends and who were her enemies. The Empress Niuhuru had no interest in political power, so could be discounted. But Tzu-hsi gave orders immediately that Su Shun, the wealthy man behind the assassination plot, was to be decapitated and his supporters ordered to commit suicide. She grabbed his estates and laid the foundations of an immense fortune.

Civil war at its most terrible raged through five provinces and 20 million people died in the first years of her reign, as the Taiping rebellion continued to run its terrible course in the mountains of the north. During these years she relied heavily on the wisdom of Prince Kung. He saw her every day, taught her state craft and did his best to curb her war-like tendencies.

At first their meetings were conducted with the strictest formality and etiquette. As time went by, however, Prince Kung became a little too familiar for Tzu-hsi's liking. She had had enough of the pupil-teacher relationship and decided to get rid of him.

Her moment came in the fourth year of her regency. One day Prince Kung absentmindedly started to rise from his knees during a long and tedious audience. (A judicial rule of etiquette forbade anyone to stand in the sovereign's presence to safeguard against attack). Tzu-hsi shrieked for help, worked herself into a terrible rage and claimed that he had moved towards the throne to attack her. He was seized by eunuchs, dragged from her presence and stripped of all honours and duties.

Later, probably because she could not do without him, she extended her forgiveness and he was re-admitted to the Grand Council. But she had made her point. She had brought down the most powerful man in the country, and subjugated him to her will.

Her private life became more and more extravagant and she encouraged her officials to increase taxes on an already impoverished Chinese people in order to keep the Dragon Court in feudal magnificence. Still not satisfied she began selling all positions of authority for large donations to her coffers.

Meanwhile, the young Emperor, Tung Cheh, was being brought up in a hot-house environment dominated by painted concubines and eunuchs. It was as though Tzu-hsi was plotting his downfall from the very beginning, looking ahead to the day when he assumed power and she would no longer be needed. She indulged the eunuchs and took no notice of the terrible influence they had on him from the earliest age. By fifteen it was obvious that he had all his father's ambi-sexual tastes and was steeped in debauchery. The eunuchs planned orgies and she encouraged them to introduce him to the whores in the back streets of Peking.

By 1872, when he was 16, he was considered old enough to marry and daughters of Manchu officials were ordered to appear at the Palace. He chose as his bride a beautiful 18-year-old girl called Alute who proved to have brains as well as looks. Tzu-hsi became fiercely jealous of her and extremely angry when she realized that Alute was encouraging the wretched Tung Cheh to think for himself and resist the influence of the eunuchs. But it was too late.

When the time came for the young Emperor to assume the throne officially and for Tzu-hsi to retire and do her embroidery, her chagrin was felt in every corner of the Forbidden City. She gave orders that the old Imperial Summer Palace, destroyed by the British and French, should be rebuilt for her in all its glory. Vast sums were raised for the purpose but many, Prince Kung among them, complained of such extravagance while China was still suffering from the terrible results of the Taiping rebellion. The rebuilding was abandoned and Tzu-hsi shut herself away in fury.

She did not have long to wait. The Emperor's exploits with the whores and transvestites of Peking were beginning to take their toll. He was found to be suffering from venereal disease then his weakened frame succumbed to smallpox. Little was done to help him. In the flowery language of the court, he 'Ascended the Dragon' on 13 January 1875. He was only 19.

His loving Empress, Alute, had never left his bedside. Tzu-hsi hearing her complain to him of her overbearing ways flew into one of her terrible rages and ordered the eunuchs to take her away and beat her. Alute was pregnant and there was no doubt among court officials that Tzu-hsi had made up her mind to get rid of the girl before the birth of her child.

On the day of her son's death, sitting on the Dragon throne with the compliant Niuhuru by her side, she called a Grand Council. Tung had left no heir. An Emperor had to be chosen. Sweeping aside all tradition she insisted it should be her nephew, the son of her only sister. She was flagrantly manipulating the ancient dynastic law and only ten men dared to defy her. She made a note of their names. She could not stand opposition and had unscrupulous methods of getting rid of those who stood in her path.

She immediately adopted her nephew, Kuang-hsu. The thin, delicate three-year-old was fetched in the middle of the night, hastily dressed in imperial robes and taken to pay homage at the bier of his dead cousin. On 25 February 1875 he became Emperor. Tzu-hsi knew she could remain in power as regent for another decade at least. The neglected, humiliated Empress Alute, denied the succession for her expected child and made ill by her mother-in-law's treatment, killed herself with an overdose of opium. It was even said in some quarters that Tzu-hsi had ordered her to commit suicide because her presence was repugnant to her.

With the arrival of Kuang-hsu unexpected rivalry grew up between the two regents. The child was obviously terrified of Tzu-hsi and much preferred the gentle Niuhuru. Stories vary as to the actual nature of the dispute which finally brought about the latter's death, but it is known that one afternoon Tzu-hsi sent her some rice cakes, and by the evening she was dead.

After that the Dragon Empress ruled alone as regent for six years, her constant companion being the chief eunuch, Li Lien Ying, a corrupt, avaricious, cruel man who was, nevertheless, utterly devoted to her. She totally dominated the young emperor, a languid, listless youth with 'a voice like a mosquito'. He was said to have been frightened of her and one can understand why. A court official, describing her rage said; 'Her eyes poured out straight rays, her cheekbones were sharp and the veins on her forehead projected. She showed her teeth....'

In 1887 Kuang-hsu attained his majority and the regent, now 55, went into retirement. She chose a luxurious retreat just outside Peking, where she could keep a close watch on him. What she saw amazed her. The Emperor was not the puppet she had supposed. He had, in fact, a thirst for Western knowledge and ideas and visions of ending the repressive regime he had inherited and creating something nearer to European democracies. Tzu-hsi had married him to her niece, a bad tempered, plain girl who created trouble from the start. He much preferred his two senior concubines, Pearl and Lustrous, who were educated women and had sympathy with his ideas.

Though he always treated her with great respect, Tzu-hsi came to hate him for his outward looking politics. There was only one sort of China for her and that was the China of her ancestors. She set her chief eunuch to spy on him and blamed him for China's humiliating war with Japan whereas the blame in fact lay at her doorstep for she had ruined the navy by taking funds.

Great bitterness developed between Tzu-hsi and her nephew. At last he decided the only solution was to kill her favourite, Jung Lu, and imprison her. But he was betrayed by officials who feared what changes the coup might bring and instead found himself a prisoner.

The Dragon Empress

The enraged Dowager Empress as she was now called, dared not kill him but had all his attendants put to death or banished and replaced them with her own. Pearl, Kuang-hsu's concubine, knelt before her imploring her to spare the Emperor further humiliation. She even dared to suggest that as Kuang-hsu was the lawful sovreign anyway she had no right to set aside the mandate of heaven. Tzu-hsi dismissed her and had her imprisoned.

As for the pitiful young Emperor with his dreams of a better world, his reign was virtually ended. She kept him in solitary confinement and re-instated herself as regent. But the rest of the world was becoming interested in China, which had been a closed book for centuries, and there was great sympathy for Kuang-hsu. The British Minister went so far as to say that foreign countries would view with displeasure and alarm his sudden demise. She was incensed by this sympathy for him and her old hatred of 'foreign devils' began to fester.

The Boxer movement started among gangs of reactionary youths in the Kuan district of Shantung. They were violently anti-foreign and derived their name from the gymnastic exercises and shadow boxing they performed to work themselves into a frenzy. Their blood chilling rites and ceremonies were accompanied by cries of 'Exterminate the barbarians.' But as they were fiercely loyal to the Ch'ing Dynasty and fanatically nationalistic, Tzu-hsi chose to regard them as a 'people's army' and gave them support.

Soon the killing and the burning began. No missionary or Chinese convert was safe. Some of her ministers dared to warn all Europeans to get out while they could; they were beheaded. When a dispatch came from the foreign ministers demanding her immediate abdication and the restoration of the Kuang Emperor she roared 'How dare they question my authority – let us exterminate them.'

Appalled by what was going on, foreign governments made plans to invade China and rescue those who were holding out, mostly in the only important European building left standing – the British Legation. An international force landed and captured Tientsin, then started moving up the railway line to Peking. The Dowager Empress watched with dismay as turmoil grew in the city and people began fleeing to the hills. As foreign troops drew nearer she made no attempt to control what was happening but made plans to leave with the Emperor.

All the concubines were ordered to appear before her, the Emperor's favourite, Pearl, among them. The unfortunate girl who had still not learned her lesson, suggested that the Emperor's place was in Peking. Tzu-hsi was in no mood for argument. 'Throw this wretched minion down the well' she ordered. Pushing aside Kuang-hsu who fell on his knees pleading with her to spare the concubine's life, she ordered 'Let her die at once.' There was certainly no time to waste. The enemy was at the gates. Dressed as peasants and riding on an old cart, Tzu-hsi and her nephew fled Peking.

For the first time in her life the Dowager Empress began to experience what it was like to live as an ordinary Chinese. During the first days in exile she had to sleep like the poorest traveller in wretched, flea-ridden inns and eat the coarse common porridge made from millet. She saw the suffering of peasant families and professed pity for them, handing out gifts of money, and saying she had not appreciated their plight in the seclusion of her palace.

But she did not have to share their life for long. Even in exile she was soon surrounded by luxury. With great relief she heard on 1 June 1901 that peace terms had been agreed and she could fix a date for the court's return. Fully convinced that she would be exempt from blame, she left for Peking in a blaze of pageantry with silk banners, painted lanterns and flowers. Before she entered the city she made offerings to the river god.

She gradually managed to convince herself that she had nothing to do with the atrocities and greeted every foreigner she met with the utmost charm and civility. She demanded that history be rewritten and all decrees favouring the Boxers wiped from the records. At last she realized the full power of the western world and in the last few years of her life issued edicts that brought about major reforms that even Kuang-hsu would have approved.

The Emperor had been badly treated ever since their return from exile. He was given insolent eunuchs to serve him, provided with stale and unpalatable food and when the rest of the palace was converted to electricity, his apartments were left out.

But the end was very near for both of them, an extraordinary end that could have been a twist of fate but was more likely due to human venom.

In the summer of 1907 the Dowager Empress suffered a slight stroke and the following year became weak and ill with dysentry. Her usually robust health seemed to be failing. As she took to her bed, the Emperor became desperately ill and took to his. He was suffering from a disease of the kidneys and his health was ruined, but the doctor who was fetched to see him found him writhing in agony and suffering from symptoms he had never seen before. Kuang-hsu lay back on his satin cushions and died early in the morning on 14 November 1908. Before he died he scribbled a curse on the woman who had put him on the throne.

Twenty-four hours later Tzu-hsi asked for the traditional robe of longevity, turned her face to the south, and died. Those present said when told of the Emperor's death she had seemed relieved. Had she, in a last act of hatred had him poisoned? No one could be quite sure.

She was buried with great splendour. Twenty years after her funeral bandits broke into her tomb and stole the treasure that had been buried with her. Her body was carelessly flung to one side.

The Rat Poisoner
LYDIA SHERMAN

Wherever Lydia Sherman went she found buildings infested with rats. Or at least that was the story she told the neighborhood druggists from whom she bought her poison.

The arsenic soon eliminated the rats and, as it turned out, some of the human beings she considered a nuisance, too. As many as 42 people are believed to have died by Lydia's hand.

Married to patrolman Edward Struck of the New York Police Department, the sturdy but attractive housewife kept a low profile until 1864. Then Struck was sacked by the police for a shabby display of cowardice and promptly turned into an unemployed drunk. Lydia put him to bed one evening with a lethal snack of oatmeal gruel and rat poison.

Puzzled as to the manner of his death, the doctor blamed it on 'consumption' but made up his mind to ask for an official investigation. But Lydia had ensured her husband had a quick burial and the authorities saw no reason to intrude on her 'grief'.

One by one Lydia's children died – Mary Ann, Edward, William, George, Ann Eliza, and finally the widow's namesake, tiny toddler Lydia. In every case she shrewdly called in a different doctor, all of whom obligingly took her word for the cause of death.

When the people of San José, California, heard the fate of local kidnap victim Brooke Hart, they decided to seek vengeance. In 1933, Brooke Hart, a 22-year-old heir to a hotel chain, was kidnapped by garage worker Thomas Thurmond and his old schoolfriend John Holmes. The pair attacked him with a brick, weighted him down and threw him into the sea. To their amazement Hart came to and began yelling, so they shot him.

Thurmond and Holmes demanded $40,000 from Hart's father for the 'safe return' of his son. But the police traced the kidnappers' phone calls and the evil couple were arrested. When Brooke Hart's body was discovered, a raging mob broke into Santa Clara Jail, put out one of Holmes' eyes and then hung him and Thurmond from nearby trees.

An ex-brother-in-law went to the authorities swearing Lydia was 'full of black evil' and demanding that the bodies be exhumed. But the bored bureaucrats refused to budge.

Lydia moved from one job to another. In 1868 she married an aging and rich widower named Dennis Hurlbut. With rat poison available at 10 cents a package, he was soon out of the way.

That left her free to marry Nelson Sherman, who took her with him to his Connecticut home. There she had problems, including a suspicious mother-in-law and the four Sherman children by a previous marriage.

Two of the children she disposed of at once. Mourning the death of his 14-year-old daughter, Addie, Nelson Sherman turned to alcohol and thus signed his own death warrant.

'I just wanted to cure him of the liquor habit,' Lydia said.

A Connecticut doctor was suspicious and insisted that his stomach and liver be analyzed. Toxicologists found enough arsenic to kill an army. The vital organs of the two children were also permeated with poison.

Pleading that she had murdered out of human compassion – 'all those people were sick, after all' – the fashionably dressed widow cut an impressive figure at her trial in New Haven, Connecticut. And in a way, her luck held. Amazingly gentle with the not so gentle murderess, Judge Park instructed the jury to consider only charges of second-degree murder.

Sentenced to life in Weathersfield Prison, she vowed she would never die in jail. But there her luck did end – she was still behind bars when she died in 1878.

Livia

Livia was one of the most cruelly ambitious women the world has ever known. Her portrait was painted with fine precision by Robert Graves in his book '*I, Claudius*' as the she-wolf of all the Roman Empresses.

She was the wife of the great Caesar Augustus, who owed at least some of his glory to her, but her passion for personal power led her to such acts of treachery that she stands alone.

Her family was one of the most illustrious in Rome and her ancestral stock more ancient than Rome itself. She had a high bred kind of beauty and a disdainful air that came naturally to her. Her mind ranked as one of the finest but when she chose to she could ensnare men with her seductive manner.

When she was at the height of her beauty and married to Tiberius Nero, Augustus became intrigued by her. Caesar was then in his prime, a splendid looking man with fair, tightly curled hair, a typical Roman nose and sparkling eyes. He was also blessed with an affable temperament, except when at war when he was as cruel as any. He found Livia, with her satin smooth charm, vastly different from his wife, the odd and gloomy Scribonia.

Livia could not have left Augustus in doubt for long about her own feelings for she was soon pregnant and general gossip assumed the child to be his. Unfortunately Tiberius Nero was an old enemy and could not be bought. So, taking the bull by the horns, Augustus asked Tiberius to give him his wife and left him in no doubt as to what would happen if he refused. It did not take the lady long to assess who would further her ambitions better.

Augustus consulted the oracles pretending to be anxious about whether he might marry a woman already with child. The oracles were favourable, so the wedding took place. Tiberius was asked to give her away and, perhaps to soothe his ruffled ego, was guest of honour at the great feast that followed.

Three months later Livia had a son who was named Drusus. Augustus sent the baby to be brought up by Tiberius in case it should be thought his own, but ribald jokes about who was really the father caused a great deal of laughter among the ordinary people.

Two historic battles soon separated the Emperor of Rome and his new Empress. In the first he defeated the great Roman general, Pompey, in one of the bloodiest battles known at that time. He went on to bring an end to Mark Anthony at the famous battle of Actium, after which Cleopatra took the asp and killed herself rather than be taken back to Rome in triumph.

Augustus returned home to be loaded with honour and glory and Livia basked luxuriously in its reflection. A town called Liviada was built in her honour. She was given the most pompous titles, poets celebrated her in verse and temples were erected in her name.

Victory meant a time of peace. In Rome Augustus anticipated all her wishes so that in time her authority was as absolute as his own. She always showed great tenderness towards him, but there was also a great deal of art and cunning in her behaviour, which he did not find out until it was too late. She took care at that stage that nobody should have anything to reproach her with. One day, some young men, sporting about, had appeared before her stark naked. They were condemned to death but she had them pardoned saying that a naked man made no more impression on the imagination of a virtuous woman than a statue.

Her two sons, Tiberius by her former husband, and Drusus, grew to be men. She saw to it that they were given important status in the Roman army and that their victories, however trivial, were treated as triumphs. Tiberius was cruel and arrogant and addicted to debauchery of the worst kind. Augustus gave his opinion that if he ever came to power he would cause the greatest misery and suffering. Drusus, on the other hand, was such a fine man that the Emperor would have liked to have named him as his successor but felt it would confirm peoples' suspicions that he was his own son.

As it was he chose his nephew and son-in-law, Prince Marcellus as heir presumptive, a soldier he considered to have noble qualities. This was not what Livia had in mind. Her one aim now was to pave the way to the throne for her son, Tiberius. Soon after Augustus had made his announcement, Prince Marcellus died in great agony. Livia had struck her first blow.

As if in answer, fate threw a tragedy across her path. Her son Drusus was killed on his way back to Rome after a battle. Her grief was so great that philosophers were sent for to give her what comfort they could. From then on she became more deadly and doubled her efforts for Tiberius. With Prince Marcellus out of the way she thought matters could be arranged quite easily for she had advised Augustus so skilfully in other matters that he began to think her always right. But then he took the step of marrying his daughter, Julia, widow of Prince Marcellus, to Agrippa. She gave birth to two sons, Gaius and Lucius, both in direct line to the throne. For a time there was nothing Livia could do.

But as the years passed and Augustus grew older she determined afresh to get rid of any obstacle that stood between her son and the throne. She made her plans without any outward show of treachery or violence, like a snake creeping up in the night. By now the Emperor was completely under her domination and her word had become, if anything, more respected in Rome than his. People did not dare disobey her.

The day came when the two young princes Gaius and Lucius met sudden and tragic ends, the first in Lycia as he was returning from war, the second in Marseilles. People were aghast at the awfulness of the tragedy and Augustus could not be comforted. Feeling that soon he would have no kin of his own left in the world, he adopted his daughter's youngest son, Agrippa, together with Tiberius. This step divided the Empire between his own grandson and Livia's son. He thought she would be pleased, but she was furious that all her well laid plans had ended in this. Agrippa had to be got rid of but another death, so soon, would not be satisfactory. She set to work to poison the Emperor's mind with malicious talk and rumours about his grandson, none of which were true. But Augustus, believing her implicitly, wept and had him banished to the island of Planasia. To all Rome the punishment seemed unjust and cruel. Agrippa had not the polished style of the other princes, but as far as anyone knew, this was his only crime.

Augustus often complained of his cruel destiny in losing one by one so many members of his family. He began to think back on all that had happened and suddenly longed to see Agrippa, the grandson he had exiled. He made up his mind to go to his island prison. He kept his visit a secret from anyone, even Livia, for perhaps at last he was beginning to have suspicions. Only his friend Fabius Maximus knew. But this man told his wife and his wife told Livia. This produced such venom, such anger, that Caesar should have acted without her knowledge, that she made the most terrible decision of all – to kill Augustus and his grandson.

Even with her smooth tongue she could not conceal her true feelings on his return, when she told him there was 'no occasion for all this secrecy.' One day at his palace in Nola, lying in the very room where his father, Octavius, had died, she brought him a dish of figs. He ate them with pleasure, but they were full of poison. As he died, Augustus spoke to Livia with words of tenderness, but those close enough thought they saw a light of dawning horror in his eyes.

His death was kept secret for some time because Tiberius was absent. Livia fretted and paced her palace floors willing her son to come home. As soon as he arrived, the death of Augustus and the succession of Tiberius were announced simultaneously. Poor Agrippa was murdered. Livia said that Augustus had ordered it in his will but everyone knew this was just another of her crimes.

The Romans, by now afraid of this she-wolf, lavished fresh honours and titles upon her. This was just what she had schemed for. Now, the glory of being mother of the Emperor would give her even greater stature. But she had not reckoned with Tiberius. She had bred a son worthy of her.

He was jealous of her honours, looking upon them as diminishing his own stature. He gave orders that her household was not to be increased by a single

Livia

officer. He was in fact indifferent to her. She irritated him by constantly reminding him that he owed his throne to her.

This ingratitude did not stop her. She took every step necessary to ensure that he should reign without trouble or threat. She persecuted all those of Augustus's family she had still left alive. However, there was still Prince Germanicus, her own grandson, who, like his father, Drusus, was brave and honest. Tiberius himself was jealous of his fame, hated hearing of his triumphs and resented his victories. Orders were sent to Syria where he was in charge of the army and he was killed by poison.

Mother and son grew further apart. Tiberius hated Livia's boundless ambition. The pomp and magnificence with which she surrounded herself were anathma to him. He was just in time to stop her putting her name before that of Augustus on a memorial dedicated to the great Caesar.

Finally, to escape her, he left Rome and went to Capri where he spent the rest of his life indulging his taste for nameless debauchery. Livia reigned absolute in his place. She enjoyed herself and lived until she was 80. When news of her end was carried to Tiberius in Capri he said he could not go to Rome. He excused himself with weak stories of ill health and other difficulties, but it was thought he dared not let it be seen how terribly his appalling life had aged him.

Livia was placed in a mausoleum with Augustus, and her grandson, Caligula, pronounced her funeral oration. The senate wanted to make her a goddess, but Tiberius, in a fit of retaliation would not allow it. He said he did not think she would want such a thing. At that, she must have stirred in her grave.

Elizabeth Bathory

The Countess Elizabeth Bathory who lived in the Carpathian mountains in the 16th century was one of the original vampires who inspired Bram Stoker's legend of Dracula.

She was Hungarian by birth. Records give her entry into the world as

Countess Elizabeth Bathory

1561. As a girl she was beautiful with long fair hair and an exquisite complexion. She was married off to an aristocratic soldier when she was fifteen and became mistress of the Castle of Csejthe in the Carpathians.

Life in the dark, gloomy Csejthe Castle, while her husband was away on his various military campaigns, became very boring indeed. She was determined to liven things up.

First she gathered round her a sinister band of witches, sorcerers and alchemists who taught her the black arts. Then, armed with her special flesh-tearing silver pincers, a manual of tortures her husband had used when fighting the Turks and a taste for flagellation learned from her aunt, she set out to indulge herself and while away the lonely hours.

When her husband died in 1604 she had reached the difficult age of 43. She longed for a new lover to replace him but her reflection in the mirror showed her that time and indulgence had not improved her looks. One day she slapped the face of a servant girl and drew blood with her nails. She was convinced that that part of her body where the girl's blood had dripped was much fresher and younger than before. It only needed the alchemists to add their opinion and she was convinced that drinking and bathing in the blood of young virgins would preserve her beauty for ever.

So, at the dead of night, the Countess and her cronies would tear about the countryside hunting for girls. They would be taken back to the castle, hung in chains and their blood used for the countess' bath, the finest saved for her to drink.

The terrible woman carried on like this for five years until she began to realize the blood of peasant girls had not been terribly effective. In 1609 she turned to the daughters of her own class. Offering to take in 25 girls at a time to teach them social graces, she soon had a flourishing academy.

Helped as usual by her peasant procuress, Dorotta Szentes, know as Dorka, she treated the 'pupils' with the same inhuman cruelty as she had treated the others. But this time she became too careless. The bodies of four girls were thrown over the castle walls. Before she realized her mistake villagers collected them and took them away to be identified. Her secret was out.

News of her reign of terror finally reached the ears of the Hungarian Emperor, Matthias II. He ordered that the Countess be brought to trial. But as an aristocrat she could not be arrested, so Parliament passed a new Act so that she would not be able to slip throught their hands. At her hearing in 1610 it was said she had murdered 600 girls.

Dorka and her witches were burnt at the stake. The Countess escaped execution because of her noble birth. But she was condemned to a living death – walled up in a tiny room of her castle and kept alive by scraps of food pushed through the bars. She died four years later without a word of remorse.

The Missing Mormon

If a Mormon missionary were suspected of raping a beauty queen, the affair would provide ample material for sensational news treatment. But when, in 1977, a beauty queen was suspected of raping a Mormon missionary, the case had all the makings of a grand press block-buster. The newspapers went wild over the saga of Kirk Anderson and Joyce McKinney, devoting such an acreage of newsprint to it at one stage that the *Daily Mail* was constrained to advertise itself as 'The Paper *Without* Joyce McKinney'.

The story first broke in September 1977, with the disappearance and subsequent reappearance of American missionary Kirk Anderson. The *Sunday Times* noted on the 18th of that month:

> The Mormon missionary missing in Surrey turned up yesterday and said he had been kidnapped and held handcuffed and manacled for three days – it is believed on the orders of a wealthy, lovesick woman.
>
> Kirk Anderson, 21, was released unharmed near Victoria Station in London and telephoned Scotland Yard to say he was returning to his home at Milton Gardens, Epsom, by train. However, he boarded the wrong train and ended up at Sutton a few miles away, and had to call the police to pick him up.

That slip-up by the luckless missionary was a portent of stranger things to come. Anderson told the police of how he had long been persecuted by a 29-year-old former girlfriend named Joyce McKinney. They had had a brief affair in Salt Lake City, the Mormons' worldwide headquarters, and when he broke with her she had begun to harass him. The missionary alleged that windows at his home had been smashed, car tyres ripped up and a car he was driving in was rammed. He moved from Utah to California – the girl followed him. After continued harassment, the Mormon asked to be sent to Britain to avoid her. But she would not give up. Anderson kept on running: from East Grinstead, to Reading and finally to Epsom.

It was at Epsom, the Mormon claimed, that the kidnapping had occurred. 'This seems to have been a case of hell hath no fury like a woman scorned', said the detective who had headed the search for Anderson. At Orem, in Utah, Anderson's parents declared their relief on hearing that their son was safe. 'We don't know anything about this girl', said Mrs Anderson. 'I personally think he has been living very close to the Lord.'

Joyce McKinney was arrested some time later, with a male accomplice named Keith Joseph May, aged 24. They were charged with abducting

Above: McKinney outside Epsom Court; Right: Anderson leaving court

Anderson, and, on a second charge, accused of possessing an imitation .38 revolver with intent to commit an offence. It was made known that Joyce McKinney had entered Britain on a false passport. Yet the first press accounts gave the impression of a tearful ingénue. From the back of the prison van taking her to court, the girl protested her innocence, handing out messages written on pages of the Bible. One read: 'Please ask Christians to pray for me.'

It was at a preliminary hearing in November that the salacious details on the affair started to hit the headlines. The 'Sex-in-Chains' case swept all other issues from the front pages of the popular press.

Opening for the prosecution, Anderson's counsel described the couple's brief affair in Utah in 1975, and Joyce McKinney's subsequent persecutions. He alleged that on 14 September, the girl and her accomplice had forced Anderson into a car outside his church, using an imitation revolver and a bottle of chloroform. The car sped off to a cottage in Devon where it arrived some five hours later. Miss McKinney had then told her captive that she was not going to let him go until he agreed to marry her.

There was no doubt that sexual intercourse had taken place at the cottage. Nor was there any doubt that Anderson was tied to a bed while the act took place. The point at issue was that Anderson claimed to have been the victim of forced sex, while McKinney alleged that the shackles were merely instruments of bondage games.

In Anderson's version, Keith May had fastened him to the bed with chains and a leather strap. 'Joy told me if there was to be a ransom, the ransom would be that I would have to give her a baby.' Asked how female rape could have occurred, Anderson replied: 'She had oral sex'.

On the third night of his captivity, the missionary said, he was completely spread-eagled on the bed: 'When she came into the room there was a fire in the fireplace and she put some music on. She was wearing a négligée. She came to me as I lay on the bed. I said I would like to have my back rubbed. She proceeded to do that but I could tell she wanted to have intercourse again. I said I did not.' She left and returned with Keith May who used chains, ropes and padlocks to tie him down on his back to the four corners of the bed. She tore the pyjamas from his body and had her way with him.

Anderson firmly refuted the suggestion that the bondage equipment was for sex games. But the back rub? Wasn't that highly erotic, and bound to court temptation? Anderson was aggrieved: 'I do not look at a back rub like that. My mom gives me a pretty good back rub, but that does not mean that I want sex with her.'

During cross-questioning, Anderson alluded to a bizarre accessory of his own – an article of clothing unknown to the general public. This was the Mormons' sacred undergarment.

Not only had Miss McKinney torn off his pyjamas; she had also violated a special one-piece undergarment which acted as a kind of male chastity belt. Anderson had since burnt the article. 'They are so sacred to me that anytime they are desecrated in any way the proper method to dispose of them is to burn them.'

Joyce McKinney's statements presented a very different version of events. Anderson had made love willingly, she said. They had indulged in oral sex and bondage games to sort out his sexual difficulties; he was lying, now, because he feared excommunication from the Mormon church.

'Mr Anderson lay willingly while I tied him up,' she said. 'If he had not, this little 120 lb girl could not have tied up a 250 lb, 6 ft 2 in man.' She was, in fact, terrified of Anderson's strength: 'His legs are as big round as my waist.' The missionary had revelled in the proceedings, and lay on the bed 'grinning like a monkey' and moving his hips with her.

McKinney invoked her own religious faith in her defence, claiming that back in Utah she had prayed for 'a very special boy' to come into her life. Anderson had 'teased me and kissed me until I was out of my mind.' In a much-quoted phrase, she declared: 'I loved Kirk so much I would have skiied down Mount Everest in the nude with a carnation up my nose.'

What was the public to make of it all? On the one hand, McKinney's protestations that 'this little girl' could not have tied down and ravished the hulking missionary carried some weight. But then, if Anderson was willing, what was Keith May's role in the affair? Her accomplice remained a somewhat shadowy figure. May's own counsel claimed that the Devon escapade was seen by his client as 'a rescue operation from the oppressive and tyrannical organisation' (the Mormon Church).

In all events, May and McKinney were granted bail prior to the trial proper, on condition that McKinney stayed indoors from 21.00 to 09.00 every night. On 13 March 1978, the conditions were eased so that the two defendants could go to the cinema in the evenings. The prosecution objected on the grounds that they might skip bail and flee the country. Nonsense, a spokesman for Miss McKinney insisted: 'She wants to remain in this country to clear her name.'

On 16 April, however, the world learned that the *Sex-in-Chains Girl* was missing. The police searched high and low – but to no avail.

What had happened was that, posing as a deaf mute, Joyce McKinney had fled to Canada. Safely across the Atlantic, having lost none of her old flair, she came out of hiding dressed as a nun.

The whole furore erupted again. Newspapers battled for exclusive interviews, and a legal war was waged between *Penthouse* (which claimed her own story) and the *Daily Express* (which published photographs and stories before the magazine reached the bookstalls). May 22 became Joyce McKinney Day as far as the popular press was concerned. The *Daily Mirror* managed to obtain a photograph of her in the nude. Lacking a comparable illustration, *The Sun* improvised by mocking up a montage of its own. Joyce McKinney's head was shown superimposed on the body of a naked woman skiing down snowy slopes – a carnation, of course, was shown protruding from a nostril.

'The gospel according to Mormon sex-in-chains girl Joyce McKinney is: Give a man what he wants,' blared the paper, and quoted the fugitive as saying, 'I'm a very old-fashioned girl. I believe that a man's home is his castle and that a husband should be pampered. All I wanted to do with Kirk was to satisfy and pleasure him. But he had deep inhibitions due to his upbringing. I wanted to get rid of those guilt feelings by doing sexually outrageous things to him in bed. I thought I had succeeded, but in the end the Mormon Church won.'

In reality, Joyce McKinney emerged as an all-American product. She was still remembered in North Carolina as a 'fine, fine girl', who had been a regular attender at Bible camp. As for being a beauty queen, the most that could be said was that she had once been elected Miss North Carolina High School. Her own account of her early affair with the missionary was described in true teen-magazine style. She had been out driving with a friend in her new Stingray convertible when the Mormon put his head through the window. 'I found myself gazing into the deepest pair of baby-blue eyes. He put Paul Newman to shame. My heart did flip-flops. I turned to my girlfriend and said: "Hey, get out – I'm in love"'. And of the affair which followed, Miss McKinney said: 'It was bombs, firecrackers, the Fourth of July every time he kissed me'.

Even her subsequent pursuit of the missionary seems to have been undertaken with a kind of blue-eyed innocence. According to a friend, she had visited skin-flicks and live sex acts in order to pick up tips on arousal. Then she placed an advertisement in an underground paper asking for 'a muscle man, a pilot and a preacher to help in a romantic adventure.' The proposed team was never assembled, but she managed to finance the trip to England with $15,000 paid to her by an insurance company for injuries received in a car crash.

Joyce McKinney's crime, if crime it was, had an ancient pedigree. She loved, not wisely, but too well. And after the last great orgy of confessions and interviews, the story died practically overnight. As far as the legal position was concerned, the fugitive forfeited her bail money, but proposals to extradite her for trial were abandoned.

For seven years, the case was almost forgotten. Then, in June 1984, newspapers announced, 'SEX-IN-CHAINS JOYCE IS AT IT AGAIN.' Incredibly, Joyce McKinney had hit the headlines for a new alleged harassment of Kirk Anderson. She was arrested in a car outside the ex-missionary's office at Salt Lake City, charged with disturbing the peace and giving false information to the police.

Anderson had married since the alleged kidnapping episode, and now worked for an airline company in Utah. It was the first time he had seen her in seven years. Anderson claimed that he had noticed Joyce shadowing him over the weekend and had stalked him to his office. He told police that he was very concerned she might be planning to snatch him again. A police spokesman said, 'When we arrested her we found a notebook detailing his every move. There were also pictures of Kirk and his wife Linda.'

A man was with Miss McKinney when the police swooped, but he was not arrested. Her lawyer, Jim Barber, said, 'She only wanted to see him for old times sake. She is writing a screenplay about her experiences and wanted to find out how the story ended.'

Alice Kyteler

In the dusty, mouldering pages of some 14th century archives lies the story of a beautiful woman, rich, influential, probably of Anglo Norman stock. She lived in the town of Kilkenny in Ireland where, it was recorded, she had been married to three wealthy husbands in succession and in the year 1324 was about to lose her fourth. Her name was Lady Alice Kyteler and she was one of the most sinister figures of her time.

Lady Alice was not popular with her neighbours partly because of her inordinate wealth, partly because of her arrogance and haughty, overbearing manner.

There were also rumours that her Ladyship was involved in the practice of witchcraft and sorcery, though no one could prove it.

Her first husband had been one William Outlawe, a banker and money lender who died before 1302. Then she married Adam le Blund of Callan who expired by 1311 to be followed by Richard de Valle who also went to his maker rather quickly.

Two of these husbands had been widowers with children who lost their inheritance when the besotted fellows left everything to Lady Alice. If they suspected foul play, they said nothing at the time.

However, when Lady Alice's fourth and latest husband, Sir John le Poer fell dangerously ill in 1324 with a wasting disease which made his nails fall from his fingers and toes and caused his hair to come out in handfuls, the children began to hint that their fathers had died from equally strange illnesses with similar symptoms.

Sir John, in love with his wife, did not want to hear what they were implying. But when one of his maid servants began to give such broad hints that it would have been foolish to ignore her, Sir John decided it was time for him to act.

He demanded his wife's key to her room. When she refused he seized her and after a struggle, wrenched it from her belt. A search soon brought to light a number of boxes and chests, all heavily padlocked. Forcing them open the wretched man found inside all the evidence he needed to prove that his wife was a poisoner and deeply involved in witchcraft.

Sir John gathered together all the strange powders, phials and potions, the wicked looking instruments and wafers of sacramental bread inscribed with the name of Satan and sent them, in the safekeeping of two monks, to the Bishop of Ossory, whose diocese it was. The Bishop was to prove a formidable prosecutor.

He was an English Franciscan named Richard De Ledrede, known to be a fanatic in hunting out those who dabbled in sorcery and a man greedy for funds. Should Lady Alice be found guilty her wealth would be confiscated by the church.

After an investigation the Bishop accused her of being involved in 'divers kinds of witchcraft' and ordered her arrest along with eleven accomplices including her own son William Outlawe and her personal maid, Petronilla de Meath.

The Bishop's indictment contained no fewer than seven formidable charges to which the inhabitants of Kilkenny listened with fascinated horror. Lady Alice, it emerged, had crept from her home in the dead of night to hold meetings with her accomplices in local churches where religious ceremonies were mocked and appalling rites performed. Living animals were sacrificed to the devil then, torn limb from limb, scattered at the cross roads. She had been expert in making charms and ointments from such hideous ingredients as the hair of criminals who had been hanged, nails from dead men's fingers, the intestines of animals, worms, poisonous herbs and flesh of babies who had died unbaptised.

All these things she was said to have boiled together in the skull of a robber who had been beheaded.

The indictment also included 'an unholy and obscure association' between Lady Alice and a demon called Robert Artisson who was described as her familiar and who would appear sometimes in the shape of a huge cat, at others like a shaggy beast or yet again in the disguise of a black prince with two tall companions, each carrying a rod in his hand. Lady Alice was said by her maid to have had sexual intercourse with this 'apparition'. Who was this creature?

Under the influence of witchcraft he was believed to be supernatural but in fact he was probably a fellow practitioner from another town or village. The Bishop cast his net wide to try to trap him, but he never succeeded. It was rumoured he must have been an educated man or a noble for no peasant would have had the wit or resource to have escaped Ossory's Inquisition for long.

That she had used her potions to kill her former husbands and to bring Sir John to the point of death was soon obvious. She had an insatiable greed for money. Her only true allegiance was to her favourite son, William Outlawe, who had proved a willing disciple in her diabolical craft. She used to perform a rite which was meant to make him rich. She would take a broom out into the streets of Kilkenny at sunset and raking all the dirt and dust towards the door of her son's house chant:

> 'To the house of William my son
> Hie all the wealth of Kilkenny town!'

It was one thing for the Bishop to order Lady Alice's arrest, quite another to take her into custody. He found himself obstructed on every side. Up to this time sorcery had been a secular crime, not under the jurisdiction of the Church so the Bishop had to ask the Lord Chancellor of Ireland to issue a writ for the arrest of the accused.

Unfortunately, the Chancellor was one Roger Outlawe, a kinsman by her first marriage who supported her.

Taking the law into his own hands, the Bishop sent two representatives to call her in person before the court of the Bishopric. She refused to accept his jurisdiction. The ecclesiastical court, she said, was not empowered to judge her or anyone else on a matter of this kind. Nevertheless, the court sat and the Bishop excommunicated her.

Her supporters took revenge by making him a prisoner in Kilkenny Castle for eighteen days and while he fretted and fumed the accused coolly indicted *him* in a secular court for defamation of character.

All this only served to stiffen the Bishop's resolve to get 'the Kyteler' in the end. Time after time he was asked to leave secular courts where he demanded her arrest. When at last, after being obstructed at every turn, permission came to bring the accused sorcerers to trial in an ecclesistical court, it was too late. The bird had flown. Helped by fellow aristocrats, the Lady Alice had gathered up her jewels and escaped to England where she lived for the rest of her days.

Her fellow witches were left to face the fire. Bishop Ossory found an ally in Lady Alice's husband, Sir John, who helped him to arrest William Outlawe. This gentleman begged to be reconciled with the church and pardon was granted him as long as he fulfilled certain penances and paid for the re-roofing of St Mary's Cathedral in Kilkenny.

Lady Alice's maid, Petronilla de Meath, eventually brought to trial with the other accomplices paid the greatest price. She was the first witch to be burned in Ireland. Yet, she declared, compared with Lady Alice she was a mere novice. Her mistress had taught her everything. She believed there was no more powerful witch in the world than her Ladyship, Alice Kyteler. The abandoned and unrepentant Petronilla went to the stake and was burned on 3 November 1324.

Lady Alice was tried and found guilty 'in absentia', but she remained safe as long as she stayed away from Ireland. The Kyteler case nevertheless became something of a landmark, not only because it was the first trial of its kind in Ireland.

The dusty, 14th century records also showed that by her instruction and teaching Lady Alice Kyteler had set out the complete witch creed for centuries to come.

The Fall River Axe Murders

LIZZIE BORDEN

According to the immortal rhyme, Lizzie Borden took an axe and gave her mother forty whacks; when she saw what she had done she gave her father forty one. But according to American justice, the 32-year-old spinster was not responsible for the bloody slaughter of Andrew J. Borden and his wife Abby. She was acquitted after a ten-day trial, and the courtroom rang with applause at the verdict. Ever since, the world has wondered why.

The Borden household at 92 Second Street in the Massachusetts cotton spinning town of Fall River had never been a happy one. Andrew was a crusty, puritanical character whose one aim in life was making money, and holding on to it. He had amassed half a million dollars from shrewd business dealings, first as an undertaker, then as a property speculator and banker. His first wife, Sarah Morse Borden, died in 1862, two years after giving birth to his second daughter, christened Lizzie Andrew because Borden wanted a boy. Borden married again two years later, but it was no love match. Abby Durfee Gray was a plain, plump woman of 37, more of a housekeeper than a wife. And there was no love lost between her and Borden's two girls. The elder sister Emma called her Abby. Lizzie called her Mrs Borden, refused to eat at the same table as her, and spoke with her only when it was essential.

Despite Borden's wealth, the family lived in conditions worse than many of the town's humble millworkers. The unsanitary whitewood house had staircases at the front and back, which was as well, because the friction in the family meant that bedroom doors upstairs were kept locked at all times, the parents reaching their room via the rear stairs, the girls using the front ones.

Lizzie's resentment of her stepmother, and the way they lived, boiled over when her father, whom she loved dearly, put up the money for Abby's sister, Mrs Whitehead, to buy the house from which she faced eviction. Borden presented the title deeds to his wife, and when Lizzie found out, she regarded it as further proof that Mrs Borden was only after her father's riches. Shortly afterwards, Mr Borden arrived home from business to be told by Lizzie that his wife's bedroom had been ransacked by a burglar. He reported the incident to police, but soon cut short their inquiries when it became clear that Lizzie herself had done the damage during 'one of her funny turns'.

Lizzie was plain, introspective and repressed with genteel pretensions. The curly-haired redhead had a small circle of very close friends. Though she belonged to the Women's Christian Temperance Union, was treasurer and secretary of the local Christian Endeavour Society, and taught a Sunday School of Chinese men at the local Congregational church, she spent most of her time in more solitary pursuits – fishing, or merely brooding at her bedroom window. There was plenty for her to brood about.

In the summer of 1892 Fall River sweltered in a heatwave. In May the tedium of the Bordens' lifestyle was interrupted when intruders twice broke into outhouses at the bottom of their garden. Mr Borden's reaction was somewhat bizzare. Sure that the intruders were after Lizzie's pet pigeons, he took an axe to the birds and decapitated them.

By August the heat had become so bad that Emma left to stay with friends in the country at Fairhaven, 20 miles away. Lizzie stayed at home for a special meeting of the Christian Endeavour Society. The weather made no difference to Mr Borden's plans for running an economical household. The family sat down to a monstrous joint of mutton, cooked by their only servant, an Irish girl called Bridget, and served up in various guises at every meal. Everyone except Lizzie was violently ill.

Although 4 August dawned as the hottest day of the year, the family routine went on just the same. After breakfast Mr Borden set out to check on his businesses; John Morse, brother of his first wife, who was staying for a few days, left to visit other relatives; Mrs Borden began dusting the rooms, and Bridget, still queasy from food poisoning, washed the windows. Lizzie came down later than the rest, and was soon seen ironing some clothes in the kitchen.

Shortly after 09.30, Mrs Borden, on her knees dusting in the spare bedroom upstairs at the front of the house, was struck from behind with a hatchet. It was a

---

Mystery will always surround 44-year-old Gilles de Rais, branded one of history's most shocking sadists. Once a lieutenant of Joan of Arc and a Marshal of France, he turned a life of near obscurity to one of notoriety.

He derived pleasure from sexual attacks on children and occasionally heightened the excitement by torturing or decapitating them first.

More than 120 children came into his evil clutches – all were first kidnapped then brutally murdered. After each of his sadistic adventures he sank into a coma. Finally, in 1440 he was sentenced to be strangled and then burned.

The axe allegedly used by Lizzie Borden

crushing blow to the head, and killed her instantly. But 18 more blows were inflicted on her before she was left in a room awash with blood.

Just before 11.00, Mr Borden arrived home to find the front door locked and bolted. Bridget the maid, by now cleaning the windows inside the house, went to let him in, and expressed surprise that the door was double locked. She heard a laugh behind her, and turned to see Lizzie coming down the front staircase, smiling.

Mr Borden was nearly 70, and walking in the morning heat had clearly tired him. Lizzie fussed round him, told him his wife had gone out after receiving a note about a sick friend, and settled him on the living room settee where he began to doze, his head resting on a cushion. Lizzie went back to the kitchen, and chatted to Bridget about some cheap dress material on sale in town. But Bridget was still feeling unwell, and decided to retire to her attic bedroom for a while. She heard the clock strike 11.00 as she went up the back stairs.

Ten minutes later she dashed downstairs again. She heard Lizzie shouting: 'Come down quick. Father's dead. Someone came in and killed him.' Lizzie would not let the maid into the living room – she sent her across the road to fetch the local doctor, a man called Bowen. He was out on a call. Lizzie then sent Bridget to fetch Alice Russell, one of her closest friends. By this time, the maid's rushing about had attracted the attention of neighbours. Mrs Adelaide

Churchill, who lived next door, spotted Lizzie looking distressed, and asked what was wrong. She was told: 'Someone has killed father.'

Mr Borden had been hacked to death in exactly the same way as his wife, though his head had been shattered with only ten blows. The hatchet had landed from behind as he slept, a tricky task as the settee was against a wall. Blood had splashed everything – wall, settee, floral carpet. Dr Bowen arrived and examined the body. The blows seemed directed at the eyes, ears and nose. He was completely satisfied the first blow had killed the old man. He placed a sheet over the body.

Mrs Russell and Mrs Churchill did their best to comfort the bereaved Lizzie, fanning her, dabbing her face with cold cloths, rubbing her hands. But both noticed that she did not really need comforting. She was not crying or hysterical, and she assured them she did not feel faint. She was still strangely calm when the police arrived, declining their offer of delaying the necessary interview until she had had a chance to rest.

At first suspicion fell on John Morse, who behaved strangely when he returned to the house. Though a large and excited crowd had gathered in front of the building, he was seen to slow down as he approached. Then, instead of going inside, he wandered round to the back garden, picked some fruit off one of the trees, and started munching it. Inside the house, his alibi came so glibly, in the most minute detail, that it almost seemed too perfect. But when tested it was found to be true.

Attention then turned to Lizzie, whose behaviour had been equally strange, and whose statements were not only curious but contradictory. When Bridget had asked her where she was when her father was killed, she replied: 'I was out in the yard and heard a groan.' When Mrs Churchill asked the same question, she said: 'I went out to the barn to get a piece of iron.' She told the same story to the police, saying she had eaten three pears while searching in the attic of the barn. But a policeman who checked the attic found no cores, only undisturbed dust.

Mrs Churchill also recalled the extraordinary reply Lizzie had given when she first arrived, and asked where her mother was. Lizzie said: 'I'm sure I don't know, for she had a note from someone to go and see somebody who is sick. But I don't know perhaps that she isn't killed also, for I thought I heard her coming in.' It was some minutes before Mrs Churchill and Bridget began to search for Mrs Borden. They knew she was not in her own room, for the sheet that covered her husband came from there. So they started climbing the front staircase. Halfway up, Mrs Churchill glanced through the open door of the spare bedroom, and saw the body lying on the floor beyond the bed.

Why had Lizzie not seen it there when she came down the stairs to welcome her father home? Why had she been trying to buy prussic acid, a lethal poison, only the day before from shops in town? And why, the previous evening, had she visited her friend Mrs Russell, told her of the food poisoning episode, and complained about her father's brusque way with people, saying she was afraid one of his enemies would take revenge on him soon?

Those were the questions police asked themselves as they pieced together the clues, and studied Lizzie's statements. They were sure that the murders had been committed by someone in the household. Though neighbours had noticed a young man outside the Borden home at 09.30, looking agitated, they had not seen him go in. And police thought it unlikely that a killer could hide in the house for 90 minutes between the murders while Bridget and Lizzie were going about their chores.

Bridget was considered as a suspect and dismissed. Neighbours had seen her cleaning the windows. Some had even seen her vomitting because of the food poisoning. And she had no known reason for killing her employers. But Lizzie had motives in plenty. The tension in the family, the quarrels about money, the hatred of the stepmother, were all well known in the area. She was warned that she was under suspicion and told not to leave the house. She accepted the conditions, in the arrogant, off-hand way that she had dealt with all the police's questions.

The police obtained a warrant for her arrest, but did not serve it until after the inquest. Though they had found an axe-head that had recently been cleaned in the cellar of the Borden house, they had no proof that it was the murder weapon, or that Lizzie was the murderer. Once she was arrested, she could use her legal right to silence. It was important to hear her evidence at the inquest.

More than 4,000 people attended the funeral of Mr and Mrs Borden. The two heads were cut off before burial, and the battered skulls sent for forensic examination. A few days later, the inquest opened. It was held in secret, conducted by the public prosecutor, who gave Lizzie a tough time in cross-questioning. And once again she started contradicting herself.

She claimed now that she had not been on the stairs when her father arrived home shortly before 11.00, but was downstairs in the kitchen. Asked why she had changed her story, she explained: 'I thought I was on the stairs, but now I know I was in the kitchen.' She also denied saying she heard her stepmother returning to the house. The public prosecutor was certain she was guilty of the killings. So were the newspapers, which daily poured out torrents of emotional calumny on Lizzie, adding smears and lies to the known facts. But it was one thing to obtain a conviction in print, quite another to win one in a court of law. And the public prosecutor confided in a letter to the Attorney General that he was not confident.

His fears were well founded. The tide of anti-Lizzie propaganda in the press turned public feeling in her favour. How could such a God-fearing, quiet,

Lizzie Borden

> **Brush manufacturer Henry Wainwright tired of his mistress, slit her throat and shot her. Then he buried her in his shop. When he became bankrupt a year later he dug up her body and to his horror found she was still 'intact'. He had buried her in chloride of lime instead of quicklime. Wainwright then meticulously chopped up the body and put the pieces into parcels to await disposal. But when he went in search of a London cab, a workman picked up one of the parcels and a hand fell out. Wainwright was executed at Newgate in 1875.**

respectable girl do such horrible and bloody deeds? Flowers and good luck messages began pouring into Fall River for her from all over the country. Suddenly the state was the villain of the piece for persecuting her.

Lizzie had something else on her side also. She hired the best lawyer in Massachusetts, George Robinson, a former governor of the state. One of the three trial judges was a man Robinson had elevated to the bench while governor. He owed the defence lawyer a favour – and he delivered. The judges refused to allow evidence of Lizzie's attempts to buy prussic acid, saying it was irrelevant to the case, and they ruled that transcripts of her questioning at the inquest were inadmissible.

Lizzie's friends also rallied round. Both Emma and Bridget gave favourable evidence, playing down Lizzie's enmity for her stepmother. Mrs Russell admitted that Lizzie had burnt one of her dresses the day after her parents' funeral, but insisted there were no blood stains on it. Lizzie, too, played her part perfectly in court. When she fainted halfway through the hearing, there was an outcry at the way she was being tortured. And as she stood in the dock, modest, refined, neatly dressed, it was easy for George Robinson to say to the jury: 'To find her guilty, you must believe she is a fiend. Gentlemen, does she look it?'

The jury agreed she did not. After a ten-day trial her ordeal was over, and she was whisked off for a lavish celebration party, laughing at newspaper clippings of the hearing that friends gave her. She was now very rich, able to inherit her murdered father's wealth, but surprisingly she chose to stay on in Fall River, buying a larger house in the better part of town. Bridget, whom many suspected of helping Lizzie to dispose of clues to the killings, returned to Ireland, allegedly with a lot of money from the Borden bank account. She later returned to America and died in Montana in 1947, aged 82.

For a while Emma shared the new home with Lizzie, but the sisters quarrelled, and Emma moved out. Lizzie became something of a recluse, living alone, unloved and whispered about, until she died in 1927, aged 67. Emma, nine years older, died a few days later. They were both buried in the family plot, alongside their real mother, their stepmother, their father and their sister Alice, who had died as a child.

Can Lizzie rest in peace beside the victims of that hot morning in August, 1892? No-one else was ever arrested for the murders. No-one else was even seriously suspected. The case has become one of the most intriguing unresolved mysteries in the annals of crime. Five stage plays, a ballet, and countless books have been written about it. Opinions range from those who say she was a cunning, calculating killer who twice stripped naked to ensure her butchery left no blood-stained clothes, to the Society of Friends of Lizzie Borden, which still exists today to persuade us she was innocent.

Perhaps, in a way, she was. In her book *A Private Disgrace*, American authoress Victoria Lincoln argues convincingly that Lizzie committed the murders while having attacks of temporal epilepsy, the 'funny turns' her family were accustomed to. Lizzie suffered attacks four times a year, usually during menstruation. Miss Lincoln says: 'During a seizure, there are periods of automatic action which the patient in some cases forgets completely and in other remembers only dimly.' That could explain Lizzie's confusing statements and her coolness when accused of the killings.

Miss Lincoln even suggests the trigger to Lizzie's attacks. A note was delivered to 92 Second Street on the morning of 4 August, but it was not from a sick friend. It was to do with the transfer of a property to Mrs Borden's name. The first such transaction had driven Lizzie to vandalism. Did the second drive her to murder?

Messalina

The Roman Empire, in its heyday, produced a bevy of women whose exploits chilled the blood. Livia, Agrippina and Poppaea were bad enough, But the monster of them all was Messalina, wife of the gentle Emperor, Claudius.

Her power over him was such that for years he went in ignorance of her cruelty, debauchery and avarice. When he began to suspect the truth, he was too timid to act. Beautiful to look at, she always knew how to soothe and flatter him, how to twist the truth and lull his fears.

Her education in the darker side of life began very early for her mother, Lepida, was a vicious woman who dabbled in magic as well as prostitution and carried on an incestuous relationship with her own brother.

Messalina married Claudius before he became Emperor. She was his fifth wife. They had a daughter, Octavia, later to marry the Emperor Nero and a son, Britannicus, born within the first few weeks of his reign. But she was a woman of such passionate desires that she could never remain faithful.

Claudius became Emperor in a coup that surprised him as much as the rest of Rome. He was bookish, some thought simple, with an easy, indolent nature, much addicted to the pleasures of eating and gaming. Every day he gave sumptuous feasts to which as many as 600 people were invited. He never troubled his head about what was going on in his household.

His wife, with her silky brown limbs and provocative eyes, had no difficulty attracting lovers. Only later, when her true nature was known, did those who were fascinated by her, think twice. When she first became Empress she carried on her love affairs secretly and with discretion but as she began to realize that no one dared oppose her, she flaunted her passions as she chose.

Ironically, her cruelty was first brought to light by a fit of jealousy. Her victim was Princess Julia, daughter of Germanicus and sister of the terrifying Caligula. This Princess and her sister had been banished by Caligula to the island of Pontia after he had abused and raped them both. Claudius, touched by their plight, recalled them from exile and restored them to their estates and former splendour.

Julia was a fascinating woman but unfortunately, as it turned out, being descended from the Caesars, had inherited a haughtiness and noble bearing which Messalina detested. It was also obvious that the Emperor seemed to have a great regard for her and they spent a lot of time together.

Mistaking her husband's regard for love, Messalina began to look upon the handsome Julia as a rival to be got rid of. She brought about her downfall by accusing her of crimes she could not possibly have committed. Claudius believed what he was told and Julia was banished. Soon after, through Messalina's agency, she was killed.

From now on anyone who stood in her way became the victim of her cruelty. She had only to accuse them of treason or an equal crime, and they were put to death without mercy. Her word became law. Appius Silanus was one of the first to die in this way. He had married her mother, Lepida, and become a close friend to Claudius. He was universally well thought of and expected to achieve high office. But he had the misfortune to be found attractive by Messalina. She made advances to him which he repelled, reminding her of their family relationship. Humiliated, she swore to destroy him.

Claudius had a superstitious belief in dreams so when Messalina's servant, Narcissus, told him, on her instructions, of a dream in which he saw Silanus plunge a dagger into the Emperor's heart, he was disturbed. It only needed Messalina to add that she too had had the same dream several nights in succession, and Claudius fell into the trap set for him. Believing he was about to be assassinated, he gave orders for Silanus to be killed.

This served as a strong warning to the senate as to what they could expect from their Emperor under the spell of his evil wife. Several leading senators determined to get rid of Claudius and had plans for the Emperor of Dalmatia, with his vast army, to take over in Rome.

The plans came to nothing, but gave Messalina the opportunity for the violence she had been waiting for. Claiming to be acting for the good of the state she hunted down the guilty senators, in Claudius' name. Estates were confiscated, men tortured, anyone remotely connected with the plot put to death. Things came to such a pitch that many preferred to commit suicide rather than risk capture. She was intoxicated by her power and had reached a point at which she believed the least resistance to her should be punished.

She had a ravenous physical appetite, and heaped rewards on those who joined her in debauchery. Not being content with her own degredation, she forced women of rank to prostitute themselves. If they refused, she had them raped in front of their husbands. She ordered a room in the palace to be fitted up like a brothel, had the name of the most notorious whore in Rome inscribed over the top and amused herself by impersonating her, giving herself to every man that came.

Her infamy was common knowledge yet, incredibly, kept from Claudius. Messalina could make him believe what she wanted to and sometimes made a fool of him. This was so in the affair of Mnester, the most famous dancer in Rome. She was so madly in love with him that she had statues of him erected all over the city, but he did not give in to her being afraid of what would happen to him if the Emperor found out. She pursued him until at last he said he would do whatever she pleased as long as the Emperor consented. Messalina went to Claudius and 'after a thousand deceitful caresses' complained that Mnester had refused to obey her over some petty business. She asked Claudius to give directions that her orders were to be treated with more respect. Claudius sent for the dancer and told him, in future, to obey Messalina implicitly. He obeyed and became her lover.

Greed was another of her vices. For years she had coveted the beautiful Gardens of Lucullus owned by Asiaticus, a senator of great distinction. As she

Messalina

could get them no other way she accused him of being responsible for Caligula's murder, saying he had boasted of the assassination. To everyone, it was obvious he was innocent, but by trickery she had him condemned and he was forced to choose his own death.

There was still one more outrage for her to commit – but it was the one which brought about her end. Passionately in love, yet again, she saw no reason why she should not have two husbands. Her lover was Gaius Silius, a strikingly handsome man who had already been appointed Consul for the following year. By now, drunk with power, she decided to marry him in public and forced him to send away his own wife.

She heaped honours and favours upon this 'husband to be' and stripped the palace of costly hangings, furniture, silver and statues to enrich his house. Silius himself, now trapped, was far from easy in his mind. Although bewitched by the Emperor's wife, he was increasingly aware of the danger to which he was exposing himself.

Messalina chose a weekend when Claudius was away in the country for the celebration of their wedding. It was an affair of great magnificence for which she was dressed as a bride and the feast which followed it went on for days. Claudius knew nothing of it. The truth was broken to him through Narcissus, Messalina's former servant, who hated her and vowed to ruin her. Silius, he was warned, was practically Emperor and Rome in chaos. His initial astonishment and fear gave way to rage. His friends warned him to deal with the couple at once and ensure his safety.

Word soon got back to Rome that Claudius was coming to punish his wife. Hoping to move him to compassion, Messalina sent their children, Octavia and Britannicus, to meet him. She was still sure she could save herself if only she could be alone with him. Narcissus made sure they did not meet. He took the Emperor to see the love nest, sumptuously furnished with his own fine things. Silius was put to death immediately.

But Claudius did not act instantly with regard to his wife. He ordered her to present herself next morning to justify her behaviour. Those around him decided they must act. Centurions were ordered, in the name of the Emperor to find her and put her to death.

Messalina had fled to the Gardens of Lucullus. Her mother, Lepida, was with her. The centurions broke open the gates of the garden and the captain presented himself to her, without a word. He handed her a dagger, giving her the chance to kill herself but she couldn't do it. To make an end of it quickly, he ran her through with his sword.

Claudius was given news of her death but did not seem to take it in. For some time after he would plaintively ask why the Empress Messalina did not come.

Ulrike Meinhof

Early in the evening of 16 June 1972 a tense German policeman, acting on a tip-off, knocked at the door of a flat in the suburban village of Langenhagen, near Hanover airport.

The door was opened by a sullen looking woman with straggling hair, who immediately realized her mistake. Suddenly police were swarming everywhere. She struggled hysterically, fought and shouted obscenities. But it was all over for Ulrike Meinhof.

After the biggest and most sustained search in German police history, the middle class anarchist who had come to be regarded as the most dangerous woman in Europe, was in their grasp. As she was led away they opened one of her suitcases, packed for a flight from Hanover airport. They were not really surprised to find it contained three 9 mm pistols, two hand grenades, one submachine gun and a ten pound bomb.

With university drop-out, Andreas Baader, as her partner, Ulrike had been waging war on the established order for nearly three years. The terrorist group they formed committed so many crimes, ranging from murder to forgery, that it needed 354 pages to list them when they came to trial. Baader and two other gang leaders were already in prison. But until that June evening when Ulrike Meinhof was captured, the authorities could not rest for she was undoubtedly the intellect, the driving force behind everything.

Ulrike Meinhof was born into an intellectual, upper middle class family at Oldenburg, Lower Saxony, on 7 October 1934. Both her parents were art historians but her father died when she was only five, her mother when she was 14. During her formative years she was fostered by her mother's friend, Professor Renate Riemeck, an intellectual woman of strong radical views. It was said that Ulrike learned from her many of her socialist ideas and the importance of never accepting the edicts of authority without first questioning them.

The attractive, red haired girl soon showed signs of academic brilliance. In 1957, when she was 23, she went to Munster University to study sociology and philosophy. She campaigned against the atom bomb, the Americans in Vietnam and most of the burning issues that radical minded students were interested in.

One day she was introduced to a thin faced, handsome man called Klaus Roehl. He ran a lively, left wing magazine called *Konkret* and when he asked her to join its staff she agreed.

Before long Ulrike had acquired a reputation as a first class radical journalist, writing columns of such brilliance that she began to be talked about in circles outside the university. She probed into the economy of Germany, dealt with social questions many people felt were being brushed under the carpet and wrote about the misery that existed among those who had no part in Germany's so called Economic Miracle.

Klaus Roehl made her his editor and his wife.

The magazine was successful enough in its own way, but not a best seller. When Roehl hit on the idea of adding sex to the political content, it took off. They made a lot of money, lived in a fashionable house and drove round in a large white Mercedes.

Ulrike, now the mother of twin daughters, found herself the darling of radical chic society and became a familiar face on television. But the success and the gloss were superficial and inwardly Ulrike was burning with resentment. Her husband, she had discovered, was a womaniser. His affairs became too much for her and after seven years together, they were divorced.

She gave up her job with her marriage, moved to Berlin and put her daughters, Regine and Bettina, into an old fashioned, strict discipline boarding school. This left her free to mix with a group of well-off young people with extreme radical views, who believed the only way to change society was through violence. The idea took root. She was soon publicly defending arson, violent protest and the crimes of urban guerillas. But before she acted politically she had to get rid of some personal bitterness. She started a campaign against her husband and his magazine which culminated in a night of fury in which she and her friends vandalised the home in which she had once taken such a pride.

Through the grapevine she heard a lot about a young agitator and arsonist called Andreas Baader who was serving a prison sentence for his part in burning down a Frankfurt department store. One day she met Baader's 'revolutionary bride', a tall, blonde girl called Gudrun Ensslin, a pastor's daughter, who had studied philosophy. Gudrun told her his friends were determined to get him out and they wanted her to help. On certain days he was allowed to work outside the prison in a Berlin library, and it was decided to 'spring him' from there. On 14 May 1970 Ulrike led the raid with a gang of armed terrorists, leaving the librarian severely wounded and several prison guards with bullet holes. The violence had started.

After Andreas and Ulrike had had time to sum each other up, they agreed to form the Baader-Meinhof gang with a hard core of about 24 fellow anarchists. Apart from themselves the leading members would be Baader's girl friend, Gudrun, and Jan Carl Raspe, who became Ulrike's lover.

Andreas Baader was officially the leader of the group. He was a dark,

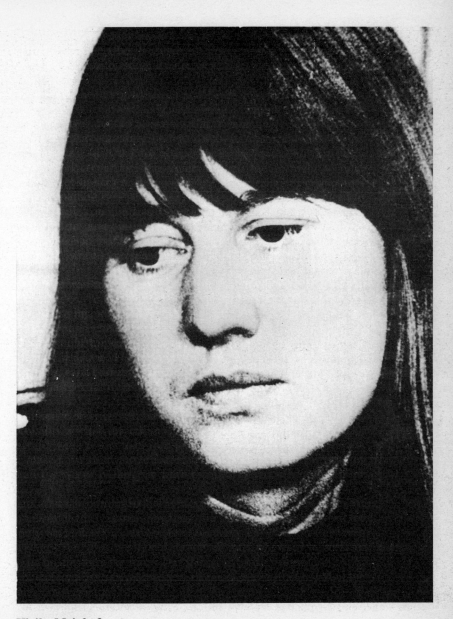

Ulrike Meinhof

brooding, handsome man, attractive to women, who based his image on the young Marlon Brando. He was also indolent, spoiled and aggressive. Ulrike Meinhof supplied the drive and the brains in their partnership.

The four of them managed to flee the country after the raid and turned up in the Middle East to train with the Palestine National Liberation Front. But the Germans and Arabs did not get on too well, each accusing the other of being cold and arrogant. The two women were considered domineering and a damned nuisance and before long the PLO decided that their trainees were rebels without a true cause and asked them to leave.

Ulrike remained passionately pro-Palestinian. On her return to Germany she made the shocking decision to send her two small daughters to a refugee camp in Jordan to be trained along with Palestinian children to become *kamikaze* fighters against Israel. Fortunately for them, her plans went wrong. Karl Roehl had been scouring Germany for his children and had even engaged private detectives. He was tipped off just in time and they were snatched from a hideout in Palermo. They hated him at first because their mother's indoctrination had been very thorough. But for all his faults he was a good and devoted father and won back their affection.

The gang grew to be about 150 strong all told. Most of its members were from quite prosperous backgrounds, the only two working class recruits being garage hands, useful for dealing with stolen cars.

They were armed to the teeth with small fire arms, submachine guns, hand grenades and bombs and set out on a series of bank raids and robberies to raise funds to buy more. There was one particularly terrible assault on a branch of the Bavarian Mortgage and Exchange Bank in the small provincial town of Kaiserslautern, 35 miles west of Heidelberg, in which a police officer was murdered with callous deliberation.

Taking part in the raid was a new recruit, a long haired blonde called Ingeborg Barz. The girl was so horrified by the bloodshed that she made up her mind to go home. She telephoned her parents in Berlin. It was the last they ever heard of her. According to Gerhart Muller, who turned state witness, she was summoned to a meeting with Ulrike Meinhof then driven to a remote spot near some gravel pits where she was executed.

Violence piled upon violence while the ordinary man in the street watched with horror. During two years of urban terror five people were shot or blown to bits, there were 54 attempted murders, countless vicious assaults and a series of bombings directed against the American Army in Germany. Ulrike had developed a complete disregard for human life and categorized some people, including policemen, as 'pigs'.

The police put all their manpower into an attempt to crack the terrorist hold on West Germany and their chance came one day early in 1972 in a quiet Frankfurt Street. They had received an anonymous tip that a garage there was stuffed with ammunition. They drove up in two lorries, loaded with sandbags and began to build a wall – but because they were dressed in overalls they looked more like corporation gardeners delivering bags of peat. After a time a smart lilac coloured Porsche drew up. Three young men in leather jackets climbed out. Two of them went into the garage, the third, waiting outside on the pavement was grabbed by the police. They found they had got Carl Raspe the arch terrorist who was also Ulrike's lover. After a long, tense seige, first a gang member called Holger Meins was brought out. Then, after a brief exchange of fire the police dragged out a dark young man writhing with pain from a bullet in the thigh. It was Andreas Baader.

Not long after Gudrun Ensslin was captured in a Hamburg dress shop when a shop assistant discovered a gun in her jacket and phoned the police. Ulrike began to feel very much alone. As the months went by she found that even her friends from the trendy left felt she was too dangerous to be associated with.

Then came the night in June when she decided to head for Hanover airport. She knew a left wing teacher who had a flat nearby and turned up on his doorstep with several suitcases. He was in a terrible dilemma. He now held a respected position as Federal President of the Teachers' Union. The last thing he wanted was Ulrike Meinhof as house guest. He went to seek the advice of some friends and they urged him to phone the police at once. He made the phone call and stayed clear of the flat. . . .

The rest of Ulrike's life was to be spent in prison or in the courtroom where she yelled and shouted abuse at her judges. The trial of the Baader-Meinhof gang was considered so potentially explosive that a fortified courtroom and special cells were built at the top security prison at Stammheim in Stuttgart. There was great fear that reprisals and counter measures would be launched by terrorists still outside.

Though members of the gang were kept apart she became aware as the trial went on of the enmity of the others, especially in the case of Gudrun Ensslin. Solitary, apart from her typewriter and her books, she began to brood. Eventually the pressure must have become too great. On the morning of 9 May 1976 she was found hanging in her cell.

Her followers refused to believe that she had committed suicide and for a time insisted she had been murdered by the authorities. Four thousand people marched in the cortège at her funeral in Berlin, many of them masked to avoid identification. The police felt they were watching over a time bomb and later they had to deal with revenge terrorist attacks.

But of Ulrike Meinhof a priest who knew her said afterwards 'I think she finally decided she had come to the end of the wrong road. . . .'

Madeleine Smith

The sensational trial of Madeleine Smith which kept staid Edinburgh in a ferment for nine days in July 1857, has always divided people into two camps. There are those who believe that Madeleine was a cunning, cold-hearted poisoner who, once she had tired of her lover, killed him so that she could marry someone socially superior. And there are those who consider her a pathetic victim of blackmail, driven to despair by Emile L'Angelier, the man she once loved, but totally innocent of his death.

When the jury returned a verdict of 'Not proven' Madeleine Smith, who, throughout the trial had shown interest, but no concern, was seen to sigh heavily, then smile. Wild cheering echoed through the court. But the fact remained that L'Angelier had died an agonising death with eighty two grains of arsenic in his stomach, enough to kill a dozen men, and nobody knew how it had got there.

Before having an opinion one way or the other it is necessary to know something about the background of this handsome, languid girl from a middle class Victorian home and her suitor, an impoverished but dapper young packing clerk who desperately wanted position and respect and 'a lady' for his wife.

Madeleine was the elder daughter of a highly successful Scottish architect, James Smith, who was one of the pillars of Glasgow. He had offices in Vincent Street, a solid family house in India Street and a somewhat over-ornate country residence on the Clyde. She was not beautiful but her lustrous eyes, luxuriant brown curls and graceful carriage made her very attractive. Her father was a typical Victorian papa who provided a prosperous household with six servants for his family, but expected his word to be taken as law. She emerged in her finery most evenings to attend some function or other but the days could be tedious with little to do but occupy herself with typical Victorian hobbies thought suitable for a young lady such as painting on vellum, making feather flowers and creating pictures from seaweed. What no one knew, until she met Emile, was that behind the facade of demure respectability was a vibrant, sensual woman crying to be let out.

Emile L'Angelier was a total stranger to her sort of world. His father was a nurseryman in Jersey and he had been sent to Scotland to work with a firm of seedmen, with the object of improving his status. When Madeleine met him, however, he was still a packing clerk, earning very little, but with rather grandiose ideas about his future. However his employer seemed to consider him industrious, honest and sober and if he was somewhat vain, perhaps that was because he was French.

She first saw him staring at her as she was strolling in Sauchiehall Street with a friend. Their eyes met, and he bowed. He discovered someone at his work who knew her and who promised he would introduce Emile at the first opportunity. When that moment came he took the opportunity of giving her a note, a *billet doux*, which expressed his feelings in flowery terms. Madeleine told him she had worn it next to her heart at the ball that night. So began the vast correspondence that was later to prove so damning. The letters showed that by April 1855 he had gained her affections but was not sure of them. Twice during the year she tried to break off their relationship but he was persistent. He made it clear he was not a man to be so easily dropped. In a copy of a letter written as early as 19 July 1855 he showed what he was capable of. 'Think what your father would say if I sent him your letters for perusal....'

She had poured out all her suppressed sensuality on paper, writing him love letters that made people gasp with shock, for it was a period at which women were supposed to suffer sex, not enjoy it. Later, when L'Anglier's lodgings were searched over 500 letters from Madeleine were discovered and sixty of them were read out in court.

Their go-between was a friend of Emile's called Mary Perry who seems to have been fond of him without expecting a relationship. She was perfectly satisfied to be a letter carrier between her friend and this fine lady and let them use her house for their secret meetings.

Once they had declared their love for each other in fulsome romantic terms they became 'engaged' and obviously slept together. On 7 May 1856 Madeleine wrote him this letter:

'My own beloved husband:

I trust to God you got home safe, and were not much the worse for being out. Thank you, my love, for coming so far to see your Mimi. It is truly a pleasure to see my Emile. If we did wrong last night, it must have been in the excitement of our love. I suppose we ought to have waited till we were married. Yes, beloved, I did truly love you with my soul. I was happy; it was a pleasure to be with you. Oh, if we could have remained, never more to have parted! Darling Emile, did I seem cold to you last night? Darling, I love you, my own Emile. I love you with all my heart and soul. Am I not your wife? Yes, I am; and you may rest assured that after what has passed I cannot be the wife of any other....'

Madeleine had obviously made up her mind to introduce Emile to her father, but James Smith had no intention of letting his daughter marry a penniless little foreigner. 'Do keep cool when you see him, I know his temper – every inch like my own' she advised Emile. But the meeting never took place. Emile's pride was wounded and the hurt is reflected in a letter he wrote to his beloved in which he fumes and fusses about the treatment he has received.

'Never fear my own beloved husband' she wrote to console him 'I shall be quite ready whenever you fix our marriage day. . . . I am quite sure when they hear we are married they will all give in.'

When the family moved down to Row, their country house on the Clyde she asked for a ground floor bedroom. This meant she just had to step out of her window to meet him. Throughout that summer of 1856 she abandoned herself to her love. Emile seems to have accepted that they were betrothed and that they would eventually be married.

But he had also noticed that a certain name seemed to have crept into her conversation and her letters with a frequency that alarmed him. The name was William Minnoch. This gentleman had for some time admired Madeleine and wanted her for his wife. He was a short, fair complexioned business man in his thirties, well educated, successful and well liked by James Smith who considered him an ideal son-in-law. He began calling, with obvious intent, but Madeleine said she did not find him in the least attractive and was not interested in him. 'Don't give ear to any reports you may hear . . . there are several going about regarding me getting married . . . regard them not' she told Emile.

When the Smith family returned to Glasgow secret meetings were made more difficult than before. They moved to a different house and this time Madeleine's bedroom was in the basement with the bedroom window at street level covered by bars. There was no chance of her slipping out without being detected. They would sometimes have a whispered conversation through the bars but it was not very satisfactory. Emile began to feel depressed.

Still, nothing had prepared him for the shock which came in her next letter. She talked of their love as though it was in the past. 'We shall often talk over all our past performances – it really has been quite a small romance' she said lightly. He was devastated. He began to see his dream of being someone of consequence fading rapidly as he woke to the reality of her increasing coldness towards him.

She had been seen in public with Minnoch and her letters to Emile became shorter and shorter and were signed simply 'Yours devotedly'. There was no doubt that she had enjoyed being escorted by someone as well regarded and socially acceptable as William, as she now called him, and on 28 January she made up her mind to accept his proposal of marriage.

First, she had to bring an end to her affair with the little Frenchman. Emile

The trial of Madeleine Smith

played into her hands by indulging in a petty little habit with which he showed her his displeasure. He returned one of her letters. Her response, considering the passionate abandon of her previous correspondence was brutal.

'This may astonish you, but you have more than once returned me my letters and my mind was made up that I should not stand the same thing again. And you also annoyed me much on Saturday by your conduct in coming so near to me. Altogether I think owing to coolness and indifference (nothing else) that we had better for the future consider ourselves as strangers. I trust to your honour as a gentleman that you will not reveal anything that has passed between us.... I shall feel obliged by your bringing me my letters and likeness.... I trust you may yet be happy, and get one more worthy of you than I.'

It became evident that he would not give her up without a fight. Nor would he give up the letters and threatened to show them to her father. His friend Tom Kennedy, who was cashier at Huggins, where he worked, tried to persuade him to behave like a gentleman and let the whole affair come to an end. Weeping, Emile told him 'No, I shan't; she shall never marry another man as long as I live...' He also said miserably 'Tom, it's an infatuation; she shall be the death of me.'

When Madeleine realized that he was not going to return the letters and might, in his present state, pluck up the courage to show them to her father she became frantic. 'Emile will you not spare me this – hate me, despise me – but do not expose me. I cannot write more. I feel ill tonight.'

She asked him to come to the house, where she could talk to him through the bedroom window. He kept the appointment on 11 February 1857 and she appears to have agreed to a wedding the following September.

On the morning of 20 February when Emile's landlady, Mrs Jenkins went to call him for breakfast, she found him very ill. He said that on the evening before as he was returning home he was seized with violent spasms in the stomach and thought he was going to die before he could reach his bed. During the night he had been very sick. Four days later Mrs Jenkins was wakened at four in the morning by groans and cries from his room. The symptons were the same as on 20 February, but this time Emile was shivering and complained that he was cold and thirsty. The doctor who was fetched to see him, decided it was a bilious attack and prescribed accordingly. He advised him to take a short holiday.

At about this time Madeleine had been shoping for arsenic in Sauchiehall Street. She went into a chemist and asked for sixpence worth of poison. Asked for what purpose she needed it she replied 'For the garden and for rats at our country house.' The arsenic was sold to her mixed with soot according to the law and she seemed concerned about the colour of it. The chemist admitted afterwards he did wonder why if she was only giving it to rats.

She had written to Emile showing concern about his bilious attacks, addressing him as 'My dear, sweet Emile' and sending him love and kisses. She assured him she loved no one else in the world but him. Emile, by now wary of her passionate outpourings, asked her to give him some plain answers to his questions. Nevertheless, he signed himself 'your ever affectionate husband – Emile L'Angelier'.

Emile was feeling a little better and went to see his friend and go-between, Miss Perry. He told her he had seen Madeleine then remarked 'I can't think why I was so unwell after getting coffee and chocolate from her on the two occasions we met.' He even went as far as to say he thought the drinks might have been poisoned, but obviously, did not consider that had anything to do with the woman he loved.

She was very much occupied elsewhere. She had gone up to Bridge of Allan in Stirlingshire to make arrangements for her marriage to William Minnoch. She seems to have forgotten that she had promised to marry Emile in September. Before she left Glasgow she had been shopping again. This time she asked for an ounce of arsenic 'for rats in Blythwood Square' (their Glasgow home). But Christina Haggart, the Smith's maid swore she had never seen a rat in that house.

Madeleine continued to write Emile affectionate letters: 'I long to see you, to kiss and embrace you, my own, only sweet love. Miss me my sweet one – my love, my own dear sweet little pet'. Why she insisted on sending him these sugary epistles while demanding the return of her other letters is hard to guess.

Emile got leave from work and caught the train to Bridge of Allan hoping to catch Madeleine but she had already returned to Glasgow. He had missed a letter she had written asking him to meet her on 19 March and another letter containing an urgent summons was sent on to him by his landlady. He read the note eagerly: 'Why, my beloved, did you not come to me. Oh beloved are you ill? Come to me sweet one. I waited and waited for you, but you care not. I shall wait again tomorrow night same hour and arrangement. Do come sweet love, my own dear love of a sweetheart. . . .' He caught the first train back.

When he arrived back at his lodgings in Franklin Place on the evening of 22 March he told his landlady that he would be very late that night. He went out, presumably to see Madeleine. He did not return until half past two in the morning and rang the bell violently. Mrs Jenkins found him doubled up with pain on the doorstep. He told her all the old symptons had returned and she helped him to his room where he again vomited a greenish substance. By four in the morning he was so bad Mrs Jenkins herself ran out to fetch the doctor, who said he would visit him in the morning, meanwhile she was to give him a few drops of laudanum and a mustard plaster. But two hours later in response to urgent pleas from Mrs Jenkins he stirred himself and hurried round to Franklin Place to give his patient a morphine injection.

When Mrs Jenkins drew back the curtains in Emile's room at nine o'clock the next morning he looked so pale that she asked if he would care to see anybody. He asked for his friend, Miss Perry, but before she could be fetched the doctor arrived. When he lifted Emile's head from the pillow, it fell back limply. He was dead.

When they came to look through his belongings they found a letter which began 'Why, my beloved, did you not come to me? ...'

Nothing now could stop the relentless stream of inquiries and of course they led straight to Madeleine, to her love affair with Emile and to the letters she had written him. An autopsy had revealed that Emile's stomach had contained enough arsenic to kill 40 men and the position of the poison in his body showed that it had been ministered more than once.

One morning when the maid servant went to waken Madeleine, she found her bed empty. It was thought that she had probably gone to their country house and Minnoch set off with one of her brothers to fetch her back. They caught up with her on the Clyde steamer but the tactful husband to be asked for no explanations.

On Tuesday 31 March Madeleine, showing great composure, made a statement to the Sheriff of Lanarkshire telling the whole story of her relationship with Emile L'Angelier and even admitting that they had plans to marry. But she insisted the last time she saw him was three weeks before his death.

When the trial began on 30 June all eyes were fixed on the trapdoor leading down to the cells. There was a gasp from the public gallery as the prisoner came up and moved towards the dock. She was tall, elegantly dressed with a fashionable bonnet, and exuded an air of nonchalance that some observers thought indecent. She was veiled and carried a lace edged handkerchief and a bottle of smelling salts. She rose, threw back her veil and in a clear voice declared herself 'Not Guilty'.

She was asked why she had bought arsenic and, contrary to what she had told the chemist she explained to the court that it was purely for cosmetic purposes, to soften her hands and improve her complexion. Victorian women often did this, though it was obviously unwise. Madeleine said she had diluted it with water and used it on her face, neck and arms. The prosecution made a great deal of the fact that she had given one reason for purchasing arsenic to the Glasgow chemist but quite a different one to the court. It was however essential to show that she had arsenic at the right time and also the opportunity for administering it at that time. Could she have laced the coffee and cocoa she handed to Emile through her bedroom window? It was very hard to prove.

On the fifth day of her trial the letters were produced and read out in a thin voice by the aged clerk. The Lord Advocate ordered that passages that were particularly offensive should be omitted. She did not show a scrap of emotion as she heard evidence of her passionate love for the dead man.

When it came to the summing up the Lord Advocate for the prosecution, said he would show that Madeleine had got herself into such a position that murder was the only solution. She had, he said, the means, the opportunity, the motive and the cool character that was perfectly compatible with murder. But Dean Inglis of the Faculty of Advocates, for the defence, put Madeleine's case in a masterly speech. He presented Emile as vain, pretentious and conceited, a seducer who had corrupted an innocent girl. He had also at one time boasted of being an arsenic eater and there was evidence he had been a frequent sufferer from stomach ailments. 'Think you' the Dean demanded 'that without temptation, without evil teaching, a poor girl falls into such depths of degredation? No! Influence from without – most corrupting influence – can alone account for such a fall.' He appealed to the noblest instincts of all those listening to consider the awful fate of this girl if found guilty.

The jury was out for 25 minutes before bringing in their 'Not Proven' verdict. It may have been popular with the crowds but it was noticed that the usually courteous Dean Inglis left the courtroom without so much as a glance at his client. Only when it was all over did they begin to think of her total lack of emotion. One newspaper commented that she had demeaned herself as if L'Angelier had never had a place in her affections. 'If it had been a trial for poisoning a dog, the indifference could not have been greater.'

Her indifference towards William Minnoch was equally noticeable. The whole business had made him ill with grief but when told he had been ill she commented 'My friend I know nothing of. I have not seen him. I hear he has been ill, which I don't much care.' Minnoch had had to make a very brief appearance as a witness for the prosecution and was never forgiven.

The 'Not proven' verdict was not a comfortable one to live with in Scotland. It really meant that some parts of the evidence were too doubtful to risk a conviction. Madeleine moved to London where she married an artist, bore him three children and lived an interesting life. Her last days were spent in America where she died at the great age of 91, protesting her innocence to the end.

Chapter five

FRAUDS AND SWINDLERS

Like it or not, the rascals, scoundrels and rogues of this world are generally more interesting characters than the good guys. What follows is a compilation of shady men and women who, for whatever reason, became notorious for their fraudulent, swindling ways.

The master-faker who even took Goering for a ride

How many of the treasures of the world's museums and art galleries are genuine and how many fakes will probably never be known. The art forgers are just too clever for most experts.

According to ex-forger David Stein, 'I can open an art catalogue anywhere in the world and recognize my own work.' Master-faker Elmyr de Hory said of the experts: 'They know more about fine words than fine art.' And Hans van Meegeren described them as 'arrogant scum'.

Van Meegeren is recognized as the greatest art forger of all time. But his criminal career was revealed only through the most amazing sequence of events. . . .

After the fall of Nazi Germany in 1945, Hermann Goering's priceless collection of old masters was uncovered at his Berchtesgaden mansion. Most had been looted from churches, galleries and private collections during the German march through Europe. A few, however, had been honestly purchased, and one of these was a painting entitled *Woman Taken in Adultery*. It was signed by Jan Vermeer, the 17th-century Dutch master.

In those first days after the war's end, the hunt was on throughout newly liberated Europe for collaborators. And when it was discovered that Goering's agents had paid £160,000 for the painting from a dealer in Amsterdam, Dutch police thought they had found someone who had been too generous to the Nazis. That someone was van Meegeren.

At that time van Meegeren was a rich nightclub owner who had amassed a small fortune by selling previously undiscovered old masters to major art galleries. Apart from the painting purchased by Goering, he had sold six other works signed by Vermeer to Dutch galleries.

Van Meegeren was arrested and thrown into prison to await trial as a collaborator – a charge which could carry the death sentence. He was interrogated daily for three weeks without changing his story. Then, when he was finally brought to court, he came up with the most astonishing defence.

He said that, far from collaborating with the Nazis, he had actually duped them. He had not sold Goering a Vermeer but a van Meegeren – the old master's work was a fake he had painted himself. And he had sold dozens of others for vast sums around the world.

At first the judge did not believe him. But he gave van Meegeren a chance. Placed under guard in his Amsterdam studio, he was told to paint another

Hans van Meegeren

Vermeer that would fool the experts. He did so – it was titled *Jesus Among the Doctors* – and he was freed.

The master-forger's freedom was, however, short-lived. For as more and more van Meegerens came to light, he was brought to trial again, this time charged with deception. He was jailed for 12 months, but died of a heart attack six weeks later at the age of 57.

What made van Meegeren embark on his career of forgery? Surprisingly, in view of the huge sums his fakes fetched, the motive was not money. Van Meegeren was a relatively successful painter who had his first major exhibition at The Hague when he was 33. It was a sellout, yet the critics slated it.

Foremost among them was a pompous professor, Dr Abraham Bredius, who dismissed van Meegeren's work with contempt. Over the years, the struggling painter's pent-up anger and frustration over Bredius's attacks found an outlet. Van Meegeren began to paint copies of the works of the artist whom Dr Bredius admired most of all: Vermeer.

Throughout 1936 van Meegeren remained in self-imposed exile in a rented villa in France, working on his masterpiece, a perfectly executed 'Vermeer' which he titled *Christ and the Disciples at Emmaus*. He 'aged' the painting 300 years by a process he had painstakingly developed.

In 1937 he put the painting on the market through a Paris lawyer, claiming that it had been in the possession of a Dutch family living in France. The family, so the story went, had fallen on hard times and now needed to sell their heirloom.

Naturally enough, the lawyer first approached Dr Bredius who, as the world's leading authority on Vermeer, could vouch for the painting's authenticity. He had no hesitation in doing so.

But not only did Bredius give his stamp of approval to the painting, he also – to van Meegeren's great delight – claimed the work as his own discovery. Bredius urged that it be bought for £50,000 by Rotterdam's Boyman's Museum. Bredius would often go there to study it – and van Meegeren to gloat over it.

Busting out all over

Perhaps the most prolific forger of sculptures was Giovanni Bastianini who before his death in 1868 turned out terracotta busts by the dozen under contract to an art dealer. They were considered to be perfect examples of Renaissance sculpture, and the Florentine faker's works appeared in museums around the world. There are still two in London's Victoria and Albert Museum.

Disgust at the ignorance of art 'experts' and anger at the dishonesty of dealers prompted another artist, Elmyr de Hory, to go into the faking business.

De Hory, a stateless Hungarian, received the greatest accolade of all when another famous faker, Clifford Irving, the American author later jailed for his forged biography of Howard Hughes, wrote a book about the artist entitling it simply *Fake*.

It was reported that paintings by the stateless Hungarian artist were among millions of dollars' worth of fakes sold to a Texas millionaire. The ensuing scandal made de Hory famous, although he insisted that he had never tried to pass his own work off as that of someone else. He said he had never put a famous signature to one of his own paintings – even when that painting was in the precise style of a sought-after artist.

In 1974, at the age of 60, de Hory was taken from his home on the Spanish island of Ibiza and jailed on Majorca. There was no formal charge, and the artist was out again after four months.

Like so many with his talents, he never disguised his contempt for the international art pundits who 'know more about fine words than fine art'. He claimed he could paint a portrait in 45 minutes, draw a 'Modigliani' in 10 and then immediately knock off a 'Matisse'.

'The dealers, the experts and the critics resent my talent,' he said, 'because they don't want it shown how easily they can be fooled: I have tarnished the infallible image they rely upon for their fortunes.'

Almost as quick on the draw as de Hory, but displaying rather more daring, was another brilliant artist, David Stein, who for a brief but mind-boggling four-year reign was undisputed king of the art forgers.

He was a talented painter in his own right, but the high prices paid in the art world were too great a temptation to resist. Working in watercolours or oils, he recreated the styles of some of the world's best-known artists – living and dead.

The dead gave David Stein no trouble, but the living led to his downfall. Pressed for time one day, he rushed off three watercolours he had promised a dealer. Working furiously in his New York apartment, the whole fateful operation took just seven hours. At six in the morning he was lying in bed dreaming up ideas for the paintings. At one o'clock the same day he was handing a satisfied art dealer the 'genuine' works of French artist Marc Chagall, each with its own certificate of authentication.

In those seven hours he had treated the paper he used with cold tea to give it the impression of ageing, executed the watercolours, forged the certificates of authentication and Chagall's signature, and had the pictures professionally framed.

The art dealer was delighted when Stein handed over his 'find'. He examined the three forged Chagalls and, without ever suspecting the truth, began

Michelangelo's 'Antique'

There is nothing new about the forgery of art-works. Michelangelo himself is reputed to have raised much-needed funds as a struggling young man by selling to a Rome cardinal a statue of Cupid which the artist had first stained and buried to age it into an 'antique'.

haggling with Stein over the price. Eventually a cheque for $10,000 changed hands.

The dealer was so proud of his new acquisitions that he determined to show them to someone who had newly arrived in New York – Marc Chagall himself. For, while Stein had busied himself with the forgeries, Chagall had been flying into the city to supervise the installation of two huge murals he had painted in the Metropolitan Opera House.

The dealer had already fixed an appointment to see Chagall and, at their meeting, expected that the great artist would be delighted to see three of his earlier works again. Chagall's reaction at first bewildered then horrified him. 'Diabolical!' said the Frenchman, 'They are not mine.'

Had 31-year-old Stein stuck to Cézannes, Renoirs or Manets, he would have got away with it. As it was, the police came to arrest him that evening. The daredevil forger said afterwards: 'As they arrived at my front door, I left through the back with a glass of Scotch in my hand!'

He made his way to California and it was there that his luck ran out. He was arrested and confessed all. 'If only I had stuck to dead men,' he moaned when he was later indicted on 97 counts of grand larceny and counterfeiting.

While in jail, Stein shared his knowledge of faking with the New York Police Department, helping them create a special art forgery squad. With remission, he served just 16 months and, on his release, he left his three American galleries and half-a-million dollars a year income to return to his native Europe.

This was when the half-French, half-British Stein made his second mistake. He had not realized that the French police also wanted to ask him a few questions. That error cost him another two-and-a-half years in jail.

In the early 1970s, a free man at last, Stein decided to forget the old masters and stick to painting Steins. His fame as a brilliant forger aided his success and he later set up businesses and homes in both London and Paris.

But Stein was still angry at those people he regarded as the real fakers of the art world, the band of ignorant people who claim to be experts.

'A lot of the art world is fake,' he said. 'About two or three hundred of my forgeries are still on the market listed as originals.'

Hans van Meegeren.

Kings of the art forgers

Fake 'Old Masters' have fooled dealers and even museums

Brimming with confidence, David Stein walked into the shop of a well-established New York art dealer one afternoon with three water-colours under his arm.

The dealer stood back and admired them. He carefully studied the certificates of authentication and was impressed by the signatures on them – 'Marc Chagall'. There was some discussion over money, and a cheque for $10,000 was handed over.

Both men parted happily – the dealer because he had bought the paintings so cheaply, Stein because he had got rid of three more fakes.

Those three 'Chagalls' had not even existed seven hours before. Stein had awoken in his New York apartment at six o'clock that morning and remembered that he had an appointment with the dealer at one in the afternoon. So he had decided to get down to a bit of quick forging.

He had 'aged' three sheets of paper with cold tea. Then, after dreaming up suitable subjects, he had polished off the three paintings without a break. He had rushed out to have the paintings framed and, while waiting, had written himself three certificates of authentication. Then he had gone off to keep his appointment with the dealer.

That day's forgeries had been in the style of Chagall, but they could equally have been based on the work of a dozen artists from Renoir to Gauguin. Stein could turn his hand to them all. And that is where he went wrong.

'If only I had stuck to dead men,' he lamented later. For at the very time that he was selling his three fake water-colours, Chagall was in New York. The Russian-born artist had arrived to see two of his enormous murals erected in the Metropolitan Opera House. The dealer had an appointment to visit him, and he took along the three paintings to show the old artist. Chagall took one look at them and declared: 'Diabolical.'

The police came for Stein that same night. 'They arrived at the front door, and I left through the back with a glass of scotch in my hand,' he said. Stein fled to California, where he was arrested and decided to confess all.

The four-year reign of Stein, king of the art forgers, was at an end. The suave, sophisticated, 31-year-old man-about-town spent 16 months in a New York jail after being indicted on 97 counts of counterfeiting and grand larceny. While inside, he helped the police to form an art-forgery squad.

When he came out of jail in 1968, Stein, who was half-British, half-French, decided to put all such risky ventures behind him. He said goodbye to his three American galleries, his New York apartment and his art earnings of up to $500,000 a year, and returned to Europe. Unfortunately, he did not realise that further charges were awaiting him, and he was sentenced to two-and-a-half years in a French prison.

By the time he came out again, Stein was famous throughout the art world. His bogus Old Masters were much sought after. But he decided to paint and

---

Railway staff at Wolverhampton station picked up from the platform a note which had been thrown from the window of a passing train.

It read: 'Mr. Russell, of 32 Vale Road, Bloxwich, Staffs, has left the kettle on the stove. Please inform the police.'

The police, duly informed, called at Number 32 to find the kettle on the stove but the gas unlit.

David Stein signing one of his paintings with others in the background.

sell his own works in his own style. He was instantly successful, and set up homes and businesses in Paris and London.

Stein remained bitter about the people he saw as the real fakers – the pretentious phoneys of the art world.

'People who buy a painting and find out that they have made a mistake are angry because they have displayed their own ignorance,' he said. 'About two or three hundred of my works are still on the market as originals. I see them in dealers' catalogues, in salerooms and even in museums. A lot of the art world is fake.'

Just how much of the contents of museums and art galleries is fake, and just how much is genuine, we shall never know. The art forgers are just too clever for most experts.

America's Cleveland Museum of Art had to remove from display one of its most prized possessions, a wooden Madonna and Child, supposedly carved in Italy in the 13th century. In fact, it was carved around 1920 by an Italian art restorer, Alceo Dossena. His fake was only discovered in 1928 when the sculpture was X-rayed and modern nails were found to be imbedded in the wood.

The museum put the Madonna and Child in its basement and looked around for other works to replace it. Three weeks later it bought a marble statue of Athena for $120,000. It too was a Dossena fake.

In 1918 the New York Metropolitan Museum of Art paid $40,000 for a seven-foot statue of an Etruscan warrior which had supposedly been buried since pre-Roman days. One arm of the warrior was missing, as was the thumb of his other hand.

In 1960 Alfredo Fioravanti confessed to the museum that he was one of six men who had created the statue between them 50 years earlier. He produced the warrior's missing thumb to prove it. The thumb fitted perfectly.

In 1975 the same museum had to withdraw from display a beautiful 'Greek' bronze horse when it was shown to be a fake. The horse had been one of the museum's most popular attractions.

Among the most renowned art forgers of this century was the hard-drinking Dutchman, Hans van Meegeren. His exploits came to light after World War Two, when he was put on trial for helping the Nazis. He had sold to Hermann Goering for $150,000 an exquisite painting purporting to be by the Dutch master Vermeer.

Van Meegeren's answer to the charges of complicity made against him was that he had not sold a Vermeer but a Van Meegeren. The painting was a fake – and it was only one of dozens that he had sold for vast sums around the world.

At first, the judge did not believe him. But he gave the painter a chance to prove his boast. Van Meegeren was placed under guard in his Amsterdam studio and told to paint another Vermeer that could fool the experts. He did so, and was freed.

The master forger's freedom was short-lived, however. As more and more Van Meegerens came to light he was brought to trial again – this time on a charge of deception. He was jailed for 12 months, but died before he could complete his sentence.

Even the grand old master Michelangelo is reputed to have raised much-needed funds as a struggling young man by selling to a Rome cardinal a statue of Cupid which the artist had first stained and buried to age it into an 'antique'.

Perhaps the most prolific forger of sculptures was Giovanni Bastianini, who, before his death in 1868, turned out terracotta busts by the dozen under contract to an art dealer. They were considered to be perfect examples of Renaissance sculpture, and the Florentine faker's works appeared in museums around the world. There are still two in London's Victoria and Albert Museum.

In 1977 a beautiful wooden carving of a kneeling stag was given pride of place in the antiques department of Harrods, the department store in London. It was reputed to have come from a French château and to have been carved around 1580. The price tag was £9,800.

Then Frank Sedgwick, a 47-year-old ex-fitter whose hobby was woodwork, walked into the store and said: 'That's mine.'

What was claimed to be a fine example of 16th-century craftsmanship had been knocked up by Sedgwick in a fortnight. He had carved it five years earlier at his home in the Kent village of Petham and had sold it for £165. It had changed hands several times since, and each time its antiquity and its price had grown – until Harrods accepted it for sale. After Sedgwick's visit, they removed it.

Famous faker Clifford Irving (see page 144), the American author jailed for his forged biography of Howard Hughes, once wrote another biography, entitled *Fake*. It was about the exploits of a stateless Hungarian, Elmyr de Hory, whose paintings have hung in dozens of galleries around the world.

The book reported that De Hory's paintings were among millions of dollars'

In 1928, Liberian President Charles King put himself up for re-election. He was returned with an officially stated majority of 600,000 votes. King's opponent in the poll, Thomas Faulkner, later claimed that the election had been rigged. When asked to substantiate his allegations, Faulkner pointed out that it was difficult to win a 600,000 majority with an electorate of less than 15,000.

The Reverend Edgar Dodson, of Camden, Arkansas, chose for a sermon the theme 'Thou shalt not steal'. While he was preaching, someone stole his car.

---

worth of fakes sold to a Texan millionaire. The ensuing scandal made De Hory famous, although he says firmly that he had never tried to pass his work off as someone else's: that is, he has never put a famous signature to one of his own paintings, even when that painting has been in the precise style of a sought-after artist.

In 1974, at the age of 60, De Hory was taken from his home on the island of Ibiza and put into jail in Majorca. There was no formal charge, and he was out again after four months.

Like so many with his talents, he never disguised his contempt for the international art pundits who 'know more about fine words than fine art'. He claimed he could paint a portrait in 45 minutes, draw a Modigliani' in ten, and then immediately produce a 'Matisse'.

'The dealers, the experts and the critics resent my talents,' he said, 'because they don't want it shown how easily they can be fooled. I have tarnished the infallible image they rely upon for their fortunes.'

Even distinguished experts of the most famous art gallery in the world, the Louvre, in Paris, have been taken for a costly ride. The gallery's worst blunder was revealed in 1903 when a Parisian painter claimed that he was the creator of one of its most treasured possessions – a beautifully intricate golden head-dress called the Tiara of Saitaphernes.

The claim was untrue. The tiara was a fake, sure enough. But the man who had made it was not the Parisian painter. Its creator was a Russian goldsmith, Israel Rouchomowsky – and he did not want the false claimant to take credit for his work. So Rouchomowsky travelled to Paris to put the record straight. The administrators of the Louvre continued to deny that the tiara was a fake, until the old Russian produced the original designs he had drawn for the headdress eight years earlier – and, to rub salt into open wounds, began working on a new tiara, as intricate in every detail as that in the Louvre.

In the Louvre today hangs what must be the best-known and best-loved painting in the world. It is also one of the most copied. It is the Mona Lisa. In 1911, the famous smiling lady was stolen. Three thieves, dressed as workmen, had walked casually into the gallery before it shut one evening and had hidden in a basement room. The next day, the Louvre was closed for cleaning. The 'workmen' wandered into the hall where the painting was hung, took it off the wall and walked out of the gallery carrying it, frame and all.

Of the three men, only one had been in this line of business before. He was Vincenzo Perugia, an Italian burglar. The other two were art forgers Yves Chaudron and Eduardo de Valfierno, who had developed their forgery techniques in South America. There, they would interest a crooked dealer or collector in a particular painting at a gallery and promise to obtain it for him, at the right price. The two would then present themselves at the gallery as art experts and take the painting down in order to study it. They would then produce an exact copy, attach it to the back of the genuine painting, and invite their prospective buyer to the gallery to put his mark surreptitiously on the back of the canvas. Later they would remove the fake from the original and take it to the client. There, on the back of the canvas, the buyer would see the mark he had made – the 'proof' that he was getting the genuine article.

In each case, the gallery experts were none the wiser – they still had their original – and the buyer, when he discovered he had been tricked, could hardly complain to the police.

Chaudron and Valfierno switched their operations to the world's art capital, Paris. There, they went one stage further with their elaborate deceptions. They printed phoney pages of newspapers, which included stories about valuable paintings having been stolen. They would show the stories to gullible collectors and then sell them forgeries of the 'stolen' works.

Finally, the tricksters decided that they were ready for their biggest coup. They would forge the Mona Lisa. But this time they would make sure that the buyers would never later be confronted by the genuine article and discover they had been tricked. For this time Chaudron and Valfierno would steal the original.

They recruited Perugia into their gang and, within months of pulling off their amazing robbery, they had forged six Mona Lisas and sold them to gullible Americans for $300,000 each.

Chaudron and Valfierno still had the genuine treasure hidden, but whether they planned to destroy it, sell it, or even return it, will never be known. Their accomplice, Perugia, stole it from them and fled to Italy, where he clumsily tried to sell it himself.

The gang were uncovered and the Mona Lisa was returned to the Louvre, where, under heavy guard, behind a thick glass panel, and surrounded by electronic alarms, it remains today.

STRIP CLUBS SHOCK.
MAGISTRATES MAY ACT ON INDECENT SHOWS.
                                                    – *Daily Mirror*

The great Howard Hughes rip-off

It was billed as the publishing coup of the decade. But it proved to be the literary hoax of the century. The project was the 'autobiography' of the richest eccentric in the world, the legendary multi-millionaire recluse Howard Hughes.

The man behind this ambitious venture was an author named Clifford Irving, a man who, despite never having met Hughes, planned to write the mystery man's life story and sell the book to a publisher as being Hughes's own words.

Hughes was a sick, semi-senile man, possibly drug-addicted, and a fanatical recluse. He would allow nobody near him apart from the tight circle of Mormon male nurses who tended his needs in a succession of hotel-suites around the world.

Clifford Irving was an altogether different character. Born in New York in 1930, he was an incurable adventurer. Educated at art college and Cornell University, he sailed the Atlantic and lived with California's beatniks and Kashmir's drop-outs. He ended his ramblings when he married a pretty, slim blonde named Edith and settled down to write on the Mediterranean island of Ibiza.

His New York publishers, McGraw-Hill, encouraged him in his work and he attained moderate success. It was to McGraw-Hill that Irving turned when he wanted to sell his 'publishing coup of the century'.

Irving's amazing lie was this. . . . He had sent a copy of one of his own books to Howard Hughes for his critical comments. Hughes had replied in the kindest terms. The two had hit it off so well that Irving had boldly suggested 'ghosting' a Howard Hughes autobiography. And, to Irving's surprise, the old recluse had agreed.

McGraw-Hill fell for the bait. They agreed that Hughes would receive a hefty payment for allowing a series of tape-recorded interviews with Irving. And, of course, the author himself was to get large advances on the project. The total sum: one-and-a-half million dollars!

None of this went to Hughes. Roughly half of it was paid out – and all went into Irving's pocket. Not that it stayed there for long. The spendthrift author splashed out on luxury trips around the world. Wherever he went, he claimed to be keeping secret appointments with Hughes or his associates.

McGraw-Hill constantly fired off telegrams to Irving enquiring about the progress of the book. The author would reply from one five-star hotel or another, stressing the extreme difficulties of his task and Hughes's paranoid insistence on secrecy. Craftily, he maintained the publishers' interest by mailing them sample sections of the manuscript and providing letters supposedly sent to him by Hughes.

The sample chapters contained tantalizing quotations supposedly transcribed from tape-recordings made by Irving with Hughes. Some conversations were said to have taken place over the phone, others in person. The contents of the texts were mainly lies – but lies cleverly intertwined with rumour and half-truth and embroidered with the gleanings of newspaper libraries.

Irving's art-school training came in useful at this stage. For the letters signed by Hughes were in reality written by Irving to himself. The forgeries were so perfect that they fully satisfied the more doubtful sceptics at McGraw-Hill. At one stage, when the publishers became worried about the delay in receiving substantial parts of the manuscripts, they secretly took the Hughes letters to New York's leading handwriting analysts – who confirmed without doubt that they were indeed written by the old man.

Not all of Irving's work was pure fiction, however. The author had a secret source of hitherto unpublished revelations about the recluse. The source was Hughes's former aide, Noah Dietrich, who had made copious notes about his long liaison with the billionaire. Dietrich had been planning to turn this material into a book of his own. But Irving secretly borrowed the aide's notes, copied them and proceeded to lift from them some of the more interesting tit-bits.

McGraw-Hill were well and truly hooked. Tempted by fantastic stories of Hughes's secret World War Two missions, of his friendship with novelist Ernest Hemingway and of his glamorous, globe-trotting life-style, they kept the money pouring in. It arrived by post in the form of cheques made out to Hughes. They were paid into a Swiss bank account but the money did not remain there for long. The account, in the name of H. R. Hughes, had been opened by Edith Irving, using a passport forged by her husband.

Irving must have known that his amazing confidence trick could not last for ever. But when the crash came, it was from the most unexpected direction. By an amazing coincidence, someone else had been plotting a similar scheme to Irving's. A rival publishing house had taken the bait and proudly announced that an authorized biography of Hughes was shortly to be printed.

For a while, panic reigned at McGraw-Hill. The scene of confusion was repeated at the Time-Life organization which had agreed to buy the serialization rights to the Irving book. But the man at the centre of the storm remained as cool as ever. Irving produced a new forged letter from Hughes denouncing the rival book as a fake – and demanding more money for his own.

Raising the price was a master-stroke. McGraw-Hill once again fell for Irving's tale. But for the first time they had to show their own hand and announce the existence of the Irving book.

That sealed the conman's fate. Hughes ordered his lawyers to hold a press conference at which reporters who had followed the astonishing saga of the billionaire recluse were allowed to question Hughes by telephone. The Irving 'autobiography' was denounced, yet the trickster continued his protestations of innocence.

The man who finally shattered Irving's story was Robert Dolan Peloquin, a super-sleuth who had won the title 'Sherlock Holmes of the jet age'. This handsome 6ft 1in American lawyer had spent 16 years in the service of the US Government, taking on the con-men of the Mafia and the sophisticated criminals of the computer world. He was one of Bobby Kennedy's closest aides when the assassinated politician was America's Attorney-General.

Peloquin later left Government service to become president of Intertel, a private international intelligence agency based in Washington DC, with branches throughout the world. Ex-Scotland Yard head of CID Sir Ranulph Bacon joined him on the staff of what has been called 'the world's most formidable private investigating firm'.

It was at Intertel that Peloquin took a call from Chester Davis, lawyer for legendary recluse Hughes, who was alarmed at impending publication of the 'autobiography', and wanted Peloquin to prove the book was a fraud.

This meant knocking holes in publisher McGraw-Hill's claim that Hughes had collaborated with Irving. They based their claim on cheques made out to and endorsed by H. R. Hughes, and deposited in a numbered Swiss bank account. McGraw-Hill said handwriting experts had verified the signatures on them as that of Howard Hughes. But they refused to let Intertel see the cheques for themselves.

The controversy over the book was headline news. And that helped Peloquin get the evidence he needed. An executive of McGraw-Hill went on America's early-morning Today TV programme, brandishing three cheques worth a total of $650,000 and cashed by H. R. Hughes. Peloquin immediately obtained a video tape of the show, froze the frames where the cheques appeared, and had enlargements made of the prints.

It was just possible to see the name of the Zurich bank which had endorsed the payments. Peloquin was on the first available plane.

In Zurich, he was told that H. R. Hughes was a woman. Her description gave him a hunch. He phoned his Washington HQ and asked for a photograph to be wired to him. Four hours later he was back in the bank. The woman in the picture had her hair in a different style, but officials were almost sure she was H. R. Hughes. The picture, of course, was of Irving's wife.

Clifford Irving with his wife Edith and their two sons

Within minutes, the information had been cabled to Chester Davis, who called in the US Attorney in Manhattan. Irving and his wife were arrested.

Irving denied all until the very end. But his lies were finally seen for what they were when internationally famous singer Nina, the beautiful blonde half of the Nina and Frederick folk duo, revealed that at a time when Irving had supposedly been closeted with Howard Hughes, the author had really been with her.

In 1972, Edith Irving, distraught over the stories of her husband's womanizing, was sent to jail for two years in Switzerland. After hearing her sentenced, Irving sobbed: 'I have put my wife in jeopardy. She has suffered terribly. I have heard her cry herself to sleep at night.'

Then he too went down. After cracking and confessing all, Irving was fined

Shock of recognition

Swashbuckling silent screen hero Douglas Fairbanks senior was a great hoaxer. He had a special chair electrically wired to give mild electric shocks to anybody who sat in it. But he came unstuck once when a female fan sat in the chair. He applied the current but she showed no reaction. When he asked if she was feeling all right she explained: 'I thought one always felt like this when meeting a wonderful movie star like you, Mr Fairbanks.'

$10,000 and sentenced to 30 months' jail in the US. He was also ordered to pay back some of the $500,000 he owed McGraw-Hill.

Edith Irving served only 14 months of her sentence and her husband 17 months. But they were never reunited. Edith won a divorce and remarried her husband's former tennis partner. Clifford himself moved down to Mexico with a young woman friend.

There he set about writing another book, legitimately this time. It was a detailed, dramatic account of how he pulled off his $1½ million superhoax. He needed it to sell well in order to pay off his huge debts. And, ironically, the book was given a huge and topical sales boost soon after with the death in 1975 of the one man whose fabulous wealth had made the hoax of the century possible – Howard Hughes.

The politician who faked his own death

Sixty-five-year-old Mrs Helen Fleming was happy to help the pale Englishman who approached her on Miami Beach on a grey, blustery day in November 1973.

Mrs Fleming who ran the Fontainebleau Hotel beach office, had already talked to him some ten days before. He had then told her that he was in Florida on business and that on a previous trip all his possessions had been stolen from the beach. That was why he now asked Mrs Fleming to be good enough to look after his clothes while he went for a swim. The old lady was glad to oblige such a polite, well-spoken gentleman.

The Englishman also impressed on Mrs Fleming his name. He mentioned it

several times, and she had no trouble in recalling it later. The name was . . .
John Stonehouse.

Stonehouse, 48-year-old Member of Parliament, strolled down the beach to
the choppy sea – and vanished. He left behind him a wife, two children, a
mistress, a constituency, several ailing companies and debts of about £800,000.

Next morning, James Charlton, a director of one of Stonehouse's companies,
who had travelled to Miami with him, reported to the police that his partner
had not been seen all night. A search was organized but no body could be found.
It was assumed by everyone that he had drowned.

But John Stonehouse had not drowned. His 'death' was simply the final step
in an amazingly devious plot.

At the time of his supposed death, Stonehouse was in fact strolling along
Miami Beach to a derelict building near the Fontainebleau. There he
retrieved a hidden suitcase containing clothes, money, travellers' cheques,
credit cards and a passport – all in the name of Joseph Markham. He took a cab
to Miami International Airport, boarded a plane to San Francisco and booked
into a hotel there under his assumed name.

Over the next week he made his leisurely way by air to Australia. From room
1706 of the Sheraton Hotel, Honolulu, he made two phone calls to his beautiful
mistress, Sheila Buckley at a London hotel. He went night-clubbing in Honolulu,
sight-seeing in Singapore, and on November 27 flew into Melbourne.

There, in the heat of a southern summer, 'Joseph Markham' lazily acquired a
suntan, planned a reunion with his young mistress, and congratulated himself
on the success of the most brilliantly executed and foolproof deception of the
decade . . . or so he thought.

John Thomson Stonehouse had always been an arrogant man. His conceit
made him few friends as he carved a career in politics and business. He wanted
to be a millionaire but he ended up in debt. He aimed to be Prime Minister but
he ended up in jail.

Stonehouse first entered the House of Commons as a Labour MP in 1957,
and subsequently held various ministerial posts, including Postmaster General.
But when Labour lost power in 1970 he was offered only a minor post in the
shadow cabinet. He turned it down and decided to use his political contacts to
enter the business world and 'make a million'.

Financial independence, he told his beautiful wife Barbara, would allow him
to return full-time to politics and make an attempt at the Labour leadership.
But again his ambitions outstripped his ability.

Stonehouse formed 20 companies in five years, including a merchant bank.
One by one they ran into trouble. His little empire only lasted as long as it did
because of the way he manipulated funds between one company and another.
Whenever the accountants were due to inspect the books of one company, cash

would be pumped into it from another so that trading figures looked good.

It was a survival system that could not last. Finally, Stonehouse owed more than £1 million. Banks and credit card companies were demanding £375,000 and he had signed personal guarantees, that he had no chance of honouring, to the tune of £729,000.

By 1974 Stonehouse knew that a Department of Trade investigation was imminent. It would expose him as a liar and a cheat, signal the collapse of his companies, and lead to personal ruin, disgrace – and possibly prosecution for fraud. So he turned to the only ally he could fully trust – his mistress.

Mrs Buckley, 20 years younger than her lover, first worked for Stonehouse as his secretary when he was Minister of State for Technology. With her long black hair, full lips and flashing eyes, the 22-year-old beauty was a popular figure in the Commons. But she had eyes only for her boss. Separated from her husband, in 1973 she moved into a nearby apartment and became Stonehouse's mistress. Her pet name for him was 'Dum Dum'.

After her divorce in 1973, on the grounds of her husband's adultery, Sheila Buckley and her 'Dum Dum' set in motion a plan to salvage as much as possible from what remained of Stonehouse's companies. His eventual aim was to tuck away a nest-egg of more than £100,000 in banks in Switzerland and Australia and use the money to establish himself and his mistress in a new life together with fresh identities in New Zealand.

But first John Stonehouse had to 'die'. . . .

The initial step was to find someone else, someone who was *really* dead, so that he could assume that man's identity. As MP for Walsall, Staffordshire, Stonehouse tricked a local hospital into giving him details of men of his age who had died in the wards. He told them he had money to distribute to widows and that he was carrying out a survey. They gave him two names.

He used the same cover story when he called on Mrs Jean Markham and told her how sorry he was that her 41-year-old husband Joseph had died some weeks earlier of a heart attack.

He extracted from Mrs Markham all the information he needed for his plot to steal her dead husband's identity – particularly the fact that since Mr

---

Thieves in a flap

Cat burglars couldn't believe their eyes when they found a giant 2½ ft dog flap in the back door of a house they were about to rob in Berkshire, southern England. They crawled through, subdued a 4-ft Great Dane called Jasper and fled with £5,000 of jewellery.

Markham had never travelled abroad he had not needed a passport.

Then Stonehouse repeated his act with Mrs Elsie Mildoon, whose husband Donald had also died in the same hospital.

Everything was now ready. Stonehouse obtained copies of the two men's death certificates. Then he applied for a passport in Markham's name. He had himself photographed in open-necked shirt with hair brushed straight back, large spectacles, and a wide grin to distort his features.

He signed copies of the photograph, certifying it to be a true likeness of Joseph Markham, in the name of Neil McBride MP. Stonehouse knew that McBride was fatally ill with cancer. He died two months later.

On August 2, 1974, the Passport Office issued British Passport Number 785965 in the name of Joseph Arthur Markham. Stonehouse had his new identity.

In order to establish Markham as a real person, he got him a private address in a cheap London hotel and a business accommodation address as J. A. Markham, export-import consultant. He opened a bank account as Markham, deposited sums of money in it, then transferred the money to another Markham account with the Bank of New South Wales in London. He flew to Switzerland and put large sums in special Markham accounts there; and he obtained an American Express credit card in the dead man's name.

By November 1973 Stonehouse had no fewer than 27 different accounts in his own name in 17 banks, as well as nine accounts in the names of Markham or Mildoon. The ground plans had been well laid for his disappearance. But there was still one more major test to make.

On November 6 Stonehouse flew to Miami, supposedly to try to raise a big investment to save his ailing merchant bank. On the beach he chatted with Mrs Fleming. He travelled out under the name of Markham, even buying his plane ticket with a Markham credit card. No one was suspicious. The dummy run was a success.

Ten days later he was back in Miami on his final business trip – this time travelling on his own passport – and it was then that he performed his vanishing trick on Miami Beach. A day later the Miami Beach Police Department contacted London with the message: *John Stonehouse presumed dead*.

And 'dead' John Stonehouse might have stayed – but for the most astonishing stroke of bad luck.

The day after his arrival in Australia, Stonehouse called at the Bank of New South Wales in Collins Street, Melbourne. There he checked that Aust. $24,000 had been transferred from London in the name of Markham. He withdrew $21,500 in cash and walked down the road to the Bank of New Zealand, where he introduced himself as Donald Mildoon. He said he was planning to emigrate to New Zealand and wished to deposit $21,500 in cash.

John Stonehouse surrounded by crowds as he leaves Brixton prison

The teller to whom he handed the money was 22-year-old Bryan King. Later, returning from lunch, Mr King spotted Mr Mildoon emerging from the Bank of New South Wales. Mildoon strolled down the street to the Bank of New Zealand. There he deposited another $2,200 in cash.

The young man was suspicious. He told his boss, who telephoned the Bank of New South Wales. 'No,' he was told, 'We have no customer by the name of Mildoon. But we do have a newly arrived British immigrant named Markham who has been drawing out large sums of money in cash.'

The bank notified Victoria State Police and from that moment Stonehouse, alias Markham, alias Mildoon, was watched. The police did not have to wait long for his next move. For the following day Stonehouse boarded a plane at Melbourne Airport and flew to Copenhagen for a secret meeting with Sheila Buckley.

On December 10 he was back in Melbourne. While he was paying a call on his bank, Stonehouse's apartment was visited by Detective Sergeant John Coffey of the Melbourne Fraud Squad. He found nothing incriminating – but a book of matches caught his eye. They came from a hotel which Coffey had once photographed while serving as a steward on a cruise liner almost 20 years earlier. The hotel was the Fontainebleau, Miami Beach.

Coffey had Stonehouse closely tailed 24 hours a day. His actions were entirely unsuspicious. The only regular event in his life was his daily walk to buy *The Times*: but he could never wait until he was home to begin reading it. He always searched through it intently as he stood on a street corner.

Coffey bought copies of the newspaper, trying to discover what the Englishman was looking for. All that he found were reports about the disappearance of another Briton, Lord Lucan, wanted for the murder of his family's nanny.

Coffey naturally assumed that Mr Markham and Lord Lucan were one and the same man. But three days later he read about inquiries into the affairs of another missing Englishman, John Stonehouse MP, who had vanished from the Fontainebleau Hotel, Miami Beach. Coffey remembered the book of matches.

Victoria police called Scotland Yard and asked them urgently to airmail photographs of both Lucan and Stonehouse. The Yard also supplied the information that Stonehouse had a long scar on his right leg.

Early in the morning of Christmas Eve, Coffey and other detectives, armed with revolvers, arrested 'Mr Markham'. At first Stonehouse refused to answer questions. But when his right trouser leg was raised to reveal a scar described by Scotland Yard, he admitted his real identity.

In the fugitive's pocket was a letter addressed to Donald Mildoon. It read: 'Dear Dums, do miss you. So lonely. Shall wait forever for you.' It was from Sheila Buckley – one of many she wrote to Stonehouse while he was on the run.

> ## Nothing to declare
> A customs officer was suspicious about a lorry that had just driven off an English Channel ferry at Dover, Kent. He sauntered up to it, knocked on the side and shouted: 'Are you all right in there?' Back came the reply from 22 illegal Asian immigrants: 'Yes!'

On the day of his arrest in Melbourne, Stonehouse telephoned his wife Barbara. Unknown to either of them, the call was recorded. Stonehouse apologized to her, describing what had happened as a 'brainstorm' and explaining that by adopting another identity he hoped to set up a new life.

He concluded with an amazing request. He asked his deserted wife to fly out to Melbourne and to bring his mistress as well. 'Bring Sheila,' he said, 'and we'll link up. If the Australian authorities will allow it, I will remain here and start a new life. . . .'

Stonehouse then spoke to his 14-year-old son, Matthew, telling him that he would understand it all one day and urging him to be brave.

He ended the call with a final plea to his wife to fly to his side with Sheila Buckley in tow: 'Please tell her . . . and try to persuade her. I know she'll need enormous support. The poor girl's been going through hell like you have. I feel for you both.'

Incredibly, wife and mistress flew out separately to join Stonehouse who was by now out on bail. But after an emotional scene, with Stonehouse threatening to commit suicide, Barbara returned home. Sheila Buckley stayed on in Australia with her lover – a sort of phoney honeymoon for them both – until in April 1975 an extradition order was signed. Three months later the couple were flown back to Britain. Finally, in April 1976 their trial began at the Old Bailey.

It cost the British taxpayer an estimated £750,000 to bring John Stonehouse to justice. There was a six-week preliminary court hearing, six barristers involved in the 68-day trial, and a subsequent civil enquiry cost £100,000.

For almost two years an eight-man Scotland Yard fraud team had been tied up sifting through mountains of documents. They had visited America, Australia, Switzerland, Holland, Hawaii and Liechtenstein. Witnesses were brought from Australia and Hong Kong; altogether more than 100 people gave evidence in court.

On August 6, 1976, guilty verdicts to 14 charges involving theft, forgery and fraud rang out in the Old Bailey's historic Number One Court.

Jailing Stonehouse for seven years, the judge, Mr Justice Eveleigh, said: 'You are no ill-fated idealist. In your evidence, you falsely accused people of cant, hypocrisy and humbug – when your defence was all these things.'

Sheila Buckley collapsed in tears as she was given a two-year suspended sentence for helping her lover spin his web of fraud. Throughout his years in prison, she stood by him. He suffered two heart attacks and for several days seemed close to death in a prison hospital. Sheila Buckley visited him regularly.

Stonehouse served only three years of the seven-year sentence. And when he left jail, sick, bankrupt and broken, Sheila and he moved in to a small £13-a-week love-nest in an unfashionable area of London.

In February 1981 the couple married at a secret ceremony in the small Hampshire town of Bishop's Waltham. Perhaps at that ceremony the new Mrs Stonehouse recollected the words she spoke to reporters after her lover's arrest in Australia in 1974 . . . 'If I had the same decisions to make all over again tomorrow, I feel certain that those decisions would remain the same.'

The faker famous for his 'Sexton Blakes'

Brilliant faker Tom Keating rocked the art world he despised with his amazing imitations of the works of great masters. In 1979, at the age of 62, he went on trial at the Old Bailey for forgery. But all the charges were dropped when his health deteriorated.

Keating, a big bearded ex-naval stoker, called his fakes, in Cockney rhyming slang, 'Sexton Blakes'. At first he painted them to get even with the dealers who had, he reckoned, exploited him.

As a young man, he had lived in a damp prefab with his wife and two children, and was paid £5 a time to copy other artists. He angrily quit the job when he found his paintings on sale in galleries for £500.

'Those dealers are just East End blokes in West End suits,' he said. 'They

Artist, Tom Keating

Fake Madonna

America's Cleveland Museum of Art had to remove from display one of its most prized possessions, a wooden Madonna and Child, supposedly carved in Italy in the 13th century. In fact, it was carved around 1920 by an Italian art restorer, Alceo Dossena. His fake was only discovered when in 1927 the sculpture was X-rayed and modern nails were found to be embedded in the wood.

The museum put the Madonna and Child in its basement and looked around for other works to replace it. Three weeks later it bought a marble statue of Athena for $120,000. It, too, was a Dossena fake.

don't give a damn about the paintings. All they're after is the profit.'

In the 1950s his marriage broke up and he went to Scotland to restore murals. While he was there he began imitating the works of other painters and sending them to auction.

He returned to London in 1960 for his most important commission – restoring the pictures in Marlborough House which had been empty since the death of Queen Mary in 1953.

One day he met Queen Elizabeth while carrying out the restoration of a giant painting by Laguerre of the Duke of Marlborough.

In his book, *The Fake's Progress*, Keating recalls: 'The Queen came up the stairs and gazed at it in astonishment. She turned to me and mentioned that she had run up and down the stairs hundreds of times as a little girl but had not been aware these beautiful pictures were on the wall. "Well they are madam," I said. "And there's a lot more under the black varnish on the other walls."'

Then, according to Keating, the Queen watched him use a solvent to clean a section of the painting.

The work at Marlborough House was an isolated job for hard-up Keating. Most of his time would be spent turning out his 'Sexton Blakes' by the score, giving most of them away but selling others through auction rooms.

In 1963 he read a book on the 19th-century artist Samuel Palmer and became captivated by him. He scoured the art galleries looking for examples of Palmer's work to copy. At the Tate, said Keating, he touched one 'and a strange sensation went through me like an electric shock'.

Keating was a perfectionist. He was always careful about selecting the right paper or canvas. And he claimed that the spirit of Palmer would guide his hand.

'I'd sit in my little sketching room waiting for it to happen,' he explained. 'I have never drawn a sheep from life but then Palmer's sheep would begin to appear on the paper. Then Palmer's *Valley of Vision Watched Over by the Good Shepherd in the Shadow of Shoreham Church*. With Sam's permission I sometimes signed them with his own name, but they were his, not mine. It was his hand that guided the pen.'

It was also in 1963 that Keating met Jane Kelly, a pretty convent-educated schoolgirl busy studying for her exams. In Bohemian coffee bars, she and her friends would cluster round the painter, treating him almost as a guru.

Jane was 17, Keating 46. Yet, after the death of her boy-friend in a road accident, they fell in love – and the impressionable teenager became the painter's mistress. They moved to historic Wattisfield Hall in Suffolk, where Jane restored pictures and Keating embarked on a prodigious output of fakes.

When, at the Old Bailey in 1979, Keating was shown his most famous fake – a sepia, ink-wash of *Sepham Barn* sold for £9,400 as a genuine Palmer – he told the jury: 'I am ashamed of this piece of work.'

He had no recollection of painting it, he said. It had, however, been done using modern materials, the main figure of a shepherd was 'un-Palmerish' and the flock of sheep 'unsheep-like'. It was the sort of painting, he confessed, that he would normally have burnt or thrown away.

Looking at another work subsequently sold for £2,550, Keating appeared bemused and said: 'That must have taken me about half an hour. It's just a doodle. It has the ingredients of Palmer but not his technical ability of aesthetic appeal'.

The 'doodle' was of a barn at Shoreham, which had been sold at a country auction for £35. It was later sold by a London gallery to Bedford Museum for £2,550 after restoration work by the National Gallery.

Bemusing the Met

In 1918 the New York Metropolitan Museum of Art paid $40,000 for the 7-ft statue of an Etruscan warrior which had supposedly been buried since pre-Roman days. One arm of the warrior was missing, as was the thumb of his other hand.

In 1960 Alfredo Fioravanti confessed to the museum that he was one of six men who had created the statue between them 50 years earlier. He produced the warrior's missing thumb to prove it. The thumb fitted perfectly.

In 1975 the same museum had to withdraw from display a beautiful 'Greek' bronze horse when it was shown to be a fake. The horse had been one of the museum's most popular attractions.

After the sale of *Sepham Barn*, Keating and Jane went to live in Tenerife. There, Jane met a Canadian with whom she fell in love and whom she later married. The nine-year affair between Jane and Keating was over. They met again seven years later – when Jane gave evidence at the Old Bailey about Keating's famous fakes. The scandal, which ruined many reputations in the art world, broke after an expert had written in *The Times* suggesting *Sepham Barn* was not genuine.

By Keating's own rough count, no fewer than 2,500 of his fake pictures are hanging in galleries or on collectors' walls. No one will ever know which are fakes and which are old masters. Not even Tom Keating who, after his trial was stopped, continued turning out his paintings – at a price.

Because of his notoriety, Keating's works became highly prized. 'Suddenly everyone wants to own a Keating,' said one gallery owner. 'Prices have doubled in a month. His paintings are going round the world.'

Keating was offered a £250,000 contract from one London gallery and a £30,000 commission for a single portrait. He turned both down.

'I have enough work to make me rich beyond my wildest dreams,' he said. 'But I've met many millionaires and they have all been miserable. All I have ever wanted to do is to paint. I would give all the damn things away if I could afford to. Painting is God's gift, not mine, and it should be used to bring pleasure.'

At the height of his fame, a television film was made about the master-faker's life and work. Director Rex Bloomstein got to know him well. He said of Keating:

'He was a very emotional man. When painting, he would cry and shiver. He said he felt the artist come down and guide his hand. he was the most fascinating, complex person I have ever met.'

Crowning jest

In 1902 hundreds of upper-crust Americans received invitations to the Coronation of Edward VII and Queen Alexandra of England. Attached to each invitation was a set of instructions about the proper attire for the Coronation. Wealthy Americans were asked to turn up in costumes typifying the origins of their titles. Coal barons might wear miners' helmets, judges might carry six-shooters, and railway tycoons might sport guards' whistles. The invitations were, of course, a hoax. But they were cleverly adapted facsimiles of the genuine articles.

Never give a sucker an even break!

Phineas is an unusual name. Biblically, it means 'he with a brazen mouth'. In the case of Phineas T. Barnum, the greatest showman the world has even seen, it was extremely apt.

Big-mouthed Barnum would tell the most outrageous lies to lure his American audiences. They were persuaded to pay to view his 'cherry-coloured cat' – only to find themselves staring incredulously at an ordinary black alley cat which, according to the sign, was 'the colour of *black* cherries'! They would queue to see 'the horse with its tail where its head should be'. Spectators would be led into a tent where a perfectly ordinary horse would be tethered in a stall – back to front, with its tail in the feeding trough!

Phineas Taylor Barnum, born July 5, 1810, lured millions of sensation seekers to his museums and circus tents by creating and exhibiting well-publicized fakes and phonies such as these.

There was his 'Feejee Mermaid' which he claimed had been fished from the Pacific in 1817. Thousands paid their 10 cents to see this marvellous freak that in reality was the result of a taxidermist's art and Barnum's imagination. The upper part of the mermaid was a monkey and the lower part a fish.

In 1841 Barnum opened the American Museum in New York. It housed a permanent exhibition of art, curiosities and natural history, and Barnum boasted: 'I mean people to talk about my museum, to exclaim over its wonders, to have men and women all over the country say that there is no place in the United States where so much can be seen for 25 cents as in Barnum's American Museum.'

Most of the exhibits really were remarkable . . . and quite genuine. There was a fantastic working model of the Niagara Falls and the first Punch and Judy show ever seen on that side of the Atlantic. There was also a live hippopotamus and a flea circus. But such was Barnum's distaste for plain speaking that he billed the hippo as 'the Great Behemoth of the Scriptures' and the fleas were advertised as 'insects that can draw carriages and carts'. Of course, the carriages and carts were suitably insect-sized.

Another of Barnum's attractions was an African elephant which had been a big draw in the London and Paris zoos. It was called Jumbo and it has given its name since to everything from jumboburgers to jumbojets. It died in 1885 after being struck by a train during a tour of Canada.

At the other end of the size scale was mighty midget 'General' Tom Thumb.

Barnum's half-brother Philo mentioned to the showman that the five-year-old phenomenon was being exhibited at Bridgeport, Connecticut. Barnum dropped everything, raced to see the tiny fellow and signed him up on the spot to work for him at $3 a week.

Tom Thumb, born January 4, 1838, had weighed more than 9 pounds at birth and had developed normally until the age of six months. Since then he had not grown another inch. At the age of five he still stood just 2 ft 1 in tall.

Anyone else might have thought this extraordinary enough in itself. But not Barnum. He billed the lad as 'General Tom Thumb' a dwarf of 11 years of age, just arrived from England'. He trained the midget to be 'autocratic, impudent and regal' and made him learn by heart appalling, stilted, pun-filled speeches which he recited to enrapt audiences. Barnum dressed him at different times as Napoleon, a Roman gladiator and Cupid. Tom Thumb became Barnum's roving ambassador (and publicity agent) and during a British tour was even introduced to Queen Victoria.

Phineas T. Barnum is credited with coining the phrases 'There's a sucker born every minute' and 'Never give a sucker an even break'. It has also been suggested that the following famous words, generally attributed to Abraham Lincoln, were in fact spoken by Barnum: 'You can fool all the people some of the time and some of the people all of the time, but you cannot fool all the people all the time'.

Barnum learned these elementary rules of showmanship at an early age. In his home town of Bethel, Connecticut, he worked in a barter store, where goods were paid for not in cash but in kind. So much suspect merchandise was offered to the store that the rule of the house was to make sure of a good bargain by automatically offering faulty goods to the customer in return. 'Everything in that store,' said Barnum, 'was different from what it represented.' Burnt peas were sold as coffee beans and cotton offered in place of wool.

Barnum learnt a few useful lessons in Bethel. But he earned little money. So in 1843 he took his family to New York and established a sideshow. His very first exhibit secured his fortune. Posters plastered all over Manhattan announced:

'The greatest curiosity in the world, and the most interesting, particularly to Americans, is now exhibiting at the Saloon fronting on Broadway; Joice Heth, nurse to General George Washington, the father of our country, who has arrived at the astonishing age of 161 years, as authentic documents will prove, and in full possession of her mental faculties. She is cheerful and healthy though she weighs but 49 pounds. She relates many anecdotes of her young master . . .'

Barnum had not invented Joice Heth. She really existed. She was a hideously ugly old negress whom Barnum had come across in a sideshow in Philadelphia. She was blind and partly paralyzed, but Barnum borrowed money to buy her from her exhibitor and put her on show in New York. Joice would answer

Phineas Taylor Barnum, the great American showman

questions from the audience about her supposed career as Washington's nurse; any errors in her replies—and there were many—were excused on the grounds of her failing faculties.

So astute was her new owner that he even wrote anonymous letters to the newspapers calling into question the veracity of the old lady's claims. His reasoning, echoed by many a publicity man since, was that it is better to have people talking about you than not. Bad publicity is still publicity.

Joice Heth died in 1836. And Barnum, of course, found a way of making mileage of the event. He engaged a leading surgeon to perform an autopsy on the raddled old hag—in front of an invited audience. Unfortunately for Barnum, the surgeon's verdict was that Joice Heth was no more than 80 years old. Barnum was labelled a charlatan but he protested that he had been duped just like everyone else. It kept his name in the news!

Barnum's career in conmanship continued for a further half-century, with only one major setback. In 1865 fire destroyed his fabulous American Museum. A fireman single-handedly carried the 400-pound Fat Lady to safety but the 7ft 11in World's Tallest Woman had to be rescued by crane along with her friend the Human Skeleton. Wild animals escaped through the streets of New York and an orang-utan caused havoc in a nearby block of offices. It was big news, Barnum made sure of that.

The damage was put at $500,000 and Barnum was insured for only a tiny fraction of it. Yet by the time of his death in 1890, he had recouped his fortunes. He left $5 million—proving that 'there's a sucker born every minute'.

The bank robber aged nine

A nine-year-old freckle-faced youngster munched a chocolate bar in a New York court in March 1981, as a judge heard evidence that he was America's youngest bank robber.

The boy was said to have walked into a bank, pulled out a toy cap-pistol, held up a clerk, and walked out with just over $100.

If he hadn't been so small, the security cameras might have detected him in time. As it was, he skipped out a good few steps ahead of the guards. With the FBI and the police on his trail the boy spent all but $20 of his loot on hamburgers, chips, three picture shows and a wrist watch which played a tune. Then he turned himself in.

His lawyer said that the boy was brought up on a constant diet of TV crime shows. The day after watching *FBI* and *Policewoman* he got out his toy gun and went to the bank.

The unbelievable Horatio Bottomley

As we have seen from the unsuccessful racecourse fraud described in the previous chapter, Horatio Bottomley had the gift of the gab. He could charm people into parting with their money – and often talk his way out of trouble afterwards.

Bottomley was born in London's East End in 1860 but he rose to become a Member of Parliament and a conman with few rivals.

From an early age he knew what he wanted – money, fame, women and a successful political career. After first working as a solicitor's clerk and then a shorthand writer at the Law Courts in London, he turned his attentions to making money – big money – by fraud.

Together with friends, he launched a publishing company. Through another friend he bought some properties, including a printing works in Devon, for more than £200,000. Then he sold them to the publishing company for £325,000.

The trouble was that most of the properties were worthless. Bottomley knew it but the directors of the publishing company had been taken in by him.

Charged with fraud and sent for trial, Bottomley defended himself with such skill that he won. He so impressed the trial judge that he suggested that Bottomley should consider becoming a lawyer!

Bottomley's next move was into the Australian gold boom. By 1897 he had made a small fortune from promoting gold mines. Despite his success, his firms failed regularly and he was constantly being served with writs for bankruptcy.

Yet the public continued to pour their money into his ventures.

His method was simple. He would start a company, declare high dividends and as a result the price of the shares would rocket. Then he and his conspirators would sell the shares at the inflated price.

When the company started to sink, as it invariably did, up would pop Bottomley with a new company, offering to take over the old firm, backed, of course, by more funds from the unsuspecting shareholders.

Bottomley was instrumental in founding the *Financial Times* newspaper and the jingoistic magazine *John Bull*; he was elected to Parliament to represent the London constituency of Hackney South.

Although married, he kept a succession of young mistresses in love nests throughout the country.

At his home in Upper Dicker, near Eastbourne, Sussex, he lived the life of the local squire. But in 1912 he suffered a major setback when forced to resign from

Horatio Bottomley in 1927

Parliament because of a bankruptcy case.

Undeterred, he carried on as usual with his business enterprises and when hostilities broke out in 1914 used his demagogic powers in *John Bull* to support the war effort. He also made stirring recruiting speeches up and down the country – for which he charged a fee!

In 1918, with the war over, he was re-elected to Parliament for his old constituency. One year later he launched his biggest swindle and sealed his own fate . . .

Victory Bonds had been issued by the Government with a face value of £5, although investors could buy them at a discount price of £4 15 shillings. For ordinary working people this was still a lot of money; so Bottomley launched his Victory Bond Club. People were able to invest as little or as much as they wanted and the club would buy the bonds for them.

Bottomley was hailed as the friend of the little man – an image he loved to cultivate. What the investors didn't know was that their hero had siphoned off about £150,000 of the estimated half-million pounds that had flowed into the club in six short months.

The beginning of the end came when Bottomley started and then dropped a criminal libel case against one of his former partners, Reuben Bigland, who had accused him of a swindle.

By this time, the Chancery Court was investigating his empire and in 1922 he was prosecuted at the Old Bailey for fraudulent conversion of the funds of the Victory Bond Club.

This time Bottomley's glib tongue didn't sway the jury. After hearing evidence that he had used the money from the club to pay off £10,000 worth of debts, spent £15,000 on his burning passion for horse-racing and another £15,000 to buy and exhibit a German submarine, they took just 30 minutes to find him guilty. He was sentenced to seven years penal servitude but was released on licence in 1926. He tried to restore his old lifestyle, but in vain.

Horatio Bottomley, ex-millionaire, died in poverty in 1933.

Tea break

A woman who was picking blackberries from a cluster of brambles growing along the wall of London's Wormwood Scrubs prison noticed a rope and a wooden ladder drop down the side of the wall. Three men followed. 'I didn't raise the alarm,' said the woman. 'They told me they were nipping out for a cup of tea and planned to go back later.'

The bouncing Czech who sold the Eiffel Tower at a knock-down price!

The idea came to Victor Lustig in a flash. There he was lounging in his Paris hotel room in March 1925 idly perusing the newspapers when he came across an item that made his eyes widen. The Eiffel Tower, said the report, was in need of major renovation. It had even been suggested that the city's most famous landmark should be demolished and rebuilt. . . .

To an artist, inspiration can come in a flash – and Victor Lustig was nothing if not an artist. The only difference was that his art was outside the law – he was a genius at deception. And the news item in that Paris paper opened up the opportunity for the coolest confidence trick of the present century.

First, Lustig (or 'Count Lustig', as he styled himself) acquired some printed notepaper from the French Ministry of Posts, which was responsible for maintaining the monument, and invited five French businessmen to a secret meeting at the Crillon Hotel, Paris.

When they arrived, they were ushered into a private suite by Lustig's 'ministerial secretary', a fellow con-man named Robert Tourbillon. The five were then sworn to secrecy and told the terrible news: that the Eiffel Tower was in a dangerous condition and would have to be pulled down.

There was sure to be a public outcry over the demolition of such a well-loved national monument, so the French government had to ensure total security. This was why five highly respectable and trusted members of the business community had been specially chosen for their loyalty and discretion.

The five flattered fools fell for Lustig's ruse completely. They each agreed to submit tenders for the value of the 7,000 tons of scrap metal that would be produced by demolishing the tower. Then they went away to make their calculations.

Lustig, however, had already picked out his candidate, a scrap metal merchant named André Poisson, one of the provincial nouveaux riches anxious to make a name for himself in the Paris business world. When, within the week, all five bids were in, Lustig accepted Poisson's and invited him back to the hotel to give him the good news.

It was then that the con-man played his master-stroke. He asked Poisson for a bribe to help the deal go smoothly through official channels. The duped dealer agreed willingly, and gave the back-hander in cash. If he had ever had any suspicions, they were now allayed. After all, a demand for a bribe meant that Count Victor must be from the Ministry!

Poisson handed over a banker's draft. In return, he received an utterly worthless bill of sale.

Lustig and Tourbillon were out of the country within 24 hours. But they stayed abroad only long enough to realize that the outcry they had expected to follow their fraud had not materialized. Poisson was so ashamed at being taken for a ride that he never reported the hoax to the police.

The 'count' and his partner returned to Paris and repeated the trick. They sold the Eiffel Tower all over again to another gullible scrap merchant. This time the man did go to the police, and the con-men fled. They were never brought to justice, and they never revealed just how much money they had got away with.

To a man like Lustig, proud of his art, selling the Eiffel Tower not once but twice was the pinnacle of a long career in confidence trickery. Born in Czechoslovakia in 1890, he had worked his way through Europe, using 22 aliases and being arrested 45 times.

He emigrated to America – but found the pickings so rich among the wealthy passengers on his Atlantic liner that he returned to make the transatlantic trip over and over again!

During the roaring Twenties, when 'making a fast buck' seemed to be all that life was about, Lustig preyed on the avarice of the greedy and gullible.

His cardinal rule when setting up a 'prospect' was to listen. Lustig never sold hard; he always let his victim do the talking, while the con-man showed deep interest. He would seek out his victim's political views and religious preferences and concur wholeheartedly to make him feel he had found a kindred spirit. But at the end of the day, the most crucial common interest would always be money.

Rags-to-riches multi-millionaire Herbert Loller had amassed all the money he could ever need. But he still wanted more, however dubiously it was acquired. Lustig demonstrated to him a machine which duplicated banknotes, and sold it to him for $25,000. Of course, it never worked. But by the time Loller discovered the fact, Lustig had disappeared to the next town, with another name and a new identity.

In the bootlegging days, Lustig insinuated himself into the company of Al Capone. It took a very brave, or perhaps foolhardy, man to tangle with the Chicago gangster, but Lustig actually tried to swindle him out of $50,000. The con-man told him he had a system that would ensure he doubled his money on Wall Street within two months.

Lustig took the money but after a while even he got cold feet and returned the $50,000 intact to Capone. The gangster must have taken a liking to the genial

Victor Lustig

fraud, because he forgave him and even gave him a $5,000 'tip' for his troubles.

Lustig's associations with the Capone gang continued for several years and led the trickster into an area of crime in which he found himself out of his class. That crime was counterfeiting.

By 1934 a special team of federal agents had been assigned to capture Lustig and his old Capone associate. William Watts and to stem the flow of forged $100 bills which the pair were producing at the rate of $100,000 a month.

After tapping their phones for several months, the agents thought they had enough evidence. The pair were arrested and, although Lustig offered to reveal the whereabouts of all the counterfeit engraving plates if he were freed, he was thrown into New York's dreaded Tombs prison.

He didn't remain there long. One morning wardens found his cell empty and a sheet missing. They discovered it dangling from a window. Lustig had gone to ground again.

The master fraud may well have learned his lesson by now. After his jailbreak he fled to Pittsburgh and took on identity number 23 – that of quiet, retiring Mr Robert Miller. But luck was against him. A tip-off led police to his apartment and, after arrest number 47, he was put back in jail to await trial.

The outcome was the worst Lustig could have expected. In December 1945 he was found guilty of distributing a staggering $134,000,000 in counterfeit bills and was sentenced to 20 years imprisonment – the first part of it to be served on the escape-proof island of Alcatraz.

'Count' Victor Lustig, king of the con-men, served only 11 years of his sentence. He died in Springfield Prison, Missouri, in March 1947.

But what of Lustig's partner, Robert Arthur Tourbillon, the man who acted out the role of his 'secretary' in the greatest confidence trick of the century, the sale of the Eiffel Tower? Tourbillon, or 'Dapper Dan Colins' as the police knew him, had almost as amazing a career as Lustig himself.

Born in 1885, Tourbillon's first job was as a lion-tamer in a French circus. His act was called the Circle of Death and it involved his riding a bicycle around a pride of lions. Circus life was too tame for him, however, and at an early age he turned to crime.

He was 23 when he emigrated to America and was 31 when he first went to jail – for, of all things, 'white slavery'. He emerged from prison four years later determined to stick to the one crime he was best at: fraud. Until then, he had been known among the criminal fraternity as The Rat (after his initials) but he now styled himself 'Dapper Dan Collins', bought himself the smartest clothes in New York and set sail for his homeland, France.

He lived for several years in Paris, mainly off the proceeds of rich, old ladies who fell for the Casanova charm of this suave 'American'. In 1925 he and Victor Lustig pulled off their Eiffel Tower fraud and afterwards both men went to ground.

Further bad luck brought Tourbillon to the end of the road. Two American detectives who were in Paris with an extradition warrant for another crook heard about the suspicious exploits of 'Dapper Dan', sought him out – and recognized 'the Rat'. They arrested him and returned him to New York aboard the liner *France*. It was an amazing voyage. Tourbillon was given the freedom of the ship and, on his money, the trip turned into one large party for passengers, crew, criminal and detectives.

Amazingly, when the liner reached New York and Tourbillon was arraigned before a court, the robbery charges that had been brought against him failed to stick and he was freed. But not for long. . . .

In 1929, Tourbillon was charged with defrauding a New Jersey farmer out of $30,000 savings and was jailed for two years. He served 16 months and left jail vowing to return to France. Whether he did so or not, no one knows – for after speaking to reporters outside the jail, Tourbillon was never heard of again.

The 'professor' with an academic act

Thousands of former American college students owe their qualifications to the professor who never was. They were guided to examination success by a man who hoaxed his way into a series of top university posts – and proved he was suited for the job he had no right to hold.

Marvin Hewitt, born the son of a Philadelphia policeman in 1922, was a loner as a child. He discovered advanced mathematics at the age of 10, and was soon so well versed in the subject that neither his family nor his playmates could understand a word of what he was talking about.

He yearned to continue his studies at university, but could not qualify because routine schoolwork bored him. He left secondary school early, at 17, and for six years worked unhappily in factories and freight yards.

Then a newspaper advertisement caught his eye. A military academy needed a senior preparatory school teacher. Hewitt applied, claiming he was a Temple University graduate, and landed the post.

For the first time in his life he felt at home – admired and respected by pupils and fellow teachers alike. When the spring term finished, he decided to further his own education – as an aerodynamicist at an aircraft factory. He picked out a name from a universities' *Who's Who* list and landed a job on the strength of the borrowed qualifications. With his knowledge of advanced mathematics, even the most complex tasks were simple.

That summer, growing in confidence, he chose a fresh name for another post in education. Julius Ashkin was about Hewitt's age, had had a promising career at Columbia University and was about to start work as a teacher at the University of Rochester.

Hewitt usurped his name and qualifications, and applied to Philadelphia College of Pharmacy and Science for a job as physics teacher. He got it, at $1,750 a year. Students watched with admiration as their new master did complicated calculus in his head. And at the end of the year his classes did as well as any others in departmental examinations.

The only dark cloud on Hewitt's horizon was his salary. He felt Ashkin was entitled to better things. So he began writing to other colleges, enhancing his prospects by introducing the Christie Engineering Company in his list of references. This was a simple matter of getting letterheads printed, and hiring a secretarial service to handle mail.

Soon the Minnesota Bemidji State Teachers College sent Christie an inquiry about physicist Ashkin. They received a glowing testimonial – and Hewitt landed a job at $4,000 a year.

On the strength of his new-found means, Hewitt married. His wife Estelle was unperturbed by his bizarre explanation that because he had qualified under an assumed name he had to continue using it. She was even prepared to have all her 'Mrs Hewitt' mail delivered to a post-office box, and to put off her parents when they wanted to visit the couple.

Despite such precautions, Hewitt was running into problems. The president at Bemidji had also attended Columbia University, and was ever-ready to discuss mutual friends and acquaintances with 'Ashkin', a fellow campus old boy.

It was time to move on, and Hewitt decided to return to higher education, where he could mix with minds he considered more his equal.

Out came the Christie notepaper again, and back came an interview offer from the physics department at St Louis University. Hewitt was too scared to go, and wrote excusing himself, saying he could not get away on the suggested date. To his surprise, he was offered the post anyway, at $4,500 a year.

Now Hewitt was in his element. He was teaching graduate courses in nuclear physics, statistical mechanics and tensor analysis. He was proud of lecturing at Ph.D. level. Students liked him and fellow staff respected him, even if some did comment on inexplicable gaps in his knowledge of basic physics.

But again the close links between colleges and academics put his future in peril. A professor who travelled occasionally to Argonne National Laboratory, Chicago, for research, returned one day to tell Hewitt that he had run into an old friend who had worked with Ashkin at Columbia – and remembered him well.

Hewitt was now living on his nerves every time his colleague went to Chicago. But amazingly, the conversations at Argonne, faithfully reported on the professor's return, did not give the imposter away.

In the spring of 1948, Hewitt got another shock. An article appeared in the journal *Physical Review* – written by the real Julius Ashkin. Hewitt dashed to see his professor, and explained that he had written the paper, but signed it from Rochester University because that was where he had done the work on which it was based. Although his explanation was accepted, Hewitt wisely decided that there was a limit to how long his luck could last at St Louis.

He applied to the University of Utah at Salt Lake City, and received the red carpet treatment when he arrived for his interview. Glowing references from St Louis and Columbia backed up the good impression he made. Nobody realized that they were references for two different men. And nobody checked with Rochester University.

A dean at Columbia had even given Hewitt a quite unexpected 'insurance' bonus. He told Utah there had been two Ashkins on his books.

The Utah authorities were so delighted to get their man, they appointed him to a $5,800-a-year position as full professor. Hewitt had now overtaken the man whose qualifications he had borrowed. The real Ashkin was still an assistant professor at Rochester. It was the moment he had dreamed of. But his joy was not to last for long.

A month after he began work as head of department, a letter arrived addressed to 'Dr Julius Ashkin (?)'. It demanded that the masquerade be ended, but added:

'Let me assume that you are versed in theoretical physics and that you are a fundamentally decent man. I should then be willing to help you to relieve yourself of what must have become an almost unbearable burden. It is on these assumptions that I have decided not to take any immediate steps to notify university officials.'

The letter was from the real Julius Ashkin. And though he kept his word, one of his colleagues at Rochester was less merciful and tipped off the authorities. Hewitt was hauled before the Utah president and had to admit the truth. Generously, the authorities offered him the choice of staying on as a research fellow, to qualify for the degrees he needed to hold his position legitimately, or of transferring to another college to qualify.

But Hewitt was too shaken by events to take up either offer. He slunk back disgraced to his mother's home in Philadelphia, and for 18 months laid low, supported by his family and in-laws.

Then, in the spring of 1950, he launched a new bid for bogus academic fame. He wrote to a teachers' placement agency, announcing that George Hewitt, D.Sc., John Hopkins, was available for a posting. Qualifications included work as research director for the giant RCA communications company.

Hewitt had invented an RCA vice-president, and given him an address in Camden, New Jersey where letters could be sent – and answered by Hewitt.

The dead-letter ploy worked again. Hewitt took up an appointment teaching electrical engineering at Arkansas University's college of engineering, and flung himself into the work. Apart from lessons, he gave a local engineering society a lecture on 'The Orthogonality Property in Microwave Transmission.' He also presented a paper on 'The Theory of the Electron' at the Arkansas Academy of Science, and worked on two research programmes.

Then an RCA chief came to the university seeking engineering recruits. 'We have your former research director here,' he was told.

'Oh yes, who's that?'

'George Hewitt.'

'Who?'

It was back to Philadelphia for Hewitt. But by now he had twin baby sons to support as well as a wife. So he became Clifford Berry, Ph.D., Iowa State College, and took a post at New York State Maritime College.

Bored by teaching undergraduates, he tried to gatecrash technical industry. But this proved a tougher nut to crack than colleges. So he became Kenneth Yates, Ph.D., Ohio State University. And in January 1953 he began work teaching at the University of New Hampshire.

Again he was unmasked. One of his students in theoretical physics and relativity became suspicious of lapses in his tutor's knowledge. Checking a copy of the *American Men of Science* catalogue, he found the real Yates was working near Chicago for an oil company.

Confronted by the facts, Hewitt again owned up and quietly resigned. 'I always do all I can to straighten things out,' he said. But this time, any hopes he had of reappearing quickly in a new area were dashed. The news leaked to a newspaper, and quickly his career as a bogus boffin was splashed over every front page in the country.

Hewitt had always caused more trouble to himself than to anyone else. He said wistfully: 'If they'd only let me be a professor, I'd never want anything else or lie. I lied only to get those jobs. I was a good teacher, I've never really hurt anyone.'

Going cheap – some of the world's best-loved landmarks

In 1925, within the space of a few weeks, a plausible Scottish rogue named Arthur Furguson sold off three of London's best-known landmarks to gullible American tourists. Buckingham Palace went for £2,000, Big Ben fetched £1,000 and Nelson's Column was sold for £6,000.

That anyone could fall for such obvious confidence tricks seems beyond belief. Yet Furguson was a past master at the art of gentle persuasion, thanks to his training as an actor. He appeared in repertory company melodramas throughout Scotland and northern England, once acting the role of an American conned by a trickster. Perhaps it was this part which inspired him to move south to London to try his hand in earnest at the con game.

The ex-actor would take up his position near a London monument, studying it with an air of rapt concentration. Soon a tourist would make an inquiry about the history of the monument and Furguson would engage him in conversation.

Once, while pacing around Trafalgar Square, he was approached by an American tourist from Iowa. Yes, said Furguson, the tower in the centre of the square was Nelson's Column, erected in honour of the great admiral. But sadly, he said, it would not be there for long. It was to be sold and dismantled along with several other landmarks to help repay Britain's vast war loan from the United States. And it was he, Furguson, who as a ministry official had been given the task of arranging the sale.

Yes indeed, Furguson informed the gentleman from Iowa, he was reluctantly authorized to accept a bid for the column even at this late stage. Furthermore, since the tourist was so obviously a lover of great art, he could arrange for him to jump the queue.

A cheque for £6,000 promptly changed hands and the American was left with a receipt and the address of a demolition company. It was only when the demolition company refused to consider carrying out the job of knocking down one of London's most historic sights that the American at last began to suspect that he had been taken for a ride.

Furguson used much the same ploy to dispose of the Big Ben clock tower and the King's royal residence of Buckingham Palace. Then, encouraged by his success in extracting cash from trusting Americans, he emigrated late in 1925 to enjoy this fount of easy money.

Within a few weeks he was back in action. In Washington DC, he met a Texas cattleman admiring the White House. Pretending to be a government agent, Furguson spun a slender yarn about how the administration was looking for ways of cutting costs. Now, if the Texan would care to lease the White House at a knockdown rent of $100,000 a year . . .? Furguson was in business again.

Moving on to New York, the wily Scotsman explained to an Australian visitor that, because of a proposed scheme for widening New York Harbour, the Statue of Liberty would have to be dismantled and sold. A great loss to the US, but would it not look grand in Sydney Harbour . . .? The Australian immediately began to raise the $100,000 that the con-man asked for the statue. But his bankers advised him to make a few further inquiries, and the police were tipped off.

This time Furguson had really slipped up. He had allowed the Australian visitor to take a souvenir snapshot of himself with the Statue of Liberty in the background. Police were immediately able to identify him as a man they had been watching.

Furguson was arrested, and a court sentenced him to five years in jail. When he came out, the master-hoaxer retired from the ancient monuments business and, until his death in 1938, lived in California – languishing in luxury on his ill-gotten gains.

The Balfour snowball

J abez Balfour started with nothing and ended with nothing. But in between he made millions – by getting the public to invest cash in fraudulent companies.

Balfour became one of the most respected men of the late Victorian era. He was a Justice of the Peace, Mayor of the London suburb of Croydon and Member of Parliament for Burnley, Lancashire. He was on the point of landing a top Government job when his empire crashed and he was forced to flee the country.

Balfour is said to have originated the snowballing technique (whereby one company finances another) when, in 1868, he set up the Liberator Building Society. Over the next few years there followed a succession of companies such as the Lands Allotment Company, George Newman and Co. and the Real

Jabez Spencer Balfour

Estates Co. In 1882 he founded the London and General Bank with the main aim of processing the mass of dubious cheques that flowed from one into another of his companies.

While his companies bought and sold land and properties to one another – always of course with huge profits for Balfour and his cronies – the subscriptions poured in from the unsuspecting public.

The small investors believed in Balfour. Every year, regular as clockwork, they got eight per cent interest on their savings. Each time Balfour floated a new company it would be oversubscribed as the public flocked to invest.

Balfour was a success and they wanted to be part of it. What they didn't know was that their dividends were being paid out of new subscriptions and were not derived from any real company profits.

As the years passed, the snowball gathered speed and Balfour's business transactions became more and more complicated, his money-spinning schemes even bolder. He not only captivated his devoted investors but also dominated his business colleagues and employees, some of whom were genuinely honest men, others out-and-out villains.

Unlike some of his fellow con-men, there had never been a breath of scandal about Balfour. He had had a strict non-conformist upbringing and he carried this image of trust and respectability into his business and political life.

Large snowballs may take time to melt – but melt they do.

Suddenly in 1892, one of his companies collapsed, owing £8 million. It came out of the blue, quite stunning the financial world, so accustomed to Balfour's successes. Investors, and indeed the entire nation, were shocked at the news.

The only person not caught by surprise was Jabez Balfour. He was well prepared. While Britain was counting the cost of his 20 years of scheming and stealing, he was heading for South America, where he disappeared for three years.

Then, unhappily for him, he was recognized by a visitor to the little Chilean town of Salta. The man reported his discovery to the British Consul who eventually, after a long struggle, managed to extradite Balfour back to Britain to stand trial at the Old Bailey.

Some of the top legal brains of the time were lined up against Balfour. Masses of papers and legal documents were piled high on the court benches as they fought to show how he had swindled his way to millions.

It didn't take long for the jury to decide that he was guilty. He was sent to prison for 14 years with the words of the judge, Mr Justice Bruce, ringing in his ears: 'You will never be able to shut out the cry of the widows and orphans you have ruined.'

Balfour served his time and was planning to start up in business again when he died of a heart attack.

Bank busters extraordinary

Innumerable con-men have tried and failed to get the better of the mighty Bank of England. But it took four American financial wizards just six weeks to swindle 'The Old Lady of Threadneedle Street' out of £100,000 at the height of the Victorian era.

Their method was simple and it made George Macdonnel, Edwin Noyes, George Bidwell and his brother, Austin, rich men. But not for long.

They took advantage of a banking procedure that differed from the American system. The Bank of England had a well-established business in buying bills of exchange at discount rates.

The owner of a bill could take it to the Bank and exchange it for cash before it was officially due to be bought back by the finance house that issued it to raise capital. The Bank kept the bills until the end of the financial quarter when they were due to be repaid in full by the finance houses.

Macdonnel discovered that the Bank did not check whether bills were genuine before buying, as was done at home in America. He knew that a forgery would not be discovered until the end of a financial quarter, allowing the conspirators plenty of time to get away.

He sent word to his friends, the Bidwells, who joined him in London to launch the scheme in November 1872. Austin Bidwell opened an account under a false name at the Bank of England's branch in London's smart West End. Austin Bidwell must have been a very persuasive character, or the branch officials very gullible, for the Bank did not even check his identity, references or address. They seemed more than happy to have £2,000 on deposit from the smooth-talking American 'businessman'.

The conspirators' next move was to pay £8,000 in foreign currency into Bidwell's account. Any doubts entertained by the branch manager, Colonel Peregrine Francis, were surely allayed by the knowledge that his American customer was credit-worthy. Bidwell announced that he was planning to open a

---

What a gas!
Ronald Carr's gas-meter fiddle was a double disaster. He altered the meter the wrong way, so he ended up paying more instead of less. And in court at Rochdale, Lancashire, he was fined £75 for trying to steal the gas.

factory in Birmingham and might need to be granted credit. Francis quickly agreed. In order to strengthen confidence in Bidwell, the conspirators set about trading with genuine bills of exchange.

By the New Year of 1873 the time was right for the conspirators to move in for the kill. Bidwell informed Francis that his Birmingham factory had started to thrive and that he expected to be involved in some large financial transactions over the next few weeks.

Meanwhile, the men had been making faithful copies of their genuine bills of exchange. At this point they brought in from America Edwin Noyes, the fourth conspirator. His task was to present the bills of exchange and to help the gang change gold sovereigns for paper money which could be transported more easily.

In the six weeks up to the end of February 1873, Noyes exchanged a total of 94 bills, totalling £102,000. The plot came to light when the gang thought they still had three weeks of safety before the end of the financial quarter. In his haste to forge exchange bills, Macdonnel had failed to put dates on two of them. Bank manager Francis returned the bills to the finance houses that had supposedly issued them, to find that he had been duped. Noyes was the only member of the gang still in Britain and he was arrested as he went to close his bank account. Austin Bidwell was arrested in Cuba, his brother George was caught in Edinburgh and Macdonnel was extradited from New York.

When the case came to trial at the Old Bailey in August 1873, the evidence against the four men was so overwhelming that the defence lawyers did not even bother to address the jury. All four men were sentenced to penal servitude for life. Austin Bidwell was released after 17 years, Macdonnel and Noyes after 18 years. But George Bidwell, a con-man to the last, convinced the prison doctor that he was near to death and was released on compassionate grounds after only six years in jail. As soon as he was released, he made a remarkable recovery from his mystery illness.

A bevy of bottoms

Dozens of seemingly unrelated people received special invitations to a surprise dinner at a top London hotel. Nobody knew anyone else at the dinner but, as they introduced each other, they discovered that the guest list was made up of Winterbottoms, Sidebottoms, Littlebottoms, Witherbottoms, Highbottoms, Lowbottoms and plain ordinary Bottoms. One of these many Bottoms had called all the other Bottoms together for a joke.

The £32 million 'mouse'

Lowly clerk gambled away a giant bank's assets

F ew people in the world of high finance had heard of Marc Colombo. There was no reason why they should have done. He was just one of 59,000 names on the payroll of Lloyds Bank, a lowly foreign-exchange dealer in the Swiss backwater of Lugano.

But in September 1974, Colombo hit the headlines all over the world in a way that left hard-headed money experts open-mouthed in amazement. Lloyds Bank International announced that 'irregularities' at Lugano, the smallest of their 170 overseas branches, had forced them to suspend both Colombo and branch manager Egidio Mombelli – and had cost the bank a staggering £32 million.

It was the biggest loss ever announced by a bank in Switzerland, and a loss unprecedented in the history of British banking. The news wiped £20 million from Lloyds' London shares and left their top officials in despair over the loop-hole that had allowed it to happen.

What had the handsome 28-year-old wheeler-dealer been up to? And how had he got away with it?

Colombo was a little man with big ideas. He watched as the world's leading currencies daily changed their values on the foreign-exchange market, offering enticing opportunities for men shrewd and brave enough to buy when the price was right and sell at a profit. He decided to grab a piece of the action for his bank.

The 1973 Middle East War and the subsequent Arab oil embargo had sent exchange rates haywire, and Colombo was convinced that the dollar would lose value against the strong, stable Swiss franc. So, in November 1973, he plugged into the international phone network of money dealers and struck what is known as a forward deal.

He contracted to buy 34 million U.S. dollars with Swiss francs in three months' time. If, as he expected, the dollar was worth less when the time came to settle, he could buy back his francs with cheap dollars. But the dollar's value did not tumble. It went up. And Colombo lost seven million francs on the deal – about £1 million. A lot of money to a £9,000-a-year clerk, but not a lot, he reasoned, to a bank which had just announced half-year profits of £78 million.

Colombo, who had worked at the branch for less than a year, knew that reporting the loss to his boss, Mombelli, would probably get him the sack.

So he decided to increase his stake, and go for double or nothing.

So he began an amazing gambling spree. Without Lloyds suspecting a thing, he used their name and risked their money to set up transactions totalling £4,580 million in just nine months. At first, he was betting that the dollar would lose value. It did not. So he switched to gambling that it would go on rising. It did not.

In most offices, a checking system would soon have put a stop to Colombo's antics. Because most foreign-exchange deals are by phone, they are difficult to monitor, so confirmation in writing is usually sent to a third party at the contracting dealer's office. This ensures that holdings of different currencies can be balanced and risks minimised.

But Lugano had a staff of only 16, and no one, including Signor Mombelli, suspected that Colombo was anything other than a diligent, honest employee.

Colombo continued making deals he was not authorised to make with banks he should not have been dealing with. He was blatantly ignoring the £700,000 daily limit on debts or holdings laid down by head office. He was not covering his gambles on buying with counter-balancing orders to sell. He was using inter-bank swap arrangements to borrow cash to cover up losses. And instead of declaring his transactions in records sent to head office and the Swiss authorities, he was logging them in his diary.

Such madness could not go on forever, and the day of reckoning came in August 1974. A senior French banker mentioned casually to a Lloyds man in London that Lugano 'has reached its limit with us'. Alarm bells began ringing at Lloyds' offices in Queen Victoria Street. A phone check with a German bank revealed that it, too, had had massive unauthorised deals with Lugano.

Top executives left London secretly next morning. Unannounced, they confronted Colombo, Mombelli and Karl Senft, the man in charge of all three of Lloyds' Swiss branches. They seized all the papers they could find and flew back to London with the three Swiss employees.

Painstakingly, officials worked all weekend, unravelling the intricate and costly web Colombo had woven. To their horror, they found that he had contracted speculative forward deals worth £235 million which were still unpaid. And he had not hedged his bets. He had committed the bank to

---

A Louisiana firm was given an old mattress to renovate. The workers had already thrown away and burned a lot of the old stuffing when they came across $20,000 hidden in the remainder. They returned this money to its forgetful owner; the other $6,000 he had hidden they had burned.

risking a sum 'largely in excess of the combined capital and reserves of all three banks in Switzerland'. Yet the official ledgers showed deals worth only £36,000.

With special permission from the Governor of the Bank of England, Lloyds transferred huge sums of money to Lugano to cover the promises Colombo had made. Then the bank's international money market director, Robert Gras, spent three weeks trying to minimise the damage – secretly, for any leak would have made the delicate operation more difficult and expensive. It was a mammoth task. When at last the books were in order, and all debts had been settled, Lloyds had lost £32 million.

When the bombshell news was announced by chairman Sir Eric Faulkner, Colombo and his wife had fled their luxury villa on a mountainside above Lake Lugano. Mombelli too had disappeared on an 'extensive holiday'.

But a year later they were both in court in Lugano, facing charges of criminal mis-management, falsification of documents and violations of the Swiss banking code. Colombo admitted exceeding his authorised dealing limits and conducting transactions with unauthorised banks, but denied accepting illegal commissions and criminal intent.

The prosecution described Colombo as the mouse that made Lloyds tremble, and accused him of gambling wildly like a man at a casino. He replied: 'Being a foreign-exchange dealer is always a hazardous operation. It is a gambler's profession.'

When questioned about how his losses had snowballed, he said: 'There was the pride of the foreign-exchange dealer who will not admit failure. I was at all times convinced that I could recoup my losses, but it only takes a little unforeseen something to upset the market. I was a prisoner of events.'

Mombelli, 41, made no secret of the fact that, all along, he had not really understood what was happening. He had initialled papers without realising their significance. The judge described him as 'a disaster, a bank manager without brains'. But Mombelli said after the trial: 'It's a foreign-exchange Mafia. For every dealer you need at least four administrators to check what he is doing. They do things that no ordinary banker understands.'

Lloyds in London were astonished when the two men walked free from the

---

In accordance with his usual custom, an unknown benefactor walked into the Church Army offices, handed over a cheque for £500 and left without waiting for thanks.

As large numbers of these parasites are around at this season, it may be useful to give some hints as how to exterminate them.

– *Western Daily Press*

court. Colombo was given an 18-month suspended sentence and Mombelli one of six months, and they were fined only £300 each, because the judge accepted that they were not lining their own pockets.

Colombo's only motive seems to have been to boost his own ego. Even if his wheeler-dealering had ended in profit, he would still have faced dismissal for unauthorised use of the bank's money. And a profit, after all, had not been an impossible dream for the young Colombo. . . . He later claimed that if his deals had been allowed to stand they would, through later developments on the foreign-exchange market, have netted Lloyds Bank £11 million profit.

Madame Rachel

Like a black satin spider Madame Rachel sat in her exotic Bond Street beauty parlour waiting for vain little society flies to become her victims. She lured them in with the promise of everlasting youth and the opportunity of purchasing her fabulous preparations. Miracles, she assured them, could be performed with her royal Arabian soaps, her luxurious Circassian baths, her peach bloom lotions and alabaster creams. Wrinkles and other tiny signs of age could be banished for ever with her greatest discovery of all – magnetic rock water dew from the sands of the Sahara.

Unfortunately many gullible women in the 1860's found Madame Rachel's advertisements for her famous beauty salon quite irresistible. What they did not know until they were trapped in her web was that the lotions and creams were a cover for a far more lucrative profession. Once Madame had chosen her victims she proceeded to strip them of their money and their reputations and to blackmail them with great cunning.

Many dared not tell their husbands how foolish they had been until it was too late. Fear of scandal, even when there was no truth in the allegations, was like a disease in Victorian England. It was a brave man who eventually exposed the truth and wrought Madame to her deserved end. Not, though, until she had brought havoc in some quarters of London society.

Typical of her method was that used on a woman of wealth and position who had been wheedled into taking a course of baths under Madame's personal supervision. One day this lady removed some diamond ear-rings and valuable rings she was wearing and slipped them into a drawer in the dressing room before stepping into the Circassian waters. On her return she found her jewels had gone. She rang the bell and told Madame Rachel of her loss. The old virago fell into a towering rage and declared she did not believe the lady had any jewellery with her. When she persisted Madame ranted: 'It's no use giving yourself airs here. I have had you watched. I know where you live. How would you like your husband to know the real reason for your coming here? What if I tell him about the man who has visited you. . . .' The wretched woman crept home in despair. Though there was not a word of truth in the allegations she did not dare tell her husband the story until after Madame had been arrested.

Sarah Rachel Russell was born into a Jewish theatrical family about the year 1806. Though in her later years she was said to resemble a somewhat dissipated Queen Victoria, in her youth she was good looking with a magnificent head of hair. She was first married to an assistant chemist in Manchester, then to a Mr Jacob Moses who went down with the wreck of the Royal Charter off Anglesey in 1859 leaving her a young family to provide for, and finally to a Mr Philip Leverson who gave her more children but removed himself from the scene by the time she was operating in Bond Street.

In her early days she was a clothes dealer and used to be allowed to take her goods back stage at the London theatres. But she added procuring to her business activities and was thrown out of Drury Lane for making an insulting proposition to one of the dancers, who threw a pot of ale in her face.

Soon after marrying Leverson she fell desperately ill with an unspecified fever. She was taken to King's College Hospital where her head was shaved and she lost every bit of her beautiful and abundant hair. Her distress was so acute that the doctor treating her gave her some lotion to rub on her scalp which, he promised, would produce an even finer crop of hair than she had before. To her amazement his promise came true and she begged him to give her a copy of the prescription. He did so gladly. That prescription was probably the scientific basis of all the lotions and creams which she later described as 'the purest and most fragrant productions of the East!'

By 1860 she was ready to launch out with her new skills. She opened a shop in Bond Street for the sale of cosmetics and other toilet requisites but the venture was a flop and she found herself in the Insolvency Court and later the debtors' prison. Nevertheless she knew she was on to something good and determined to try again, this time using her genius for self publicity and her florid imagination.

The new business was launched with a pamphlet entitled *Beautiful for Ever*. It was snapped up by every woman in London who cared about her looks and had money to spend. Its language was wildly romantic and idiotically far-fetched but it worked. Madame claimed to be the sole possessor of the delicate and costly arts whereby the appearance of youth could be produced in the face and figure of an older woman. The secret? Her magnetic rock dew water of the Sahara at two guineas a bottle. She gave her customers an insight into how this magic liquid was obtained: collected in the early morning it was carried from the Sahara to Morocco on swift dromedaries there to be used exclusively by the ladies of the court. She had gained the sole right of importation from the Sultan of Morocco himself 'at an enormous outlay'. As it was guaranteed to 'increase the vital energies, restore the colour to grey hair and remove wrinkles, defects and blemishes' it sold like a bomb.

She offered her customers about 60 preparations including her own special brand of face powder. One shade was called 'Rachel' and brunettes still buy powder of that name in the shops today to suit their darker skins. Her most expensive treatment was the *Complete Royal Arabian Toilet of Beauty* which, she claimed, she had planned for the Sultana of Turkey with marvellous results. She did not say how much the Sultana paid but she charged ordinary mortals around 200 guineas.

However, word had begun to spread that beauty treatment was not all that Madame had to offer at her Bond Street establishment. Business flourished and soon she had enough money to take and furnish an elegant house in Maddox Street and to reserve a box at the Opera, which cost £400 for the season. Creams and lotions did not pay for such luxuries. Procuring, fraud and blackmail did.

Sometimes she played for the highest stakes. At others she would risk everything for a relatively small sum. One day the wife of an admiral called at her salon to buy perfume. Madame, singularly plausible, persuaded her to call again, then again. Each time the Admiral's wife bought a few small items. Eventually she received an exorbitant bill. She managed to pay but stopped calling in at Bond Street. Madame did not intend to let her escape so easily. She sent a bill for £1,000 to the Admiral, claiming she had cured his wife of an unpleasant skin affliction. Protests only brought further demands and a threat that unless the bill was settled promptly details of a scandal concerning his wife would be spread throughout London. Fortunately the Admiral went straight to his lawyers and refused to pay a penny. Madame dropped the claim.

The victim who eventually turned on Madame Rachel was a weak, vain little woman of almost unbelieveable gullibility, called Mary Tucker Borradaile. The widow of an Indian army colonel she lived alone in London on her military pension and the modest interest on her investments. She was thought to be about fifty though she refused to reveal her age even in court. She had an almost morbid desire to cling to the pretence of youth and by the autumn of 1864 it seemed she had found the answer to all her problems. She read an advertisement for Madame Rachel's fabulous oriental treatments for enhancing youth, beauty and grace and decided to consult her at all costs.

Madame looked at her new customer with satisfaction. She was 'a skeleton apparently encased in plaster of Paris, painted pink and white and surmounted by a juvenile wig'. Her voice was childish and affected, her lack of brains sadly evident. Madame smiled sweetly and assured her of complete and lasting rejuvenation.

On her first visit Mrs Borradaile spent a modest £10 though in the twelve months following her treatment added up to £170 and she paid out other sums of money for cosmetics. By the Spring of 1866 it was obvious that despite all the baths, creams and lotions Mrs Borradaile looked pretty much the same. Disappointed and peeved she told Madame she had expected to see a better result for her money.

Madame decided she had better move on to the second part of her plan. She informed Mrs Borradaile that a nobleman, Lord Ranelagh, had seen and fallen in love with her. A few days after this extraordinary announcement when they were both sitting in Madame's parlour a tall, elegant man came into the shop. Madame addressed him as Lord Ranelagh. 'Are you *really* Lord Ranelagh?' asked the bemused widow. He bowed, presented her with his card and left. On several occasions after that she saw his Lordship in the shop and once he bowed to her.

His Lordship, it appeared, had first seen her in the days of her beauty when her husband was still alive, and her impression had been imprinted on his heart, only to be revived when he saw her again in Madame's parlour. He begged her to allow Madame to proceed with her 'Beautiful Forever' programme. This meant an immediate outlay of £1,000 to which the widow at first objected but seeing that she could not be brought to the pinnacle of perfection required by her suitor for less, the silly woman agreed to foot the bill.

Madame now began to bring her letters from Lord Ranelagh, which she explained, would be signed 'William' for the sake of discretion. All their courting would be done by letter and they were eventually to be married by proxy.

His Lordship had requested his beloved to deliver up to Madame all her jewels as they were not worthy of her future rank. More costly pieces would of course be provided by him in the future. Meanwhile he advised her to buy a few diamonds for their wedding. A coronet and a necklace were ordered from a New Bond Street jeweller for £1,260 and as the widow hadn't got that much in cash she sold some property in Streatham to pay for them. The money was handed to Madame Rachel, never to be seen again. Nor did she see the diamonds. Lord Ranelagh, it seems had needed the cash for some project he had in mind and had suggested that a coronet which had belonged to his mother might be altered for her.

The letters which Lord Ranelagh continued to send to his future wife were extremely coy but included phrases like: 'My own sweet love I am worried to death about money matters. . . .' He claimed he had tried to see her, referring to Madame in a conspiratorial way as 'Granny'. It was obvious, from the letters, that his Lordship was most anxious to preserve an amiable relationship between his fiancée and 'Granny'. If she once jibbed at the demands made on her purse he was quick to reply: 'My own darling Mary, why don't you do as Granny tells you. . . .'

Even the bride to be could not help but notice that sometimes the letters appeared to be written in a different hand. Often there were spelling mistakes and grammatical errors she did not expect from such an aristocratic fiancé. Once the writer inexplicably signed himself 'Edward'. Madame hastily assured her that Lord Ranelagh had not lost his memory but had injured his arm and had had to ask a friend to write the letter for him.

As the wedding day approached it was suggested that she should visit a coach builders in New Bond Street to select a carriage for herself and also a quantity of silver and plate. All her own things, even rings, brooches and trinkets had been packed away by Madame Rachel – they were not considered suitable for her future station in life.

Finally, having stripped the poor creature of everything she owned apart from the clothes she stood up in Madame dealt the final blow. She had her arrested for debt and taken to Whitecross Street prison where she could only obtain her release by making over to her 'creditor' her pension of £350 per annum.

That, according to Madame's calculations, should have been the end of the affair. But the worm turned. Poor, brainless Mary Borradaile wanted revenge. She made contact with her brother-in-law, a Mr Cope, and he came to her rescue. Having obtained her release he instituted proceedings against the woman who had ruined her.

On 20 August 1868 the case of the Queen v Leverson came before the Central Criminal Court in London and provided entertainment for days as the whole ludicrous story spilled out. There were in fact two trials, the jury at the first having failed to agree. Mary Borradaile, it had to be admitted, was hardly a credible witness, tottering into the box with her yellow wig awry and giving her evidence in a childish, lisping voice while Madame, resplendent in black satin and ostrich plumes, watched her through narrowed eyes. Even *The Times* called her a 'self confessed idiot'. But by the time the second trial started on 22 September, Mrs Borradaile had got her spirits up and at one point, when she was being cross examined by Mr Digby, Seymour cried out:

'She's a vile and wicked woman and you are bad too!'

Madame Rachel, accused of obtaining money by false pretences, claimed in her defence that her client was in fact having an affair with a man called William, that she had concocted the story of her engagement to Lord Ranelagh herself and that all her money had been squandered on her real lover. She had merely been a go-between and had helped Mrs Borradaile to deceive her relations out of the kindness of her heart.

There was a great stir when Lord Ranelagh entered the box. He said he recalled meeting the lady in question on two occasions. He had been introduced to her by Madame but had never had the slightest intention of marrying her and had never corresponded with her in any way. He was extremely embarrassed.

Mr Digby Seymour, summing up for the accused, failed to convince the jury that the pathetic widow was the loose conniving woman he would have them believe. The appearance in the witness box of Madame Rachel's two daughters did nothing to help her. In spite of their charm and good looks it soon became obvious that they were lying for all they were worth and the court came to the conclusion that the younger of the two had in fact written the 'William' letters.

The jury was only out for 15 minutes before returning a unanimous verdict of 'Guilty' sending Sarah Rachel Leverson to prison for five years. She was, said one counsel, 'a most filthy and dangerous moral pest.'

Madame served her time in jail then emerged, apparently undaunted, to start up business again as 'Arabian perfumer to the Queen'! No longer welcome in exclusive Bond Street she established herself in a shop at 153, Great Portland Street where she was soon up to her old game. Her sign caught the eye of a young woman called Cecilia Maria Pearce, wife of a Pimlico stockbroker, who though she was only 23 was dissatisfied with her complexion. Before long the old rogue had her deeply involved. This time, however, she had not taken on a fool but a bright young woman who soon realized she was in trouble and consulted her eminent solicitor, Sir George Lewis. For the third time a warrant was issued for Madame Rachel's arrest. She was tried at the Old Bailey in April 1878 and sentenced to five years imprisonment, the judge regretting he could not give her more. But Madame did not serve out her term. She died in Woking jail on 12 October 1880.

Perhaps the evidence given by Sabina Pilley, one of her assistants, finished her off. For Sabina had torn aside the veil of mystery and divulged her exotic secrets. The fabulous Arabian complexion treatment, for instance, consisted of starch, fuller's earth, pearl ash and water with a dash of hydrochloric acid. As for the Royal Arabian and Circassian baths, so much enjoyed by the Sultana of Turkey. Alas, they were just hot water and bran.

Chapter six

THIEVES AND VILLAINS

A fantastic pageant of thieves and villains are assembled in this chapter. Men and women whose deeds, although never laudable, nevertheless make compelling reading. Some are malicious criminals, but others are somehow admirable even though you may never approve of their misdeeds.

The Glamorous Lovers
BONNIE PARKER AND CLYDE BARROW

Despite the popular image of Bonnie and Clyde as glamorous, rather hard-done-by bank robbers, the reality was very different; they were extremely vicious thieves and murderers.

Handsome Clyde Barrow was born on 24 March 1909 to a poor Texas farmer. Even as a young child he displayed sadistic tendencies, taking great delight in torturing farm animals.

Bonnie Parker born in 1911 came from a devout Baptist family. Her father died when she was four and the family then moved to Cement City, Texas. She was a pretty, petite girl with blue eyes and fair hair. Bonnie had married a Dallas tearaway named Roy Thornton when she was only 16 but the marriage had ended when he was sentenced to 99 years' jail for murder. Her mother was delighted when she met Clyde Barrow because she felt he would help Bonnie to get over her broken marriage. Bonnie was then nineteen-years-old and Clyde twenty-one.

Their relationship did not get off to a good start. The first night that Clyde visited Bonnie's house he was arrested on seven accounts of burglary and car theft. He was given a sentence of two years, but escaped when Bonnie smuggled a gun into the jail. He was recaptured after robbing a railway office at gunpoint, only a few days after his escape. Clyde Barrow was sentenced to prison for fourteen years.

Life in Texas prisons was brutal and extremely tough. Desperate to get out,

---

Charles Arthur Floyd, a strapping farm worker from Okalahoma, felt that he had suffered enough poverty in his life – so he took to robbing banks and machine-gunning guards. A madam of a whorehouse in Kansas City nicknamed him 'Pretty Boy' Floyd and the title stuck to him throughout his criminal career.

During one bank robbery getaway he killed a policeman and was sentenced to 15 years. But he escaped from the train taking him to jail and went on to commit numerous other robberies and at least two more murders. An FBI bullet finally struck him down in a field at East Liverpool, Ohio, in 1934.

Bonnie Parker and Clyde Barrow

Blackbeard was the monster of the Spanish Main whose overpowering 2 metre (6ft 4in) frame put the fear of God in both foes and allies. He had no hesitation in shooting his men – just to let others know who was in charge.

Despite his Latin looks, Blackbeard was born Edward Teach in Bristol, England. He fed his sexual appetite with a bevy of 14 wives and mistresses. And when he was in a flirtatious mood, he would adorn his twisted black beard with silk ribbon. When a price of £100 was put on the scoundrel's head, he met his match in Lieutenant Maynard, captain of a British boat. In 1718 Maynard cornered Blackbeard's boat and he and his men fired 25 shots into his body. Maynard celebrated his victory by flying the murderer's beard from the bowsprit.

Clyde persuaded another prisoner to cut off two of his toes with an axe. He was released on crutches and headed straight back to Bonnie.

To please Bonnie's mother he took a job in Massachusetts in an attempt to make an honest living. However, he could not bear being so far from home and was soon back in West Dallas. Bonnie left home just three days later, to embark on a life of robbery and murder. The couple were joined by a friend of Clyde's called Ray Hamilton, and two other men.

The first murder was committed in April 1932 for the paltry sum of $40 when they shot a jeweller named John W. Bucher in Hillsboro, Texas. Bonnie was in jail at the time on suspicion of having stolen a car, but she was released three months later without any charges having been made. During that time Clyde and his associates brutally gunned down a Sheriff and a Deputy-Sheriff outside a dancehall.

The gang's biggest ever haul was $3,500, stolen from a filling station at Grand Prairie. Bonnie and Clyde decided to celebrate with a motoring holiday around Missouri, Kansas and Michigan, staying at top hotels and eating at expensive restaurants.

Not surprisingly, the money did not last long. They reverted to petty crime, murdering for surprisingly small amounts of money. Bonnie coolly shot a Texas butcher three times in the stomach before robbing him, and William Jones, a 16-year-old member of the Barrow gang, shot dead the son of the owner of a car they were caught stealing. Shooting to kill was now an automatic reflex.

In March 1933 the gang was joined in Missouri by Clyde's brother, Buck, and Blanche, Buck's wife. They narrowly escaped arrest from the apartment they were all staying in and shot dead two policemen in their escape bid.

It was now no longer safe for the fugitives to stay anywhere and they fled from town to town, robbing and killing as they went. They were both very aware that they would not remain at liberty for much longer and, indeed, Bonnie predicted their deaths in her poem, *The Story of Bonnie and Clyde*. Their greatest fear seemed to be that they would not see their parents again, to whom they were both deeply attached.

Near Wellington, Texas, their car plunged to the bottom of a gorge. Clyde and Jones were thrown clear but Bonnie was trapped and seriously burned when it caught fire. She was rescued, with the help of a local farmer. The gang were sheltered for a few days by the farmer and his family who soon became suspicious and called the police. Once again, the fugitives escaped at gunpoint, and were rejoined by Buck and Blanche. Bonnie was still seriously ill.

In July the gang decided to rest at a tourist camp in Missouri. Again, the police surrounded them. Although they shot their way to freedom Buck had been hit through the temple and Blanche was blinded by glass. Desperately hungry, with the two women seriously ill and Buck dying, they stopped to buy food. Within minutes the police were upon them and Buck was shot in the hip, shoulders and back. The police had found him, after the shoot-out, with his wife crouched over him, sobbing. Buck died in hospital six days later and Blanche was given a 10-year prison sentence.

Bonnie and Clyde spent the following three months desperately running from the police, but their luck could not hold out. On 23 May 1934 their Ford V-8 sedan was ambushed by six police officers. Their car was pumped full with 87 bullets and they died immediately, their bodies bloody and broken. Clyde was 25 and Bonnie just 23.

Incredibly, the glamorous legend of the two ruthless lovers had already begun. Vast crowds flocked to their funeral in Dallas, snatching flowers from the coffins as souvenirs. Time has done nothing to erase their memory, and despite their callous, cruel deeds, they are remembered by many as folk heroes.

The Great Train Robbery

How the perfect crime became the great foul-up

It was high summer in the heart of the English countryside. The date was August 3, 1963, the place Bridego Bridge at Sears Crossing, Buckinghamshire – the setting for a crime that was to capture the world's imagination and to become known as the Great Train Robbery.

It was shortly after three o'clock in the morning on that August day that 15 men loaded 120 mailbags into a lorry after robbing the Glasgow-to-London night mail train. The mailbags contained £2½ million.

AUGUST 3 1963

The Great Train Robbery was almost the perfect crime. Almost. For due to a monumental blunder, it turned into a disaster that made the villains who pulled off the robbery the most notorious criminals in the world.

The plan for the raid was hatched in January 1963. It all began with a meeting between a London solicitor's clerk and Gordon Goody, one of the leading lights of a South London 'firm' of criminals. The rendezvous, cheekily enough, was the most famous court in the land, the Old Bailey. There, the clerk boastfully confided to Goody that someone he knew had information about where a vast sum of money could be 'lifted'.

Goody was interested. He called in his friend, Ronald 'Buster' Edwards. And through a string of contacts and secret meetings over the next few days, the incredible project was outlined to them.

Every night, according to the informants, old banknotes from all the banks in Scotland were sent by train to London to be destroyed. The money was always in what was called the High Value Packages Coach which formed part of the night mail train from Glasgow to Euston. There were usually five Post Office workers in this coach, which was always next-but-one to the diesel engine. The other coaches further down the train were manned by dozens of mail sorters. But the coach next to the engine contained only parcels. It was unmanned. The amount of money being carried in the High Value Packages Coach varied from day to day but always rose dramatically after a bank holiday. On August 6, for instance, it might be as much as £4 million. The problem was how were they to rob the train?

However the job was to be tackled, Goody and Edwards realised that it was going to be too big a task for them alone. Through the spring of 1963, the gang grew as more and more tough and specialised criminals were recruited. The team even included members of a rival 'firm' then operating in London.

The gang contained a colourful bunch of villains. Principal among them were: Goody, a tough 32-year-old loner with a sharp taste in clothes and girls; Edwards, aged 30, an overweight but likeable club owner who was a devoted family man: Bruce Reynolds, also 30, married but fond of high living: Charlie Wilson, 32, a resourceful criminal friend of Reynolds: Jimmy White, a quiet, 42-year-old ex-paratrooper: Bob Welch, 34, a South London club owner and one of the top men in the second 'firm': his friend Tommy Wisbey, a 32-year-bookmaker: and Jim Hussey, aged 30, who ran a restaurant in London's Soho.

The gang also brought in three specialists: 'wheel man' Roy James, 23, a silversmith and racing driver, winner of several major races: Roger Cordrey, a 38-year-old florist who was an expert at 'adjusting' railway signalling equipment: plus a retired train driver. At the last minute, they also recruited a small-time thief and decorator, with a pretty wife, an engaging smile and a yearning for the luxury life he could never afford. His name was Ronald Biggs.

Bridego Bridge carries the main Scottish railway line over a winding back road through Buckinghamshire farmland. It was at this spot that the gang had decided to rob the train. By August 2, they had all assembled at a large and lonely farmhouse, Leatherslade Farm, 26 miles from the bridge. They were dressed in an assortment of commando gear. They decided that it would be a good cover if they looked like soldiers out on a night exercise. To complete the picture, they had two Land-Rovers and a lorry painted army green.

At around midnight, these motley 'soldiers' of fortune set out from the farm

---

The career of outlaw Jesse James ended in a shoot-out at Northfield, Minnesota, in 1876. The gunfight began when a bank cashier refused to open a safe. One of the James gang fired at the cashier, alerting the townsfolk who put the bandits to flight. It was later discovered that the safe had not been locked.

in convoy and drove to Bridego Bridge to prepare the amazing ambush. They were armed with pickaxe handles, coshes and an axe to break down the door of the coach. Cordrey, the diminutive rail-equipment fixer, organised the switching of the two warning lights – one several hundred yards up the track and another closer to the bridge. The first warning light, sited beside the track, would cause any train to slam on its brakes. The second, on a gantry above the line, would bring the train to a full stop. The gang also cut the lines to trackside emergency telephones and to nearby farms and cottages. Then they waited.

The train was due to come into view from the bridge at 3 a.m. The timing had been checked night after night on dummy runs by the gang. On the morning of August 3 it was right on schedule. The look-out man alerted the rest of the gang by walkie-talkie, and they all took up positions on the embankments beside the line.

On the train, driver Jack Mills looked out for the usual green trackside light. But tonight it was amber. He put on the brakes and throttled back the mighty diesel. The overhead signal gantry came into sight. It was showing a red light. Mills stopped the train directly under it and asked his fireman, David Whitby, to use the emergency telephone beside the gantry to find out what was going on.

Whitby vanished into the darkness. Mills heard him ask someone: 'What's up, mate?' Then nothing. Whitby had encountered Buster Edwards walking down the track, had asked his innocent question – and found himself bundled down the embankment and pinioned to the ground by some of the burliest, most villainous-looking thugs he had ever seen.

Back in the cab of the train, driver Mills was being attacked from both sides. He kicked out at the men trying to climb up into the cab but he was overpowered from behind and hit twice across the head. Blood poured down his face, and the next thing he remembered was being handcuffed to fireman Whitby.

The gang had got their train but they still had not got at the money. The next step was to separate the engine and the two front coaches from the rest of the train and drive the engine forward from the gantry to Bridego Bridge, where the cargo was to be unloaded.

The 'heavies' in the gang then launched themselves against the High Value Packages Coach. With axe, crowbar and coshes, the door and windows were smashed in, and the five petrified Post Office workers inside were suddenly faced with what must have seemed like the advance force of an army. The postal workers were made to lie down on the floor while the gang unloaded the mailbags through the shattered coach door and along a human chain which led down the embankment and into the back of their lorry.

Then, sweating but jubilant, the gang drove back in their military convoy to Leatherslade Farm. The operation had gone exactly according to plan, but for the knock on the head received by driver Mills. In time, it proved to be a big 'but' – for the violence used against him weighed heavily at the robbers' trial, and his death some years later brought claims from his family that his health had deteriorated dramatically after the raid.

But, for the moment, as the mailbags were piled up in the living room of Leatherslade Farm, the future for the gang looked rosy. They spent the rest of the night counting out the money. They set aside sums for major bribes and backhanders, and shared out the rest. In all there was £2½ million.

Years later, in a remarkable book about the robbery*, Goody related how he had sat with a bottle of whisky in his hand listening to the police wavebands on his VHF radio. He heard one policeman tell a colleague: 'You're not going to believe this, but someone's just stolen a train.'

The gang members had all concocted their alibis and made arrangements to salt away their shares of the loot until the hue and cry was over. They left the

* *The Train Robbers* by Piers Paul Read (W. H. Allen, the Alison Press and Secker & Warburg, 1978)

The mail train at Bridego Bridge, the pick-up point for the lorry.

farm and went their separate ways brimming with confidence. It was short-lived. . . .

Most of the gang had left damning evidence behind them at Leatherslade Farm. There were fingerprints, clothing and vehicles. But the robbers had not been over-worried. They had arranged for an associate to stay at the farm after they had moved out and to clean it from top to bottom so that not even a hair from their heads would be found if the police ever searched the place.

The job was never done. The contract was bungled. The 'perfect crime' became the ultimate criminal foul-up.

When the police found the farmhouse hideout, most of the robbers went on the run. Detectives knew who they were from the fingerprints and palm prints they had left. One single Monopoly board was a mine of information to forensic scientists. Soon the faces of the robbers were on posters all over Britain.

Within a year of the robbery, most of the gang were in jail. The 30-year sentences which were meted out for 'a crime against society' shook the thieves – and even created a measure of public sympathy for them. Goody, Welch, James, Wisbey and Hussey all got 30 years, although they were eventually released after serving 12 of them. Cordrey got 14 years and was freed after seven. But the robbers who gave police the most trouble were Reynolds, Buster Edwards, Wilson, White and Biggs.

With his paratrooper's training, White went on the run in England, taking with him his wife and baby son. He evaded capture for three years but, with his money stolen or blackmailed from him by 'friends', he was almost glad to be caught. He was captured while working as an odd-job man on the Kent coast, and in 1965 was jailed for 18 years. He eventually served only nine of them.

Reynolds and Edwards also evaded arrest, even though their names and faces were known to every policeman in Britain. They hid out in London for almost a year, then fled with their wives and children to Mexico City. Edwards even underwent plastic surgery to alter his appearance. But their money was being spent at a frightening rate and their life as exiles began to pall.

Both eventually returned to Britain. At the end of 1966 Edwards gave himself up to police. He was given a 15-year sentence and served nine years. Reynolds was arrested in Torquay, Devon, in 1968 – five years after the robbery. Chief Superintendent Tommy Butler of the Flying Squad knocked on the door of the Reynolds' home at 6 o'clock on a November morning and said: 'Hello, Bruce – it's been a long time.' Two months later Reynolds appeared in court and was sentenced to 25 years in jail. He was released in 1978.

Life in prison was never easy for any of the train robbers. They were all kept under the closest security because of two sensational escapes. Wilson was sentenced, along with the rest of the gang, to 30 years' imprisonment in 1964.

He remained in jail for just one year. He escaped, with outside help, from Winson Green Prison, Birmingham, and joined Reynolds and Edwards in Mexico City. But, like his friends, he tired of the place and settled down under a false name with his wife and three daughters in a smart suburban home near Montreal, Canada. But early in the morning of January 25, 1968, Chief Superintendent Tommy Butler arrived at the front door. Behind him, and surrounding the house, were 50 men of the Royal Canadian Mounted Police. Wilson was flown back to England to continue his 30-year sentence. He was also released in 1978.

Apart from the few members of the gang who had never been caught and convicted, the arrest of Wilson and Reynolds and the surrender of Edwards left only one man still wanted by the police – Biggs, the small-time crook who had been lured by the glittering promise of the crime of the century was sentenced to 30 years' jail along with Goody and the rest. In July 1965 he was out of prison again – 'sprung' by an armed gang who broke into London's Wandsworth Prison. He fled to Australia with his wife and children. But later, with the police not far behind him, he moved on to Brazil, leaving his family in Melbourne.

Early in 1974 a reporter of a London newspaper tracked down Biggs and set about writing his story. Unbeknown to the reporter, however, the newspaper's executives had tipped off Scotland Yard about the scoop they were about to break. As a result, on February 1, 1974, Chief Superintendent Jack Slipper and another police officer arrived in Rio de Janeiro to arrest Biggs.

The former Train Robbery Squad officer was soon given a new title by the British press: Chief Superintendent Slip-up. For Brazil had no extradition agreement with Britain, and the Rio police refused to hand over Biggs. Then Biggs's young Brazilian girlfriend announced that she was pregnant. The father of a Brazilian child could not be deported. After his much-publicised swoop, Slipper flew home empty-handed. And the last – though probably the least – of the Great Train Robbers went free.

Police in Venezuela issued a warrant for the arrest of a known criminal. Unfortunately for them, the man's house was built slap across the Venezuela-Colombia border.

When they called to arrest him, he ran into his bedroom, locked the door and phoned his lawyer. The bedroom was in Colombian territory, and the offence with which he was to be charged was not punishable in that country.

The Venezuelan police gave up.

The Mafia:
Network of Evil

The newspapers of the time reported it in typically racy, lurid terms, as befitted the occasion . . . 'Mafia Godfather Carmine Galante was shot dead over a plate of spaghetti in New York's Knickerbocker Avenue last night. The cigar-chewing 'boss of all bosses' was sipping chianti as two black limousines drew up outside Joe and Mary's Italian restaurant. Four neatly dressed men strolled calmly from the cars into the eating house and opened fire.

'Galante, who rubbed out all gangland opposition to become America's most powerful mobster since Lucky Luciano, tried to rise from his chair but was cut down in a hail of bullets. His bodyguard Nino Copolla also died instantly. The restaurant owner and his 17-year-old son were also wounded, and the boy died later in hospital.'

A typical gangland killing of the 1930s? A regular act of savagery from the days of prohibition, bootlegging, tommy guns and Al Capone? No, that report appeared in the London *Daily Express* of 13 July, 1979 – a full 50 years after the infamous St Valentine's Day Massacre which first brought the full horrors of mobster rule to the shocked attention of the world.

In those 50 years and more, organized crime has become bigger and bigger business. But, as evidenced by the shooting of Carmine Galante, its face is just as ugly. And, as ever, this sordid sub-culture and black economy is run by the same, sinister, all-encompassing organization . . .

They may call it 'The Mob', 'The Syndicate', or 'The National Network of Organized Crime'. Older and more sentimental members call it 'Cosa Nostra' – literally, 'Our Thing'. Most people, however, know it simply as The Mafia.

Its roots are as shadowy as its present-day operations. Even the derivation of the word Mafia is unknown. It may come from a Sicilian dialect term for bravado or possibly from an Arabic word, mehia, which means boastful. All that is certain about the Mafia's origins is that it was formed in the thirteenth century as a patriotic underground movement to resist Sicily's unwelcome rulers, the French. And on Easter Monday, 1282, these freedom fighters led a bloody massacre of the foreign invaders as the bells of the capital, Palermo, rang for vespers.

A similar society, the Camorra, was founded later in Naples. Over the centuries both flourished as secret brotherhoods vowed to protect the local populace from the despotic rulers of their regions. But, almost inevitably, both abused their autocratic powers to exploit and subjugate their people rather than protect them.

America's Italian immigrants took both societies across the Atlantic with them in the last century – and it was in the city slums of the U.S. that the two groups merged. An early boost to the fledgling 'families' in exile came in 1890 when 11 immigrant Mafiosi were lynched in New Orleans. The government paid $30,000 compensation to the widows and families of the hanged men. But the money was expropriated by the criminal brotherhood.

With further massive influxes of southern Italians around the turn of the century, the Mafia took its hold on immigrant ghettoes of the major cities. At first, they were a protection agency – at a price. Then their activities spread to illegal gambling, loan sharking, prostitution and finally drugs.

The introduction of Prohibition in 1920 was probably the biggest single factor in the success story of the Mafia. The market in bootleg liquor to help America

La Cosa Nostra	**literally translates as 'This Thing of Ours'**
Capo di Tutti Capi	**boss of bosses, the Godfather**
consigliore	**counsellor, a family leader's chief of staff**
caporegima	**leader of a family's bodyguard, muscle squad or hit men**
soldier	**rank-and-file strongarm man or hit man**
regime	**a group of such soldiers**
going to the matresses	**going to war with another group**
Moustache Pete	**derisive term for old-style, trigger-happy Mafia gangster**
making his bones	**murder carried out to prove loyalty**
omersa	**Mafia vow of silence**
bootleg	**illicit, as in bootleg booze – a boot being the ideal place to hide it**
hijack	**'Hi, Jack' was the greeting when a bootleg liquor truck was being held up**
speakeasy	**bar selling bootleg liquor – so-named because customers didn't speak of it too loudly**

drown its sorrows through the Depression was seemingly limitless. Every one of the several, fragmented, ill-organized Mafia families spread across the nation worked together to fulfil that demand . . . at enormous profits.

When Prohibition was repealed in 1933, the profits dried up and new forms of investment had to be found. Loan sharking, the numbers games, 'protection' rackets and prostitution kept the money rolling in. But new areas of exploitation were needed.

The growing drugs market was one of the most potentially lucrative and the Mafia built up French and Far Eastern Connections. Another was legal gambling, with the golden boom in casino cities like Las Vegas, Reno and more recently Atlantic City. The third was the labour movement.

Trade unions were cynically milked for the funds that could be misappropriated and, more importantly, for the 'muscle' they could lend to any extortion situation where a strike could prove costly.

Early this century, the trades unions were manipulated by New York Mafia boss Jacob 'Little Augie' Orgen, whose labour rackets earned him a huge fortune until his death at the hands of gunmen in 1927. Such Mafia notables as Albert Anastasia, Vito Genovese, Meyer Lansky and Lucky Luciano all worked for and learned from Orgen in those early days.

If Orgen's operation was the training ground for union corruption, Jimmy Hoffa's was the finishing school. No trade union has been infiltrated to a more infamous degree than the Teamsters Union. And Hoffa, the Teamsters boss, was its notorious leader.

Hoffa appointed a number of aides who had criminal records. Many were chosen for their expertise in terror and extortion. He also poured millions of dollars into his own pockets and then bought a Miami bank to look after the money. When the crusading Robert Kennedy became chairman of the Senate Rackets Committee, Hoffa became his prime and very personal target. He described Hoffa's leadership of the Teamsters as a 'conspiracy of evil.'

Because of the shady deals revealed by the committee, Hoffa was jailed in 1967, sentenced to serve 13 years for jury tampering and defrauding the union's pension fund of almost two million dollars. Four years later President Nixon issued a pardon and freed Hoffa on condition that he held no union office until 1980. That was not good enough for the still-ambitious Hoffa, who fought in the appeal court for the lifting of the ban.

Nixon's orders were not Hoffa's only problem. While in jail, he had appointed his long-time ally Frank Fitzsimmons as president of the union in his stead, on the firm understanding that he was no more than a 'caretaker' until the former boss was freed. But Fitzsimmons came to enjoy his taste of supreme power and had no intention of giving up the job. The union's Detroit headquarters became the battleground for the feud between Fitzsimmons and Hoffa.

James – 'Jimmy' – Hoffa

Although Hoffa had many allies within the union ranks, observers believed that his outlandish style no longer suited the 'respectable' image required by the shadowy figures who wanted to get their hands on the union's purse strings. Jimmy Hoffa was an embarrassment.

Shortly after midday on 30 July, 1975, Hoffa got into his bullet-proof car to drive to a mysterious luncheon meeting. An anonymous telephone caller later told the police where they could find the car. It was empty. Jimmy Hoffa was never seen again.

Hoffa's crime in Mafia eyes was that he had broken the rule of silence. The low-profile approach ordered by the families since the last war was being endangered by the loud-mouthed union boss.

The Mafia always had a vow of silence. A new recruit would hold a scrap of burning paper in his hand while he recited the oath: 'This is the way I will burn if I betray the secrets of the family'. But beyond this natural secrecy lay a more productive lesson for the Mafia chiefs – that they could operate more effectively, more profitably and with less interference from law enforcement agencies if they did not advertise their shadowy organization's existence with public killings and scandals.

Salvatore Maranzano was first to see this. The first man to claim the title Il Capo di Tutti Capi – The Boss of All Bosses – Maranzano called a conference of the major families in 1931 and proposed a constitution that would end the bitter rivalries within their ranks. But he was ahead of his time. Within five months, he and 40 of his men were murdered.

Gang warfare on such an overt scale alerted Americans to the magnitude of the crime problem in their midst. It also alerted the Mafiosi themselves to the dangers of advertising their power in blood.

The man who ordered Maranzano's killing, Meyer Lansky, learned the lesson best of all. He took up his assassinated rival's theme of cooperation. Lansky and his contemporaries, 'Lucky' Luciano and Vito Genovese, made themselves millions by adopting the low-profile approach to organized crime.

If Maranzano first voiced the new Mafia philosophy and Lansky espoused it, then Carlo Gambino perfected it. Gambino was the inspiration for the character featured as Il Capo di Tutti Capi in the novel and film *The Godfather*. Under the iron rule of this frail old man, the Mafia flourished. By 1976, when Carlo Gambino died peacefully in his bed at the age of 73, the Mafia had apparently vanished into the woodwork.

But there was just one more act necessary to make the transformation complete. And that was the removal of ambitious, brutal, old-time mafioso Carmen Galante, who saw himself as the new Godfather following Carlo Gambino's death

Galante's life story is almost the story of the American Mafia itself. His parents

A tough, fresh 'super-cop' was called in by New York's
police commissioner in 1911 and given a brief to close down
the city's illegal gambling joints. The man entrusted with
this task was Lieutenant Charles Becker – the most corrupt
policeman on the force. Within months, Becker was running
his own gambling club and taking a rake-off for 'protection'
from several others.

Becker's eventual downfall was his greed. He fell out with
a partner over his share in a casino and had the man
gunned down outside a restaurant. The gunmen were
hauled in by a police team untainted by Becker's
corruption. They all implicated the lieutenant in the crime.
Becker went to the electric chair in 1915.

were Sicilian immigrants who settled in the tough East Harlem district of New
York. He never weighed more than 10 stone 10 lbs but his usefulness with a gun
quickly won him respect among mobsters as a 'good soldier'.

On Christmas Eve 1930 he was involved in a shoot-out in which a detective
and a six-year-old girl were wounded. He was jailed for 15 years but was released
after 12 and returned to the Mafia brotherhood.

Galante was a man of contradictions and surprises. He made a subordinate
marry his mistress of 22 years so that her children by him would be legitimate.
He was responsible for destroying thousands of lives with the drugs he made
available. He ordered countless killings. Yet he loved kittens and was a keen
gardener. He controlled prostitutes and a pornography empire but was furious if
he heard a man use bad language in the presence of a woman.

Galante's specialized business interests were drug peddling to teenagers,
organized prostitution, loan sharking and crooked gambling. He was instrumental in setting up the 'French Connection' to flood the East Coast of the USA
with hard drugs from Marseilles.

He had always lived by the gun and it was this loud, loutish and overtly brutal
approach that brought about his premature demise at the age of 69.

Believing that no one would dare stand in his way after the death of Carlo
Gambino in 1976, Galante began to encroach on the territories of other Mafia
families. He was thought to be trying to amass a $50 million personal fortune to
pass on to his relatives. To this end, he risked warfare with other families and
put his own gang at risk from the police and the FBI.

In January 1979 he was told to give up his leadership but he refused. The
decision meant that he had signed his own death warrant.

That was why Galante's assassins, carrying scatter-guns and wearing ski masks, visited Joe and Mary's restaurant on 'unlucky' 13 July 1979 and killed him so quickly that his trademark cigar was still clenched at a jaunty angle in his mouth as he hit the floor. Then a .45 bullet was calmly fired into his left eye – a traditional Mafia calling card.

Less than a mile away from the bloody scene, when the news was brought that Galante was dead, 20 ruthless Mafia bosses raised their glasses in a macabre toast. They had gathered at another New York restaurant to discuss underworld strategy following the removal of their former associate.

A senior detective on the case said: 'It shows you how cold-blooded and businesslike these people are'.

The FBI first got wind of the underworld summit meeting when a Mafia chief from California flew into New York. They saw him rent a car and tailed him to a restaurant in a seedy Brooklyn side-street. To their astonishment, it was lined with gleaming black Cadillacs and Lincoln Continentals.

Among those at the meeting was Frank 'Funzi' Tieri, boss of New York's Genovese family. Galante had been pushing hard to take over the Genovese mob and police believed that Tieri, 74, had a part in the assassination. He certainly reaped the benefits . . . for he was shortly afterwards voted the new Godfather.

Tieri had done similar 'business' in the past. He had taken control of the Genovese family seven years earlier after the shooting of the former boss Tommy Eboli – a killing that police also put down to Tieri.

The style of Frank 'Funzi' Teiri was much more suited to the new image of Mafia business-men. Unlike Galante, he could keep his nose clean, his mouth shut and maintain a low profile. He had learned his trade as a lieutenant of the infamous Vito Genovese in the bloody 1950's gangster battles for control of the lucrative empire of Lucky Luciano after he was deported to Italy. But since then he had turned to the more orthodox range of Mafia rackets – with the exception of drugs, which he declined to touch.

The Mafia was called in by the CIA spy agency to assassinate Cuban leader Fidel Castro, according to a self-confessed Cosa Nostra gangster. Jimmy Fratianno claimed in 1981 that the plots suggested included poisoned cigars and a Capone-style machine-gun ambush. There was even a suggestion that he could be publicly humiliated by exposing him to powder that would make his beard fall out.

His legitimate businesses included a sportswear firm, a sales corporation and companies operating school bus services.

Shortly after coming to power, Tieri was described by New York Police Department as the biggest loan shark in the country. They said: 'He controls most of the gambling and loan sharking in the Bronx, East Harlem, Brooklyn and Queens. And he controls gambling in New Jersey, Florida, Puerto Rico, California and Las Vegas'.

Tieri's lifestyle suited the mob. He lived in a neat, three-storey house on a tree-lined street in a middle-class suburb. Every morning he would kiss his wife (her first name was, strangely, America) and leave for work wearing a conservative business suit. He would then be driven by his chauffeur one mile to the home of his mistress, Rita Perelli, from where he ran his operation.

He was said never to use the telephone and never to commit any note of his activities to paper. And he kept the loyalty of his criminal family not by threats but by a profit-sharing scheme. The Mafia's transformation from a gang of gunfighters to a band of multi-million-dollar businessmen was complete.

By the 1980s the Mafia had infiltrated almost every area of American business life. The U.S. Justice Department named the following industries as having the biggest Mafia involvement: music, video recording, haulage, garbage collection, clothes manufacturing, commercial banking, insurance, meat supply and processing, hotel and casino operation, funeral parlours, tobacco distribution, building construction, baking, cheese making, cooking oil wholesaling and pizza retailing.

Today an American may start his life wrapped in a Mafia nappy, listen to rock music from a Mafia record company, dine out on a Mafia steak, drive a car bought on a Mafia bank loan, holiday at a Mafia hotel, buy a house in a Mafia development and finally be buried by a Mafia funeral service.

Ralph Salerno, a leading US authority on organized crime, has said: 'If New York's five Mafia families conspired to paralyse the city, they could halt every car, taxi, bus, truck, train, ship and plane. They could also shut down literally thousands of wholesale and retail businesses. And they could close down services like laundering, dry cleaning, catering, garbage collection and dozens more.

It is no exaggeration to say that in New York every morsel of food you eat at home or in a restaurant, every item of clothing you wear and every journey you make is tainted by The Mob'.

The influence of the Mafia is now so all-pervasive that more than 2,000 past and potential witnesses to Mafia crimes are being guarded by the Witness Protection Program of the US government. The bill for keeping these 'squealers' safe from Mafia hit-men is currently $20 million a year.

At one time, the Mafia was estimated to have between 3,000 and 5,000 criminals working for it across the country. Nowadays this is a small proportion of the payroll, compared with the thousands of 'front men' and perfectly honest employees who look after The Mob's business interests. A *Time* magazine survey put profits from the Mafia's 10,000-plus legitimate firms at $12 billion a year – five times as high as the profits of America's largest industrial corporation, Exxon. Add to that the Mafia's profits from crime: an estimated $48 billion.

Such fabulous rewards come mainly from extortion. Companies are forced to buy Mafia products or shut down.

The US Justice Department believes that the cost of bribing a government meat inspector in New York is as low as $25 a day. For that, he will say that kangaroo- or horse-meat is '100 per cent beef'. It is then sold, not to pet food manufacturers for whom it was intended, but to market traders and restaurants. Similarly, Mafia vegetables often seem crisper – but only because they have been treated with a chemical that can cause cancer.

The Mob controls the supply of goods to companies by its union power. Mafia men stand for election as union officials – rival candidates being discouraged with baseball bats, knives or guns. A company which resists Mafia extortion can easily have its supplies cut off by a strike or union blacking. Few can afford to resist. Most, whether they know it or not, are contributing generously to the Mafia's billion-dollar profits.

Jacob Orgen and Jimmy Hoffa may be dead. But their methods are reaping fortunes of which even they never dared to dream.

The reach of the Mafia can sometimes be longer than the arm of the law. In 1984 a Mafia gang leader was incarcerated in a Spanish jail in Barcelona. Every evening, the prisoner, 34-year-old Raymond Vaccarizi, was visited by his wife, who stood in the street below his cell and called up to him. Vaccarizi would lean out of the window for a half-hour's chat.

The prison authorities knew of this innocent arrangement and allowed it to continue. Unfortunately, the Mafia also knew about it . . . and they were concerned that their colleague might begin to talk more than sweet nothings after his expected extradition to France to face murder, robbery and arms charges.

One sultry evening in July, the wife made her usual visit. Vaccarizi leaned out of the cell window – and two shots rang out from a high-powered rifle. The prisoner was hit in the heart and the face. He was dead before he hit the cell floor.

Meyer Lansky, 'Lucky' Luciano and Victor Genovese: The First Mob Magnates and Founders of Murder Incorporated

Meyer Lansky, born Maier Suchowjansky, was a respectable 16-year-old Polish immigrant who had settled with his family in New York and taken a job as an engineering apprentice. One day he passed a doorway on the city's lower East Side and saw a girl being assaulted. Lansky rushed to her rescue, fists flying.

In the ensuing fight, police were called and all three men were arrested and kept in prison 48 hours for brawling. They were 48 hours that changed Meyer Lansky's life.

The girl's two attackers were young thugs named Salvatore Lucania and Benjamin Siegel . . . who later preferred to be known as 'Lucky' Luciano and 'Bugsy' Siegel. Despite his attack on them, they took Lansky under their wings and Luciano, in particular, tutored him in a life of crime.

Luciano was five years older than Lansky. A Sicilian immigrant, he had been in and out of trouble ever since his arrival in New York at the age of ten. He was first arrested within hours of disembarking from his migrant ship – for stealing fruit from a handcart. His life of petty crime led him to jail for the first time in 1915 for drug peddling, and shortly after his release he met and teamed up with Meyer Lansky.

Luciano was at first Lansky's mentor and later his associate. They controlled a number of New York gangs, mainly Italian and Irish, involved in robbing homes, shops and warehouses.

But there was an area of crime in which Luciano specialized and which Lansky abhorred – prostitution. The Jew would have no part in the vice trade because, when a teenager, he had fallen desperately in love with a young prostitute – then found her one night in an alley with her throat cut, probably by her pimp.

Between 1918 and 1932 Lansky was arrested seven times on charges ranging from disorderly conduct to murder. But he had to be released on every one because of lack of witnesses.

Luciano was more successful in keeping out of police custody. He and Lansky had both become members of the gang of Jacob 'Little Augie' Orgen, who made a fortune from union and organized labour rackets. While Lansky concentrated on less violent crimes, Luciano became New York's most feared hit-man, whose favoured weapon was an ice pick. His reward was a string of Manhattan brothels which, by the mid-Twenties, were estimated to be earning him more than $1 million a year.

In 1920 came the ill-judged turn of events that was to turn Luciano, Lansky and others into multi-millionaires . . . Prohibition.

The soft-spoken Lansky paved the way for a new breed of tommy-gun wielding thugs to take over the illegal liquor business in the north and ensure the supply of whiskey to New York. Principal among these was Alfonso 'Al' Capone, who was fiercely loyal to Lanksy and Luciano.

In 1927, Luciano and Lansky were joined by a third ruthless killer and future crime czar, Vito Genovese. Born in Naples in 1897, Genovese had been a friend and neighbour of Luciano since the former's arrival in New York at the age of 16. A petty thief with only one arrest, for carrying a revolver, he too had graduated to organized crime while working 'under contract' to Jacob Orgen.

Despite the combined reputations of Lansky, Luciano and Genovese, the gang of three were still not the most powerful mobsters in New York. That accolade was being fought for between two old-style Mafia leaders, Salvatore Maranzano and Giuseppe Masseria, bitter rivals whose territorial battles had left as many as 60 of their 'soldiers' shot dead in a single year.

Both gang bosses tried to woo Luciano, Lansky and Genovese to their side, probably fearful of the trio's growing power. They refused. By way of persuasion, Maranzano lured Luciano to an empty garage where a dozen masked men lay in wait. Maranzano had him strung up by his thumbs from the rafters and punched and kicked until he lost consciousness. Luciano was repeatedly revived so that the torture could continue anew. Finally, Maranzano slashed him across the face with a knife. The wound required 55 stitches.

Not surprisingly, Luciano told his tormentor that he had changed his mind and was now happy to join the Maranzano mob. He was offered the Number Two job if he would first wipe out the Mafia rival, Masseria.

Luciano invited Masseria for a meal, pretending that he was now keen to join forces with him. They sealed the deal and toasted one another across the table at Scarpato's Restaurant, Coney Island. But when Luciano retired to the lavatory, four gunmen burst into the dining-room. Masseria must have known his fate the moment he saw them. They were Vito Genovese, Bugsy Siegel and two other Lansky men, Albert Anastasia and Joe Adonis. Masseria tried to flee but was cut down in a hail of 20 bullets.

Which now left only Maranzano between the Lansky gang and the pinnacle of power in the U.S. underworld.

Maranzano, aged 63, could have claimed to have been the first true Capo di Tutti Capi. After Masseria's death, this elegantly dressed Sicilian, who had once trained to be a priest, called a meeting of the New York families in a hall where the walls were hung with crucifixes and other religious emblems. He drew up a constitution of what he termed La Cosa Nostra and proclaimed himself its effective Godfather. Lansky and his associates had other ideas and in September 1931 he helped Luciano settle his old score with Maranzano.

One morning four 'taxmen' called at Maranzano's real estate agency on Park Avenue. His bodyguards kept their guns hidden as the four identified themselves as Internal Revenue Service investigators and demanded to see the books and the boss. Ushered in to his private office, the four revealed themselves as Bugsy Siegel, Albert Anastasia, Red Levine and Thomas 'Three Fingers' Lucchese. All four drew knives.

Just five months after pronouncing himself Godfather, Maranzano was killed – stabbed several times and then shot for good measure. Over the next few days about 40 more of Maranzano's team and their associates were systematically eliminated.

The mob magnates – Lansky, Luciano and Genovese – were now firmly in power. Gone were the old-style trigger-happy Mafioso leaders derisively termed 'Moustache Petes'. In came the accountants and corporate executives, still backed of course by the ultimate persuaders, the hired killers. One arm of the operation was labelled the National Crime Syndicate, the other was called Murder Incorporated.

Helping set up this mercenary death squad was Albert Anastasia, one of the killers of both Giuseppe Masseria and Salvatore Maranzano. Known as New York's 'Lord High Executioner', he meted out murder on contract for a quarter of a century, becoming head of one of the city's five Mafia clans, the Mangano family.

His growing power finally became too much of a threat to his principal New York rivals, including Genovese, two of whose henchmen followed Anastasia to his barber's shop one morning in 1957. As a warm towel was draped over his face, he did not see the two gunmen position themselves behind the barber's chair. Then they calmly blew his head off.

It was a scene of which Meyer Lansky probably disapproved. He was the man who, more than any other, welded previously fiery-tempered Mafia families

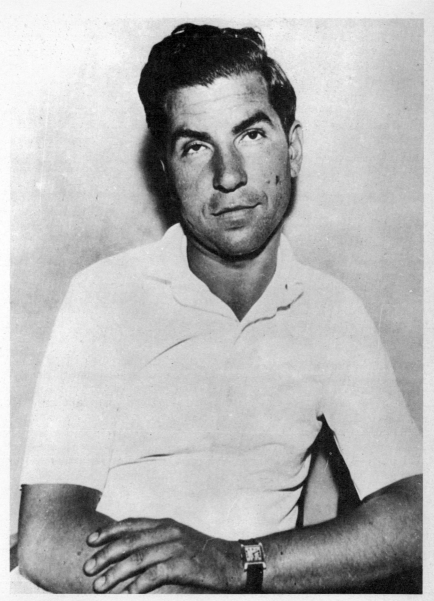

'Lucky' Luciano

scattered around the nation into a 'federal' unit. Autonomous in their own area, they nevertheless came together to seek agreement on major policy issues. Above all, they maintained a low profile; the days of street warfare were over for good.

In their book *Meyer Lansky: Mogul of The Mob*, authors Dennis Elsenburg, Uri Dan and Ell Landau quote their subject as saying: 'Crime moved out of the small ghettoes and became nationwide.'

An associate, Joseph Doc Stacher, says of Lansky and Luciano: 'They were an unbeatable team. If they had become President and Vice-President of the United States, they would have run the place far better than the idiot politicians'.

Lansky was certainly a wily politician within the crime syndicate. Despite being a Jew in a predominantly Italian society, he became trusted as an 'independent' Mafia mogul, more concerned with money-making than internal power struggles. His value to his associates was his ability secretly to invest the mob's ill-gotten gains in respectable industries and in the gambling casinos of Las Vegas, Cuba and the Bahamas.

Lansky made millions for the Mafia and an estimated personal fortune of $300 million. Seemingly safe from criminal charges, his main concern in his old age was the taxman. He even left the United States on one occasion – to live in an hotel he owned in Israel, much to the displeasure of the Israeli government. But he returned to America to spend his last years in the land that had made his organization fabulously rich. As he himself described it: 'We're bigger than U.S. Steel.'

Like Lansky, his old friend Vito Genovese also seemed to lead a charmed life. Before World War Two he salted an estimated $2 million into secret Swiss bank accounts and fled to Naples. A vociferous supporter of Mussolini (he contributed generously to fascist funds), he switched sides hurriedly when the tide of war changed and offered his services to the occupying American forces.

Genovese pinpointed black-market operations in post-war Italy and helped close them down. He then resurrected them with one of his own 'front men' in charge. His Italian Connection came to an end when he was extradited back to the U.S. to face an old murder charge. It failed to stick after the principal witness was shot dead, and Genovese returned to his New York stamping ground.

His former lieutenant, Albert Anastasia, having been eliminated along with other rivals, Genovese savoured the fruits of power for only a year before being jailed in 1959 for drug smuggling. He had served ten years of a 15-year sentence when he was found dead from a heart attack.

The third of the triumvirate, 'Lucky' Luciano, did not always live up to his name. He must have thought his luck had finally run out when he was sent to jail to serve a 30- to 50-year sentence for 90 vice offences. Then, in November 1942, he got a visit from his old friend Lansky.

'Lucky' Luciano – dead of
a heart attack

All the pomp of an
Italian funeral for
Luciano

Lansky told him that he had just done a deal with U.S. naval intelligence who were concerned that information about Allied convoys was being leaked by pro-Mussolini Italian immigrants working on the New York waterfront. The fears seemed to have been confirmed by the burning of the French liner *Normandie* at its moorings in New York. So many fires had broken out at the same time that the U.S. Navy, which was due to use the ship to carry troops and supplies to Europe, was certain Italian saboteurs were to blame.

The deal Lansky had struck was that the Mafia, under Luciano's direction from his prison cell, would work in conjunction with a special unit of naval intelligence to flush out Italian spies and saboteurs. In return, Luciano would win his freedom after the war. He readily agreed.

At least one other Mafia man was immediately freed from jail at Luciano's request. He was Johnny 'Cockeye' Dunn who was responsible for the no-questions-asked removal of two suspected German spies. Apart from keeping peace on the waterfront, the team was also credited with pinpointing an enemy submarine off Long Island. Four German spies were captured as they came ashore from it and, under interrogation, revealed a North American network of Nazi agents.

Before the Allies invaded Sicily, Luciano sent word to local Mafia leaders that all help should be given to the Americans. Four Italian-speaking U.S. naval intelligence officers joined up with the Sicilian Mafia and successfully raided German and Italian bases for secret defence blueprints. Later, in Rome, the Mafia foiled an assassination attempt against Britain's General Sir Harold Alexander and, as a footnote to history, seized Mussolini's entire personal archives.

The American authorities kept their part of the bargain and, in 1945, within a few months of the war in Europe ending, Luciano was freed from jail but was told he was to be deported to Italy.

His comrade in crime, Lansky, was there to bid him farewell – after first giving him $500,000 to help him start his new life. He lived in Rome for a while but grew restless for the 'big time' and shortly afterwards turned up in Cuba. Luciano issued an invitation to leaders of U.S. organized crime to meet him in Havana. But before his empire-building in exile could begin, U.S. pressure on Cuba's President Batista forced his dispatch back to Italy.

On 26 January 1962, Luciano went to Naples airport to await the arrival of an American producer who was considering filming the Mafia chief's life. But Luciano's luck had at last run out. He dropped dead of a heart-attack in the airport lounge.

Extraordinarily, after a lifetime of corruption, torture and violent death, America's three moguls of organized crime – Meyer Lansky, Vito Genovese and 'Lucky' Luciano – all died of natural causes.

Al Capone and the Chicago Mob

A l Capone, 'Legs' Diamond, 'Machine Gun' McGurn, 'Bugs' Morgan, 'Dutch' Schultz . . . they are names that have gone down in America's violent folklore. In books, films and TV series, they have been dramatized, often glamorized and sometimes turned into heroes.

But the stark truth about these gangsters of the Twenties is far from glamorous. They lived tawdry lives and, in the main, died violently. A principal exception to that rule was the most infamous gangster of the age, Al Capone himself. He died peacefully but deranged, from syphilis.

Alphonse Capone, born in New York in 1899, was one of nine children of Italian immigrants. A street-fighting thug, he gained his lifelong nickname, Scarface, while working as a bouncer for a Brooklyn brothel.

This small-time hoodlum could have faded into criminal obscurity but for a strange quirk of fate. Capone urgently needed to get out of New York where he was wanted for questioning over the death of a policeman. He contacted Chicago gangster Johnny Torrio, who remembered the young thug from his own street-fighting days in New York and immediately invited him to join his team.

Capone arrived in Chicago in 1919 to find Torrio working for old-time mafioso tycoon 'Diamond' Jim Colosimo. This strange character, so called because of his penchant for jewellery, ran just about every brothel in the city, as well as various labour rackets. Torrio, a cousin of Colosimo's wife, was his principal lieutenant, sworn to guard his boss with his life. It was no informal oath of allegiance: Torrio, like the rest of Colosimo's hired army, had to swear fidelity to their leader on his family Bible.

Colosimo, with his second wife, singer Dale Winter, held court nightly at his retaurant on South Wabash Avenue, surrounded by unsavoury 'heavies' as well as by politicians and entertainers. With the introduction of Prohibition, Torrio tried to persuade Colosimo to expand his business to take advantage of the new market in illicit liquor. The older man refused.

On 11 May 1920 Torrio asked Colosimo if he would be at his restaurant at a particular time to sign for a delivery of whiskey. As Colosimo waited in the empty restaurant, Al Capone stepped out of a phone booth and, acting on Torrio's orders, shot Colosimo dead then took his wallet to make the killing look like a robbery. An hour later he was back at Torrio's side ready to shed tears and swear vengeance upon receiving the news of their boss's death. Torrio and Capone took over the Colosimo crime empire, added bootleg liquor to it and began to amass a fortune.

In the early Twenties, Chicago's underworld was split between the Torrio-Capone mafia axis and the mainly Irish gang of Charles Dion 'Deanie' O'Bannion.

O'Bannion was perhaps the most remarkable of all the hoodlums of his day. Angelically baby-faced, an ex-choirboy once destined for the priesthood, O'Bannion fell into crime almost by accident. He worked for William Randolph Hearst's newspaper the *Herald Examiner* while moonlighting at night as a singing waiter in a club which was the haunt of criminals. It was these villains who introduced O'Bannion to the richer pickings on the wrong side of the law.

'Deanie' O'Bannion was a criminal with a great sense of humour and a considerable style. Unlike his Italian rivals in neighbouring parts of Chicago, the Irishman would not allow brothels in his area, refused to sell any but the finest liquor from his chain of breweries and distilleries and ran his business from the grandest flower shop in Chicago, catering for the city's high society weddings and funerals.

O'Bannion laughed at the crudities of the Italian overlords. But in 1924 he cracked his most costly joke at their expense – he sold Johnny Torrio a half-share in a brewery for half a million dollars. He did not tell Torrio that he had received a tip-off that the brewery was about to be raided. The police swoop left O'Bannion in the clear. But Torrio, who had been meticulous in his efforts to avoid any police record, was booked. Furious, he sought instant revenge.

On 10 November 1924 three men called at O'Bannion's flower shop to buy a wreath. The baby-faced proprietor did not realize who the wreath was for. The men, Alberto Anselmi, John Scalise and Frank Yale, were killers hired by Torrio and Capone. Yale held O'Bannion down while the others shot him dead.

O'Bannion's funeral was the grandest Chicago had seen. The rich and the famous mingled with murderers, thieves and bootleggers to pay their respects to the supplier of the best booze in town. 'Deanie' would have been proud of the floral tributes. The wreaths alone were worth $50,000.

O'Bannion's funeral was the first of many over the next few years. Torrio and Capone had started a gangland war that they could not finish. Before the Twenties were out, more than 1,000 bodies were to end up on the streets of Chicago in a string of bloody reprisal raids. And the first raid was against Torrio himself.

O'Bannion's loyal henchmen, Hymie Weiss and George 'Bugs' Moran, ambushed Torrio as he left home. They gunned him down and left him for dead. But he survived, was himself arrested over the illicit brewery raid and was jailed for nine months.

The following year, shaken by events in Chicago and doubtless concerned that Capone's own ambitions may not have included him in future plans, Torrio 'retired' at the age of 43. Pursued first out of Chicago and then Florida with Weiss and Moran on his tail, he settled in Naples until he felt safe enough to return to New York in 1928. He worked behind the scenes for Meyer Lansky until 1939 when he was jailed for two years for non-payment of taxes. He died of a heart attack in 1967.

Torrio's flight from Chicago in 1925 meant that Capone was now lord of the richest territory in the underworld. Torrio had taken with him a 'golden handshake' estimated at more than $50 million but that still left a thriving empire in prostitution, bootlegging, gambling and extortion which Capone ran in a grandiose manner.

But Capone's showmanship almost cost him his life. He controlled his $5 million-a-year business from the Hawthorn Hotel in the wholly corrupt Chicago suburb of Cicero. In September 1926, 'Bugs' Moran and Hymie Weiss, having failed to settle their score with Johnny Torrio, attempted to wipe out his successor. They drove in a motorcade past the Hawthorn Hotel and sprayed it with hundreds of rounds of submachine-gun fire.

Astonishingly, Capone was unhurt. But his pride was ruffled. He had Weiss gunned down in the street at the first opportunity. Moran, however, proved more elusive. Capone had to wait another two years to attempt revenge on him in the infamous St Valentine's Day Massacre.

But first there were other items of business Al Capone had to clear up. The Genna family, a gang led by four Sicilian brothers, were Capone's main suppliers of rot-gut whiskey and gin. The liquor was cheap, foul and dangerous. Produced at 40 cents a gallon, it was sold to Capone at two dollars and passed on to drinking dens at six dollars. Many of the customers who drank it were blinded and some even died.

Capone fell out with the influential Gennas, not over the quality of their whiskey but because they were vying with him for power and influence among the Italian criminal fraternity. One by one, the Gennas and their gang were gunned down until the remaining members of the family fled, some to Sicily, some to other parts of the United States.

Another victim of this war was a crook-turned-politician called Joseph Esposito. Nicknamed 'Diamond Joe' because of the $50,000 worth of gems studded into his belt, Esposito was Committeeman for Chicago's notorious 19th Ward where he controlled police, politicians and union leaders – as well as running a string of distilleries for Capone. Caught up in the Capone-Genna war, he was gunned down in the street by unknown assailants in 1928.

Another supplier of bootleg liquor to Capone was policeman's son Roger Touhy. Capone wanted him out of the way so that he could take over his

Al Capone, the head of the Chicago mob

business. First he kidnapped Touhy's partner Matt Kilb, held him to ransom and, when Touhy paid the $50,000 asked, shot him anyway. When Touhy still held out against Capone's demands, he was framed for a kidnapping and sentenced to 199 years imprisonment. He served nine years before escaping and proving his innocence. Within days of finally winning his freedom, he was shot dead in a Chicago street.

Capone's blood-letting stretched to New York where Frank Yale, one of the men who had been hired to assassinate Dion O'Bannion, was thought by Capone to have cheated him on liquor deals. In 1927 Yale was lured to a fake appointment in Brooklyn where he was machine-gunned to death from a passing car.

But Capone's most longed-for victim was still 'Bugs' Moran, the O'Bannion aide who had tried to kill Johnny Torrio in that first round of revenge shootings back in 1924. For the task, Capone employed the most deadly hit-man of them all, 'Machine Gun' Jack McGurn.

McGurn's real name was James Vincenzo de Mora, born in Chicago's Little Italy in 1904. A professional boxer, his connection with Capone was through his father who worked in one of the Genna family's distilleries. When his father was killed by Genna lieutenants, McGurn joined Capone as a hired gunman. His reputation was fearsome. His trademark was a nickel coin pressed into the palm of the victim's hand. By 1929 at least 15 bodies had been found with McGurn's 'calling card'. His fees for such contract killings were high and allowed him to buy shares in a number of Chicago clubs. He married one of his club's showgirls. In 1927 when a comedian, Joe E. Lewis, refused to work at one of the clubs, he was beaten up by McGurn and had his vocal cords cut.

On 14 February, St Valentine's Day, 1929, Jack McGurn was ordered by Capone to rid him finally of his arch enemy Moran, who had recently been publicly bad-mouthing 'Alphonse The Beast'.

Moran's gang were expecting a liquor delivery that day at a garage at 2122 North Clark Street. Seven of Moran's men were inside the garage when three 'policemen' burst in carrying machine guns. They ordered the bootleggers to line up with their faces against a wall and mowed them down in a hail of bullets. The 'policemen' were Capone's men – one of them McGurn.

'Bugs' Moran was not among the victims, however. He turned up late for the liquor delivery and fled when he witnessed the supposed police raid.

The St Valentine's Day Massacre, as the newspapers labelled it, at last brought the measure of public outrage that forced politicians and police – even the crooked ones – to act to curb the violence on Chicago's streets. 'Machine Gun' McGurn, whose role in the slaughter was well known, was no longer wanted as a hired gun by Capone. He was simply not good news to have around.

McGurn believed he could hang up his gun and make a good enough living out of his clubs. But the Depression put paid to that. Hard-up but still flashily dressed in three-piece suit, white spats and highly polished shoes, McGurn was walking down a quiet street on 14 February 1936, seven years to the day after the St Valentine's Day massacre, when two gunmen approached and blasted him. When police arrived at the scene they found a nickel pressed into his palm and a cut-out valentine heart by his side.

McGurn's killers were never traced but it is believed that one of them was

'Bugs' Moran. O'Bannion's loyal Irish lieutenant had disappeared from public view after his men were massacred in the garage on North Clark Street. After the war he turned up again in Ohio where he was arrested for bank robbery. He died in Leavenworth Jail in 1957.

'Bugs' Moran had survived almost every other member of the Chicago gangs of the bloody Twenties. And he had outlived by ten years the most notorious of them all, Al Capone.

After forcing Moran to flee for his life following the 1929 massacre, Capone had taken over control of the entire criminal network of the city of Chicago. But his victory was short-lived . . .

In 1931, what the police failed to achieve in a decade the taxman achieved in a few weeks. On 24 October after a speedy trial, Al Capone was found guilty of tax evasion. He was fined $50,000 and ordered to pay $30,000 costs – chickenfeed to him. But he was also sentenced to a jail term of 11 years. It broke him.

When he was released in 1939, he was already sliding into insanity from sylphilis. He hid himself away on his Florida estate, shunned by his neighbours and by the new breed of Mafia leaders who wanted nothing to do with the loud-mouthed, brutish scar-faced relic of a bloody past best forgotten. Al Capone died alone in 1947.

'Bugsy' Siegel: the Hollywood Gangster

It wasn't a pretty sight when they found the bullet-riddled body of 'Bugsy' Siegel. And that wouldn't have pleased the man who had the reputation of being the Casanova of the Mafia.

Siegel was gunned down as he sat on a sofa in his girlfriend's house. A final bullet was fired into his left eye – the coup de grâce that was the Mafia's 'calling card'. Tall, good-looking, well-groomed and smartly dressed, 'Bugsy' would have abhorred such messy methods. He would have preferred a more dignified death.

Benjamin Siegel, born in Brooklyn in 1906, had always been convinced that he was headed for the big-time. But he started small – stealing cars, driving trucks of illicit liquor and guarding illegal gambling houses.

It was when, in his teens, he teamed up with the much lighter, more calculating Meyer Lansky that his fortunes changed. He called his group of small-time criminals the Bug And Meyer Gang and, by the mid-thirties, through his loyalty to Lansky, became a trusted associate of the top racketeers on America's east coast.

In 1935 Siegel was indicted in New York for shooting a rival gang member, one of 'Dutch' Schultz's men. Lansky decided his friend must leave town, so he set him up with a £500,000 investment and sent him to California to team up with local mobster Jack Dragna.

Life in the Californian sunshine was paradise to the impetuous Siegel. Soon after his arrival, he was seducing one starlet after another. A millionairess divorcée, Countess Dorothy Di Frasso, took him under her wing. She travelled with him to Italy, where they met Mussolini. Siegel and the countess launched an expedition to seek Spanish treasure on the Cocos Islands – but after blasting an island with dynamite they returned empty-handed.

In Hollywood, Siegel was on first-names terms with stars like Jean Harlow, Gary Cooper and Clark Gable. But his greatest friend was actor George Raft, famous for his film gangster roles. He and Raft went on a gambling spree on the French Riviera – until Siegel got a cable from Lansky ordering him to 'stop acting like a movie star' and get back to work.

But it was not all play for Siegel. He and Dragna operated a string of illegal Los Angeles gambling houses and offshore casino ships, as well as drug smuggling operations and even a wire service. The money rolled in throughout World War Two, and in 1945 Lansky helped organize for him a $3 million loan to build a casino hotel in Las Vegas – forerunner of the many monolithic emporia that were to make the desert town into a mobsters' Mecca.

Siegel matched $3 million of his own money with the crime syndicate's stake and started building The Flamingo, a name chosen by his girlfriend of the moment, Virginia Hill. But, during construction, large sums of money were salted away into Swiss bank accounts, some of them said to be in the name of Miss Hill.

In late 1946 many of America's leading gangsters, including Siegel's east-coast associates Lansky, 'Lucky' Luciano and Vito Genovese, met at a hotel in Havana to spend a holiday, to attend a Frank Sinatra concert and to discuss the problem of the errant 'Bugsy'. Lansky, who considered Siegel a blood-brother, argued the case for his friend. But he was over-ruled. It was decided that Siegel be asked to repay with interest all of the syndicate investment as soon as the hotel was open. If he failed, then . . .

'Bugsy' Siegel's luck was out. He opened the Flamingo Hotel on 26 December 1946 with Virginia Hill at his side. The event was a disaster. Bad weather grounded planes in Los Angeles and few of the invited famous faces turned up. The razmatazz of the grand opening fell flat, publicity was scant, interest dimmed and the punters stayed away. For two weeks Siegel struggled on. The casino alone lost more than $100,000 before he ordered it closed.

The demands for repayment of the Mob's loan became more and more insistent. But Siegel's money was largely tied up in the hotel, and the sums siphoned off to Switzerland did not add up to what the syndicate demanded. Siegel thought he could bluff his way out of the crisis, under the protection of his old friend Lansky.

Lansky, however, had reluctantly washed his hands of him. 'Lucky' Luciano, who had known 'Bugsy' even longer than Lansky, accepted the task of arranging his execution. He asked for the money one last time. Siegel refused.

On the night of 20 June 1947 Siegel was sitting on the sofa in the living room of Virginia Hill's rented house in North Linden Drive, Los Angeles, when an unknown killer or killers fired five bullets at him.

His rich and famous friends steered well clear of Benjamin 'Bugsy' Siegel once his fame had turned to notoriety. There were only five mourners at his funeral.

'Legs' Diamond and 'Dutch' Schultz: the New York Bootleggers

Jack 'Legs' Diamond and 'Dutch' Schultz were two hoodlums who brought an unwelcome taste of Chicago-style gang warfare to the heart of New York. Both thought themselves smart, stylish, wise guys. Both changed their names to glamorize their image. Both died by the gun – cold-bloodedly executed by their own kind.

Jack 'Legs' Diamond was born John Noland in 1896 in Philadelphia. Moving to New York in his teens, he followed the classic criminal pattern of street-fighting, theft and 'protection'. In the early Twenties he worked for racketeer Jacob 'Little Augie' Orgen, carrying out inter-gang killings at his behest.

The money he earned from Orgen was spent on a lavish lifestyle. Although married, he supported a string of mistresses and earned the nickname 'Legs' from a brief spell as a professional dancer. He bought shares in a number of nightclubs and eventually purchased a top nightspot of his own.

Everything had come easily to Diamond. But in 1927 'Little Augie' Orgen was assassinated and Diamond wounded. He backed out of the impending inter-gang warfare and instead set himself up in the bootlegging business. He went into partnership with an already established bootlegger calling himself 'Dutch' Schultz.

Schultz's real name was Arthur Fliegenheimer, born in New York in 1902 and following the same criminal path as 'Legs' Diamond. Perhaps they were too much alike – for as partners, Diamond and Schultz made great adversaries. They seemed incapable of keeping their bargains with one another.

When Diamond fled the scene after killing a drunk at his club, Schultz took over much of his business. Diamond retaliated by hijacking Schultz's liquor trucks.

Diamond had felt safe in his activities as long as he had the patronage of his new gangland protector, New York gaming club and brothel owner Arnold Rothstein. But just as he had lost a friend in the assassinated Orgen, so he did again in 1928 when Rothstein was found dying in a gambling club after refusing to pay a $320,000 debt due from a single poker game.

Schultz deemed it a safe time to get rid of Diamond. A hit squad dispatched to kill him found Diamond in bed with his mistress and sprayed the room with gunfire. Five bullets entered his body but he survived. Two further attempts on his life failed. But on 17 December 1931 Schultz's gangsters finally got their man.

Diamond had been celebrating his acquittal from charges that he had beaten up two rival bootleggers, and in the early hours visited a girlfriend's apartment. From there, he went home. As he lay in bed, the door was shattered from its hinges and 'Legs' Diamond was finally shot dead.

'Dutch' Schultz now had a free hand to run his liquor, gambling and protection rackets which together brought in an estimated $20 million a year. But his gun-slinging style of business was inimical to the new, rising breed of Mafia leader such as 'Lucky' Luciano, Vito Genovese and Meyer Lansky.

After a sensational tax evasion case, in which Schultz was acquitted after having the trial moved to a small and 'manageable' upstate courthouse, Luciano and his associates decided to spare the Mafia further embarrassment. On 23 October 1935 'Dutch' Schultz was dining with three friends at a Newark, New Jersey, restaurant when a man with a machine-gun entered and shot them all.

The last of New York's old-style gun-slinging gangsters was out of action for good.

The great pretender who duped a city's mayor

Few rogues in history have won the same fame and affection as Wilhelm Voigt. But then few have managed so successfully to poke fun at arrogance and pomposity.

It is Germany 1906. The Kaiser, his army and government officials are all-powerful, and too many soldiers and bureaucrats are too full of their own importance.

Voigt, a cobbler by trade, but a man who has spent almost half of his 57 years in jail, is free again after serving 15 years for robbery. The authorities have taken away his passport and identity card, and, in an authoritarian state, there is not much you can do without them.

But he is not one to buckle down to the system. He ponders an audacious idea. But because of the Prussian awe of authority, it is one that just might work.

Voigt buys a second-hand army uniform in a Berlin shop, and instantly turns himself into a captain in the service of the Kaiser. Next item on the agenda is some soldiers to command. Standing outside a barracks, he watches a corporal marching along with a squad of five privates.

'Corporal, where are you taking those men?' barks Voigt.

'Back to barracks, sir,' says the corporal.

'Turn them round and follow me,' snaps Voigt. 'I have an urgent mission for them on direct orders of the Kaiser himself.'

Voigt leads his little army back up the road. On the way, he orders four more soldiers to fall in and follow him. With nine men to back him, he is now a force to be reckoned with. So commandeering a bus is an easy task.

Their destination is Kopenick, an outlying district of Berlin. Once there, Voigt lines his troops up for inspection, then marches them off to the town hall. There, they burst through the door of the mayor's parlour, and confront the startled civic leader. 'You're under arrest,' snarls Voigt.

One of eight bell-ringers involved in a marathon peal at a church in Buckinghamshire, England, lost his trousers. The 56-year-old man asked if he could stop pulling on his rope to pull his trousers up. But he was told he must continue ringing for another 5,040 chimes.

'Where is your warrant?' whimpers the mayor. 'My warrant is the men I command,' roars the imperious 'captain'.

The mayor is himself a reserve officer, so he is not going to argue with orders, even if the captain's badge is on upside down, and the captain looks a little old.

Dispatching some of his men to collect the mayor's wife, Voigt turns his attention to the borough treasurer's office. There, he arrests the custodian of the town's cash, and announces: 'I am ordered to confiscate all your funds.' Meekly, the treasurer unlocks his safe and hands over 4,000 marks, worth about £650. Voigt signs a bogus receipt.

Ordering his men to hold the prisoners outside, Voigt now ransacks the office looking for a passport and identity card. But he is out of luck.

Still, he does have 4,000 marks. And he has succeeded in making a mayor, a treasurer and the army look pretty foolish. Well content with his day's work, Voigt scurries away to the railway station.

In the station's left-luggage office is a bundle of civilian clothes he took the precaution of leaving before the escapade began. Voigt heads for the lavatory. Moments later, he is in his own clothes, the uniform neatly parcelled under his arm, and on a train back to Berlin.

Next day, the newspapers are full of the exploits of the mystery man who took authority down a peg or two. Voigt is delighted. But as the days pass, and still no culprit has been arrested, he begins to feel cheated of the recognition he has earned. So he plants a photograph to help police find their way to him. And after ten days, the officers arrive to arrest him at his breakfast.

The trial is a sensation. Voigt, the man who pricked the pomposity of both army and government, is almost a national hero. And there are rumblings of discontent when the judge hands out a four-year sentence. It seems harsh.

Voigt was not to serve the full term. The Kaiser, who was said to have muttered 'amiable scoundrel' when told of his exploits, gave way to public sympathy and affection by pardoning him after 20 months.

Voigt retired in comfort to Luxembourg – on a life pension given to him by a rich Berlin dowager, who was captivated by the sheer audacity of his deeds. He died in 1922.

Joseph Samuels, convicted of killing a man in cold blood, was sent to the gallows in Sydney, Australia, in 1803. But as the trap-door opened and Samuels took 'the drop', the hangman's rope snapped and the killer survived. The hangman tried a second time, but on this occasion the trap-door only half-opened. At the third attempt, the rope broke yet again. Samuels was reprieved.

Curious Crime

T he title of Britain's Most Optimistic Burglar was awarded by the *Sunday Times* to a Yorkshireman with a withered hand, an artificial leg and one eye missing who was advised by magistrates to take up 'a more rewarding occupation' after his seventh conviction, in March 1977.

Thieves come in all shapes and sizes, and people will steal practically anything. In August 1982, for example, *The Times* reported from Washington that: 'The Smithsonian Institution has found the bottom half of George Washington's stolen dentures but the FBI is still hunting the uppers.'

Obsessive would-be doctors and dentists are a recognized type of criminal impostor. In March 1981, a particularly bizarre case was reported. A hospital filing clerk had become so obsessed with surgery that he built a secret operating theatre in an attic. He fitted it out with £3,000 worth of medical equipment stolen from the Warwick hospital in which he worked. There were scalpels, clamps, oxygen cylinders, trolleys, chemicals and hundreds of other surgical accessories. In this weird 'Aladdin's Cave of appliances, the man carried out experiments on rats and rabbits. He was caught when a porter at the hospital saw him loading an anaesthetic trolley into a car.

The Trouser Thief of Toronto was apprehended in 1938. For 33 years he had stolen nothing but trousers. 'His record goes back to 1905,' said the prosecutor, 'and only once, in 1907, did he lapse from his standard and steal anything but a pair of trousers. On that occasion it was a shirt.'

The Trouser Thief was a specialist. So too was Peter Kelly, 'a most horrible annoyance', whose arrest was reported in *The Times* of 12 October 1837. The report is worth quoting verbatim for it shows that however times and crimes may change, the newspapers' interest in off-beat episodes has remained unaltered over the years:

'Peter Kelly, a pauper of St Sepulchre's parish church, was charged with having undressed himself for the purpose of exciting the charitable feeling of the public more effectually.

'A constable stated, that to his great astonishment he saw the prisoner go up stark naked (with the exception of the abdomen, round which was tied a piece of old rag) to a hall in Finsbury Circus and knock boldly. The females all ran away the moment they beheld such an object, for he was not only destitute of clothing, but he had not shaved for six months. Upon being repulsed at one door, the prisoner went up to another, and the witness learned that he asked for charity wherever he knocked.

'Mr Miller, one of the parish officers, said, that the prisoner had been a pauper all his life, and had been in every prison within 50 miles of London. The plan he adopted of going naked was very ingenious, and sure to tell among the humane, who would drop a few pence and run away.

The Lord Mayor – He looks like an idiot.

Mr Miller – he is about a quarter of a fool and three quarters of a knave, and he is the most horrible annoyance, for when he fancies getting money, he tears his clothes off and knocks loudly at the doors of the most respectable houses. When we catch him at such tricks we generally put him in a sack, with his head through one hole and his legs through two others.'

Kelly's defence, incidentally, was that he considered it quite warm enough to go about the streets with no clothes on. In modern days, he might have made a passably good insurance swindler. Certainly he could have fared no worse than the motorcyclist whose case came up in September 1982. He tried to swindle £100,000 out of an insurance company by getting his girlfriend to chop off his foot. Phase One of the master plan was successful – the foot came off. Phase Two was less so – nobody was fooled. The man was jailed in San José, California.

Reflecting on his misfortunes, the footloose defrauder might do well to consider a career as a drug smuggler. Or perhaps not. One 46-year-old thought he would be free from suspicion because of his physical handicap. But when he stepped of a plane from Caracas, Venezuela, he was arrested by narcotics agents in New York.

The agents came up empty-handed when they searched his luggage. Then, noticing his wooden leg, they took him to the nearest hospital and removed it in the presence of a doctor. Hidden in a compartment in the leg, neatly encased in a plastic bag, was 18 ounces of cocaine, worth $65,000.

The man pleaded guilty to drug possession and was sentenced to four years in prison. While serving his term, the smuggler made an appeal against the validity of the search, claiming that federal agents had violated his right to

---

The World's Most Determined Murderess

This title belongs to a **36-year-old American woman** who devised a series of bizarre schemes to murder her husband, finally succeeding at San Diego, California. The case was reported in January 1978.

She put LSD in his toast, served him blackberry pie containing the venom sac of a tarantula spider, placed bullets in the carburettor of his lorry, tossed a live electric wire into his shower, and injected air into his veins with a hypodermic needle to induce a heart attack.

She finally succeeded by dropping tranquillizers into his beer and smashing his skull with a steel weight.

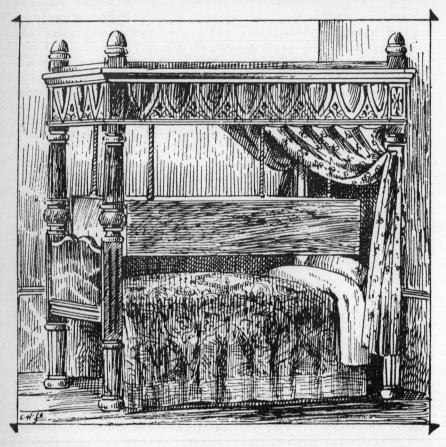

Nightmare device – the suffocating bedstead

privacy. The appeal was launched with a cheerful optimism and it was turned down.

A 45-year-old Düsseldorf man lodged no such appeal, but then his plan had been twice as ambitious. In 1978, in Bangkok, he was jailed for five years for trying to smuggle about 2 lb of morphine out of Thailand in his two artificial legs.

Criminal ingenuity knows no bounds. The *Strand Magazine* of 1894 illustrates a suffocating bedstead devised by the landlord of a wayside coaching inn. It comprised a massive wooden box which was lowered over sleeping travellers to imprison them in an air-tight cavity. Their possessions could then be stolen without risk, and the bodies disposed of afterwards. The means by which a Brooklyn housewife was killed in May 1982 was equally macabre. A package arrived at her home, and when she opened it in her kitchen she found a volume entitled *Quick and Delicious Gourmet Cookbook*. She lifted the cover. Immediately, there was a blinding flash and two .22-calibre bullets tore into her chest; she died three hours later. 'It took a lot of thinking to make that bomb,' an inspector later commented. The cookbook was only $1\frac{1}{2}$ in thick, but it had been hollowed out to enclose a six-volt battery wired to a charge of gunpowder and three bullets. At the time of writing, neither motive nor murderer were known for sure.

How unfeeling the modern criminal can be! In September 1982, the *Daily Mirror* reported: 'A group called the Pixie Eradication Society has been smashing garden gnomes on Dartmoor "to rid the national park of these distasteful little objects".'

The action of a Philadelphia banker was more curious still. He shook hands with a Philadelphia woman after church service. The alleged atrocity was committed in 1975. Two years later, the woman claimed, her hand still hurt and she brought a suit against the banker for $10,000 damages. Her husband launched a related suit on his own behalf, seeking $10,000 for himself because he had been 'deprived of his wife's assistance in society'; the case of the Golden Handshake?

The banker was accused of negligence in 'pulling, squeezing and shaking the woman's hand' without considering the strength and power of his hand grip. The case of two senior citizens of Cleveland, Ohio, provides a finale for this chapter on crime. The men must be classed as the World's Worst Gunslingers. After the event, which occurred in 1981, they were released having signed papers saying that they did not wish to press charges against one another and their names were not released. One, however, was aged 77 and the other 76.

The men had a grudge that went back a long way. They lived in flats opposite one another and began quarrelling, as they had often done before, in the narrow hallway of an apartment house one Tuesday morning. On this occasion, however, mere insults could not quench their rage. Each went back to his apartment block and returned brandishing a venerable six-shooter. Then they began to blaze away.

Both shot their full load – 12 bullets were fired in all – and alarmed residents called the police. 'There were bullet holes above, bullet holes down, and bullet holes all over the hallway,' said a detective. But every one had gone astray. Police suggested that the gunslingers missed because one needed a cane to prop himself up and the other had trouble seeing because of a glaucoma. They were standing just five feet apart during the duel.

The Kray Twins: the 'Mafia' of London's East End

When London gangsters, the Kray twins, were sentenced in 1969, the judge Mr Justice Melford Stevenson told them with scornful understatement: 'In my view society has earned a rest from your activities'. These activities included theft, extortion and finally murder, in a reign of terror that marred the memory of Britain's 'swinging sixties'.

The Krays held London's underworld in a mafia-like grip. In their heyday, they were feted by showbusiness personalities. They were photographed with the famous. They were generous in their support of charities. And they were feared like no other criminals. In every way, they were a British version of America's thirties gangsters, whose exploits they studied avidly and emulated slavishly.

Even after the full extent of their crimes was revealed in court and the pair were jailed for life, many people in the East End of London still spoke affectionately of the Krays. Some regarded them as 'Robin Hood' characters. Others, more realistically, saw them as people who maintained gangland peace and kept the seedy streets safe. Few at the time asked any questions as to how such a peace was being maintained and by what sort of men.

The Kray twins were born on 17 October 1933 at Hoxton in the East End. Ronnie was the elder. Reggie arrived 45 minutes later. They also had an older brother, Charles.

The boys had Jewish, Irish and Romany blood in their veins. Their father Charles, who was 25 at the time of the twins' birth, was a dealer in old clothes, silver and gold. Their mother Violet was just 21.

Just before the war, the family moved to one of the toughest, most run-down areas of Bethnal Green, shortly to become even more decrepit thanks to visits from the Luftwaffe. Ronnie and Reggie became known as the Terrible Twins because of their love of fighting – at first with fists and later with bicycle chains and flick-knives.

By the age of 16, they were carrying guns. A year later, they made their first appearance in court. They were accused of seriously beating up a 16-year-old rival but the case was dismissed for lack of evidence.

The twins were fighters in every sense. At 17, they became professional boxers. A year later they were called up for their National Service and punched the recruiting corporal on the nose. Much of their subsequent military service was spent in jails.

After their dishonourable discharge in 1954, they went into the protection business. If a bookmaker, store or club owner wanted to ensure 'no trouble', a weekly payment to Ronnie and Reggie would do the trick. As the easy money rolled in, so their gang of collectors grew. Their territory covered the East End and much of North London.

They founded their own clubs – at first in the East End, where a sports hall provided a front for their rackets, and later in fashionable Knightsbridge where the West End found the pair a rough and ready attraction.

By now, Ronnie was known as 'the Colonel', Reggie was 'the Quiet One' and their home in Vallance Road termed 'Fort Vallance.'

The Krays could be magnanimous, loyal and charming. They could also be frighteningly, unpredictably brutal. But mainly it was Ronnie who took the lead, egging his brother on to prove himself by being tough enough to follow his lead.

In 1956 Ronnie shot a man in the leg. When picked out at an identity parade, he avoided being charged by claiming he was Reggie – thus making nonsense of the evidence. Later that year Ronnie was caught and convicted. He received a three-year sentence for stabbing a man with a bayonet in a raid on a rival gang's territory.

It was at this time that Ronnie Kray's dangerous instability became apparent. He went berserk in jail. He became obsessively fearful that someone was trying to have him 'put away'. He even had to be shown his reflection in a mirror to prove he was still in one piece. Finally, he was sent from prison to a mental hospital where he was certified insane.

In true flamboyant Kray style, the family moved in to help – and Ronnie moved out. Reggie paid a visit to the mental hospital and swapped clothes with his brother. When Ronnie was safely away, Reggie owned up to his little trick.

Ronnie remained free for some weeks, during which time his sense of bravado induced him to make surprise calls on East End pubs to taunt the police. But his strange state of mind worried his family and, after a suicide attempt, they allowed the police to recapture him. After further treatment, he was deemed fit to be released, in 1958.

But Ronnie Kray was far from cured – and no one knew it better than his brother. Reggie had a good business brain, and the family's commercial enterprises had flourished during Ronnie's spell in jail. There was the original 'Double R Club' in Bow, a new club in Stratford, a car sales business and even an illegal gambling club a stone's throw away from Bow police station. But

The Kray twins, Reggie (left) and Ronnie (right), with brother Charles

Ronnie's return from prison also meant a return of the heavy-handed gangsterism that put such businesses in peril.

The brothers argued about their 'firm'. But when in 1960 Reggie was jailed for 18 months for demanding money with menaces, it was his brother's turn to have a free hand at running the business.

Ronnie took a contract from the notorious slum landlord, Peter Rachman. The Krays' hoodlums would guard Rachman's rent collectors in return for a healthy commission. The result was not only added riches for Ronnie but his introduction to a more sophisticated society. His new Knightsbridge club, 'Esmerelda's Barn', became a favourite rendezvous for entertainers and sports people. It also became a haven for penniless young men on the make . . . for Ronnie was by now openly homosexual.

Reggie was otherwise inclined. When released from prison in 1961, he fell hopelessly in love with a 16-year-old East End girl. For the first time in their lives, the brother's lifestyles were now widely different – Ronnie veered towards his swinging friends 'up West' while Reggie returned to his roots on the east side of town. Largely thanks to Reggie's business acumen, the Krays added a restaurant and several other clubs to their empire. And Reggie got married – tragically for his teenage bride who could not cope with the gangster's crazy world and eventually committed suicide in 1967.

It may have been due to the strain of Reggie's failing marriage or it may have been due to the Al Capone fantasy world of brother Ronnie, but the regime of the Krays took an even more violent turn in the second half of the Sixties.

There were beatings, brandings and knifings. One former friend who drunkenly insulted Ronnie needed 70 stitches to face wounds. There were also at least three unsuccessful attempts on the Krays' lives, and Ronnie took to sleeping with a gun under his pillow.

Warfare flared between the Krays and Charles Richardson's gang, based in south London but intent on muscling in on West End protection rackets.

In March 1966, a small-time 'heavy' working for Richardson strayed into Kray territory. The brothers were told that George Cornell had been announcing to East Enders that 'Ronnie Kray is a big, fat poof and don't take any notice of him . . . He can't protect you from anything.'

Ronnie was tipped off that Cornell was in a well-known Whitechapel pub called the Blind Beggar. Ronnie walked calmly into the bar and, as he later described in his own words, 'put a gun at his head, looked him in the eyes and pulled the trigger. Then I put the gun in my pocket. His body fell off the stool and I walked out.'

Later he justified the murder by saying: 'Cornell was vermin. He was a drunkard and a bully. He was simply nothing. I done the Earth a favour ridding it of him.'

The following year, Reggie made his own violent contribution to the murder statistics.

By now, the brothers' business had expanded to drugs and pornography, areas that did not endear them to their traditional East End friends. Ronnie's homosexual proclivities were the talk of their 'manor' – quite apart from his by-now obvious paranoia. And Reggie 'the Quiet One', following his wife's suicide, had taken to drink and to shooting at the legs of people who gave him offence.

The Krays were becoming bad news. They were being shunned by the rich and famous as well as by the poor and infamous. They were trouble. The twins became concerned about their 'image' and decided to hold a test of their 150-strong gang's loyalty – a meaningless murder.

The victim was to be Jack 'The Hat' McVitie, so called because of the hat he wore to hide his baldness. McVitie's crime was to owe the brothers £500 and to have insulted them in their absence during a drunken binge.

Four of the Krays' men lured McVitie to a 'party' in a borrowed house in Stoke Newington where Ronnie, Reggie and two henchmen lay in wait. As their victim entered he realized his impending fate and turned to flee. Ronnie pinned him against a wall and told him: 'Come on, Jack, be a man.' McVitie said: 'I will be a man but I don't want to die like one.'

Ronnie led him into a basement room where the killing became near-farcical. As McVitie walked through the door, Reggie pointed a gun at his head and pulled the trigger . . . nothing happened. Ronnie then picked up a carving knife and thrust it at McVitie's back. But it failed to pierce his thick coat.

McVitie made a dash for the window. He dived through, only to be grabbed by his feet and hauled back in. Ronnie pinioned his arms from behind and screamed at his brother: 'Kill him, Reg. Do it. Don't stop now.' Reggie picked up the knife and stabbed his pleading victim in the face and then through the throat. The knife passed through his gullet and pinned him to the floor.

McVitie's body was never found.

Flushed with their success, the twins decided to form a Murder Incorporated organization along the lines of the American model. But, by now, every move they made was being monitored by a Scotland Yard team led by Detective Superintendent Leonard 'Nipper' Read.

Plans were laid to kill a minor crook who was appearing as a witness at an Old Bailey trial. The murder weapons were a crossbow and a briefcase with a hidden hypodermic syringe filled with cyanide. Another plan was for the contract killing of a gambler who owed an unspecified debt to the Krays' prospective paymasters in Las Vegas. A third plot was to be the murder of a Maltese club owner by blowing up his car with dynamite.

Detective Superintendent 'Nipper' Read's case against the Krays was now strong. But he knew that, unless the twins were safely behind bars, prospective witnesses would suffer 'memory loss' or simply vanish.

Then the police got lucky. A Kray associate was stopped while about to board a plane from Glasgow to London. He was carrying four sticks of dynamite, presumably destined for the Maltese club-owner's car. Detectives raided his home and found the crossbow and briefcase complete with poisonous syringe.

On the night of 8 May 1968 Ronnie and Reggie went drinking at the Old Horn pub in Bethnal Green. They went on to the Astor Club in fashionable Berkeley Square, returning to their mother's new council flat in Shoreditch at four in the morning. Reggie went to bed with a girlfriend, Ronnie with a boyfriend. At dawn 'Nipper' Read's men swooped on the flat and arrested them.

The Kray twins were charged with the murders of George Cornell and Jack McVitie. Eight other members of their 'firm', including their brother Charles, were charged with various lesser crimes.

The twins pleaded not guilty but after a sensational 39-day trial at the Old Bailey, they were jailed for life with a recommendation that they should serve no less than 30 years. They were 35 years of age when the trial ended on 8 March 1969, which meant that they would be pensioners before they were released.

Ronnie and Reggie were sent to separate top-security prisons. In 1972 they were briefly reunited at Parkhurst jail on the Isle of Wight. But in 1979 Ronnie was again certified and sent to Broadmoor hospital for the criminally insane.

Reggie found his sentence harder to take than his brother. He was classified as a Category A prisoner – highly dangerous and liable to escape. Shadowed at all times by two prison officers, his movements were logged and monitored while his visits were screened and limited. While of Category A status, no parole board could consider his case. All his appeals fell on deaf ears. In 1982, he unsuccessfully attempted suicide by cutting his wrists.

Ronnie was luckier in his time behind bars. Being an inmate of Broadmoor, he was allowed more privileges than his brother. He received visits from old East End associates and from showbusiness and sporting friends. They brought him parcels of food from Harrods – smoked salmon and game pie – and classical records for the hi-fi in his cell. He also had a colour television set.

Ronnie Kray would regale visitors with details of his exploits in the days when he and his brother wrote headlines in blood. In 1983 he told a visiting journalist, long-time friend Brian Hitchen: 'We never hurt ordinary members of the public. We only took money off other villains and gave a bundle of that away to decent people who were on hard times.

'I look back on those days and naturally remember the good times. Then, people could take ladies into pubs with them without the risk of their being insulted. Old people didn't get mugged, either. It couldn't have happened when we were looking after the East End.'

About life in Broadmoor he said: 'There are some really bad ones in here,

Brian, some really bad ones. But they are all some mother's sons – and that's where the heartbreak is. Because no matter what they've done or how bad they've been, the mothers don't stop coming and don't stop loving them. When I see these mums, I feel really sorry for them having to come here.'

In 1982 the twins' strongest link with the outside world ended. Their most constant visitor, their mother Violet, died one week before her seventy-third birthday. Violet Kray had become an East End legend in her own right and was said to have been the only person on earth who had any control over the twins.

Ronnie and Reggie were allowed out for a day to attend her funeral, which was turned into a star-studded East End occasion.

Reggie said after his return to Parkhurst jail: 'It's so lonely without visits from our mum. They were always the best ones. I shall miss her so much. Throughout the funeral, Ronnie and I were handcuffed to police officers who must have been 6ft. 3ins. (1.9 metres) tall. But they needn't have worried. Violence is not part of my life anymore.

'I get angry when I read about the way things are in the East End nowadays – like those attacks on old ladies. Years ago, if we saw an old lady we would help her across the road and wish her goodnight. Now they rape 80-year-old women and kill them for their pensions. It makes me sick.'

And of the hopelessness of life in jail, he said: 'You can so easily give up after all these years. They have passed quickly. But it is only when I see the youngsters come in here that I realize what a terrible waste of life it is.'

The Palace Intruder

The *Daily Express*, which broke the story, called it 'the most gross and scandalous lapse of security in her 30-year reign'. Queen Elizabeth II of England had, in the early morning of 9 July 1982, been abruptly awakened by an intruder at Buckingham Palace. The man was barefooted, wearing jeans and a scruffy T-shirt. He had sat on her bed cradling a broken ashtray in his hands, and dripped blood onto the royal bedclothes.

For an eerie ten minutes, the man had engaged his sovereign in conversation, making no threatening moves but preferring to chat about the coincidence that each of them had four children. The Queen was finally saved when a chambermaid entered the royal bedroom, took one look at the prowler and blurted: 'Bloody hell, Ma'am! What's he doing in here?'

What *was* he doing in there? How had he got into the bedroom? Where were the guards? And where, for that matter, was Prince Philip? The full story of the sensational incident emerged only over several weeks, following a police investigation and the intruder's trial on a charge quite separate from the events of 9 July.

The prowler's name was Michael Fagan, aged 33, an unemployed decorator from North London. Fagan was never brought to court for the incident in the royal bedroom. Instead, he was charged for an earlier misdemeanour. Incredibly, Michael Fagan had been into the Palace before, on the night of 7 June. And for that offence, he was charged only with stealing half a bottle of wine.

At a preliminary hearing on 19 July, the court was packed. Fagan entered with his hands behind his back and strutted into the dock. He constantly turned and smiled towards members of his family. Propping stockinged feet on a wrought iron rail at the front of the dock, he laughed and waved to his wife Christine and his mother Ivy. Fagan appeared to be enjoying himself. Only when the name of the Queen was mentioned did he bristle: 'I told you not to fetch her name up,' he glowered at his solicitor. 'I would rather plead guilty than have her name dragged into this.'

Indeed, throughout the whole bizarre affair, one thing emerged very clearly, Fagan practically worshipped his monarch.

Fagan behaved in the same eccentric way when brought for trial proper. He smiled and winked at reporters, waggling his eyebrows and groaning theatrically from time to time. At one point he even took out his upper set of dentures, grinned and picked a piece of prison food from them. When asked to take the oath, he replied: 'I'm not religious, Your Worship' (he called everyone 'Your Worship', even the lady usher). Fagan was allowed to read the oath for atheists, and read it he did, starting right from the top:

'Please read your name clearly', he boomed, reciting the instructions at the top of the card. Even the judge permitted himself a smile.

Fagan told the jury that he broke into the Palace on that first occasion because 'a little voice in my head' told him to do so. His defence was that he did it as a favour to the Queen. 'Her security was no good, and I proved it,' he said. 'I wanted to show the Queen was not too safe . . . I could have been a rapist or something.'

Having climbed over railings he had shinned up a drainpipe and emerged at the window of a housemaid's bedroom. The maid herself had just returned to the Palace from a seance. She almost fainted when she saw the intruder's gaunt features at the window. But when she reported her experience to Palace staff, they refused to believe that anyone could have made the perilous climb to her window. 'You saw a ghost,' they mocked. (Her story was later confirmed, however, when pigeon repellent from window ledges was found on a carpet.)

Fagan, meanwhile, wandered around the palace 'to look at the paintings and take the place in'. He told the court: 'I walked past a couple of rooms – one said "Princess Anne" and the other said "Mark Phillips". I thought they was asleep so I did not disturb them.' He saw another door marked 'Prince Philip', and then entered the room of Prince Charles's private secretary. There he waited for half an hour, expecting to be arrested.

In the room was a pile of presents for the newborn baby of Prince Charles and Lady Diana. And nestling beside a pair of baby bootees, Fagan found a bottle of cheap white wine. (The label read Vache Tomocula California Johannesburg Reisling 1981 – the bottle appeared in court.) Fagan took the bottle, pushed the cork down with a pair of scissors so that it bobbed around inside, and then poured himself two glasses. 'I was thirsty,' he explained. 'I had done a hard day's work for the Queen.' All the time he was waiting for someone to come and arrest him. Finally, however, he thought, 'Sod this, there's no-one here.'

Despite the very full account which Fagan gave of this first visit, the jury found him not guilty. It was an extraordinary decision: 'Bonkers!' the *Sun* called it, in a banner headline splashed across its front page. 'Next time you are walking along The Mall and feel thirsty, why not pop into Buckingham Palace

---

Early Intrusions

The affair of Michael Fagan prompted the press to examine earlier cases of royal intrusion. A Maidenhead man wrote to *The Times* to say that his late mother, when a teenager, had been smuggled into the royal apartments at Windsor by an infatuated footman. She had been concealed behind a curtain for the sole purpose of watching the old Queen Victoria eating a solitary meal. 'Nearly 90 years later,' the man wrote, 'I still grow cold when I think of the dire consequences if my mother had been discovered.'

If intrusions were not new, neither was lax security. A former Grenadier Guards officer, who had done royal service in World War Two, told the *Daily Telegraph* that he had found guardsmen and police playing gin rummy, smoking, chatting and reading comics instead of guarding the royal family at Windsor. Disturbed by what he had seen, the officer took to cycling silently around the grounds at night, wearing plimsolls instead of the regulation hob-nailed boots. His tours of inspection had their effect: 'Soon everyone was absolutely on their toes,' he wrote. 'But what did the police do? They complained to the Governor that under an 1890 regulation bicycles should not be ridden on the terraces. I was pulled up in front of the Governor, made to write an abject apology and promptly sacked.'

for a glass or two?' it suggested. Fagan had clearly not entered the Palace *in order to* steal the wine, but the decision remained astonishing.

It appeared that through a vagary of English law, Fagan could not be charged with trespass for his second visit; when he entered the royal bedroom.

Much, nonetheless, was revealed about the incident. Fagan, the press discovered, had told his sister that he had a girlfriend in the West End called 'Elizabeth Regina'. The sister had not grasped the significance of the name. On the night of 8 July, a friend of Fagan's told reporters: 'He said he was restless and could not sleep so I invited him in for a drink. We had a couple of whiskies and Coke and played some records. We chatted about children and family – nothing very serious that I can recall. He left about 5 a.m. but did not say where he was going. Certainly there was no mention of royalty or Buckingham Palace.'

It was, nevertheless, to Buckingham Palace that Fagan repaired. And a Scotland Yard investigation revealed precisely how somnolent the Queen's supposed protectors had been.

Fagan got inside by climbing a railing near the gates to the Ambassadors' Entrance at 6.45 a.m. He was spotted by a policeman but, in the first of a startling string of gaffes, the police control room let the warning slip.

Through an unlocked ground floor window, Fagan climbed into the Stamp Room, where the extensive royal stamp collection is displayed. An alarm was set off – but it was ignored. Fagan then went back out the same window, shinned up a drainpipe, removed his socks and sandals and climbed in another window which had just been unlocked by a maid. For a quarter of an hour, he prowled around the Palace corridors unchallenged.

One member of the Palace staff remembered seeing him, but did not consider his behaviour sufficiently suspicious to cause alarm. The intruder slipped through various warning devices which had been badly adjusted. Finally, he found the private apartments by 'following the pictures' along the gallery that connects to the Queen's quarters.

Fagan spotted an ashtray, and thoughts of suicide occurred to him. He smashed the article and, at 7.15 a.m., entered the Queen's bedroom carrying a sliver of the broken glass. He intended to slash his wrists with it in front of the Queen, and made his way in, already bleeding from a cut right thumb.

The royal chambermaid called during the weird interview, only after the Queen had made several attempts to summon help.

There followed scenes of careful manoeuvring to remove the intruder, which might have come straight from the script of a theatrical farce. The Queen told the chambermaid to take Fagan out of the room and give him a cigarette. The servant accordingly led him into a large pantry opposite the bedroom. By now, the footman had returned (he had been walking the corgis), and the Queen

**Michael Fagan,
intruder**

quickly informed him of the situation. She herself took charge of the dogs, while the footman went into the pantry to help deal with Fagan. He offered the intruder a cigarette, and gave him a whisky. Fagan repeatedly tried to get back into the bedroom, but the footman blocked his path.

The chambermaid, meanwhile, slipped away and dashed along the corridors to the police lodge, and eventually a constable arrived.

In the storm of publicity which ensued, some rather off-beat discoveries were made about the domestic life of the royal family. The *Sun*, for example, regaled its readers with reports from Fagan's wife about the eerie interview in the royal bedroom. The Queen, it appeared, had been wearing a shortie nightgown at the time; she had the figure of a 16-year-old and her wig was allegedly sitting in her room. Many papers dwelt at length on the fact that Elizabeth and Philip obviously had separate bedrooms. 'Separate beds:' mused the *Daily Mirror*. 'How important is it to cuddle up together?'

The inefficiency of the security services were, of course, the subject of much outraged comment. *The Times* observed: 'So much for the guards at Buckingham Palace. The ceremony of Changing the Guard will never be quite the same again . . . All that array of scarlet tunics, burnished brass and polished leather, and still an intruder could stroll into the Queen's bedroom without being detected.'

The Prime Minister, Mrs Thatcher, went in person to Buckingham Palace to apologise to the Queen on the Government's behalf. Home Secretary William Whitelaw, meanwhile, faced an indignant reception in the House of Commons, and was greeted with mocking jeers when he announced: 'In recent years a number of additional security measures have been introduced at Buckingham Palace. But this latest incident shows that the position is still not satisfactory.'

Satisfactory it certainly was not, despite all the guardsmen, police, servants, surveillance cameras and electronic devices maintained at immense cost. It was found that Fagan's expeditions were not unique. During the previous year or so three other incidents had already occurred (though only Fagan managed to penetrate the Palace itself). In June 1981, three young German tourists had climbed the Palace wall and camped for a night in the royal gardens, thinking they were a park. Two months later, a 25-year-old man was found wandering in the palace grounds; he told police he was very fond of Princess Anne and had hoped to see her. In June 1982, another man had burst into the palace courtyard brandishing a commando-style knife.

The newspapers dug up Palace intrusions from the past, and noted that lax security was not a new phenomenon. And yet Fagan's expeditions remained unique in their bizarre quality, and the scandal which ensued.

Following his apprehension on 9 July, Fagan remained in police custody, even after his acquittal on the wine-stealing charge. It was felt that his state of mind was such that his movements and actions were totally unpredictable. Clearly he had both personal problems, and suicidal tendencies. In October 1982, he was brought to trial on a charge unconnected with the Palace – that of taking away and driving a car that did not belong to him. Following the pattern of his previous court appearances, his behaviour was somewhat wayward: 'Burn the bastards to hell!' he bellowed. 'This is a Fascist country!' The judge ordered him to be taken from the dock and removed to the cells. 'Sieg Heil!' the intruder roared as officers grabbed him.

Although Fagan was not present for the duration of the hearing, he did leave a statement drawn up while awaiting trial. Remorseful in tone and clearly authentic in sentiment, it provided a curiously sad epitaph on the whole sensational affair:

'Along with everyone else in the world, I love Her Majesty the Queen. I have the deepest respect, the deepest respect for her. I would do nothing to embarrass her. I know she likes to help people and I thought she would like to help me. And I have admired her for eternity.

'I understand that I should have written to her rather than gone to see her, and that by doing so I have caused her unwelcome and inaccurate publicity which I do not wish her to have. There is nothing I could do now to put the clock back although I wish I could. Anything that I can do to make up for the embarrassment I have caused I would do.

'Your Majesty, please excuse my intrusion into your privacy – I didn't realise it would become a world topic. All I wanted to do was discuss my personal problems, but the way I went about it has embarrassed Your Majesty's family.

'You were wonderfully understanding with me and I know you will accept that this apology is written with all sincerity.

Humbly, Michael

In his absence, Fagan was ordered to be sent to a high security mental hospital for an indefinite period. The intruder's solicitor accused the authorities of being too harsh, and indeed, considering how his most sensational exploits had gone unpunished, there was a curious irony in the court order. As the solicitor pointed out, never before in British history had anyone been sent to a high security mental hospital for taking away a car.

Ice-cool crooks

Ice-cool nerve seems to be the principal qualification for a life of crime. It was certainly needed in the case of The Great Frozen Asset Robbery.

In 1980, staff at pubs and clubs in Camden, North London, were baffled by the pools of water which appeared under their cigarette machines. They discovered that an ingenious crook had got away with thousands of cigarettes by making ice 'coins' and putting them in the slots. Then he would vanish with his loot while the evidence literally melted and evaporated.

The coolest courage, plus a dash of sheer daring, helped a thief who had been caught red-handed by a woman as he fled from her house carrying a shotgun and the family silver in a plastic bag.

With police patrol cars and a Royal Air Force helicopter on his tail, the fugitive raced away on foot, abandoning his getaway car. Then, on a sudden inspiration, he stopped to seek sanctuary – at a police college.

The brazen bandit knocked on the door of the college at Bramshill, Hampshire, and asked if he could use the phone. He called a cab – and disappeared.

Even more daring were the thieves who stripped the lead from the roof of a police station in Coventry. The building, which the police authority was trying to sell at the time, had to have £5,000 spent on it to make the roof waterproof again.

'If you can lift it, take it' seems to be the motto of the criminal crowd. A banner advertising a crime prevention week in Reading, Berkshire, was stolen. And another thief took the trouble of removing a cardboard cut-out of a Canadian Mountie from a police exhibition at Aylesbury, Buckinghamshire.

A couple who broke into a chemist's shop in Ilkeston, Derbyshire, made a bed from disposable nappies, downed a bottle of energy-giving drink and made love before leaving with goods worth £144.

A gang broke through an elaborate security system to raid the home in Turin, Italy, of a wealthy businessman who earned his fortune making burglar alarms.

After a bigger haul were the three men who boarded an El Salvador Airlines DC-6 jet at Miami airport in 1979. They filed a flight plan for Haiti and took off, stealing the plane. The theft was discovered when the real crew arrived.

One crook who made a clean break was the 23-year-old convict who literally swept out of a Paris jail. He was given a broom and carried on brushing, unnoticed, through the gates and away.

But for sheer cheek, there is no case to beat that of the British bridegroom who invited his boss to the wedding. The bridegroom, a 34-year-old chauffeur, for once did not have to take the wheel, as he and the guests – boss included – were whisked by limousines to the church in Grimsby.

Two of the bridegroom's best friends, however, were not invited to the wedding. They had a prior engagement that very day. For while the bridegroom stood at the altar saying 'I do', his two friends were hard at work – snatching a safe, containing between £15,000 and £20,000, from the boss's home.

The chauffeur, however, did not long enjoy wedded bliss. The conspiracy was uncovered and he was jailed for three years.

The underground 'mole' behind the world's biggest bank robbery

The 1976 raid on the Nice branch of the Société-Générale was the biggest bank robbery ever. Afterwards, owners of rifled strongboxes put in claims totalling £6 million, but French police believe the haul could have been nearer £50 million.

Most of the raiders, who tunnelled from a sewer into the bank's vaults, were never caught. The mastermind, Albert Spaggiari, was arrested but escaped from a courtroom and was believed to have headed for South America. To the French, he became something of a cult hero. He even wrote a book about the robbery, which was made into a film.

Spaggiari evidently set his heart on big-time crime in his teens. At 16 he applied in writing to join a group of Sicilian bandits, but received no reply. Two years later he joined the army and served as a paratrooper in Indo-China, where he had three citations for bravery in action. But after staging a robbery at a nightclub he was court-martialled, jailed and dishonourably discharged.

He then joined the OAS and went to Algeria. The OAS hated France's President, General de Gaulle, and Spaggiari claimed to have organized an assassination attempt – along the lines of the one featured in Frederick Forsyth's thriller, *Day of The Jackal*. When de Gaulle visited Nice, Spaggiari had him in the sights of a rifle from the upper window of his mother's shop. The reason he did not fire was that his OAS chief failed to give the order.

A year later Spaggiari was arrested with four accomplices for printing and distributing right-wing pamphlets. Police searching their print shop and homes discovered an illegal cache of arms and ammunition. Because of his previous record, Spaggiari got four years' imprisonment, while his friends were put on probation.

After his release, he became a photographer, opening a shop and specializing in smart weddings and pictures of the rich and famous who pass through Nice.

His work brought him in contact with the town's top people, and he cultivated a friendship with the mayor, Jacques Médecin. Later Médecin became France's Minister of Tourism and took Spaggiari with him on a tour of Japan as his official photographer.

Spaggiari used the profits from his photographic business to invest in a chicken farm in the hills. He lived there with his wife Baudi, his collection of German imperial army spiked helmets and an armoury of guns, ammunition and explosives. It was at the farm that he and his accomplices plotted the biggest bank raid ever.

Spaggiari, lean and handsome and always smoking a big Dom Miguel cigar, was a popular and respected character in Nice.

The city was considered by many to be the crime capital of southern France, having inherited the dubious honour from Marseilles. Violence and gang warfare were a part of everyday life. At stake were the rich pickings from drugs, vice and robberies.

Much of the illicit profit ended up in safe-deposit boxes in bank vaults. Other boxes in the vaults of the Société-Générale would have held assets undeclared for tax reasons. Many victims of Spaggiari's raid claimed much less than they had lost – for fear of attracting the attention of the tax inspectors or the police.

Some of the boxes broken open by the thieves held humble secrets. One was filled with coffee, sugar and biscuits, presumably hoarded in case of the outbreak of World War Three. Others held chocolates, toffees, cigarettes and flasks of alcohol, belonging to secret smokers, drinkers and dieters who could not resist the occasional lapse.

Spaggiari is thought to have got hold of a map of the town's sewer system with the help of a highly placed town hall official. He rented a safe-deposit box at the Société-Générale to note the layout and security system.

To check for electronic sensors, he left a wound-up alarm clock in his box, to see if its ringing set off detectors. It did not. There was no alarm system in the vaults because they were considered impregnable. The walls were 5 ft thick.

Spaggiari decided to tunnel from the nearest sewer to the vaults, then break through the masonry walls with electric drills. After 18 months' planning, the gang entered the sewer system via a small underground river.

They reached the vaults of the Société-Générale by digging a tunnel 24 ft long and 4 ft high. It took them two months, working by night and laboriously carrying their equipment in and out every evening and morning. They carried the soil away in plastic sacks, to dump in the hills above Nice. The tunnel, supported at the correct intervals by jacks, was constructed so professionally that when police discovered it they first checked on ex-miners.

The gang broke through to the vaults on the evening of Friday, July 20, 1976. They brought in an air pump to set up a ventilation system. Then they opened safe-deposit boxes with jemmies, taking notes, gold and jewellery, and scattering share certificates and private documents over the floor.

The gang could have worked undisturbed until the early hours of Monday morning but for one piece of bad luck – rain.

Their getaway sewer was a main storm drain. A heavy downpour threatened to flood it and on Sunday the gang made a hurried escape in rubber dinghies after rifling 317 of the 4,000 deposit boxes in the vaults.

Before leaving, they welded shut the door leading to the bank to give themselves a few more hours before the robbery was discovered. A bank employee who tried the door on Monday morning assumed it was stuck and it was not until lunchtime that a professional was called in to cut through it.

In their haste, Spaggiari and his gang left behind thousands of pounds' worth of equipment. Police found heavy-duty blow torches, 27 gas cylinders, 11 crowbars, pit-props, sledgehammers, jemmies, bolt-cutters, lamps, hacksaws, rope, pliers, hammers, spanners, drills, cooking stoves, eating utensils, empty wine bottles and the remains of meals. On one wall was scrawled the message: 'Without anger, without violence, without hatred'. Above it was the peace symbol.

While bank employees were still trying to free their welded-up vault door, the raiders were counting and sharing their loot, a task which took them from Monday morning until Wednesday evening.

Spaggiari was eventually traced through a shop from which he had bought equipment for the raid – and by the Dom Miguel cigar butts found in the vaults.

On March 10, 1977, Spaggiari was being questioned by an examining magistrate about the disposal of the loot, which he steadfastly claimed to have handed over to an underground OAS-style group. The prisoner complained to the magistrate that the room was stuffy and moved towards a window, apparently for some fresh air. He threw the tall casement open and jumped.

Spaggiari fell 20 ft, landed with an expert paratrooper's roll on a parked car, and sprang on to the pillion of a waiting motorbike. As he sped away, he turned and made a rude gesture to the police. After a 15-minute journey to the airport, he caught the early evening flight to Zurich.

After his escape, sightings were reported in Spain and South America. But it was felt in France that some police were only half-hearted in their efforts to catch the thief whom many regarded as a folk hero.

How Black Bart's one-man gang kept Wells Fargo on the run

Astagecoach robber of the Wild West who stood apart was Black Bart. He was always courteous, never hurt anybody and stole only from the treasure box and mailbags – never from the passengers.

Bart's first hold-up was on a blazing hot day in 1875 when he stopped a Wells Fargo stagecoach near Sonora, California. As the horses struggled up a hill, a strange gunman jumped out from the bushes. He wore a flour sack on his head, with holes cut out for the eyes, and a long, white coat.

He told the driver to throw down the box and mailbags, and he ordered his supposedly hidden accomplices to shoot if anyone offered resistance. The driver saw six guns poking out from the bushes. They were all trained on the stagecoach.

What followed on that day has passed into Western folklore. For when a petrified woman passenger threw her purse at Bart's feet, he calmly picked it up. With a gracious bow, he returned the purse and said he was interested only in the treasure box and mailbags, not passengers' money or valuables. This strange robber took his loot and told the driver to continue his journey.

For several years, Black Bart robbed in his cavalier manner. His reputation and courteous ways became the talk of California. And he never earned more than £250 from each of his stagecoach robberies, since most gold and valuables were by then transported by train.

The man given the task of nailing Black Bart was Jim Hume, Wells Fargo's chief detective. He soon realised that Bart was a cunning and resourceful robber. When Hume visited the scene of that first robbery, Bart's 'gang' was still there – six sticks poking through the bushes.

Hume learned little about Bart. He left no clues, his trail just petered out and he seemed to walk everywhere rather than ride. Bart became bolder and even left Hume his name and a poem at the scene of one of his hold-ups. But then he began to slip up. . . .

After a series of hold-ups, Hume visited houses in the area and learned that a grey-haired hitch-hiking stranger with a grey beard, white moustache and two missing front teeth had stopped to have dinner. A picture of the hooded raider was at last emerging.

It was a laundry mark on a handkerchief that finally led to Black Bart's capture in 1882. The thief had managed to escape unharmed when he had been interrupted by a young gunman as he was about to rob a coach, but he had blundered by leaving behind his sleeping-roll and handkerchief.

Hume had no trouble tracing the laundry mark to a San Francisco laundry – and that led him to a Mr. Bolton. He was an elderly man, softly spoken, with grey hair, grey beard, white moustache and two missing front teeth.

Mr. Bolton explained his frequent absences from home by saying that he had to make visits to his mine. But there was no mine, and Hume knew that he had his man when Black Bart's clothes were found at Mr. Bolton's home.

Black Bart was arrested and, courteous to the end, he returned much of the money taken on his raids. For their part, Wells Fargo made charges on only one hold-up and forgot about the others.

By now, the gentlemanly thief had become a popular hero. The judge must have had a soft spot for him, too. Black Bart was jailed for only six years.

Defectors: Unexpected Bonuses

Western newspaper readers could be forgiven for thinking that Russia and her allies always win in the espionage war. Successive spy trials and scandals since 1945 have shaken public confidence in all NATO nations. But for every Western traitor unmasked, there are at least two defectors from Russia or her Warsaw Pact partners. Often the West's recruitment of a disillusioned Communist renegade or a carefully-cultivated double agent goes unpublicized for years, for good reason. The significance of what they reveal could be lost if the Soviet Union learns of the leaks, and takes precautions to guard its operations. And Russian defectors live in real fear for their lives. Moscow justice is usually meted out not by judges and juries, but by assassins.

Most defectors are minor agents of limited immediate value to Western spymasters. Their information about codes and how the KGB works forms part of a jigsaw which, when pieced together with facts from other sources, can lead to a breakthrough in the cold war. Others have priceless secrets to trade for asylum. And very occasionally, high-ranking Soviet intelligence officers betray their masters in a way which changes the balance of espionage power.

In 1953, the CIA recruited Lieutenant Colonel Yuri Popov in Moscow. For five years, until he was shot after betrayal by British traitor George Blake, Popov, an officer with GRU, the Soviet military intelligence organisation, gave the Americans the code names of nearly 400 Russian moles in the West. Many of them were identified and rounded up.

In 1960, another top man approached the West. Colonel Oleg Penkovsky said he turned traitor because he feared Russian leader Nikita Khruschev would plunge the world into nuclear war. He identified hundreds of Soviet agents abroad, including Eugene Ivanov, the spy in the Profumo affair. He handed over 5,000 documents about Russian military plans and weapons, especially rockets. He gave prior warning of the building of the Berlin Wall. But most important, he marked President Kennedy's card in the Cuban missiles crisis.

The world held its breath during October and November 1962, as the American and Russian leaders played what seemed to be a deadly game of brinkmanship. Khruschev had installed missiles in Communist Cuba, only 322 km (200 miles) from the American coast, and aimed at every major US city. Kennedy blockaded the island and demanded that the missiles be dismantled and removed. For days the battle of nerves seemed likely to unleash a third global war or even a nuclear holocaust. Then Moscow appeared to back down. The weapons were withdrawn in return for an American pledge not to attempt any repeat of the Bay of Pigs invasion adventure. What no one knew at the time was that Oleg Penkovsky had warned of the missile plan as early as April 1961, and kept Washington informed of Soviet decisions at every stage of the confrontation, giving Kennedy the confidence to make a tough stand.

Weeks later, Penkovsky and his British contact, Greville Wynne, were arrested. At a Moscow show trial early in 1963, the Russian was sentenced to death, and Wynne to eight years in prison. He served only 18 months before being exchanged, haggard and thin, for Gordon Lonsdale, mastermind of the Portland spy ring. Wynne claimed at his trial that he was an innocent businessman. But once safely back in Britain, he published two books bragging about his espionage exploits.

In one book, Wynne alleged that when Penkovsky came to England escorting a trade mission, he insisted on seeing the Queen and was introduced to Lord Mountbatten. The Russian also wanted to parade round London in a British uniform, and demanded £1,000 in cash to buy gifts for friends in Moscow. Such tales of bizarre behaviour helped raise doubts, not only about Wynne, but about Penkovsky. If the stories were true, how had the Russian survived as a spy for nearly two years?

In his book, *Inside Story*, published in 1978, espionage writer Chapman Pincher described Penkovsky as 'far more valuable (to the West) than Philby ever was to Moscow'. But by 1981, when Pincher published *Their Trade Is Treachery*, Penkovsky had become, 'in the minds of many members of MI5 ... a Soviet plant, the key figure in a disinformation exercise of the highest political consequence.' Now the suggestion was that Penkovsky was not shot. Nor, as Wynne claimed, did he commit suicide in his cell. Instead he was living in retirement, having fooled the West into believing that the Cuban missiles were important to Khruschev. In fact, according to the new thinking, the object of the crisis exercise was to protect Fidel Castro's Cuba as a centre for Communist subversion in South America – an object allegedly achieved by the American promise not to invade.

Such re-evaluations are not uncommon in espionage, where time can put a different perspective on events, where the borders between heroism and villainy are often blurred, and where suspicious minds are the first line of defence. The West has been conned by defectors who were not what they seemed. But in Penkovsky's case, the repercussions in Moscow after his arrest point to him being a genuine Western coup. General Ivan Serov, appointed GRU chief after the Popov affair, was axed along with several top assistants,

---

A disgruntled Soviet defector betrayed a Russian masterspy in 1955. Rudolf Abel, a KGB colonel with more than 30 years experience, arrived in New York in 1948 to build a replacement network for the Yakovlev spy ring blown by Igor Gouzenko. He established himself in Brooklyn as Emil R. Goldfus, an artist, photographer and radio enthusiast, and quickly impressed Moscow with his flow of secrets on nuclear weapons and rockets. In 1954, the Kremlin sent Reino Hayhanen to America to help with communications. But the newcomer was a reluctant spy and an alcoholic. Tired of his moaning, and afraid it would lead to a security breach, Abel arranged for Hayhanen's recall. But the espionage assistant defected rather than face the wrath of his masters. Abel was arrested on the basis of Hayhanen's evidence, and in October 1957 was sentenced to the electric chair. Appeals commuted this to 30 years in jail, and in February 1962, he was sent back to Russia in exchange for Francis Gary Powers, the U2 spy-plane pilot shot down over Sverdlovsk two years earlier.

A press officer for the World Health Organisation in Geneva defected to Britain in March, 1980. Ilya Grigorivich Dzhirkvelov was a KGB officer who had served three years in the Swiss city – a vital espionage nerve centre. After a carefully planned escape with his wife and seven-year-old daughter, he compromised scores of Soviet agents in Western Europe, especially in France and Belgium.

and the KGB took tighter control of GRU activities. Many agents were recalled or left without instructions for months while counter-espionage experts tried to assess the damage Penkovsky caused.

Nine years later, Soviet leader Leonid Brezhnev cut short a tour in Eastern Europe to attend a hasty meeting at Moscow airport with KGB spymaster Yuri Andropov and other top Communist party officials. As a result of their discussions, key spies were ordered home from Mexico, Canada, Finland, Greece, Germany, France, Nigeria and the Far East.

The cause of the Kremlin's consternation was the unprecedented mass expulsion of 105 Russian diplomats and trade officials by Britain on 24 September 1971. MI6 and the CIA were already aware that most of them were spies. But it was the defection of Oleg Adolfovitch Lyalin which revealed the full extent of their espionage activities. For Lyalin was an officer in the KGB's Department V, responsible for sabotage and assassination. And his evidence so enraged Prime Minister Edward Heath and Foreign Secretary Sir Alec Douglas Home that they warned Moscow that if any reprisals against Western envoys followed the exit orders, even more Soviets would be kicked out.

Lyalin arrived in London in 1969, with the cover of an official at the Soviet trade delegation based in Highgate. The security services soon discovered that, although he was a married man with a family in Russia, he was having an affair with his secretary. He also showed a liking for the luxuries of Western life, particularly drink. And in August 1971, two police officers stopped his car after seeing it being driven erratically. A blood-alcohol test proved positive. Lyalin had no diplomatic immunity. The consequences of a court case and return to Russia in disgrace were pointed out to him. In return for plastic surgery to protect him from possible assassination attempts, he agreed to cooperate with the authorities.

He revealed staggering details of what Attorney General Sir Peter Rawlinson later described in Parliment as 'the organization of sabotage within the United Kingdom and the elimination of individuals judged to be enemies of the USSR.'

Teams of saboteurs had been prepared to exact maximum damage on British radar stations, communications centres and other sensitive defence complexes in the 24 hours before any surprise attack by the Soviet Union. Lyalin's specific target was to blow up the Fylingdales early warning system in Yorkshire, on constant watch for missile attacks. He had maps showing where he was to link up with Russian commandos on the coast.

Lyalin also outlined plans for specially-adapted Aeroflot airliners to drop mines into the Clyde Estuary, trapping the nuclear submarine fleet at Holy Loch; for the London Underground system to be flooded; and for teams of already-recruited British traitors to attack British and American air bases, using arms and equipment from clandestine stores already established in the countryside. Since NATO contingency plans consider Britain an off-shore aircraft carrier for American reinforcements in the event of conventional warfare anywhere in Europe, the implications of a strong subversive army ready to strike at the defences from behind were horrific. Sadly for MI6 and the CIA, Lyalin knew few names of those involved. And he warned of a parallel network of GRU agents working separately from the KGB teams.

Britain made a formal protest to Soviet Foreign Minister Andrei Gromyko, circulated a full list of all the expelled Russians to friendly countries, and followed up Lyalin's leads as best it could at home and abroad. Specific details about the extent of Soviet preparations to attack other countries in peacetime were not released to the public, possibly for fear of causing too much alarm. But the counter-espionage forces of the West were left in no doubt that their task had taken on a sinister new dimension.

In the 1950s and early 1960s, most Iron Curtain defections were handled by the Americans. The CIA had a far bigger budget than MI5 or MI6, and could afford the time and money for the long, delicate task of 'turning' a Soviet agent. Also, many of the spies fleeing from the KGB or agencies of Russia's satellite countries insisted that the CIA keep Britain in the dark because both MI6 and MI5 had been infiltrated by Moscow moles. The 1945 Volkov debacle, detailed earlier, had taught subsequent defectors a lesson. Igor Gouzenko, Anatoli Golitsin, and Polish defector Michal Goleniewski were just three Communist renegades petrified of betrayal by a British spy chief. The 1971 defection of Oleg Lyalin in London was taken as evidence that MI6 and MI5 were now mole-free. And 11 years later the British landed an even bigger fish.

Vladimir Andreyevitch Kuzichkin was described by one intelligence source as the West's most precious catch for 30 years when he arrived in London with bulging dossiers of Soviet secrets in October 1982, and was taken to a Sussex hideaway for debriefing by British and American inquisitors. The Russian vice consul in the Iranian capital Tehran was really the KGB's spymaster in the Middle East, and brought with him a breakdown of the espionage network both there and in Western Europe, complete with code-names, code systems, the identities of agents and sub-agents, and details of KGB operations.

More inspired intelligence leaks were forthcoming about Kuzichkin than most defectors, possibly because the espionage organizations were still stung by the publicity battering they had taken over the Geoffrey Prime case, to be discussed later in this book. The West needed a morale booster – and Kuzichkin was it. Hints were dropped that he had worked as a double agent for Britain for up to five years, that he was lured by the love of a beautiful Egyptian-born MI6 girl working in Tehran, that his usefulness to Britain and America was on a par with Philby's value to Moscow at the height of his powers.

Kuzichkin's main task in Tehran was to infiltrate agents into the Iranian Communist party, the Tudeh, to foment subversion against the regime of Ayatollah Khomeini, which was proving less than pliable to the Kremlin's will. But he had access to sensitive KGB material affecting espionage throughout the Middle East and the NATO countries. Then, in June 1982, his British controllers learned he was about to be unmasked as a traitor. Unable to spirit him secretly out of Iran, they struck a deal with Khomeini's security police. Kuzichkin was delivered to them, and provided enough evidence for the arrest of Tudeh leader Hassein Zadeh and hundreds of his followers. Soviet influence inside Iran was effectively smashed. Then the defector was taken to Paris, and handed to the British. His wife elected not to follow him.

In accordance with diplomatic protocol, the Russian ambassador in London was allowed to request a meeting with Kuzichkin. But the spy who came in from the cold war was not interested. He knew that his information would force the KGB to completely reorganize their operations in at least ten countries. And for that, they were hardly likely to thank him.

The most wanted men in the West

What was the truth about the Wild West? Our ideas tend to have been formed by characters like Tom Mix, Gene Autry, the Lone Ranger and Roy Rogers. Screen idols through the years have portrayed the cowboy as a slick, good-looking, gun-totin', lariat-twirling goodie in a white hat, or scheming, scowling baddie in a black hat.

Hollywood took the names of men like Billy the Kid, Jesse James and Butch Cassidy and turned them into heroes. But few of the folk who lived and died in the 19th-century West would have agreed. . . .

Baptist minister's son Jesse Woodson James strolled into the Clay County Savings Bank in Liberty, Missouri, on February 13, 1866, and took the liberty of relieving cashier Mr Greenup Bird of $60,000.

It was the start of a bloodthirsty war that the James boys and their daring cousins, the Youngers, waged throughout Kansas and Missouri. They got away with gunning-down train guards and bank tellers because nobody knew what the villains looked like – since none of them ever had his photograph taken.

Jesse would openly stroll around Nashville and Kansas City, calling himself Mr Howard, and on one occasion even bought a drink for a Pinkerton Agency detective searching for him.

Detective Bligh confided to 'Mr Howard' that his last wish would be to confront Jesse James. Later James sent him a note: 'Go ahead and die. You've seen Jesse James.'

Jesse loved playing to the crowd. On one occasion during a Missouri train hold-up, he personally presented the guard with his latest press cuttings.

The day Jesse and his boys slipped up was when they tried to rob the First National Bank in Northfield, Minnesota. The townsfolk had been tipped off that the gang were on their way, and as they arrived in town they were met with a hail of bullets, grapeshot and even bricks. Two of the gang were blown to pieces, three Younger brothers were captured, but Jesse got away.

The man who finally put paid to Jesse James was a gunslinger named Bob Ford, who joined the gang after secretly agreeing with the authorities to assassinate James for a free pardon and part of the reward money.

On April 3, 1882, Jesse, then aged 35, got up to straighten his favourite 'Home, Sweet Home' picture on the wall of his bunkhouse abode. Ford blew off the back of his head, and his brains scattered across the floor.

The owner of the house where Jesse died, at St Joseph, Missouri, chopped up

The only authentic portrait of Billy the Kid

the floor and sold the blood-stained wood-shavings for five dollars a time.

The James gang's greatest partners in crime were the Younger family. Cole Younger, then 28, first teamed up with Jesse's gang in Logan County, Kentucky, in 1868, to rob the local bank.

Cole had already met Jesse as one of Quantrill's Raiders at the massacre of Lawrence, Kansas, where, in one of the most unparalleled acts of savagery in the West, 150 men and boys were shot by William Quantrill's Confederate guerillas.

Cole had a passionate love affair with Myra Belle Shirley, the 18-year-old daughter of a Dallas horse-breeder. After two disastrous marriages, she went on to achieve notoriety as Belle Starr.

The other Younger brothers – Bob, 18, Jim, 26, and John, 28 – later joined Cole in the James gang. John died from a Pinkerton bullet and the surviving three were captured and jailed for life after the Northfield, Missouri shoot-out.

Butch Cassidy and the Sundance Kid were turned into posthumous superstars thanks to one successful film. In real life, neither were heroes – although a cut above some of the other crooks of the age.

Butch Cassidy was born Robert Leroy Parker in 1867 in Beaver, Utah, but later changed his name as a token of respect to his idol Mike Cassidy who taught him the arts of rustling and horse stealing.

In his youth, Butch was involved in everything from petty larceny to train and bank hold-ups. But it wasn't until he was released from Rawlings Penitentiary, Wyoming, that he decided to get his own gang together. They soon became known as the Wild Bunch.

Legend has it that Butch, eulogized by contemporary posters as a cheery, affable character, never shot directly at a man. When pursued by a posse he would always fire at the horses.

Trains were the speciality of Butch and his Wild Bunch. One day they scooped $30,000 from a Union Pacific express by detaching the last car and blowing it and the safe inside to smithereens. They followed this success with three more train raids until Pinkerton agents got on the gang's trail.

The Pinkertons and the railroad's own crime fighters forced the gang to seek refuge in South America. Around 1909 (some say in Bolivia, others in Uruguay), Butch and his chief cohort in crime, Harry 'Sundance' Longbaugh, either committed suicide or were shot dead in a battle with troops.

Harry Longbaugh had got his nickname when, as a boy, he served 18 months in jail at Sundance, Cook County, Wyoming, for horse stealing. Thereafter, he called himself the Sundance Kid.

The Kid had no raindrops falling on his head – only 'wanted' posters. In late 1901, Sundance and his lady love, Etta Place, sailed for Buenos Aires after being run out of the US by the Pinkertons.

The Wild Bunch. Butch Cassidy is seated on the right and the Sundance Kid on the left.

He continued robbing banks and trains, managing to keep one step ahead of the law by hiding out among local Indians, until his death alongside Butch Cassidy.

The most famous gunfighter of the West was a soft-spoken, agreeable young man named William Bonney, better known as Billy the Kid. Believed to have been born in New York, he moved west with his family and became a cowboy in Lincoln County, New Mexico. There he worked for an English ranch owner John Tunstall, who befriended him.

In March 1878, two killers riding with the posse of corrupt Sheriff Brady of Pecos blasted Tunstall to death. When Bonney, then aged 19, heard of his benefactor's death, he grabbed a pair of Colt 44s and went looking for the two killers.

Billy found them and shot them dead. Then, with a price on his head, he teamed up with a gang whose members put paid to Sheriff Brady.

By now, Bonney's fame was spreading. People began talking about a gunslinger named Billy the Kid.

State Governor Wallace tried to con Billy into giving himself up. Wallace hired the Kid's one-time friend, Pat Garrett, who persuaded Billy to testify at an inquiry into gang warfare in Lincoln County in exchange for a light sentence.

The Kid walked smack into the trap – but shot his way to freedom. Unknown to Billy, Garrett was made Sheriff of Lincoln County in recognition of his treachery.

Still trading on their old friendship, Garrett guessed that eventually the Kid would head towards the hideout of a mutual friend, Pete Maxwell.

Garrett got there first, urging Maxwell to persuade Billy to surrender. But as they were talking, Billy walked in – straight into two slugs from Garrett's Colt.

Billy the Kid, 21, sprawled dead with 19 notches on his gun. But he could never add up. He had actually killed 21 people in less than two years to avenge his friend and earn himself a place in American legend.

The Wild West is packed with stories of vicious outlaws. But one robber who stood apart was Black Bart. He was always courteous, never hurt anybody and stole only from the treasure box and mailbags, never from the passengers.

Bart's first hold-up was on a blazing hot day in 1875 when he stopped a Wells Fargo stagecoach near Sonora, California. As the horses struggled up a hill, a strange armed man jumped out from the bushes. He wore a flour sack on his head, with holes cut out for the eyes, and a long, white coat.

He ordered the driver to throw down the box and mailbags, and he shouted to his hidden accomplices to shoot if anyone offered resistance. The driver saw six guns poking out from the bushes. They were all trained on the stagecoach.

What followed that day has passed into Western folklore. For when a petrified woman passenger threw her purse at Bart's feet, he calmly picked it up. With a gracious bow, he returned the purse and said he was interested only in the treasure box and mailbags. Not passengers' money or valuables. The strange robber took his loot and told the driver to continue his journey.

For several years, Black Bart robbed in his cavalier manner. His reputation and courteous ways became the talk of California. And he never earned more than £250 from each of his stagecoach robberies, since most gold and valuables were by then transported by train

The man given the task of nailing Black Bart was Jim Hume, Wells Fargo's chief detective.

He soon realized that Bart was cunning and resourceful. When he visited the scene of that first robbery, Bart's 'gang' were still there – six sticks poking through the bushes.

Hume learned little about Bart. He left no clues, his trail just petered out and he seemed to walk everywhere rather than ride.

Bart became bolder and even left Hume his name and a poem at the scene of

Charles E. Bolton, alias Black Bart

one of his crimes. Then Black Bart began to slip up.

After a series of hold-ups, Hume visited houses in the area and learned that a grey-haired, hitch-hiking stranger with a grey beard, white moustache and two missing front teeth had stopped to have dinner. A picture of the hooded raider was at last emerging.

A laundry mark on a handkerchief finally led to Black Bart's capture in 1882. The thief managed to escape unharmed when he was interrupted by a young gunman as he was about to rob a coach. But he blundered by leaving his sleeping-roll and his handkerchief.

Jim Hume had no trouble tracing the laundry mark to a San Francisco laundry – and that led him to a Mr Bolton. He was an elderly man, softly spoken, with grey hair, grey beard, white moustache and two missing front teeth.

Mr Bolton explained his long absences from home by saying that he had to make frequent visits to his mine. But there was no mine, and Jim Hume knew he had his man when Black Bart's clothes were found at Bolton's home.

Black Bart was arrested and, courteous to the end, returned much of the money taken on his raids. For their part, Wells Fargo made charges only on one hold-up and forgot about the others.

By now, the gentlemanly thief had become a popular hero. The judge must have had a soft spot for him, too. He was jailed for six years. It could have been worse.

Black Bart Bolton may have been one of the last stagecoach robbers – but he is remembered first and foremost as the outlaw who wouldn't hurt a fly.

Swallows: From Russia With Love

Major James Holbrook turned away from the window of the small hotel room and gazed again at the beautiful girl stretched out on his bed. She made it hard for the American military attaché to concentrate on the task which had brought him from the embassy in Moscow to the small town of Rovno, a few miles east of the Soviet border with Poland. He was supposed to check rumours that Russia was preparing to invade its neighbouring satellite, plunged into turmoil in 1981 by Solidarity demands for economic and political reform. Then he had met the girl . . .

He returned to her inviting arms. Holbrook, 41, had never met anyone so skilled at loving, so ready to pander to his every whim. Her embraces were a lonely man's only comfort in such a bleak outpost. But as they clung together again, the door was abruptly kicked down, camera flashbulbs exploded harshly, and a Russian colonel known to the American walked into the room. He gently pointed out that, as a married man with two children, Holbrook had seriously compromised himself. However, his Soviet friends could ensure that his wife and the embassy never heard of the incident if Holbrook cooperated by providing Moscow with a little information.

Holbrook was no naïve amateur in the espionage game. He courageously confessed his indiscretion to his superiors and was recalled to Washington. An intelligence spokesman there said:

> 'We can only guess that the Russians got wind of the fact that Major Holbrook was being considered for a new job as military adviser to Vice President George Bush at the White House. He would have had access to the most highly secret material of President Reagan's administration.'

Holbrook had been hooked by a 'swallow', one of the hundreds of stunningly lovely Russian girls ruthlessly trained at specialist camps to cold-bloodedly seduce Westerners. And the fact that an agent well-versed in KGB espionage techniques could be tempted proved how effectively the beauties learn their lessons. But Moscow leaves nothing to chance in its efforts to recruit shamed victims of sex traps as spies. Targets are meticulously scrutinized for 'personality defects'. If a man has an eye for a pretty girl, the KGB provides one exactly suited to his tastes. And it has plenty of erotic experts to select from.

Indonesian President Achmed Sukarno had a worldwide reputation as a womaniser, so it was only natural that the KGB should try to blackmail him with a sex trap when he visited Moscow. He was introduced to a stream of expertly-trained beautiful swallows, and filmed making love to all of them in his hotel suite. But when the evidence was shown to him prior to a blackmail bid, Sukarno amazed the Soviet agents by asking for copies of the films to take home for public showing, adding: 'My people will be really proud of me.' The recruiting attempt went no further.

In his book *Sexpionage*, author David Lewis tells of an interview he had in Tunisia with Vera, a swallow who defected. She told him how the KGB recruited intelligent and attractive girls from schools and colleges with promises of salaries and privileges superior to those of most Russians in return for unspecified duties for the state. They were then taken to heavily guarded camps in remote areas for a de-humanizing course, designed to rid them of all inhibitions. First they watched films of every sexual activity, including perversions. Then they were ordered to strip in front of other women. Later men watched them undress, and caressed and criticised their bodies. Then coachloads of soldiers arrived, and the girls were ordered to make love to the complete strangers. Their performances were filmed for group discussion later. After several weeks, the girls lost all shame, and were ready to fall in with any suggestion for group or single sex.

As Vera told Lewis:

> 'We were told we should remember that we were soldiers fighting in the front line of a bitter ideological battle. In war soldiers were often ordered to do things which, as individuals, they would find repulsive; but hard sacrifices were essential. Our bodies were weapons to be used in a cause. By the time our training was completed, we were hard, cynical, sophisticated young women capable of bedding any heterosexual man authority selected for us, and giving him the time of his life.'

Top politicians and diplomats are not the only victims of Soviet swallow sex traps. Ordinary Western workers on assignment behind the Iron Curtain can have their lives disrupted by amorous agents. In July 1979, the 54-year-old wife of British engineer Richard Clasper received a manila envelope at her Tyneside home. It contained photographs of her 57-year-old husband making love to a beautiful young brunette. Mrs Clasper collapsed with shock and was rushed to hospital. Her husband told reporters that, despite warnings from Special Branch detectives before he left for Russia, he succumbed to loneliness at the remote building site where he was working, and went to bed with a 27-year-old interpreter. A mysterious stranger then arrived, asking him to spy on Russian workers at the site, but he refused. Clasper added: 'It was the first time I had been unfaithful in 31 years. This has wrecked my marriage, broken my wife and ruined me.'

Vera said she became sickened by her role as a sexy spy in 1963, after seducing a young Frenchman about to get married. He was told his bride-to-be would learn of the liaison unless his father, an influential chief in the mining industry in France, passed over commercial secrets. The boy killed himself by walking in front of a car in Moscow's Red Square, unable to cope with the shame of his seemingly 'innocent affair'. Vera then seduced a senior KGB official in return for official papers allowing her to visit East Berlin, where she defected.

The French, with their traditional partiality for *amour*, have been special targets for swallows. And it was the suicide of another sex trap victim, Moscow air attaché Colonel Louis Guibaud, that prompted the defection in London in 1963 of Yuri Krotkov, a film scriptwriter used by the KGB to set up seductions, often using actresses as bait. What disillusioned Krotkov told MI5 stunned his interrogators and rocked the French establishment. For he revealed that France's ambassador to Russia had been compromised by at least two swallows.

Maurice Dejean arrived in Moscow with his pretty young wife in 1955, and was quickly picked out by KGB sex trap mastermind Lieutenant General Oleg Gribanov as a likely target. His roving eye made him vulnerable. Krotkov, who had previously compromised Mexicans, Indians, Pakistanis, Americans and Britons, decided to win the ambassador's trust by charming his wife, Marie Claire. After engineering a meeting at a diplomatic reception, he cultivated the acquaintance by inviting her on river cruises, providing tickets to the ballet, and picking up the bill for lavish dinners. Eventually Dejean joined them on the social outings. Krotkov introduced him to a buxom, sophisticated interpreter called Lydia. Then, after arranging for Madame Dejean to enjoy a day away in the country, he invited the ambassador to an exhibition of paintings.

The lovely Lydia just happened to be admiring the pictures when they arrived. Within hours, she and Dejean were lovers.

Having photographed the event, the KGB already had a hold on the French envoy. But Lydia was known to be divorced. To spring their trap, the Russians needed another swallow. Lydia was sent out of Moscow 'to film on location' and Dejean was introduced to another actress, Larissa. Within days they too were bed partners. But in June 1958, the amorous ambassador received a nasty shock. Two burly men burst into Larissa's love nest. One played the part of an outraged husband. Dejean was left in no doubt that he would hear more about his adultery.

Worried, he consulted one of the friends Krotkov had introduced to him – Gribanov himself. He was reassuring, promising to try to pull strings. Within days, he was able to set the ambassador's mind at ease. The 'husband' had agreed not to press charges. But Dejean was now dangerously entangled. One day, the KGB would expect repayment for this 'favour'.

After Krotkov's defection, Dejean was recalled to Paris by his close friend, President De Gaulle, and grilled by counter-espionage men. It seemed the KGB had never called in the debt. De Gaulle dismissed him with the words, 'So Dejean, you enjoy the company of women.' It turned out he was not the only ambassador to share this hobby.

A blonde Russian swallow brought the distinguished diplomatic career of Sir Geoffrey Harrison to an abrupt end when she seduced him in Moscow. Sir Geoffrey was recalled to London in 1968, and it was thought at the time that the departure of Britain's ambassador was a protest at Russian intervention to crush liberalism in Czechoslovakia.

Only 13 years later was it revealed that he had had a torrid affair with a chambermaid called Galia at the embassy. When shown photographs of himself with her, and invited to become a Soviet spy, he wisely confessed to his Foreign Office bosses.

Sir Geoffrey said after a Sunday newspaper disclosed his secret:
> 'I did not ask Galia if she worked for the KGB, but the assumption was there. I regret it, of course I regret it. I was warned before I went to Moscow about this sort of thing – anyone going to the Iron Curtain countries is warned this can happen. It was a very silly thing for me to do.'

His replacement as ambassador to Moscow, Sir Duncan Wilson, said:
> 'Galia was a blonde, buxom girl and very attractive. There was no doubt she was one of the Russians' top drawer girls. She was clearly in a completely different class from the rest of the domestics, but I have no idea how good she was at housework – I dismissed her a few days after I arrived.'

Sir Duncan was astonished to receive a phone call days later from the Australian ambassador. 'It appeared Galia had gone straight round and asked him to give her a job, and he wanted to know if I could give her a reference,' he said. 'I made it quite clear she would not be at all suitable.'

How many Britons, Americans and West Europeans have been inveigled into espionage by the attentions of captivating Russian swallows? Commander Anthony Courtney, a former Naval Intelligence officer who later became a Conservative MP, has estimated the total of silent, shamed moles in the NATO countries at 10,000. And he says there are at least 50 in the British Foreign Office.

His opinions have particular relevance. For Commander Courtney was the first known victim of a sex trap used to discredit rather than recruit. In 1961, shortly after the death of his first wife, he was befriended on a business trip to

Anthony Courtney

Moscow by beautiful swallow Zina Volkova, who was working as an Intourist car rental assistant. Largely at her instigation, he took her back to his room in the National Hotel, and found comfort in her arms. Two years later, back in London, the Commander made a series of speeches in Parliament questioning the diplomatic immunity of employees at Soviet bloc embassies, and claiming that 20 chauffeurs at the Russian embassy in Kensington were KGB officers.

In August 1965, copies of intimate photographs of Courtney and Zina were delivered to influential MPs, the *News Of The World* newspaper and the Commander's second wife. Courtney was able to explain them to his wife and the security services, but the public were less reasonable. He lost his job as MP for Harrow East, and his political career was finished. Moscow does not usually take such drastic steps over critics on the back benches at Westminster, and many believe the public shaming of Courtney was a warning to somebody even better placed in the power structure, to toe the Kremlin line or else.

George Blake: Deadly Deceptions of a Double Agent

The British public was stunned in May 1961 when it was announced that a spy called George Blake had been jailed for 42 years. It was an astonishing long sentence compared to those imposed on Nunn May, Fuchs and the Portland spy ring. What had Blake done? The trial had been held in secret, in the interests of 'national security', and Prime Minister Harold Macmillan refused to divulge the facts of the case despite repeated attempts by the Labour opposition to raise the matter in Parliament. Eventually he agreed to a confidential briefing for three Labour Privy Councillors, so minds could be put at rest. But what he told them had the opposite effect.

Blake was born in Rotterdam in 1922, the son of Albert William Behar, an Egyptian Jew who held a British passport, and his Dutch wife. The teenage George Behar joined the Dutch Resistance to Nazi occupation, but was eventually forced to flee to Britain, where he enrolled in secret organizations to carry on the war against Germany, finally changing his name to Blake, and working as an intelligence officer with the Royal Navy Volunteer Reserve.

After the war he transferred to the Foreign Office, where his brilliance as a linguist' was quickly recognized. The Fuchs case brought in new rules, insisting that all civil servants should be British born, but by then Blake was already in the fold, working as a vice consul – and MI6 agent – in Korea. He was captured by the Communists and held in a North Korean interrogation camp for some months. Later suggestions that he was brainwashed at this stage were contradicted by fellow prisoners, who said Blake stood up bravely to his jailers.

By 1953, he was in Berlin for MI6, with instructions to infiltrate the Soviet spy set-up in the city that was, throughout the 1950s, the frontline flashpoint of the cold war between East and West. For more than four years, London was satisfied with his work in the complex, confused, murky waters of double agent espionage. Naturally, to win the trust of the Russians, he had to provide certain secrets, but MI6 remained confident they were getting more than they were giving. In fact, they were being duped.

In 1961, the arrest of a German spy and the defection of a Pole both provided evidence, too late, that Blake had turned triple agent. The spy was then based in Beirut. Interception of his message to Moscow, warning that Gordon Lonsdale was about to be arrested, was the final proof MI6 needed. An agent was sent to Lebanon to discuss a new job for Blake in London. It was the technique used with Kim Philby two years later. Philby fled to Russia. Blake, presumably unaware he had been unmasked, returned to England – and arrest.

The Macmillan government tried to justify the secret trial on the grounds that agents betrayed by Blake were still being withdrawn from behind the Iron Curtain. In fact, by then, they had all been rounded up and either shot or imprisoned. More than 40 anti-Communist agents around the world had been compromised. There were more secret shocks in store for the Labour Privy Councillors – leader Hugh Gaitskell, deputy leader George Brown and ex-minister Emanuel 'Manny' Shinwell – as they were briefed by Mr Macmillan and his Cabinet Secretary Norman Brook.

In Berlin, Blake had photographed almost every secret document that crossed his desk and handed the snaps to the KGB. He had hidden in the office when it was locked by a security man for the lunch hour, and worked undisturbed. He had informed the Russians of the whereabouts of prominent East Germans who had defected to the West, allowing the KGB to kidnap them and whisk them back behind the Iron Curtain. And he had betrayed one of the West's most expensive and ambitious projects, Operation Gold.

This was a joint project between the CIA and MI6 to build a tunnel to tap East German and Russian messages in East Berlin. It was conceived in December 1953 and took three months to dig. It began on the site of a new radar station near a cemetery at Rudow, in the Western sector of Berlin, and stretched nearly 0.8 km ($\frac{1}{2}$ mile) under the barbed wire of the border, 7.3 m (24 ft) below street level.

Huge iron pipes, 2.1 m (7 ft) in diameter, linked large chambers containing monitoring equipment, a telephone exchange switchboard and an air-conditioning plant. Highly sophisticated microphones, amplifiers, tape-recorders, teleprinters and transformers made it possible for the American, British and German eavesdroppers to listen in to 400 conversations at any one time. Lines were tapped from East German government offices, the KGB HQ in Karlshorst and the Soviet Army command post, with links to Moscow and other Warsaw Pact capitals.

During the first winter, heat rising from the tunnel began to melt snow on the ground above. A refrigeration system was quickly installed along the ceiling, and work on de-coding messages carried on inside the electrically-sealed security doors of the clandestine chambers.

Then, on 22 April 1956, East German border guards and Soviet intelligence staff began digging above the eastern end of the tunnel. Alarms gave the eavesdroppers time to escape, but the Western secret services had to watch mortified as the Russians milked every ounce of propaganda out of their 'discovery', giving guided tours to an estimated 40,000 people.

In fact, the CIA had suspected for some months that the tunnel had been detected. Telecommunications traffic from the tapped offices had dropped dramatically. Their suspicions were confirmed after Blake's arrest. He later claimed that he told Moscow about the project as soon as it was given the go-ahead. Had the West been deliberately misled for nearly three years?

Blake's treason continued in the Middle East. In 1958, the Egyptians exposed the entire British spy network in the area. Some agents were arrested. Others under diplomatic cover in embassies had to be hurriedly withdrawn, and President Nasser threatened to name every spy over Cairo Radio. He never did, but it took years for a replacement network to be set up.

Nasser had no reason to love the British. Two years earlier, Prime Minister Anthony Eden had sent troops ashore in the Suez crisis, and there are suspicions that MI6 was involved at the time in a plot by Egyptian rebels to assassinate their leader – a plot that was never put into action. But the reason for the 1958 clear-out was not primarily revenge. The Kremlin was about to supply Nasser with arms, and did not want British spies around to report the fact. Thanks to Blake, they were not.

Were Blake's superiors at fault, allowing him to know too much? Critics of MI6, while acknowledging that a double agent has to sacrifice some secrets, say that to feed him too many vital ones makes him vulnerable to blackmail or torture if captured – and the spymasters culpable if he proves a traitor. Colonel Charles Gilson, head of the Russian section of MI6 on the Continent until about 1958, shot himself in Rome after retiring. Money problems were the official reason.

George Blake

Blake, who was second only to Kim Philby as MI6's most damaging traitor, served just a fraction of his 42 year sentence. On 22 October 1967, he kicked out a weakly-cemented window bar at Wormwood Scrubs Prison, London, and vanished, resurfacing soon afterwards in Moscow. Once again, the KGB had looked after one of their own – and he had had time to write an ironic farewell. It was Blake's job to look after administration in the prison canteen. On the day of his escape, he had entered all the expenses and income in the accounts ledger, then added a note of apology – he had not had time to add up the totals.

William Vassall: Auntie Vera at the Admiralty

William John Christopher Vassall, the British Admiralty spy jailed for 18 years in 1962, said after his release: 'Traitor is not a word I associate with myself. I was simply a victim of circumstances.' And he added: 'If the attitude towards homosexuality had been as tolerant then as it is today, I would not have acted as I did.'

In retirement, former Prime Minister Harold Macmillan could probably sympathize with those words. But at the time, the storm created by Vassall's conviction, and the inquiry into the security services which followed, only added to the seemingly-endless series of scandals which rocked his Tory government in the early 1960s. Only later was it seen that Vassall was different from George Blake, Gordon Lonsdale, Klaus Fuchs and Kim Philby. They were dedicated spies or misguided intellectuals, doing what they did for ideological reasons. Vassall was just a pathetic, frightened man forced to betray his country by a cunning, perfectly-sprung trap.

The 29-year-old vicar's son was quickly spotted by the Russians as a likely blackmail target when he arrived as a junior clerk at Britain's embassy in Moscow in 1954. The KGB had agents in the building working as doormen or interpreters, and watched carefully as the lonely, slightly effeminate newcomer was snubbed by class conscious diplomatic types who viewed his attempts to socialize as social climbing. There was a strict pecking order among the snobs, and they constantly reminded Vassall that minor officials had to keep to their station.

The KGB moved tentatively at first. They engineered a restaurant meeting with a lively, attractive girl. Vassall showed little interest. They tried again with a male companion. Vassall was clearly more keen on him. The KGB knew he could be snared. But for a year they left him alone, to settle into the job and become a trusted member of the embassy staff. He was befriended by Sigmund Mikhailski, one of the KGB men on the embassy staff, who provided tickets for the Bolshoi ballet and the opera, and introduced the lonely Briton to Russian friends, some of them homosexual.

During Vassall's second winter in Moscow, one of the new companions invited him to a party in a private apartment at the Hotel Berlin. Vodka, wine and brandy flowed freely until Vassall felt quite dizzy. He was led to a curtained recess, undressed, and laid on a divan. He was vaguely aware of other men undressing, of photographs being taken ...

Two months later, a Russian army officer on leave invited Vassall to his apartment in the city. There was instant mutual attraction, or so it seemed. The men were naked on the bed when the door burst open and two KGB officers entered the room. The army man quickly dressed and left without a word. Terrified and humiliated, Vassall was shown the photographs taken at the Hotel Berlin. He was told he had been followed since arriving in Moscow. He had committed a serious crime against Soviet law. However, no one need hear of it, if he was prepared to cooperate.

Vassall was trapped and he knew it. Exposure could lead to prison, in Moscow or London, where homosexuality was then still a criminal offence. There would also be social disgrace and a possible international incident. He meekly agreed to become a spy.

At first his new masters nursed him, asking for names and jobs about which they already knew, just to check his truthfulness. At Christmas, 1955, they gave him 2,000 roubles, about £50. More envelopes crammed with cash followed. He could no longer have second thoughts and confess. 'It was like a spider's web,' Vassall was to say later. 'It was done very, very cleverly. At no time could I have escaped. I just got more and more entangled.'

In July 1956 the Russian investment really began to pay off. Vassall returned to London as acting personal assistant to the deputy director of the Admiralty's Naval Intelligence Division. The files in his drab office in Horse Guards Parade, overlooking the garden of No 10 Downing Street, were packed with high-security information, and fresh intelligence crossed his desk every day.

Each evening, as the civil service army headed home to suburbia, Vassall would have something more to do. He never carried a briefcase – the KGB had told him not to, because the chance of being stopped in spot searches was greater. Instead he slipped secret documents between the pages of *The Times* newspaper that he always carried, neatly folded, under his arm.

Then the £14-a-week Whitehall clerk would take a taxi to his £10-a-week Dolphin Square flat in trendy Pimlico, adorned with expensive antiques. He would take a special paper knife from his desk drawer, insert it into a hidden slot in his bookcase, and slip open a concealed drawer. There was the miniature camera, bought with KGB money in the duty free shop at Rome airport, with which he recorded every item he thought of value to the Soviets.

It was not time-consuming work – the Russians rarely asked him for specific documents – and he had plenty of opportunity to cut a dash around town in his 19 Savile Row suits, enjoying evenings at the opera, and West End theatre, a quiet drink at his club, dinner with a few discreet friends, or a visit to one of the twilight clubs which catered for his kind.

At weekends he went 'off to the country', usually visiting elderly ladies who

William Vassall

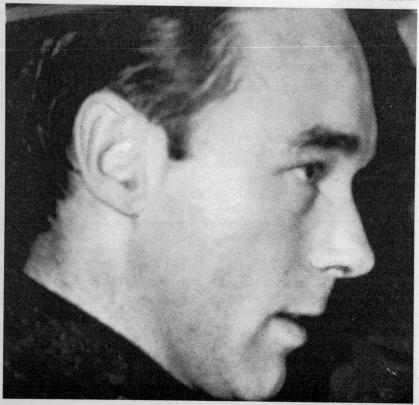

were enchanted by his fastidious charm, and thought he was 'something at the Foreign Office'. Vassall encouraged the air of mystery, dropping hints about legacies and private means to explain his apparent affluence. The same tactics worked at the office. The nickname Vera had followed him from Moscow, with Auntie added as a term of abuse. He was tolerated as a possible homosexual who kept himself to himself. Nobody really considered him a security risk.

Vassall was to describe his exploits later as 'not exciting, but terrifying'. And never more so than on the night he met his KGB contact, Gregory, at the King's Head public house in Harrow-on-the-Hill. After a few drinks in a quiet corner, Vassall went to fetch his coat, which had a spool of film in the pocket. His coat had gone, with a similar one left in its place.

Vassall tried not to panic. He left his name with the pub manager. Next day he telephoned. Yes, someone had called to say he had taken the wrong coat. Vassall dialled the number he was given. A man answered. He said he worked at Scotland Yard.

The reluctant spy walked to the Trafalgar Square rendezvous fearing arrest. He met the man he had spoken to on the phone. They exchanged pleasantries and coats, and parted. Vassall felt in his pocket. The precious film was still there.

When the Portland spy ring arrests hit the papers, Vassall met his contact on the Embankment by the House of Commons, and was told to stop operations. Nobody knew how much MI5 had learned from Lonsdale, Houghton, Gee and the Krogers. The Admiralty clerk treated himself to foreign holidays and invested in savings certificates and stock market shares. He was still picking up his KGB salary.

After a year, the Russians ordered him to start work again. By now, he had been promoted to assistant private secretary to the Civil Lord of the Admiralty, Thomas Galbraith, with access to the most recent developments in submarines and sonar detection. But Vassall's days were already numbered.

In December 1961, the American CIA had acquired an important defector in Helsinki, later revealed to be KGB Major Anatoli Golitsin. He was the man who brought conclusive proof of Kim Philby's treachery. And he also revealed that the Kremlin was receiving a steady flow of top quality British naval intelligence

Armed with this information, it did not take long for the security services to narrow the field down to Vassall, still living above his visible means. Surveillance confirmed the suspicions. On 12 September 1962, Vassall prepared to leave his office to pick up currency for another holiday in Italy. Looking out of the window, he spotted an unfamiliar car in the official car park. Inside, three men were staring hard at the Horse Guards Parade entrance he always used.

He hurried to another way out of the building, but it was too late. 'There were more cars and more men with cold unkind faces,' he wrote later. 'They moved in on me. I was trapped.' But there were other emotions, too. 'It was the most wonderful relief,' he admitted. 'I hadn't the power or the strength to do it on my own. It wasn't exactly as if someone had come to help you. But it was what you had wanted to happen for such a long time.'

The trial, for recording secret official information useful to an enemy between 18 August 1956 and 11 September 1962, was a formality, and Vassall began an 18-year prison sentence. Then, in January 1963, a three-man Tribunal headed by Appeal Judge Lord Radcliffe began an investigation of the security aspects of the case. Newspaper reports had suggested that the existence of a spy in the Admiralty had been known for 18 months, since the Portland arrests, yet nothing was done. There were also suggestions of an over-friendly relationship between Vassall and his boss Galbraith.

The tribunal was able to give the lie to both allegations and clear both Galbraith and Lord Carrington, First Lord of the Admiralty, of negligence. But in the course of its hearings, two journalists were jailed for refusing to disclose their sources, ensuring that the embarrassing Vassall affair stayed in the front page headlines.

The spy himself was released on parole from Maidstone jail in 1972, and disappeared into the obscurity of a Sussex monastery under an assumed name. He re-surfaced briefly in 1980 when his story was shown in a television series on spies. He was remarkably philosophical about what had happened, saying: 'I don't hate anybody, even the KGB. They were just doing their job, and we have people like that too, don't we. What happened to me wasn't anything personal.' But he was bitter over one thing – how Anthony Blunt had been allowed to enjoy his freedom for 15 years after confessing his spying. Vassall said: 'I would like to lead my life the way he has been allowed to lead his.'

A KGB agent bugged the bed used by the British Queen during her tour of West Germany in 1965. Martin Margraf, who posed as a freelance waiter, was working at the luxurious Petersburg Hotel, beside the Rhine near Bonn, when the Queen and her husband, Prince Philip, arrived. He concealed a tiny microphone behind the headboard of their double bed, and retrieved it after they left.

He escaped to prove his innocence

Alfie Hinds was the Houdini who ran the police ragged in the 1950s when he escaped three times from prison. He broke out each time to protest his innocence of a robbery conviction which landed him 12 years in jail.

Alfie's running battle with the police and the whole legal system began in 1953 when he was convicted of taking part in robbing London's big department store, Maples, of £30,000 in wages.

Alfie, who was born in 1917, had a criminal past. He had been to approved school and Borstal, and during the Second World War had deserted from the army.

But after his marriage in 1947 to Peg Stoodley, a docker's daughter, Alfie went straight. He opened a business dealing in war surplus goods and second-hand cars, and handling demolition work. Peg and Alfie had a son, born in 1948, and a daughter born in 1951.

Throughout his trial at the Old Bailey Alfie protested his innocence. The police claimed he had led a gang which blew open the safe and escaped with the wage money. Alfie said he was at home with Peg when the store was robbed.

But the jury didn't believe him and the judge, Lord Goddard, sentenced Alfie to 12 years preventive detention.

Alfie, describing the trial as a 'farce', was determined to fight back. The campaign to prove his innocence was to involve him in 31 court appearances between the time of the Maples robbery in 1953 and the final hearing in 1965.

His first appeal for a fresh hearing was rejected by the courts. So Alfie decided he must get out to draw the public's attention to his case.

In 1956 he was cooped up in Nottingham Prison, studying law with a driving determination to use every twist and turn of the legal system in his fight for freedom.

His plan was to escape to Eire where he believed he could convince an Irish jury of his innocence.

There were two escape plans then being hatched at Nottingham – one a mass break-out and another involving just one man – a smash and grab driver who was serving eight years.

Alfie said: 'I did not join the mass attempt. My problem was that if I broke prison I was committing a crime. The golden thread which ran through all my years of imprisonment was that I must not commit one crime in order to prove that I was innocent of another.'

He discovered that if he escaped at the same time and by the same route as another prisoner, but provided he had not been involved in any planning, all he could be accused of was 'escape from lawful custody', which was not a criminal offence.

Alfie knew of the one-man escape plan but never let on. When his fellow prisoner made his break, Alfie simply tagged along.

Reunited with Peg, he moved to the Clapham area of London. He bombarded the newspapers with letters explaining the reason for his escape. He even promised to give himself up if he could get an inquiry.

Despite the publicity, no new hearing was promised. So Alfie took the ferry to Ireland. Then he contacted Peg, getting her to send over some money to buy a cottage a few miles south of Dublin.

But in August 1956 it all went wrong. Alfie was arrested as he went to pick up a consignment of tools from a Dublin shipping company.

Back in Pentonville, Alfie spent two years in fruitless legal wrangles trying to prove that he had been unlawfully brought back from Eire and that the Maples case should be reopened. But even as he made a succession of court appearances, a second escape plan was forming in his mind.

Alfie decided to make his getaway during one of his many visits to the Law Courts in London. Each time he arrived, his escorts removed his handcuffs, took him for tea in the staff canteen in the basement and then upstairs to the lavatory before his hearing started.

Alfie arranged with an old friend, due for release from Pentonville Prison, to make a key for the lavatory and leave it taped to the underside of one of the canteen tables.

On the day he planned to escape, Alfie was escorted as usual to the Law Courts. Down in the canteen, his trembling fingers groped beneath the table – and closed round a packet. It was unexpectedly big for a key but he managed to slip it into his pocket without arousing the suspicion of the prison officers.

Warily he undid the package in his pocket. Inside, to his surprise, was a padlock. What was it for?

Tea finished, Alfie and his guards made their way up the stairs to the court and the lavatory. One glance at the door showed Alfie that the plans had changed. 'There', in his own words, 'were two of the biggest and brightest nickel-plated screw-eyes I had ever seen, one on the door itself and the other in the right-hand jam.'

'I assumed my prison friend had been unable to fit the lock and that this was his solution.'

Rushing ahead of his escorts, the padlock gripped firmly in his right hand, Alfie opened the door to the lavatory with his left hand. As they entered, he

Alfie Hinds on his way to prison accompanied by a huge police guard

slammed it shut.

Within a second, the padlock was in place and Alfie was away again, down the stairs and out into the street. There, waiting to take him to London Airport was his brother Bert and a friend, Tony Maffia.

At the airport they found they had missed the Dublin flight. So they drove to Bristol. There, as a result of a circulated description, Bert was mistakenly arrested as the escaper. Alfie, sitting quietly in the airport lounge, was picked up as a suspected accomplice. But at the police station a prison officer arrived and identified the right man. Back went Alfie to Pentonville.

In June 1958 Alfie made his final escape – this time from Chelmsford Prison in Essex. As with his first break-out, he waited until just one man was on his way 'over the wall' – and followed him.

This time his fellow escaper was Londoner Georgie Walkington, serving seven years, who planned to escape from the prison yard with the aid of some keys.

Once outside, both men made a dash for a waiting car and were away before police had time to set up road blocks. They stayed together in a caravan in Kent before going their own ways.

Georgie was caught at a London dog track but Alfie reached Ireland by boat from Liverpool. Using assumed names, he set himself up as a car dealer in Dublin.

Things went well – until Alfie was caught smuggling cars across the border between Northern Ireland and Eire. His fingerprints were sent away for identification and the startled Customs men only then discovered that their smuggler was none other than the king of the escapers.

He was sent to prison for six months in Belfast for smuggling before being returned to Britain in November 1960 to finish his 12-year sentence.

Within a month Alfie was making legal history. An appeal to the House of Lords was finally under consideration. In December he made several visits to the House Appeals Committee – the first time that a prisoner had been permitted to argue in person before the noble peers.

Hoodwinked

A raider put a pillowcase over his head and held up a store in Riverside, California. But after blundering around and knocking into display counters, the bandit got the message that it is always best to cut eye-holes in the mask! He raised a corner of the pillowcase to find his way out of the store, was instantly recognized by a customer, and was later arrested by police.

But again his hopes were dashed. His application for leave to appeal to the Lords was thrown out.

A few days later Alfie was on his way to the top security prison, Parkhurst, on the Isle of Wight.

Then, in 1962, he got his lucky break. Ex-Chief Superintendent Herbert Sparks, who had investigated the Maples robbery, had written a series of articles for a Sunday newspaper. One of them told how he had caught Alfie Hinds. It implied, of course, that Hinds was guilty. In January 1963 Alfie issued a writ for libel against the detective. Just over a year later the case was heard. Alfie spent six days in the witness box.

In his summing up the judge, Mr Justice Edmund Davies, asked the jury: 'Has Hinds spoken with the voice of truth about the Maples robbery, or is he a plausible liar who appears to have attracted to himself in some quarters wholly unmerited sympathy and support?'

After five hours of deliberation the jury found for Alfie and awarded him £1,300 damages.

The following day Alfie heard that the Home Secretary, Henry Brooke, had ordered his immediate release.

Despite his lawyer's advice, Alfie refused to stop battling to completely clear his name. He still insisted on a retrial and in November 1965 his appeal opened at the Court of Criminal Appeal. But it was to be the old disappointments all over again. His appeal was dismissed by the court and later by the House of Lords.

Alfie had won his case with the libel jury but had been unable to get the original conviction against him removed.

He went to live in semi-retirement with Peg in St Helier on the island of Jersey, becoming a do-it-yourself property developer, buying up old properties and renovating them himself.

His keen and agile brain, which had become sharpened through endless hours of battling in the courts, earned him a place in the Channel Islands Mensa Society – an organization for people of super-intelligence.

Warm thanks

A 27-year-old pregnant Swedish girl named Else Haffner won the sympathy of magistrates when she appeared before them on a shoplifting charge. They put her on probation – but their character judgement was soon shown to be faulty. As Else left the court at Malmo, Sweden, she was arrested again . . . and charged with walking out in a fur coat belonging to one of the magistrates.

Chapter seven

SPIES AND SPYMASTERS

Few real spies or secret agents have a licence to kill like Ian Fleming's fictional hero, James Bond. Nonetheless espionage can still be a deadly business. Spying traverses many territories, it is a worldwide occupation involving thousands of agents, a great deal of money and much advanced technology. Although it wasn't always like that...

Satan in satin

When his Great Army of the Potomac was crushed at Bull Run, Abraham Lincoln knew there had been treason in his government – and that behind the treachery was a beautiful but deadly woman. He called on General George B. McClellan to take command of the shattered Union Army. And together they turned to Allan Pinkerton, founder of Pinkerton's Detective Agency and internationally known manhunter. Now he was to become a hunter of women. Specifically, his prey would be Mrs Rose O'Neal Greenhow – 'Rebel Rose' – whose Washington spy ring was like a noose around the Union throat.

Rich, brilliant and seductive, the 44-year-old widow lived in an elegant mansion that had become the favourite gathering place of Washington's elite. She made no secret of her Southern sympathies or her flaming love affairs. She claimed to have been James Buchanan's mistress and the power behind his presidency. She also boasted that her current affair with Senator Harold Wilson had led to the trapping of Union forces at Manassas and the Bull Run catastrophe. There would later be documentary proof of her claim when Rebel archives were taken after the fall of the Confederate capital of Richmond, Virginia.

As chairman of the Senate's Military Affairs Committee, Wilson knew Lincoln's secret war plans. He had confided those secrets to Rose Greenhow, who routed them to another of her lovers in the Confederate high command, using as courier a female operative who crossed Union lines disguised as a farm-girl.

The contest between Rose and Pinkerton became a classic duel of wits. Rose made the first move, inviting him to a lavish house party where she tried every blandishment on the no-nonsense Scot. But when Pinkerton failed to take the bait, she became his deadliest enemy.

In the weeks that followed, Pinkerton and his men kept a constant watch on her home. Rose knew of the surveillance and openly laughed at it. Her own female operatives, all stunningly beautiful, continued to pass in and out of the house, and the great of Washington still vied for her favours.

The treacherous Wilson was a constant caller, and General McClellan angrily told Pinkerton that military secrets were reaching the enemy daily. Without further delay, Pinkerton arrested Mrs Greenhow in her home. Under the lady's furious eyes, he ordered a search of the premises and turned up damning evidence.

There was the cipher by which she had communicated with the enemy.

Rose O'Neal Greenhow with her daughter in the courtyard of the Old Capitol Prison

There were Senator Wilson's passionate love letters. There was a list of Rose's couriers and fellow conspirators, most of them wealthy and powerful. Worse, there were copies of official information on the movement of troops, the sizes and quantities of ordnance, and blueprints of the forts defending the city.

The grim-faced Pinkerton wanted Rose and her co-conspirators hanged, but Lincoln and McClellan vetoed the idea. Some of the traitors were so highly placed that the already shaky administration could have toppled.

For five months Lincoln wrestled with the problem, while Pinkerton kept Rose under house arrest in her home. But on January 18, 1862, she was transferred to Washington's Old Capitol Prison.

No spy in history has enjoyed kinder prison treatment. With the Greenhow fortune still at her disposal, she was given a suite of rooms on the second floor where guards brought her catered meals and champagne from her own cellars.

In Rose's case, prison discipline was suspended entirely. Her powerful friends came and went at will, and the guards retired politely when Senator Wilson was a guest. Another frequent caller was Gustavus V. Fox, Assistant Secretary of the Navy, who was reckless enough to divulge the government's naval plans.

To everyone's surprise, Rose had taken up knitting, and balls of coloured wool were delivered to her through the Provost Marshal's office. She turned out an endless supply of socks, sweaters and tapestries and presented them as gifts to some of her callers.

Suspicious, Pinkerton intercepted one of the female visitors and took a close look at her tapestry. It held a cunningly concealed message for the Confederates – a coded outline of the information Rose had gleaned from Fox.

Even Lincoln agreed now that a woman who could spy from behind bars was too dangerous a prisoner to keep.

In June 1862, Pinkerton escorted her to Fortress Monroe, where she signed a pledge 'not to return north of the Potomac' until the war was over. 'But then I shall return,' she assured him. 'And after we have burned your White House to the ground, I think we shall hang Old Abe in my yard to frighten away the crows.'

In fact, she was never to return.

Jefferson Davis, President of the Confederate States, sent her from his capital of Richmond to London in order to recruit money and sympathy for the Rebel cause. There she published a book of memoirs reviling Allan Pinkerton and detailing her affairs with Lincoln's traitorous friends. Suppressed in the United States, her book was an overnight sensation in England.

But on Rose's return voyage, the blockade runner carrying her was grounded on a shoal off the coast of Wilmington, North Carolina.

Too impatient to wait for rescue craft, Rose set out for shore in a small boat. The boat capsized in heavy seas, and her body was never found.

> ## Double Deutsch
> **The Oxford University dons who turned up for a lecture by the eminent psychologist Dr Emil Busch were puzzled but impressed. The man they had come to see after answering an advertisement in an Oxford newspaper had a flowing beard, a strong German accent and a strange way of haranguing his audience so that most of what he said was unintelligible. They later learned that 'Dr Busch' was one of their undergraduates, and his entire speech had been gibberish.**

She left many questions behind her.

Never exposed during his lifetime, Harold Wilson went on to become a Vice-President of the United States. Gustavus V. Fox escaped without a rebuke. And though he knew their identities well, Lincoln took no action against any of the traitors who had worked so intimately with Rebel Rose.

It may have been a fatal mistake. Historians agree that these same conspirators could have been in league with John Wilkes Booth, the demented actor who brought Lincoln's life to a violent end.

Vernon Kell: Curse of the Kaiser

German agents began infiltrating Britain to prepare for World War 1 as early as 1902. The authorities took little interest. Then, with the setting up of MO5, later renamed MI5, the police at last found someone who took their espionage warnings seriously. And Vernon Kell, taking on the might of German intelligence single-handed, realized Scotland Yard's Special Branch men were vital allies. He started close co-operation with Superintendent Patrick Quinn. It paid off just 12 months later.

Kaiser Wilhelm II came to London in 1910 for the funeral of King Edward VII. In his party was a naval captain known to be a spymaster. He was trailed to a seedy barber's shop run by Karl Gustav Ernst in the Caledonian

The Kaiser

Road. It was an unlikely choice for a gentleman who only wanted a haircut. Kell applied for permission to intercept the barber's mail. He discovered that Ernst was Germany's intelligence post-master. Berlin sent him packages containing individual letters of instructions for their agents, to be posted in London. The agents sent back their reports via Ernst's shop.

Kell and Quinn now played a waiting game. Detectives kept watch on every agent unmasked, but it was vital not to alert them to this fact because the Germans would then replace them, or find new ways of contacting them. It was also important to trace every member of each agent's network. Only when it became obvious that crucial secrets were about to be relayed to Berlin did the counter-espionage forces strike. Where possible, information and instructions were merely doctored by the interceptors, sometimes using expert forgers from Parkhurst jail. But some arrests were essential – if there were none the Germans might smell a rat.

One of Kell's problems was that espionage was not taken seriously by the law. German army lieutenant Siegfried Helm, caught red-handed making detailed sketches of Portsmouth's dockyard defences, was merely bound over to keep the peace and released by a court. Spying in peacetime was not considered an offence.

Kell campaigned for changes in the Official Secrets Act, and in 1911 it was amended to cover collection of information which might be useful to an enemy in future wars. Kell could now prosecute such spies as Dr Armgaard Karl Graves, jailed for 18 months at Edinburgh for snooping on the Navy's Rosyth base and collecting information about weapons from Glasgow companies; Heinrich Grosse, tried at Winchester in 1912 after amassing a huge dossier on ships, submarines and artillery at Portsmouth; and Frederick Adolphus Schroeder, imprisoned for six years in April 1914. As Frederick Gould, he used German intelligence funds to buy the Queen Charlotte public house in Rochester, near the top-secret Chatham dockyard, in 1902. Kell had known about him since 1911, but only pounced when his wife set out by train for Brussels with sensitive data on guns, cruisers and minefields in her bag.

Kell's finest hour came when war was declared on 4 August 1914. Before dawn on the following day, he and the Special Branch, now led by Sir Basil Thomson, had arrested Ernst the barber – paid £1 a month by the Germans – and 23 other spies. Germany's entire intelligence network in Britain was wiped out as agents were seized in London, Newcastle, Barrow in Furness, Portsmouth, Southampton, Brighton, Falmouth and Warwick. German armies battling the French near Mons were amazed to encounter British troops when they tried to outflank their enemy. The British Expeditionary Force had slipped unnoticed across the Channel to the trenches. The furious Kaiser exclaimed: 'Am I surrounded by dolts? Why have I never been told we have no spies in England.' Gustav Steinhauer, who called himself the Kaiser's Master Spy, had no answer.

The Germans tried to form a new network, but with little success. Kell and Thomson supplemented their vigilance with newspaper propaganda campaigns whipping up spy hysteria, and reports of suspect neighbours flooded in. One spy, posing as a Norwegian journalist, was suspected because he was too quiet in his rooms. Detectives discovered invisible ink in a bottle marked gargling lotion.

Two Dutchmen arrived in Portsmouth, posing as cigar salesmen. Their reports to Rotterdam were disguised as orders, 5,000 Coronas representing five warships about to sail. Kell's postal censors were puzzled by the sudden popularity of cigars in Hampshire and detectives were called in. The two spies were arrested and shot. Another agent toured Britain as a music hall trick-cyclist. Censors discovered messages in invisible ink on English songsheets he was sending to Zurich.

Kell made brilliant use of another detected spy. Carl Hans Lody, a German naval reserve officer who had been living in America, landed in Scotland posing as an American tourist in September 1914. He immediately sent a telegram to his contact in Sweden saying, 'Hope we beat these damned Germans soon.' It was a suspicious communication between representatives of countries supposed to be neutral. Lody was tailed as he travelled round England. The watchdogs could not believe their luck when they discovered he was sending to Germany as fact a British propaganda story stating that Russian troops were landing in Scotland to reinforce the Allies in the European trenches. Lody was later nicknamed the spy who cost Germany the war. Two divisions were withdrawn to watch Channel ports for the Russian arrival, weakening the Kaiser's forces for the vital Battle of the Marne which the Germans might otherwise have won. Lody was eventually arrested and shot at the Tower of London in November 1916.

British intelligence also detected the amorous activities of over-rated sex spy Mata Hari. Gertrud Margarete Zelle, born in Holland, took the name Mata Hari (it meant Eye of the Morning) when she became an erotic dancer in Paris. During the war, she cashed in on the pleasure sex gave her by sleeping with important military figures on both sides, and selling what they told her to the enemy. In Paris, Berlin and Madrid, she plied her erotic espionage trade, though the secrets she passed were seldom of much value. In 1916, her ship to Holland docked at Falmouth, and she was escorted to London for interrogation. If she persisted in consorting with the Germans, she was warned, she would be in trouble. Mata took no notice. She was later arrested by the French, and shot on 15 October 1917.

Only one spy escaped the notice of Kell and Thomson – they only learned about him when he wrote his memoirs back in Germany in 1925. Jules Silber could pass as an Englishman after travels in India, America and South Africa. He fought for the British in the Boer Wars, which helped gain him a job in the postal censor's office when he turned up in London in 1914, offering his services. He regularly sent the Kaiser dossiers on what he learned from reading other people's letters. His own mail went undetected because he could stamp it 'passed by the censor'. Silber's most spectacular success was warning Germany about the Q-ships. A girl wrote that her brother was involved in a strange scheme to put guns on old merchant ships. Silber posed as a censor to call on her and warn against future indiscretions. Before he left,

Mata Hari

she had revealed all he needed to know about the innocent-looking cargo carriers camouflaged to protect Atlantic convoys against German submarine attack.

Silber's information was a rare naval coup for the Kaiser's fleet. For most of the war, British Naval Intelligence under Admiral Sir Reginald Hall – nicknamed Blinker because of a nervous tic in one eye – ruled both the ocean and air waves. Hours after hostilities began, a British ship sliced a hundred yards of cable out of Germany's main under-water telecommunications link with the outside world. This forced the Kaiser's forces to send messages by radio, which could be intercepted at listening stations along the English south coast. The messages were then decyphered in Room 40 of the Admiralty building in London, using naval code books taken during an engagement with the German cruiser *Magdeburg* on 26 August.

Hall got his hands on the enemy's diplomatic code when a German guerrilla harrying British forces in Turkey fled abandoning his baggage. When a new German transmitter began broadcasts from Brussels, using another code, Naval Intelligence learned that the staff included a British-born cypher clerk called Alexander Szek, who still had relatives living near Croydon in London. Szek agreed to copy the code book, piece by piece. When he completed the task, he vanished. Mystery still surrounds exactly what happened. The British said the Germans discovered his treachery and executed him. French sources claimed a British agent smuggled Szek out of Brussels to prevent the Germans learning their code was broken, then pushed him off ship in the middle of the English Channel to ensure he stayed silent. Another version is that he died in a hit-and-run 'accident' in a Brussels side street. Whatever the cause, Szek's death proved that the British no longer considered espionage a game. It was now a matter of life and death.

Control of the German codes enabled Admiral Sir Reginald Hall to fool the Kaiser with deliberately false messages. In September 1916 he arranged for one of his agents to leak an emergency code to the Germans, then signalled that ships were sailing from Dover, Harwich and Tilbury with troops to invade the north Belgian coast. To authenticate the information, he had 25 special editions of the *Daily Mail* newspaper printed, with a spurious story about preparations at 'an East Coast base'. Copies were smuggled to Holland, and passed surreptitiously to German agents. The ploy worked almost too well. The German High Command detached a large force from the trenches and moved it to the coast. But a War Office agent, not told of the subterfuge, warned Whitehall the movement heralded a plan to invade England. The War Office started preparing to evacuate south-east England until it was let in on Hall's secret.

Hall's most significant part in winning the war was the Zimmermann Telegram. The code Szek provided enabled Room 40 decipherers to read a message from the German Secretary of State, Arthur Zimmermann, to his ambassador in Mexico City in January 1917, warning that unrestricted submarine attacks on neutral Atlantic convoys were about to start, and instructing the envoy to organise Mexican attacks on the southern United States if America entered the war. Hall ensured that the message reached the White House in a way which clearly proved it was not a British invention. Together with the sinking of the liner *Lusitania*, the telegram forced the United States to abandon its policy of isolation three months later. It was the turning point in Allied fortunes.

Hall, Thomson and Kell had done as much as anyone to earn the victory that finally came on 11 November, 1918. They were abetted by Commander Mansfield Cumming, first chief of the Special Intelligence Section, later MI6, which was founded in 1912 for offensive espionage abroad. One of his agents is said to have alerted Hall's Naval Intelligence to the possibility of using Alexander Szek to obtain the Kaiser's code. His name was Sidney Reilly ...

Reckless Reilly: Ace of Spies

The history of espionage has produced no greater enigma than Sidney Reilly. Both his birth and death are shrouded in mystery. But his achievements were unquestionable. Beyond doubt he was a ruthless agent and a relentless womanizer whose exploits put even the fictional adventures of 007 James Bond in the shade. Bond's creator Ian Fleming said: '007 was just a piece of nonsense I dreamed up. He was not a Sidney Reilly, you know.'

Though he later carried passports giving his birthplace as Tipperary, Ireland, Reilly was probably born in southern Russia, near Odessa, on 24 March 1874. At 19 he is said to have discovered that the Russian army colonel married to his mother was not his father. He had been conceived during her affair with a Viennese doctor, and his real name was Sigmund Georgievich Rosenblum. The shock of finding he was Jewish, made the youngster flee anti-semitic Russia. He stowed away on a British boat to South America, and worked as a docker, road-mender and plantation hand. Then, according to his own story, he was recruited as cook for a British expedition into the wilds of the Amazon. When natives attacked the camp, Reilly's sharpshooting scared them off.

Impressed by his courage, and his fluency in several languages, including Russian and German, the leader of the party, Major Fothergill, gave him £1,500 and offered him a secret service post. Reilly began work as a freelance.

He took the name Reilly from his first wife. Margaret Reilly Thomas was 23, lively and attractive when the spy met her in Europe. She was touring with her dour, bad-tempered husband Hugh, a Non-Conformist minister

Sidney Reilly

from Wales. He was wealthy, 60 years old, and, Margaret told Reilly, a sadist who beat her viciously. Reilly started staying in hotel rooms just across the corridor from theirs. Margaret slipped into his bed surreptitiously as her husband slept under the influence of increasingly large doses of laudanum from Reilly, who was posing as a medical expert. When the Reverend Thomas fell seriously ill at his London home, Reilly suggested a Continental trip to get him away from prying neighbours. At Newhaven, en route to the Europe ferry, Thomas died. Margaret inherited £8,000. Five months later she became the first Mrs Reilly. She was not the last. And Thomas was not the last man Reilly murdered.

The new century found him in Holland, posing as a German, checking Dutch aid to the Boers in South Africa. Reilly had an uncanny knack of being able to see the world's trouble-spots and getting in early. He realized the potential of the oil discoveries in the Middle East. Britain, he warned, was in danger of missing out. He went to Persia and discovered the Shah had granted development rights to an Australian, William D'Arcy, who was in Cannes discussing financial backing with the wealthy Rothschilds. Reilly disguised himself as a priest and walked brazenly on to the family yacht in the French harbour, touting for charity cheques. While the hosts wrote them out, he drew D'Arcy to one side and promised that the British government would top any offer the Rothschilds made. In May 1905, D'Arcy was given £900,000 of shares in the company formed to cash in on the opportunity Reilly provided – British Petroleum, better known today as BP.

Reilly spent the next few years in the Far East gathering details of Russia's naval strength and eastern defences.

But by 1914 he was back in Europe, embarking on a series of missions which almost defied belief, and earned him the British Military Cross. Before war broke out in 1914, he secured a job at the giant Krupp armaments factory in Essen under the alias Karl Hahn. He volunteered for extra night shifts, and broke into the top-secret drawing offices to scrutinize every detail of the weapons' production schedule. When he was discovered, he killed two watchmen to escape.

Back in Russia, he posed as a wealthy businessman and organised the St Petersburg flying week. German visitors eagerly confided secrets of aircraft development. The extraordinary spy then persuaded German naval builders Blohm and Voss to make him their sole agent for exports to Russia. He earned huge commissions as a salesman, and was so successful that Britons in St Petersburg complained to their ambassador that he was robbing British companies of orders. Reilly became rich, and London received blueprints and specifications of the Kaiser's most up-to-date warships.

The British secret service was getting so much priceless information from

Reilly that it had to accept him on his own terms. Spy chiefs knew, or suspected, he was selling the intelligence he sent them to other powers, particularly Russia and later France. And they were powerless to prevent him taking the audacious risks which earned him the nickname Reckless Reilly. They even had to turn a blind eye to his bigamous marriage when Margaret refused a cash offer to agree to a divorce. Reilly forced her to leave St Petersburg, then married Countess Massino, ex-wife of a Russian government minister.

By 1917, Reilly was back in London. Though over 40, he volunteered to pioneer a new kind of espionage parachuting behind enemy lines to collect information. He was dropped near Mannheim, with forged papers claiming he had been invalided out of the German army, and in three weeks picked up vital data about the offensive planned by the Germans for 1918. The attack, which might have won the war, was countered. Reilly later posed as a German officer, and spent several days in a mess at Konigsberg, East Prussia, collecting the latest war gossip. And his greatest triumph was to sit in at a High Command conference attended by the Kaiser himself.

Reilly had somehow established himself as driver to an officer on the staff of Prince Rupprecht of Bavaria. As they drove to the war council, the British spy pretended there was an engine fault, and lifted the car bonnet to investigate. When the impatient officer joined him in the dark of the lonely forest road, Reilly quietly killed him with a blow to the head, donned his uniform, and drove on to the meeting, coolly making apologies for his late arrival by saying his driver had been taken ill. He then sat taking notes of all future battle plans, and was able to warn the British Admiralty of a submarine offensive to cripple Atlantic supply lines. U-boat commanders found their targets protected by heavily armed convoys.

In April 1918, Reilly was sent back to Russia. The Bolsheviks had seized power the previous year, and seemed likely to make peace with the Germans, freeing the entire might of the Kaiser for an offensive on the Western Front. British Prime Minister David Lloyd George sanctioned an attempted overthrow of the communists to prevent the pact, and Reilly was the only man who might just bring it about. Using a pass provided by a contact in the new Soviet secret police, the Cheka, Reilly set about organizing cells of resistance. He raised more than two million roubles from White Russian sympathizers, and also used £120,000 of the British government's money to bribe influential figures.

The bizarre plan was to kidnap Soviet leaders Lenin and Trotsky and parade them through the streets in their underpants, objects of ridicule. Reilly even selected an alternative government, with himself as prime minister. But the congress at which the leaders were to be seized was unexpectedly postponed. Then another anti-Bolshevik, Dora Kaplan, tried to kill Lenin. He survived, though hit twice by her bullets, and a savage purge by the Cheka was launched. Most of Reilly's accomplices were rounded up.

Reilly was at the British consulate at St Petersburg when the Cheka called. A courageous naval captain called Cromie died holding them at bay with two pistols long enough for Reilly to flee through a window. Though the Bolsheviks put a price of 100,000 roubles on his head, Reilly survived for two months, posing as a Russian peasant, a Greek traveller and a Turkish merchant before reaching safety aboard a Dutch trading ship.

Back in London, Reilly divorced Nadine and married actress Pepita Bobadilla, again bigamously. He remained obsessed with the need to overthrow the Russian regime, and began working with Boris Savinkoff, once a revolutionary but now one of Lenin's fiercest foes in exile. Both men were intrigued at the emergence of The Trust, said to be an organization of influential Russians committed to overthrowing Lenin and restoring democracy. Savinkoff went to Moscow to find out more about the rebels. A year later, in 1925, Reilly followed. He was never seen in the West again.

At first it was thought he was shot trying to cross the Finnish border into Russia. His new wife inserted a death notice in newspapers, saying Soviet troops killed him near Allekul on 28 September. But she believed he was still alive. The notice was an attempt to force a statement from either the British or Russian authorities. Both stayed tight-lipped. Over the next five years, refugees from Soviet oppression spoke of seeing Reilly inside Butyrski prison hospital. Some said he was insane after torture. Then more sinister leaks began emerging. A Finn claimed the master spy knew The Trust was a Soviet scheme to entice enemies of the state into the Cheka's grip, but was hoping to 're-organize Bolshevism if he could not defeat it'.

During World War 2, Soviet defector Walter Krivitsky alleged information from Reilly helped Russia penetrate the British secret service and Foreign Office. 'He thought by telling us a little he could help Britain and save himself.' said Krivitsky. 'In the end he did not help Britain and he did not save himself.' In 1966 a Russian magazine said Reilly, when arrested, offered to tell all he knew about British and American intelligence networks. And in 1972, a Paris newspaper claimed Reilly was a Soviet agent all along.

Only the KGB's files are likely to ever unlock the last riddle surrounding Reilly. A television series on his life, shown in Britain in 1983, described him as the ace of spies. No agent has ever achieved so much so audaciously, even though security in every state was far less efficient than it is today. He was a legend in his own lifetime – and may have left a devastating legacy. If, as Krivitsky and others claimed, he told the Russians, either voluntarily or under torture, how to infiltrate the British Establishment, Sidney Reilly laid the foundations for a spy ring whose exploits almost matched his own . . .

Moscow Mole Philby Burrows Deep

C ambridge University was for decades a bastion of privilege, a stepping stone for the moneyed elite progressing from public school to public office. In a rarified atmosphere, snugly shielded from the harsh realities of life, bright young things whiled away three years study with the self-assured arrogance of a class whose right to rule the country had never been questioned. But in the 1930s a new breed with a new creed began to graduate from the cloistered quadrangles. They were the Communist super spies – Guy Burgess, Donald Maclean, Kim Philby, Anthony Blunt and a fifth man who, according to espionage experts, is only protected from the disgrace he deserves by the libel laws.

The damage the infamous five inflicted on Britain, America and totally innocent third parties has still not been fully assessed, 50 years after they espoused the Soviet cause. One British Foreign Office spokesman said: 'Philby robbed European countries of their freedom.' A CIA man told journalists: 'From 1944 to 1951, the entire Western intelligence effort, which was pretty big, was what you might call a minus advantage. We'd have been better off doing nothing.' Yet, incredibly, not one of the five was ever brought to justice. Burgess, Maclean and Philby all fled to Moscow. Blunt was allowed to keep his job – Surveyor of the Queen's Pictures – and his knighthood for 15 years after he confessed his treachery in 1964. And the fifth traitor, whose exposure must wait until his death, was also offered immunity from prosecution in return for information.

The master moles thrived, condemning hundreds of people to death, because the Establishment could forgive almost any behaviour as long as a chap had the right pedigree. Reliability revolved around parentage, schools, universities, clubs and regiments. All the super spies qualified for trust on those grounds.

Harold Adrian Russell Philby, nicknamed Kim, was the meticulous rather than brilliant son of an Arabian adventurer who had also been involved in British India. In 1929 Kim arrived at Trinity College, Cambridge, to read history and economics. A year later, Guy Francis de Moncy Burgess, the larger-than-life eccentric son of a naval commander, moved into rooms just down the corridor, studying history. And in 1931, Donald Maclean, the shy, clever son of a puritanical Liberal cabinet minister, arrived to read French.

Cambridge had changed since their fathers' days. The Depression brought disillusion. Jobs were scarce, even for people with degrees. The great hope for change, the Labour government, was voted out in 1931. The crisis of faith in capitalism went hand-in-hand with worries at the war clouds gathering over Europe. Britain seemed unwilling to stand up to the rising tide of fascism. Would it side with Nazi Germany against Russia? Anti-Fascist students later fought and died for the Republican cause in the Spanish Civil War. Others chose a more clandestine way to channel their disgust. Soviet recruiters were taking full advantage of students' anxious anger.

At Cambridge, Donald Maclean wrote an article in a magazine denouncing 'the whole crack-brained criminal mess' of capitalist society which was 'doomed to disappear'. Yet in 1935 he successfully passed entrance examinations for one of the pillars of capitalist society, the British Foreign Office, and was posted to the Paris embassy where he quickly established himself as one of the rising stars of the diplomatic profession.

At Cambridge, Guy Burgess organized a strike by college staff, and was prominent at demonstrations against war and high housing rents. But after a trip to Moscow in 1934, he too was in London seeking an institutional niche. When he failed in attempts to join Conservative Central Office and *The*

Cambridge University

Times, he pulled strings to become personal assistant to Conservative MP Jack Macnamara, and accompanied him on three trips to Hitler's Germany.

At Cambridge Kim Philby became a committed but discreet Communist. In 1934, he went to Vienna, and was an eye-witness to bitter bloodshed in the streets as the Austrian government tried to put down Socialist attempts to challenge the old order. He helped Communists escape what he saw as police persecution, and married his landlord's daughter, Alice Litzi Friedman, a Soviet spy, to help her flee as a British subject. But by 1936, he was attending meetings of the right-wing Anglo-German Fellowship in London, and editing its pro-Hitler magazine.

All three men were carefully cultivating conservative backgrounds, changing their image to bury a rebel past. All three were under orders to penetrate the Establishment as Soviet Trojan horses. And the Establishment clutched them to its heart.

In February 1937 Philby left for Spain to cover the civil war from the Franco side. At first as a freelance reporter, then as *The Times* special correspondent, he made a big impression with his accurate, impartial reporting. He also made important contacts with British intelligence. And since the Russians were backing the Republicans, he was able to feed Moscow with secrets from the opposition.

Soon after he arrived, Philby narrowly escaped death in a horrific incident which nearly saved Western spycatchers a 26-year nightmare. The car in which he was travelling was hit by a Russian-made shell. Three journalists with him died. Philby escaped with head wounds. Three months later came a solemn ceremony laced with irony. General Franco, the arch-Fascist Philby secretly opposed, proudly pinned on his chest the Red Cross of Military Merit. There was another wry confrontation when Philby returned to England in 1939. He was interviewed about his Spanish adventures on BBC Radio – by Guy Burgess.

Burgess, a brilliant conversationalist, was able to make friends with the rich and influential despite his outrageous drinking and blatant homosexuality. He was combining his work for Macnamara with a new job at the BBC, and both roles brought him important contacts, in Britain and in Europe. Winston Churchill gave him an autographed set of speeches. And as war approached, he became a secret courier of messages to French leader Edouard Daladier and Italian dictator Benito Mussolini when Neville Chamberlain, the British Prime Minister, tried to initiate new dialogues outside normal diplomatic channels in a desperate last-ditch bid for peace.

Apart from keeping the Russians informed of crucial developments, Burgess was using high society gossip and his European trips to ingratiate himself with British Intelligence. They paid him for each tip-off, and in January 1939, his devious diligence paid off. MI6 offered him a full-time staff job.

The secret service was hopelessly understaffed for war, and one of Burgess's tasks was to recruit men to make up the numbers. His hunting ground was the plush clubs and society parties of London's West End. In August 1940, a new man just back from reporting the war in France was introduced by Burgess. It was Kim Philby, who had separated from wife Litzi to cut his known Communist connections.

Philby's efficiency made a quick impression on spymasters more used to the plodding efforts of former members of the British police in India. He was given a key post in MI6's Iberian section, with orders to counter the Nazi spy threat in neutral Spain and Portugal, and protect vital Allied shipping in the Mediterranean and Atlantic. It was a job he did well – with one exception.

In 1943 top German army officers and the Abwehr secret service chief, Admiral Canaris, were said to be losing faith with Hitler and his Nazi henchmen. An MI6 man working under Philby wrote a paper which suggested exploiting the split to end the war before Germany was driven to unconditional surrender. If the ploy had worked, thousands of lives could have been saved, and Eastern Europe would have been spared Russian enslavement. But Philby stopped the paper circulating to those who might have followed it up. He knew Russia wanted Germany destroyed, and divided, unable ever again to threaten the Soviet Union.

When *The Times* asked if Philby might rejoin their staff, the editor was told it was impossible 'because his present work is so important and he performs it with such exceptional ability'. Philby, like Burgess and Maclean, had burrowed deep inside the Establishment citadel. And as the end of the war neared, the trio stood poised to wreak even more serious damage.

What does Kim Philby's son John, born in 1944, think of his father? Soon after visiting him in Moscow in 1975, he said: 'My father is nearly always described as a traitor, yet in no way was he a turn-coat. Neither was he even a double agent. At a very early age he made a conscious decision and he stuck by it. He believed he had a higher loyalty and for that he fought, often at very great cost to himself. It is said he betrayed a group of Albanian exiles backed by the West and parachuted into Albania in 1949. Probably this is true. But the men sent in were armed to the teeth. They were not there on a package holiday. Spying is a dirty business. In cold wars, as in hot wars, people get hurt.'

Philby Looks After His Friends

In August 1945 the newly-appointed Russian consul in Turkey approached British diplomats offering a potentially devastating deal. Konstantin Volkov, who claimed he was area head of Soviet intelligence, wanted £27,500 and asylum in the West. In return, he was prepared to reveal every detail of Russia's espionage operations in Turkey, plus the lowdown on how the Moscow spy network operated. And he would name three Russian agents working inside the British government, two in the Foreign Office and one in counter-espionage. It was too hot a potato for the diplomats in Istanbul to handle. They had to pass the offer to London, and Volkov agreed to wait 21 days for a decision.

Twenty days later a British intelligence official arrived in Turkey. Kim Philby apologized for the delay, blaming vacation arrangements. He waited a few days, but Volkov never made contact. Weeks after Philby returned to London, the reason for the defector's silence become clear. A Soviet military plane touched down unannounced at Istanbul airport. A car raced towards it across the tarmac. A heavily bandaged figure was lifted aboard the plane on a stretcher, and the aircraft took off again. Volkov had been betrayed by one of the Moscow moles he was seeking to unmask.

To the Kremlin's delight, MI6 had unwittingly appointed Philby head of espionage directed at Russia in 1944. By the end of the war, he had a staff of 100 working for him. But his treachery was making all their efforts meaningless. British agents sent behind the Iron Curtain were caught and shot. Russia's spies in British institutions had a highly-placed defender.

The two Foreign Office men Volkov would have named were Burgess and Maclean. The former had entered the diplomatic service via the press department. But by 1946 he was secretary and personal assistant to Hector McNeil, a friend from his BBC days, and now deputy Foreign Secretary. Burgess, privy to Tory secrets before the war, was now close to the heart of the new Labour administration. He accompanied McNeil on official visits to Paris and Brussels, was his aide at the Council of Foreign Ministers, and shared cabinet confidences.

Maclean was even better placed. In 1944, he had been appointed Head of Chancery at Britain's American embassy in Washington DC. Secret communiques between Prime Minister Churchill and Presidents Roosevelt and Truman crossed his desk, detailing war tactics and later the groundwork for the NATO alliance. And from February 1947, Maclean was secretary of the combined Policy Committee, dealing with classified atom bomb information from America, Britain and Canada. He knew who was doing what where, and how much uranium the Allies were buying. The Russians had scientists spying for them – one, Allan Nunn May, whose story will be told later, was a Cambridge contemporary of Maclean. From what the diplomat told them, they could work out exactly how many bombs the West was making. Maclean had another advantage. He was given a permanent pass which allowed him to enter the US Atomic Energy Commission headquarters unaccompanied. It was a privilege even the commander of the American atomic effort did not enjoy.

Both Burgess and Maclean were showing signs of strain under the burdens of their double lives. They were drinking with increasing ferocity, and making highly indiscreet comments about themselves and British policy. But instead of sacking them, the Foreign Office gave them new chances. When Maclean's anti-American stance became intolerable in Washington, he was 'promoted' to a top job in Cairo, where he had access to confidential dispatches from key embassies all over the world. When his drinking there became inexcusable – he was arrested by Egyptian police – he was whisked back to London, and given six months to sort himself out. Then he was appointed head of the American Desk at the Foreign Office, which gave him the chance to tell Moscow of America's crucial decision to limit involvement in the Korean War.

Burgess, too, lived a charmed life. He was removed from a Far East propaganda operation for being 'dirty, drunk and idle'. Recuperating in Gibraltar after a fall at a restaurant, he insulted and scandalized diplomats

---

An unnamed Cambridge contemporary of Guy Burgess confessed to *Daily Mail* reporters in 1979 that he had organized an underground group in the Bletchley area of Buckinghamshire during World War 2 while working for the Ministry of Food on emergency feeding plans. 'I was to lie low and be ready to organize resistance if the Germans invaded,' he said. 'I managed to gather a great deal of useful information. One of my sources was a comrade who was a ticket collector on trains. He used to listen to the conversations of girls on their way home from war jobs – they used to speak rather freely and he picked up a lot.'

and tourists alike with his unwary outbursts about homosexuality and politics. But as in Maclean's case, loutish behaviour was punished only by a change of scene. Burgess was posted to Washington as First Secretary in August 1950. It was a catastrophic appointment for Anglo-American relations. But it caused even more trouble for Kim Philby and the Russians.

Philby had reached the pinnacle of his espionage career, officially and unofficially, a year earlier. He preceded Burgess to Washington, as MI6 liaison man with the CIA. American agents who had learnt to respect Philby as a colleague in London during the war had no qualms about letting him in on every major operation. CIA director Bedell Smith often briefed him personally. And Philby pretended to be as puzzled as the Americans when a series of top operations turned sour.

The two agencies launched a major attempt to foment a revolution in Russian-influenced Albania in 1949. Exiled King Zog offered his battle-hardened royal guard, and other volunteers, as guerrilla fighters. But for three years, every attempt to infiltrate men into Albania by submarine or parachute ended in disaster. The Russians were always waiting with ambushes. They even knew the emergency radio drill when one captive Albanian tried to stop a follow-up party falling into the trap. The operation cost 300 Albanian lives.

The same thing happened when the CIA and MI6 muscled in on a modestly successful venture by dissident Ukrainians – smuggling arms into Soviet-run Ukraine, and literature out. Couriers began to go missing, and the flow of literature became Russian propaganda. After two disasters, both Britain and America fought shy of further meddling behind the Iron Curtain.

Philby was not only betraying infiltration operations and CIA agents all over the world; he was also able to tell Moscow how much the CIA knew of Soviet operations. And by 1949 the CIA thought it knew a lot. In a brilliant code-breaking operation, Russian messages taped during the war, while priority was given to German and Japanese intercepts, were finally

Official files on the defection to Moscow of Burgess and Maclean should have become available to public scrutiny late in 1981 under the 30-year rule on historic documents. But Mrs Thatcher's government held them back. Labour MP Stanley Newens commented: 'I suspect that details of the investigation into the defection would be embarrassing to people still alive. There are also people now dead whose reputations might have to be re-evaluated if the documents were published.'

TV personality Malcolm Muggeridge worked under Kim Philby during his war-time service as an MI6 agent' 'I was always delighted to see him, I enjoyed his company,' he recalled years later. Once, when both were 'quite plastered' after a good dinner in Paris, they walked up and down in front of the Russian embassy in the Rue de Grenelle, discussing how they could penetrate it. Muggeridge also met Burgess at his Bentinck Street flat in London. He was with Blunt, and Muggeridge took an instant dislike to the 'comically pernickety and gentlemanly homosexual' art historian. He said: 'It is extraordinary for a brilliant art scholar like Blunt to be a devoted slave, to the point of betraying his country, to the most philistine government, aesthetically speaking, that has ever existed.'

unravelled. Fuchs, the Rosenbergs and Harry Gold, atom bomb spies whose exploits are covered later in this book, were all tracked down after the Soviet backlog was decoded, though the CIA invented or hinted at alternative methods of detection to try to keep their cypher triumph secret.

The Russians told Philby not to bother saving spies who had already served their purpose. But he sat on a report naming Bruno Pontecorvo, an Italian born nuclear scientist who later defected to the Soviet Union. And he also protected a high-level political spy code-named Homer. Philby was supposed to help to track him down from a field of 700 suspects. But he knew from the start who he was – Donald Maclean.

When Guy Burgess arrived in Washington, unkempt, unreliable and utterly unsuited to diplomacy, Philby surprisingly took him under his own roof for nearly a year. It was a mistake that almost cost his career when, in February 1951, he asked Burgess to run a vital errand.

Philby knew the net was closing in on Maclean in London. He was one of the final four Homer suspects. But the Russians could not allow him to be arrested. The ravages of spying, drinking and repressed guilt had left him unable to withstand interrogation. He would crack, putting at risk the espionage network so carefully built up over 20 years. It was also important for the Russians to prove to other moles that a spy in trouble could rely on help from Moscow. Maclean had to be spirited out of harm's way.

Burgess was a friend Maclean would trust. Though notorious for eccentricity, he was not suspected of spying. America was only too glad to see the back of Burgess, whose buffoonery was no longer a joke. But to ensure a plausible reason for departure, Burgess went driving in Virginia and was stopped three times for speeding. With him in the car was a well-known homosexual, which further enraged the Americans. Burgess sailed home on the liner *Queen Mary*.

He contacted Maclean early in May, and both men became aware of MI5 counter-espionage men trailing Maclean. But it seemed there was no rush to leave. Burgess plunged back into his social whirl, Maclean continued to provide the Russians with updates from the American Desk in Whitehall. Then, on the morning of Friday 25 May 1951, Foreign Secretary Herbert Morrison signed a paper authorizing the interrogation of Maclean.

The fateful Friday was Maclean's 38th birthday, and he allowed himself a leisurely lunch with friends during a routine office day. But Burgess had no time to relax. He was tipped off about the interrogation within minutes of the go-ahead being signed. Hastily, he told a friend he could not make a planned weekend trip to the Continent. In fact, he needed the friend's ticket for Maclean. He packed, hired a car, and drove to Maclean's house in Kent, arriving as Maclean returned from his office. They shared a meal with Maclean's wife Melinda, then drove to Southampton. As they boarded the 23.00 ferry to Europe, one of them called to a docker: 'Back on Monday.' But Burgess and Maclean were never to set foot in Britain again.

The diplomats' vanishing act puzzled the public. There was no mention of espionage for years, and even when the two men were at last paraded in public by the Soviet Union, in 1956, both claimed they were not spies, merely 'peace lovers' disillusioned with the West.

But a more enduring mystery was why Burgess fled with Maclean. Philby had specifically told him not to go, realizing his disappearance would focus suspicion on his friends, particularly friends who had shared their Washington homes with him. Had he panicked, knowing his Foreign Office career was over? Had he too broken under the strain of drink, debauchery and a double life? Or had Maclean refused to go alone to a cold, forbidding country where he knew no-one? Had the Russians decided they could not trust Maclean to make the journey on his own? The West has still not found a conclusive answer.

Burgess helped the Russians assess British political news and Maclean was given a desk job at the Soviet Foreign Office. But neither was really happy in his new homeland. Burgess, homesick and out of place in a puritanical country, died in 1963, when his drinking finally caught up with him. Maclean, who lost his wife to Kim Philby, lasted until 1983. His status as a top spy was confirmed in 1956, when the CIA is said to have seriously considered kidnapping him to find out exactly what secrets he had betrayed.

Meanwhile, in June 1951, the third man they left behind was fighting for his espionage life . . .

Philby's Flight
Spares British Blushes

Kim Philby was instantly suspected of aiding the Burgess-Maclean escape, just as he and the Russians expected. He was one of the few who had links with both men – he was in on the secrets of Maclean's surveillance, and Burgess had been his house-guest. Moscow was gambling on Philby's ability to bluff his way out of trouble. And the master spy justified that faith in a way even the Russians could hardly believe.

MI6 chief Sir Stewart Menzies summoned Philby to London for a clear-the-air confrontation. Many colleagues refused to accept that calm, capable, well-connected Kim could be a Moscow mole. But top officers in their counter-espionage counterpart, MI5, had no doubts. They were re-evaluating Philby's career record and asking awkward questions, particularly about the Volkov incident. CIA chiefs were also certain of his guilt. They told Menzies: sack Philby or we end all intelligence co-operation.

Philby was not escorted home, but he resisted the temptation to flee to Russia. His ice-cold, calculating brain needed to learn how much his bosses knew. He resigned from the Foreign Service – with a £4,000 golden handshake. His resignation meant he could no longer be posted abroad under diplomatic cover, but did not rule out other kinds of undercover work.

In June 1952, MI5 pressure resulted in a 'secret trial' for Philby. For three days, Helenus Milmo, a former secret agent who later became a judge, grilled him about his past in front of assessors. Philby stalled, using his lifelong stammer to disrupt the rhythm of cross-examination and give himself time to think. He denied everything while carefully analysing exactly what his interrogator knew. It was soon clear that MI5 had only circumstantial evidence which would never stand up in court without a confession. Philby was not prepared to make one, and the trial ended inconclusively.

Philby had been mentioned as a possible director of MI6 during his heyday in Washington. Now he tried a succession of less glamorous jobs. He went to Spain as a reporter for *The Observer* newspaper, worked for a while in the City of London, and even became a toothbrush salesman. It is also possible he was used from time to time by MI6. He was seen in Cyprus, mixing with Armenians exiled from their Iron Curtain homeland, and spotted by scientists at a lonely outpost on the Russo-Turkish border. Friends in the service helped him out when he was short of cash, even paying school fees for some of his five children by second wife Aileen. But he made no attempt to rebuild his career. He seemed to be waiting for something to happen. In September 1955, it did.

At long last, the government published a White Paper on the disappearance of Burgess and Maclean. It was a 4,000 word whitewash. One MP dismissed it as 'an insult to the intelligence of the country'. But an MI5 man, furious at the omission of Philby's name, decided to force the facts into the open another way. Nobody could call Philby a spy outside Parliament without receiving a writ for libel. But statements in the House of Commons carry privilege, allowing newspapers to report them, however libellous. So journalists approached by the MI5 man briefed opposition MP Marcus Lipton. He asked Tory Premier Sir Anthony Eden: 'Have you made up your mind to cover up at all costs the dubious third man activities of Mr Harold Philby, who was First Secretary at the Washington embassy a little time ago?' Philby's link with the two runaways was finally established. Publicity next day made a full Parliamentary debate inevitable.

Philby later claimed it was 'the happiest day of my life' when Lipton asked his question. And in the debate on 7 November, Foreign Minister Harold Macmillan – the man with overall responsibility for MI6 – told MPs: 'I have no reason to conclude that Mr Philby has at any time betrayed the interests of this country, or to identify him with the so-called third man, if indeed there was one.'

Knowing that such official blessing made it unsafe for anyone to repeat Lipton's accusations, Philby held a jaunty press conference three days later, building for himself the image of a wholly innocent man whose career had crashed because of misguided friendship for the no-good Burgess. Even Macmillan knew that was not true. He was scrupulously fair to Philby in Parliament because he knew he could not be proved guilty. But he ordered MI6 never to use Philby as an agent again. Astonishingly, the order was ignored. Whether through illogical loyalty to a friend, or to keep him in the fold where he could be watched, Philby was sent to Beirut, a crucial espionage centre in the Middle East, where the Russians were currying favour in Egypt, Syria and the Gulf states.

Philby was using a foreign correspondent job for both *The Observer* and the *Economist* magazine as his cover, and filed impressive stories from the Lebanese capital. But the CIA were keeping tabs on his movements. He was

---

Writer Goronwy Rees, an Army intelligence officer during World War 2, met Kim Philby. He said of him: 'There was in him a streak of cruelty, malice and brutality which was never far beneath the surface and made him, one suspects, positively enjoy his life of treachery and betrayal.'

Papers discovered when MI5 men searched Guy Burgess's flat in 1951 led to the discovery of a mole in the British Treasury. But it was December 1979 before the public learned that John Cairncross had spied for the Russians after being recruited to the Communist party by his teacher at Cambridge in the 1930s – Anthony Blunt. Cairncross claimed he 'just let Burgess see some notes I had made, general summaries of discussions and that sort of thing'. In fact, the papers were comprehensive briefings on Britain's attitude to Hitler and assessments of whether war with Germany was likely – crucial information which led to Russia's two-year pact with the Nazis in 1939. After being unmasked in 1952, Cairncross went into exile in Rome, working for the United Nations Food and Agriculture Organization.

travelling far more than was reflected in his journalistic output.

In 1962, the American agency wiped out any lingering doubts MI6 held about Philby's guilt. The CIA sent over the detailed debriefing of a Russian defector, Anatoli Golitsin, who identified Philby as the man who tipped off Burgess and Maclean – and as the organizer of a KGB operation against Arab states in the late 1950s. At around the same time, a woman friend of Philby's second wife told MI6 he had admitted being a long-term Soviet agent.

Sir Dick White, MI6 chief since 1956, decided to send one of his agents, Nicholas Elliott to confront Philby in Beirut. But first he agreed with the Attorney-General, Sir John Hobson, that the spy could be offered immunity from prosecution in return for a full confession. Elliott arrived in Lebanon early in January 1963 – but according to espionage expert Chapman Pincher in his book *Their Trade is Treachery*, the KGB had beaten him to it. Yuri Modin, the Russian who ran Burgess and Maclean in London and organized their flight, had already alerted Philby to Elliott's visit and prepared an escape route for him. Philby could not defect before the interrogation because he would endanger the source who told the Russians about it.

Philby drank more heavily than usual in the weeks before Elliott's arrival. But he was sober when he met his former friend, and said: 'I was half expecting to see you.' Elliott told Philby there was new evidence against him. According to Pincher, Philby then began a careful confession, without even asking what the new evidence was. He said he was recruited by the Russians in Vienna in 1934, had sabotaged the Volkov, Albanian and Ukrainian operations, and sent Burgess to warn Maclean. But there were other misleading sections of the admission which, says Pincher, point to it being a KGB exercise to protect other Soviet moles in Britain. Philby signed a two-page typewritten resumé of his statement, and Elliott flew to America to check it with the CIA.

Ten days later, on 23 January, Philby and a female friend were on their way to a dinner party when Philby stopped the taxi and got out, saying he had to send a cable to London, and would join the party later. It was six months before he was seen again in public – in Moscow. And like Burgess and Maclean, he left behind more questions than answers.

The Russians knew MI6 wanted Philby back in London for more thorough questioning. Could they allow that, realizing that he was feeling the strain of nearly 30 years spying? Or did they arrange his getaway because, with his MI6 prospects completely blown, he was of more use to them in Moscow? Did they also know that the CIA, learning at last the full extent of Philby's treachery, had sent a team to Lebanon to assassinate him? And did MI6 connive at the escape, frightening Philby into defection? Certainly by 1963 the government, already embarrassed by a spate of spy trials, to be discussed later in this book, would be glad to forego the blushes of another. And MI6 would not have to explain publicly why it continued to employ a suspected Russian agent for 12 years, in direct contravention of orders.

Philby said on arrival in Russia that he had 'come home'. He soon settled to a new life as a senior KGB officer in the Moscow headquarters at 2, Dzerzhinsky Square. He was given the Order of the Red Banner and Russian citizenship, and helped himself to Melinda Maclean, who had followed her husband, Donald, into exile. Later he ditched her too and married a Russian girl. His only contact with Britain was a daily copy of *The Times* – a special privilege from the Kremlin, so he could keep up with the English cricket scores. Western intelligence agencies have detected his hand in the planning of some KGB offensives in Europe, notably an attempt to steal NATO secrets in 1968. In June 1979, he was spotted in Damascus, Syria – his first known excursion outside the Soviet Union in 16 years.

What drove Philby to a career which, at its zenith, doomed every Western spying mission, offensive and defensive, before it began? Was it a life-long, unsuspected Communist conviction which nevertheless did not stop him enjoying the full fruits of capitalist society? Was it a desire for adventure inherited from his father? The experts are undecided. And Philby the mystery man says only: 'Knowing what I did, I could not have done anything else.'

The Establishment took belated revenge on the insider who betrayed its trust by withdrawing his OBE and striking him off the membership list at London's Athenaeum club. Little did it realize that, for 44 years, it was harbouring another Russian spy who had climbed even higher up the ladder . . .

Anthony Blunt: Traitor on the Queen's Payroll

Anthony Blunt joined Russia's 'Cambridge Circus' of spies even before Donald Maclean. Guy Burgess, himself enlisted by Kim Philby, recruited his fellow homosexual in 1935. But it was November 1979 before he was publicly unmasked as a traitor by Prime Minister Margaret Thatcher. Though he had confessed to the espionage authorities 15 years earlier, he went unpunished. For the spy who betrayed His Majesty's forces during World War 2 was, by 1964, Sir Anthony Blunt, Surveyor of the Queen's Pictures. And in 1946 he had spared royal blushes with a delicate, top-secret mission to Germany.

Blunt preceded his fellow Soviet agents to Trinity College, arriving in 1926. The London vicar's son proved such a brilliant scholar that he was offered a teaching post, and was a Fellow of the college when Burgess reached Trinity. The two soon became friends, and Blunt readily agreed to Burgess's suggestion that he work for the Russians to fight the spread of Naziism. When his Soviet spymaster ordered Burgess to London, Blunt took over his task of spotting other talented students likely to join the cause.

By 1939 Blunt too was in London as deputy director of the prestigious Courtauld Institute of Art. When war broke out he volunteered for military intelligence. He was rejected because of his Marxist past. Astonishingly, he was then accepted by MI5 on the recommendation of an art chum. For the next five years he undermined the counter-espionage operations of Britain's secret services just as effectively as Kim Philby was wrecking MI6's overseas efforts. Blunt the spy had caught the spycatchers on the hop.

One of his first acts was to tell Moscow that, for seven years, someone in the office of Politburo member Anastas Mikoyan had been feeding information to MI5. The mole's supply of information stopped immediately. Then Blunt revealed that MI5 had bugged the HQ of the British Communist party. And he kept the Russians informed about the names and duties of every MI5 officer – he was even in charge of the surveillance roster for a time, able to tell Moscow exactly who was watching whom.

Later Blunt worked closely with Guy Burgess in operations against the neutral embassies in London. Burgess was recruiting Spanish, Portuguese and Scandinavian envoys as agents for MI5. Blunt was involved in the clandestine monitoring of diplomatic pouches and telephone messages. He was thus able to spot likely collaborators for MI5 – and the Russians. The two men met regularly in Blunt's rooms at the Courtauld Institute in Portman Square, preparing reports for their Soviet contact and providing secret documents for him to copy. Late in the war, these included plans for Operation Fortitude, a vital propaganda ploy to persuade the Germans that the D-Day landings would be at Pas-de-Calais, not the real target, Normandy. The Russians had an interest in prolonging the war on the Western Front – they could then grab more of Eastern Europe. Fortunately for thousands of Allied lives, they made no use of Blunt's information.

Unusually, the Russians let Blunt leave MI5 at the end of the war. Normally a spy infiltrated into such a useful position would be left in place until discovery loomed, and it was later surmised that Blunt was freed only because there was an equally effective mole in MI5 to provide the service the Kremlin required in the cold war years. But Blunt did not leave the service of Moscow. His new job, as Surveyor of Pictures for King George VI, was perfect cover for his activities as a courier. Nobody would suspect him of running messages for Soviet spies, collecting information and leaving money in secret hiding places for other agents, passing on titbits of information gleaned in casual chats with former MI5 colleagues. All of these tasks Blunt now performed. He became an indispensible back-up to Russia's front line agents. He even saved Philby's skin when Burgess and Maclean fled.

After the diplomats' disappearance in 1951, security forces wanted to inspect Burgess's London flat. Blunt had a key, and let them in. While they searched for incriminating evidence, Blunt noticed three letters implicating both Burgess and Philby in traitorous activities. He quietly pocketed them.

The Russians knew Blunt would be questioned after the disappearance of his former colleague Burgess, and they told him to defect. Blunt, delighted with his new post and prestige as Buckingham Palace adviser, declined, saying he was confident of surviving any interrogation. Again, the Russians let him have his way. And despite 11 MI5 grillings over the next 12 years, he lived up to his promise. He was even able to continue to run messages for the Soviets, helping to re-activate Philby in 1954, and visiting him in Beirut.

Then, in 1963, his luck ran out. A brilliant young American recruited by Moscow at Cambridge in the 1930s was offered an art consultancy job in Washington by President Kennedy. Though he turned it down, he took the opportunity to clear his conscience. He admitted providing the Russians with personal appraisals of American attitudes, and named Blunt as the 'known Soviet agent' who had enlisted him and others.

In April, 1964, Blunt was confronted with this information by MI5 interrogator Arthur Martin. Then he was told that the Attorney General Sir John Hobson, had authorized his immunity from prosecution if he confessed.

Anthony Blunt

Without knowing what Blunt had done, and forgetting the Attorney General's rider – immunity from prosecution only if he had stopped spying in 1945 when Russia was still an ally – MI5 had wiped Blunt's slate clean. Now he was able to confess, which he did, and name some people he had recruited. He was also able to give misleading information to protect others.

Why was immunity so readily given? It is true MI5 had no hard evidence on which to base a successful prosecution, and could justify allowing one spy off the hook if he led them to more. But no-one at that stage knew the enormity of Blunt's crimes which, if detected in war time, would have sent him to the gallows for treason. The real reason for the unpublished 'pardon' was Blunt's royal connections.

In 1946, Buckingham Palace asked MI5 to nominate a trustworthy volunteer for a delicate mission in Germany. Blunt was no longer on the secret service staff, but agreed to undertake the task. He never revealed what it entailed, but the following year, having accomplished it, he was presented with the Commander of the Royal Victorian Order award. The mission may also have been a factor in his knighthood, awarded in May, 1956. In January 1983, Chapman Pincher reported in the *Daily Express* that MI5 officers believed the task was to retrieve records of possibly embarrassing conversations between Hitler and the Duke of Windsor – the present Queen's uncle – during the Duke's visits to Berlin in 1937. Blunt next day denied the report, claiming, rather implausibly, that he merely collected letters Queen Victoria wrote to her daughter, Empress Frederick of Prussia. He did not explain why it was so vital to collect them so soon after the war, half a century after they were written.

Clearly, dragging the Royal Family into a spy trial in the early 1960s, when there were more than enough spy trials anyway, was not in anyone's interests. So while less significant Soviet agents like Vassall began 18 year jail

---

Philby, Burgess, Maclean and Blunt continued spying for the Russians even though they knew that in 1938, the Soviet agents who handled them, a Hungarian called Theo and a Czech named Otto, were recalled to Moscow and shot in one of Stalin's bloody purges. Theo and Otto were both 'illegals' – secret agents working on false passports and false identities in other countries. After 1938, the 'Cambridge Circus' spies were controlled by 'legals' – Soviet spies working under diplomatic cover from their embassy in London.

sentences, Blunt retained his Palace job, his prestige and his reputation until, in 1978, author Andrew Boyle published his book, *The Climate of Treason*. Blunt was not named, but his exploits were. And public opinion was so outraged at the new revelations in the Burgess, Maclean, Philby saga that Mrs Thatcher was forced to act and Blunt was finally, publicly unmasked. He died in March 1983, aged 76, unloved and unmourned, stripped of his titles and totally disgraced.

Blunt gave interrogators many names of other Russian agents, mainly minor and no longer operating, but he always denied there was a so-called Fifth Man in the 'Cambridge Circus'. According to Chapman Pincher, the security authorities know there was – and know who he is. In his book *Their Trade Is Treachery*, he reveals that the spy was recruited by Burgess and Philby in Cambridge after Philby returned from Vienna, that he hid his Communist convictions to gain work at a government defence station as a scientific civil servant, and that he knew two top Russian controllers, Yuri Modin and Sergei Kondrashev, who was sent to Britain specifically to handle the scientist and George Blake.

In 1966, when confronted with evidence about his Communist past and offered immunity from prosecution, he declined to confess. As he was near retirement, he was allowed to qualify for his pension on non-secret work. Exactly who he was, and the damage he did, will have to wait, according to Pincher, until death renders the libel laws irrelevant.

Dr Allan Nunn May: the Treacherous Scientist

Igor Sergeievitch Gouzenko was a worried man. After two years as principal cypher clerk to the military attaché at the Russian embassy in Ottawa, he was about to be recalled to Moscow, and he knew life there could not compare to the luxury and freedom he, his wife Svetlana and young son Andrei were enjoying in Canada. Gouzenko began secretly copying documents to earn asylum in his new country. Their contents were to shock the governments of Canada, Britain and the United States, and expose what was later described as the greatest treachery of the century – the atom bomb espionage of Klaus Fuchs, Allan Nunn May, and Julius and Ethel Rosenberg.

The race to develop the atom bomb had begun in 1938, when refugees from Nazi Germany revealed that chemist Otto Hahn had successfully released an immense amount of energy by splitting the nucleus of the uranium atom. Realizing the horrifying potential of such a weapon in Hitler's hands, the British Prime Minister instantly set up a priority research programme, and sent teams of commandos to Norway to destroy a hydro-electric plant producing heavy water, essential to A-bomb experiments and then under Nazi control. In 1942, Britain and America agreed to pool their scientific resources to speed up production of the deadliest weapon the world had seen, but, though Russia was by then an ally in the war, the two Western powers agreed, largely at Churchill's instigation, not to share their progress with the Kremlin.

On 16 July 1945, a blinding flash, a tremendous bang heard 200 miles (320 km) away, and a multi-coloured spume of cloud stretching 40,000 feet high above the desert at Alamogordo, New Mexico, signalled the success of the Anglo-American team. Less than a month later, on 6 August, an American bomber unleashed the new bomb on the Japanese city of Hiroshima. It killed 78,150 people, effectively ended the war in the Pacific, and was hailed by the American President, Harry Truman, as 'the greatest thing in history'.

The Allies' sense of triumph was shortlived. On 6 September, when British envoys in Ottawa were still planning a victory garden party, Igor Gouzenko, then 25, tried to hand over his documents. At first nobody wanted to know. The local newspaper declared them too hot to handle. Officials at the Justice and External Affairs Departments stalled him while alerting Prime Minister W. L. Mackenzie King. It was decided the risk of a diplomatic break with

Russia – then still considered a friend and ally by Canadians – outweighed the value of Gouzenko's information and the possible danger of returning him to the people he had tried to betray. Only after four Soviet security men were caught ransacking Gouzenko's flat were he and his family whisked into protective hiding and his revelations taken seriously. They showed that:

American Secretary of State Edward Stettinius had been surrounded by spies.

Soviet vice-consul Anatoli Yakovlev was running sophisticated espionage networks from New York, sending military secrets to the Kremlin, laundering money for European operations and controlling his agents in Washington via courier Elizabeth Bentley.

Canada had been infiltrated by at least 20 Soviet agents, including two cypher clerks, Emma Woikin at the Canadian External Affairs Department, and Kay Willsher at the British High Commission in Ottawa, who had access to all highly-sensitive messages. And, most crucially; two Britons working on the atomic bomb in North American research laboratories were Soviet agents, and had passed secret materials and calculations to the Russians.

The scope of the clandestine operations staggered the Canadians, who quickly passed news of the bombshell on to the White House and 10 Downing Street, by now occupied by Labour Premier Clement Attlee. Throughout the war Churchill had counselled against trusting Stalin and the Russians. Now he was proved right. Far from reciprocating friendship, it seemed the Soviets were preparing for a new war. While counter-espionage services in the three countries began checking out Gouzenko's leads, the three leaders, Mackenzie King, Truman and Attlee, agonized over a response. The atom bomb leaks were clearly the biggest eye-opener.

Gouzenko knew the scientific traitors only by the code-names Alek and Golia. Alek was readily identifiable, thanks to a telegram sent to Moscow by

Dr Allan Nunn May was released from Wakefield Prison on 29 December, 1952. The British Cabinet considered depriving him of remission his good behaviour had earned, and keeping him locked up until 1956. They feared he would take his expertise behind the Iron Curtain. But Nunn May had learned his lesson. He went back to Cambridge, where years earlier he had gained a brilliant double first degree, and researched metal fatigue until 1962, when he went to Africa to become professor of physics at Ghana University.

Clement Attlee

Gouzenko's embassy boss Colonel Nikolai Zabotin, ostensibly military attaché but really a Russian spymaster in Canada. It revealed that Alek was transferring to work in London at King's College in the Strand. Inquiries at the Montreal branch of the Atomic Energy Division research laboratories established that Dr Allan Nunn May, a British physicist who had flown west to join the Allied nuclear programme in January 1943 was moving to London.

Since the telegram also revealed details of pre-arranged meetings between Nunn May and a Russian courier in London, the authorities decided to let him take up his new job, in the hope of tracking down more Soviet agents. Nunn May was to be in front of the British Museum on 7 October, carrying a copy of *The Times* under his left arm. His contact, holding the magazine *Picture Post* in his left hand, would ask for the most direct route to the Strand, and the scientist would offer to show him, adding: 'Best regards from Mikel.'

In the event, Nunn May never kept his secret rendezvous. 'I decided to wash my hands of the whole business' he told interrogators later, but on 15 February 1946, he was picked up by Scotland Yard Special Branch men for questioning in a coordinated trans-Atlantic swoop on the spies Gouzenko unmasked. At first he denied everything. But when confronted by evidence of his links with Soviet agents, he confessed to providing information and uranium samples to the Russians in return for 'some dollars (I forget how many) and a bottle of whisky which I accepted against my will'. He added: 'The whole affair was extremely painful to me and I only embarked on it because I felt this was a contribution I could make to the safety of mankind. I certainly did not do it for gain.'

Nunn May's motives were outlined at length by his defence counsel, Gerald Gardiner KC – later the Lord Chancellor – during his trial at the Old Bailey in May 1946. He said that, like doctors, some scientists 'take the view, rightly or wrongly, that if they have discovered something of value to mankind, they are under an obligation to see that it is used for mankind, and not kept for any particular group of people'. In addition, said the barrister, when the acts were committed, in February 1945, the Russians 'were customarily referred to as allies, and no one at that date referred to them as enemies or potential enemies'.

But Mr Justice Oliver was having none of that. Dismissing the attempt to portray Nunn May as 'a man of honour who had only done what he believed to be right' he made it clear he agreed with the prosecution, led by Attorney-General Sir Hartley Shawcross, who described the whole affair as 'a somewhat squalid case' of a man who made himself more important than his country's laws and policy. The judge jailed the traitor for ten years, saying he had shown 'crass conceit and wickedness' in compromising 'one of the country's most precious secrets'.

Back in Canada, the Soviet spymasters had fled home to Moscow.

While the police rounded up and put on trial their quota of the people Gouzenko named, his wife came out of hiding to go into hospital to give birth to her second child, a girl. She was booked in as the wife of a Polish immigrant farmer, and visited each day by her devoted 'husband' – a Royal Canadian Mounted policeman who had taken lessons in the art of speaking fractured English.

Gouzenko, Svetlana and the two children were later settled, under an assumed name and under RCMP protection, in a Canadian home known only to a select few. Over the years he occasionally appeared on TV to comment on subsequent spy scandals, always covered by a hood to prevent identification. He also wrote two books based on his experiences. But long before they were published, the counter-intelligence net was closing in on the other scientist traitor, Golia. Professor Israel Halperin, identified by Gouzenko as a spy, was acquitted by a Canadian court. But in investigating him, government agents had discovered an interesting name in his address book ... that of Klaus Fuchs.

Emil Klaus Julius Fuchs: the Nuclear Spy

Of all the atom spies, Emil Klaus Julius Fuchs is generally regarded as the most valuable to the Russians, and the most traitorous to the West. Accepting sanctuary in Britain after fleeing Nazi oppression in his native Germany, he betrayed those who trusted him by actually volunteering his services as a spy, then giving the Kremlin the secrets of how to make the atom bomb.

Fuchs, a brilliant but reticent nuclear scientist, was born on 29 December 1911 – eight months after Allan Nunn May – in the village of Russelsheim, near Darmstadt. His father was a Protestant pastor who later turned Quaker, and the boy's pious but poor upbringing led him to membership of the Communist party. At the University of Kiel, he was beaten up by Nazi Brownshirts for his beliefs.

On 27 February 1933, Hitler's agents burned down the German parliamentary building, the Reichstag, and named the Communists as culprits. It was the prelude to a vicious purge. Fuchs, in Berlin for a conference, immediately went underground, made his way to Paris, and then, using a cousin's girlfriend as his contact, got in touch with a Quaker family in Somerset. They invited him to England, where he was befriended by academics and allowed to continue his studies in mathematical physics at Bristol University free of charge. He was the perfect student, quick and conscientious, and after obtaining his doctorate at Edinburgh, he was awarded a research scholarship.

With the outbreak of war with Germany, Fuchs, like all aliens, came under close scrutiny. But when he appeared before a tribunal in Edinburgh in November 1939, he was cleared to continue his work. Exactly five years earlier, the German consul in Bristol had told the local chief constable Fuchs was a Communist. But since he had not joined the British Communist party, and was not involving himself in overt Communist activities, the report was dismissed as a Nazi attempt to discredit him.

By May 1940, however, the Nazis had invaded Holland and Belgium, and Fuchs was interned with other hitherto trusted aliens. He was shipped to Canada, and was lucky to survive – another boat with internees on board was sunk by a U-boat. While in a prisoner-of-war camp there, he received newspapers and magazines from Professor Israel Halperin, a friend of Fuchs'

Dr Klaus Fuchs

sister, then living in America. But by 1941, Fuchs was back in Britain, freed because of strings pulled by his friends, notably his Edinburgh professor, Max Born.

That May, Fuchs had to sign the Official Secrets Act. German-born Dr Rudolf Peierls, the mathematical physics professor at Birmingham University, offered him a poorly-paid secret job connected with the war. Fuchs again passed a security vetting because the German warning about his Communist past was ignored. Peierls and his wife took the newcomer under their own roof for 18 months, until he moved into lodgings. They were among the influential figures who backed his application for naturalisation, which was essential for top secret work of national importance. On 7 August 1942, Klaus Fuchs formally became a British citizen, swearing an oath of allegiance to King George VI.

But Fuchs knew that oath was worthless. So did his Soviet spymasters because the German refugee from Naziism had volunteered his services to Moscow soon after arriving in Birmingham. Through a friend in the British Communist Party, he had contacted 'Alexander' – Simon Davidovich Kremer, the military attaché's secretary at Russia's London embassy – and at several weekend rendezvous in the Kensington area, he handed over carbon copies of his official reports, and handwritten notes on subjects about which the Soviets wanted more information. Fuchs knew exactly what he was doing: he even rang the Russian embassy to check that 'Alexander' was not a British counter-espionage agent.

Later, a German-Jewish refugee codenamed Sonya was given all the latest data on Anglo-American progress over the atomic bomb. She was Ruth Kuczynski, a Russian spy working from Oxford. She and Fuchs met in country lanes outside Banbury. Then he was posted to America to continue the work of nuclear collaboration. Sonya gave him precise instructions for a meeting with a Soviet agent in New York.

Emma Woikin, jailed in Canada for 2½ years after being named by Russian defector Igor Gouzenko as a Soviet spy in the Canadian External Affairs Department, told a Royal Commission investigating Gouzenko's revelations that she passed on secrets via the lavatory at her dentist's surgery. She left documents concealed there when she had an appointment for treatment to her teeth. The secrets were collected by the chauffeur of the Ottawa spymaster Nikolai Zabotin.

> **Innocent men lost their jobs after the treachery of Klaus Fuchs was revealed. To tighten security, it was ordered that , in future, all civil servants with access to secret material had to be British born, preferably of British parents. Dr Boris Davison, who also worked at Harwell, had to quit because his parents were still behind the Iron Curtain, and could be used in an attempt to blackmail him.**

Fuchs was given automatic security clearance by the Americans – not to do so would 'insult our principal war ally', a spokesman said later – and began work on a gaseous diffusion plant. But one Saturday in January 1944, he made his way, as arranged, to a street on the lower East Side of the city, carrying a tennis ball. A man called Raymond was waiting for him, carrying a book with green binding and two pairs of gloves. It was the start of a relationship which was to give Moscow the means to catch up in the nuclear race.

'Raymond' was Swiss-Jew Heinrich Golodnitsky, who had taken the name Harry Gold when his parents arrived in America in 1914. Fuchs never learned his true identity, nor that he worked as a biochemist for the Philadelphia Sugar Company, nor that he was a vital link in the espionage chain supervised by the Russian vice-consul, Anatoli Yakovlev, the spymaster named by Gouzenko. But he did know what he told 'Raymond' was reaching the Russians. And he told him all he knew, including details of a bomb-producing plant near Knoxville, Tennessee, and plans for the actual construction of the uranium bomb. The secrets were handed over at furtive meetings all over the city.

Then, late in 1944, Fuchs failed to keep two appointments. He had been instructed to join Dr Robert Oppenheimer and his old Birmingham chief Dr Peierls at Los Alamos air base near Santa Fe, New Mexico, for final assembly and testing of the bomb.

But he had not had time to tell Gold, who now worried that something had gone wrong. After checking Fuchs' apartment, he called on Fuchs' sister, living at Cambridge, Massachusetts, and left his telephone number. It was January 1945 before Fuchs travelled north and rang Gold's number. But the news was worth waiting for. The scientist wrote down all he learned at Los Alamos, and disclosed a second type of A-bomb, using plutonium. Details of design, components and manufacture were included in the dossier, together with information on a new implosion lens which triggered the bomb by exploding inwards.

Estimates of the amount of time Russia's spies saved in developing the bomb vary from 18 months to 5 years. And the West can only guess at how much money was saved because Allan Nunn May, Klaus Fuchs, David Greenglass and other traitors obviated the need to explore alternative avenues in nuclear research. Russia exploded its first bomb in September, 1949, four years after the first American blasts. Britain, which had cooperated in producing the US weapon, and then been denied access to it by the McMahon Act, had to wait until 1952 for its initial explosion – even though it had paid the wages of two of the scientists whose knowledge saved Russia so much.

Gold arranged the next contact for June in Santa Fe. There, sitting in a car on the Castillo Bridge, Fuchs revealed that the first test was due next month, and he would be watching it. He refused Gold's offer of $1,500, saying he did not need money.

When the men next met, in September, America had successfully exploded the bomb at Alamogordo, and dropped others on Hiroshima and Nagasaki. Fuchs gave an eye-witness account of the test blast, admitting he had under-estimated the Allies' abilities to create the weapon in time to use it against the Japanese. He also passed on all he knew of the bombs dropped on the two cities – size, materials, how they were detonated.

Harry Gold now dropped out of Fuchs' life. The scientist applied for, and won, the job of chief of theoretical physics at Harwell, the British atomic research establishment. Fuchs had mixed feelings about going 'home'. He had heard of Allan Nunn May's arrest, and though there was no direct link between the men, counter-espionage was sure to be on the lookout for more spies. In addition, the British, not the Red Army, had taken Kiel, the town where Fuchs had been to university. Would they find the German records of his early Communist connections?

The McMahon Act, passed by isolationist American senators, had cut Britain off from sharing American nuclear information, and Harwell was set up to develop an independent atomic weapon. Fuchs threw himself into his new job, recruiting staff, setting up programmes, sitting on almost every committee, even representing Britain in 1947 at a conference in Washington to decide what nuclear knowledge could be made public, and what could not. Ironically, Fuchs, the man who had given all of it to the Russians, argued against releasing too much to Western audiences.

For more than a year, Fuchs made no contact with the Soviets and they did not bother him. He was now of only minor value to them and, as became clear later, they had other sources of information. Donald Maclean and Kim Philby were both still in Washington, and Maclean attended the 1947 conference as the British embassy's political advisor on atomic energy.

Early in 1947, however, Fuchs did re-establish his links with the Russians. In a North London public house, he accepted £100 in notes, the first time he had taken any money other than his expenses. It was, he said later, a formal act to bind him to the cause, and over the next few months he passed secrets about the new Windscale nuclear reactor plant in north-west England, and information about British development of the bomb.

But for the first time Fuchs was beginning to withhold some facts. He also failed to turn up for some meetings. He was suffering what he later described as 'a controlled schizophrenia', in which his Marxist philosophy and acquired isolation from society – essential for the successful spy – were at odds with the friendships he was forging with the 'decent people' at Harwell.

In October 1949, a month after American planes detected the first Soviet atomic bomb blast, Fuchs went to Harwell's security officer, Wing Commander Henry Arnold, with 'a personal problem'. His father had become professor of theology at Leipzig University, in the Russian zone of Germany. They could use him as a lever to extract information about Harwell. Should he, Fuchs, resign?

Arnold stalled, saying he was not competent to advise. Then he contacted Service chiefs in London, saying Fuchs was suffering a crisis of conscience, and might be ripe for interrogation. Unknown to Fuchs, America's FBI and the British MI5 and MI6 had realized his treachery two years earlier. The clues had come in 1947 at a United Nations discussion on controlling atomic energy, when Soviet delegates clearly knew American techniques and codes, and from an intercepted message from the Soviet embassy in Washington to Military Intelligence HQ in Moscow. This narrowed the field to a British scientist at Los Alamos. By checking the movements of all Britons there it was possible to establish the spy's identity – Fuchs. But there was no evidence which would stand up in court.

Arnold's report triggered the big attempt for a confession. William James Skardon, a persistent but patient interrogator who was later to quiz Kim Philby, was sent to Harwell to question Fuchs. For the first two meetings, Fuchs denied being in touch with Soviet officials in America. Then, at the third meeting on 13 January 1950, the scientist abruptly changed his story, and decided to confess 'to try to repair the damage I have done ... to make sure that Harwell will suffer as little as possible and to save my friends as much as possible of that part that was good in my relations with them.'

Skardon was astonished when Fuchs admitted spying for seven years. Nobody had realized the extent of his betrayal. And he was appalled when Fuchs told him he considered the worst thing he had done was to tell the Russians how to make the atomic bomb.

Long, painstakingly detailed debriefings followed, and on the basis of what he said, the FBI were able to arrest Harry Gold.

Fuchs signed his confession on 27 January and seemed to think that, having cleared his conscience, he could return to work at Harwell. The authorities had other plans. On 2 February he was lured back to London and arrested by Commander Leonard Burt of Scotland Yard. Like Allan Nunn May, he was charged under the Official Secrets Acts with communicating information which might be useful to an enemy, and remanded in custody.

The arrest caused a sensation on both sides of the Atlantic. At a committal hearing, Mr Christmas Humphreys, prosecuting for the Attorney General, described Fuchs as a unique Jekyll and Hyde character, saying:

'Half of his mind was beyond the reach of reason and the impact of facts, the other half lived in a world of normal relationships and friendships with his colleagues and human loyalty. The dual personality had been consciously and deliberately produced. He broke his mind in two.'

But if the packed No. 1 court at the Old Bailey expected to see some kind of monster in the dock, they were disappointed. The nondescript, bespectacled defendant pleaded guilty to four separate specimen breaches of the Official Secrets Act, and made a brief statement in which he thanked the court and the staff of Brixton Prison for fair treatment, and was ready to serve his sentence to atone for his crimes.

Lord Chief Justice Goddard glared unmercifully at him. Hinting that hanging would suit the offences – 'Your crime to me is only thinly differentiated from high treason ... but you are not tried for that offence' – he said:

'You took advantage of the privilege of asylum, which has always been the boast of this country to people persecuted in their own country for their political opinions. You betrayed the hospitality and protection given to you by the greatest treachery.'

One hour and twenty minutes after the trial began, Klaus Fuchs left court to start a 14 year jail sentence – the maximum penalty under the law on which he was charged – in Wormwood Scrubs. On 12 February 1951, the Home Secretary formally stripped him of his British nationality 'on grounds of disloyalty'. As a stateless person, he could not be deported when he left Wakefield jail on 22 June 1959, having served nine years and earned full remission for good behaviour, but he chose to leave the country, and was driven to London, and put on a plane to East Berlin.

The Russians had publicly denied any knowledge of Fuchs at the time of his arrest. Intelligence experts later speculated that the Kremlin had set him up for arrest, since his worth to them had fallen, and a big spy trial would embarrass both Britain and America, and jeopardize future cooperation in high-security areas. Now they welcomed him back, approved the granting of East German nationality, and installed him as £12,000-a-year deputy director of the East German Central Institute for Nuclear Physics at Rossendorf, near Dresden.

In September 1964, he took over as director ... when his boss, Professor Heinz Harwich, defected to America.

Julius and Ethel Rosenberg: Traitors or Victims?

Were Julius and Ethel Rosenberg, as they claimed, 'the first victims of American fascism', condemned to death by 'the most monstrous frame-up in the history of our country'? Or were they, as President Dwight Eisenhower declared, master spies who, 'by immeasurably increasing the chances of atomic war, may have condemned to death tens of millions of innocent people all over the world'? It is a controversy which even America's new Freedom of Information Act has so far failed to resolve conclusively.

The Rosenbergs went to the electric chair in New York State's Sing Sing Prison just after 20.00 on 19 June 1953. It was the first daylight execution anyone could remember, to avoid the Jewish Sabbath which began at sundown. It was the first execution of a woman for a federal offence since the death of Mary Surratt for complicity in the assassination of Abraham Lincoln in 1865. And it was the first – and only – peacetime execution of civilians in America for espionage. What had they done to earn such an unenviable place in history?

It was a time of national paranoia about Communists and Communism. A wave of hysteria, fuelled by the Igor Gouzenko revelations and spy trials, was spearheaded by the Senate Committee for Un-American Activities, later led by the notorious Joseph McCarthy. Reds were suspected under every bed, and careers, notably in Hollywood, were wrecked on the flimsiest of evidence of left-wing leanings. Better dead than red was the watchword of the witchhunt leaders. And woe betide anyone who refused to answer correctly the universal question: 'Are you now or have you ever been a Communist?'

Less publicly than McCarthy, but equally assiduously, J. Edgar Hoover, ambitious and powerful ruler of the FBI, was waging war on Communist sympathizers. Once in his hands, there was only one way a red could make life easier for himself – by unmasking more 'commies'. Since Gouzenko had revealed Russian vice-consul Anatoli Yakovlev as a spymaster in New York, the FBI had managed to turn his courier, Elizabeth Bentley, into an informer, and in the course of investigating one of her tip-offs, they interviewed Harry Gold. Three years later, on 23 May 1950, he was arrested in Philadelphia in connection with his contacts with Klaus Fuchs. Gold made no secret of the fact that he had spied for the Russians since the 1930s and began naming more names, hoping cooperation would make his punishment lighter.

He revealed that, when he went to New Mexico to meet Fuchs in June 1945, he also contacted an American soldier working at the Los Alamos base. The soldier was carrying half of a torn packet top from a Jello pack which matched the half Yakovlev gave Gold in New York. Gold had to say 'Julius sent me'. The soldier then gave him details of the A-bomb implosion lens Fuchs had told the Russians about, and Gold handed over $500.

Gold was able to identify the soldier, from photographs the FBI showed him, as David Greenglass. He and his wife Ruth were already under suspicion for Communist sympathies. Greenglass was then working at a Brooklyn engineering firm with Julius Rosenberg, the son of Russian immigrants, who had married Greenglass's sister, Ethel. The FBI knew Rosenberg had been discharged after five years service in the US Signals Corps for belonging to an illegal organization, the Communist party.

Greenglass was arrested on 16 June 1950, and under questioning by an assistant attorney, admitted not only handing secrets to Gold, but giving information and sketches about the A-bomb to his brother-in-law in New

---

Harry Gold, the Russian agent involved in both the Klaus Fuchs and Rosenberg spy operations, was jailed for 30 years in 1951, but released on parole in 1965. The Kremlin, delighted with his efforts on the Soviet Union's behalf, awarded him the Order of the Red Star. But he died in Philadelphia in 1972 before he could take advantage of one of the benefits the Order gave him ... free rides on the Moscow buses.

Julius Rosenberg

York on two occasions in 1945. He said Rosenberg told him they would go to 'his friends' the Russians. He also revealed that, after Gold's arrest, Rosenberg had advised Greenglass and his wife to flee to Mexico, and offered money to help them go. Other associates of Rosenberg, including a former college friend Morton Sobell, had escaped there, said Greenglass.

Julius Rosenberg was arrested the following day, even though he told the FBI: 'I didn't know anything about the atomic bomb until it was dropped on Japan.' His wife Ethel was arrested six days later, and on 18 August Morton Sobell was held in Laredo, Texas. He was allegedly deported by the Mexicans, though there was a firm suspicion that FBI agents kidnapped him and brought him north of the border to restore him to US jurisdiction.

Greenglass, Gold, Sobell and the two Rosenbergs were indicted, along with Yakovlev – then back in Moscow – on espionage conspiracy charges. Only Gold and Greenglass pleaded guilty. Ruth Greenglass was not indicted, even though her husband claimed Rosenberg sent her to Los Alamos to persuade him to spy. The reasons for her exemption only became clear years later, when FBI papers on the case were released to the public. Greenglass's attorney, O. John Rogge, had done a deal. Greenglass agreed to testify against his brother-in-law as long as Ruth was given immunity, and as long as the prosecution recommended a sentence for him of less than five years. Needing positive evidence against Rosenberg, the authorities agreed.

At that stage, Greenglass's statements had not implicated Rosenberg's wife Ethel. Now both David and Ruth made new admissions, stating that when they gave information to Rosenberg, he handed it to Ethel to type up for the Russians. The significance of this was revealed later when a note written by FBI chief Hoover to Attorney General Howard McGrath came to light. It read: 'There is no question that if Julius Rosenberg would furnish details of his extensive espionage activities, it would be possible to proceed against other individuals. Proceeding against his wife might serve as a lever in this matter.'

The FBI knew from an intercepted Soviet radio message that a husband-and-wife team in New York were involved in espionage. Their surveillance of Rosenberg convinced them he was a vital part of the Russian spy ring. And though they knew that the Greenglasses had been committed Communist workers since their early 20s, they were prepared to allow them to go to court with a story of being lured into espionage by David's brother-in-law.

Apart from the Greenglasses, Harry Gold and Elizabeth Bentley, the prosecution had another witness, Jerome Eugene Tartakow. He befriended Rosenberg over games of chess in the New York House of Detention, where Rosenberg was held pending his trial. Tartakow, also a known Communist, claimed Rosenberg revealed details of his espionage, and how he had taken care of some friends when he realized 'he had played the game and lost'. Rosenberg took a liking to his new young friend, who was serving two years for car thefts, and after his release, got him a chauffeur's job with his defence attorney. Rosenberg realized too late that Tartakow was an FBI informer.

When the hearing against Gold, Greenglass, Sobell and the Rosenbergs began on 6 March 1951, Judge Irving Kaufman quickly made it plain that any evidence about Communist connections was very welcome, despite defence protests that such testimony was no proof of espionage. Greenglass and Gold repeated their versions of the atom secrets hand-overs, Elizabeth Bentley told of telephone calls from a man calling himself Julius, and an electronics engineer, Max Elitcher, admitted acting as a courier between Sobell and Rosenberg.

Royal Navy Sub-Lieutenant David James Bingham was the spy nagged into treachery. Beset by money worries and a fiercely ambitious wife, he agreed in February to her suggestion that he sell secrets to the Russians. Bingham, 31, a £1,843-a-year electronics expert on the anti-submarine frigate *Rothesay,* received £5,000 for telling Moscow in detail about the latest nuclear depth charges, six underwater sonar eyes – recognized as the most advanced submarine detectors in the world – and Naval and NATO tactics and strengths. He gave himself up on 31 August 1971, claiming his conscience was troubling him after being promoted to a hush-hush Anglo American torpedo project. In fact a day earlier, Russian spy Oleg Lyalin had defected, and Bingham knew the game was up for him and his spymaster, Russian embassy assistant naval attaché Lory Torfimovich Kuzmin. At Bingham's trial in Winchester during March 1972. Mr Justice Bridge denounced his 'monstrous betrayal' and Attorney General Sir Peter Rawlinson said he had sold secrets 'almost beyond price'. Bingham was jailed for 21 years, but served only 7, being released on parole. His wife Maureen, 34, who admitted; 'I nagged him into becoming a spy and the Russians gave us money like water' was imprisoned for 2½ years. The couple divorced while in jail, and their four children were taken into local authority care.

Then Rosenberg took the stand. He denied any knowledge of espionage. When asked whether he was a Communist, he invoked the Fifth Amendment of the Constitution, refusing to answer 'on the grounds that it might incriminate me'. But he did admit to admiring Russian achievements, adding: 'I felt and still feel that they contributed a major share in destroying the Hitler beast who killed six million of my co-religionists, and I feel emotional about that.'

Ethel Rosenberg was equally vehement in denying any connection with espionage, and non-committal when Communist associations were aired. In his closing speech, the couple's attorney, Emanuel Bloch, urged the jury to believe his clients rather than the Greenglasses, who had 'put it over on the government'. He added:

> 'David Greenglass was willing to bury his sister and her husband to save his life. Not only are the Greenglasses self-confessed spies, they

are mercenary spies. They'll do anything for money. Any man who will testify against his own flesh and blood, his own sister, is repulsive, revolting, and is violating every code of civilization that ever existed. He is lower than the lowest animal I have ever seen.'

It was all to no avail. The jury found both Rosenbergs and Morton Sobell guilty. Sobell was jailed for the maximum 30 years, with a recommendation against parole. Both the Rosenbergs were condemned to death. The judge told them:

'I consider your crime worse than murder. In murder a criminal kills only his victim. Your conduct in putting into the hands of the Russians the A-bomb years before our best scientists predicted Russia would perfect the bomb has already caused, in my opinion, the Communist aggression in Korea, with the resultant casualties exceeding 50,000 and who knows but that millions more innocent people may pay the price of your treason. Indeed, by your betrayal you have altered the course of history to the disadvantage of our country.'

The two Rosenbergs were taken down to separate cells below the courtroom. There followed an incredible interlude which stunned jailers and fellow prisoners alike. Ethel sang Puccini's aria from *Madame Butterfly*, 'One Fine Day He Shall Return'. As applause rang round the cells, Rosenberg requested another song from the same opera. Ethel sang it, and responded to shouts from other prisoners with more songs, ending with 'The Battle Hymn Of The Republic'.

Emanuel Bloch lodged appeals, telling Rosenberg: 'You are two straws buffeted about by the political winds.' All his efforts were rejected by the courts. Eminent Nobel prizewinners Harold Urey and Albert Einstein aired their doubts in letters to newspapers, saying there was evidence of a family feud between the Greenglasses and the Rosenbergs, and pointing out that, while Greenglass and Gold, who confessed to spying, were jailed for 15 years and 30 years respectively, the only defendants to consistently maintain their innocence had been condemned to die – on the testimony of people who stood to profit from such a verdict.

Three times the campaign to reprieve the Rosenbergs reached President Eisenhower. On 11 February 1953, rejecting petitions for a new trial, he said: 'By their act these two individuals have betrayed the cause of freedom for which free men are fighting and dying at this very hour.' On 16 June he met a delegation of clergymen representing 2,300 church ministers and rejected a petition for executive clemency, admitting in a letter to his son John, serving in Korea, that, although it 'goes against the grain to avoid interfering' when a woman's life was at stake, he considered Ethel the stronger partner in the spy partnership, and added that if he commuted her sentence alone, 'the Soviets would simply recruit their spies from among women from here on'.

Finally, as protests against the deaths reached a crescendo on the actual day of execution, the President issued this statement five hours before the couple were due to walk to the electric chair:

'I am not unmindful of the fact that this case has aroused grave misgivings both here and abroad in the minds of serious people. I can only say that, by immeasurably increasing the chances of atomic war, the Rosenbergs may have condemned to death tens of millions of innocent people all over the world. The execution of two human beings is a grave matter. But even graver is the thought of the millions of dead whose deaths may be directly attributable to what these spies have done.'

Throughout the two-year ordeal of appeals, as each fresh hope was raised and dashed, the Rosenbergs kept each other's spirits up with letters that included expressions of tender love and angry denials of any guilt. There were also poignant scenes when they were allowed visits by their children, Michael and Robert, who were aged eight and four respectively when their parents were sentenced. Rosenberg wrote that he 'broke down and cried like a baby

Dwight and Mamie Eisenhower

> **Giorgio Rinaldi and his wife Angela Maria used their skills as parachutists to spy for Russia. The Italian skydivers travelled throughout the NATO countries giving aerobatic displays, and during rehearsals often photographed secret missile sites or sensitive airport installations. After their arrest in 1967, 29 other Soviet spies in 7 countries were rounded up as a result of Giorgio's admissions.**

because of the children's deep hurt' after one such visit. Finally, after a second plea to the Supreme Court was rejected by five votes to four, the execution date was set for 18 June – the Rosenbergs' 14th wedding anniversary. In the event, the end was delayed by 24 hours.

There remained one way to avert the execution. It was spelled out to both Rosenbergs by James Bennett, federal director of the Bureau of Prisons, on behalf of the Attorney General, Herbert Brownell. Cooperate fully with the government, he said, and we have the basis to recommend clemency.

Ethel asked Bennett if he wanted her to concoct a pack of lies. Julius likened the 'cooperate or die' ultimatum to the rack and screw of medieval torture chambers. And, through his lawyer, he told the world:

'By asking us to repudiate the truth of our innocence, the government admits its own doubts concerning our guilt. We will not help to purify the foul record of a fraudulent conviction and a barbaric sentence ... History will record that we were victims of the most monstrous frame-up in the history of our country.'

A special telephone line to Sing-Sing was kept open right to the last, in case either of the Rosenbergs 'changed their minds'. It remained unused while Ethel wrote her final letters, telling her children: 'Always remember that we were innocent and could not wrong our conscience. We press you close and kiss you with all our strength.' To Emanuel Bloch, charged with guardianship of the children, she wrote: 'You did everything that could be done. We are the first victims of American fascism.'

Julius Rosenberg died first, a flicker of a smile on his lips as he stared calmly in front of him. He did not say a word. As Ethel walked to the electric chair, the rabbi accompanying her made one last plea: 'For the sake of the children who still need you, will you say something which can save you? Must this tragedy be completed?' She replied calmly: 'I have nothing to say. I am ready.' She was 37, her husband two years younger.

Their deaths did not end the agonizing over their guilt. David Greenglass, released in 1960 after serving less than two-thirds of his sentence, was reunited with Ruth. They changed their names to start a new life in anonymity. He stuck to the version of events he had given in court. The FBI also maintained their conviction that the Rosenbergs were major figures in a prime espionage ring whose activities extended far beyond the offences for which they were convicted.

Emanuel Bloch, who died of a heart attack 8 months after the executions aged 52, said at the emotional funeral: 'Insanity, irrationality, barbarism and murder seem to be a part of the feeling of those who rule us.'

Michael and Robert Rosenberg continued to campaign about the innocence of their parents in association with the National Committee to Reopen the Rosenberg Case, and in 1975 Robert wrote a book in which he saw the Watergate scandal under President Richard Nixon as a natural development from the 'showcase trial' of his parents, which he blamed on government abuse of power.

But perhaps writers Sol Stern and Ronald Radosh came closest to the truth of the Rosenberg affair when they wrote in *New Republic* in 1979 of FBI documents 'demonstrating that Ethel was included in the indictment only as a hostage against her husband; and that she was ultimately convicted on tainted evidence obtained at the eleventh hour. The purpose was to pressure her husband into revealing details of his post-war espionage work.'

A dirty trick? Perhaps but then, as we shall see, the intelligence services of the West are far from alone in employing them ...

Cynthia: the Spy They Couldn't Resist

The night-watchman at the French embassy in Washington was wary. He did not trust the couple who pleaded to be allowed to spend nights of passion inside the building. The man said he was married, and had nowhere else to pursue his affair. He always gave generous bribes. But two days earlier, the champagne with which they plied him had made him strangely drowsy. He had slept like a baby all night. Now they were back again. The watchman decided to check what they were really up to. He crept to the door of the room where they were. Gingerly he peeped inside – then backed away. The girl, a green-eyed, auburn-haired beauty, was completely naked, stretched seductively across a couch. Little did the guard at the Vichy French mission realize that his eyes had just feasted on the body of the most successful sex spy of World War 2, a woman whose espionage exploits made those of Mata Hari pale into insignificance.

Amy Elizabeth Thorpe was American-born, but had married British diplomat Arthur Pack during the 1930s. He was a dry, pompous man, completely unsuitable for a girl with her looks and spirit of adventure, but she stuck with him as his work took him to Chile, Spain and finally Poland. There she was at last given the chance of some excitement. In 1937, British intelligence invited her to become an agent. She accepted readily.

Soon Amy – codenamed Cynthia during the war – was the mistress of a well-placed official at the Polish Foreign Ministry in Warsaw. He told her of developments in Germany and Czechoslovakia, useful inside information for the British. But more important, she learned of Polish engineers working on a version of the German Enigma cypher machine. It was the first step in an operation which led to Britain acquiring the code which cracked Hitler's secret communications.

By 1941, Cynthia was in New York, the prize agent in the star-studded pack at British Security Coordination. William Stephenson needed someone to lure secrets from the embassies of the Italians and Vichy French. Cynthia's successes in Poland made her ideal. She was established in a comfortable home in Washington, and joined the cocktail party circuit in the American capital, renewing acquaintance with an old flame, Admiral Alberto Lais, now Mussolini's naval attaché in the USA.

Unlike later sex spies, Cynthia made no secret of her intentions. She blatantly told Lais she needed Italian codes and cyphers to help Allied intelligence in the war effort against his country. He was so besotted by her beauty that he provided them for copying. Even BSC veterans were stunned. One said: 'It seems fantastic that a man of his experience and seniority who was by instinct, training and conviction a patriotic officer, should have been so enfeebled by passion.' The Italian codes helped the outnumbered British fleet outwit Axis ships in the Mediterranean, and were of priceless value in the Allied invasions of North Africa. But once Lais had served his purpose, Cynthia threw him over. She told the FBI about his knowledge of sabotage in American ports, and he was sent home as an undesirable.

Her next target was the embassy of Vichy France, the pro-Nazi puppet government set up after Hitler's occupation of the country. Captain Charles Brousse, a former naval pilot, was the ambassador's press officer. He had worked with British intelligence before the war, but was sickened when British ships attacked the French navy at Oran in 1940 to prevent the fleet being used by the Germans. He was also no friend of Americans, believing them vulgar, with no understanding of the political realities of his country.

Slowly, seductively, Cynthia won him over. She was as smart mentally as she was attractive physically, and Brousse was captivated. He even agreed to her moving into the hotel where he lived with his third wife. He told her about a cache of French gold hidden on the Caribbean island of Martinique. BSC sent agents to locate it and prevent it falling into Nazi hands. Stephenson then cheekily used control of the gold as security in negotiations for badly-needed loans from America for the British war effort. Cynthia also learned of more Nazi plots against Allied shipping. And she was told of German agents in North and South America funded via the French legation. Then came a difficult order – get hold of new French naval codes.

These were locked in a strongroom at Vichy France's embassy in Washington. Even Brousse had no access to them. Together they planned

---

Wing-Commander Forest Frederick Yeo-Thomas was awarded the Military Cross and George Medal for his adventures with the British Special Operations Executive in occupied France. Once, ordered back to London when the German presence around Arras became too strong, he travelled to the plane pick-up point hidden under flowers in a funeral hearse, gripping a sten-gun to defend the secrets he was carrying home concealed in the coffin should German troops halt the cortège.

their love tryst deception of the night watchman. Generous tips and the 'nowhere to go' sob story made their faces familiar. Then came the night when they brought the bottles of champagne. The watchman's suspicions were correct. While he slept off drugs in the booze, Cynthia and Brousse let an expert locksmith in through a side door to study the vault where the codes were kept. And on the night the watchman peeped at naked Cynthia, BSC experts were at the vault copying the vital cyphers.

Like Cynthia's work on Enigma and the Italian codes, it was an espionage coup that changed the course of the war. In 1945, official BSC papers said the powerful and intoxicating hold Cynthia established over worldly wise men 'opened the way back into France and ultimately into Germany'. And when H. Montgomery Hyde, Stephenson's official biographer, asked Cynthia years later whether she was a little ashamed of her sexual antics, she replied: 'Ashamed? Not in the least. My superiors told me that my work saved thousands of British and American lives.'

Cynthia volunteered for further service in Europe. She wanted to be parachuted behind the German lines as a secret assassin. Though she had taken risks before, this time spymasters ruled it was too dangerous. After 1945, Brousse divorced his wife, and Cynthia's husband Arthur Pack was found shot dead in Argentina. He had been in poor health. The way was clear for Cynthia to marry Brousse, which she did. They lived in a castle in the South of France until 1963, when the world's most successful amorous agent died of cancer. Brousse died ten years later.

Eric Erickson: Oil Salesman Extraordinary

American spies monitoring German manoeuvres before the decisive Battle of the Rhine in 1945 stared in astonishment as Hitler's on-the-run army prepared for its last stand. Horses were pulling ammunition trucks to the front. And tanks were being dragged into position by oxen. It was final proof of the success of one of the most dangerous espionage exploits of the war. Businessman Eric Erickson had fooled the Nazi top brass for more than three years. Travelling freely through Germany, once on a pass personally provided by SS supremo Heinrich Himmler, he located and inspected vital oil and synthetic fuel refineries, then told Allied bombers the best way to destroy them. But his triumph was achieved at a tragic price. To maintain his cover, Erickson was forced to watch helplessly as a firing squad slaughtered the girl he loved.

Erickson, born in Brooklyn, New York, had become an international oil dealer and a Swedish citizen by the time war broke out. During his world-wide travels, he was often in Germany and had noticed with concern the rise of the Nazis. Then, over dinner in Stockholm with an old acquaintance, Laurence Steinhardt, the American ambassador to Russia, he was offered a way of hitting back. Steinhardt knew that, sooner or later, America would become embroiled in the fighting. Already its secret services were preparing for the day. But they needed information on the Nazi oil supply lifelines. Erickson, with fluent German, established contacts in the Reich and good reasons for going there on business, could provide it. Would he? Erickson quickly agreed to try.

For 18 frustrating months he carefully cultivated a new image. He alienated all his old friends by angrily denouncing their anti-Nazi opinions, often in public. He hung pictures of Hitler in his office and home. Gradually he built up contacts at the German Legation. As a final coup de grâce, he persuaded Prince Carl Gustav Bernadotte, nephew of King Gustav, to forfeit popularity in neutral Sweden by pretending to sympathize with the Nazis. The Prince, convinced that Erickson's mission might shorten the war, bravely agreed to dine with local German big-wigs and flatter their snobbish egos. In September 1941, Erickson was at last allowed a visa for a business trip to Germany, having overcome all distrust at his American origins. Only one other Swede knew he was playing a role – his new bride, Ingrid.

The Gestapo were waiting when his plane touched down at Berlin's Tempelhof airport, and Obersturmbannführer Baron Franz von Nordhoff gave him a severe grilling about his attitudes to Hitler, the Nazis, America and the possibility of a Nazified Sweden. The smooth-tongued spy eased his way out of every tight corner, and was allowed to continue with his tour, ostensibly to buy German oil for his country. He memorized everything that might prove useful to the Allies. He also recruited a network of 12 trusted old friends to provide him with information about the oil plants where they worked. It took time to convince them he was really working for the Americans, and was not a Nazi agent provocateur. Many demanded a slip of paper, signed by Erickson, to prove to the Allies after the war that they had helped the cause. Erickson knew that each document would be his death warrant if it fell into German hands, but he had no choice but to sign.

Erickson travelled from Berlin to Hamburg, and on to Halle and Hanover. He memorized the exact layout of refineries, production details, nearby

> **Secret American bomb-sights helped the Luftwaffe blitz London and other cities during the Battle of Britain. Blueprints were stolen by ardent Nazi Hermann Lang while he worked at the Norden engineering works in Long Island, and were handed to an Abwehr agent in America. Delighted Luftwaffe chief Marshal Hermann Goering gave Lang 10,000 marks. He was arrested after an FBI spy infiltrated the Nazi secret service in America, and jailed for 14 years in 1941. He returned to Bavaria in 1950.**

landmarks, the site of anti-aircraft batteries and fighter plane airfields. And on his return to Sweden, he poured the detailed data into a Dictaphone tube provided by American agents. Soon the oil Erickson had bought in exchange for iron ore credits began to arrive. Unknown to the Nazis, some of it was used to fuel British patrol boats which were running the German naval blockade of Scandinavia to collect Swedish ball-bearings and other precious parts needed in the war effort.

When the Japanese attack on Pearl Harbour brought America into the war officially, Erickson came under more severe pressure. Some of his relations in the US cut all connections with the 'Nazi-lover'. The Gestapo checked him out again, even taking the trouble to collect his records from Cornell University where he had taken an engineering degree in 1921. Once more he was able to set their minds at rest, and throughout 1942 he made several trips to Germany, sometimes with Prince Carl. He also began visiting countries under Nazi occupation, inspecting refineries commandeered for the Reich war effort. On 12 June his information was acted on for the first time. American B-24 bombers flew from Egypt to attack the vital oil base at Ploesti, Rumania. Thereafter the businessman-spy spent hours in air raid shelters during his trips to Germany as the US Eighth Air Force accurately blasted refineries in Hamburg, Hanover, Marienburg and Ludwigshafen. During the summer of 1943 177 heavy bombers attacked Ploesti again. Erickson and his network were able to report that they had knocked out more than 40 per cent of the plant's refining capacity.

Erickson was living on a knife-edge. Apart from the possibility of being killed by the planes his intelligence was guiding, there was the constant fear of betrayal to the Gestapo, either by one of his agents or by accident. A crisis blew up when Hamburg contact Otto Holtz, one of the men who demanded a potentially lethal slip of paper, died unexpectedly. Erickson had to fly to Germany and retrieve the evidence from the bank vault before the man's pro-

Nazi widow or son found it. It took two nerve-racking days of tact and subterfuge.

There was little escape from the relentless pressure. Erickson dared not let himself relax for a moment. When forced to share rooms at crowded hotels with other travellers, he took pills to stay awake, afraid of giving himself away by talking in his sleep. Then, late in 1942, he met attractive brunette Marianne von Mollendorf, another secret Allied agent. He became a courier to smuggle her secrets out of Germany, and she advised him on oil contacts and political changes. At first they pretended to be lovers as cover for clandestine meetings. Later they no longer needed to pretend.

In May 1944 waves of Allied bombers began blitzing refineries throughout the Reich. German fighters sent up to fend them off were ruthlessly shot down, 2,500 in one month alone. As the Luftwaffe ran short of planes, Nazi oil production was cut by half and more than 100,000 men diverted to repair work. The damage was a significant factor in the success of the D-Day landings and the long haul to Berlin. But it also gave Erickson a problem. The Germans now had no surplus oil to sell to Sweden. The excuse for his business trips had vanished. Then he came up with a brilliant solution. Instead of buying oil, he would pose as a seller. He offered to build a synthetic fuel refinery in Sweden, safe from the bombers, to supply the creaking Nazi war machine.

German officials in Stockholm were impressed by the carefully forged dossier of plans and bogus pledges of financial backing from influential Swedes. They forwarded them to Berlin, and Erickson followed to wine and dine decision makers. It took time to convince them, and required several trips to the German capital. Late in 1944 he flew into Templehof again – and was whisked off to the worst moment of his life.

Gestapo men, waiting as usual, drove him away, but not to their massive

---

American cryptographers broke the Japanese Purple Code after the disaster of Pearl Harbour. In May 1942 it enabled them to gain revenge and turn the tide of war in the Pacific. Admiral Chester Nimitz learned of a planned Japanese invasion of an island codenamed AF. He was certain the target was Midway, but just to make sure, he ordered the commander there to radio HQ that he was running short of water. Three days later, Japanese radio traffic revealed the water shortage at their target, AF. When the attack came, American reinforcements inflicted a shattering defeat.

grey HQ at 8 Prinz Albrechtstrasse. This time the destination was Moabat jail. Erickson was convinced his espionage had been discovered, and he knew, from past warnings, how the Nazis dealt with those who betrayed their trust. Gloomily, he watched from a cell window as a guard loaded a machine gun in the prison courtyard. Then he was led out into the sunshine. With relief he saw he was just one of a group of foreign visitors privileged to witness some executions. But when the condemned prisoners were led out, his heart turned to stone. Among them was Marianne von Mollendorf.

Fury and fear fought within him. Did the Nazis know of their liaison? Would Marianne think he had betrayed her? Could he, even at this late stage, do anything to save her? Was this all a charade to trap him into incriminating action? Their eyes met, but Marianne showed no flicker of recognition. Erickson steeled himself, battling for self-control, as she stood proudly in line. He forced himself to watch as the machine gun cut her and the other prisoners to ribbons.

Erickson went through the motions in the days that followed. And before the end of the week he was granted an interview about the proposed Swedish refinery by SS chief Himmler himself. It was soon clear that the Reichführer was as mentally unstable as rumours suggested, but Erickson cautiously managed to persuade him of the need for a personal inspection of German synthetic fuel plants to establish exactly what would be required in Stockholm. He was given a pass which allowed unrestricted travel.

Erickson began his tour, but was quickly aware, despite Himmler's words, that the Gestapo were tailing him. It was important to let them do so. As a businessman he was not supposed to know about espionage techniques, but it meant adapting rendezvous tactics. Information had to be left in the form of seemingly innocent notes on restaurant tables, slipped to contacts at fleeting meetings on street corners, whispered in the darkened corridors of bordellos. Finally, in Leipzig, Erickson's luck ran out. He was recognized by Franz Schroeder, an ardent Nazi who remembered the Swede's pre-war, pro-Jewish attitude. Erickson took him for beers at a tavern to try to explain his change of heart, but he could see Schroeder was unimpressed. When they parted, Erickson knew the German would alert the Gestapo. He had to be silenced. But first the spy had to shake off his SS shadow.

Darting through a nearby hotel, he leapt into a taxi, flashed his authority from the Gestapo chief, and ordered the driver to take the road down which Schroeder had walked. He soon spotted his quarry, and paid off the taxi to follow on foot. Schroeder went into a telephone box, and Erickson crept closer. Sure enough, the German was phoning an SS friend about his suspicions. Before he could go into details, Erickson pounced, driving his pocket knife into the back of the man's head, and wresting the phone from him. Memories of Marianne's death flashed through his mind, strengthening his resolve, somehow hardening his heart against natural repugnance at killing for the first time. As the body slumped to the floor of the kiosk Erickson vanished into the shadows.

Convinced that it would not take his Gestapo shadow long to make a connection between the body and the man Erickson had met, the Swede cabled Prince Carl, using the code which signified an emergency. By return came a telegram saying Erickson's wife was seriously ill, and he should come to Stockholm immediately. Sending his apologies to Himmler, who was due to meet him again, Erickson took the first available flight out of Germany. His American controllers agreed he could risk no more trips. But already he had done enough.

Bombing raids continued to sap the strength of Hitler's forces. Now the chemical plants Erickson reconnoitred were targets. The Nazis retreated through Europe, abandoning tanks, trucks and jeeps to conserve fuel. The Luftwaffe cut back on training time for pilots and tests on aircraft engines for the same reason, with catastrophic results. And munitions factories using the by-products of the synthetic fuel process ran short of raw material for shells and bombs.

In Stockholm, Erickson and Ingrid devoured every report of Allied advances, and rejoiced on 7 May 1945 at the German surrender. But they remained outcasts for another month. Then the cream of Swedish society were invited to a party at the American embassy. As they sipped their cocktails, the guests of honour were announced – and in walked the Ericksons and Prince Carl. Gasps of shocked disgust soon turned to humble apologies as the truth behind their pro-Nazi stance was at last revealed. And within days newspapers throughout the world were hailing the secret heroes who had done so much to crush Hitler.

Robert Lee Johnson: GI with a Grudge

S ergeant Robert Lee Johnson was one of life's misfits, a coarse, hard-drinking, gambling soldier. But the GI with a grudge was to provide Moscow with a rich harvest from seeds sown in unlikely ground and patiently nurtured for ten years.

Johnson was a military clerk with the US Army in Berlin in 1952. When passed over for promotion he developed an obsession to get even with his superiors. The best way, he decided, would be to defect to the Russians, and become a radio star, broadcasting propaganda to the West. But the Soviet officials he approached soon realized he was not the sort of citizen the Kremlin would welcome. They suggested another way to avenge his injustices – spying.

At first Johnson was enthusiastic. He photographed almost every paper he could find. The Russians, overwhelmed, asked him to desist, and instead suggested specific topics in which they were interested. Johnson, who had minimal security clearance, found such documents hard to come by. He lost interest in espionage, and when he transferred to a French posting of no interest to Moscow, the KGB ceased contact. In 1956, Johnson left the Army and returned to America. He lost what money he had gambling, and was living off the immoral earnings of the Viennese prostitute who had become his wife when, in January 1957, the Russians reactivated him. He was offered £150 a month for details about American rockets. Johnson applied to the Army and he was accepted at his old rank. He was posted as a guard to the Palos Verdes missile base in California.

Johnson pleased his KGB masters, providing drawings and photographs of missiles, overheard comments on their capabilities, and even a sample of rocket fuel. He continued to spy when transferred to a base at El Paso, Texas. Then he was sent overseas again, to Orléans in France. And there the Russians stepped up the pressure on their avenging soldier.

Johnson's wife had a nervous breakdown – the first of several – in 1960, and was admitted to an army hospital in Paris. Vitali Sergeevich Orzhurmov, Johnson's Soviet spymaster, suggested he apply for a job in the French capital on compassionate grounds. And in March 1961, he became a clerk-guard at the Orly airport Armed Forces Courier Centre.

This compact concrete bunker behind barbed wire in a remote corner of the airfield was closely guarded round the clock, every day of the year. It was one of the most sensitive mail clearing houses in the world. Vital military and diplomatic documents passing to and from Washington were delivered here. Orders and code changes to the US Mediterranean fleet and American Army bases, plus NATO up-dates on strategy for defending Europe, all passed through the bunker's steel vault, guarded by two steel doors. The Russians had long schemed how to have a look inside the 'impregnable' citadel of secrets. Now the unlikely Johnson was to be their passport.

A rule that French nationals could not be interrogated in US security clearance checks helped Johnson win the job. There was no major blemish on his past Army record, and officers appointed him, unaware that neighbours had heard Johnson's wife accuse him of espionage during their frequent and loud domestic disputes. Once their man was safely on the staff, the Russians questioned him closely on routine at the Centre. Johnson explained that the first door to the vault was secured by a metal bar with combination locks at either end. The inner door had a sophisticated lock opened by a key – but no one, not even a general, could open it unaccompanied.

Johnson was told to lie low and learn more about the vault without arousing suspicion. He volunteered to re-decorate the white-walled inner sanctum when the task came up, and was able to report that there was no secret alarm system inside. Months later, a young lieutenant momentarily left him alone as they sorted through a delivery to the vault, and Johnson took an impression of the inner door key in modelling clay the Russians had provided. He obtained the combination of one of the metal bar locks when a new officer carelessly wrote it down to memorize it, then discarded the scrap of paper in a wastepaper basket. But the other combination proved elusive.

Johnson now volunteered for all the unpopular overnight and weekend shifts, when only one man was left on guard. He explained that he needed midweek days free to visit his wife in hospital. The Russians gave him a Minox camera to take pictures of the combination lock from every angle. Later, they provided him with a circular metal plate and a metal cone 22.8 cm (9 in) long. He was to connect them either side of the lock, and stand clear for 30 minutes because the lock-picking computer was radio-active. Johnson completed the operation during his regular 18.00 hours Saturday to 06.00 hours Sunday duty. Three weeks later his Soviet controller handed him the necessary numbers to open the combination.

By now Orzhurmov had been joined in Paris by Feliks Aleksandrovich Ivanov, another diplomat who was really a KGB agent. The Johnson operation had become one of Moscow's top priorities, and they needed two men to ensure no unforeseen hitches. A routine was carefully rehearsed. Johnson was to take documents from the vault and deliver them to one of his

A British MP was charged with spying for an Iron Curtain country in 1970. Will Owen, 68 and Labour MP for Morpeth until he resigned his seat when charged, admitted receiving £2,300 from a man at the Czech embassy he knew to be a spy, in return for giving him confidential information he acquired as a member of the House of Commons Estimates Committee. Though acquitted by the jury, who argued that such information was not covered by the Official Secrets Act under which he was charged, Owen was ordered to pay £2,000 towards the cost of the trial. And Josef Frolik, the Czech defector who led MI5 to Owen, maintained the MP handed over secret military facts during a 15-year espionage career in which he was paid up to £500 a month. Owen died in April, 1981.

controllers on a lonely service road at 00.15 hours. He was to collect them again in a deserted lane near a cemetery 8 km (5 miles) away at 03.15 hours and replace them in the vault. If the overnight operation was undiscovered, he was to drop a Lucky Strike cigarette packet marked with an X by a telephone box on his way home.

The Russians had left nothing to chance. They showed Johnson two identical Air France flight bags. He was to deliver the documents in one, and receive in return the other containing a drugged bottle of Cognac and four antidote tablets. If anyone arrived unexpectedly at the Centre before his delivery or pick-up rendezvous, Johnson was to offer him a drink to knock him out for a few hours. If Johnson, too, was forced to drink from the doctored Cognac, the pills would prevent the drug affecting him. Johnson was also rehearsed in a getaway scheme should anything go wrong. Using a Canadian passport in his name, hidden along with money and instructions inside a hollow 'rock' in a field 16 km (10 miles) outside Paris, he was to flee to Brussels. He would be contacted there at Chaussée de Fôret using a recognition code based on identical 1921 American silver dollars.

Johnson first plundered the vault on 16 December 1962. It took him just two minutes to open the three locks and select a bagful of large manila envelopes bearing red and blue seals. A team of Russian specialists at the Soviet embassy in Paris, specially flown in via Algeria, carefully opened each one, copied the contents, and resealed them while Johnson sat at the Centre, watching the clock until his 03.15 replacement run. The plot worked perfectly, as did a re-run the following Sunday. And soon after Christmas, his Russian spymasters told him the Kremlin was so delighted with his efforts that he had been made a major in the Red Army, and given a US $2,000 bonus. Some of the most interesting documents had been read by Nikita Khruschev personally.

Flattered by such praise and appreciation, Johnson felt that at last he was really getting even with the Army. Now the vault was to be raided only at four to six week intervals, each time with the approval of the Politburo. This spy was too valuable to take any chances which might expose him to discovery.

To Moscow's consternation, things started to go wrong, despite the meticulous planning. At one 03.15 pick-up in February, Johnson's old Citroen car refused to start, and he and his Soviet contact spent 20 minutes making increasingly desperate attempts to get it going before succeeding. Johnson was given the money to buy a Mercedes. Then the whole escape network was alerted because Johnson forgot to drop his all-clear cigarette packet. It meant two days of writing explanatory reports for his long-suffering Russian minders. In April there was an even worse slip-up. Johnson fell asleep before the 03.15 rendezvous. Panic-stricken, Ivanov took the risk of driving to the Centre, and dropping the air flight bag packed with secrets in Johnson's car. The slovenly spy woke just in time, and was re-locking the last combination when his relief guard arrived.

Johnson told the Russians he was unable to get away because a courier arrived who refused his offer of the Cognac. But his spymasters knew he was lying. Couriers never arrived on Sunday mornings. They feared he had been detected and 'turned' by the Americans, so all operations were called off for the summer. Johnson was told it was because the nights were too short. In September, the vault plundering would begin again.

It did not, simply because Johnson was at last promoted and transferred, first to Seine Area Command HQ, then back to Washington, where his wife had been sent for further psychiatric treatment. The Russians hoped they could use him again later if he landed a posting in the Pentagon. But Johnson's unstable home life made that too impossible. In October, 1964, after yet another bitter row with his wife, he left their Arlington home for a gambling spree in Las Vegas. As an Army deserter, Johnson was investigated by the FBI. When agents questioned his wife, she accused Johnson of spying.

Johnson, who had surrendered to police, drunk and penniless, at Reno, Nevada, at first offered to become a counter-spy for the FBI. His offer was treated with contempt. Then he opened up with details of his espionage 'revenge' on America.

A Federal Court at Alexandria jailed him for 25 years on 30 July 1965. Johnson pleaded guilty, so the American public learned little of what he had done. Even US espionage experts could not estimate the exact extent of the damage he had caused. They had to assume the Russians might have seen every document that passed through Orly between 16 December 1962 and 21 April 1963. The Defence Department admitted: 'Our losses are enormous. Some are irreparable and incalculable. Had we not discovered the losses and had there been war, the damage might very well have proved fatal.'

Soon after the trial, authentic-looking US contingency plans began arriving at newspaper offices in Italy and Germany, purporting to show eventualities in which NATO would wage bacteriological and nuclear war against civilians in Western Europe and the Middle East. The scare reports were the more alarming because Johnson's theft of real documents had helped make the forgeries perfect.

At least four of the Soviet team involved in running Johnson received Russia's highest decoration, the Order of Lenin. But Johnson's story ended in the sordid fashion that he had lived his life. On 18 May, 1972, his son Robert, a Vietnam veteran, visited his 52-year-old father in Lewisburg Penitentiary, Pennsylvania, and plunged a knife into the spy's chest. Johnson died within an hour.

Chapter eight

UNSOLVED CRIMES

Occasionally there is a crime committed that cannot be solved. The massive manhunts and painstaking investigations lead nowhere. A cheat, thief or maniac may go free. A cunning criminal may live to strike again. Or, even when apprehended, a villain may leave an agonizing question mark over his or her foul deed.

The World's Last Airship

I t was a monster of the skies, a wonder of technology and engineering. The giant airship *Hindenburg* was more than 245 m (800 ft) long and stabilized by a tailfin as high as a ten-storey building. Its four powerful diesel engines gave it the power to cruise effortlessly above the clouds at 36 metres per second (80 mph.). The airship could carry 100 passengers through the atmosphere for a week in a style as opulent as any ocean liner.

When all the 16 bags inside its 22.8 m (75 ft) diameter frame were filled with hydrogen, the airship would wrench itself away from the ground with a lifting force of 239 tonnes (235 tons), enough to raise a modern jumbo jet. Admittedly the properties of hydrogen gas, lighter than the surrounding air, which gave the *Hindenburg* the lift to soar into the sky, brought the risks and dangers of explosion. But with more than a quarter of a century of hard-won experience, the Zeppelin Company was confident that no mishap would endanger their new flagship. They knew that the hydrogen in the gas bags, more than 230,000 cubic metres (7,200,000 cubic feet) of highly inflammable gas, would erupt in a devastating explosion if it was ever ignited. But the design, they said, was flawless. Only an act of God, or deliberate sabotage by a madman, could damage the *Hindenburg*.

And when the *Hindenburg* was consumed in a fire-ball over New Jersey on 6 May 1937, killing 13 of its passengers, 22 of its crew and 1 ground control worker, both the American Goverment and Hitler's Nazi regime conspired to cover up any clues to what may have been the biggest crime in aviation history.

While the fledgling airliners of the 1920s and 1930s were plagued by bad weather and mechanical breakdowns trying to operate services between towns only a few hundred miles apart, the monster airships of Germany appeared regularly over the skyline of Rio de Janeiro and New York.

They had become known simply as Zeppelins, after their brilliant but eccentric designer, the Graf Ferdinand von Zeppelin. Born into a noble Prussian family in 1838, he was an adventurous 23-year-old when he obtained an introduction to US President Abraham Lincoln during the American Civil War and joined the Union Army as a 'guest' cavalry officer.

But the young soldier soon became bored by the slow pace of the war and joined a civilian expedition to explore the sources of the Mississippi River. On a scouting mission at St Paul, Minnesota, he took his first ride in a tethered balloon to survey miles of countryside in one brief flight.

If only balloons could be powered and steered, he enthused, what a perfect gun platform and bombing weapon they would make, soaring safely over the slogging infantry and cavalrymen on the field. His vision of giant balloons or dirigibles as weapons of war never left him but he stayed an earthbound cavalry officer until the end of his military career at the age of 52.

Within a few years of retiring, he had applied for a patent for an airship and began experimenting with the designer, Dr Hugo Eckener, an experienced sailor and meteorologist, at their little workshop near Lake Constance in southern Germany.

By 1909 Zeppelin had formed the world's first airship passenger service, Deutsche Luftschiffahrts Aktien Gesellschaft – DELAG. Operating flights between Berlin, Frankfurt, Hamburg and Dresden, his airships carried 32,750 passengers on 1,600 flights in 5 years without a single accident.

Then came 1914 and the Zeppelins went to war.

The Zeppelin raids over England caused little material damage but they raised panic among the population of London. The sight of the dreaded airships caught in the searchlights, cascading their bombs on to the capital, brought Londoners out into the streets, screaming and shaking their fists impotently in the air.

But within two years the British air aces in their tiny biplane fighters were more than a match for the Zeppelin monsters. In their hydrogen bags the Zeppelins carried the seeds of their own destruction. It took only one hit from the newly developed ZPT tracer bullets coated in burning phosphorus, to turn the airships into flying holocausts.

Graf von Zeppelin died in 1917, just as it was proved that his airships were too vulnerable to gunfire to be machines of war.

But Dr Hugo Eckener struggled through the post-war economic ruin of Germany as chairman of the Zeppelin Company, dreaming of a peaceful future for the airships as transatlantic transports.

In July 1928, the world's most advanced passenger airship, the *Graf Zeppelin*, made its maiden flight on the 90th anniversary of the old Count's birth. Three months later, with 20 passengers aboard, it made its first transatlantic voyage to New York where Eckener and the crew were treated to a ticker-tape welcome. In the next five years of operation on regular services to North and South America, the *Graf Zeppelin* established an unrivalled airship mastery of the skies.

The prestige of this achievement was not lost on the new Nazi masters of Germany. Eckener was not popular with the new regime. Before their rise to power he had made radio broadcasts in Germany condemning their brutality. But with the Nazis controlling the purse strings of German industry, including the Zeppelin Company, he was powerless to stop the traditional black, white and red livery colours of the Zeppelins being repainted with the swastika, the symbol of Hitler and his Nazis.

Eckener, a stubborn 68-year-old, was defiant when he was summoned before Dr Joseph Goebbels, the Propaganda Minister, in 1936 when his newest airship, the biggest, fastest and most powerful, was unveiled.

The airship must be called 'Adolf Hitler', he was told by the Nazi minister. 'No,' Eckener replied. 'I warn you the sight of the swastika on our airships is already provoking hostility when we dock in the United States. If the new airship is called "Adolf Hitler" it will be the target for hatred and sabotage.'

Eckener won the day, but Goebbels decreed that in the German press and on radio the new airship would not be referred to by its Zeppelin Company name, *Hindenburg*. In the Nazi press it was referred to by its works design title – LZ 129.

When the *Hindenburg* began its regular services from Frankfurt to the Lakeheath Naval Air Base in New Jersey it received a rapturous welcome. But as the trickle of persecuted refugees from the Nazis reached a flood-tide on America's shores, Eckener's fears of flaunting the swastika proved to be well founded. In August 1936 more than 100 American demonstrators, posing as celebrating visitors, boarded the German liner *Bremen* as she lay at a pier in New York and sparked off a riotous protest against Hitler's involvement in the Spanish Civil War.

Security was stepped up at the liner berths and at the *Hindenburg*'s hanger across the river at Lakeheath. The American government was concerned by reports that the *Hindenburg* had even been the target of riflemen who had fired potshots at the Zeppelin from atop the Manhattan skyscrapers and from the open fields of New Jersey.

The German ambassador in Washington had received hundreds of threatening phone calls and letters from opponents of the Nazis who were determined to destroy the *Hindenburg* and keep the swastika out of American skies.

Aware of the serious blow to their regime's prestige if the *Hindenburg* was sabotaged, the Sicherheitsddinst, the security élite of Hitler's SS, began to conduct searches of the *Hindenburg*'s hangar in Frankfurt, and the airship itself, before each flight.

On Monday 3 May 1937, Colonel Fritz Erdmann, the new chief of Special Intelligence for the Luftwaffe, was ordered to SS headquarters in Berlin for a briefing on the *Hindenburg* flight due to leave that day.

Erdmann and the two junior officers who were to accompany him in civilian clothes on the flight to America were startled by the briefing given to them by SS Sturmbannführer Major Kurt Hufschmidt. He told them: 'We have reliable information that an attempt will be made to destroy your flight.

The *Hindenburg* in flames

The sabotage will come by bomb, probably after the *Hindenburg* has arrived over American soil. This attack is designed to make the Fatherland look vulnerable in the eyes of our enemies, disloyal Germans, Jews and troublemakers in the United States.'

The ss man also revealed that in March 1935 a bomb had been discovered in the main dining saloon of the *Graf Zeppelin*, hidden underneath a table by one of the passengers. The bomb had been defused safely.

He also told of a Gestapo search of a Frankfurt hotel room for a mysterious passenger who had just arrived from America on a *Hindenburg* flight. The man had travelled on a forged Swedish passport and although he eluded the Gestapo, they searched his room and found detailed technical drawings of both the *Graf Zeppelin* and the *Hindenburg*.

Erdmann was given a rundown on suspect passengers who were making the flight with him. They included: a German couple, both journalists, who were known to have a Jewish writer as a friend, a young photographer from Bonn whose cut-price fare had been arranged by a senior Zeppelin executive since sacked for having Jewish ancestry, a 36-year-old American advertising executive who was known to be a spy for US intelligence, and Joseph Spah, a 35-year-old music hall entertainer from Douglaston, Long Island.

Spah was a comedian and acrobat who travelled on a French passport and had an American wife. But to the humourless ss man he was a suspect because his music hall act, popular in parts of Berlin, was known to contain jokes against people in authority.

At the departure hanger in Frankfurt, all passengers and their luggage were thoroughly searched. Security men confiscated all the young photographer's flashbulbs, fearing they could be used to start a deliberate fire. They also X-rayed a small Dresden china souvenir doll brought on board by Spah.

But the Luftwaffe intelligence officer accepted the assurance of the *Hindenburg* captain, Ernst Lehmann, that the two married journalists were both personal friends who were writing his biography. And Captain Lehmann insisted that the American spy working for the advertising agency had been under close surveillance and posed no threat. The intelligence officer accepted his explanation.

Joseph Spah, according to the captain, was no more than a nuisance. He had brought along a frisky young German shepherd dog which was travelling with him in order to become part of his new act at Radio City Music Hall in New York. The dog travelled in the freight compartment at the rear of the airship and twice Spah had been found unsupervised in the area, away from the authorized passenger lounges. But they accepted his explanation that he must personally feed the nervous young dog during the two-and-a-half-day journey.

Colonel Erdmann reassured the captain: 'Any of our passengers sabotaging the *Hindenburg* on this voyage would be committing suicide. I think the attempt will come after we have moored at Lakeheath. Then it will be the responsibility of the ground staff to ensure the safety of the airship.'

But according to many investigators and historians, a bomb was already on board. An incendiary device, wired to a darkroom photographic timer powered by two small batteries was hidden inside the explosive hydrogen atmosphere of Gas Cell Four, near the tail of the *Hindenburg*.

The *Hindenburg* was due to moor at Lakeheath at 06.00 on 6 May. But the night before it ran into strong headwinds over Newfoundland and the airship radioed it would not arrive until 18.00. The *Hindenburg*'s docking was always made precisely at 06.00 or 18.00 to allow definite working times for the ground crew.

A small reception committee waiting at Lakeheath for the *Hindenburg*'s arrival took advantage of the postponement to go off for dinner in the nearby town of Toms River. They included broadcaster Herbert Morrison, who was preparing to record a commentary on the airship's mooring for the listeners of station WLS in Chicago.

By mid-afternoon on 6 May the *Hindenburg* had passed Long Island sound and the sight of the giant airship with its glittering swastikas brought traffic to a halt in Manhattan. As it crossed the baseball stadium at Ebbet's Field in Brooklyn, the game between the Brooklyn Dodgers and the Pittsburgh Pirates was suspended while players and spectators alike gaped in admiration at the pride of Hitler's Germany.

Just before 16.00 the airship arrived over Lakeheath, but Captain Lehmann set a southerly cruising course to ride out the stormy winds for two hours until the ground crew mustered for his appointed time of arrival.

At 17.22, the *Hindenburg* was being advised by ground control to keep circling ahead of an approaching storm front. And it was then, it is believed, that a timer on the detonator of the fire-bomb hidden in Gas Cell Four was set – for two hours hence.

An hour later Lakeheath radioed: 'Advise landing now' and the airship headed for the airfield. At 19.05 the *Hindenburg* crossed the south fence of the airfield. As 92 US Navy men and 139 civilian workers prepared to reach for the mooring lines which would be dropped from the *Hindenburg* to secure the airship, radio reporter Herbert Morrison could see cheerful passengers at the open promenade deck windows waving at him.

At 19.22 the *Hindenburg* lowered the mooring lines and gave one last burst of her engines to line the airship up with the 61 m (200 ft) mooring tower.

If the airship had been on schedule, all the passengers would have disembarked and it would have been floating at the mooring mast with only a skeleton crew... But the timer on the bomb had been set to the original schedule.

At 19.22 there was a puff of flame and a fire-ball 122 m (400 ft) across erupted from the linen-covered framework of the *Hindenburg*.

Herbert Morrison had been describing the scene as the airship docked:

> What a sight it is ... a thrilling one ... a marvellous sight. The sun is striking the window of the observation deck on the westward side and sparkling like glittering jewels on the background of dark velvet. Oh, oh, oh ... it's burst into flames. Get out of the way please. Oh my, this terrible – it's burning, bursting into flames, it's falling. Oh, this is one of the worst, oh, all the humanity ...

His voice trailed off in tears.

When the film from the newsreel cameras which recorded the fire-ball were processed, it showed that it took only 34 seconds from the first explosion of flame until the glowing framework of the *Hindenburg* hit the ground. The millions of cubic feet of hydrogen had flamed off in less than a minute, although the blaze of engines, fuel oil and framework lasted for hours.

The crew men on the ground, holding the mooring lines underneath the burning giant, scattered and ran for their lives.

One of them, Allen Hagaman, tripped over the rails surrounding the mooring tower and the glowing framework of the airship crashed down on him. He was identified the next day by the scorched remains of his wedding ring.

But in the few seconds as the *Hindenburg* fell from the sky, there were miraculous escapes as passengers and crew leaped from the crashing airship, or simply stayed inside the burning wreckage until it settled on the ground and ran to safety through the white-hot hoops of the *Hindenburg* framework. Joe Spah was one of those who survived. He jumped more than 9 m (30 ft) from the burning airship and, with his acrobat's training, landed apparently unhurt. Luftwaffe intelligence colonel Fritz Erdmann, who had predicted an attack would come after the *Hindenburg* had landed, perished in the flames. Of the 36 passengers, 13 died. Of the 61 crew members, 22 died.

In the commission of inquiry that followed, German experts were invited to join the investigation as 'observers'. Most of the commission's discussions were 'off-the-record' talks between American government officials and high ranking German diplomats.

Documents now filed in the National Archives in Washington show that the American and German technical experts agreed not to consider sabotage as a cause of the disaster – at least in public.

The archives show that senior officers of the American Departments of Commerce and the Interior warned the commission solicitor Mr Trimble Jr that 'a finding of sabotage might be a cause for an international incident, especially on these shores'. The commission ignored a written report by Detective George McCartney of the New York Police Department bomb squad, who analysed the wreckage and reconstructed technical details of a firebomb which he believed had been placed in Gas Cell Four. And the chief of the Luftwaffe, Hermann Goering, ordered the German technical advisers to the commission not to cooperate with any avenue of investigation that hinted at sabotage by any member of the crew.

After a month-long hearing, the commission reached a conclusion backed by both the Americans and Germans. The hydrogen fire-ball had been sparked off, they claimed, by a freak spark of static electricity, an unfortunate phenomenon not seen before and not seen since. Hermann Goering concurred: 'It was an act of God. No one could have prevented it.'

But behind the scenes in Germany, the Gestapo were ruthlessly interrogating the families and friends of every one of the *Hindenburg* crew and passengers. Their suspicions eventually focussed on 25-year-old Eric Spehl. As a rigger on the *Hindenburg* he was one of the crew responsible for checking the gas bags for leaks.

Spehl had been a devout Catholic, never a fervent supporter of the Nazi regime. And he had one great weakness, a passionate love for a divorced woman ten years older than himself who had become his mistress.

Gestapo agents, who checked the gossip with Spehl's neighbours in Frankfurt, found that the young man had gone through a traumatic meeting with his mistress's ex-husband just before the *Hindenburg*'s last voyage. The man had come to Spehl's flat. He was an artist, he was haggard and half crazed with fear. He was on the run from the Gestapo and needed money to escape.

Spehl gave him all the money he had ... and then tipped off the Gestapo. The Nazi torturers arrested the artist and crushed his fingers one by one in a vice until the bones showed through his knuckles. Spehl was reported to be infuriated by the sight and still seething with anger when he boarded the fatal *Hindenburg* flight.

The Gestapo searchers in Frankfurt ripped Spehl's apartment to pieces. They could find no sign of his mistress, who had fled the city. And they could find no trace of Eric's beloved new gadget for his photographic darkroom, his two-hour timer.

Neither could they interrogate Eric Spehl. He died, horribly burned, in the emergency field hospital set up at Lakeheath, beside the glowing embers of the world's last great airship.

The Arm in the Shark Case

The story hit the headlines on Anzac Day – 25 April 1935. It was labelled in shrieking type across the front pages as 'The Arm In The Shark Case'. To incredulous newspaper readers that day, to police and forensic experts, it was one of the most bizarre mysteries ever.

The mystery began in the Sydney seaside suburb of Coogee. Fisherman Bert Hodson had set out in his small boat to examine lines he had baited with mackerel about 1.5 km off shore. He was after shark. Hodson was in luck: he found not one but two of the dread killers. One small shark was already firmly hooked to one of his lines. Another, a 4.2 m (14 ft) tiger shark, was in the process of devouring the smaller one. The fisherman hauled in the line and found the tiger shark was now firmly ensnared. Turning his boat for the shore, he headed home with the creature in tow.

Hodson would normally have killed the shark and hung it on the boathouse scales. But the fisherman's brother, Charles, ran an aquarium at Coogee and Bert knew that the prize tiger shark would provide an excellent attraction for the paying customers who crowded down from the city.

And so it proved. The shark circled menacingly round the aquarium to the delight of the trippers for a few days. Then, on 25 April the fascination on the faces of the visitors turned to horror as they witnessed the most astonishing spectacle. The tiger shark went into convulsions. It surged around the water, disgorging the contents of its stomach: rats, birds, parts of the smaller shark – and a human arm.

Charles Hodson acted swiftly. He fished out the arm and telephoned the police. They found the grisly specimen to be the left arm of a man, with a tattoo of two boxers slugging it out. Attached was a length of rope.

At first, police put the case down as a shark attack on a lone swimmer or yachtsman until, over the days, their suspicions became aroused. No one had been reported missing off a Sydney beach. And a police surgeon who examined the arm claimed that it had not be bitten off by a shark but cleanly amputated with a sharp knife.

Fingerprints were taken of the hand and, although they were blurred, experts were able to match the prints of the thumb and ring finger with those of a man in police files. They belonged to James Smith, who ran a billiard room grandly titled the Rozelle Sports Club, and who had once been arrested for illegal bookmaking. Smith had been missing from his home for 28 days. His brother, Edward, positively identified the arm but was unable to give any hint as to Smith's movements. And all that the victim's wife, Gladys, knew was that her husband had left home saying that he was taking a party on a paid fishing trip.

The police sought out Smith's friends. One of them John Brady, was not easy to find for he was wanted by Tasmanian police on a forgery charge. But he was eventually run to ground on 17 May, living with his wife in a small flat in north Sydney. Under interrogation, Brady admitted having stayed with Smith in a cottage at Cronulla, on the same stretch of coastline as the shark had been caught, but denied knowing anything about the crime.

Over the next few months, divers and chartered aircraft searched the waters of Gunnamatta Bay, near Cronulla, hoping to find further clues.

The police had a theory, however. They believed that Smith went to stay with Brady at Cronulla to plan their next fraud, but that the two men fell out over the sharing of the loot. Brady, they believed, killed his accomplice and hacked up the body. He placed the remains in a metal trunk – but could not fit in the arm. So he roped it to the outside of the trunk and dumped the terrible evidence into the sea. A small shark, attracted by the blood, attacked the trunk, severing the rope with its razor-sharp teeth. As the arm floated free, the shark swallowed it whole.

The shark's next meal was the mackerel on Bert Hodson's line. And that was when the shark became a meal for the larger tiger shark.

The police theory sounded far-fetched. But the 'Arm In The Shark Case' was soon to prove that fact can be even stranger than fiction.

The crime that detectives believed Smith and Brady had been plotting was an insurance fraud over a yacht that had apparently disappeared. Police interviewed the yacht's former owner, whom they regarded as a key witness. But the day before an inquest was due to be held into Smith's death, the witness was found shot dead in his car beneath the approaches to Sydney's famous Harbour Bridge.

The following day, detectives received another blow. The coroner who was to have held the inquest ruled that he could not do so without a complete body. Nevertheless, Brady was charged with murder and sent for trial.

The trial lasted only two days. The judge refused to admit as evidence signed statements that had been taken from the witness before he was found shot dead. Without this evidence, the jury was directed to acquit Brady. Two men were charged with murdering the witness, but they too were acquitted.

Brady continued his career of crime. In all, he spent more than 20 years of his life in jail. During all that time, the only person who knew the full facts of the 'Arm In The Shark Case' never once hinted at what the truth might be.

And the full story never will be known. John Brady suffered a heart attack at the age of 71 in a prison repatriation hostel. His secret died with him.

The Black Perambulator

The woman was found in a Hampstead street, lying on a heap of builders' rubbish. Moonlight played softly on her black jacket with its trimming of imitation Astrakhan. Her skull was crushed, and head itself had almost been severed from the body – it remained attached only by a sliver of skin and muscle.

The date was 24 October 1890, and rumours soon started to circulate. It was whispered that the murder was the work of Jack the Ripper, the phantasmal figure who had stalked the East End only two years earlier. Had the Ripper now returned to claim victims in North London?

A mile or so away was an abandoned perambulator whose cushions were soaked with blood. And the following day, detectives made another grim discovery. The corpse of an 18-month-old baby was recovered from waste ground in Finchley. It was not very long before the three gruesome finds were connected.

The murdered woman was found to have the initials P.H. embroidered on her underclothes. The fact was reported in a morning newspaper which caught the attention of a certain Clara Hogg, who lived in Kentish Town. She knew that her sister-in-law, Mrs Phoebe Hogg, had gone out on the afternoon of 24 October with her baby. She had not come back that night. The initials fitted the missing woman, and Clara went with a friend to the mortuary where the body had been taken. There, choking back her nausea, Clara recognised her sister-in-law as the grisly figure on the slab.

What puzzled the police was the behaviour of Clara's friend, a tall redheaded woman named Mary Pearcey. She insisted that the corpse was not Phoebe Hogg's; she became hysterical and tried to drag Clara away. It was, in fact, to visit Mary Pearcey that Phoebe Hogg had set out on the fateful afternoon. Yet the russet-haired Mary first denied the fact; then admitted that the visit had taken place.

Clearly, Mary Pearcey's role in the affair needed some investigation. And it did not take much probing for detectives to discover a familiar geometry in the mystery – the geometry of a love triangle.

Frank Hogg, husband of the murdered Phoebe, turned out to be a man with an eye for the ladies. A bearded and jovial furniture remover, he had lived with his wife at Prince of Wales Road, Kentish Town. But Frank also possessed the latchkey to Mary's home at Priory Road nearby. He was a regular visitor there, and had been since before his marriage.

Probing deeper, the police discovered that the marriage itself was a forced affair. While he was still a bachelor in 1888, Frank had been seeing both women. His true affection was for the strong-willed and vivacious Mary Pearcey. It was, however, the meeker Phoebe Styles who became pregnant by him. Although leading a double love-life, Frank was a regular church-goer who knew which course he ought to pursue. He wrestled for some time with his conscience, at one point proposing to abandon the whole mess by making a new life abroad. It was Mary Pearcey who told him not to emigrate, but to marry the pregnant Phoebe. The redhead wrote him passionate letters which expressed little jealousy of her rival: 'Oh, Frank! I should not like to think I was the cause of all your troubles, and yet you make me think so. What can I do? I love you with all my heart, and I will love her because she will belong to you.'

Again: 'Do not think of going away, for my heart will break if you do; don't go dear. I won't ask too much, only to see you for five minutes when you can get away; but if you go quite away, how do you think I can live? I would see you get married 50 times over – yes, I could bear that far better than parting with you for ever . . . you must not go away. My heart throbs with pain only to think about it.'

Mixed in with these protestations of love were phrases culled from the romantic novelettes which Mary read avidly. One has an especially ironic ring in retrospect: 'In this false world we do not always know who are our friends and who our enemies, and all need friends . . .'

In the end, Frank did marry Phoebe Styles, settling down with her, his mother and sister Clara at Prince of Wales Road. Phoebe seems to have known all about her husband's liaison with Mary, but raised no strong objections to it. Curiously, the two women were friends, and when Phoebe's second child miscarried, Mary even nursed her rival through the pain and trauma. As for the first baby, Mary doted on it, almost as if she shared in the motherhood of the infant in every way.

To this day, what triggered the bloody climax remains a mystery. The police did determine, though, that on the day before the fateful visit, Mary sent Phoebe a note: 'Dearest: come round this afternoon and bring our little darling, don't fail.' On that occasion, the blinds at Mary's house were seen to be drawn down as if in preparation. As it happened, Phoebe Hogg was unable to go round that day, but after receiving a second note she went to the house the following day.

Mary did admit to police that Phoebe arrived with the baby in the pram, but claimed it was only to borrow some money. Asked why she had first denied the visit, she replied improbably: 'I did not tell you before because Phoebe asked me not to let anybody know that she had been here.' Later, to a police matron, she was to hint that there had been an argument: 'As we were having tea Mrs Hogg made some remark which I did not like – one word brought up another. Perhaps I had better not say any more.'

The neighbours had heard screaming in Mary Pearcey's house at 16.00 – screaming, and the smashing of crockery.

The police produced a search warrant and examined the premises. They found that they had been recently cleaned, but not very thoroughly. Spatters of blood could be seen on the walls and ceiling; the poker had blood and hairs on it. In a dresser drawer was a carving knife, also stained with blood. A skirt, an apron, curtains, a rug – all bore tell-tale stains.

Mary Pearcey sat at a piano during the search, and tinkled out nursery rhymes. When asked why so many bloodstains were to be found about the place she continued to play at the keyboard, eerily chanting, 'Killing mice, killing mice, killing mice!'

Later, the police discovered that Mary was wearing two wedding rings; no ring had been found on the body of Phoebe Hogg.

Arrested and charged with murder, 24-year-old Mary Pearcey was tried at the Old Bailey in December 1890. Throughout the proceedings, the accused woman protested her innocence, but the circumstantial evidence against her was overwhelming. Some two hours after the cries were heard at her home, a neighbour had seen Mary Pearcey pushing the perambulator, draped with a black shawl, along Priory Road. Night had now fallen, and she was hunched over the vehicle as if hoping not to be recognised. The pram itself appeared heavily laden, with something strangely bulky crammed up towards the hood . . .

The extraordinary journey which followed covered a circuit of some six miles. The murdered woman was found at Crossfield Road, Hampstead, and the baby was abandoned off Finchley Road. There was no evidence of violence being done to the infant, but its clothing was stained with blood. The impression was that it may have been suffocated by the weight of the corpse above it. As for the perambulator, it was found abandoned in Hamilton Terrace, St John's Wood, its grim freight shed at last.

Frank Hogg admitted to the police that he had gone round to Priory Road late that night, and let himself in with his latchkey. When he found the place empty, he pencilled a brief note: 'Twenty past ten. Cannot stay.' Had he lingered, he might have encountered Mary Pearcey returning from her macabre excursion.

The jury took only an hour to consider its verdict and found Mary Eleanor Pearcey guilty of murder. Asked if she had anything to say why sentence of death should not be passed, she swiftly answered: 'Only that I am innocent of the charge.'

Now wretched and reviled, Frank Hogg refused to see his mistress in the condemned cell, a rebuff which Mary lamented: 'He might have made death easier to bear.' On 23 December 1890 she was led to the scaffold and she faced her end with great calm and composure. To the prison chaplain accompanying her, she observed enigmatically: 'The sentence is just; the evidence was false.'

A puzzling remark. And it is just one of the untidy strands left in the Pearcey case. Some have doubted whether Mary could have accomplished the crime alone: Phoebe had been clubbed senseless and had her head severed by a knife drawn across the throat several times. It was done with such force that it cut clean through the vertebrae. Then there was the business of cramming the corpse into the pram. This was a formidable task even granted the point made by F. Tennyson Jesse in her *Murder and Its Motives*: 'the matter was made easier by the fact that there was nothing to prevent the head being doubled right back.'

What provoked the maniacal assault? Was it premeditated, or sparked by that 'remark which I did not like'? And if the evidence was false, who had falsified it?

London in the 1890s was the city of yellow fog and gaslit streets known to readers of Sherlock Holmes stories. And for afficionados of great unsolved murder mysteries there is one tantalizing postscript piece which in no way fits the jigsaw.

It emerged at the trial that Mary Pearcey's true name was Mary Eleanor Wheeler. She had taken her surname from that of a carpenter, John Charles Pearcey, with whom she had once cohabited. He stated at the trial that they were never formally married, and that he had left Mary because of her roving eye. But some mysterious figure seems to have occupied a special place in her affections. For on the day of her execution, Mary instructed her solicitor to place the following advertisement in the Madrid newspapers: 'M.E.C.P. Last wish of M.E.W. Have not betrayed.'

There is little doubt that Mary Pearcey lured Phoebe Hogg to Priory Road and there killed the unfortunate woman. The motive seems clearly to have been rooted in jealous love. Who then was M.E.C.P.? And what was the secret they shared? The puzzle has prompted one fantastic solution: that Mary was a member of a nefarious secret society, and liquidated Phoebe when she found out about it. More prosaically, it has been suggested that Mary was secretly married as a teenager to a man whose name she did not want sullied at the trial. Finally, it is possible that the novelette-reading Mary simply invented a little enigma to lend romance to her appalling crime.

We simply do not know. But reading and re-reading the last cryptic message you cannot help believing that a fascinating dimension to the case of Mary Pearcey may have dropped into the void when the hangman's fatal trap was sprung.

Who was R. M. Qualtrough?

William Herbert Wallace was a drab, colourless, boring man who lived a drab, colourless, boring life. He was thrifty and hard-working, mild mannered and a little snobbish, soberly dressed and utterly, utterly respectable. His idea of a night out with the boys was his regular fortnightly visit to a local café to take part in chess tournaments. A swinging party at home with his mousy wife, Julia, usually consisted of the couple playing duets on violin and piano.

Herbert's meek and unassuming manner was greatly appreciated by his employer, a solid dependable insurance company who employed him as a collector and agent. In 15 years in their employment he had proved to be utterly trustworthy. He was diligent and he never pushed for promotion.

His admirable personal qualities and those of his shy little wife made them ideal neighbours in their neat terraced house in Wolverton Street, Anfield, Liverpool. He was never known to show outbursts of exuberance or bad temper.

In fact, the jury at his trial decided, Herbert Wallace had all the characteristics of a sadistic brutal murderer.

His wife had been battered to death so violently that her brains had spilled out on to the floor. She had died at the hands of a man who deliberately laid a meticulous trail of false clues to throw the police off his scent.

There was no real evidence to connect her husband with Julia Wallace's death. In fact he had a near-perfect alibi. But then Herbert Wallace was a man who ordered his life with pedantic attention to detail.

He was too good to be true. The jury's verdict seemed to be that Wallace was so absolutely ordinary that he had to be capable of great evil ...

In spite of flimsy police theories which hardly stood up to defence cross-examination, in spite of a complete lack of motive on the part of the accused man, in spite of a summing-up by the trial judge who virtually begged the jury to acquit him, Wallace was found guilty of his wife's murder.

He sat impassively in the dock when the verdict was returned. It was this same lack of emotion which had led him there in the first place. 'I am not guilty. I cannot say anything else,' he whispered plaintively to the court as the judge prepared to pass sentence.

The judge, Mr Justice Robert Alderson Wright, showed more distress than the convicted man. But he had no option under law. Shaken by the jury's verdict, he donned his black cap and passed the only sentence open to him: to be hanged by the neck until dead.

And the mystery man who actually bludgeoned Julia Wallace to death heaved a deep sigh of relief. He had got away with the perfect murder.

The first sign that Herbert Wallace's humdrum life was about to be shattered came with a telephone call from a complete stranger to the City Cafe in North John Street, Liverpool, at 19.15 on Monday 19 January 1931. Herbert Wallace was due at the cafe that night to exercise his rather mundane skill as a chess player. He was taking part in a tournament aptly named 'The Second Class Championship'.

But the 52-year-old insurance agent was not there to take the telephone call. A waitress answered the phone and passed it to Samuel Beattie, Captain of the chess club, who explained that Wallace had not yet arrived. Did the caller want to phone back later?

The voice on the other end of the line asked to leave a message for Wallace. The caller identified himself as 'R. M. Qualtrough' and requested that Wallace should call on him at his home at 25 Menlove Gardens East, Mossley Hill, the following night to discuss some insurance business. Beattie wrote the message on the back of an envelope.

About the same time Herbert Wallace was setting off from his home at 29 Wolverton Street to catch a tram to the City Cafe for the chess club meeting.

The Wallaces had been married for 18 years, after a two-year engagement in their home town of Harrogate, Yorkshire. Herbert had a worthy, but lowly paid, job as political agent for the local branch of the Liberal Party. When the meagre party funds could no longer support his salary, he moved to the quiet suburb of Anfield in Liverpool.

Julia, five years younger than her husband, set about making their new home in Wolverton Street neat and tidy, just like their lives. In her earlier years she had spent some time in the genteel studies of music and painting, and a small upright piano took pride of place in the parlour of their trim terraced house. As Herbert settled in to his new job as a collector for the Prudential Insurance Company, the childless couple could afford little luxuries like the £80 which Mr Wallace had spent on a microscope.

He prided himself on being a diligent amateur scientist. He even lectured part-time in chemistry at Liverpool Technical College and often he and Julia would spend the evening in the little laboratory he had built just off his bathroom, examining slides on the microscope. At the age of 50, Herbert had even started to learn the violin and accompanied Julia on the piano.

His job paid him an annual salary of £250 and the thrifty couple lived quietly within their means. Herbert had a bank savings account of £152 and Julia had her own modest savings of £90.

The Wallaces' home

As Herbert Wallace wrote in his diary: 'We seem to have pulled well together and I think we both get as much pleasure and contentment out of life as most people.'

The only times he left Julia alone were his visits to the chess club and his lectures at the technical college. But when he stepped out that night to catch his tram to the café, there was a nagging worry in his mind. There had been a spate of burglaries in Anfield in the past few weeks and Wallace often kept large sums of his insurance company's money at home. 'Don't open the door to any strangers while I'm gone, dear,' he reminded Julia as he left.

Samuel Beattie never actually saw Wallace arrive at the City Cafe but shortly after the phone call he saw him seated, taking part in a game, and he passed on Qualtrough's message.

Wallace seemed puzzled by the telephone call. He did not know any Mr Qualtrough. The address was on the other side of the sprawling Liverpool suburbs, quite outside his normal insurance sales territory. On the way home from the club that night, he quizzed other members about the location of Menlove Gardens East. Which tram should he take to get there? How long would the journey take?

The following day Wallace set out, regular as clockwork, on his appointed rounds in Anfield, collecting a premium of a few pence here, paying out a claim of a few pounds there. He returned home punctually for lunch at 14.00, went back to work for the afternoon and finished in the evening at 18.00. While Julia prepared tea, Wallace went upstairs, washed and changed and filled his jacket pocket with insurance quotation and proposal forms.

At 18.30, their meal over, Julia Wallace answered a knock at the door. It was the milk boy, 14-year-old Alan Close. He handed Mrs Wallace a pint container of milk and she took it into the kitchen to empty the contents into her own jug, returning to the front door to give the boy the dairy's can. That was the last time she was seen alive.

About 15 minutes later Herbert Wallace left the house. He walked a few hundred yards and boarded a tram in Belmont Road for the first leg of his journey to meet the mysterious Mr Qualtrough. At 19.06, after travelling a mile and a half, he switched to a second tram in Lodge Lane. His behaviour was unusual for the normally reserved Herbert Wallace. He chatted amiably to the tram conductor Tom Phillips about his high hopes of selling a big insurance policy at his destination. At 19.15 he arrived at Penny Lane and switched to a third tram to complete his five mile journey. He asked conductor Arthur Thompson to let him off at the stop nearest Menlove Gardens East.

'Don't know it,' Thompson admitted. 'But we stop in Menlove Avenue. Just ask around, it's bound to be near there.'

For the next half hour Wallace tramped busily around the streets of Mossley Hill. He found Menlove Gardens North. He found Menlove Gardens West and Menlove Gardens South. But no Menlove Gardens East. He knocked on the door of Mrs Katie Mather at No 25 Menlove Gardens West and she told him there was no Menlove Gardens East. He remembered his Prudential Insurance supervisor, Joseph Crewe, lived nearby and found his home and knocked on the door. He got no reply.

He met Police Constable James Sargent on his beat in nearby Allerton Road and was advised to go to the local post office to check a street directory for Mr Qualtrough's address. Wallace agreed. Then he remarked on the late hour.

'Yes, almost eight o'clock', the policeman agreed. There was no directory available at the post office and Wallace found a newsagent's shop. He pestered the owner, Mrs Lily Pinches, into checking the names of customers on the shop's newspaper delivery round, explaining his errand to her in great detail. No, she confirmed, there is no Menlove Gardens East.

Wallace gave up and went home.

He arrived back at Wolverton Street shortly before 21.00 and his neighbours, John Johnston and his wife Florence, saw him struggling with the handle of his back door. Finally he managed to get the door open and went inside. The Johnstons were still watching as Wallace emerged a few moments later and calmly invited them in. 'It's Julia,' he explained flatly. 'Come and see, she has been killed.'

Within minutes the police were summoned. Julia Wallace was dead. Her skull had been battered by ten separate blows, any single one of which would have been fatal. There was blood everywhere. A total of £4 was missing from the little cash box in the kitchen cabinet. She had been killed, the forensic experts decided later, between 18.30 and 20.00 that night.

Herbert Wallace appeared to be almost unmoved by the sight of his dead wife. Later that night he left the murder house and moved in with his brother's family a few miles away. The detectives, meanwhile, moved in to 29 Wolverton Street. And the tongues wagged furiously.

Why had Herbert Wallace talked of his business so freely to tram conductors and total strangers in his quest to find Menlove Gardens East? Had he deliberately drawn the patrolling policeman's attention to the time? And who was R. M. Qualtrough, whose call the night before had lured him away from home? If the address in Mossley Hill never existed, did R. M. Qualtrough exist?

On 2 February 1931, a week after the body of Julia Wallace was buried in Anfield Cemetery, Herbert Wallace was charged with her murder. Cautioned by the police, he said simply and sadly: 'What can I say in answer to a charge of which I am absolutely innocent?' The press headlines had become so sensational and strident that when the trial opened at St George's Hall seven weeks later, even the prosecution made little objection to a defence request that no residents of the city of Liverpool should sit on the jury.

The prosecution made much of a key piece of evidence. They had traced the source of the call from 'R. M. Qualtrough'. By sheer chance, the call to the City Cafe the night before Julia Wallace's murder had to be routed through a telephone supervisor because the coin mechanism in the public phone box had been faulty. The call and the defect were duly logged. The call had come from Anfield 1627, a kiosk in Rochester Road, only 400 yards from Wallace's home.

Of course Wallace was not at the café to receive the call from 'Qualtrough', prosecuting counsel Edward Hemmerde, explained triumphantly. For the same reason, 'Qualtrough' couldn't phone back later to speak to Wallace after he arrived at the chess club, because Herbert Wallace was 'R. M. Qualtrough'.

Wallace, Hemmerde claimed, had made the telephone call himself then sprinted for a tram and arrived at the café to receive the message he had phoned through as 'Qualtrough'.

His pestering inquiries of tram conductors, the policeman and the residents of Mossley Hill the following night were all part of the plan to establish his alibi, the prosecutor insisted. And Wallace's unflurried demeanour when he returned home and found his wife's body was the action of a man who already knew murder had been committed.

Herbert Wallace's defence counsel, Roland Oliver, outlined his case simply. His client had not committed the murder and it was not for the defence to prove who had wielded the murder weapon. Wallace was not 'Qualtrough' and the defence did not need to establish the identity of the mystery man. Wallace made a fuss of finding Menlove Gardens East, he explained, because it was a break from his usual routine, a chance to earn the unexpected bonus of a sale. He was displaying an emotion that was rare for him: excitement. He had only reverted to character when he found his wife's body. He became placid and introspective. Wallace had no motive for killing his own wife.

By all the rules of criminal law, Roland Oliver was absolutely right. The police had no evidence, only suspicions. Herbert Wallace had to be presumed innocent. But on the fourth and final day of the trial, the jury took only an hour to reach their verdict: Guilty.

It is almost routine for a judge to express his agreement with a jury's verdict in a complex, tasking case. Mr Justice Wright, however, did not even offer them a word of thanks for their efforts. He pronounced the mandatory sentence of death by hanging.

The defence lodged an immediate appeal and a week after he should have been hanged Wallace was taken from the condemned cell to London, to appear at the Royal Courts of Justice in the Strand. Far from the hysteria and prejudice of Liverpool, three judges sifted through the hard evidence against Wallace. After a two-day hearing they retired for 45 minutes and pronounced their verdict: Appeal allowed, conviction quashed.

Wallace left the courtroom free – but spiritually broken.

Two days later when he returned home, Liverpool police pointedly announced they would not be re-opening their investigation into Julia Wallace's murder. The cruel implication was not lost on Wallace's hostile neighbours and his workmates. The insurance company gave him a desk job to try to shield him and a year later he retired on a pension.

In February 1933, just over two years after the death of his wife, Herbert Wallace became ill with a recurring kidney disease and died in a local hospital. Five days later he was buried in Anfield Cemetery beside his beloved Julia.

So who murdered Julia Wallace? Who was R. M. Qualtrough? There were only 14 people in the whole of Liverpool with the name Qualtrough and the police interviewed and cleared them all. In the atmosphere of outrage which followed the murder, Liverpool police reached the single-minded conclusion that Wallace was guilty. Squads of detectives armed with stop-watches and timetables spent days riding on trams and walking briskly around Anfield trying to demolish his timing of events.

Herbert Wallace had his own suspicions. In the long nights of lonely agony after his wife's murder, he wondered which of his small circle of acquaintances knew he was due at the City Cafe that fateful night and left the tantalising telephone message for him. Julia, he knew, would only have opened the door to a familiar face. Even facing the hangman's noose, shy Herbert Wallace could not bring himself to scream in righteous anger and point a forceful finger of accusation.

He apologetically mentioned the names of two men to the Liverpool detectives investigating the case. Both men were in their early twenties and both were former employees of the insurance company. At different times, they had both parted company from the insurance firm after cash shortages were found in their accounts. On separate occasions, they had filled in for Wallace on his rounds when he was ill. They knew all about his social routine, about his chess club meetings. And they knew that on some Tuesday nights, as on the night Julia was murdered, the cash box in the kitchen could hold as much as £50. Indeed when they stood in for him they had been inside his home and had handled the cash box. Julia would have readily opened the door to them, knowing they were former colleagues of her husband.

Police records show that detectives only interviewed one of these men – and even then accepted without question his assurance that he had an alibi for the night of the murder.

The police concentrated all their energies on the man they wanted ... the mousey little insurance agent whom everyone so desperately wanted to believe was a murdering monster.

Advertisement of Death

The voice on the telephone was smooth, fluent and persuasive ... and instantly Josephine Backshall was cocooned in a web of friendly familiarity. She knew the caller's voice well and had been longing for him to ring. After all, he was helping her to earn £100, a big enough sum of 'pin-money' to make a world of difference to the family budget.

There was nothing in the least shady about the job as a part-time model that Josephine was beginning to enjoy. In fact, the thought that the small advertisement she had placed in the local paper could be misconstrued in anything like an unseemly light had never crossed the mind of the house-proud, 39-year-old mother-of-three, who sang for the local church choir and was a leader of the town's Brownies troupe. And the idea that there could be anything sinister about the man who answered her advertisement and, in a 'trial session', had photographed her on the front lawn of the family's tidy, middle-class semi-detached home in Maldon, Essex, would have seemed too outrageous to contemplate.

The man, she told her husband Mike, seemed like a 'good sort'. And, as she spoke to him again on the 'phone, she realized that what he was offering her would be her biggest job so far: £100 for a day's work – probably, she thought, modelling for something no more glamorous than a cheap cosmetic firm.

The caller talked on, cool, collected, giving the impression of a very pleasant personality. A meeting was arranged for that evening and, after kissing her husband goodbye, she walked through the front door of their spruce home for the last time.

Three days later, at about 12.00 on Friday, 1 November 1974, she was found strangled to death.

Her body had been dumped in a shallow pond by the side of a lonely lovers' lane. Her hands were bound in front of her with a length of cord strapped tightly to her wrists. An identical cord was lashed to her neck.

Josephine Backshall, the church-going good neighbour who enjoyed an innocent life of simple pleasures, was killed because she put her faith in a confidence trickster. She trusted a mystery man whose identity the police have spent more than 100,000 man-hours trying to discover, with not a single clue to put them on the trail of a quarry whose disappearance has made the Josephine Backshall case one of Britain's most perplexing unsolved crimes.

No fewer than 40 detectives were assigned to the case in the first year of one of the biggest, yet most baffling, investigations of its kind. More than 19,000 members of the public were interviewed. All of them had either the Christian name of Pete or Dave, or the surname of Thomson or Johnson. It was a combination of those names that fitted the clues that Josephine had given her family and friends. It was to them that she had spoken of the man with the camera who was setting her up not, as she believed as a part-time model, but as a victim of brutal murder, even the motive for which has never been established.

Thousands of car registration plates were later painstakingly checked and rechecked by police trying to find the killer's car – possibly a blue Ford which was seen pulling away from the Fountain public house in Good Easter, Essex, on the night Josephine kept her fateful rendezvous with her killer.

Detectives established that Josephine and the man she so easily trusted did stop for a drink – one half-pint of beer each – at the Fountain about an hour after she had left her home. He was presumed to have picked her up nearby and taken her there after a 'business dinner' at a Chinese restaurant – an assumption based on the fact that forensic experts discovered the remains of Chinese food in her stomach.

Publican's wife Joan Jones became the last witness to the rendezvous of a killer and his victim when she saw the couple in the Fountain's saloon bar. 'I caught only a fleeting glance of him,' she says. 'He was a tall man. His head touched a line of beer mugs hanging over the bar. He never actually seemed to face me and, on reflection, it seemed almost as though he was trying to not let anyone get too close a look at him'.

Mrs Jones identified Josephine from a cine film containing family holiday shots which detectives showed her. 'I remembered her at once,' she says. 'She was an attractive woman. She had sat in the corner of the bar with the man and had seemed totally at her ease.'

For months, police kept details of the Fountain meeting secret in the hope that the killer would retrace his steps. It was a forlorn hope.

The only other potential lead detectives had to go on was a 'French connection'. A keen-eyed policewoman found a cosmetics sample in Josephine's bedroom which was one of a very limited batch which had been imported from France prior to a sales drive. Could the killer, detectives pondered, have been using Josephine to model this new range?

Inquiries again, however, came to nought – as did a scrupulous check on every photographic studio in both England and France from which a killer might have been tempted by Josephine's original advertisement, which read:

'Lady, late 30s, seeks part-time employment. Own transport. Anything considered. Previous experience: banking. Able to type.' Underneath was her home telephone number.

Josephine Backshall

It was the sort of advertisement often used to skirt the law as a method of offering sex-for-sale. A senior officer on the case later described it as 'positively naive'. He added:

'We all know what the phrase "anything considered" is taken to mean. The great irony and tragedy of this case is that any innuendo couldn't have been further from the truth. Mrs Backshall was a God-fearing woman – and that sort of interpretation of her advert simply wouldn't have occurred to her. It seems more than likely that her own innocence – a rare attribute in this day and age – may have, tragically, led her to set herself up as a victim of murder.'

Other senior officers have described the Josephine Backshall case as the 'most frustrating' they have ever worked on. But, as far as has been possible, they have managed to piece together this diary of death:

A few days after Josephine placed her ad, a male caller telephoned to offer her work 'modelling for cosmetics'. An appointment was made for a week later, 15 miles from Josephine's home, at Witham, Essex. The man never showed up. He 'phoned the following day, rearranged the appointment, and again failed to appear. Two weeks later, the 'phone rang once more – and Josephine happily arranged yet another meeting.

This time, the couple did meet. The 'photographer' took a series of pictures of Josephine on the front lawn of her home during the day. By that stage, Josephine's husband had begun to believe her part-time job would come to nothing and, ironically, expressed mild doubt as to the authenticity of the cameraman who was promising his wife tidy sums for what seemed simple work. Josephine allayed those fears, saying that the man seemed perfectly genuine and, indeed, a 'good sort'.

The telephone rang again on Tuesday, 29 October 1974 and the last, fateful meeting was arranged. Josephine left the family home in Norfolk Close, Maldon at about 18.00, driving to Witham in her red Ford Cortina, registration number BVW 374L.

Detectives have established that she was seen at Witham's Colingwood Road car park between 18.30 and 19.00. A passer-by told them her car may have broken down, because he saw her looking into the engine with the bonnet raised close to the car park entrance. Some time before 19.00, however, she must have met her killer.

There is a time gap between then and three days later, when a telephone line worker made the gruesome discovery of her body in the ditch at Bury Green on the Essex and Hertfordshire border.

The killer had left no clue behind. Chief Superintendent Jack Moulder, who still keeps the Josephine Backshall case file open, can only say: 'Someone, somewhere must know him.'

Doctor Death

An 84-year-old retired doctor died in July 1983 in the genteel Sussex seaside resort of Eastbourne. His passing might have warranted no more than a paragraph in the local paper, but for one thing ... The doctor, John Bodkin Adams, was believed by many to be a man who literally got away with mass murder. And it was only upon his death that newspapers could safely produce their dossiers on the astonishing case, in which Adams was tried at the Old Bailey for the murder of one of his patients, Edith Morrell, a 72-year-old widow. If he had been convicted he would have been charged with further murders. Two other charges had been prepared and the Crown believed it had sufficient evidence to prosecute three other cases.

Early in the investigation one of the policemen involved, Scotland Yard Detective Chief Superintendent Charles Hewitt, believed Adams killed nine of his elderly patients. He later increased his estimate to 25, believing that Adams had probably 'eased' many others out of this world after influencing them to change their wills in his favour.

But none of this came to light at the Old Bailey. Adams was acquitted after a classic courtroom duel between the then Attorney-General, Sir Reginald Manningham-Buller QC, and a brilliant defence lawyer, Geoffrey Lawrence.

Lawrence disliked his client intensely but he fought tigerishly, turning the Attorney-General's over-confidence against him in a brilliant tactical coup which is still recalled and admired by lawyers. Manningham-Buller was certain he would destroy Adams once he had him in the witness-box. Lawrence simply told Adams to exercise his right to remain silent – and thus avoid cross-examination. It was that, the police and prosecution believed, that saved him from the rope. For with the linchpin of the Crown's case snatched away, the jury took just 45 minutes to find him not guilty.

The trial was such a disaster that the Director of Public Prosecutions lost confidence that a conviction on any other charge could be procured. So he announced there would be no further action.

What the jury never knew – and could not in law be told – was that the police had investigated the deaths of a further 400 of his patients. They had also exhumed the bodies of two of the women who had not been cremated. They had prepared cases on the deaths of nine patients and had evidence pointing to the murder of many others.

The police knew that over his 35 years of practice in Eastbourne, Adams had been the beneficiary of 132 wills, amassing £45,000 in cash – worth ten

Dr John Bodkin Adams

times that today – antique silver, jewellery, furniture and cars, including two Rolls-Royces, from the bequests of dead patients.

So was John Bodkin Adams merely a plausible rogue or was he the most cunning mass murderer of the century?

He was certainly the most fashionable doctor in Eastbourne, a town where the elderly could spend their last days peacefully in genteel retirement. He had arrived there virtually straight from medical school in his native Northern Ireland and built up a good practice with the cream of the town as his patients.

He was an ugly man, only 1.7 m (5 ft 5 in) tall and weighing almost 114 kg (18 stone), with a pink fleshy face, small eyes and thin lips and a rolling chin that sagged over the celluloid collars he wore. But to his elderly women patients he was charming. He caressed their hands and combed their hair.

However, the picture painted by the year-long investigation by Mr Hewitt, then a sergeant, and his 'governor' Detective Chief Superintendent Bert Hannam of the Yard's Murder Squad, was this:

Adams made his victims dependent on his drugs. They craved his morphine and heroin and became addicts. He influenced them to change their wills in his favour. Then they died.

His method, the police claimed, was not startling, shocking or gory. He eased them gently out of life with an overdose of drugs.

Scotland Yard's investigations showed that of all the patients for whom Adams signed death certificates, he explained an improbable 68 per cent as being due to either cerebral haemorrhage or cerebral thrombosis.

Even before the war there was gossip that Adams did his rounds with a bottle of morphia in one pocket and a blank form in the other. In 1936 he had been the beneficiary in the will of Mrs Alice Whitton, to the extent of £3,000 – a substantial amount then. Her niece contested the will in the High Court but Adams won and kept the money.

The tongues continued to wag into the mid-1950s. But it was not until 1956 that police investigations actually began and the evidence started to build, much of it circumstantial.

There was the case of William Mawhood, a wealthy steel merchant, who was such a long-standing friend of Adams that he lent him £3,000 to buy his first house. As Mawhood lay dying, Adams asked his wife Edith to leave the bedside for a moment. She heard Adams say: 'Leave your estate to me and I'll look after your wife.'

Mrs Mawhood rushed back into the bedroom. She said later:

'I grabbed my gold-headed walking stick and struck out at the doctor and chased him around the bed. He ran out of the room and as he dashed down the stairs I threw my stick at him. Unfortunately it missed, and broke a flower vase. I shouted to him to get out of the house. It was the last I wanted to see of him. I certainly would not tolerate the idea of Adams trying to get into my husband's will.'

There was the case of Emily Mortimer, whose family had a strict tradition, designed to keep its fortune intact. Whenever a Mortimer died, the bulk of the estate was divided among the surviving members of the family.

Adams persuaded Emily to break the tradition. In the year she died, she added a codicil to her will, transferring £3,000 worth of shares from the family to the doctor. Shortly before her death, she changed the will again so that Adams received £5,000 and members of the family were cut out. Adams signed the death certificate – the cause of death 'Cerebral thrombosis'.

Police discovered the case of the two old women who were persuaded by Adams to let him sell their house and move into a flat for the good of their health. He then refused to hand over the money from the house sale until forced to do so by a writ two years later.

Statements from local solicitors and bank managers on the doctor's insistent concern with the wills of his patients revealed a host of questionable activities. Visits to banks with patients to change details of wills already made; telephone calls to solicitors insisting on their immediate attendance to change or draw up a new will; a comatose patient who signed his altered will only with an X; wills changed on several occasions so that the deceased were cremated instead of buried as originally stipulated; and 32 cheques for the doctor amounting to £18,000 drawn on one old lady's account in the last few days of her life – and with highly suspect signatures.

Odious as such unprofessional behaviour was, it was not evidence of intent to murder. There was, however, plenty of other evidence . . .

Clara Neil-Miller was an elderly spinster who had lived in genteel retirement with her sister Hilda for 13 years. When Hilda died she left everything to Clara. When Clara died, 13 months later, she bequeathed the bulk of her estate – £5,000 – to Adams.

Three years later the police exhumed both bodies and the post-mortem showed that Clara had died of pneumonia, not coronary thrombosis as Adams had put on the death certificate. Then one of the other guests in the rest home for the elderly where she died told the police:

'Dr Adams was called to Miss Clara the night before she died. She was suffering from influenza. He remained in her bedroom for nearly 45 minutes before leaving. I later became worried as I heard nothing from the room. I opened the door and was horrified by what I saw.

This was a bitterly cold winter's night. The bedclothes on her bed had been pulled back and thrown over the bedrail at the base. Her nightdress had been folded back across her body to her neck. All the bedroom windows had been flung open. A cold gush of wind was sweeping through the room. That is how the doctor had left her.'

Police found that, in addition to the £5,000 bequest, Clara had, in the weeks before her death, made out cheques for £300 and £500 to the doctor. The purpose was not clear. It could not be for medical treatment as, apart from the flu, she was not ill. Nor did she receive much in the way of medicines.

Adams had a financial interest in the rest home and sent many patients there. A potential key witness was the woman who ran it, Mrs Elizabeth Sharp. Ex Detective Chief Superintendent Hewitt recalled:

'Mrs Sharp was on the point of talking when we left Eastbourne for a week's conferences with the Attorney-General in London. She was the witness we needed. She knew much of what went on between Adams and his patients. She knew where the bodies were buried and she was scared and frightened. When we left, she was about to crack.

One more visit was all we needed, but when we were in London she died. When we got back to Eastbourne and heard the news, she had already been cremated on the doctor's instructions.

I always had a feeling, but no positive clue, that Adams speeded her on the way. It was too much of a coincidence when she died.'

Then there was the case of Julia Bradnum, a strong and healthy 82-year-old until one morning when she woke up with stomach pains. The doctor was called and remained in the room with her for five minutes. Ten minutes later she was dead.

Her body was also exhumed but it was too decomposed to show much more than that she had not died of the cerebral haemorrhage Adams' certificate claimed.

Only a few weeks before she died Adams had brought her a new will. He said something about her other will not being legal, she later told a friend, Miss Mary Hine. 'She asked me if I would witness the new one,' Miss Hine said. 'Dr Adams pointed to a spot on the paper where I was to sign. I turned over the paper to see what I was witnessing, but Dr Adams put his hand on the writing and turned it back.'

Another of the doctor's patients was Harriet Maud Hughes, aged 66, whom Adams had started to treat only three months before her death of 'cerebral thrombosis'. She spoke of changing her will in his favour. A few weeks before her death, she became ill but then recovered sufficiently to go to her bank with the doctor, who asked the bank manager in her presence to make him the executor of her will. Afterwards, she told her domestic help:

'You should have seen the bank manager's face. He was most surprised at my choice of executor.'

After her death it was discovered that she had added two codicils to her will. The first that she should be cremated. The second, added a month later, left £1,000 each to a Mr and Mrs Thurston, acquaintances of Dr Adams. After the death, the police discovered Adams received 90 per cent of the bequests – giving the Thurstons 10 per cent for the use of their name.

Then there was the case of James Priestly Downs, a wealthy retired bank manager and widower who in his last days tried nine times to sign his will while in a drugged state. On the tenth occasion he signed it with an X. Adams guided his hand. The will left the doctor £1,000. All Mr Downs was being treated for was a fractured ankle. After a fortnight of the treatment, however, he was in a coma. A month later he died.

Annabelle Kilgour was a widow who had been ill for several weeks and was being looked after by a State Registered Nurse, Miss Osgood. One night Adams arrived and said he would give an injection to help her get a good night's sleep.

The nurse was astounded as she watched the doctor give what she regarded as being greatly in excess of the normal dose. 'This will keep her quiet,' he said, and left.

It did. She immediately fell into a coma and died the next morning. When Adams arrived, the nurse told him: 'Mrs Kilgour is dead. You realize, doctor, that you have killed her?'

The nurse later told the Yard men: 'I have never seen a man look so frightened in all my life.'

Once again Adams gave the cause of death as cerebral haemorrhage. In her will, Mrs Kilgour left the doctor a sum of money and an antique clock.

Margaret Pilling, a member of one of Lancashire's richest cotton families, was suffering from nothing more serious than flu when Adams was called to her. Within a fortnight she was practically in a coma. But her family insisted she should go to stay with them.

Her daughter, Mrs Irene Richardson, said later:

'At first we thought she was dying of cancer and that the doctor was being kind by not telling us. But we held a family conference and decided we were not satisfied with the treatment. Whatever her illness, she was definitely being drugged. Her condition was deteriorating rapidly.'

We took a house for her at Ascot, near one of her relatives. Within a fortnight she was on her feet and at the races. Had I not taken her away, I am quite satisfied she would have died.

But the case that really clinched the matter, as far as the police were concerned, was when Bobbie Hullett, a friend of the Chief Constable Richard Walker, died. Mrs Hullett, a vivacious woman of 49 widowed four months earlier, was not even really ill.

Late in 1955 her husband Jack, a retired Lloyds underwriter, became ill. 'Thank God I have a good doctor,' he told one of his nurses. When he was stricken by a heart condition one night in March the next year, the 'good doctor' sat on his bed and injected a dose of morphia. Seven hours later Jack Hullett died. In his will he left Adams £500. The residue went to Bobbie, who was shocked and grief-stricken. Friends rallied round – none more so than Adams, who prescribed drugs to help her sleep. In four months she was dead.

Perhaps in the beginning the sleeping drugs were a wise practice. But as the weeks passed the dosage was not cut down. The domestic staff said later: 'She staggered downstairs most mornings as though she was drunk.'

One of her closest friends was comedian Leslie Henson. He said: 'Her death shocked me greatly. My wife and I saw her turning into a drug addict. We invited her to our home to get away from everything, but she rushed back after 24 hours to get to her pills again. We saw her disintegrating mentally through them.'

After her death another of her friends, Chief Constable Walker, began to make a few discreet phone calls. It was established that two days before Bobbie fell into the coma from which she never recovered, she gave Adams a cheque for £1,000. He immediately drove to the bank and asked for a special clearance. Within hours the amount was credited to his account. At the time, Dr Adams' bank accounts had £35,000 in them. With his investment holdings amounting to a further £125,000, he was not exactly in urgent need of money.

At the inquest, Adams was severely criticized by the coroner for his diagnosis and treatment. A number of penetrating questions were asked. Why had he not told his co-doctor, called in as a second opinion, of his patient's depressive medical history? Why had he failed to get proper daytime medical attention for her or had her put in a nursing home? Why, after 34 years as a doctor, did he take the advice of a young house surgeon in administering a new drug? Why had he failed to call in a psychiatric consultant? And why had he persisted in his diagnosis of a cerebral catastrophe after a pathologist had suggested it might be poisoning?

The doctor replied: 'I honestly did what I thought was best for her.'

The coroner was unimpressed. 'There has been an extraordinary degree of careless treatment,' he said.

And that was the moment that Chief Constable Walker called in Scotland Yard.

So what went wrong? Why, in the face of all this evidence, was John

Bodkin Adams not charged with other offences? Why did the prosecution choose to concentrate on the case of Edith Morrell, the 72-year-old widow of a wealthy Liverpool shipping merchant?

One prosecution lawyer said afterwards: 'We chose it because it was such a clear and obvious case of murder that I should have thought no jury could have regarded it in any other way.'

But Mr Hewitt says:

'Adams was allowed to escape because the law made an ass of itself. I will never forget that conference we had with Manningham-Buller in the Attorney-General's office at the House of Commons. Bert Hannam and I felt sick with disbelief when he announced he was going for Mrs Morrell. It was madness when we had so many better cases, with more specific evidence – and, what's more important, with bodies.

Mrs Morrell had been cremated. This meant we could not use evidence of the best forensic scientist of the day, Dr Francis Camps. But Manningham-Buller was so arrogant he would not listen to his junior counsel, Melford Stevenson and Malcolm Morris, or Mr Leck of the Director of Public Prosecutions' office.

He knew the doctor was a worried man and he would destroy him in the witness-box. But it never happened because Manningham-Buller never considered for a moment that Adams might not be called to give evidence.'

Adams came to trial on 25 April 1957 – six years after Mrs Morrell's death. Prosecution witnesses testified that over a period of six weeks, Adams had prescribed a massive dose of more than 4,000 grains of barbiturate and heroin for Mrs Morrell.

The British Pharmaceutical Association's recommended maximum daily dosage was a quarter morphia grain. But in the last day of her life Adams injected into his barely conscious patient 18 grains of the drug, they said.

But Geoffrey Lawrence managed to discover the nurses' daily record books which gave a more accurate account of the medicine Adams prescribed than the memories of the nurses themselves. Then came his master stroke of not putting Adams into the box.

Three months after his acquittal Adams appeared at Lewes Assizes and pleaded guilty to 14 charges, including the forgery of National Health Service prescriptions and failing to keep a record of dangerous drugs. He was fined £2,400 and ordered to pay costs. In November that year he was struck off by the General Medical Council.

On 22 November 1961, at the age of 62, he was readmitted to the medical register, an event which went largely unnoticed. Only the Home Office retained some doubts: his licence to dispense dangerous drugs was never returned.

His practice in Eastbourne picked up again, although never to its previous size. In 1965, a grateful patient left £2,000 to Adams in her will.

Shortly before his death Adams was interviewed at his Eastbourne home. He refused to talk about his personal life. 'I don't want any more publicity,' he said. 'I have had too much of it. God knows, I have.'

The Nazis' Gold

War is the ideal cover for crime. World war provides an even more effective diversion. While the Nazi war machine fanned across Europe in World War 2, a criminal operation was carried out on the most colossal scale ...

Quite simply, Adolf Hitler and his generals set about systematically stealing the untold wealth of conquered countries in an orgy of blatant crime-for-profit. Like 20th-century pirates, they planned to make themselves rich in plunder at the expense of their victims. They stole not only the few miserable possessions of the millions of Jews they sent to the death camps. They literally stripped sovereign nations of their entire wealth – billions and billions of pounds in gold and diamonds and works of art. From the treasure houses of the former Czars, deep inside Russia, to the art galleries of Paris and the bank vaults of Rome, the Nazis stole and stole and stole.

Even decades after the end of the war, many governments still refuse to admit the extent of the fortunes stolen from them by the Nazis. Intelligence experts on both sides on the Iron Curtain estimate that as much as £50 billion worth of gold is still unaccounted for and that hundreds of Nazi crooks and their families are leading lives of luxury on the proceeds of the biggest robbery in history.

Much of the missing billions is still probably hidden inside Germany, sunk out of reach at the bottom of lakes or in the depths of collapsed mine shafts. Fortunes in gold were certainly channelled through Swiss bank accounts into the coffers of South American governments who charged £5 million a head to give sanctuary to fleeing Nazi criminals at the end of the war. But stunned and sickened by the debris of the war, grimly completing the task of counting the toll in death and destruction, the Allied forces gave a low priority to tracking down stolen cash and bullion. By the time they started trying to recover the astronomical sums of wealth stolen by the Nazis, the fortune had vanished into the creaking remains of the international banking system. Stolen Nazi gold is undoubtedly the basis for many of the multi-national businesses which flourish today.

In their panic-stricken flight, however, many Nazis found the sheer bulk of their loot impossible to move and they literally dumped billions by the roadsides of Europe. Even now those caches of casually hidden treasure are being uncovered. In June 1983 workmen renovating the well of an abandoned monastery in northern Italy, near the Austrian border, found the shaft blocked by heavy metal chests. They finally raised them, and counted 60 tons of gold, worth more than £540 million at 1983 prices.

An embarrassed Italian government then admitted publicly for the first time that the Nazis, their wartime Allies, had emptied the Central Bank of Rome in 1944 and had made off with 120 tons of gold. The scramble to prove ownership of the gold brought a counter-claim from neighbouring Yugoslavia that the bullion was just part of the reserves from their own national bank in Zagreb, looted by Nazi occupying forces and loaded into a convoy of trucks to be driven back to the Fatherland.

Throughout the history of warfare, victorious soldiers have plundered and looted their vanquished opponents. The looters have ranged from humble infantrymen who 'liberated' enemy wine cellars to high-ranking officers who commandeered whole castles for their private estates. Their motto: To the victor belong the spoils.

For Adolf Hitler's Third Reich, however, there was to be no petty thieving. With Teutonic thoroughness, the thefts were to be carried out on a grand scale, meticulously planned and on the direct orders of the Führer himself. Organized bank robbery was as much a declared war policy of the Nazis as the conquest of Europe and the mass murder of the Jews. The formation of an official looting department in the Nazi government was born out of Hitler's smouldering resentment of his fellows.

As a brooding teenager, Adolf Hitler moved to the Austrian town of Linz in 1903, after the death of his father in their home town of Braunau, some 20 miles away. He struggled through school, ignored by teachers and disliked by his fellow pupils, nursing only an ambition to become an artist. When his mother died in 1908, Hitler, then 19 years old, felt free to leave Linz and take his meagre talents to the glittering Austrian capital of Vienna. He marvelled at the city's splendid galleries and museums and his first call was on the Academy of Fine Arts where he applied for enrolment as a student. The

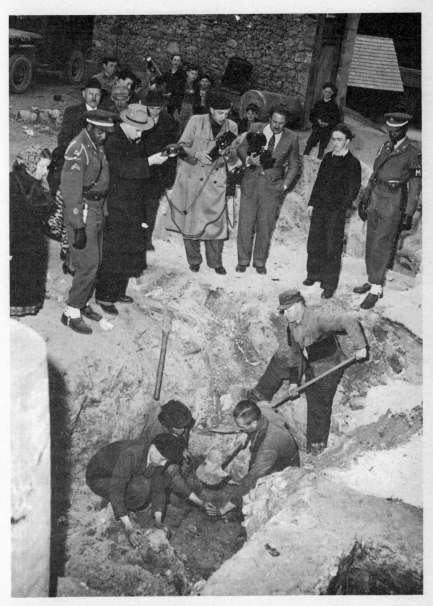

Priceless treasure is unearthed at Hermann Goering's castle

Academy examiners were unimpressed with his barely competent portfolio of drawings and recommended he try for training elsewhere, perhaps in the less demanding profession of apprentice draughtsman.

For the next few years, until he left for Munich in 1913, Hitler seethed with anger as he scraped a miserable living in doss-houses, selling his poorly painted watercolours to bar-room patrons who pitied him because he looked so ragged and pathetic. The experience left him with a sense of humiliation which remained with him for more than 20 years, until he became the all-powerful Führer and annexed Austria into the Greater Germany. That is when Hitler became master of Vienna – and had his revenge on the city he despised.

As he planned to launch war on the rest of Europe, so Hitler also planned his artistic revenge on the cultured city of Vienna. In March 1938, while

Recaptured treasure is inspected at New York's United Nations Galleries

basking in a rapturous welcome from the citizens of the drab town of Linz, his adopted home, he summoned the director of the town's provincial museum, Dr Karl Kerschner. 'I will make Linz the art capital of the world,' he promised him. 'It will have the finest treasures all of Europe can provide. I will make those ungrateful peasants of Vienna feel they are living in a slum.'

Then Hitler, the failed artist, began to sketch out his amateur architectural plans for rebuilding the city, centred around his dream of a Führermuseum which would be crammed with paintings and sculpture, tapestries and rare books, and all the golden treasures he could loot from the four corners of Europe. He sent for his squat, bloodthirsty deputy, Martin Bormann, and instructed him: 'Wherever German tanks roll, I want them to bring back to Linz all the treasures they can carry.'

And so was formed Sonderauftrag Linz – the Linz Special Mission – history's only example of a select gang of gold bullion robbers, diamond, jewel and art thieves, armed with bombers, tanks, high explosives and carte blanche to murder on behalf of their Government. But before the looting gangs bothered to turn their attentions to the treasure houses beyond Germany's boundaries, they first set out ruthlessly stripping the fortunes of their own tortured Jewish population.

While Hitler ordered vaults to be built inside the air-raid shelters of Munich as temporary store-rooms for the Linz collection, his special squad began to 'confiscate' the belongings of Jewish families. Their first target was Baron Louis von Rothschild, the richest man in Austria. Rothschild was arrested by the Gestapo and interrogated by Hitler's roving art and bullion assessor, Dr Hans Posse of the Dresden Art Museum.

Baron Louis was stripped of all his possessions, as a colossal ransom to allow him and his family to leave the country and escape from Nazi persecution. His priceless collection of gold coins was seized, together with all his valuable works of art including paintings by Van Dyck, Holbein, Tintoretto and Gainsborough.

Fortunes fell into Nazi hands even before their armies began to cross the borders into the Netherlands, Belgium and France. As fear and panic spread through the wealthy and well-to-do classes of Europe, Jews and non-Jews alike, homes and possessions were sold at give-away prices and the dwindling assets of great merchant families began pouring into the banks of neutral Switzerland.

Martin Bormann was one of the Nazi hierarchy given the task of trying to harass and bully the Swiss bankers into handing over the accounts of clients whose funds had been earmarked for seizure by the German government. Scornfully oblivious to the wrath of the Nazis, the bank managers of Geneva and Basle stood firm. They would not even discuss the identities of their clients. Ironically, a few years later, that lesson was not to be lost on the Nazi leaders who had cursed the tight-lipped Swiss money men.

As Hitler's war machine rumbled through Europe, with the Führer's hand-picked vultures following in their tracks, the section leaders of Sonderauftrag Linz were swamped. They could no longer cope with the tidal wave of treasure which began piling up in the Munich air-raid shelters. They were furiously building new offices to house the records of their glittering hoard when the most glittering prize of all fell into their hands – Paris.

Enough gold and works of art had already been allocated to the Linz project to transform the town many times over. And now the untold wealth of the Louvre, the Palace of Versailles and the vaults of the Bank of France were at their mercy. Even veteran looter Hans Posse was overwhelmed. So another unit was established specially to supervise the pillage of Paris. Art expert Alfred Rosenberg was given his own top priority organization to strip France of its national heritage and to transport the country's wealth back to Germany.

Rosenberg, son of an Estonian shoemaker, set about his task with gusto, hampered only by the overwhelming greed of the obese Luftwaffe chief Hermann Goering. The air marshal could not resist setting out to build up his own personal fortune, diverting train loads of looted art works and gold to his own private estate, Karinhall, near Berlin.

For four years the Nazi leaders stole everything they could lay their hands on. From Russia came the treasure of the palaces of Emperor Alexander and Empress Catherine. While German infantrymen died of starvation and exposure trying to capture the cities of Stalingrad and Leningrad, the looting sections plundered a total of 427 museums and banks, transporting their booty back to Berlin in fifty special trains each month.

The bank vaults of Poland and Czechoslovakia were stripped and two thirds of the national wealth of Belgium and Holland were stolen. By 1944 it was estimated that the Nazis had plundered a staggering total of £15 billion from occupied countries, worth about twenty times that amount at present-day prices. Goering's own personal fortune was built on his share of 21,903 objects of art shipped back from France.

Then the tide of war turned against the Nazis.

Hitler's dream of his Imperial Museum at Linz began to crumble as Allied bombers hit deeper and deeper into the heart of Germany. With defeat staring them in the face, the Nazis scrambled to dispose of their loot. The salt mines of the remote Austrian village of Alt Ausee were crammed with art treasures and gold, the Hohenfurth monastery, just inside the Czech border, was filled with diamonds and the castle of Schloss Neuschwanstein, near Fussen, Bavaria, packed with bullion. For the demented Führer there was no

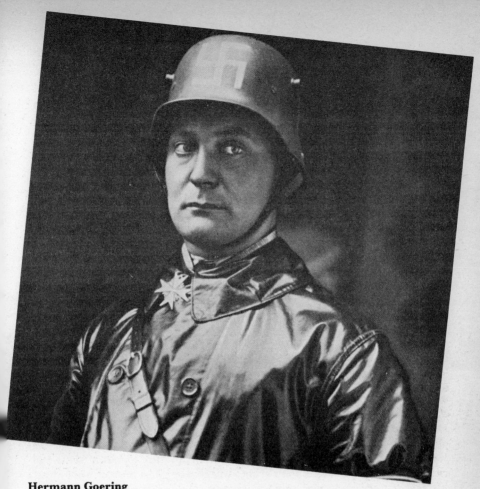

Hermann Goering

hiding place where he could scuttle for safety. But those of his accomplices who thought they could save their own skins met in Berlin to form the secret organization Odessa, devoted to financing the escape of the most wanted men in Europe. At their disposal were billions of pounds. War criminals like Bormann, death camp doctor Joseph Mengele and extermination leaders Adolf Eichmann and Walter Rauff began to bless the secrecy of Swiss banks. Using the same well-oiled banking system which had helped to protect some of their victims a few years earlier, the Odessa men funnelled gold through secret accounts to buy themselves new identities and safety in South America. Vast ranches and villas throughout Argentina, Bolivia, Paraguay and Chile were established on the stolen wealth of the men who were never caught, whose crimes are still unpunished. Odessa spent recklessly to finance its fugitives, but it is certain that pockets of Nazi gold still lie undiscovered throughout Europe.

In 1982 Danish naval divers trying to locate sunken Nazi gold in Lake Ornso, in central Jutland, came under sniper fire. The theory police came up with at the time was that it was from a former Gestapo informer who feared the hoard might reveal details of his collaboration in looting Danish banks.

During the final collapse of Germany in May 1945, the most bizarre bank robbery in history took place as American and Russian troops raced each other into the heart of Berlin. The Americans were ordered by General Eisenhower to storm the Reichsbank in Berlin, blow the vaults and transport the contents by jeep and truck back behind American lines for safekeeping. The troops responded enthusiastically, but some £200 million in gold and negotiable Swiss securities went missing on the journey back to American headquarters. Three and a half decades later, in April 1979, three men in Ontario, Canada, were jailed for trading in some of those missing war-time securities. It is also estimated that American soldiers and stragglers from the German Army helped themselves to £90 million in gold bullion, foreign exchange and jewels from the bank. Not a penny was ever recovered and not a single soldier charged with robbery.

But South America was not the only final resting place for missing Nazi gold. In the United States and Europe the fortunes of respectable business empires thrive today on the proceeds of the Nazi looting during World War 2. Yet the wartime Allies have decided that the scandalous details of history's most massive unsolved robberies will never be published. At the headquarters of the British secret service and the World War 2 Records Division of the National Archives in Washington, the files holding the names of the worst criminals and the details of their crimes will remain Most Secret until at least the 21st century – and probably well beyond.

Conviction Without the Corpse

Life as the wife of a high-powered newspaper executive gave Muriel McKay all the trappings of suburban luxury – elegance a million miles removed from the street-wise world of the popular press in which her husband had made it to the top. Her world revolved around a genteel neighbourhood where every home had been built with the wealthy in mind and through whose letter-boxes you would hardly expect to find the daily diet of sin, sex and sensation which was the trademark of husband Alick's down-market journals of mass-appeal. But on the evening of Monday 29 December 1969, the McKays' world was turned, ruthlessly and without warning, upside down ...

Alick McKay, number two to newspaper tycoon Rupert Murdoch and deputy chairman of the huge-circulation *News of the World*, returned home shortly before 20.00. From the outside, everything looked normal at St Mary House in Arthur Road, Wimbledon, south-west London. It was only after he had rung the doorbell a second time and discovered that the front door was unlocked – alarming in itself since the couple had agreed to take special care following a burglary a few months previously – that he began to realize that something was seriously wrong.

His worst suspicions were confirmed as he stepped into the hallway. Muriel's black handbag was lying open with its contents strewn half-way up the flight of stairs; the telephone had been hurled to the floor; on the hall table was an opened tin of plasters, a bale of thick twine and a rusty, wooden-handled meat-cleaver. Instinctively, Alick picked up the cleaver and raced upstairs, yelling his wife's name, fearing the intruder or intruders were still in the house.

But Muriel McKay, and whoever else had invaded the family home, had gone. Within minutes, Alick, trying to remain calm, discovered that several items of jewellery, including an eternity ring, a gold and pearl pendant, three bracelets and an emerald brooch, and a small amount of money were missing from Muriel's handbag. His mind racing, Alick ran to a neighbour's to see if anyone had heard or seen what had happened. No one had, and from the house next door he phoned the police.

In similar cases the police approach is generally low-key at the outset. Every possibility has to be examined and, in most cases, the most tangible one is that the person missing has put himself or herself on the missing persons list voluntarily – by simply walking out. And, in an overwhelming number of cases, if there is a culprit to be found, then it is more often than not the spouse who is 'left behind'.

But any thoughts that this was such a case were soon dispelled when, at 01.15 on Tuesday 30 December, the telephone rang at St Mary House. A detective who answered the call beckoned Alick to take the phone as he hurriedly picked up an extension. This was the chilling conversation that followed . . .

Caller: This is Mafia Group 3. We are from America. Mafia M3. We have your wife.

McKay: You have my wife?

Caller: You will need a million pounds by Wednesday.

McKay: What are you talking about? I don't understand.

Caller: Mafia. Do you understand?

McKay: Yes, I have heard of them.

Caller: We have your wife. It will cost you one million pounds.

McKay: That is ridiculous. I haven't got anything like a million.

Caller: You had better get it. You have friends. Get it from them. We tried to get Rupert Murdoch's wife. We couldn't get her, so we took yours instead.

McKay: Rupert Murdoch?

Caller: You have a million by Wednesday night or we will kill her. Understand?

McKay: What do I do?

Caller: All you have to do is wait for the contact. That is for the money. You will get instructions. Have the money or you won't have a wife. We will contact you again.

The line went dead as the caller rang off.

Further evidence arrived with the morning post, in a letter sent 12 hours previously from Tottenham, north London. Inside, in faltering handwriting on a piece of blue, lined paper, was a pathetic message. Alick McKay recognized at once the writing of his wife: 'Please do something to get me home. I am blindfolded and cold. Please cooperate for I cannot keep going. I think of you constantly and the family and friends. What have I done to deserve this treatment? Love, Muriel.'

The Muriel McKay case had begun to escalate into a major investigation. And with it came the attendant media 'circus'. As the McKay family closed ranks in the house at Arthur Road, one story upon which the press pack thrived was a call to Gerard Croiset, the world-famous Dutch clairvoyant who counted among his more spectacular successes the accurate pinpointing

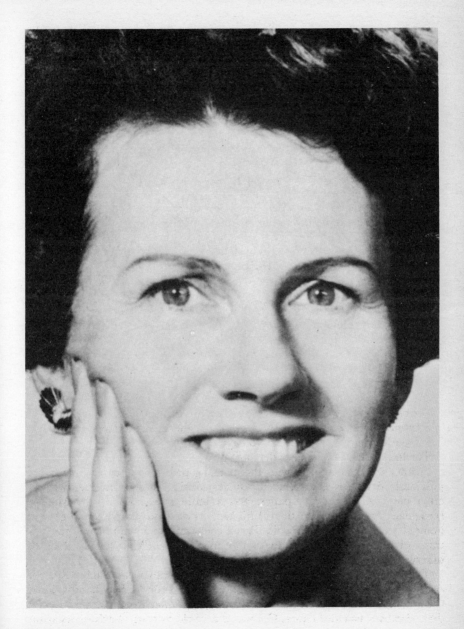

Muriel McKay

of the graves of murdered schoolchildren in Britain's notorious Moors Murders case. Croiset's unique powers enabled him to point to an area on a map which was, although largely ignored by police at the time, to prove of great significance: the border of Essex and Hertfordshire, some 40 miles outside London.

By the time a full week had elapsed, however, the police, who by then had a 30-strong team of detectives working full-time on the investigation, were still perplexed. Not one positive lead had emerged, despite the usual combing of underworld contacts and a check of hundreds of jewellers to discover whether Mrs McKay's missing possessions had been 'fenced'. The newspapers were running headline stories such as 'The Case That Does Not Add Up', and the crank callers and con-men, one of whom was later fined for trying to extort money from Alick McKay, were hampering what few inquiries could reasonably be made.

By 6 January every Metropolitan Police officer had been issued with a full description of Muriel McKay, her photograph had been posted on 'Wanted and Missing' boards at police stations throughout the country, Interpol had been alerted and a special watch was being kept on all entry points to Australia, the McKays' country of origin.

The breakthrough came a fortnight later. A large envelope posted from Wood Green, north London, contained another letter from Muriel, which read:

'I am deteriorating in health and spirit. Please cooperate. Excuse writing, I'm blindfolded and cold. Please keep the police out of this and cooperate with the gang giving Code M3 when telephoning you. The earlier you get the money the quicker I may come home or you will not see me again. Darling can you act quickly. Please, please keep the police out of this if you want to see me. Muriel.'

Also in the envelope was the ransom demand for one million pounds.

Three more telephone calls from the so-called M3 group came the following day. As the kidnap gang issued a series of demands, rendezvous points and instructions, Alick McKay desperately pleaded for some form of proof that his wife was still alive.

The gang responded with a further letter, accompanied by three pieces of material – one from the green woollen two-piece outfit Mrs McKay had been wearing, another from her black top coat and a snip of leather cut from one of her shoes. From the fourpenny stamp on the envelope, police scientific experts were able to remove a thumb-print. It did not belong to Mrs McKay. Much later it was matched to the thumb of a man called Arthur Hosein.

Police began to plot the ransom handover. It was to be made in two stages – apparently of £500,000 a time. But only £300 of the money, borrowed for the operation from Alick McKay, was to be genuine. The rest would be duds.

A series of attempted drops of the 'ransom money' followed over the next few days, resulting in some farcical mix-ups. The tolerance of the kidnap gang was wearing thin. And to the police, the gang's indecisive, amateurish handling of the actual ransom forced them to consider the possibility that the kidnappers were 'first-timers'.

The crucial day was Friday 5 February. A final call came from the gang: 'If you do not drop the money, she will be dead. You must trust M3. We deal with high-powered telescopic rifles. Anyone trying to interfere with the cases – we will let them have it.'

An elaborate plan was agreed whereby, after a supposedly monitored journey by tube-train and taxi, the money was to be dropped off by a hedge close to a garage on the Bishop's Stortford road in Hertfordshire. This time the plan went like clockwork, with police 'staking out' the drop, ready to swoop on whoever collected the ransom.

It transpired that no one did. But the police, mercifully, had their first stroke of luck. A Volvo 144 car – registration number XGO 994G – was spotted twice circling the drop-off point. It was the same vehicle that had turned up on an earlier, abortive delivery run. It belonged to Arthur Hosein.

Hosein, a Trinidad-born immigrant tailor, had, he believed, finally found his niche in English society when, in 1967, he purchased for the modest price of £14,000 Rooks Farm in Stocking Pelham, Hertfordshire. Two years after he moved in with his German-born wife Else, his younger brother Nizamodeen joined them. They were, from the start, a bizarre family, constantly at odds with their rural neighbours.

Villagers remember how quickly Arthur became known as 'King Hosein', because of his incredible arrogance and boasts that it was his intention to become 'an English gentleman and a millionaire'. It was patently clear, even then, that he exerted an eerie, Svengali-like influence over his younger, easily-dominated brother. Arthur would talk expansively of his 'estate' – and if Nizamodeen ever dared remind him of the more mundane reality of failing, neglected Rooks Farm, he would be severely castigated.

Despite his Walter Mitty existence, however, Arthur did realize that his dreams of vast wealth were unlikely to be fulfilled were he simply to rely on his ailing smallholding. Then, two months before Christmas 1969, an idea for actually making that million took root in the brothers' minds.

They were watching television when they saw what they believed to be the answer to all their problems: the affluence of Rupert Murdoch. The press tycoon was a guest on the popular David Frost show, talking of his newspapers' involvement in the exposé of the notorious Christine Keeler sex-and-politics scandal. References were made to Murdoch's beautiful blonde

Arthur and Nizamodeen Hosein

wife Anna, as well as the sort of enormous sums his newspaper, the *News of the World*, was willing to part with in exchange for exclusive stories.

A crude, but seemingly foolproof plan was hatched to abduct Anna Murdoch and hold her to ransom for one million pounds. The plan was put into operation just after the Christmas break. Only it was Muriel McKay, the wife of Murdoch's second-in-command, who became the target, purely by accident when the bungling brothers got the addresses of the two executives mixed-up; they followed Rupert Murdoch's Rolls-Royce which was being used by the McKays while Murdoch was away.

At 08.00 on the misty morning of 6 February, a squad of 20 detectives, armed with a search warrant obtained by Chief Superintendent Smith of Wimbledon police in west London, walked up the short driveway to the house at Rooks Farm in Stocking Pelham. They told Arthur Hosein's wife Else, who answered the door, that they were making inquiries about a cache of jewellery which had been stolen in London 39 days previously.

At first, Arthur Hosein remained cool enough to cast doubt in the searchers' minds as to whether he might, indeed, be their man. His wife, who seemed understandably irritated at having so many men trample around her home, also showed no signs of stress. And Arthur himself, when questioned about the missing jewellery, calmly replied: 'I know nothing. I earn over £150 a week. I do not deal in stolen property. You can look where you like.'

Look the detectives did. Methodically, painstakingly they began their search of Rooks Farm. It was only a matter of minutes before a vital shred of evidence – the first of many – came to light. From an upstairs bedroom, a young detective constable emerged with some blue and yellow slips of paper, cut into the shape of flowers for the Hosein children, which were identical to scraps found at one of the earlier ransom drop-offs.

A writing pad, on which could be made out the indentations of words that had been written on a previous page, was taken away. Experts later matched the indentations to one of the pathetic letters Muriel McKay had been forced to write by her captors. More sinisterly, a shotgun, the double-barrels of which had been sawn down in the fashion now favoured by criminals, was discovered. Moreover, it had recently been fired. Later, a key witness was to say he had heard a single shot ring out from the direction of Rooks Farm several days earlier.

The mounting evidence then took a nightmarish turn – one which was to lead to the most grisly of theories and seal forever the mystery which surrounds the Muriel McKay case. Police discovered a billhook, recently used to slaughter animals, in the farmhouse. At the time of this sinister discovery, Arthur Hosein casually commented: 'I borrowed it from a farmer friend. I wanted to chop up a calf. It was Nizam [Arthur's pet name for his brother] who did the chopping. We fed it to the dogs and put the bones and head with the rubbish.'

The information was not, perhaps, sinister in itself. But allied to the fact that the Hosein brothers had recently sold a number of pigs at market, and that traces of bone were found in the fire at their house, police began to ponder the dreadful theory that Muriel McKay may have been murdered ... and then fed to the pigs.

Had they ever been able to trace the livestock the brothers sold, they might have found the traces of cortisone – a drug Mrs McKay had been prescribed by the family doctor – which would have proved the unthinkable. But the body of Muriel McKay never was discovered. Exactly how she died, where she died and when she died remains unsolved. The considerable efforts of the police to elicit a full confession from the Hosein brothers proved – and still prove – futile.

The brothers were found guilty of the murder of Muriel McKay, even in the absence of her body. The massive weight of circumstantial evidence which the police collected against them was compounded by the matching of Arthur Hosein's fingerprints to those not only on the letters from the 'M3 gang' to the McKay family, but also on a copy of the *Sunday People* newspaper which, ironically, the brothers had dropped in the drive of the McKays' house when they staged the kidnap.

During three days of intensive interrogation at Kingston Police Station in Surrey, the true characters of the Hosein brothers emerged. Weak, easily-dominated Nizamodeen cracked quickly, and twice tried to take his own life. At one stage, when asked where he was on the night of 29 December 1969, he replied in a state of panic: 'Oh, my! What has Arthur done to me? Where did Arthur say I was? I was with my brother Arthur.' Later, he threw his arms around a detective's shoulders and sobbed: 'Kill me. What have I done? Arthur always gets me into trouble. Kill me now.' Nizamodeen's defence lawyers even found it difficult to communicate with him. In deep shock, he completely refused for six weeks even to discuss the murder case with them, until finally they persuaded him to study statements made by the prosecution witnesses.

In contrast, Arthur, while never confessing to the murder of Mrs McKay, put on a show of bravado. Described by one senior officer as 'an aggressive psychopath', he would sit in the interview room dictating statements at a ferocious pace. At one stage he boasted to his interrogator that he intended to write a book about the McKay case and turn it into a film, starring Richard Burton as the policeman in command and Sammy Davis Junior as himself. Arthur's bombast and apparent unconcern at the charge of murder he was facing astonished detectives.

Even during their trial at the Old Bailey eight months after their arrest, the brothers played out their completely contrasting roles. Nizamodeen, pale and trembling, could barely be heard giving evidence in the witness-box, even with a microphone strapped around his neck. Arthur, on the other hand, was full of himself as ever. Having convinced himself he would be acquitted – a belief he confided to cellmates and police alike – he launched into an astonishing diatribe when convicted by the jury, yelling at the judge, Mr Justice Sebag Shaw: 'Injustice has not only been done, it has also been seen and heard by the gallery to have been done. They have seen the provocation of your lordship and they have seen your immense partiality.' Unmoved, the judge passed life sentences on both brothers, with further 25-year and 15-year sentences of imprisonment on Arthur and Nizamodeen respectively for the other charges relating to Mrs McKay's abduction.

During the months between the Hoseins' arrest and their trial, the police continued their desperate, fruitless search for the body of Muriel McKay. One inmate who shared a cell with Arthur while on remand claimed that he had told him that the body was disposed of in a reservoir. Police drained the huge site Arthur had named but, again, to no avail. The story was dismissed as having been either another instance of Arthur's many fantasies or an attempt by his fellow prisoner to swap phoney evidence for some sort of remission deal.

Eventually the police were forced to abandon their search – leaving forever three vital, unanswered questions. They are still unsolved: how was she murdered, when was she murdered and where was she murdered? Was she, it is still suggested, the victim of an indescribable fate and fed to the pigs of Rooks Farm? Only two men know the answers: Arthur and Nizamodeen Hosein.

In a final, heart-rending postscript to one of Britain's most perplexing, unsolved cases, the *Sun* newspaper published a statement from Alick McKay the morning after the trial of the Hoseins ended. It said:

'One can accept death in the ordinary way. It is something which has to be faced and one has to adjust one's life to take account of it.

But in these circumstances, one is unable to accept the explanation of death without finding a body, although I am convinced Muriel is never coming home again. I must face this situation of course and face my life as best I can.

I suppose I do not want to know the brutal facts really, and yet I must always ask, how did she die, what happened to her, where is her body?

However much I try to escape the tragedy and hurt of it, I suppose I really would like to know the answers ...'

The Harry Oakes Affair

T he sub-tropical paradise of the Bahamas boasts 700 islands and rocky
      islets or cays, most of them uninhabited, surrounded by the sparkling
      blue-green waters of the Gulf Stream. Only 80 km (50 miles) away
across the horizon is the millionaire's paradise of Miami and all the brash
excitement of Florida, Land of the Stars and Stripes.

The Union Jack flies in Nassau, capital of the Bahamas, testimony to its
position as an outpost of British civilization and administration, a veneer of
respectability over its fabled history as a haven for buccaneers and rum
runners, adventures and soldiers of fortune.

But to Edward Albert Patrick David, Duke of Windsor, former monarch of
the British Empire, life in the Bahamas had held all the appeal of exile in an
Arctic waste. His appointment as Governor General in August 1940 was seen
as a deliberate punishment by the wartime cabinet of Winston Churchill.

For four years, since his abdication as King Edward VIII, the headstrong
and impetuous duke had been a grave embarassment to his government and
loyal subjects. He had provoked a constitutional crisis and world-wide
scandal when he abdicated his throne to marry the woman he loved,
American divorcee Wallis Simpson. A year after their marriage the duke and
his restless American duchess had even visited Nazi Chancellor Adolf Hitler
in Germany while he was arming his nation for war against Britain. The duke
quickly became a propaganda pawn for the Nazis.

The duke had only set foot on English soil once since his marriage before
being caught up in the roaring tide of war as the Germans invaded France
and sped towards the Windsors' new adopted home in Paris.

The former king and his wife fled south to neutral Spain and sought safety
in Madrid. Fearful that the duke might be the victim of a kidnap and used as
a hostage, Churchill asked him to return home by flying boat to Britain.

But the Duke of Windsor, resentful that his wife would not be accorded any
privilege or status as a member of the royal family, refused. He chose the only
alternative Churchill gave him, the post of Governor General of the Bahamas,
thousands of miles across the Atlantic where he could be safely isolated from
the intrigues of wartime Europe.

Lonely and ostracized, the Windsors arrived in Nassau to be greeted by the
Bahamas' most prominent citizen, Sir Harry Oakes. Sir Harry's title was no
genteel hereditary honour from a long line of ennobled forefathers. He was
reputedly one of the richest men in the Empire, a newly created baronet, a

self-made multi-millionaire. He was a ruthless businessman who had battled and bullied his way to the top from a hell-raising existence as a Yukon and Alaskan gold prospector. This hardened man of the world swiftly became the Duke of Windsor's close friend.

Their social and personal lives became entwined and Oakes even turned over his palatial home in Nassau to the Windsors while the Governor General's mansion was refurbished. The two men were constant drinking and dining companions on their frequent trips to the American mainland where Oakes introduced the duke to his social and business acquaintances.

The duke's lifetime of royal grooming as a man born to handle the gravest of personal and national crises helped him maintain his composure on the morning of 8 July 1943 when his equerry roused him from sleep and told him that Oakes was dead. He had been savagely beaten and stabbed, his skull had been fractured and an attempt had been made to burn his bloodstained body beyond recognition.

The former king quickly invoked his authority under the Emergency War Powers Act, using his powers of censorship to insist that news of Sir Harry's murder should be hushed up. A few hours later he belatedly put the wheels of legal investigation into motion – by calling in a personal contact in the Miami police.

The duke made the baffling request to Miami Police Department: 'I think one of our leading citizens has committed suicide. Can you come and confirm this?' In fact Sir Harry Oakes's 'suicide' had all the hallmarks of a Mafia gangland contract killing.

Harry Oakes had not been born a British subject. The son of a schoolteacher in Sangerville, Maine, he was a daydreamer who spent his college days boasting of the great fortune he planned to amass. After two years as a student doctor at Syracuse he gave up college. Harry told his fellow students, all dedicated young medical men: 'You can make a good living, but you'll never get filthy rich as a doctor. I want to be filthy rich.'

Harry put his medical training to use as a hospital orderly in the prospecting camps of the Canadian north, treating frostbite and gangrene and malnutrition, while he gleaned every scrap of information he could from experienced old panhandlers.

For 14 years he followed the restless waves of prospectors chasing every elusive strike from California to Yukon, Australia and the Congo. His dogged persistence paid off in 1910 when, with a partner, he finally struck gold at Kirkland Lake in northern Ontario. It was the second largest gold find in North America and over the next 12 years he connived and wheedled and spent part of his growing fortune to buy out his partner's interests and gain sole control.

Oakes was a crude and ruthless tycoon by 1923 when, at the age of 48, he married Australian bank typist Eunice MacIntyre who he met on a cruise liner. To strengthen his links with the country which provided his massive wealth, Oakes renounced his American citizenship and became a naturalized Canadian.

But Harry Oakes became disenchanted with his adopted country as his tax bill climbed higher and higher and he found himself paying 85 per cent of his income to the taxman.

On holiday with his wife and five children at one of his homes in Palm Beach, he met real estate promoter Harold Christie who boasted of the tax advantages of the Bahamas, where the British administration charged no income tax or death duties. It did not take Oakes long to decide to protect his fortune by moving to Nassau and he became a grateful benefactor. He poured millions of pounds into the islands, buying hotels and landscaping golf courses, funding charities to provide milk for children and hospitals for the poor.

His generosity soon spilled over into Britain itself where he bestowed £250,000 on one hospital. A grateful King George VI, the Duke of Windsor's younger brother who had succeeded to the throne after the Abdication, conferred a baronetcy on him in 1939.

The colourful and brash businessman who greeted the Windsors on their arrival set about making himself the power behind the Duke of Windsor's new 'throne'. All major legislation required the consent of the Governor General – the duke – and Sir Harry had him eating out of his hand.

This was the cosy relationship that real estate developer Harold Christie had to explain to his business associate when they met in Palm Beach, Florida, to discuss the prospect of opening a casino in the Bahamas.

He had already ingratiated himself with the duke and had his tacit endorsement. But Sir Harry was blowing hot and cold about the plan. Harold Christie may have wanted to apply some more gentle persuasion to the cantankerous old tycoon when he met him on the night of 7 July 1943 at Sir Harry's palatial home 'Westbourne' in Nassau.

Sir Harry was due to leave in two days time to join his family at yet another holiday home, in Maine, and Christie could not afford to miss the opportunity for some business talk. Sir Harry had guests to a small dinner party that night but they left at 23.00.

Then, according to Harold Christie, he went to bed and Christie retired to another bedroom further down the corridor. Neither man left the house again that night, Christie claimed, and although wakened during the night by the thunder of a tropical storm, he heard no sound from Sir Harry's bedroom.

When he rose for breakfast at 07.00 he strolled along the balcony to the screen door leading to the master bedroom and called out for Sir Harry. There was no reply, so he waited a few seconds and stepped inside.

Christie chilled at the sight that greeted him. The room was filled with smoke, but there was no fire. Sir Harry Oakes lay on his back on the bed, his face caked with blood, his skull fractured with four puncture marks, his flimsy pyjamas burned off and sticking to the open blisters on his charred skin.

Christie's calls of alarm alerted a housekeeper and within minutes he made the first of his frantic telephone calls to the Island Police Commissioner and to the Governor General, the Duke of Windsor.

The Bahamas police were no experts in matters of sudden, violent death and it was not entirely without relief that the commissioner received the news that the duke had asked for help from the Miami Police Department to confirm Sir Harry's 'suicide'.

The duke had spoken to Captain Edward Melchen, chief of the homicide bureau, a policeman who was also a personal friend, having acted as a bodyguard for the duke on his frequent visits to Miami. Within hours, Melchen arrived in Nassau accompanied by another trusted detective, Captain James Barker. The two men made one cursory inspection of the blistered body on the smoke-blackened bed.

'Face up to it,' Melchen told the Duke. 'This is no suicide.'

Throughout the following day, while the two Americans set up a temporary headquarters at 'Westbourne' interviewing members of the staff and the dead baronet's family, Christie and the Duke of Windsor kept in constant touch with each other by telephone. That afternoon the duke visited the murder house himself to see the scene of the gruesome crime and he spent some twenty minutes alone with Captain James Barker.

Two hours later, a suspect for the murder of Sir Harry Oakes was arrested.

Alfred de Marigny was a lean, lanky 36-year-old with a dark complexion, a native of the Indian Ocean island of Mauritius. He was also Sir Harry Oakes's son-in-law.

De Marigny had been married and divorced twice before he began his courtship of 17-year-old Nancy, Sir Harry's eldest daughter. He had been living in the Bahamas squandering the divorce settlement from his wealthy second wife when he set his sights on Nancy, and the locals all agreed he was a shiftless gigolo.

His relationship with his mercurial father-in-law had been stormy ever since de Marigny's marriage to Nancy in New York two days after her 18th birthday ... two days after becoming old enough to marry without her parents' consent.

At the time of her father's death, Nancy de Marigny had been in Florida for medical treatment and Alfred had thrown a dinner party with his houseguest and 'hanger-on', fellow Mauritian playboy George de Videlou.

Alfred left the house at 01.00 to drive two of his guests home. His route could have taken him past 'Westbourne' in the middle of the night, the prosecution insisted at his trial.

And there was evidence to link him with the murder, prosecuting attorney Eric Hallinan claimed. Whoever killed Sir Harry tried to spread flames around the room to burn evidence of the crime. And when de Marigny was examined by police, it was found the hairs on his right arm had been singed and burned.

More importantly, according to the prosecution de Marigny's fingerprints was found on an ornamental Chinese screen in the murder bedroom.

The importance of the singed hairs on de Marigny's arms was quickly squashed by defence counsel Godfrey Higgs who extracted testimony from a witness, one of de Marigny's dinner guests, that Sir Harry's son-in-law had scorched his arm trying to light a candle inside a lantern on the dinner table.

The evidence of the fingerprint became the crucial turning point in the case and highlighted some inexplicably inept investigation. Miami cop Captain James Barker testified that he had 'lifted' a fingerprint of Alfred de Marigny from the Chinese screen. He had used a gummed strip of rubber to obtain the imprint of the moist fingermark – at the same time destroying any permanent evidence that the print had been on the surface of the screen.

The space where de Marigny's print was alleged to have been was blank. Captain Barker, whose evidence became more hesitant, admitted he had not brought his own camera with him from Miami to photograph fingerprint evidence 'in situ'. He told the court, quite reasonably: 'I thought I was coming to confirm a suicide. The fingerprint camera didn't seem important.'

Barker's credibility was finally demolished by the defence's own expert, Maurice O'Neil of the New Orleans Police Department, a past president of the International Association of Identification. He examined a photograph of the sharp contours of de Marigny's fingerprint and declared it could not have been lifted off the screen without being superimposed on the pattern of intricate etchings which also covered the screen.

De Marigny's fingerprint, he deduced, had been lifted from a smooth surface, possibly from a tumbler or a cigarette packet the accused man had handled in Sir Harry's bedroom long after the murder when he was invited to the house by the American detectives.

Defence attorney Higgs never made any suggestion why he thought Captain Barker should give such blatantly phoney evidence. And there was little explanation for another crucial piece of cross examination . . .

Harold Christie, the property developer who slept in the murder house, swore on oath that neither he nor Sir Harry had left 'Westbourne' after 23.00

that night. Then Higgs called to the witness stand Captain Edward Sears, a reliable Bahamian policeman, assistant superintendent in charge of traffic.

Sears, who had know Christie since their schooldays together, confidently testified that he had seen him in George Street, Nassau, at 01.00 on the night of the murder. Christie had been a passenger in a station wagon speeding away from the direction of Nassau harbour. Sears could not identify the other man in the car, the driver. He only knew he was a white man, a stranger to the islands.

The jury retired for two hours to consider their verdict. They found Alfred de Marigny not guilty of the murder of his father-in-law.

No one else was ever charged with the murder of Sir Harry Oakes.

One blood-spattered clue to the identity of the man who may have murdered Sir Harry was uncovered nearly ten years later in Miami, on 26 December 1952, when Captain James Barker was killed by a .38 bullet from his own revolver.

The trigger was pulled by his son who tearfully told Dade County Court that Captain Barker had become a violent drug addict, corrupt and depraved. The policeman's slaying at the hands of his son was ruled 'justifiable homicide'.

It came as no surprise to his colleagues who had known for years that Barker was on the payroll of Meyer Lansky, the tough and ruthless gangster who ran the Mafia crime syndicate in Florida and Cuba.

At the time of Sir Harry's death, Lansky desperately wanted official approval to open a lucrative gambling casino in Nassau. He pulled every trick he knew and used the services of any influential people in the Bahamas he thought could be won over to his cause.

Lansky told his henchmen that one obstinate man was standing in his path and would have to be taught a lesson.

To this day people in the Bahamas still talk about the powerful motor cruisers which used to slip in and out of Nassau harbour any time they pleased, without bothering with customs and immigration formalities. They were the ships of Lansky's fleet, crewed by gun-toting skippers who knew the waters between Miami and Nassau from the days of Prohibition, when they ran illicit booze from the liquor warehouses of the British Bahamas to the speakeasies of Florida.

If Harold Christie was seen sitting as a terrified passenger in a car speeding from the docks the night Sir Harry Oakes was murdered, had he been to a meeting aboard one of those boats? Had Sir Harry been with him?

Was Sir Harry's bleeding body hunched in the back of the station wagon, fatally beaten after telling Lansky's emissaries that nobody pushed Harry Oakes around, not even the Mob?

The unidentified white man seen by police Superintendent Sears ... was the man Meyer Lansky sent to Nassau to teach Sir Harry Oakes a lesson?

Did Captain James Barker, the Miami policeman on Lansky's payroll, have orders to find a scapegoat? Did he try to frame the hapless de Marigny to shift suspicion from a contract killer?

As soon as decently possible after the end of World War 2 the Duke of Windsor left the Bahamas, hurrying back to a civilized European exile in Paris. He never discussed the Oakes murder.

Harold Christie was later knighted for his services to the Government of the Bahamas. He died in September 1973 while travelling in Germany.

Killings in the Congo

Assassination is the murder which touches the lives of millions and changes the course of history. The life of a national hero is ended by a bullet from a telescopic rifle, or a tyrant and his entourage are swept away in one blast from a hidden bomb.

The motives of a single assassin can be complex, from a madman harbouring a murderous grudge for some imagined injustice, to a lone patriot willing to sacrifice his own life to end the rule of a dictator. Often assassination is murder by committee, by a political group who want to wrest power from their opponents by destroying their figurehead.

Almost always assassination is an open outrage. The murder of a public figure usually has to be carried out in a public place, a factor dictated by the need to catch the victim when he is most exposed and vulnerable – and often a grisly ploy by the assassins to demonstrate their power and determination before a stunned audience. Assassins plot murder in secret and kill in public. And they are not slow to accept the responsibility for their crime. The lone madman is rewarded with the public platform he seeks, the political committee want to announce their success widely and clearly.

But the deaths of two prominent political figures within nine months of each other in 1961 may have provided rare case histories of assassinations unadmitted and undeclared.

Both deaths are linked together in the turbulent world of African politics. One was explained away as an unplanned, unfortunate killing. The other was

Patrice Lumumba shows his wrist which was injured during imprisonment

neatly catalogued as a fatal flying accident, the understandable failure of man and machine on a tricky night flight. Doubts still linger about the real causes of the deaths of firebrand African revolutionary Patrice Lumumba and international statesman Dag Hammarskjoeld, the peace-making Secretary General of the United Nations.

Patrice Emergy Lumumba was a fiery, erratic orator, a 35-year-old inexperienced politician with a driving, ruthless ambition. His lust for power and his ability to whip up an emotional crowd made him a force to be reckoned with in 1960 when the colonial rulers of the vast tract of the Belgian Congo felt the wind of change sweeping through Africa.

Foreseeing the explosive force of rising African nationalism, the Belgians had no great wish to pay the heavy price for hanging on to their African colony. But neither could they see any prospect for a smooth transition to independence as they began to hand over power to the people of the Congo in the elections of 1960. They were dismayed by the growing support for rebel leader Moise Tshombe who was leading the movement to wrench his own rich Katanga Province from the new independent Congo into a separate nation. But they watched most closely two political rivals who both swore to force Katanga to stay within the new Congo and who would hold the balance of power between them.

The Belgians were quietly satisfied when the election returned the quiet, educated civil servant Joseph Kasavubu to the post of President. They saw danger signs in the wave of popular support which swept Patrice Lumumba, a rebellious postmaster, into power as Prime Minister. Lumumba, they knew, had courted the promise of military backing from the Soviet Union to help him win office.

The new Prime Minister, expelled from a Roman Catholic mission school as a teenager for sexual promiscuity and later jailed for two years for embezzlement, confirmed their worst fears. Within weeks the enthusiastic and naive Lumumba found he had unleashed forces he could not control. The political theorists and policy managers of Moscow supervized his every move as the Congolese began to feel they were being freed from one foreign colonial ruler just in time to inherit another. Lumumba's reaction was to begin a bloody purge against dissident tribesmen using the resources of the teams of Russian technicians and military advisers pouring into the country.

Lumumba personally directed his troops to carry out the massacre of 3,000 Baluba tribesmen, flying his army to the scene in 19 Ilyushin jet transports provided by the Russians.

Some international observers condoned his ruthlessness as the brute force needed to weld the newly born country together. Others saw him provoking an increasingly bitter civil war.

Under pressure from the Belgians, President Kasavubu had Lumumba arrested and removed from office. There followed a cat and mouse game in which Lumumba escaped from house arrest and, according to his supporters, was greeted by cheering crowds in every village he visited.

The departing Belgians, who wanted to have a stable ally in the new Congo Republic to protect their commercial interests, were angered by Lumumba's freedom, although they seemed to regard him more as a nuisance than a serious menace, a naive troublemaker who would soon outlive his usefulness to his political controllers.

Lumumba was re-arrested in January 1961 and sent to an area where he could not expect any cheering crowds of villagers, the rebellious province of Katanga. Within a week he was dead, together with his two trusted followers Joseph Okito and Mauruce Mpolo.

But that was not the way the story was told ... Initially, Patrice Lumumba was reported to have escaped from custody yet again. A poker-faced Katanga Minister of the Interior Paul Munungo held a brief press conference to show newsmen the hole in the wall where he claimed Lumumba and his accomplices had tunnelled their way to freedom from their villa in Elisabethville, under the noses of their guards. 'We are offering a reward for their capture,' he explained.

His next press conference, three days later, was equally brief and subdued. Lumumba, according to the minister, had escaped from Elisabethville by car, travelling more than 321 km (200 miles) through unfriendly country, and stopped at a remote settlement in the bush outside the town of Kolwezi. There the villagers, anxious to claim the £3,000 reward, had promptly hacked him and his companions to death. A Katangese official had visited the site and confirmed the three men were buried in an unmarked grave.

All pressure from the journalists for further details was brushed aside.

'We forgot to specify on the reward posters that we wanted Lumumba captured alive', the Minister apologized. 'So the villagers are not to blame for his death. Besides he was a criminal so there's no harm done.'

And the location of the un-named village? It had to be kept secret, was the reply, to prevent any potentially ill-advized pilgrimages by Lumumba supporters. Lumumba's untimely death was doubtless a relief to the harassed Belgians. But the Russians who had been seen to be powerless to protect their protégé, were furious.

'Assassination' they cried and grandly set about planning a university for African revolutionaries in Moscow, to be named as a memorial to Patrice Lumumba. In the meantime they demanded the resignation of the Secretary General of the United Nations, the international body which was overseeing the Congo's transition to independence.

The wreckage of Dag Hammerskjoeld's aircraft

Being the target of scathing abuse and demands that he quit his job were nothing new for Dag Hammarskjoeld. The Scandinavian elder statesman suffered the violent criticism of Western leaders who claimed he was not making enough use of the multinational UN armed forces at his command to speed up the creation of the new Congo state. Eastern leaders complained bitterly that he interfered too much.

When Gurkha troops provided by India for the UN peace-keeping operation beat and killed hundreds of Katangan rebels, Hammarskjoeld shouldered the responsibility, burdened by the sharp condemnation of world leaders who were appalled by his mishandling of the delicate situation. Russian premier Nikita Krushchev branded the UN official: 'A bloody handed lackey of the colonial powers'.

Hammarskjoeld simply went about his job as he saw it, impartially trying to be a peaceful midwife in the bloody and painful birth of the new Congo.

He seems not to have hesitated when he received the invitation from the Katangan rebel leader, Moise Tshombe, to meet him for talks on a possible peace initiative in the battle between the breakaway province and the rest of the Congo. The talks were to be held in neutral territory, in Ndola in Rhodesia, the neighbouring country to Katanga.

From the outset, the flight was surrounded in furtive secrecy and disastrous planning. Hammarskjoeld planned to fly from Leopoldville in a DC4 Skymaster plane, specially prepared at the airport for him. At the last minute, to avoid the waiting packs of journalists, he switched to another aircraft, a DC6 airliner.

The DC6 was certainly better equipped. It was the personal plane of General Sean McKeown, commander of the UN forces in the Congo. With its four powerful engines it had a comfortable cruising range of more than 4,000 km (2,500 miles).

But 24 hours before, the DC6 had come under attack as Congolese soldiers had blasted one of its engines with anti-aircraft fire. The DC6 had been hastily repaired and left unguarded in a dispersal bay at Leopoldville Airport.

The pilot, Per-Erik Hallonquist, added to the confusion, designed to throw journalists off the track, by filing a flight plan for a journey to a small airport in Kisai Province, about halfway along his secret route to the Rhodesian border town of Ndola.

He took off in mid-afternoon, with 15 other people on board, including a radio operator with no flying experience. Only minutes before becoming airborne did he realize that the page of maps and instructions giving details of his approach to Ndola, was missing from his flight briefing book.

The flight, however, seems to have begun uneventfully. After four hours flying, around his expected time of arrival, Hallonquist contacted Ndola air traffic control, asking about weather and runway conditions and reporting his intention to descend from high altitude to 9,700 km (6,000 ft), obviously preparing to begin his approach to the airport.

The control tower responded and waited. And waited and waited ...

Two and a half hours later, the controllers were startled to see the DC6 approach the airfield from the south-west, flying from deep inside Rhodesian territory as if it had overshot its destination by 160 km (100 miles) and was retracing its route. There had been consternation over the non-arrival of the DC6 but no panic. The aircraft still had enough fuel to stay aloft for another seven hours.

Hallonquist radioed again, with matter-of-fact calmness. 'I have your runway lights in sight ... Overhead Ndola ... Now descending.' Without the benefit of radar coverage, the air traffic control staff peered into the night, beyond the runway, waiting for a glimpse of the DC6. They saw only a sudden brilliant flash of flame. Then darkness. The DC6, turning on its final approach, had struck a tree with its wingtip and plunged burning into a forest close to the airport.

In the confusion, darkness and thick jungle, it took almost two hours for the first rescue team to locate the aircraft. They found bodies scattered all round the strewn wreckage. And they found the macabre clues which seemed to show that the final fatal plunge of the DC6 might not have been a simple misjudgement by its pilot.

The fuselage, near the flight deck, was peppered with bullet holes. The body of Dag Hammarskjoeld lay sprawled in the aisle between the twisted seats. A few feet away was a revolver. And tucked into the lapel of his jacket was a playing card, the Ace of Spades.

Only one man was found alive that night, security officer Harry Jullian, an American. He was unconscious, suffering broken limbs and burns to 50 per cent of his body.

The next day the investigators began to piece together the evidence. Hammarskjoeld had not died instantly of his injuries and he had not been shot. But the long delay in reaching the crash site meant that he died without being able to tell anything about the final few minutes of the flight.

Smashed bottles of whisky and brandy had been found in the wreckage, adding weight to reports that many of the flight crew and and security escort had boarded the plane weary and staggering after an all-night binge in a Leopoldville drinking club.

Technical experts found that the plane's altimeter had an inexplicable mechanical error of 37 m (1,200 ft), giving the pilot a deceptively safe reading of his height above the ground.

And one witness had reported hearing the whistle of jets above the airport only minutes before the DC6 crashed. The only jets within flying distance were the fighter aircraft of the rebel Katangese, 160 km (100 miles) away in Elisabethville.

Later that day Sergeant Jullian recovered consciousness. The investigators sat by his bedside.

'Where had you been during the missing two hours?' they asked. 'Why didn't you arrive when you were expected?''

'Mr Hammarskjoeld told us to turn back, he didn't say why,' was all the injured man could reply. He died two days later without speaking again.

A Rhodesian inquiry firmly blamed the crash on pilot error. Later a five-man UN Commission sifted through the evidence, considering sabotage and gunfire, and concluded that the cause of the crash still remained unexplained.

The Katangese, who had bitter memories of their treatment at the hands of the UN's Gurkha troops, refused to take part in any investigation.

If Dag Hammarskjoeld's plane was brought down by a time delay bomb or a gunfight in the cabin or an attack by jet fighters, no one gloated openly or took the blame for killing him.

But who put the mark of death, the Ace of Spades, across the chest of the dying statesman? Could it have been someone who shared that last flight with him?

France's Uncrowned King

Before the revolutions of peasants and elected parliaments began to sweep through Europe in the 18th and 19th centuries, the royal dynasties of kings and princes jealously guarded their awesome power with strict codes of bloodline and heritage and succession.

The rulers who claimed a God-given right to govern millions of subjects, built their fabulous fortunes on elaborate rules of royal lineage. Loyal courtiers were always on hand to advise on the interpretation of the laws of succession in the tangled web of regal inter-marriage, first-born sons, feuding cousins and charlatan pretenders to great thrones and titles.

Often when powerful monarchs passed from the gilded stage and their relatives fell to squabbling among themselves, the line of succession could pass the mantle of power to tiny babies, first-born crown princes not old enough to walk or talk.

Jealous royal power brokers would often cast an envious eye on the cradle of some child-king, knowing that in many cases a quirk of fate, like a bout of fatal chicken pox, could swing an empire into the hands of a rival relative. Sometimes they were not slow to realize the advantages of giving fate a helping hand. Snatching a kingdom from a child, taking the royal candy from a baby, was fair game, even if the infant was a close blood relative.

When little Charles Louis was born into the royal family of Bourbon in 1785, he seemed set for a life of luxury. He was the younger of two royal children, but as the male heir, the Dauphin, he took priority over his older sister Marie Thérèse. His destiny was to rule France as the inheritor of its palaces and grand estates. But the overburdened French peasants had other ideas. Louis was only four years old when the Revolution burst on to the streets of Paris and the mobs began to howl for an end to monarchy.

The little Dauphin's parents, Louis XVI and Marie Antoinette, whose free spending lifestyle had so outraged their poverty stricken subjects, were soon prisoners of the Revolution. For two years Louis and Marie and their children were kept under house arrest as French democracy went through its own turbulent infancy, ruling the country in a confusion of committees and assemblies.

Luck ran out for King Louis and his Queen in 1793 during the session of the newly appointed Convention which unleashed the infamous Reign of Terror. Louis and Marie became just two of the stream of doomed French nobility whose lives were ended by the guillotine.

While the members of the Convention transferred the little Dauphin and his sister to the Temple Prison in Paris, the exiled royalists who had fled abroad immediately proclaimed the seven-year-old boy their new King, Louis XVII.

There is little doubt that many of the fiery members of the new Republic's National Assembly would happily have guillotined the boy king and his sister. But they could not overlook his potential as a pawn in the bargaining game they had to play with their hostile neighbours of Austria, Prussia and Spain, where the ruling royal families, fought frequent invasion skirmishes with the French to try to restore the monarchy. As long as the Dauphin and his sister remained prisoners in the Temple, their continued safe-keeping had some value if the National Assembly used them as hostages to buy off the pressure from threatening outsiders.

In the meantime, the royalists in exile and their sympathizers inside Paris, began a whole series of plots to free the bewildered little Dauphin by bribery or subterfuge.

Even some National Assembly members, worried that the Revolution might be short-lived, considered smuggling the Dauphin to their own secret hideaways

Louis XVII

to bargain for their own lives if the royalists ever regained the upper hand. Soon all Paris was abuzz with rumours that the Dauphin had been spirited out of the temple to become a youthful figurehead for a Royalist revival.

To quell the speculation, the National Assembly appointed a team of guardians and commissoners to make regular visits to the Temple to check the well-being of the Dauphin and his sister, and to report back to them.

A puzzling report was recorded after a visit on 19 December 1794, when National Assembly member Harmand inspected the nine-year-old boy in his cell at the Temple. He noted he met a child in poor health, suffering from a disabling swelling on his arms and legs. The most bizarre aspect was the boy's responses to Harmand's inquiries about his treatment. The boy showed no signs of hearing his questions and never uttered a sound in reply. He was totally deaf and dumb. Harmond's report was quickly hushed up.

In May 1795, the boy in the Temple became seriously ill and doctors were ordered to attend him. The health of the boy, apparently still a deaf mute, deteriorated still further until the night of 8 June when he died.

Four doctors authorized by the Committee of Public Safety carried out a quick autopsy on the dead boy, removing his heart and dissecting his head. They diagnosed the cause of death as scrofula, tuberculosis of the glands of the neck.

But they never carried out an formal identification of him by his sister, Marie Thérèse, who had been kept prisoner for two years in another cell on the other side of the Temple. The body, the head swathed in bandages, was placed in a coffin and hustled off for burial in a common grave in the churchyard of Sainte Marguérite.

The next day, amid continuing rumours that another child had been switched for the Dauphin in the Temple, the Convention announced his death without making any further comment.

And so the royal house of Bourbon seemed doomed to wither as the French Republic embarked on a new era of its history under the leadership of a dynamic young Army officer from Corsica, Napoleon Bonaparte.

Napoleon took less than a decade of glorious military conquest before he tried to found his own royal dynasty, crowning himself Emperor and handing out royal titles to his own children, brothers and friends.

But after his defeat at Waterloo in 1815, the victorious allies decided it was time for real royalty to regain the throne of France. Their choice was the brother of the guillotined Louis XVI, the uncle of the Dauphin. The new monarch, next in line after the boy-king who had never ruled, became Louis XVIII. It was the sign for resurrected Dauphins to pop up all over Europe.

Dozens of 'dauphins', all about the right age of 30 and all well versed in the folklore of the alleged switch in the Temple, put forward their claims and where exposed as blatant frauds.

The most curious claim came 15 years later from a Prussian watchmaker living in London. In 1830, when another Revolution, less bloody and violent, had swept the royal family of Bourbon off the French throne of France yet again watchmaker Karl Wilhelm Naundorff came forward. He insisted he did not want to try to rule France, only to prove himself to be the missing Dauphin and to try to benefit from what little privilege was still attached to the title.

Naundorff gave a long, detailed account of how he recalled 35 years earlier being carried out of the Temple on 8 June, 1795, after being drugged with opium, and spending the next 14 years being passed from 'safe house' to 'safe house' in France, England and Germany. In 1800, he claimed, the King of Prussia had organized false identity papers for him in the name of Karl Naundorff. He then married and settled down, after serving a short prison term for counterfeiting coins.

In 1833 in France, Naundorff organized a meeting with Madame Rambaud, the dead Dauphin's former nanny, and Vicomte de la Rochefoucauld, an emissary from the Dauphin's sister, then Duchess of Angoulême. The nanny was convinced about his identity and the Vicomte reported that he was very impressed with Naundorff's claims and the watchmaker's striking physical resemblance to his 'father', the dead King Louis XVI.

But the Duchess, the Dauphin's sister, took no notice until 1836 when Naundorff tried to force her into a civil court case to prove his claim. He was arrested by French authorities and deported back to England. At home in London he set about pressing his claim, in an exhaustively researched book published later that year.

All copies of the book sent to France were seized by French customs officials at Calais. Naundorff continued to bombard the French authorities and the Duchess with petitions, undeterred by an attempt on his life at his home in Clarence Place, London. He was shot, literally with his pants down, in the outdoor toilet in his garden. He survived the wound and a Frenchman was later arrested and charged with the attack.

Two other attempts were made on his life in 1841 as Naundorff struggled to earn a living as an inventor of artillery weapons. He was badly burned in a deliberate explosion in his workshop and another arson attack on his home later that year.

With his business burned out, Karl Naundorff was bankrupt and spent four years in the grim Newgate debtor's prison in London.

Released in 1845, he travelled to Holland to try to interest the Dutch government in his designs for a new field gun. Before negotiations were complete, Naundorff died on 10 August.

The official Dutch death certificate identified him as Charles Louis de Bourbon, Duke of Normandy, Louis XVII, aged 60, son of Louis XVI and Marie Antoinette. The Dutch doctor who performed the routine autopsy noted his body bore certain marks – a mole on the thigh, triangular vaccination marks on his arm and a scar on his upper lip. The marks correspond exactly to the descriptions given by Madame Rambaud, the governess to the Dauphin Louis from his birth until 1792, the year before he was locked away in the Temple.

If Karl Naundorff was indeed the young Dauphin, the leaders of the French Revolution who locked him away as a child, without trial or charge, denied him his heritage and his chance to change the course of history.

But if his story was true, which cruel and heartless conspirators, royalists or double-crossing revolutionaries, snatched him from the Temple and left a terrified deaf mute boy to die of disease and maltreatment in solitary confinement in his place?

Death of the Black Dahlia

The corpse found on an undeveloped building site in a Los Angeles suburb on 15 January 1947 had been savagely mutilated. It was the body of a young woman, cut in half at the waist and with the initials 'B. D.' carved into her thigh.

It was the use of those initials that gave the case its notoriety. They stood for 'Black Dahlia', the nickname given to a pretty 22-year-old small-time movie actress, Elizabeth Short. She was known simply as Betty or Beth to her friends. But she also revelled in the nickname of Black Dahlia because of her liking for jet-black clothes. And, from fingerprints, the body was identified as being hers.

Elizabeth Short's brief life was not a happy one. She had been a juvenile delinquent but found love and a chance of a fresh start when she met a young serviceman. He proposed, they became engaged, then parted when he was posted overseas in World War 2.

A photo of Elizabeth Short from her family album

He never came home – and his death sent Elizabeth on a downhill path. She turned to drink and tried her luck as a bit-part actress in Hollywood. But jobs were hard to come by and she began working as a waitress by day and haunting sleazy bars and pick-up joints by night. The inevitable happened. Elizabeth started to accept money for her favours. She soon became known for her black apparel – including her black silk underwear.

The Black Dahlia had one further chance of rescue when a second lover proposed to her. Cruelly, he too died ... and Elizabeth's fate was sealed.

When the discovery of the poor girl's butchered body was reported in the Los Angeles newspapers, a strange reaction set in. Perhaps it was the photographs of the beautiful young victim – before and after death – that incited an astonishing spate of false reports and confessions.

The first came from a waitress who said she had heard two killers discussing the crime at a table. She gave the police a description – and inquiries revealed that the 'killers' were a couple of detectives having an off-duty coffee. Another tip came from a blonde dancer who told police: 'I'm meeting a man at First and Temple Streets at nine o'clock and I have reason to believe he's the Black Dahlia killer.' Detectives arrested the pair and took them in for questioning. The man turned out to be an innocent executive who had once spent a night with the blonde, following which she had been trying to blackmail him, without success. The 'tip off' to the police was just her way of applying extra pressure.

One piece of evidence the police took much more seriously was a package sent to a Los Angeles newspaper enclosing a message cut from press headlines. It said: 'Here are Dahlia's belongings. Letter to follow.' The package also contained Elizabeth's social security card, her birth certificate and an address book – with one page torn out. Police said they believed that these articles had been removed from the body – no clothing was found at the scene – and that the missing page in the address book would have revealed the name of the killer. Fingerprints were taken from the social security card but they matched none in police files.

Later, a small-time underworld figure gave himself up to police, saying 'I killed the Black Dahlia.' This time detectives thought they had solved the case, because in Elizabeth's address book had been the name of a firm the suspect had once worked for. But a lie-detector test showed he was just another crank.

Years later, a 29-year-old army corporal was held on suspicion after volunteering the information: 'When I get drunk I get rough with women.' He knew many details of the killing. But again, he was finally dismissed as being mentally unbalanced.

In all, around 50 men have claimed they committed the murder – but the case of the Black Dahlia remains unsolved.

Chapter nine

CRIMES OF PASSION

Love, jealousy, revenge and despair – they are all emotions which everyone can understand. In the following cases of *crime passionnel*, more often than not, someone feels themselves to be wronged – and someone else pays the price. But what links all these crimes is their passionate nature. Even the most coolly accomplished of them were conceived in the turmoil of hot blood.

Murder on the Opening Night

I t wasn't a very good show. Some of the biggest names in New York high society had turned up to see the new musical comedy opening on the roof garden of Madison Square Garden. *Mam'zelle Champagne* the entertainment was billed as, but its bubbles were flat and the fashionable socialites were yawning when the male lead got up to sing about love.

Then there was a gunshot; and another two shots. The orchestra stopped playing. And nobody yawned any more.

Harry Kendall Thaw, 34-year-old son of a Pittsburgh railroad magnate, was standing among the café-concert tables with a pistol smoking in his hand. Before him, Stanford White, the nation's most celebrated architect, was crumpled in his chair. Slowly he slid to the floor, blood spilling in crimson cataracts over his expensive shirt front. There were two bullet holes in his body. The third shot was lodged in his brain.

All around, people screamed and stampeded for the exits; vainly the manager called for the show to go on. The date was 25 June 1906, and the roof garden murder was to keep America reeling for months to come.

The public learned quickly that it was a love triangle killing. Thaw had publicly gunned down the seducer of his wife. 'I am glad I killed him. He ruined my wife', he had called on the fateful evening. But in this particular triangle were caught lurid shapes – of lust, sadism and madness – all refracted in the prism of big money.

The woman in the case was Evelyn Nesbit Thaw, the beautiful wife of the arrested gunman. Standards of prettiness change with the decades, but her beauty stands somehow outside time. The photographs show a pale, oval face, dark eyes, sensual mouth and lustrous curls. Frail and voluptuous, her features might have embodied the feminine mystique in a painting of any era.

In fact, Evelyn Nesbit had started out as an artist's model. But she soon moved on into the show world. At the age of 15 she was already appearing as a chorus girl in *Floradora*, a smash musical of the period. From the show one song is still well remembered: *Tell Me Pretty Maiden (Are There Any More at Home Like You?)* And from the high-kicking chorus line came another pretty maiden who appears in the pages of this book: Nan Patterson (see page 151).

Evelyn Nesbit had known the murdered architect long before she had known her husband. Stanford White was internationally respected for his building

Harry K Thaw dines in style behind bars

Stanford White

designs which included, ironically, Madison Square Garden itself. He was a large man with a florid complexion, moustachioed face and roué's lifestyle. On his first meeting with Evelyn he took her and another girl upstairs to a luxurious room in his apartment. It was equipped with a red velvet swing, and he gave the girls turns on it, pushing them right up to the ceiling where their feet reached a Japanese umbrella. But beyond his exotic décor and his playful games, White exhibited deeper passions. In his studio at the apartment, he soon had Evelyn posing for photographs in a silken kimono. On a later occasion, having dizzied her with champagne, he took her to a room whose walls and ceiling were covered with mirrors. There he seduced her while she was sleeping. She was still only 16 years old.

Evelyn went on to become one among several mistresses kept by the architect. He paid her weekly sums of money, brought her out into society and showed her off. Being married, to a very long-suffering wife, White could not offer the girl his hand. And that was one advantage which Harry K. Thaw had over the middle-aged architect.

Thaw met Evelyn Nesbit while she was going around with her seducer. And in the murder trial which was to come, his lawyers did what they could to suggest that Thaw had chivalrously redeemed the fallen showgirl. Certainly, Thaw was outraged by the story of the girl's initial seduction. He hated the architect, always referring to him as 'The Beast' and 'The Bastard'. But Thaw himself was no noble knight errant. Actually, he was a monster.

The spoiled playboy son of a millionaire family, Harry Thaw promised to marry Evelyn if she would run away with him to Europe. She accepted the offer, little knowing her admirer's sexual tastes. It was in the Tyrolean castle of Schloss Katzenstein that they were first revealed. One morning at breakfast in the rented castle, he stripped her of her bathrobe and left her naked except for her slippers. Producing a cowhide whip, he threw her onto the bed. 'I was powerless and attempted to scream,' the girl was to testify, 'but Thaw placed his fingers in my mouth and tried to choke me. He then, without any provocation, and without the slightest reason, began to inflict on me several severe and violent blows with the cowhide whip.'

She was in bed for three weeks afterwards, and other similar episodes were to occur before the marriage. It was one of Thaw's kinks, like the cocaine habit he had acquired. Other girls had received the same treatment at his hand.

Why did the chorus girl marry a man with such malevolent passions? Part of the answer must lie in the lure of the Thaw millions, amassed in railroads, coal and coke. There is evidence that some pressure was applied on Evelyn by her own family, and it is not hard to imagine their promptings: darling, your good looks won't last forever . . .

Stanford White could scarcely offer protection. In fact, he seems to have collaborated with her family in pressing for the marriage to go ahead. Whatever the reason, Evelyn Nesbit married Harry Thaw on 4 April 1905. It was a big society wedding in which the bride wore white despite the fact that the pair were known to have cohabited in New York already. The couple set up home in the Thaws' Pittsburgh mansion, and if the playboy's own family were none too happy about the marriage they made the best of it that they could.

It was Harry Thaw who became more and more unbalanced. He bought a pistol and was seen posing with it like a duellist in his bedroom. On 25 June, 1906, just over a year after his wedding, he took Evelyn to New York where they dined together at the Café Martin before going with friends to Madison Square Garden for the opening of *Mam'zelle Champagne*. Stanford White arrived later, and took a table on his own. The lacklustre performance had been going on for some time before Evelyn decided it was too dull to endure. The party rose, heading for the elevator. Evelyn in fact reached the lobby before noticing that her husband was not with the party.

Disarmed in the elevator moments after the shooting, Thaw was to explain to the District Attorney: 'I saw him sitting there, big, fat and healthy, and there Evelyn was, poor delicate little thing, all trembling and nervous.'

So spoke the sadist. The Thaw family was to spend hundreds of thousands of dollars not only on their son's legal defence, but on press campaigns to smear his victim. White, of course, presented an easy target for slander considering his roué's lifestyle. But Harry Thaw made no promising defendant either. His first trial for murder opened in January 1907 and did not end until some four months later. The jury eventually arrived at a split verdict. Seven declared Thaw guilty of first degree murder, but five held out for not guilty – by reason of insanity.

A year later, at a second trial, more was made of the issue of madness. Cases of mental disorder in the Thaw family were discussed; a brothel keeper described savage whippings that the defendant had administered to young girls. The jury on this occasion achieved a unanimous verdict. After 27 hours they voted Harry Thaw to be not guilty by reason of insanity.

Thaw was committed to the New York State Asylum for the Criminally Insane. And the story might have ended there but for the wealth and energy of his family who pressed continually for his release. Thaw did in fact taste freedom in 1913 – but not through any court decision. One morning in August he escaped the asylum, climbed into a waiting car and fled for sanctuary to Canada.

Much diplomatic pressure was exerted by the United States Government, and the fugitive was forced to return after only a month. He was jailed at Concord, New Hampshire, and eventually sent back to New York. Tirelessly, the Thaw family campaigned through their lawyers for his release. And in the end they won. In July 1915, as a result of yet another trial, Harry K. Thaw was declared both sane, and innocent of charges against him.

It was an extraordinary decision. Evelyn immediately divorced him and went off to live her own life. A free man, Harry Thaw responded to his good fortune only a few months later by kidnapping and cruelly horsewhipping a Kansas City youth who had incurred his displeasure. Again declared insane, he was again committed to an asylum. Again a court found him to be sane after all – and again, in 1924, he was released from custody.

Harry Thaw died of a coronary in Florida in February 1947. His case had made New York a Babel of gossip, loud rumour and frank accusation. But you do not have to be especially cynical to believe that, in the end, the most persuasive voice of all was the voice of money.

Harry and Evelyn Nesbit Thaw during a period of reconciliation

Wild Bill and his Women

In the old West, where female company was scarce, jealousy probably motivated more murders than cattle or bullion ever did. From bar-room brawls to main street showdowns the quarrels flared. Life was cheap, and many a legendary lawman owed notches on his gun not to zeal for the law – but to love of women.

Take Wild Bill Hickock, for example. The famed Union scout and Indian-fighter used to boast of a great Rock Creek shoot-out that began his crime-fighting career. The pistoleer claimed to have slain the ten-man McCanles gang single-handed: six bullets saw off Dave McCanles and five henchmen; he used a knife to cut down the other four villains. The West was well rid of the gang, said Hickock, for they were 'desperadoes, horse-thieves and murderers' to a man.

Wild Bill, of course, was one of the Wild West's great self-advertisers. Six foot two inches tall (wearing high-heeled shoes), with auburn curls that cascaded to his shoulders, the 'Prince of Pistoleers' made such an impressive figure that dude reporters from the East lapped up every word he said. In reality, James Butler Hickock was a drunk, a liar and a womanizer. As it happens, there was a McCanles episode – but it was not quite as Wild Bill told it.

In 1862, Hickock was working as a humble stable hand at the Rock Creek pony express station in Jefferson County, Nebraska. The manager there was a Mr Horace Wellman, and the stockkeeper a J.W. Brink. And in the offing, too, was a certain Sarah Shull (Kate Shell), something of a local belle.

Hickock stole the lady's affections from David C. McCanles, a landowner of the neighbourhood. And on 21 July 1862, the jealous McCanles rode out to the station threatening to 'clean up on the people' there. He was clearly intending a Wild-West style crime of passion, but had no cohort of desperadoes with him: just two neighbours and his 12-year-old son.

When the smoke cleared at Rock Creek that day, only the boy returned.

Years after the event, historical investigators succeeded in tracing the boy, Monroe McCanles. And he gave an account of the affair which reflected no credit on the legendary lawman. Monroe stated that when his father entered the station manager's house, Hickock shot him in the back with a rifle from a hidden position behind a curtain. Then Wild Bill turned the weapon on one of the neighbours, but only succeeded in wounding him; the man was beaten to death by Wellman who used a hoe. McCanles's second companion fled out into the scrub and was killed with a shotgun – Monroe could not say by whom.

So much for the solo slaying of ten desperadoes. Monroe's version of events

Wild Bill Hickock

was broadly confirmed in 1927, when investigators dug up court records from Nebraska. It appears that three men – Hickock, Wellman and Brink – were charged with the triple murder. The accused escaped punishment, however, on a plea of self-defence.

And did Wild Bill ride off into the sunset with the lovely Sarah Shull? Not a bit of it. He had a succession of paramours, and in 1865, his liaison with a certain Susanna Moore was to lead to the first Wild West showdown on record. A man named Dave Tutt took up with the lady and incurred the pistoleer's jealous wrath. A disputed card game provided Wild Bill with his pretext, and he challenged his rival to a gun duel in the public square at Springfield, Missouri.

The duel is an age-old means of settling a love-triangle quarrel: a kind of ritualised crime of passion. This one differed only from earlier gun duels in that the weapons were holstered. Tutt drew first, and missed. Before he had time to fire again, Hickock had put a bullet through his heart.

A Crime That Rocked a Kingdom

It was an odd, odd business. The scandal that rocked France in 1847 helped to bring down a dynasty. It involved one of the noblest families in the nation, and no *crime passionnel* in French history has provoked more discussion. There is no question about the identity of the murderer in the Praslin affair, nor of the horrific savagery of the crime. Thick dossiers of letters and statements still survive in the Paris National Archives, along with trunkloads of material evidence: a silken bell pull, bloodstained clothing, bronze candlesticks and a hunting knife among other items. But despite all that has survived and all that has been written, mystery lingers about the case, elusive as the aroma of expensive tobacco and the musk of Old French roses. Underneath, it was an odd, odd business.

The young Théobald de Praslin married Fanny Sébastiani on 19 October 1824. He was only nineteen, she was two years younger, and they were very much in love at the time. The families on both sides being of immense wealth, the wedding was a glittering occasion. The young marquis was heir to the great Praslin dukedom, and his bride was an honorary goddaughter of Napoleon. Big interests blessed the marriage, which began rich in promise as an idyl of domestic happiness.

She bore him children – nine of them in less than fifteen years – perhaps too many in the light of what was to come. For under the strain of successive pregnancies and births, the Marquise lost her radiant looks. Her dark, romantic features – inherited from Corsican blood – thickened and became swart. She grew corpulent. And her temperament, once agreeably capricious, soured into a volatile and domineering nature.

Her husband, in contrast, was a passive, introverted man little given to displays of emotion. The more she nagged, ranted and threw tantrums the more he retreated into a shell of cold reserve. Fanny continued to love Théobald in her tempestuous fashion; but on his part, love turned slowly into detestation.

Before 1839, when their last child was born, the decline in their relationship had begun. Already he had taken to shunning her bedroom, and she was writing him letters of complaint. They were eloquent letters which sprang directly from the heart, but the themes were monotonously reiterated: she regretted her fits of temper, tried to patch up the latest quarrel, craved his pity for her uncontrollable emotions. 'I am no longer the mistress of my feeling', she wrote at one point. 'Something over which I have no control takes possession of me.'

The Marquis merely became more disdainful. And in 1840, things took a terrible turn for the worse when he required her to sign an extraordinary document. By the terms of this private agreement, Madame de Praslin was to give up her natural rights as a mother. The family's governess was to have sole charge of all that concerned the children: clothes, schooling, recreation and so on. Madame de Praslin was not even permitted to see them unless in the company of the governess.

It was, by any standards, an appalling document for a mother to sign, and historians have long puzzled over its implications. Madame de Praslin wrote privately about it, claiming that she had sacrificed all to try and regain her husband's affection. But there are hints that some specific incident or discovery lay behind her renunciation. Was it some violent outburst which had frightened the children and led her husband to think them unsafe in her presence? Or was it something darker than that?

A charge of somehow 'corrupting' the children seems to have been laid against Madame de Praslin. It is known that her own governess at one time had been a certain Madamoiselle Mendelssohn, suspected of lesbian relations with her pupils. Did the Marquis suspect his wife of the same proclivities? Had she interfered with her own children?

It is just one of the affair's lingering mysteries. The contract, the shunned bedroom – all this was in private. In public, the couple continued to appear amid the plush and chandeliers of the Court, to receive guests and dispense their hospitality. In June 1841, Théobald's father died and he became the fifth Duc de Choiseul-Praslin, inheriting not only some nine million francs but the magnificent château of Vaux-le-Vicomte.

This superb building survives as one of the great splendours of French Baroque style. With its domes and towers, fountains and tree-lined avenues, it was to provide the grandest backdrop imaginable for the drama which was to unfold.

To Vaux, with the new Duke and Duchess, came a new governess only recently hired. The orphaned and illegitimate daughter of a Bonapartist soldier, she had dragged herself out of a miserable childhood to serve with a noble English family. Fair-haired, green-eyed and socially accomplished, she came to the Praslins with the best possible credentials. In due course, the whole of France was to become fascinated by the Mademoiselle: her name was Henriette Deluzy.

Partisans of the Duchess were to paint her as a scheming adventuress who brought shame to a noble household. Others saw her as a decent girl placed in an intolerable position. History's verdict must draw a little from each portrait. Henriette Deluzy did not create the unhappy marriage – it was in a disastrous state when she arrived. Nor (this seems quite clear) did she and the Duke ever become lovers in the carnal sense. But the pretty young governess was both intelligent and ambitious. Coming from her own insecure background, the splendours of Vaux, the Praslin millions, all the ranks and privileges which went with them – these lures combined with the manifest unhappiness of the Duke must surely have excited her thoughts. After all, even decent girls may dream a little . . .

Praslin told her at the outset about the contract he had made with his wife. Though it struck her as strange, it also gave her unique powers in the household. Mademoiselle Deluzy accepted the position and was soon supervising all that concerned the children. Two of the daughters, Berthe and Louise, came quickly to adore her. The young instructress was bright, vivacious and thoroughly sane – in marked contrast to their unbalanced, faintly terrifying mother.

It was not long before the Duke, too, came to seek refuge from the chill of his marriage in the governess's warm little circle. He loved his children and he loved to see them happy. Temperamentally indolent as well as reticent, the Duke spent more and more time in their company.

The Duchess, of course, was reduced to paroxysms of rage. Mademoiselle Deluzy quickly became 'that woman', and night after night in her lonely bedchamber the Duchess wrote long impassioned letters to her husband. The governess, she fumed, was 'bold, familiar, dominating, thoughtless, inquisitive, gossipy, insolent and greedy.' She had split the family, and set daughters against their mother. One accusation repeatedly made is of especial significance in the light of what was to come. The Duchess claimed that the scheming governess was deliberately *making it appear* as if she was her husband's mistress. The Duchess, however, never at any stage seems to have suspected that her rival was actually sharing his bed.

Everybody else, though, came to believe that she was. Within a year or so of Mlle Deluzy's arrival the rumours were beginning to spread. In a Paris society that drank gossip like fine wine, the scandal began to ferment. In the summer of 1844 the Duchess publicly threatened suicide, creating such an embarrassing scene that the Duke decided that a break was called for. He took three of his daughters, with their governess, off on a long Mediterranean holiday. The Duchess remained at Vaux. And for the first time in print, there appeared in a Paris gossip column, a snippet concerning the Praslin ménage. The Duke, it was said, had gone off for a vacation with his mistress.

This delicious little item did not go unnoticed. The story circulated not only around the Paris boulevards, but reached the courts of Europe as well. Mademoiselle Deluzy would have to leave the household now, all the well-informed tattlers said. But she did not. To do so would only give credence to the rumours, and the Duke determined to remain aloof from such malicious gossip.

Shamed beyond endurance, the humiliated Duchess took to eating all her

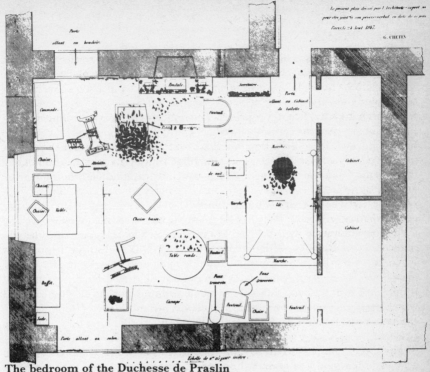

The bedroom of the Duchesse de Praslin

meals in the solitude of her bedchamber. She refused any contact with the governess and penned ever more eloquently hysterical letters to her husband.

The whole miserable business dragged on. In 1846, an unaccountable reconciliation appeared to occur, when the Duchess suddenly started making herself agreeable to the governess. It can only be explained as a change of tactics, though, for Madame de Praslin still fulminated in her letters to her husband about the 'little pair of green eyes behind your shoulder.' In reality, the mortified mother was maturing a plan for revenge.

She struck in June 1847. In that month, the Duke was suddenly but formally informed by his father-in-law that if the governess did not leave the household for good, his wife would sue for divorce and claim sole custody of the children.

The threat had terrible implications. The Duke himself clearly believed (for whatever reason) that his children were unsafe with their mother. Not only would he lose them to her, but the furore of the divorce would seriously affect his daughters' marriage prospects. The scandal would be immense, and what right-minded noble family would take on girls from this adulterous ménage? He could not doubt that Madame de Praslin would win her case – the scandal-mongering press had seen to that.

Now the governess really did have to go. After a fierce but hopeless argument with his father-in-law, the Duke regretfully informed Mlle Deluzy that she should quit the household, with a generous life pension and a good reference for future employment.

She took it badly. Whatever private fancies she may have entertained about her future at Vaux, she certainly loved her charges; for six years the Praslin girls had comprised the only family she had ever known. That night she wept uncontrollably and swallowed laudanum in quantities that nearly took her life. But the next day she recovered, and in time she capitulated. She signed the annuity agreement.

And so the whole affair might have ended, but for the dark passions which the episode had engendered. The girls, for example, were unspeakably distressed by their separation from their beloved Mademoiselle. The Duke, meanwhile, was reduced to cold fury, a refrigerated rage which chilled even the triumphant Duchess. In a private memoir she wrote: 'He will never forgive me for what I have done . . . Every day the abyss between us will grow deeper. The more he thinks about what he has done, the more he will hate me and the more he will wreak vengeance on me. The future appalls me. I tremble when I think of it . . .'

There was not much of a future left, as it transpired, for either the Duke or the Duchess.

The discharged governess sought lodgings in Paris. But wherever she was accepted she would immediately find herself thrown back out onto the street. A certain Abbé Gallard was going the rounds, warning the owners off. Mlle Deluzy, said the cleric, was an immoral woman soon to be named in a divorce court. Also, he implied that she was pregnant. The Abbé Gallard was the Duchess's confessor.

Eventually, the embattled governess found a small room at the Pensionnat Lemaire, a school for young women in one of the seedier quarters of Paris. She was desperately unhappy and wrote pitiful letters to the Praslin girls imploring them not to forget her. They answered with equal *tendresse*: they had had terrible scenes with their mother, they wrote. Also: 'You are our real mother.'

On 26 July, Mlle Deluzy briefly met two of the Praslin children with their father in Paris. His face at that time seemed to have crumpled. And during the brief meeting he told the ex-governess something about the Duchess that quite appalled her.

We do not know what that something was.

It is another of the lingering mysteries. Among all the documents preserved in the National Archives, references to the dark secret seem to have been excised. From allusions that have survived it is known to have involved '*horrors*', 'secret carryings-on' and the Duchess's 'corruption of her sons'. Horace, the ten-year-old boy, had 'confessed infamies' to his father.

Some have interpreted these elusive references in the most literal way, suggesting that the Duchess had seduced at least one of her young sons. A more probable solution is proposed by Stanley Loomis in his authoritative study of the case, *A Crime of Passion* (1967). We know that after the governess had gone, the Duchess continued to threaten the divorce unless Mlle Deluzy actually left the country. That was what lay behind the persecutions of the Abbé Gallard. And it is possible that the Duchess had persuaded one or more of the boys to speak out against his father and the governess. He might even lie, pretending, for example, to have witnessed the couple in bed. Pure speculation, of course. What we do know is that the cold, reserved and rather weak-spirited Duke now plotted the murder of his wife.

All the pent rage inside him found expression in his plan of revenge. At the great Paris residence, the Hôtel Sébastiani, he began in the most comically inept way by removing the screws from his wife's bedposts. His idea was that the vast and weighty canopy above would collapse to crush or suffocate her. There is no doubt that he entertained this bizarre project, culled from the romantic fiction of the day. After the affair had reached its bloody climax, it was found that ceiling wax had been stuffed as camouflage into the holes where the screws had been.

Nor was this the Duke's sole preparation. At the Hôtel Sébastiani, he also used his trusty screwdriver to remove the bolt by which his wife could lock her door from his own connecting suite. If the canopy failed to kill the Duchess, he would then be guaranteed of access to finish the job. His plans made, the Duke gave orders that absolutely nobody should enter the Hôtel apartments until the next visit of his family to Paris.

That visit came on 17 August. While Madame de Praslin went straight to the Hôtel Sébastiani, the Duke and four of his children repaired first to the Pensionnat Lemaire for a tearful reunion with the discharged governess. During the brief call, the Duke promised that he would try and get letters of reference from the Duchess for Mademoiselle Deluzy.

Once back at the Hôtel, father and children retired to their various quarters. The lights were out by 23.30; all looked set for a peaceful night. It was at about 04.30 that a succession of blood-curdling, barely human shrieks ripped the dawn air over Paris.

The Duke, having perhaps waited hours for the canopy to collapse, had resorted to a furtive assault. He crept stealthily into his wife's bedroom, carrying with him a pistol and hunting knife. Bruises found on the corpse the following morning indicate that he clamped one hand firmly over her mouth as with the other he tried to cut her throat. But he only half-succeeded. With blood spurting from a gashed artery, Madame de Praslin woke and grabbed the double-edged blade, cutting her hand in the process. A big, strong woman, she managed to

A contemporary print depicting the death of the Duchess

break free, to scream and to tug at the bell rope. A horrific fight and chase ensued, the Duchess staggering like a wounded animal around the room, steadying herself against the walls with her bleeding hand, frantic to escape her maniacal husband. Chairs and tables were knocked over; the bell rope was torn from its mounting. Later that morning, the copious bloodprints all around enabled the police to map the whole struggle with fine precision. It was on the sofa before the fireplace that the fifth Duke of Choiseul-Praslin finally cornered his wife. There, using a weighty brass candlestick taken from the mantlepiece, he clubbed her to the ground.

From the moment that the first terrible yelp had filled the Hôtel, servants had been trying to break into the suite. But all the doors were locked. Eventually, it was the Duke himself who admitted the staff. 'What has happened?' he asked them, feigning ignorance. The Duchess died moments later, and though the Duke tried to brazen it out by claiming that an intruder must have been responsible, his guilt was quickly established. When the head of the Sûreté Nationale first examined the appalling scene he remarked: 'This is not the work of a professional. It is the work of a gentleman.'

The Duke had had time to try and destroy the evidence, but in no satisfactory way. Smoke was seen pouring from the fireplace in his own bedroom, where he had burned bits of bloodstained clothing as well as a quantity of papers. The *robe de chambre* he was wearing was found to be damp with water applied to the red bloodmarks on the material. His hands were scratched and bitten, and the hunting knife was found concealed in his apartment.

Paris was in uproar. A crowd gathered immediately around the Hôtel, and called for the death of the murderer. For the indignant citizenry, the crime came to embody all the moral corruption with which the régime was tainted. The constitutional monarchy of Louis-Philippe was already reeling from a financial scandal in which two government ministers had been implicated. The next year the king was to be overthrown by revolution; and historians have identified the Praslin murder as being a key event which helped to trigger the insurrection.

In the public mind the issue was clear: the Duke had murdered his wife for love of an English-trained governess. And the fear was that because of his rank, the murderer would escape punishment. In reality, there was no likelihood that this would happen. The Duke was brought to trial before a Court of Peers who fully recognised the need to appease the public. In fact, the peers' greatest worry was that the Duke might commit suicide before sentence could be passed. 'What a mess!' the king was heard to exclaim as he signed the order summoning the court to convene. For the government, Count Molé wrote to a colleague: 'Impress upon the Chancellor Pasquier (head of the court) that it will be a public misfortune if this monster escapes by a voluntary death the fate which the law has reserved for him.'

In the event, however, the Duke did deprive the court of the satisfaction of dispensing its justice. While under close guard, he managed to swallow a dose of arsenic. It took him six days to die of the poison – six days of atrocious agony. He remained tight-lipped to the end, answering only evasively the questions put to him, and refusing to confess his guilt.

All the weight of public interest now fell on Mademoiselle Deluzy. She was kept in confinement for three months after the murder and subjected to the most exhaustive questioning. Had she been the Duke's mistress? Had she encouraged the crime? Throughout her ordeal, the ex-governess remained adamant in her denials. In the end she was released a free woman, but with an official proclamation hanging over her. The document acknowledged that there was no evidence to connect her with the crime. It did, however, charge her with having had a 'culpable liaison' with the Duke.

A now notorious woman, Mademoiselle Deluzy left France in 1849 to make a new life in America. Wearied by her trials but unbroken in spirit, she there married a young Presbyterian minister named Henry Field. The couple became leading lights in New York's church community, and though her past was known it was not held against her. Mrs Field died in 1875 at the age of 63. The obituaries barely mentioned the Praslin affair, but fêted her for her generous hospitality, her good works and her shining intellect. Before she died she had even written about France for her husband's religious periodical, *The Evangelist*. In her articles Mrs Field expressed her conviction that, whatever political upheavals might rock the country of her birth, one quality would guarantee the survival and well-being of France.

That quality was the strength which the nation derived from its happy family life.

Death of a Minister

Pierre Chevallier's public career had been a story of brilliant success. He came from a family of well-to-do doctors and served as a medical officer during the early months of World War Two. As a result of his bravery in tending wounded soldiers under fire he was decorated. When the Germans occupied his native city of Orléans, Chevallier continued to practise medicine by day, but by night he headed the local Resistance. Before the Allies arrived to liberate the city, Pierre Chevallier had bravely led the attack which drove the Germans out.

Elected mayor of Orléans at the age of only 30, Chevallier threw himself into the task of postwar rebuilding. So masterfully did he manage the work that Orléans was officially cited as the best reconstructed city in France. Chevallier became parliamentary representative for Orléans. And on 11 August 1951, he won an even greater honour. Aged 41, he was given ministerial rank in the new government of René Pleven.

The following day, Pierre Chevallier returned from Paris to Orléans as Under Secretary of State for Technical Education. He was driven down in a big, black limousine decorated with the official tricolor cockade. He only really came for a change of clothes – there were ceremonies to attend. His wife Yvonne was waiting at their home, and told their younger son Mathieu to run and greet him with the words, '*Bonjour, Monsieur le Ministre*' (Good day, Minister).

The child ran to the doorway with his greeting. Chevallier was delighted with the reception, and tenderly hugged his son. There were, however, no joyous greetings for his wife.

Chevallier went upstairs to change clothes in the bedroom. Yvonne followed him up. There was a quarrel – and she shot him four times with a 7.65 mm Mab automatic.

Downstairs, little Mathieu heard the shots and started crying. Yvonne went down to comfort him and hand him for care to a maid. Then she returned to the bedroom. A fifth shot was heard – and a fifth bullet drilled into her husband's corpse.

He had been a minister for precisely one day. Soon, the whole of France was to learn that behind the glittering façade of Pierre Chevallier's life lay a story of failure – the failure of a marriage.

Pierre and Yvonne had married before the war. She was a nurse of peasant background who worshipped the dynamic young doctor. From the outset, Pierre's family considered the marriage a mistake, never really accepting it. And their judgement seemed to be confirmed as Pierre's fortunes rose. Yvonne lacked the social graces, becoming tongue-tied at dinners and receptions. When the smart talk started she would fall silent. A dull girl, his colleagues would say afterwards, a bit of a liability.

In fact, she loved her husband passionately, and none of her failings need have mattered if Pierre had returned her affection. But he did not. Bit by bit, Yvonne became distanced from her husband's career and concerns. The abyss opened when one of their two sons grew ill. The child's little bed was brought into the couple's bedroom while the sickness lasted. Pierre took to sleeping in his study. And when the boy recovered, Pierre continued to sleep in his own room. He never returned to the marriage bed.

The seed of suspicion was planted in Yvonne's mind. One day, searching through his pockets, she found a love letter to Pierre signed by someone called 'Jeanette'. She strongly suspected that it was written by a mutual friend, Jeanne Perreau, who was 15 years younger than herself. After a clumsy attempt to get a sample of her handwriting, Yvonne went round and accused her rival to her face. Jeanne denied that a liaison existed and back at home, Pierre told his wife to shut up and mind her own business.

But the suspicion did not die. Jeanne Perreau was the wife of a wealthy department store owner. She was a beautiful woman with luxuriant red hair and a very opulent figure. Above all, she was witty and sophisticated, shining at precisely those functions which for Yvonne were an ordeal. In June 1951, Pierre won his parliamentary seat and gave a lavish reception. His wife saw him there flirting openly with Jeanne Perreau. Yet when Yvonne herself tried to embrace her husband, he rebuffed her in front of everybody.

There was a terrible row that night. Yvonne demanded an explanation; she begged Pierre to return to their marriage bed. He replied cruelly that not only did he not want to make love to her – he did not even think himself capable of it. She had disgraced him at the reception: 'Can you really see yourself at the big banquets in Paris?' he taunted.

Pierre said that he wanted a divorce. Failing that she should take a lover. Yvonne was outraged and refused to countenance a separation. She loved him far too much for that.

Tensions were building up now to the point where something had to give. Yvonne had, for some time, been taking drugs: tranquillisers to make sleep possible, stimulants to nerve her for the day. She drank coffee in great quantities and smoked incessantly. And it was in this state of dangerous disorientation that she took the children off for a seaside holiday. From the coast she wrote a passionate letter to her husband saying that she would try to improve herself as a wife. Pierre did not reply. And when she came back, Yvonne took poison in an attempt to end her life.

Jeanne Perreau in the witness box

Yvonne Chevallier

She only just failed, and was desperately ill afterwards. Every attempt to get through to her husband met with cold scorn on his part. Yvonne followed Pierre to Paris and tried to see him at the Chamber of Deputies. She was told, through an official, that he was too busy. Then she ransacked his flat in the city, seeking evidence of his betrayal. She found it in the form of a railway timetable. He had ticked off the times for Châtelguyon trains – Jeanne Perreau was holidaying there.

Yvonne returned in a rage to Orléans and confronted the husband of her rival. M. Perreau at first tried to soothe her fears. But after a second visit he admitted that he knew Jeanne was having an affair with Pierre. Léon Perreau was not the least distressed about it either; he was one of those curious characters beloved in French farce – a *mari complaisant* or compliant husband who simply did not mind being cuckolded.

But Yvonne was no compliant wife. Pierre had found out about her trip to Paris and phoned her to call her a 'cow' and tell her to stop ruining his life. It was after this call, and Perreau's admission, that Yvonne went out and obtained a firearms licence.

There was no problem in getting the certificate; her husband was now an important political figure and she claimed he had dangerous enemies. Armed with the certificate, Yvonne went to a gun-shop where she asked for a weapon that was guaranteed to kill. They sold her the Mab automatic.

Killing was clearly in her mind – but killing whom? On 11 August Yvonne heard over the radio that Pierre had been appointed a minister. Immediately, she sent a warm telegram of congratulation. Then she contacted a nun who was a close friend and told her that she was going to commit suicide.

The nun, of course, advised her against the act. Pierre phoned later from Paris saying that he would be coming back the next day to pick up some clothes. He did not thank her for the telegram. Perhaps it was his curt and disdainful manner that mingled thoughts of murder with those of suicide.

She spent a terrible night. The next morning, Pierre's name was blazoned across every newspaper. Chevallier a Minister! – no mention, as customarily, of the loving wife. That must have rankled. Still, she mustered up enthusiasm to get little Mathieu to say his party piece – 'Bonjour, Monsieur le Ministre.'

Having kissed his son, Chevallier went upstairs with no word of kindness for his wife. He stripped to his trunks in the bedroom, and asked her to hand him clean linen. Yvonne demanded an explanation for his liaison with Jeanne. Chevallier replied with obscenities. He was going to marry Jeanne, he said, 'and you can remain in your own filth!' Amid the curses for his wife, he gloated over his appointment: 'I'm a minister!' he kept shouting.

Pierre remained unmoved when Yvonne fell sobbing to her knees and pleaded for a reconciliation. He called her worthless, he told her she stank, he piled insult upon insult. Finally, as she reached out pleading towards him, her hand brushed against his leg.

This was the catalyst. She had dared to *touch* the Under Secretary of State. Chevallier hurled a peculiarly foul-mouthed insult at his wife and made an especially obscene gesture.

Yvonne stiffened. She warned that if he went off with Jeanne she would kill herself. 'Go ahead,' he replied. 'It will be the first sensible thing you've done in your life.'

'I'm serious,' she cried, producing the automatic. 'I will kill myself.'

'Well, for God's sake kill yourself, but wait until I've gone.'

They were the last words Pierre Chevallier ever spoke. Yvonne came towards him firing as she walked: he was hit in leg, chin, chest and forehead. Having rushed downstairs to calm the crying Mathieu, she returned to the body in the bedroom. What happened next remains something of a mystery. By Yvonne's own account, she stooped over his body intending suicide. But thoughts of her children stayed her hand. As she rose from the corpse, the gun went off by accident and a fifth bullet lodged in his back.

France was outraged by the shooting. The war hero – the dynamic young mayor with his ministerial career just opening – had been cut down by what the

Pierre Chevallier

newspapers presented as a nagging wife. Feeling ran so high in Orléans itself that the trial was held in Rheims, far from the passions of the populace.

But when the case came to court, the mood changed. In part it was due to Yvonne and the tragic figure she made in the dock. Her face was a mask of suffering, the eyes dark and sunken from evident nights of anguish and remorse. Mechanically, she knotted and unknotted a handkerchief as the defence told of the humiliations she had endured. In contrast, the *soignée* elegance of Jeanne Perreau seemed almost an insult. Hissing was heard from the public benches as she gave evidence in the box. And Jeanne's husband, Léon Perreau, made a quite ridiculous impression as the *mari complaisant* in the case. It emerged that Jeanne had told him on the very first night that she had slept with Pierre. The affair had lasted 5 years, and throughout M. Perreau had been quite acquiescent. He had even been rather flattered to be cuckolded by the up-and-coming mayor. There were positive advantages too: Perreau's brother had been decorated with the Légion d'Honneur – on Chevallier's recommendation.

What a cosy arrangement for all concerned – except poor, suffering Yvonne. Public sympathy went out strongly to the deceived wife, and the prosecution sensed the climate of opinion. For example, the prisoner was not questioned about the mysterious fifth shot fired into the corpse. This could have been exploited at length as a possible act of malice and sacrilege. Nor did the prosecution make a ritual demand for the death penalty (as in the cases of Pauline Dubuisson and Léone Bouvier). It pressed instead for a short prison sentence, suggesting two years as an appropriate penalty.

The jury was out for less than an hour, one member asking for a point of clarification. The juror wanted to know precisely what was the obscene gesture that provoked Yvonne into reaching for the gun. The accused woman had broken into hysterical sobs when the question was asked during the trial; she had not been pressed at the time. Now, the authorities privately submitted an explicit description. It must have been thoroughly outrageous, for when the jury returned it acquitted Yvonne Chevallier of every charge against her. She left the court a free woman, cheered by a large crowd outside.

Although fully exonerated for her tragic action, Yvonne Chevallier selected a punishment for herself. A few months after the trial, she took herself and her two sons off to the benighted settlement at St Laurent du Maroni. This had been the site of one of France's notorious penal colonies in the mosquito swamps of French Guiana. The prison was closed, but a ramshackle community of natives and French settlers still lived there.

Banishing herself to that tropical hell, Yvonne Chevallier took up the post of a sister in charge of the maternity wing of the hospital. She was trained for the job. Yvonne had been a midwife before meeting Pierre and participating in his brilliant career.

Off With Her Head!

K ings of the past possessed weapons of revenge unavailable to humbler citizens. A queen who took lovers threatened the royal succession. Adultery was treason, and two of Henry VIII's wives went to the block for the offence. The cases of Anne Boleyn and Catherine Howard were very different, but you could call each execution a judicial crime of passion.

Anne Boleyn was not, in conventional terms, an especially attractive woman. A contemporary described her as having a 'middling stature, swarthy complexion, long neck, wide mouth, bosom not much raised.' In fact, the observer declared, the Wiltshire girl had little to recommend her except for the king's appetite, 'and her eyes, which are black and beautiful and take great effect.'

Perhaps those dark eyes first drew Henry to her. Certainly, he wrote her some passionate love letters which have survived as evidence of real infatuation. Henry had his first marriage to Catherine of Aragon annulled in order to marry the English Anne. And though the first queen's failure to bear a male heir was a key reason for the divorce, Henry's love for Anne clearly strengthened his resolve.

When the pope refused to accept the divorce it sparked the immense upheaval of the English Reformation. And as for Henry and Anne, secretly married in January 1533, their union was not a success. The king's ardour soon cooled after the marriage and his eye started roving again. Anne bore him a daughter (the future Elizabeth I) instead of the son he desired. A second child miscarried and a third – a male heir – was dead at birth.

The stillborn child was delivered on 29 January 1536. And the unhappy event seems to have set the wheels of vengeance moving, for on 2 May, Anne Boleyn was sent to the Tower charged with adultery.

Four young courtiers were cited as her lovers: Sir Francis Weston, Henry Norris, William Brereton and Mark Smeaton. The most sensational charge, however, was that Anne had had carnal relations with her own brother, Lord Rochford; an accusation instigated by his spiteful wife. All except Smeaton protested their innocence, the latter confessing to guilt. All went to the block, Smeaton declaring on the scaffold that he 'deserved to die'.

Anne for her part persistently professed herself innocent. When she heard of Smeaton's last words she erupted with passion: 'Has he not cleared me of that public shame he has brought me to? Alas, I fear his soul suffers for it and that he is now punished for his false accusation.' She was tried and unanimously

King Henry VIII

Anne Boleyn

condemned by a court of 30 peers. The sentence carried with it an option for Henry – she could be either burnt alive or beheaded, according to the king's pleasure.

Henry, bountiful in her mercy, opted for beheading. He even had an especially sharp blade imported from the Continent for, as the queen observed with sad vanity: 'I have but a little neck.'

Anne went to the scaffold on 19 May, behaving with courage and dignity. It was said that she had never appeared more beautiful than on that fateful day. Still professing her innocence, she graciously declared that the king had done her many favours: first in making her a marchioness, second in making her a queen, third in sending her to heaven.

It is easy to imagine her a tragic victim of circumstance. Nevertheless, her own uncle presided over the court of peers which found her guilty. They saw evidence which was subsequently destroyed. And no-one, not even her own daughter Elizabeth, later tried to retrieve her reputation. Smeaton's confession, her friends' silence, the peers' unanimous judgement – all tend to suggest that she may well have been an unfaithful wife.

Still, callous statecraft clearly played its part in the affair. The king craved a male heir and did not mourn his second wife's passing. He was seen immediately after the execution wearing bright yellow garb with a feather in his cap. And the very next day he became betrothed to Jane Seymour, his third wife. She was to die not long after giving birth to the boy child he so desperately desired (the sickly Edward VI). The fourth wife, Anne of Cleves, lasted no time at all. Henry only married her to effect a German alliance, and found her so ugly on sight that he divorced her immediately. It was then that the ill-starred Catherine Howard came into his life.

Catherine was the orphaned daughter of a noble and gallant soldier, and was brought up in the household of her grandmother, Agnes, Duchess of Norfolk. The girl was pretty, young and vivacious and Henry, now 50, fell passionately in love with her. He called her his 'rose without a thorn,' and she seemed to come fresh with all the innocence of virginal maidenhood.

Unfortunately for all concerned, this was an illusion.

Catherine had committed many youthful indiscretions. And almost immediately after the wedding in July 1540, these came to the attention of the king's councillors. A former maidservant in the Duchess of Norfolk's household had confided to her brother Catherine's misconduct. The brother in turn approached Archbishop Cranmer. The queen, it appeared, had not been a virgin when she married, and the maidservant's story was as picturesque as it was disquieting:

> 'Marry, there is one Francis Dereham who was servant also in my Lady Norfolk's house which hath been in bed with her in his doublet and hose

Anne Boleyn being sentenced

between the sheets an hundred nights. And there hath been such puffing and blowing between them that once in the house a maid which lay in the house with her said to me she would lie no longer with her for she knew not what matrimony meant.'

Nor was it just Dereham who had dallied with the English rose. A man named Mannock 'knew a privy mark of her body.'

This was an awkward business. Cranmer himself had arranged the marriage and his reputation was at stake. He is said to have been 'marvellously perplexed' as to what to do about the report and called two other high officials of state who were equally troubled. Cranmer, they decided, really must inform the king, even if the story was just malicious gossip. The Archbishop agreed, but dared not face his sovereign in person. Instead he submitted a written report and waited for the storm to break.

Henry was outraged. He refused to believe it. He questioned Catherine about the allegations, and she was fierce in her denials. And though Henry desperately wanted to believe her, his obligations required that he secretly assemble a group of notables to investigate the allegations. Dereham and Mannock, the maidservant and her brother, were all tracked down and closely questioned. And when the various reports came back, the picture looked very dark for Catherine.

Henry Mannock, for example, turned out to be a musician who admitted that he 'commonly used to feel the secrets and other parts of her body.' Francis Dereham seemed once to have been betrothed to Catherine, and confessed that he had known her carnally 'many times both in his doublet and hose and in naked bed.' He also named three young ladies who had joined with them in the bedroom athletics. And he said that Thomas Culpepper, Catherine's own cousin, was another of her lovers.

Henry VIII – bold scourge of the pope and the monasteries – wept like a baby when he heard the news. For some time he was so overcome with emotion that words failed him entirely. He loved his English rose and still refused to credit the stories. But he was like a man trying to cross a muddy field in gumboots. With every step he took, the mire went on loading his feet.

As investigations proceeded, it became clear that practically the whole household of the Duchess of Norfolk had conspired to keep up a pretence of Catherine's chastity. Lady Jane Rochford (the spiteful wife of Anne Boleyn's executed brother) was reported to have encouraged Catherine's youthful frolics. She too was arrested and questioned – and was to go to the block in due course.

Bitterly galling all this must have been to the deceived monarch. But so far, the allegations all concerned Catherine's behaviour before the marriage. There was worse – much worse to come. Henry discovered that after the wedding,

Catherine had appointed the lusty Dereham to a post in her royal household. He had been writing some of the Queen's letters for her – they had been alone together in her bedchamber without the presence of servants or other members of the household.

Adulteress! The spell of the king's disbelief was broken and he had Catherine formally arrested. When questioned, she persisted in her denials until confronted with the haul of confessions from miscellaneous lovers and servants.. Faced with their frank statements, she broke down and admitted her youthful unchastity to the Archbishop. She still maintained, however, that she had been faithful as a wife.

The queen's confession was enough to seal the fates of the leading men in the case. Culpepper, a man of noble birth, was beheaded. Dereham and Mannock, both lowlier paramours, were hanged and quartered. Assorted members of the Howard family and household were arrested on the charge of misprision of treason – that is to say, concealing their knowledge of an intention to deceive the king.

Poor, wretched Catherine was now charged with adultery. But still the anguished king and his distressed councillors were reluctant to act decisively. The Lord Chancellor, for example, asked the Lords for a delay in the trial proceedings. The queen, he said, must be given a chance to clear herself of the charge. The Lords willingly agreed to the proposal. But within a couple of days, the king's own Privy Councillors pressed for a speedy resolution. They did, however, add a clause which speaks volumes for Henry's miserable state of mind. The king, they declared, need not actually attend Parliament as it assessed the evidence; he need only sign the documents when judgement was passed. This unusual arrangement was suggested because the 'sorrowful story and wicked facts if repeated before him might renew his grief and endanger His Majesty's health.'

Henry agreed to the proposal, which must have been a great relief to the Lords. They would now be able to speak their minds freely without their impetuous sovereign glowering at them from behind his beard. As in the case of Anne Boleyn, the trial records were subsequently destroyed. But it appears that Catherine did confess to 'the great crime she had been guilty of against the most high God and a kind Prince and against the whole English nation.' She asked no mercy for herself, but only for the friends and relations who had been implicated with her.

Catherine Howard was beheaded on Tower Hill on 13 February 1542. We do not know how she faced her end. But we do know that the king took no more frisky nymphs to the altar. The following year he married the patient and motherly Catherine Parr – his 6th wife – who subsequently managed to outlive him.

The Headless Wife Case

It had all the ingredients of a Gothic horror story. They included the decomposing body of the beautiful wife – kisses delivered by her husband to the corpse – the severed head saved in remembrance. The story should have been set in some dark and sinister castle. But it wasn't. The drama unfolded in tranquil West Wycombe; it was a crime for the 1980s.

Michael Telling, 34, was a member of the vastly rich Vestey family behind the Dewhurst butchers' chain. His second cousin was Lord Vestey, multi-millionaire and polo-playing friend of royalty. In terms of material advantage, Telling enjoyed immense privileges. Being a beneficiary of the Vestey Trust, he received £1,200 a month pocket money – all his bills and credit card accounts were paid on top of that.

He could afford all the expensive toys he desired: fast cars, motorcycles, guns and stereo equipment. The Vestey millions paid for holidays all around the world. But they could not pay for the one thing that Telling needed. Money never did buy love.

He had had a miserable childhood. His father was an aggressive alcoholic who chased his pregnant mother brandishing swords. The mother herself was to testify that she had rejected her son. At an early age, Michael was packed off to boarding school and there, being a sickly boy, he was bullied mercilessly. When he reacted by stealing, starting fires and playing truant, he was beaten by the staff.

He became a problem child: emotionally disturbed and barely controllable in his actions. Twice expelled, he eventually went to a special school for maladjusted children, as well as becoming an inmate at a mental hospital. At home he was kept away from the family and raised by nannies and governesses. When only nine years old he was drinking sherry and smoking heavily. He kept carving knives in his room and once threatened his mother with a blade.

It was from this wrecked childhood that he entered adult life. In 1978, Michael Telling married his first wife, 18-year-old Alison, whom he had first met in Australia. The couple had a son, but the relationship was not to last. Telling was a 'coward who was unable to face his responsibilities,' she was to say. In 1980 he went to America to buy his latest toy, a Harley-Davidson motorcycle. While trying out his new machine at Sausalito near San Francisco, he pulled up at some traffic lights and fell into a conversation with a Mr and Mrs Zumsteg. They suggested that he meet their daughter, Monika.

Within three days of the encounter, he was sleeping with Monika. And shortly after his return to England, he informed his wife that he had found another woman. In 1981, a divorce was arranged. Less than a month later, Michael Telling married Monika Zumsteg.

Much was said at the trial about his bride. Monika was headlined in one paper as a 'SEX MAD GOLD-DIGGER', and she certainly lived her life in the fast lane. Monika drove a Pontiac Firebird and drank Benedictine and orange for breakfast. She used cocaine, heroin and marijuana. In her handbag she carried a gun and a vibrator.

The couple lived at opulent Lambourn House, West Wycombe in Buckinghamshire. Luxury items included a whirlpool bath on the lawn where Monika would frolic with naked party guests. Her husband used to sit on the sidelines, drinking. She said he was only good for money. On frequent occasions, she publicly belittled his sexual efforts, boasting to him of her own lovers both male and female.

When the marriage came to its gruesome end, neighbours were to confirm the stories. Richard Richardson, for example, was an odd-job man and a friend of the Tellings. He said that Monika told him she had no intention of making a life with her husband and that 'all she wanted was his money.' Once, she told Richardson that, 'I could f . . . any man, any woman better than any man can. I am AC/DC. Man or woman – I go with anybody.' She seemed to take a vindictive pleasure out of humiliating her husband. Richardson had been present on one occasion when Monika had ordered Telling to make coffee, shouting, 'Get off your f . . . arse, you mother-f . . . Make the coffee!' Telling begged her not to talk like that and affectionately ran kisses up her arm. On another occasion, the couple had a play fight in the kitchen. Monika took the opportunity to knee Telling in the groin. 'He went white, but said nothing.'

'He worshipped the ground she walked on,' said Richardson, 'but she showed no affection. She said she would only stay with him for two years to get money out of him.' Telling had to visit his son secretly because Monika disapproved, saying that the boy was horrible and she hated him.

Telling's first wife, Alison, told much the same story. Once, Monika had visited her home, bringing a bottle of gin and a cockatoo. She smoked cannabis, drank Drambuie and took four or five pills. She complained to Alison that Michael was no good in bed, saying she did not want a divorce until she'd got some of his money. Monika said that she was prepared to get herself pregnant and go back to America with the baby to get the cash.

Telling himself was to refer to countless humiliations. Once, he had seen her frolicking half naked with another woman on the living-room floor. Yet on their honeymoon night at the Hyde Park Hotel in London, she refused to have sex with her husband. In fact, she banned sex entirely with Telling for the last seven months of her life.

Monika was doomed to become the Headless Wife. She never got a chance to defend herself against these allegations in court. But her father was to claim that the stories were outrageous: 'She was certainly not a saint, but she was nothing like she was painted. She was too flippant sometimes, like when she told a neighbour she was AC/DC. It's the kind of thing she would say for a laugh. Monika was a woman of great intelligence, kind and full of sensitivity.'

Whatever the truth, the relationship seems to have been founded on a disastrously flawed combination of personalities. She certainly liked fast living – he certainly needed love. And successive episodes illustrate how the marriage was heading for calamity. In 1982, Monika took up an Alcoholics Anonymous programme. Telling, meanwhile, underwent treatment in a psychiatric hospital. He was to claim that Monika tried to run him down with a car and attacked him with a whip. But he also admitted that he sometimes retaliated, and had attacked her on four occasions during their 17-month marriage.

The terrible climax came on 29 March 1983. By Telling's account, she was delivering a tirade in the living room, shouting that he ought to be sent to a mental hospital. The taunts finally shattered his eggshell personality. 'She came charging towards me. I thought she was going to attack me so I picked up the rifle and shot her.'

The weapon in question was a Marlin 30-30 hunting gun, and he shot her three times. She was hit in the throat and the chest. 'I kissed her then and said I was sorry. But I knew she was dead.'

If the case had ended there it would have been sensational enough. What happened next turned it into an almost unbelievable horror story. Telling left the body for two days where it was before carrying it into a bedroom: 'I went to look at her every day and kissed her often.' He also talked to the corpse as it lay on a camp bed. Eventually, he dragged the body to a summer house, a building half-converted into a sauna. And there it remained for five months.

Telling told his friends that Monika had left him to return to her native America. As 'protection' for himself, he installed an elaborate security system at his home, and even employed private detectives to find his wife.

During this period, as Monika's body lay decomposing at Lambourn House, Telling started to see a former friend called Mrs Lynda Blackstock. She spent three or four nights at his home, and he tried to woo her in his bedroom. But he could not make love successfully. 'He told me all about Monika', she was to say. 'He told me she was an alcoholic, a drug addict and a lesbian. Michael said she had gone back home to the U.S. – and he was glad.' At the trial, she was asked:

'There was not a hint that Monika lay dead in the very building you were visiting?'

Mrs Blackstock: 'Definitely not.'

Another recent girl friend, divorcée Mrs Susan Bright, also went to bed with

Telling after he had killed his wife. She slept with him several times and the couple went out for meals together. She said: 'He was very talkative, although he seemed very nervous . . . I asked him if he had heard from Monika at all and he said he thought she was in America.'

In September 1983, Telling hired a van and drove to Devon with the body. On Telegraph Hill outside Exeter he cut off Monika's head with an axe. He dumped the headless body there but could not bear to part with the head itself. Instead, he brought it home and hid it in the locked boot of his Mini in the garage. It was kept there wrapped in plastic.

Two days later, a Devon man stumbled on the headless body. Though badly decomposed by now, it still wore a distinctive Moroccan T-shirt. And although it had been decapitated, a chunk of hair and a few teeth were found at the site. The gruesome discovery made the national news, and Mrs Richardson's interest was alerted. She knew that Monika had a similar T-shirt, and was nonplussed when Telling confessed to her that he had killed his wife: 'She is in the sauna – it's stinking.'

Although Mrs Richardson did not believe him, she did eventually inform the police. At this stage, Monika was just one among many missing young women who vaguely fitted the description pieced together from the remains. But dental tests on the few teeth found revealed that the victim had suffered from a disorder of the gums. Monika, had recently undergone an operation for a gum infection.

Devon detectives went to the West Wycombe house and found the dead woman's skull in the Mini. Exactly a week after the body was discovered, Michael Telling was arrested.

He confessed the killing to the police. Asked why he had shot her he replied, 'There were 101 reasons. I can't really explain. She kept pushing me. I just snapped in the end. She was horrible in many ways.'

Horrible in many ways – the phrase might serve as an epitaph on the whole case. Asked why he had cut off her head, Telling replied, 'I did not want her identified because of my family. Even when she died I wanted her to be with me.'

The case was tried at Exeter Crown Court in June 1984. He pleaded not guilty to murder, but guilty to manslaughter by reason of diminished responsibility.

The press, of course, had a field day. 'MISTRESSES TELL OF SEX IN THE HOUSE OF HORROR' – 'SEX SESSIONS AS BODY LAY NEAR-BY', blared the headlines. The public learned that Telling had taken Mrs Bright out to a Chinese meal in High Wycombe just 24 hours after he had chopped off his wife's head.

If the press dwelled on the bizarre, macabre details, the courtroom wrangling revolved around Telling's state of mind. No-one denied that the defendant had killed his wife; he himself furnished most of the details. The question in dispute was whether he was responsible for his actions.

Michael and Monika Telling on their wedding day

The prosecution pressed for a verdict of murder. It dwelt on the 'amazing catalogue' of gruesome lengths to which Telling went to avoid detection. He had told a psychiatrist that the seed of the crime was planted four days before the event. On the evening before the killing, the time and method were, allegedly, decided. 'Despite his mental abnormality, this man determined to kill his wife. He could have prevented himself from doing so if he wished.'

Afterwards, to conceal the crime, he used his wife's Cashpoint card until the account was almost depleted, so giving the impression that she was still alive. He hired the private detectives. He made an 'elaborate pretence' of going on a camping trip when he travelled to Devon to dump the body. As for the head, the prosecution alleged, he did not take it home for remembrance – but to avoid identification of the corpse.

Set against all this apparent cunning was the testimony of psychiatrists, friends and relations. The defence stressed the defendant's maimed and disordered personality. Telling's grey-haired mother appeared in the witness box and described how as a boy he had witnessed violent arguments between herself and his alcoholic father. She told how he would run naked into the road in front of traffic; how he twice attempted suicide. She acknowledged that her son was a boy deprived of affection: 'Many of Michael's problems stem from his very lonely and unhappy childhood.'

Telling wept in the dock as his mother gave evidence, and he delayed the hearing by 15 minutes after passing a note to his lawyers asking for an adjournment. The note was strangely worded and misspelt: 'You get Mum away from this awful trial, or I will get up and let the bloddy prosoqutor hear what I think off.'

He was visibly moved too when a former school companion entered the box 'out of a sense of guilt' after reading newspaper reports. The man, Bertram Lilley, described the vicious bullying that Telling had endured: before the boys would let him join in a game they made him roll in a patch of stinging nettles until he resembled 'one large blister'.

Lilley's parents had lived in Africa at the time and he once spent a half-term at the Tellings. There was more love, he said, across the many miles to Africa 'than across the living room of that house.'

The judge in summing up reminded the court that psychiatry is not an exact science. Ultimately, the jurors were as fit as anyone else to assess whether Telling was responsible for his actions. Yet they seem to have agreed with the psychiatrist. For after $2\frac{1}{2}$ hours deliberation, the jury found the defendant not guilty of murder but guilty of manslaughter on the grounds of diminished responsibility.

Gaoled for life, Michael Telling was to remain in custody until those responsible felt it 'safe and proper' to release him.

A Tale of Two Sisters

Chronic alcoholism is a deep-rooted problem in the French countryside. Wine is cheap and the hard routines of farming life can be monotonous. To escape them, many a working man daily stupefies his senses with the bottle. M. Bouvier of Saint-Macaire came from a long line of hereditary alcoholics. His special drink was not wine, as it happens, but a crude cider alcohol distilled in the region of western France where he lived. Bouvier used to get violently drunk and regularly threatened to murder his wife and two daughters. From an early age, the girls learned to help their mother with the almost nightly ordeal of strapping him down to the bed. Someone would then run for the doctor. The doctor would give him the injections that brought a fragile calm to the household.

This is the story of those two sisters. Georgette, the older one, plays only a peripheral role in the drama. Yet it was to be intensely significant in the life of Léone, the younger girl.

The village of Saint-Macaire lies near the town of Cholet in the Maine-et-Loire department. And at the local school, Georgette showed considerable intelligence. At the age of 18 she managed to escape the household by entering a convent at Angers. Forsaking the hell of her family life, she submitted to the pious disciplines of a nun's existence. And there, for a while, we must leave her.

Léone Bouvier, two years younger, cried for a week when her sister abandoned the household. She was alone now with the wreck of her father and a mother who had also taken to drinking. Léone was not bright; in fact, her school years had left her practically illiterate. The meagre salary she earned at a local shoe factory was absorbed by the family's needs. But her mother showed no gratitude. She mocked Léone for being worthless and dull-witted. And, rejected by all those closest to her, Léone looked for love elsewhere. She turned, in particular, to men.

She was not a pretty girl. Her eyes were wide-set, her nose was large and a ragged shank of dark hair fell across her low brow. A generous heart only made her an easier prey for the local lads.

Léone lost her virginity to a fellow factory worker at a hurried coupling in the corner of a field. She saw him the next day, laughing about the episode with his mates in the factory yard. Other sad encounters were to follow until she struck up with a decent-hearted young man in the Air Force. Fate never gave Léone a break, though; not long after they arranged to be married, the youth was killed in an accident.

It was in the bleak period following the incident that Léone met Emile Clenet, a 22-year-old garage mechanic from Nantes. Their first brief encounter was at a dance in Cholet, and they made a rendezvous for the following afternoon. Misfortune was Léone's constant companion, and while cycling to the meeting she had to stop to fix a puncture. By the time she arrived, he was gone.

Six months later, however, they met again at the Lent carnival in Cholet. 'You're six months late,' joked Emile. 'But never mind, we've found each other again.' They enjoyed all the fun of the fair together and afterwards, Emile took her to a hotel room. She had never been treated to clean sheets before. She learned to love him then.

The couple fell into a set pattern of meetings. To reverse the lyrics of the popular song, it was 'Only on a Sunday' for Emile and Léone. He was a hard worker and reserved only the seventh day for his pleasures. Every Sunday, Léone would cycle to a particular spot near Cholet, and Emile would pick her up on his motorbike. After picnicing and perhaps some evening dancing, they would retire to a cheap hotel.

There was talk of marriage, and Emile took her home to meet his parents, who rather liked their son's strange little girlfriend. It is hard to determine exactly what went wrong. Perhaps Emile never seriously intended marriage. Once, there was an accident with his motorbike and Léone took a knock on the head. She suffered headaches and bouts of depression after that.

Emile could be cruel, too. Once, snapped by a street photographer, the couple went to pick up the picture. Emile took one look and said he didn't want it. When Léone asked why, he said: 'Just look at that face and you'll understand.' She hurried off to cry alone. Since meeting Emile, Léone had been taking care of her appearance, indulging in all the feminine vanities. Words like those must have wounded deeply.

The real blow came when she found she was pregnant and Emile told her to get rid of the unborn child. She did so – but the headaches and depressions grew worse after that. Then, in January 1952, she lost her job. There was a furious row in her home that night: her mother raged at her and her drunken father tried to give her a thrashing. Léone fled the household. It took her all night to cycle the 30-odd miles to Nantes where Emile worked. But when she got there in the morning, Emile was annoyed. Their arrangement was only for Sundays, he said. It was a weekday. She must leave.

Utterly abandoned, Léone spent two weeks as an outcast in Nantes, wandering the cold, winter streets. A second attempt to see Emile resulted in another rebuff. He said he was too busy to see her for the next couple of Sundays. Her money ran out. She had nowhere to sleep. And though she was never very clear about what happened during that blank fortnight, it seems she slipped into prostitution.

During the days, Léone took to standing outside gun-shop windows, gazing dazedly in at the gleaming butts and barrels. Later, she was to say that she did not quite know why she did so; perhaps suicide had been in her mind. But she remembered one incident very clearly. As she stood there, shivering in the rain, a strange young man had appeared at her side. 'Don't', said the figure, 'He is too young. He has the right to live.' Then he disappeared.

Hallucination? Léone had been a victim all her life, and perhaps her conscious mind was moving towards thoughts of self-destruction. But perhaps, too, some last instinct to survive and strike outward was prompting from within. The impulse was to murder her lover. And to redress the balance, her conscience invented the phantasmagoric young man who seemed to know her thoughts.

Whatever the truth, that voice seems to have earned Emile a reprieve. For she did not yet buy a gun. Instead, physically and emotionally exhausted, she returned to her village. Nothing had changed there. On arrival, her father was in one of his frenzies. Mechanically, she helped her mother strap him to the bed.

She had come back from one hell to another, and only thoughts of Emile sustained her. 15 February 1952 was Léone's 23rd birthday. Would her lover remember? Last year he had bought her a bicycle lamp – the only present of her adult life. She summoned up her courage, took the last of her savings, and boarded the coach back to Nantes. Humbly and apologetically she approached him at the garage and asked if they could meet on Sunday at the usual place. He showed no sign of remembering her birthday. But – to her intense joy – he agreed to meet at the rendezvous.

When he came, he brought no birthday present. Emile made love brusquely that Sunday and he did not stay the night as usual. It was on the following day that Léone went into Nantes and sought out one of the gunshops. There she bought a .22 automatic. The pistol had recently been declared a 'sporting weapon'. Léone, who could barely sign her name, did not need a license.

She lived now only for their Sundays. Léone hung around in Nantes waiting for the next meeting, living from day to day in the dockside area by taking men into hotel bedrooms. When the grey haze of waiting hours was over she hastened

---

To Have And To Hold
On 27 August 1984, Mrs Jose Kubiczek returned to her home at Saint-Amand-les-Eaux. It was to be a final visit; she came only to take custody of her son. But it seems her husband could not face the future without her. The French police reported he had strangled his wife, then dressed her in a wedding gown. He was found lying beside her corpse on the conjugal bed.

to their rendezvous at Cholet. Emile was not there. She scoured the town and eventually found his motorbike parked outside a cinema. When the film was over she ran to meet him, but he brushed her off. He had flu, he said. He was going straight home. She must wait for the coming Lent carnival.

Fate, which had dogged Léone all her life, had reserved its completing irony for this meeting. It was at Cholet's Lent carnival that the couple had enjoyed their first night together two years earlier. It was at the Lent carnival too, with its hurdy-gurdy gaiety, that Léone Bouvier was to kill her lover.

Yet it started so well. Emile roared up on his motorbike at their rendezvous and she mounted pillion on the back just as in the old days. She kissed him as they rode into the town centre to mingle with the carnival crowds. They moved gaily among the stalls, the streamers and the balloons. Emile stopped by a shooting range to demonstrate his prowess. The weapon (fate again) was a .22 automatic. And above the staccato crackle of gunshot he told her he was leaving to work in North Africa. He was going, he said, for good.'

'But what about me? We were going to get married . . .'

'So what?'

'You don't want to marry me any more, then?'

'*C'est la vie.*' Emile shrugged and mumbled platitudes, telling her she would find someone better than him. Léone was incredulous. She asked again. Again he said no, he would never marry her.

Emile drove her back to her bicycle, locked up at their rendezvous. There she implored him, 'Emile, you aren't going off and leaving me like this?'

Emile said nothing, but returned to his motorcycle and climbed on, preparing to leave. Léone took the gun from her handbag and slipped it under her coat. She came up behind him. 'Emile,' she whispered, 'kiss me for the last time . . .'

He did not respond. She put her left arm around his neck and pulled him tenderly towards her. Gently, she kissed his cheek. And as she did so she withdrew the pistol and placed the barrel-end against his neck. Then she pulled the trigger.

There was only one shot.

Afterwards she mounted her bicycle and fled, pedalling blindly to the only place she knew that offered sanctuary. It was to Angers that she cycled, to her sister's convent. She arrived there in distress, without explaining what had happened. Georgette gave her coffee and put her to bed – the poor, ruined child come like a ghost from her past.

The police came the following afternoon. Léone was arrested in the convent, but such are the procedures of French law that it was not until December 1953 that she was brought before the Assizes of Maine-et-Loire. French courts are traditionally flexible in the handling of a *crime passionnel*. Léone's misfortune was to face an unusually aggressive prosecutor and a hostile judge.

Judges play a more active role in the French courts than their English equivalents do. They may examine and cross-question a defendant at some length. And at Léone's trial in Angers, the judge showed himself entirely lacking in the subtlety associated with the French legal mind. What he had in abundance was the stubborn hypocrisy of the French provincial bourgeois.

He simply could not see that Léone's blighted childhood or her lover's callous rebuffs made one jot of difference to the case. Why did she not stay at her parents' hearth instead of wandering the dockside at Nantes? The answer should have been evident when Léone's father was brought to the witness box, sweating and shaking under the ordeal of a morning without a drink. The experts declared him an hereditary alcoholic. The mother, too, frankly admitted that they had all lived in mortal fear of his violence. But she explained that she'd done the best she could, adding the fateful reflection that her other daughter was a nun.

The judge pounced.

'You see!' he called, rounding on Léone, 'There was no need for you to go wrong. Why did you go wrong?' It is hard to exaggerate the part played by this circumstance. It seemed to nullify every mitigating factor of Léone's background. The writer Derrick Goodman has made the point eloquently: they did not come down hard on Léone because she had murdered her lover. It was because her sister was a nun.

The judge continued with his tirade, dwelling on the fact that Léone had killed Emile as she kissed him. This was a detail that seemed to him an incomprehensible outrage: *'atroce!'* he fumed, *'atroce!'*

Léone stood quietly in the dock, her head bowed low.

'Why did you kill him?' demanded the judge.

Tears were streaming down her cheeks as Léone raised her head.

'I loved him', she said simply.

The prosecution had called for the death penalty on the charge of premeditated murder. For reasons stated in the case of Pauline Dubuisson, there was no likelihood of Léone being executed. In fact, the defence had every right to expect a very lenient judgement. What was Léone's crime if not a *crime passionnel*? Middle-class ladies had walked scot-free in cases of this nature.

The jury was out for only a quarter of an hour. And it would seem that they arrived at the same formula as in the case of Pauline Dubuisson. They avoided the charge of premeditated murder, for that carried an automatic death penalty, and found her guilty of murder – but without premeditation.

The foreman complacently suggested that the prisoner be given the maximum penalty of penal servitude for life – a minimum of 20 years. The judge readily agreed. And so, with the afflictions of a simple mind and a warm heart, a horrific childhood and a succession of rejections, Léone Bouvier fell victim to the full weight of French law.

Reverend Babykins and His Gay Gipsy

O n Saturday 16 September 1922, an adultery was exposed at a lover's lane in New Brunswick, New Jersey. The Reverend Edward Wheeler Hall, Rector of St John's Episcopal Church, was found lying under a crab apple-tree with Mrs Eleanor Mills, the sexton's wife. He was 41 and balding; she a petite 34-year-old. And the couple never got a chance to defend or explain their activities. For they were found dead – murdered at their rendezvous, their bodies scattered with their torn-up love letters.

The pastor's head had been pierced by a single bullet; a bloodsoaked Panama hat lay over his face. Eleanor Mills had been shot three times; her throat, moreover, had been slashed. And as for the love letters, they told in the clearest possible terms of the special relationship which had existed between the minister and the soprano who had sung in his choir.

The letters strewn all around had been written by Eleanor Mills. Scribbled in pencil, they bore witness to intense emotions: 'I know there are girls with more shapely bodies,' the sexton's wife had written, 'but I do not care what they have. I have the greatest of all blessings, the deep, true and eternal love of a noble man. My heart is his, my life is his, all I have is his, poor as my body is, scrawny as they say my skin may be, but I am his forever.'

Someone had emptied the minister's pockets, and his gold watch had been stolen. But mere theft could not have been the motive for the killing. Propped against the dead man's foot was one of his own visiting cards, as if advertising his identity. Whoever shot the lovers had also arranged their bodies side by side in a grotesque embrace. Special savagery had been reserved for Eleanor Mills; not only had her throat been slashed but her tongue and vocal cords had been cut out. With the confetti of love letters playing about the bodies, everything pointed to a crime of passion.

·The police interviewed the dead clergyman's wife, Frances Hall. A plain, grey-haired woman nine years older than her husband, she professed complete ignorance of the liaison between her husband and his chorister. All she knew was that on the evening of Thursday 14th, her husband had received a phone call and left the house. He did not come back that night. And although it was a whole day and another night before the bodies were discovered, Mrs Hall at no stage called the police.

James Mills, husband of the dead woman, came up with a strikingly similar story. His wife had not come home on Thursday evening, but he too failed to call the police. When pressed, he said that he thought his wife might have been round at her sister's house. Like Frances Hall, he claimed to know nothing of the secret love affair.

There were many in the pastor's congregation who were not so blinkered. Rumours of the affair had been circulating in New Brunswick long before the murders took place. Perhaps one, or both, of the spouses did know of the liaison, and failed to call the police suspecting an elopement? Speculation along these lines led nowhere.

With the lack of concrete evidence, public interest in the case began to flag. But while a blameless suspect named Hayes was under investigation, a witness turned up – a colourful middle-aged Mrs Jane Gibson who came to be known as the Pig Woman.

Mrs Gibson kept pigs on a smallholding, and claimed to have seen the murder occur on the Thursday evening. Hearing noises that night, and suspecting thieves, she had mounted her mule and gone down the lane. Four figures were arguing under the crab apple-tree: two men and two women. One of these was a white-haired lady, and another a kinky-haired man. There were shouts of 'Don't, don't, don't.' Something glinted in the moonlight. Four shots rang out – and the Pig Woman fled the scene.

When questioned by the police, the Pig Woman identified Mrs Hall as the white-haired woman, and her brother Willie Stevens as the kinky-haired man.

Could the testimony be believed? The case came alive again, and the new evidence coincided with the publication of a batch of letters between Eleanor Mills and the late minister. They were all that a sensation-seeking public could have wished.

To the pastor, for example, Mrs Mills had written: 'I am on my knees, darling, looking up at my noble man, worshipping, adoring . . . I want you – your arms to hold me and hold me close if only to forget this pain for a minute. Dearest, give me some words of comfort.'

In reply, the clergyman had penned a note arranging a tryst for the following day: 'My dearest, my treasure, my anchor, my rock – oh, how I did want to fly off with you this afternoon – I wanted to get away to dreamland – heaven-land – everything seemed so sordid, earthy, commonplace . . . Dearest – love me hard, hard – harder than ever, for your Babykins is longing for his mother.'

Earthbound in New Brunswick, the clandestine lovers had allowed their fancies to roam in an illicit paradise where truth, nobility and wonder, crystal eyes and crushing embraces, were all yearned for with equal intensity. Eleanor was the pastor's 'gay gipsy' and, 'when my arrow enters your haven I am transported to ecstasy,' wrote the stalwart.

And where had this new correspondence come from? The cache of letters was sold to the press for $500 by James Mills. The transaction of course cast considerable doubt on the sexton's claim to know nothing of his wife's affair.

A grand jury was convened in November to assess the case. But the inquiry led to no indictment. For four years the case was as if frozen, neither formally closed nor under active investigation. What broke the ice was a bombshell lobbed from within the late pastor's household.

Louise Geist, who had served the Halls as a maid, got involved in a lawsuit for marriage annulment. Her husband claimed that Louise had been bribed to keep silent before the grand jury: she had in fact accompanied Mrs Hall and her two brothers to the scene of the crime and been a witness to – or a participant in – the vile deeds.

Back to the front pages came the Crab Apple-tree murder. Back to the limelight came James Mills, the Pig Woman and the rest. And into the dock went the clergyman's wife, with her brothers Willie and Henry Stevens.

The trial was held at Somerville, New Jersey, in November 1926. And it seemed at last that the solution was clear. But was it? Actually, Louise Geist repudiated her husband's claims, still insisting she knew nothing of the murder. The Pig Woman was readier than ever to point the finger at Mrs Hall and her brothers, but the hog-farming witness was now dying of cancer. She had to be brought into court on a stretcher, and her aged mother confounded everyone by constantly interrupting: 'She's a liar, a liar, a liar! That's what she is, and what she's always been.'

James Mills, meanwhile, was fiercely cross-questioned and now candidly admitted that he had known all about the affair between his wife and the clergyman. He had read the love letters and, it seemed, had quarrelled bitterly with his wife about the liaison.

Maybe Mills did it? Maybe the Pig Woman did it! (This suggestion was actually made by the defence counsel.)

At the end of the long, confused trial the jury retired for five hours. When they returned, it was with a verdict of not guilty.

Mrs Hall and her brothers were discharged, the pastor's widow becoming a recluse and dying in 1942. The whole affair had scandalised America, and remains one of crime's great unsolved mysteries. One plausible theory has been put forward by William Kunstler in his *The Minister and the Choir Singer* (1964). He suggests that the Ku Klux Klan engineered the double murder as retribution for the couple's violation of Bible teaching on adultery. Certainly, the disposition of the bodies and the mutilation of the errant choir singer suggest ritual elements in the crime. But the theory remains pure conjecture. All that can be said with certainty of the affair is that the love between Edward Hall and Eleanor Mills was true love lived in a morass of deception. And that the lovers paid a terrible price for their idyll in heaven-land.

A Life for a Life

Early in July 1955, north country publican Albert Pierrepoint received official notice that he would be needed in London on the 13th. A small, tidy man, Pierrepoint made the appropriate arrangements for a journey he had made many times before. On the afternoon of 12 July he arrived at the gates of Holloway Prison in North London. Admitted by the authorities, he was given a cup of tea and then taken to the door of a cell where, through the peep-hole, he could see a pale young woman reading a Bible.

The officials supplied the statistics he needed to know: Height – 5 ft 2 inches; Weight – 103 lbs. Albert Pierrepoint, official hangman, studied her file and proceeded to the execution chamber where, using a sandbag for dummy, he tested the spring-loaded mechanism of the trap.

At 09.00 the following morning, 28-year-old Ruth Ellis entered the chamber to become the last woman hanged in Britain. She faced the noose with the same extraordinary calm as she had exhibited throughout her trial and her ordeal of waiting. Ruth Ellis asked neither for sympathy nor for mercy. From the condemned cell she had written, 'I say a life for a life.'

The hanging was efficiently accomplished. The post mortem noted the fractures to spine, thyroid and cartilage, but reported the air passages clear. She had not been strangled like so many before her: 'No engorgement . . . No asphyxial changes . . . Cause of Death: Injuries to the central nervous system consequent upon judicial hanging.'

Yet neither the prisoner's calm, Pierrepoint's expertise, nor any amount of paperwork could mask the essential horror of what had transpired. 1955 was the year when Rock'n'Roll hit Britain; yet at Holloway Prison, a tribal retribution had been enacted upon Ruth Ellis.

Born Ruth Hornby at Rhyl in 1926, the condemned woman had led a chequered life. At 15 she had escaped from a difficult home background to start work as a waitress. In due course she found employment at a munitions factory and was already dyeing her hair with the peroxide that was to distinguish her in all the press photographs. Ruth was no shy maiden. With a slender, somewhat predatory sensuality she found it easy to acquire dancing partners among servicemen at the wartime clubs she began to frequent in London. In 1944 she had a child by a Canadian soldier, and no sooner had her figure returned than she took up a job as nude model in a Camera Club. In the years of postwar austerity, West End vice lords were already spinning their webs of sleazy excitement. Ruth became a club hostess and call girl. In 1950 she married

George Ellis, an alcoholic dentist who frequented her low-life locales. The couple had a daughter but separated soon afterwards, and Ruth returned to the circuit. It was while working as manageress at the Little Club, a seedy upstairs drinking room in Knightsbridge, that she met David Blakely, the man she was to murder.

Blakely came from a very different background. Born in 1929, the son of a well-to-do Sheffield doctor, he was given a public school education at Shrewsbury, and throughout his brief life he retained his boyish good looks. Blakely remained immature in temperament too. For all his suave charm and his well-bred accent, he never held down a steady job. Feckless, emotionally vulnerable and prone to sulks, Blakely maintained abiding enthusiasms only for alcohol, for women and – above all – for racing cars. When he drank he became obstreperous, provoking fights he was too cowardly to see through. With his women he was a braggart and a largely unsuccessful lover. And his experiences on the motor circuits were hardly any happier.

Blakely raced at Silverstone and other well-known tracks, including Le Mans in France. But though he consorted at clubs and meetings with stars like Mike Hawthorne and Stirling Moss, victory almost always eluded him. Nor did racing offer him a career. His obsession for cars, as for drink and women, was financed chiefly by private money, including a £7,000 legacy from his father.

Blakely first met Ruth Ellis in 1953. The young racing driver was drunk and insulting on that occasion, and Ruth referred to him afterwards as a 'pompous ass', telling a friend, 'I hope never to see that little shit again.' But she did – with consequences disastrous to both.

Blakely took to frequenting the Little Club, where Ruth succumbed to his charm and expensive manners. David was 'class', and before long they were sleeping together at her flat above the premises. Ruth, at the outset, was clearly the dominant partner, confident and self-possessed while he was weak and ineffectual. Moreover, as Blakely frittered away more and more of his resources, he came to depend on her to subsidise his drinking.

After having a child of Blakely's aborted in December 1953, Ruth tried to cool the relationship by cultivating a more dependable lover, company director Desmond Cussen. At about the same time she lost her job at the Little Club, partly because of the time and money she had expended on David.

Ruth first moved into Cussen's apartment, and later to a flat at Egerton Gardens. Cussen loaned her the rent and was a frequent visitor there. But Ruth could not entirely break with her younger lover. She continued to sleep with Blakely, who eventually moved in with her at Egerton Gardens. It was a period of savage quarrels and recriminations between Ruth and David. He was intensely jealous, drank heavily, and sometimes beat Ruth so badly that she had to use make-up to camouflage the livid bruises on her limbs. She had a second

Ruth Ellis

abortion by him, and under the strain of the tempestuous relationship consulted a doctor who prescribed tranquillisers for her depression. Blakely, meanwhile, had invested what little capital he possessed in building a racing car. Predictably, the vehicle broke down in practice before its racing debut.

What bonded Ruth to her young lover? Love? Social ambition, or his periodic promises of marriage? Blakely had become a liability to Ruth, yet during this period of frenzied passion, the see-saw of emotional need began to tilt. Blakely had not lost his middle-class expectations, and to friends of his, a married couple called the Findlaters, he confided his despair and his own need to make a break with Ruth Ellis. Ruth had long suspected that David was having an affair with Mrs Findlater, and the more time he spent in the company of the married couple, the more her own jealousy quickened. Ruth could dish out violence as well as take it; once, it seems, she slashed Blakely in the back with a knife.

Things came to a head at Easter, 1955. On Good Friday, 8 April, Blakely confessed to the Findlaters that he was getting frightened of Ruth. They suggested he spend the weekend with them at their apartment in Tanza Road, Hampstead. Though he was due to meet Ruth at 19.30 that night, Blakely gratefully accepted.

For two hours, Ruth waited at Egerton Gardens for her lover to turn up. At 21.30 she phoned the Findlaters to find out if David was there. The au pair took the call and told her that neither Blakely nor the Findlaters were in the flat. An hour later, Ruth phoned again, and this time Anthony Findlater answered. Though he claimed to know nothing of her lover's whereabouts, Ruth did not believe him. Again and again that night she rang Tanza Road, and in the end Findlater simply hung up the receiver whenever her voice came on the line. At the trial it was learned that Blakely was indeed at Tanza Road – shaking with fear on the couch.

Frenzied with suspicion, Ruth had Desmond Cussen drive her round to Tanza Road. When she saw Blakely's green Vanguard parked outside the flat, she ran in fury to the front door and repeatedly rang the bell. No-one replied. Eventually, she vented her spleen on the Vanguard, thumping in its side windows which were held in place only by rubber strips. The glass did not break, but the noise brought Anthony Findlater to the door in his pajamas.

There was a furious scene in the street where Ruth kept demanding that Blakely come down, and Findlater denied that he was there. Already, the married couple had prudently phoned for the police. An inspector turned up and tried to calm the situation; after warning Ruth against breaching the peace he drove away.

Findlater slammed the door, leaving Ruth still fulminating in the street. Nor did she leave at once, but kept prowling around the Vanguard until a second police visit forced her from the scene. The long-suffering Desmond Cussen, who

The Hangman's Verdict

For hanging Ruth Ellis, Albert Pierrepoint collected a fee of fifteen guineas (plus travelling expenses). He left Holloway practically besieged by a storming mob and needed police protection to get through. Pierrepoint returned to his pub, the Rose and Crown at Hoole, near Preston, and the wife who had never asked questions. And there he came to a decision: he would give up his macabre profession.

His had been an hereditary vocation, his father and uncle both having been listed as qualified executioners on the Home Office files. When the press learned of his resignation, it was rumoured that something exceptionally grim must have transpired in the death chamber. It had not – Ruth Ellis was 'the bravest woman I ever hanged' and there was 'nothing untoward'. Pierrepoint resigned because the furore caused him to examine his own conscience. Did hanging really deter murder? He concluded that it did not: 'Capital punishment, in my view, achieved nothing except revenge.'

---

had waited and watched throughout the whole performance, drove her back to Egerton Gardens.

His role in the affair deserves a word of explanation. Cussen was infatuated with Ruth but, lacking David's youth and glamour, knew he must wait until the flame of her earlier love was extinguished. For that reason, it appears, he was prepared to acquiesce with Ruth in what became an ever more obsessive quest.

Ruth did not sleep that night. Early the next morning she took a taxi to Tanza Road and kept watch on the Findlaters' from a darkened doorway. At about 10.00 Findlater emerged, and beckoned Blakely out into the street. Having examined the damaged car, the two men got in and drove off down the road.

Ruth's suspicions were confirmed – the Findlaters *were* shielding David from her. Armed with this certainty, she spent the next hours in attempts to track down her lover's movements. After lunch, she and Cussen took her ten-year-old son to the London Zoo, leaving him there with enough money for the afternoon. Then, with Cussen as chauffeur, she continued the hunt for her quarry.

Cussen drove her back to Hampstead where they located the now-repaired Vanguard outside the Magdala public house. After considerably more furtive reconnoitring, they returned to Ruth's flat, gave her son his supper and put him to bed. That night, Cussen again drove her to Tanza Road where the Findlaters

David Blakely

were holding a small party. Listening from the street, Ruth could hear David's
voice – and a woman giggling at his remarks. A new suspicion took root in
Ruth's fevered mind. David was not pursuing an affair with Mrs Findlater – but
with the couple's au pair! A trivial occurrence seemed to confirm this idea: at a
certain point, the blinds went down in what Ruth took to be the girl's bedroom;
and at the same time, she ceased to hear David's voice. The Findlaters, Ruth
convinced herself, were using the au pair to prise her young lover away from her.

Cussen drove Ruth home at about 21.00, and she spent a second sleepless
night, chain-smoking and nursing her mute fury. By the following evening, on
Easter Sunday, she must have been practically unhinged. 'I was very upset', she
acknowledged at her trial. 'I had a peculiar feeling I wanted to kill him.'

By her own account, Ruth Ellis made her way by taxi to Hampstead that evening. In her handbag she carried a heavy .38 Smith and Wesson revolver. Arriving at Tanza Road she saw no sign of the Vanguard, so she made her way on foot to the Magdala pub where she sighted David's car by the kerb. Peering through the windows of the hostelry, she could see David and a friend, Mayfair car salesman Clive Gunnell, drinking at the bar. In fact, the two men had only come to replenish stocks for an evening at Tanza Road. Having downed their drinks, they came out into the street carrying cigarettes and three quarts of light ale.

Neither noticed Ruth at first. With a quart of beer under his arm, David approached the Vanguard, fumbling in his pocket for the keys.

'David!' she called, but he did not seem to hear. Ruth approached, taking the revolver from her bag. 'David!' she called again, and this time he turned to see the blonde with the Smith and Wesson.

Immediately, he ran towards the back of the van. Two shots echoed in quick succession. Blakely was slammed against the side of the vehicle, then staggered towards his friend for cover.

'Clive!' he screamed.

'Get out of the way, Clive,' Ruth hissed in response. And as Blakely tried again to run for safety she fired a third shot that span him to the ground. Then, with every appearance of icy calm, Ruth Ellis came at her fallen lover and drilled two more bullets into his prone body. A sixth bullet ricocheted off the road to strike the thumb of a passing bank official's wife.

From the doorway of the pub, people were spilling out onto the street. An off-duty officer was among those present and he moved slowly towards her. 'Will you call the police?' Ruth asked softly as he took the gun. 'I *am* the police', he replied.

That, in bare outline, was the sequence of events that led Ruth Ellis to trial at the Old Bailey. In purely legal terms, it seemed a clear-cut case of wilful murder against which Ruth offered no substantial defence. She refused to ask for sympathy as a downtrodden mistress; in the dock she glossed over Blakely's beatings: 'He only used to hit me with his fists and hands, but I bruise very easily.' With all passion and anguish spent, Ruth Ellis *wanted* to die for the murder of her lover, and indulged in no tearful theatricals. To the disquiet of her lawyers, she even insisted on appearing in the dock with a full peroxide rinse. In the argot of the day she appeared the very archetype of a 'brassy tart'. Ruth's fate may have swung on that bottle of peroxide – with the chance injury to the bank official's wife's thumb.

In cross-examination, the prosecutor posed only one question:

'Mrs Ellis, when you fired that revolver at close range into the body of David Blakely, what did you intend to do?'

'It is obvious,' she replied with fateful simplicity, 'that when I shot him I intended to kill him.'

That, in effect, was that. The judge in summing up pointed out that jealousy was no defence under British law; the intention to kill was all-important. 'If, on the consideration of the whole evidence, you are satisfied that at the time she fired those shots she had the intention of killing or doing grievous bodily harm, then your duty is to find her guilty of wilful murder.'

Ruth herself had admitted her intention. The twelve members of the jury were out for only 23 minutes, and found the prisoner guilty of murder. Donning his black cap, the judge intoned the terrible words: 'The sentence of the Court upon you is that you be taken hence to a lawful prison, and thence to a place of execution, and that you there be hanged by the neck until you be dead . . .'

It all seemed so clear-cut. Yet, even under British law, it was not inevitable that Ruth Ellis should have hanged. Much about the case was never fully explored at the trial. Ruth's mental state, for example, was not discussed at any length: the effect of her second abortion, and the fact that she was taking tranquillisers on medical advice. The drugs, combined with alcohol she had consumed on the fateful day, may well have produced a state of serious psychological disturbance. Even on the given evidence, Blakely's violent provocations might have led the jury to recommend mercy. In the case of Kittie Byron (see page 10), such a recommendation had saved the prisoner from the gallows.

Then there was the question of the murder weapon. Ruth Ellis stated that she had been given the Smith and Wesson 'about three years ago by a man in a club whose name I don't remember.' Nobody believed this version of events even at the time. It was widely rumoured that Desmond Cussen had supplied the murder weapon, and also driven her to Hampstead on the fateful night. Interviewed in 1977, Cussen firmly repudiated the suggestions. The defence did not pursue the matter at the trial, since a hint of conspiracy to murder would have jeopardised the case for manslaughter, and the chance of a reprieve. Yet if someone did put the gun in Ruth's hand and drive her – befuddled with drink, tranquillisers and lack of sleep – to the murder scene she would have been less easily presented as a cold-hearted blonde avenger.

During the last frenzied efforts to win Ruth a reprieve, this issue became electric. On the day before her execution, Ruth Ellis made a written statement to her solicitor Victor Mishcon:

> I, Ruth Ellis, have been advised by Mr Victor Mishcon to tell the whole truth in regard to the circumstances leading up to the killing of David Blakely and it is only with the greatest reluctance that I have decided to tell how it was that I got the gun with which I shot Blakely.

The notices of Ruth Ellis's execution are posted on the prison door

I did not do so before because I felt that I was needlessly getting someone into possible trouble.

I had been drinking Pernod (I think that is how it is spelt) in Cussen's flat and Cussen had been drinking too. This was about 8.30 p.m. We had been drinking for some time. I had been telling Cussen about Blakely's treatment of me. I was in a terribly depressed state. All I remember is that Cussen gave me a loaded gun . . . I was in such a dazed state that I cannot remember what was said. I rushed out as soon as he gave me the gun. He stayed in the flat.

I had never seen the gun before. The only gun I had ever seen there was a small air pistol used as a game with a target.

Before signing the document, Ruth added:

There's one more thing. You had better know the whole truth. I rushed back after a second or so and said 'Will you drive me to Hampstead?' He did so, and left me at the top of Tanza Road.

One view of this is that Ruth Ellis had no interest in saving her life at that stage, and was only persuaded to make her statement so that her ten-year-old son should know the truth. Desmond Cussen, however, in the 1977 interview, reiterated his claim to know nothing about the revolver, adding: 'She was a dreadful liar, you know.'

With only a few hours to spare, the statement was rushed by messenger to the Home Office. Scotland Yard was notified and Fleet Street buzzed with the news. Cussen, however, could not be found to comment on the statement and lacking a confession from him, the Home Secretary refused to consider the most urgent representations.

No reprieve was granted. Early in the morning of 13 July, Ruth Ellis wrote her last note to a friend from the condemned cell: 'The time is 7o'clock a.m. – everyone (staff) is simply wonderful in Holloway. This is just to console my family with the thought that I did not change my way of thinking at the last moment. Or break my promise to David's mother.' That promise had been made in an earlier letter, in which Ruth had asked forgiveness and written, 'I shall die loving your son.'

And perhaps Ruth Ellis did die loving David Blakely. She spent her last hour in the death cell at prayer before a crucifix. Just before 09.00, the grim procession of officials entered and told her the time had come. They offered her a large measure of brandy which she gratefully accepted. Then, having thanked the authorities for their kindness, she walked steadily to the execution chamber where Albert Pierrepoint was waiting.